Frommer's®

POSTCARDS FROM

Arizona 2002

The 37-mile-long Paria Canyon trailhead follows the meandering route of a narrow slot canyon for much of its length. See chapter 7. © James Kay/Adstock Photos.

The Desert Botanical Garden in Phoenix is exclusively devoted to cacti and other desert plants. See chapter 4. © John Elk III Photography.

Horseback riding in the Superstition Mountains, which, according to legend, harbor a lost gold mine. See chapter 4. © John Elk III Photography.

The Organ Pipe Cactus is a national monument in one of Arizona's least visited and most remote areas. See chapter 10. © Tom Bean/Tony Stone Images.

Arizona draws countless visitors for its golfing alone. See chapter 1 for our favorite courses. © Richard Maack/Adstock Photos.

Biking in Oak Creek Canyon, near Sedona. Sedona offers some of the best outdoor access of any city in the Southwest. See chapter 5. © Michael Shedlock/New England Stock.

Marble Canyon and the Colorado River, viewed from the less explored North Rim of the Grand Canyon. See chapter 6. © David Muench/Tony Stone Images.

Mule riders descend to the bottom of the Grand Canyon. See chapter 6. © *Tom Bean/Tony Stone Images.*

Whitewater rafting on the Colorado River. See chapter 6. © *Dewitt Jones/Robert Holmes Photography.*

A magnificent view of the canyon from Cape Solitude on the South Rim. See chapter 6.
© *Chuck Lawsen/Adstock Photos.*

Native American crafts are ubiquitous in the Four Corners region. See chapter 7 for a primer. Top photo: Navajo rugs, like these at the famous Hubbell Trading Post, take hundreds of hours to make. © John Elk III Photography. Bottom photo: Navajo turquoise jewelry. © Dave Bartruff Photography.

A Hopi Kachina doll, used to bring rain and ensure health, happiness, long life, and harmony in the universe. See chapter 7.
© John Elk III Photography.

The dramatic landscape of Monument Valley is a favorite backdrop for Hollywood and television directors. See chapter 7. © John Elk III Photography.

Eroded soil and red color give the Vermillion Cliffs a unique appearance. See chapter 6.
© *Kerrick James/Tony Stone Images.*

Betatakin, an Anasazi cliff dwelling, is part of the Navajo National Monument. See chapter 7. © Dewitt Jones/Robert Holmes Photography.

The popular Lake Powell, created by the damming of the Colorado River at Glen Canyon, is a strange oasis in the middle of hundreds of miles of parched desert land. See chapter 7. © Nik Wheeler Photography.

Trout fishing in the Black River, near Alpine—the Alps of Arizona. See chapter 8.
© *Richard Maack/Adstock Photos.*

A spiral petroglyph in Saguaro National Park, near Tucson. See chapter 9.
© David Muench/Tony Stone Images.

The desert provides the perfect environment for hot-air ballooning—cool, still air and wide-open spaces. See chapters 4, 5, and 9 for ballooning companies in Phoenix, Sedona, and Tucson. © Michael R. Stoklos/Adstock Photos.

The Petrified Forest was once a vast, humid swamp. See chapter 7. © *Phil Degginger/Tony Stone Images.*

Legendary Route 66 symbolizes a lost America.
See chapters 7 and 11. Top: The Wigwam Motel
has been causing double takes along Route 66
since the 1940s. © *John Elk III Photography.* Right: A
self-conscious motel sign. © *Nik Wheeler Photography.*

A New Star-Rating System & Other Exciting News from Frommer's!

In our continuing effort to publish the savviest, most up-to-date, and most appealing travel guides available, we've added some great new features.

Frommer's guides now include a new **star-rating system.** Every hotel, restaurant, and attraction is rated from 0 to 3 stars to help you set priorities and organize your time.

We've also added **seven brand-new features** that point you to the great deals, in-the-know advice, and unique experiences that separate travelers from tourists. Throughout the guide look for:

Finds	Special finds—those places only insiders know about
Fun Fact	Fun facts—details that make travelers more informed and their trips more fun
Kids	Best bets for kids—advice for the whole family
Moments	Special moments—those experiences that memories are made of
Overrated	Places or experiences not worth your time or money
Tips	Insider tips—some great ways to save time and money
Value	Great values—where to get the best deals

We've also added a **"What's New"** section in every guide—a timely crash course in what's hot and what's not in every destination we cover.

Other Great Guides for Your Trip:

Frommer's Grand Canyon National Park
Frommer's Family Vacations in the National Parks
Frommer's National Parks of the American West

Frommer's®

Arizona
2002

by Karl Samson

with Jane Aukshunas

Here's what the critics say about Frommer's:

"Amazingly easy to use. Very portable, very complete."

—*Booklist*

"The only mainstream guide to list specific prices. The Walter Cronkite of
guidebooks—with all that implies."

—*Travel & Leisure*

"Complete, concise, and filled with useful information."

—*New York Daily News*

"Hotel Information is close to encylopedic."

—*Des Moines Sunday Register*

Hungry Minds™

Best-Selling Books • Digital Downloads • e-Books • Answer Networks
e-Newsletters • Branded Web Sites • e-Learning
New York, NY • Cleveland, OH • Indianapolis, IN

About the Authors

Karl Samson and **Jane Aukshunas,** husband-and-wife travel-writing team, find that the sunny winter skies of the Arizona desert are the perfect antidote to the dreary winters of their Pacific Northwest home. Each winter, they flee the rain to explore Arizona's deserts, mountains, cities, and small towns. It is the state's unique regional style, Native American cultures, abundance of contemporary art, and, of course, boundless landscapes that keep the duo fascinated by Arizona. Summers find the team researching their other books, including *Frommer's Washington*, *Frommer's Oregon*, and *Frommer's Seattle & Portland*.

Published by:

Hungry Minds, Inc.

909 Third Ave.
New York, NY 10022

ISBN 0-7645-6465-X
ISSN 1534-2123

Editor: Leslie Shen
Production Editor: Donna Wright
Cartographer: Nicholas Trotter
Photo Editor: Richard Fox
Production by Hungry Minds Indianapolis Production Services

Front cover photo: Saguaro cactus in the Sonora Desert
Back cover photo: Horseback riding in the Superstition Mountains

Special Sales

For general information on Hungry Minds' products and services please contact our Customer Care department; within the U.S. at 800-762-2974, outside the U.S. at 317-572-3993 or fax 317-572-4002. For sales inquiries and reseller information, including discounts, bulk sales, customized editions, and premium sales, please contact our Customer Care department at 800-434-3422.

Manufactured in the United States of America

5 4 3 2 1

Contents

List of Maps

An Invitation to the Reader

In researching this book, we discovered many wonderful places—hotels, restaurants, shops, and more. We're sure you'll find others. Please tell us about them, so we can share the information with your fellow travelers in upcoming editions. If you were disappointed with a recommendation, we'd love to know that, too. Please write to:

Frommer's Arizona 2002
Hungry Minds, Inc. • 909 Third Avenue • New York, NY 10022

An Additional Note

Please be advised that travel information is subject to change at any time—and this is especially true of prices. We therefore suggest that you write or call ahead for confirmation when making your travel plans. The authors, editors, and publisher cannot be held responsible for the experiences of readers while traveling. Your safety is important to us, however, so we encourage you to stay alert and be aware of your surroundings. Keep a close eye on cameras, purses, and wallets, all favorite targets of thieves and pickpockets.

New! Frommer's Star Ratings & Icons

Every hotel, restaurant, and attraction listing in this guide has been ranked for quality, value, service, amenities, and special features using a star-rating scale. In country, state, and regional guides, we also rate towns and regions to help you narrow down your choices and budget your time accordingly. Hotels and restaurants in the Very Expensive and Expensive categories are rated on a scale of one (highly recommended) to three stars (exceptional). Those in the Moderate and Inexpensive categories rate from zero (recommended) to two stars (very highly recommended). Attractions, towns, and regions are rated according to the following scale: zero stars (recommended), one star (highly recommended), two stars (very highly recommended), and three stars (must-see).

In addition to the rating system, we also use seven icons to highlight insider information, useful tips, special bargains, hidden gems, memorable experiences, kid-friendly venues, places to avoid, and other useful information:

| *Finds* | *Fun Fact* | *Kids* | *Moments* | *Overrated* | *Tips* | *Value* |

The following abbreviations are used for credit cards:

| AE | American Express | DC | Diners Club | V | Visa |
| DISC | Discover | MC | MasterCard | | |

FROMMERS.COM

Now that you have the guidebook to a great trip, visit our website at **www.frommers.com** for travel information on nearly 2,000 destinations. With features updated regularly, we give you instant access to the most current trip-planning information available. At Frommers.com, you'll also find the best prices on airfares, accommodations, and car rentals—and you can even book travel online through our travel booking partners. At Frommers.com, you'll also find the following:

- Daily Newsletter highlighting the best travel deals
- Hot Spot of the Month/Vacation Sweepstakes & Travel Photo Contest
- More than 200 Travel Message Boards
- Outspoken Newsletters and Feature Articles on travel bargains, vacation ideas, tips and resources, and more!

What's New in Arizona

The only thing constant in the world of travel is change (and we aren't just talking about fluctuating exchange rates). Room rates go up, new resorts open, restaurants and nightclubs open and close like clockwork. Arizona is no exception. The following are some highlights of what's new in the state this year.

PHOENIX, SCOTTSDALE & THE VALLEY OF THE SUN **Orientation** The Phoenix tax-the-tourists contingent has been at it again. In order to pay for the Arizona Cardinals' new football stadium, visitors to the area must now pay taxes of more than 27% on car rentals at Phoenix Sky Harbor Airport, which gives Phoenix the second highest car-rental taxes in the country (Seattle tops the list).

Where to Stay In north Scottsdale, new resorts seem to be popping up like desert toads after a monsoon rain. One of the best is also one of the smallest. **Copperwynd Country Club & Inn,** 13225 N. Eagle Ridge Dr., Fountain Hills (© 877/707-7760; www. copperwynd.com), is a 40-room boutique hotel with a dramatic ridge-top setting, luxurious rooms, and great views.

Yet another valley resort has weighed in with a major water recreation area. The trend started a few years back when a couple of Phoenix-area resorts added big, splashy pool areas similar to what you find at many ocean-side resorts. Latest to get their feet wet is the **Fairmont Scottsdale Princess,** 7575 E. Princess Dr. (© 800/344-4758;

www.fairmont.com), which has added the $4 million Sonoran Splash, with the longest resort water slide in the state.

Where to Dine Giving such established restaurants as Windows on the Green and Vincent Guerithault a run for their money is **Medizona,** 7217 E. Fourth Ave., Scottsdale (© 480/ 947-9500), which combines the flavors of the Southwest with, you guessed it, the flavors of the Mediterranean.

Seeing the Sights The Sonoran Desert is one of the greenest deserts in the world and is even more beautiful when the wildflowers bloom. Now visitors short on time can catch a few desert blooms on the new Harriet K. Maxwell Desert Wildflower Trail at the **Desert Botanical Gardens,** 1201 N. Galvin Pkwy. (© 480/941-1225; www.dbg.org), in Papago Park.

After a total makeover and expansion, the **Mesa Southwest Museum,** 53 N. MacDonald St., Mesa (© 480/ 644-2230; www.ci.mesa.az.us), is now one of the best little history and natural-history museums in the valley and is a great place to bring the kids. They'll love the animated dinosaurs.

See chapter 4, "Phoenix, Scottsdale & the Valley of the Sun," for more information.

CENTRAL ARIZONA **Jerome** Many a person passing though has been bewitched by this old mining town, which was once nearly a ghost town. With the opening of the **Connor Hotel of Jerome,** 164 Main St. (© 800/523-3554), there's one more good reason to stop and spend the night in town (as if the view across the Verde Valley weren't enough).

Sedona Enchantment Resort, 525 Boynton Canyon Rd. (© **800/ 826-4180**), which has long boasted the most unforgettable setting of any resort in the state, became an even more desirable destination with the opening of its luxurious new Mii Amo spa. With its own guest rooms and both indoor and outdoor treatment areas, it has the feel of a very exclusive health spa. You might just want to skip Canyon Ranch this year.

After years of planning and construction, the **Sedona Cultural Park** (© **800/780-ARTS;** www.sedona culturalpark.org) finally opened in the summer of 2000 on the western edge of town. With Sedona's famed red rocks as a backdrop, the cultural center's new outdoor performance space will serve as the city's primary venue for all manner of performances.

See chapter 5, "Central Arizona," for details.

THE GRAND CANYON & NORTHERN ARIZONA Expect new frustrations at the **South Rim** of the Grand Canyon this year. Now not only will you struggle to find a parking space, but you'll also have to work to find the new Canyon View Information Plaza and Canyon View Visitor Center. The well-designed new information plaza and visitor center are an excellent addition to the Grand Canyon experience and are invaluable in helping visitors plan their activities and learn about the park. However, the information plaza was designed to be accessed by a light-rail system that has not yet been built, and Congress no longer seems inclined to provide funding for the trolleys. Consequently, there are no adjacent parking lots. You'll have to park where you can and then walk or take a free shuttle bus to the plaza. See chapter 6, "The

Grand Canyon & Northern Arizona," for details.

THE FOUR CORNERS REGION: LAND OF THE HOPI & NAVAJO Winslow At La Posada, the beautifully restored historic Santa Fe Railroad/Fred Harvey hotel in Winslow, there's a new restaurant— **The Turquoise Room,** 303 E. Second St. (© **520/289-2888;** www.laposada. org). The menu combines Southwestern cuisine and items that appeared on Fred Harvey menus back in the 1920s. You won't find better food anywhere in northern Arizona.

Lake Powell & Page If you're headed to Lake Powell for a houseboat vacation, don't plan on flying into Page. Sunrise Airlines, which was the only commercial airline with regular service to and from Page has gone out of business. There are rumors of a new airline taking over the routes, so be sure to contact the Page/Lake Powell Chamber of Commerce (© **888/261-7243;** www.pagelakepowellchamber.org) for current information when planning your trip.

See chapter 7, "The Four Corners Region: Land of the Hopi & Navajo," for more information.

TUCSON Orientation If you're fleeing the rain-soaked Northwest or the congested roads of the San Francisco area for the sunny skies of Tucson, you can now get here quicker with direct flights from Seattle and San Jose on **Alaska Airlines** (© **800/ 426-0333;** www.alaskaair.com). Once you arrive in Tucson, however, expect a bit of inconvenience at the **Tucson International Airport,** which is in the midst of a $66.5 million renovation. Construction is expected to continue well into 2003. Heading to Tucson from Canada? There are now direct flights from Toronto on **America West** (© **800/235-9292;** www.americawest. com).

Visitors to downtown Tucson can now catch rides on the city's new **T.I.C.E.T.** (© **520/747-3778**) shuttle buses. There's no charge to ride these buses, the exteriors of which have been painted by local artists.

Where to Stay This past year, the **Westin La Paloma,** 3800 E. Sunrise Dr. (© **800/WESTIN-1;** www.westin. com), which sits high on a ridge in the Catalina foothills, opened an Elizabeth Arden Red Door spa. Not to be outdone, the **Omni Tucson National Golf Resort & Spa,** 2727 W. Club Dr. (© **800/528-4856;** www.omnihotels. com), spent $3 million on a total renovation of its spa.

Where to Dine Wine lovers should be sure to plan for a meal at the trendy new **Bistro Zin,** 1865 E. River Rd. (© **520/299-7799**), an upscale wine bar/restaurant in the new Joesler Village shopping plaza in the Catalina foothills. Good food and a wide range of wine flights make a meal here an educational, as well as culinary, experience.

Seeing the Sights The price of enjoying the outdoors went up this year with the implementation of a user fee at **Sabino Canyon,** 5900 N. Sabino Canyon Rd. (© **520/749-2861**). With its waterfalls, swimming holes, hiking trails, and tram rides up the canyon, this area is one of the best places in Tucson to experience the desert. The $5 fee is a small price to pay.

See chapter 9, "Tucson," for more information.

SOUTHERN ARIZONA Patagonia & Sonoita In Sonoita, **Callaghan Vineyards,** on Elgin Road (© **520/455-5322**), has moved into a new winery building just west of the village of Elgin. Also in the same area is the new **Rancho Milagro,** 11 E. Camino del Corral, Elgin (© **520/455-0381**). This B&B is a

quintessentially Southwestern place, with loads of character and a sky that could make Montana look like smallsky country.

Bisbee The town of Bisbee, everpopular as a weekend getaway for Tucsonans, took another step up the ladder of trendiness with the opening this past year of **Le Chéne Hotel & Bistro,** 1 Howard Ave. (© **520/ 432-1832;** www.lechenebistro.com). Patterned after French auberges and Napa Valley restaurants, the combination restaurant and hotel is located in a restored brick building on the corner of Brewery Gulch. The modern rooms and French cuisine make this a contender for best bet for lodging and dining in Bisbee.

See chapter 10, "Southern Arizona," for details.

WESTERN ARIZONA Kingman The town of Kingman has long played up its Route 66 heritage, and with the opening in May 2001 of the **Route 66 Museum,** 120 W. Andy Devine Ave. (© **520/753-9889**), there is now someplace for visitors to get an indepth look at the history of the famous highway. It's located in a restored powerhouse right on old Route 66 in downtown Kingman.

Yuma Yuma has long been looked upon by many Arizonans as just a place to stop and get gas when traveling between Tucson and San Diego. However, downtown Yuma is in the process of reclaiming its historic heritage, and to that end several old adobe buildings have been restored and turned into interesting shops. Also not to be missed is the **River City Grill,** 600 W. Third St. (© **520/ 782-7988**), which serves the most creative cuisine between Tucson and San Diego and has a very lively atmosphere.

See chapter 11, "Western Arizona," for details.

1

The Best of Arizona

Planning a trip to a state as large and diverse as Arizona involves a lot of decision-making (other than which golf clubs to take), so in this chapter we've tried to give you some direction. Below we've chosen what we feel is the very best the state has to offer—the places and experiences you won't want to miss. Although sights and activities listed here are written up in more detail elsewhere in this book, this chapter should give you an overview of Arizona's highlights and get you started planning your trip.

1 The Best Places to Commune with Cacti

- **Boyce Thompson Southwestern Arboretum** (east of Phoenix): Located just outside the town of Superior, this was the nation's first botanical garden established in a desert environment. It's set in a small canyon framed by cliffs, with desert plantings from all over the world—a fascinating place for an educational stroll in the desert. See chapter 4.

- **Desert Botanical Garden** (Phoenix): There's no better place in the state to learn about the plants of Arizona's Sonoran Desert and the many other deserts of the world. Displays at this Phoenix botanical garden explain plant adaptations and how indigenous tribes once used many of this region's wild plants. See chapter 4.

- **Arizona–Sonora Desert Museum** (Tucson): The name is misleading—this is actually more of a zoo and botanical garden than a museum. Naturalistic settings house dozens of species of desert animals, including a number of critters you wouldn't want to meet

in the wild (rattlesnakes, tarantulas, scorpions, black widows, and Gila monsters). See chapter 9.

- **Saguaro National Park** (Tucson): Lying both east and west of Tucson, this park preserves "forests" of saguaro cacti and is the very essence of the desert as so many people imagine it. You can hike it, bike it, or drive it. See chapter 9.

- **Tohono Chul Park** (Tucson): Although this park is not all that large, it packs a lot of desert scenery into its modest space. Impressive plantings of cacti are the star attractions, but there are also good wildflower displays in the spring. See chapter 9.

- **Organ Pipe Cactus National Monument** (west of Tucson): The organ pipe cactus is a smaller, multitrunked relative of the giant saguaro and lives only along the Mexican border about 100 miles west of Tucson. This remote national monument has hiking trails, scenic drives, even a large natural spring. See chapter 10.

2 The Best Active Vacations

- **Rafting the Grand Canyon:** Whether you go for 3 days or 2 weeks, no other active vacation in the state comes even remotely close to matching the excitement of a raft trip through the Grand Canyon. Sure, the river is crowded with groups in the summer, but the grandeur of the canyon is more than enough to make up for it. See chapter 6.

- **Hiking into the Grand Canyon or Havasu Canyon:** Not for the unfit or the faint of heart, a hike down into the Grand Canyon or Havasu Canyon is a journey through millions of years of time set in stone. This trip takes plenty of advance planning and requires some very strenuous hiking. With both a campground and a lodge at the bottom of each canyon, you can choose to make this trip with either a fully loaded backpack or just a light daypack. See chapter 6.

- **Riding the Range at a Guest Ranch:** Yes, there are still cowboys. They ride ranges all over the state, and so can you if you book a stay at one of the many guest ranches (formerly known as dude ranches). You might even get to do the *City-Slicker* thing and drive some cattle down the trail. After a long or short day in the saddle, you can soak in a hot tub, go for a swim, or play a game of tennis before chowing down. See chapters 5, 9, and 10.

- **Staying at a Golf or Tennis Resort:** If horseback riding and cowboy cookouts aren't your thing, how about as much golf or tennis as you can play? The Phoenix/Scottsdale area has the greatest concentration of resorts in the country, and Sedona and Tucson add even more options to the mix. There's something very satisfying about swinging a racquet or club with the state's spectacular scenery in the background, and the climate means you can do it practically year-round. See chapters 4, 5, and 9.

- **Mountain Biking in Sedona:** Forget Moab—too many other hard-core mountain bikers. Among the red rocks of Sedona, you can pedal through awesome scenery on some of the most memorable single-track trails in the Southwest. There's even plenty of slickrock for that Canyonlands experience. See chapter 5.

- **Bird-Watching in Southeastern Arizona:** As avid bird-watchers, we know that this isn't the most active of sports, but a birder can get in a bit of walking when it's necessary (like, maybe to get to the nesting tree of an elegant trogon). The southeast corner of the state is one of the best birding regions in the whole country. See chapter 10.

3 The Best Day Hikes & Nature Walks

- **Camelback Mountain** (Phoenix): For many Phoenicians, the trail to the top of Camelback Mountain is a ritual, a Phoenix institution. Sure, there are those who make this a casual but strenuous hike, but many more turn it into a serious workout by jogging to the top and back. We prefer a more leisurely approach to enjoy the views. See chapter 4.

- **Picacho Peak State Park** (south of Casa Grande): The hike up this central Arizona landmark is short

Arizona

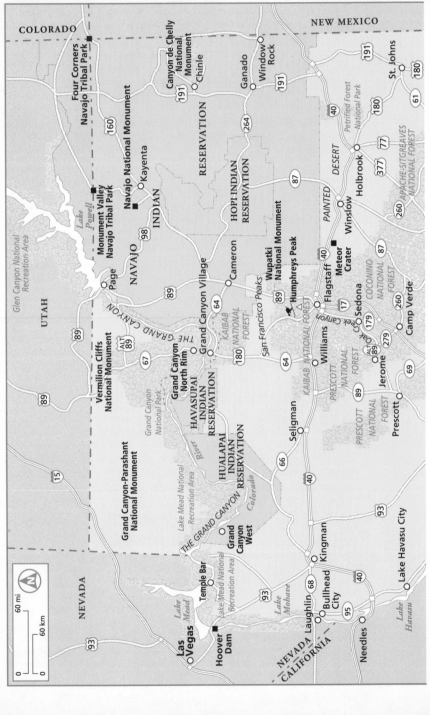

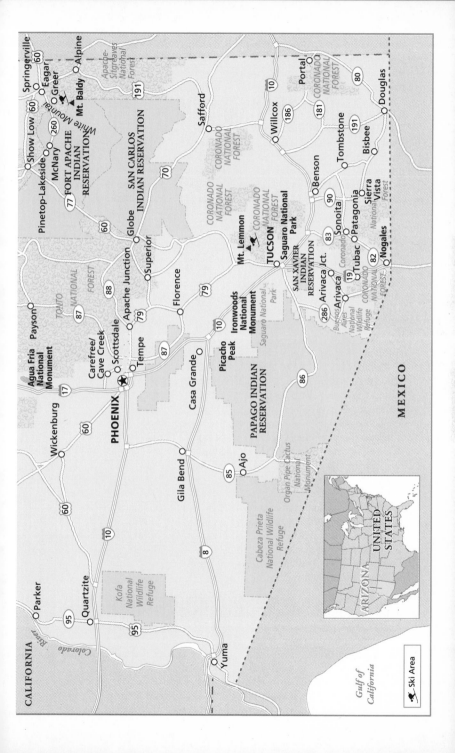

but strenuous, and from the top there are superb views out over the desert. The best time of year to make the hike is in spring, when the peak comes alive with wildflowers. Picacho Peak is between Casa Grande and Tucson just off I-10. See chapter 4.

- **The West Fork of Oak Creek Trail** (outside Sedona): The West Fork of Oak Creek is a tiny stream that meanders for miles in a narrow steep-walled canyon. This is classic canyon country, and the hardest part of a hike here is having to turn around without seeing what's around the next bend up ahead. See chapter 5.

- **South Kaibab Trail** (Grand Canyon South Rim): Forget the popular Bright Angel Trail, which is a human highway near the top. This trail offers better views to day-hikers and is the preferred downhill route for anyone heading to Phantom Ranch for the night. This is a strenuous hike even if you go only a mile or so down the trail. Remember, the trip back is all uphill. See chapter 6.

- **Antelope Canyon** (Page): More a slow walk of reverence than a hike, this trail lets you see the amazing beauty that can be created when water and rock battle each other in the Southwest. The trail leads through a picture-perfect sandstone slot canyon, which in places is only a few feet wide. See chapter 7.

- **The Keet Seel Trail** (Navajo National Monument): There is something magical and mystical about arriving at an ancient cliff dwelling after hiking 8 miles through a desert canyon. At the end of your hike, after resting for a while, you can explore the ruins. There's a campsite nearby, so you can sleep with the ghosts of the Anasazi for a night. See chapter 7.

- **The White House Ruins Trail** (Canyon de Chelly): There's only one Canyon de Chelly hike that the general public can do without a Navajo guide, and that's the 2½-mile trail to White House Ruins, a small Anasazi pueblo site. The trail leads from the canyon rim across bare sandstone, through a tunnel, and down to the floor of the canyon. See chapter 7.

- **Seven Falls** (Tucson): There is something irresistible about waterfalls in the desert, and on this trail you get more than enough falls to satisfy any craving to cool off on a hot desert day. This trail is in Sabino Canyon Recreation Area in northeast Tucson. See chapter 9.

- **Heart of Rocks Trail** (Cochise County): While the big national parks and monuments in northern Arizona get all the publicity, Chiricahua National Monument, down in the southeast corner of the state, quietly lays claim to some of the most spectacular scenery in Arizona. On this trail, you'll hike through a wonderland of rocks. See chapter 10.

4 The Best Scenic Drives

- **Apache Trail** (east of Phoenix): Much of this winding road, which passes just north of the Superstition Mountains, is unpaved and follows a rugged route once ridden by Apaches. This is some of the most remote country you'll find in the Phoenix area, with far-reaching desert vistas and lots to see and do along the way. See chapter 4.

- **Oak Creek Canyon** (Sedona): Slicing down from the pine country outside Flagstaff to the red rocks of Sedona, Oak Creek Canyon is a cool oasis. From the scenic overlook at the top of the canyon to the swimming holes and hiking trails at the bottom, this canyon road provides a rapid change in climate and landscape. See chapter 5.

- **Canyon de Chelly National Monument** (Chinle): This fascinating complex of canyons on the Navajo Indian Reservation has only limited public access because it is still home to numerous Navajo families. However, there are two roads that parallel the north and south rims of the canyon providing lots of scenic overlooks. See chapter 7.

- **Through Monument Valley** (north of Kayenta): This valley of sandstone buttes and mesas is one of the most photographed spots in America and is familiar to people all over the world from the countless movies, TV shows, and commercials that have been shot here. A 17-mile dirt road winds through the park, giving visitors close-ups of such landmarks as Elephant Butte, the Mittens, and Totem Pole. See chapter 7.

- **Up Mount Lemmon** (Tucson): Sure, the views of Tucson from the city's northern foothills are great, but the vistas from Mount Lemmon are even better. With a ski area at its summit, Mount Lemmon rises up from the desert like an island rising from the sea. Along the way, the road climbs from cactus country to cool pine forests. See chapter 9.

5 The Best Golf Courses

- **The Boulders South Course** (Carefree, near Phoenix; ℂ **480/ 488-9028**): If you've ever seen a photo of someone teeing off beside a massive balancing rock and longed to play that same hole, then you've dreamed about playing the Boulders South Course. Jay Morrish's desert-style design plays around and through the jumble of massive boulders for which the resort is named. See chapter 4.

- **Gold Canyon Golf Resort** (at Gold Canyon Ranch, Apache Junction, near Phoenix; ℂ **480/ 982-9449**): Located east of Phoenix, Gold Canyon offers superb golf at the foot of the Superstition Mountains. The second, third, and fourth holes on the Dinosaur Mountain Course are truly memorable. They play across the foot of Dinosaur Mountain and are rated among the tops in the state. See chapter 4.

- **The Tournament Players Club (TPC) of Scottsdale** (Scottsdale; ℂ **480/585-3600**): If you've always dreamed of playing where the pros play, then you may want to schedule a visit to the Fairmont Scottsdale Princess and book a tee time on the Stadium Course, which is the site of the PGA Tour's Phoenix Open. See chapter 4.

- **Troon North Golf Club** (Scottsdale; ℂ **480/585-5300**): Designed by Tom Weiskopf and Jay Morrish, this semiprivate desert-style course is named for the famous Scottish links that overlook both the Firth of Forth and the Firth of Clyde—but that's where the similarities end. Troon North has two 18-hole courses, but the original, known as the Monument Course, is still the favorite. See chapter 4.

- **The Gold Course at Wigwam Golf and Country Club** (Litchfield Park, near Phoenix; ℂ **623/ 935-3811**): If you're a traditionalist who eschews those cactus- and rattlesnake-filled desert target courses, you'll want to beg, borrow, or steal a tee time on the Wigwam Resort's Gold Course. This 7,100-yard resort course has long been an Arizona legend. See chapter 4.

- **Sedona Golf Resort** (Sedona; ℂ **520/284-9355**): It's easy to think that all of Arizona's best courses are in the Phoenix and Tucson areas, but it just isn't so. Up in the red-rock country, at the mouth of Oak Creek Canyon, lies the Sedona Golf Resort, a traditional course that's among the best in the state. See chapter 5.

- **Lake Powell National Golf Course** (Page; ℂ **520/645-2023**): With fairways that wrap around the base of the red-sandstone bluff atop which sits the town of Page, this is one of the most scenic golf courses in the state. Walls of eroded sandstone come right down to the greens, and alongside one fairway, water is pumped up the rock to create a waterfall. See chapter 7.

- **Omni Tucson National Golf Resort and Spa** (Tucson; ℂ **520/ 297-2271**): With its wide expanses of grass, this traditional course, site of the PGA Tour's Tucson Open, is both challenging and forgiving. The 18th hole of the Orange and Gold courses is considered one of the toughest finishing holes on the tour. See chapter 9.

- **Ventana Canyon Golf and Racquet Club** (Tucson; ℂ **520/ 577-1400**): Two Tom Fazio–designed courses, the Canyon Course and the Mountain Course, are shared by two of the city's finest resorts. Both desert-style courses play through some of the most stunning scenery anywhere in the state. If we had to choose between the two, we'd go for the Canyon Course. See chapter 9.

- **Emerald Canyon Golf Course** (Parker; ℂ **520/667-3366**): Canyons, cliffs, and ravines are the hazards you'll be avoiding on this very interesting municipal course way out on the banks of the Colorado River. While it may not be the best in the state, it plays through some astounding scenery and is a good value. See chapter 11.

6 The Best Offbeat Travel Experiences

- **Taking a Vortex Tour in Sedona:** Crystals and pyramids are nothing compared to the power of the Sedona vortexes, which just happen to be in the middle of some very beautiful scenery. Organized tours shuttle believers from one vortex to the next. If you offer it, they will come. See chapter 5.

- **Gazing at the Stars:** Insomniacs and stargazers will find plenty to keep them sleepless in the desert as they peer at the stars through telescopes at Lowell Observatory in Flagstaff or Kitt Peak National Observatory near Tucson. In the town of Benson, you can even stay at a B&B that doubles as an astronomical observatory. See chapters 6 and 9.

- **Sleeping in a Wigwam:** Back in the heyday of Route 66, the Wigwam Motel in Holbrook lured passing motorists with its unusual architecture: concrete wigwam-shaped cabins. Today this little motel is still a great place for anyone who appreciates retro style. See chapter 7.

- **Touring Walpi Village:** Of the Hopi villages that stand atop the mesas of northeastern Arizona, only Walpi, one of the oldest, offers guided tours. The Hopi guides share information on the history of the village and the Hopi culture. See chapter 7.

- **Digging for Artifacts at Raven Site Ruin:** Looking at Anasazi ruins is all well and good, but how would you like to get your hands dirty digging for ancient artifacts? At the White Mountain Archaeological Center near St. Johns, you can (for a fee) participate in an ongoing archaeological dig. See chapter 8.

- **A Visit to Biosphere 2:** This giant terrarium, in which humans were the residents, is a research center for understanding how the earth's ecosystems operate. The giant greenhouses in the middle of the desert are straight out of postapocalyptic sci-fi. See chapter 9.

7 The Best Family Experiences

- **Wild West Restaurants:** No family should visit Arizona without spending an evening at a "genuine" cowboy steakhouse. With gunslingers and gimmicks (one place cuts off your necktie, another has a slide from the bar to the dining room), cowboy bands, and false-fronted buildings, these eateries are all entertainment and loads of fun. See chapters 4 and 9.

- **The Grand Canyon Railway:** Not only is this train excursion a fun way to get to the Grand Canyon, but it also lets you avoid the parking problems and congestion that can prove so wearisome. Shootouts and train robberies are to be expected in this corner of the Wild West. See chapter 6.

- **Arizona–Sonora Desert Museum** (Tucson): This is actually a zoo featuring the animals of the Sonoran Desert. There are rooms full of snakes, a prairie-dog town, bighorn sheep, mountain lions, and an aviary full of hummingbirds. Kids and adults love this place. See chapter 9.

- **Shootouts at the O.K. Corral:** Tombstone may be "the town too tough to die," but poor Ike Clanton and his buddies the McLaury boys have to die over and over again at the frequent reenactments of the famous gunfight. See chapter 10.

8 The Best Family Vacations

- **Saddling up on a Dude Ranch:** Ride off into the sunset with your family at one of Arizona's many dude ranches (now called guest ranches). Most ranches have lots of special programs for kids. See chapters 5 and 9.

- **Floating on a Houseboat:** Renting a floating vacation home on lakes Powell, Mead, Mohave, or Havasu is a summer tradition for many Arizona families. With a houseboat, you aren't tied to one spot and can cruise from one scenic beach to the next. See chapters 6 and 11.

- **Lounging by the Pool:** While most Arizona resorts are geared primarily toward adults, there are a handful in Phoenix and Tucson that have extensive pool complexes. The kids can play in the sand, shoot down a water slide, or even float down an artificial river in an inner tube. See "The Best Swimming Pools," below.

- **Having a Grand Vacation:** You can spend the better part of a week exploring Grand Canyon National Park. There are trails to hike, mules to ride down into the canyon (if your kids are old enough), air tours by plane or helicopter, rafting trips both wild and tame, and even a train to ride to and from the canyon. See chapter 6.

9 The Best Museums

- **Heard Museum** (Phoenix): This is one of the nation's premier museums devoted to Native American cultures. In addition to historical exhibits, a huge kachina collection, and an excellent museum store, there are annual exhibits of contemporary Native American art as well as dance performances and demonstrations of traditional skills. See chapter 4.
- **Phoenix Art Museum** (Phoenix): This large art museum has acres of wall space and houses an outstanding collection of contemporary art as well as a fascinating exhibit of miniature rooms. See chapter 4.
- **Scottsdale Museum of Contemporary Art** (Scottsdale): This is the Phoenix area's newest museum and is noteworthy as much for its bold contemporary architecture as for its wide variety of exhibits. Unlike the majority of area art galleries, this museum eschews cowboy art. See chapter 4.

- **Museum of Northern Arizona** (Flagstaff): The geology, ethnography, and archaeology of this region are all explored in fascinating detail at this Flagstaff museum. Throughout the year, there are excellent special exhibits and festivals focusing on the region's different tribes. See chapter 6.
- **University of Arizona Museum of Art** (Tucson): This collection ranges from the Renaissance to the present, with a set of 15th-century Spanish religious panels the focus of the collection. Georgia O'Keeffe and Pablo Picasso are among the artists whose works are on display here. See chapter 9.
- **Amerind Foundation Museum** (west of Willcox): Although located in the remote southeastern corner of the state near Willcox, this museum and research center houses a superb collection of Native American artifacts. Displays focus on tribes of the Southwest, but other tribes are also represented. See chapter 10.

10 The Best Places to Discover the Old West

- **Rodeos:** Any rodeo, and this state has plenty, will give you a glimpse of the Old West, but Arizona has two that claim title to being the oldest in the country. Whether you head for the rodeo in Prescott or the one in Payson, you'll see plenty of bronco busting, bull riding, and beer drinking. See chapters 5 and 8.
- **Guest Ranches:** The Old West lives on at guest ranches all over the state, where rugged wranglers lead city slickers on horseback rides through desert scrub and

mountain meadows. Campfires, cookouts, and cattle are all part of the experience. See chapters 5, 9, and 10.
- **Monument Valley** (north of Kayenta): John Ford made it the hallmark of his Western movies, and today the starkly beautiful and fantastically shaped buttes and mesas of this valley are the quintessential Western landscape. You'll recognize it the moment you see it. See chapter 7.
- **Old Tucson Studios** (Tucson): Although many of the original

movie sets burned in a 1995 fire, this combination back lot and amusement park provides visitors with a glimpse of the most familiar Old West—the Hollywood West. Sure, the shootouts and cancan revues are silly, but it's all in good fun, and everyone gets a thrill out of seeing the occasional film crew in action. See chapter 9.

- **Tombstone:** This is the real Old West—Tombstone is a real town, unlike Old Tucson. However, "the town too tough to die" was reincarnated long ago as a major tourist attraction with gunslingers in the streets, stagecoach rides, and shootouts at the O.K. Corral. See chapter 10.

11 The Best Places to See Indian Ruins

- **Besh-Ba-Gowah Archaeological Park** (Globe): These reconstructed ruins have been set up to look the way they might have appeared 700 years ago, providing a bit more cultural context than other ruins in the state. See chapter 4.
- **Casa Grande Ruins National Monument** (west of Florence): Unlike most of the other ruins in the state, this large and unusual structure is built of packed desert soil. Inscrutable and perplexing, Casa Grande seems to rise from nowhere. See chapter 4.
- **Tonto National Monument** (east of Phoenix): Located east of Phoenix on the Apache Trail, this is one of the only easily accessible cliff dwellings in Arizona that you can still visit; you don't have to just observe from a distance. See chapter 4.
- **Montezuma Castle National Monument** (north of Camp Verde): Located just off I-17, this is the most easily accessible cliff dwelling in Arizona, although it

cannot be entered. Nearby Montezuma's Well also has some small ruins. See chapter 5.
- **Wupatki National Monument** (north of Flagstaff): Not nearly as well known as the region's Anasazi cliff dwellings, these ruins are set on a wide plain. A ball court similar to those found in Central America hints at cultural ties with the Aztecs. See chapter 6.
- **Canyon de Chelly National Monument:** Small cliff dwellings up and down the length of Canyon de Chelly can be seen from overlooks, while a trip into the canyon itself offers a chance to see some of these ruins up close. See chapter 7.
- **Navajo National Monument** (west of Kayenta): Although both Keet Seel and Betatakin ruins are at the end of long hikes, their size and state of preservation make them among the finest examples of Anasazi cliff dwellings. See chapter 7.

12 The Best Luxury Hotels & Resorts

- **Arizona Biltmore Resort & Spa** (Phoenix; ✆ **800/950-0086**): Combining discreet service and the architectural styling of Frank Lloyd Wright, the Biltmore has long been one of the most prestigious resorts in the state. This is a thoroughly old-money sort of

place, though with the recent addition of a large spa, it continues to keep pace with the times. See chapter 4.
- **The Boulders** (Carefree; ✆ **800/553-1717**): Taking its name from the massive blocks of eroded granite scattered about the grounds,

the Boulders is among the most exclusive and expensive resorts in the state. Pueblo architecture fits seamlessly with the landscape, and the golf course is the most breathtaking in Arizona. See chapter 4.

- **The Fairmont Scottsdale Princess** (Scottsdale; ✆ **800/344-4758**): The Moorish styling and numerous fountains and waterfalls of this Scottsdale resort create a setting made for romance. Two superb restaurants—one serving Spanish cuisine and one serving gourmet Mexican fare—top it off. See chapter 4.

- **Four Seasons Resort Scottsdale at Troon North** (Scottsdale; ✆ **800/332-3442**): Located in north Scottsdale not far from the Boulders, this is one of the state's newest resorts and raised the bar on luxury when it opened. The setting is dramatic, the accommodations are spacious, and the next-door neighbor is one of Arizona's top golf courses. See chapter 4.

- **Hyatt Regency Scottsdale** (Scottsdale; ✆ **800/55-HYATT**): Contemporary desert architecture, dramatic landscaping, a water playground with its own beach, a staff that's always at the ready to assist you, several good restaurants that aren't overpriced, and even gondola rides—it all adds up to a lot of fun at one of the most smoothly run resorts in Arizona. See chapter 4.

- **Marriott's Camelback Inn** (Scottsdale; ✆ **800/24-CAMEL**): The Camelback Inn opened in 1936 and today is one of the few Scottsdale resorts that manages to retain an Old Arizona atmosphere while at the same time offering the most modern amenities. A full-service spa caters to those who crave pampering, while two golf courses provide plenty of challenging fairways and greens. See chapter 4.

- **The Phoenician** (Scottsdale; ✆ **800/888-8234**): This Xanadu of the resort world is brimming with marble, crystal, and works of art, and with staff seemingly around every corner, the hotel offers its guests impeccable service. Two of the resort's dining rooms are among the finest restaurants in the city, and the views are hard to beat. See chapter 4.

- **Royal Palms Hotel and Casitas** (Phoenix; ✆ **800/672-6011**): With its Mediterranean styling and towering palm trees, this resort seems far removed from the glitz that prevails at most area resorts. The Royal Palms is a classic, perfect for romantic getaways, and the 14 designer showcase rooms are among the most dramatic in the valley. See chapter 4.

- **Enchantment Resort** (Sedona; ✆ **800/826-4180**): A dramatic setting in a red-rock canyon makes this the most distinctively—and unforgettably—situated resort in the state. Guest rooms are constructed in a pueblo architectural style. If you want to feel as though you're vacationing in the desert, this place fills the bill. See chapter 5.

- **Loews Ventana Canyon Resort** (Tucson; ✆ **800/23-LOEWS**): With the Santa Catalina Mountains rising up in the backyard and an almost-natural waterfall only steps away from the lobby, this is Tucson's most dramatic resort. Contemporary styling throughout makes constant reference to the desert setting. See chapter 9.

13 The Best Family Resorts

- **Doubletree La Posada Resort** (Scottsdale; ✆ **800/222-TREE**): With its waterfalls and swim-through cave, the pool at this

Scottsdale resort seems like it ought to be peopled with pirates and castaways. There are also horseshoe pits, a volleyball court, and a pitch-and-putt green. See chapter 4.

- **Pointe Hilton Squaw Peak Resort** (Phoenix; ✆ **800/876-4683**): A water slide, tubing river, and water-fall make the water park here the most family oriented at any resort in the valley. Throw in a miniature-golf course, a video-game room, and a children's program, and you can be sure your kids will be begging to come back. See chapter 4.

- **Holiday Inn SunSpree Resort** (Scottsdale; ✆ **800/852-5205**): If you happen to have a child who is crazy about trains, then this resort, adjacent to the McCormick-Stillman Railroad Park (which has trains to ride, model-railroad exhibits, and a merry-go-round), is the place to stay. The resort itself has big lawns and free meals for kids under 12. See chapter 4.

- **Loews Ventana Canyon Resort** (Tucson; ✆ **800/23-LOEWS**): With a playground, kids' club, croquet court, basketball hoop, and its own waterfall, this resort has plenty to keep the kids busy. There's also a hiking trail that starts from the edge of the property, and Sabino Canyon Recreation Area is nearby. See chapter 9.

- **Westin La Paloma** (Tucson; ✆ **800/WESTIN-1**): Kids get their own lounge and game room, and there's a great water slide in the pool area. In summer and during holiday periods, there are special programs for the kids so parents can have a little free time. See chapter 9.

14 The Best Hotels for Old Arizona Character

- **Hermosa Inn** (Phoenix; ✆ **800/241-1210**): The main building here dates from 1930 and was once the home of Western artist Lon Megargee. Today the old adobe house is surrounded by beautiful gardens, and has become a tranquil boutique hotel with luxurious Southwestern-style rooms and a great restaurant. See chapter 4.

- **El Tovar Hotel** (Grand Canyon Village; ✆ **303/297-2757**): This classic log-and-stone mountain lodge stands in Grand Canyon Village only feet from the south rim of the Grand Canyon. Although the lobby is small, it's decorated with the requisite trophy animal heads and has a stone fireplace. See chapter 6.

- **Grand Canyon Lodge** (Grand Canyon North Rim; ✆ **303/297-2757**): This, the Grand Canyon's other grand lodge, sits right on the north rim of the canyon. Rooms are primarily in cabins, which aren't quite as impressive as the main building, but guests tend to spend a lot of time sitting on the lodge's two viewing terraces or in the sun-room. See chapter 6.

- **La Posada** (Winslow; ✆ **520/289-4366**): Designed by Mary Elizabeth Jane Colter, who also designed many of the buildings on the South Rim of the Grand Canyon, La Posada opened in 1930 and was the last of the great railroad hotels. Today the hotel is being restored to its former glory. See chapter 7.

- **Arizona Inn** (Tucson; ✆ **800/933-1093**): With its pink-stucco walls and colorful, fragrant gardens, this small Tucson resort dates from Arizona's earliest days as a vacation destination and epitomizes slower times, when guests came for the entire winter, not for a quick week-end getaway. See chapter 9.

15 The Best B&Bs

- **Briar Patch Inn** (Sedona; ☏ 888/ 809-3030): Oak Creek Canyon, near Sedona, where this collection of luxurious cottages is located, is an oasis in the desert. Few experiences are more restorative than breakfast on the shady banks of the creek. See chapter 5.
- **Canyon Villa** (Sedona; ☏ 800/ 453-1166): Located in the Village of Oak Creek only a block away from another of the state's top B&Bs, this inn provides luxurious accommodations and fabulous views of the red rocks. See chapter 5.
- **The Graham Bed & Breakfast Inn & Adobe Village** (Sedona; ☏ 800/228-1425): With its little "village" of luxury suites, this B&B is among the most elegant in the state. Everything is calculated to pamper and put you in a mood for a romantic getaway. Forget about the red rocks; these rooms are reason enough for a visit to Sedona. See chapter 5.
- **The Inn on Oak Creek** (Sedona; ☏ 800/499-7896): Built right out over Sedona's Oak Creek, with shade trees all around and the Tlaquepaque Shopping Plaza only a block away, this inn offers a wide array of luxurious and interestingly decorated rooms, most of which have creek or red-rock views. See chapter 5.
- **Rocamadour** (Prescott; ☏ 888/ 771-1933): Set amid the rounded boulders of the Granite Dells just north of Prescott, this inn combines a spectacular setting with French antiques and very luxurious accommodations. You won't find a

more memorable setting anywhere in the state. See chapter 5.
- **The Inn at 410** (Flagstaff; ☏ 800/ 774-2008): This restored 1907 bungalow offers a convenient location in downtown Flagstaff, pleasant surroundings, comfortable rooms, and delicious breakfasts. Rooms all feature different, distinctive themes, and eight of them have their own fireplaces. See chapter 6.
- **Red Setter Inn & Cottage** (Greer; ☏ 888/99-GREER): This large, new log home in the quaint mountain village of Greer is one of Arizona's most enjoyable and romantic B&Bs. It's set on the bank of the Little Colorado River in the shade of ponderosa pine trees. The inn is also a great place for ski vacations. See chapter 8.
- **Across the Creek at Aravaipa Farms** (Winkelman; ☏ 520/ 357-6901): If you're looking for the quintessential desert B&B experience, this is it, though it isn't exactly for everyone. To reach this inn, you have to drive through Aravaipa Creek (or have the innkeeper shuttle you across). Exploring the nearby wilderness area is the main activity in this remote area. See chapter 9.
- **The Royal Elizabeth** (Tucson; ☏ 877/670-9022): Located in downtown Tucson half a block from the Temple of Music and Art, this territorial-style historic home is filled with beautiful Victorian antiques and lots of architectural details. Guest rooms have lots of touches not often seen in historic B&Bs, including "vintage" phones, TVs, fridges, and safes. See chapter 9.

16 The Best Swimming Pools

- **Hyatt Regency Scottsdale** (Scottsdale; ☏ 800/55-HYATT):

This Scottsdale resort boasts a 10-pool, 2½-acre water playground complete with sand beach, waterfalls, sports pool, lap pool, adult pool, three-story water slide, large whirlpool, and lots of waterfalls. See chapter 4.

- **The Phoenician** (Scottsdale; ✆ **800/888-8234**): This system of seven pools is as impressive as the Hyatt's, but has a much more sophisticated air about it. Waterfalls, a water slide, play pools, a lap pool, and the crown jewel—a mother-of-pearl pool (actually opalescent tile)—add up to plenty of aquatic fun. See chapter 4.

- **Pointe Hilton Squaw Peak Resort** (Phoenix; ✆ **800/876-4683**): They don't just have a pool here; they have a River Ranch, with an artificial tubing river, a water slide, and a waterfall pouring into the large, freeform main pool. See chapter 4.

- **Pointe Hilton Tapatio Cliffs Resort** (Phoenix; ✆ **800/876-4683**): The Falls, a slightly more adult-oriented pool complex than that at sister property Pointe Hilton Squaw Peak Resort, includes two lagoon pools, a

40-foot waterfall, a 130-foot water slide, and rental cabanas. See chapter 4.

- **The Buttes, A Wyndham Resort** (Tempe; ✆ **800/WYNDHAM**): A lush stream cascading over desert rocks seems to feed this freeform pool, a desert-oasis fantasy world unmatched in the state. A narrow canal connects the two halves of the pool, and tucked in among the rocks are several whirlpools. See chapter 4.

- **Arizona Inn** (Tucson; ✆ **800/933-1093**): Although the pool at this historic lodge isn't very large, it more than makes up for its size with its pleasant setting in a garden filled with fragrant flowering vines and citrus trees. See chapter 9.

- **Westin La Paloma** (Tucson; ✆ **800/WESTIN-1**): With a 170-foot water slide and enough poolside lounge chairs to put a cruise ship to shame, the pool at this Tucson foothills resort is a fabulous place to while away an afternoon. There's an adults-only pool, too. See chapter 9.

17 The Best Places to Savor Southwest Flavors

- **Café Terra Cotta** (Scottsdale ✆ **480/948-8100;** Tucson ✆ **520/577-8100**): With restaurants in both Scottsdale and Tucson, Café Terra Cotta was one Arizona's pioneers in the realm of Southwestern cuisine and continues to serve creative and reasonably priced meals. See chapters 4 and 9.

- **Roaring Fork** (Scottsdale; ✆ **480/947-0795**): Roaring Fork's chef, Robert McGrath, cut his teeth at the Phoenician's Windows on the Green and later opened this trendy downtown Scottsdale restaurant. The atmosphere is lively, and the restaurant's design is thoroughly New West. See chapter 4.

- **Sam's Café** (Phoenix ✆ **602/954-7100;** Scottsdale **480/368-2800**): The flavors of the Southwest don't have to cost a fortune, and these two restaurants are proof. Okay, so the food won't be as unforgettable as that at Vincent or Roaring Fork, but you'll get a good idea of what Southwestern cooking is all about. See chapter 4.

- **Vincent Guerithault on Camelback** (Phoenix; ✆ **602/224-0225**): The bold flavors of the Southwest are the focus of this ever-popular Phoenix restaurant, where presentation is every bit as important as taste. Even if you aren't a fan of chiles, you'll find plenty of unusual flavor combinations to tempt your palate. See chapter 4.

- **Windows on the Green** (Scottsdale; © **480/423-2530**): Over the years, this restaurant at the Phoenician resort has been a training ground for a number of the best chefs in the Phoenix metro area, and many of these chefs have later gone on to open restaurants of their own. The flavor combinations are always innovative, though not necessarily fiery. See chapter 4.
- **The Heartline Cafe** (Sedona; © **520/282-0785**): Combining the zesty flavors of the Southwest with the best of the rest of the world, Sedona's Heartline Cafe frequently comes up with surefire winners guaranteed to please jaded palates. See chapter 5.
- **The Turquoise Room** (Winslow; © **520/289-2888**): Located in the little-visited town of Winslow in the restored La Posada historic hotel, this restaurant conjures up the days when the wealthy still traveled by railroad. Rarely will you find such excellent meals in

such an off-the-beaten-path locale. See chapter 7.
- **Janos/J Bar** (Tucson; © **520/615-6100**): Serving a combination of regional and Southwestern dishes, Janos has for many years been one of Tucson's premier restaurants. It's located just outside the front door of the Westin La Paloma resort, and is as formal a place as you'll find in this city. J Bar is Janos's less formal bar and grill. See chapter 9.
- **The Tack Room** (Tucson; © **520/722-2800**): Superb service, creative Southwestern dishes, and an authentic Arizona atmosphere make Tucson's Tack Room one of the finest restaurants in the West. Although the steaks are the traditional favorite, Southwestern flavors predominate. See chapter 9.
- **Cantina Romantica** (Amado; © **520/398-2914**): Located in a historic adobe building at a remote and old-fashioned little getaway ranch, this restaurant abounds in Southwestern flavor. To reach Cantina Romantica, you'll have to drive *through* the Santa Cruz River! See chapter 10.

2

Planning Your Trip to Arizona

Whether you're headed to Arizona to raft the Grand Canyon or to golf in Phoenix, you'll find all the advance-planning answers you need in this chapter—everything from when to go to how to get there.

1 The Regions in Brief

Phoenix, Scottsdale & the Valley of the Sun This region encompasses the sprawling metropolitan Phoenix area, which covers more than 400 square miles and includes more than 20 cities and communities surrounded by several distinct mountain ranges. It's the economic and population center of the state, and is Arizona's main winter/spring vacation destination. It is here that you'll find the greatest concentrations of resorts and golf courses. It is also where you'll find the worst traffic congestion and highest resort rates.

Central Arizona This region lies between Phoenix and the high country of northern Arizona and includes the red-rock country around the town of Sedona, which is one of the state's most popular tourist destinations. The rugged scenery around Sedona played many a role in old Western movies and has long attracted artists. Today Sedona abounds in art galleries, recreational opportunities, and excellent lodging choices. Also within this region are historic Prescott, the former territorial capital of Arizona, and the old mining town of Jerome, which has now become something of an artists' community. Several ancient Native American ruins and petroglyph sites can be found here as well.

The Grand Canyon & Northern Arizona Home to the Grand Canyon, one of the natural wonders of the world, northern Arizona is a vast and sparsely populated region comprised primarily of public lands and Indian reservations. Because Grand Canyon National Park attracts millions of visitors each year, the city of Flagstaff and towns of Williams and Tusayan abound in accommodations and restaurants catering to canyon-bound travelers. North of the Grand Canyon and bordering on southern Utah lies the Arizona Strip, which is the most remote and untraveled region of the state. The Grand Canyon acts as a natural boundary between this region and the rest of the state, and the lack of paved roads and towns keeps away all but the most dedicated explorers. The newly designated Grand Canyon–Parashant National Monument lies at the western end of the Arizona Strip.

The Four Corners The point where Arizona, Utah, Colorado, and New Mexico come together is the only place in the United States where four states share a common boundary. The Four Corners area of Arizona is almost entirely Hopi and Navajo reservation land. This high-plateau region of spectacular canyons and towering mesas and buttes includes Canyon de Chelly, the Painted Desert, the Petrified Forest, and Monument Valley.

Eastern Arizona's High Country Comprised of the Mogollon Rim region and the White Mountains, this area is a summertime escape valve for residents of the lowland desert areas, and as such abounds with mountain cabins and summer homes. Most of this high country is covered with ponderosa pine forests and is laced with trout streams and dotted with fishing lakes. Although this region comes into its own in summer, it also sees some winter visitation due to the fact that it has the best ski area in the state. The Sunrise Park Resort ski area is on the White Mountain Apache Indian Reservation, which covers a large chunk of the region.

Tucson Located just over 100 miles south of Phoenix, Tucson is Arizona's second most populous metropolitan area and is home to numerous resorts and golf courses. With mountain ranges rising in all directions, this city seems more in touch with its natural surroundings than Phoenix, though traffic congestion and sprawl also plague Tucson. The city's main attractions include Saguaro National Park and the Arizona-Sonora Desert Museum.

Southern Arizona Southern Arizona is a region of great contrasts, from desert lowlands to mountain "islands" to vast grassy plains. Mile-high elevations give the southeastern corner of the state one of the most temperate climates in the world. The temperate climate has attracted lots of retirees, but it also brings in rare birds (and birders) and helps support a small wine industry. The western part of southern Arizona is one of the least visited corners of the state, in part because much of this area is an air force bombing range. You will however, find Organ Pipe National Monument out this way (wedged between the vast Cabeza Prieta National Wildlife Refuge and the Papago Indian Reservation). Tucson is at the northern edge of this region (and is not so temperate), but otherwise there are few towns of any size. However, there are a couple of interesting historic towns—Bisbee and Tuba—that have become artists' communities.

Western Arizona Although Arizona is a landlocked state, its western region is bordered by hundreds of miles of lakeshore that were created by the damming of the Colorado River. Consequently, the area has come to be known as Arizona's West Coast. Despite the fact that the low-lying lands of this region are among the hottest places in Arizona (and the warmest in winter), Arizona's West Coast is a popular summer destination with budget-conscious desert denizens. College students and families come almost exclusively for the water-skiing, fishing, and other .

2 Visitor Information & Money

VISITOR INFORMATION

For statewide travel information, contact the **Arizona Office of Tourism,** 2702 N. Third St., Suite 4015, Phoenix, AZ 85004 (© **800/842-8257** or 602/230-7733; www.arizonaguide. com). Nearly every city and town in Arizona has either a tourism office or a chamber of commerce that can also provide you with information. See the individual chapters for information on how to contact these sources.

If you're a member of the **American Automobile Association (AAA),** remember that you can get a map and guidebook covering Arizona and New Mexico. You can also request the club's free *Southwestern CampBook,* which includes campgrounds in Arizona, Utah, Colorado, and New Mexico, by calling your local AAA chapter.

MONEY

What will a vacation in Arizona cost? That depends on your comfort needs. If you drive an RV or carry a tent, you can get by very inexpensively and find a place to stay almost anywhere in the state. If you don't mind staying in motels that date from the Great Depression and can sleep on a sagging mattress, you can stay for less money in Arizona than almost anyplace else in the United States (under $30 a night for a double). On the other hand, you can easily spend several hundred dollars a day on a room at one of the state's world-class resorts. If you're looking to stay in clean, modern motels at interstate highway off-ramps, expect to pay $45 to $65 a night for a double room in most places.

It's never a problem to find an ATM when you're on the road. Throughout the state, the Star, Cirrus, and Plus networks are widely available, so you can get cash through these networks as well as with a major credit card as you travel. If you have trouble finding an ATM, call (C) **800/424-7787** for Cirrus locations, or (C) **800/843-7587** for Plus locations. Expect to pay a $1.50 service fee at most ATMs in the state.

Some people still prefer the security of traveler's checks, which are accepted at hotels, motels, restaurants, and most stores in major cities and tourist destinations. Call **American Express** ((C) **800/221-7282**) for more information.

3 When to Go

Arizona is a year-round destination, although people head to different parts of the state at different times of the year. In Phoenix, Tucson, and other parts of the desert, the high season runs from October to mid-May, with the highest hotel rates in effect during January and February. At the Grand Canyon, summer is the busy season.

The all-around best times to visit are in spring and autumn, when temperatures are cool in the mountains and warm in the desert, but without extremes (although you shouldn't be surprised to get a bit of snow as late as Memorial Day in the mountains and thunderstorms in the desert in August and September). These are also good times to save money because summer rates are in effect at the desert resorts, and the crowds aren't as dense at the Grand Canyon. This period sometimes coincides with the spring wildflower season, which begins in midspring and extends until April and May, when the tops of saguaro cacti become covered with waxy white blooms.

If for some reason you happen to be visiting the desert in July or August, be prepared for sudden thunderstorms. These storms often cause flash floods that make many roads briefly impassable. Signs warning motorists not to enter low areas when flooded are meant to be taken very seriously.

Also, don't even think about venturing into narrow slot canyons, such as Antelope Canyon near Page or the West Fork of Oak Creek Canyon, if there's any chance of a storm anywhere in the region. Rain falling miles away can send flash floods roaring down narrow canyons with no warning. In 1997, several hikers died when they were caught in a flash flood in Antelope Canyon.

One more thing to keep in mind: Sedona is just high enough that it actually gets cold in the winter—sometimes it even snows. So if you're looking for sunshine and time by the pool, book your Sedona vacation for sometime other than in the winter.

CLIMATE

The first thing you should know is that the desert can be cold as well as

ⓒ Money-Saving Tips

Planning a winter vacation in Arizona can easily induce sticker shock. However, there are a few sun-country options for vacationers on a tight budget.

- If you don't absolutely have to have all the amenities of a big resort, there are endless chain-motel options in the Phoenix and Tucson areas. Alternatively, you can get a bit more for your money if you head to such smaller towns as Wickenburg, Bullhead City, Lake Havasu City, and Yuma. If you absolutely have to be in the Phoenix or Tucson area, head for the suburbs. The farther you drive from the resort areas, the more you can save.

- You can save a substantial amount on hotel rates by joining the American Automobile Association (AAA). The savings on just a few nights' lodging can cover the cost of the annual AAA membership.

- Ask when hotel rates drop for the summer and schedule your trip for right after the rates go down (or just before they go back up in the fall). Many resorts also have a short discounted season just before Christmas.

- Pick up rental cars somewhere other than the Phoenix or Tucson airports. Rental-car companies operating inside the airport charge up to 25% in taxes and service fees. Taxes and service charges outside the airport are about half as much.

hot. Although winter is the prime tourist season in Phoenix and Tucson, night temperatures can be below freezing and days can sometimes be too cold for sunning or swimming. Although there can be several days of cool, cloudy, and even rainy weather in January and February, on the whole, winters in Arizona are positively delightful.

In the winter, sun seekers flock to the deserts, where temperatures average in the high 60s by day. In the summer, when desert temperatures top 110°F, the mountains of eastern and northern Arizona are pleasantly warm, with daytime averages in the low 80s. Yuma is one of the desert communities where winter temperatures are the highest in the state, while Prescott and Sierra Vista, in the 4,000- to 6,000-foot elevation range, claim two of the most temperate climates in the world.

Phoenix's Average Temperatures (°F/°C) & Days of Rain

	Jan	Feb	Mar	Apr	May	June	July	Aug	Sept	Oct	Nov	Dec
Avg. High	65/18	69/20	75/24	84/29	93/34	102/39	105/40	102/39	98/37	88/31	75/24	66/19
Avg. Low	38/3	41/5	45/7	52/11	60/15	68/20	78/25	76/24	69/20	57/14	45/7	39/4
Days of Rain	4	4	3	2	1	1	4	5	3	3	2	4

Flagstaff's Average Temperatures (°F/°C) & Days of Rain

	Jan	Feb	Mar	Apr	May	June	July	Aug	Sept	Oct	Nov	Dec
Avg. High	41/5	44/7	48/9	57/14	67/19	76/24	81/27	78/25	74/23	63/17	51/10	43/6
Avg. Low	14/–10	17/–8	20/–7	27/–3	34/1	40/4	50/10	49/9	41/5	31/–0.6	22/–6	16/–9
Days of Rain	7	6	8	6	3	3	12	11	6	5	5	6

ARIZONA CALENDAR OF EVENTS

January

Fiesta Bowl Classic, Sun Devil Stadium, Tempe. College football classic. Tickets go on sale in the fall. For information, call ✆ **800/635-5748** or 480/350-0900. January 1.

Phoenix Open Golf Tournament, Scottsdale. Prestigious PGA golf tournament at the Tournament Players Club. Phone ✆ **480/870-0163** for details. Mid- to late January.

Wings Over Willcox, Willcox. Birding tours, workshops, and, of course, watching the sandhill cranes at the Willcox sewage recycling ponds. Call ✆ **520/384-2272.** Third weekend in January.

February

Parada del Sol Parade and Rodeo, Scottsdale. The state's longest horse-drawn parade, plus a street dance and rodeo. Call ✆ **480/502-1880.** Early February.

World Championship Hoop Dance, Phoenix. Native American dancers from around the nation take part in this colorful competition held at the Heard Museum. For details, call ✆ **602/252-8840.** Early February.

Tubac Festival of the Arts, Tubac. Exhibits by North American artists and craftspeople. Call ✆ **520/398-2371.** Early to mid-February.

Gem, Mineral & Fossil Showcase of Tucson. Dealers from all over the world converge at more than two dozen locations around Tucson, selling everything from precious stones to dinosaur eggs; although some sell only wholesale, many offer goods to the public as well. Call ✆ **520/624-1817.** First 2 weeks of February.

Tucson Gem and Mineral Society Show. This huge show at the Tucson Convention Center offers seminars, museum displays from around the world, and dealers selling just about any kind of rock you can imagine. Call ✆ **520/322-5773** or 520/624-1817. Mid-February.

Arizona Renaissance Festival, Apache Junction. This 16th-century English country fair features costumed participants and tournament jousting. Call ✆ **520/463-2700.** Weekends from early to late February.

O'odham Tash, Casa Grande. One of the largest annual Native American festivals in the country, attracting dozens of tribes that participate in rodeos, arts-and-crafts exhibits, and dance performances. Call ✆ **520/836-4723.** Mid-February.

All-Arabian Horse Show, Scottsdale's Westworld. A celebration of the Arabian horse. For additional information, call ✆ **480/515-1500** or 480/312-6802. Mid- to late February.

Tucson Open. A major stop on the golf tour, held at the Omni Tucson National Golf Resort and Spa. Call ✆ **800/882-7660** or 520/571-0400. Mid- to late February.

La Fiesta de los Vaqueros, Tucson. Cowboy festival and rodeo at the Tucson Rodeo Grounds, including the Tucson Rodeo Parade, the world's largest nonmotorized parade. Call ✆ **520/741-2233.** Late February.

Flagstaff Winterfest. Snowshoeing and cross-country ski tours, sleigh rides, music, and family snow games. For details, call ✆ **800/842-7293** or 520/774-4505. Month of February.

March

Heard Museum Guild Indian Fair, Phoenix. Indian cultural and dance presentations and one of the greatest selections of Native American crafts in the Southwest make this a fascinating festival. The festival entrance fee includes admission to the Heard Museum. Go early to avoid the crowds. Call ✆ **602/ 252-8840.** First weekend in March.

Sedona International Film Festival, Sedona. View various new indie features, documentaries, and animated films before they (it is hoped) get picked up for wider distribution. Phone ✆ **800/780-ARTS** or 520/203-4-TIX, or go to www.sedonaculturalpark.org. First weekend in March.

Franklin Templeton Tennis Classic, Scottsdale. Top names in men's professional tennis, such as Andre Agassi and Pete Sampras, compete in this tournament at the Scottsdale Princess hotel. Call ✆ **480/922-0222.** Early March.

Wiener Dog Nationals, Phoenix. How 'bout those dachshunds? Watch this great low-ridin' action at the Phoenix Greyhound Park. You'll see the greyhounds run, too. Call ✆ **602/273-7181.** Early March.

Chandler Ostrich Festival, Chandler. Give the carnival a miss and head straight for the ostrich races. Although brief, these unusual races are something you've got to see at least once in your life. Call ✆ **480/ 963-4571.** Early to mid-March.

Scottsdale Arts Festival, Scottsdale Mall. This visual and performing-arts festival has free concerts, an art show, and children's events. Phone ✆ **480/994-ARTS.** Second weekend in March.

Wak Pow Wow, Tucson. Tohono O'odham celebration at Mission San Xavier del Bac, featuring many southwestern Native American groups. Call ✆ **520/294-5727** for more information. Mid-March.

Yaqui Easter Lenten Ceremony, Tucson. Religious ceremonies at Old Pasqua Village blending Christian and Yaqui Native American beliefs. Call ✆ **520/791-4609.** Holy Week.

Territorial Days, Tombstone. Tombstone's birthday celebration. For more information, call ✆ **800/ 457-3423.** Late March.

Welcome Back Buzzards, Superior. A flock of turkey buzzards arrives annually at the Boyce Thompson Arboretum to roost in the eucalyptus trees, and this festival celebrates their arrival. Call ✆ **520/689-2723.** Late March.

The Tradition, Scottsdale. This Senior PGA tournament at Cochise Course at Desert Mountain hosts the big names. Call ✆ **480/595-4070.** Late March to early April.

April

Maricopa County Fair, Phoenix. The Arizona State Fairgrounds hosts a midway, agricultural and livestock exhibits, and entertainment. For details, phone ✆ **602/ 252-0717.** Mid-April.

Tucson International Mariachi Conference. Mariachi bands from all over the world come to compete before standing-room-only crowds. Call ✆ **520/884-9920,** ext. 243. Mid- to late April.

Golf & Celebrity Tennis Tournament, Tucson. One of the largest celebrity tennis events in the United States, held at the Randolph Tennis Center and Starr Pass. Phone ✆ **520/623-6165.** Mid- to late April.

Plaza Suite, Tucson. Open-air jazz concerts at St. Philip's Plaza. For details, call the Tucson Jazz Society at ✆ **520/743-3399.** Sundays in April and May, September and October.

May

Cinco de Mayo, Tucson, Phoenix, and other cities. Celebration of the Mexican victory over the French in a famous 1862 battle, complete with food, music, and dancing. Call ℭ 602/279-4669 for details on the festivities in Phoenix; call ℭ 520/292-9326 for information on the celebration in Tucson's Kennedy Park. Around May 5.

Waila Festival, Tucson. A festival celebrating the social dances of the Tohono O'odham nation, featuring "chicken scratch" music—a kind of polka—and native foods. Call ℭ 520/628-5774. Mid-May.

Sedona Chamber Music Festival, Sedona. Chamber music is performed by groups from around the world at various venues. Phone ℭ 520/204-2415, or go to www.chambermusicsedona.org. Mid-May.

Phippen Western Art Show and Sale, Prescott. This is the premier Western-art sale. For information, call ℭ 520/778-1385. Memorial Day weekend.

Wyatt Earp Days, Tombstone. Gunfight reenactments in memory of the shootout at the O.K. Corral. Call ℭ 800/457-3423 for details. Late May.

Enduring Creations: Masterworks of Native American Art, Flagstaff. The finest Hopi, Zuni, Navajo, and Pai art and craft work is offered for sale in changing exhibits at the Museum of Northern Arizona. Call ℭ 520/774-5213. Ongoing event from late May to mid-September.

June

Juneteenth Festival, Tucson. Festival in Kennedy Park celebrating African American Independence Day, including food, a fashion show, and a crafts marketplace. Call ℭ 520/791-4355. Third weekend in June.

Annual Hopi Artists Exhibition, Flagstaff. Exhibition and sale at the Museum of Northern Arizona, including cultural events. Call ℭ 520/774-5213. Late June to early July.

July

Sidewalk Egg-frying Challenge, Oatman. In the ghost town of Oatman, located near one of the hottest places on earth, contestants use their own devices such as mirrors to fry an egg in 15 minutes (eggs are provided!). Phone ℭ 520/763-5885. July 4 at high noon.

Independence Day. For information on fireworks displays in Phoenix, call ℭ 602/534-FEST; in Tucson, phone ℭ 520/624-1817. In other areas, contact the local chamber of commerce. July 4.

Prescott Frontier Days, Prescott. This is the oldest rodeo in the United States. Call ℭ 800/266-7534 or 520/445-3103. First week of July.

Annual Navajo Artists Exhibition, Flagstaff. Exhibition and sale at the Museum of Northern Arizona, including cultural events. Call ℭ 520/774-5213. Last weekend in July or first weekend in August.

August

Payson Rodeo, Payson. The second of Arizona's rodeos claiming to be the world's oldest. For details, call ℭ 800/672-9766 or 520/474-4515. Mid-August.

Southwest Wings Birding Festival, Sierra Vista. Spotting hummingbirds and looking for owls and bats keep participants busy. Includes lectures and field trips. Phone ℭ 800/288-3861 or 520/459-EVNT. Mid-August.

Arizona Cowboy Poets' Gathering, Prescott. Not just traditional and contemporary poetry, but yodeling and storytelling that focuses on the cowboy lifestyle. Call ℂ **520/445-3122.** Third weekend in August.

La Fiesta de San Agustín, Tucson. Celebration to honor the patron saint of Tucson, with a Mexican fiesta theme. Call ℂ **520/762-5806.** Late August.

September

Plaza Suite, Tucson. Open-air jazz concerts at St. Philip's Plaza. For details, call the Tucson Jazz Society at ℂ **520/743-3399.** Sundays in September and October, April and May.

Navajo Nation Fair, Window Rock. A very large fair featuring traditional music and dancing by North American tribes. Call ℂ **520/871-6478** or 520/871-6703. Early September.

Harvesting of the Vine Festival, Elgin. Celebrate the harvest by stomping on grapes, listening to music, and, of course, sipping some wine. Call ℂ **520/455-9309.** Last weekend in September.

State Championship Old Time Fiddler's Contest, Payson. Fiddlers from around Arizona try their best to out-fiddle each other, along with clogging and buck dancing. Call ℂ **800/6-PAYSON** or 520/474-4515. Last weekend in September.

Jazz on the Rocks, Sedona. Open-air jazz festival held in the red rocks. For details, call ℂ **520/282-1985.** Late September.

October

Sedona Arts Festival, Sedona. One of the better arts festivals in the state. For information, phone ℂ **800/288-7336** or 520/204-9456. Mid-October.

Rodeo Showdown, Phoenix. Top rodeo stars compete in this world finals rodeo at the America West Arena. Call ℂ **800/946-9711.** Mid- to late October.

Fiesta de los Chiles, Tucson. Lots of hot chiles, served in dishes from around the world, along with crafts and music. Call ℂ **520/326-9686.** Mid- to late October.

Helldorado Days, Tombstone. Fashion show of 1880s clothing, tribal dancers, and street entertainment. Call ℂ **800/457-3423.** Third weekend of October.

Arizona State Fair, Phoenix. Rodeos, top-name entertainment, and ethnic food. Phone ℂ **602/252-6771.** Late October to early November.

Annual Cowboy Artists of America Exhibition, Phoenix. The Phoenix Art Museum hosts the most prestigious and best-known Western-art show in the region. Call ℂ **602/257-1222.** Late October.

November

Thunderbird Balloon Classic, Scottsdale. More than 150 hot-air balloons fill the Arizona sky. Call ℂ **602/978-7330** for details. Early November.

Western Music Festival, Tucson. Concerts and workshops. Phone ℂ **520/743-9794** for more information. Mid-November.

December

Festival of Lights, Sedona. Thousands of luminárias are lit at dusk at the Tlaquepaque Arts and Crafts Village. Call ℂ **800/288-7336** or 520/282-4838. Early December.

Old Town Fall Festival of the Arts, Tempe. Hundreds of artists and artisans, featuring free entertainment and plenty of food, set up along Mill Avenue. Call ℂ **480/967-4877.** Early December.

Luminária Nights, Tucson. A glowing display of holiday lights at the Botanical Gardens. Call © **520/326-9255.** First weekend in December.

Fourth Avenue Street Fair, Tucson. Outdoor arts-and-crafts festival. Phone © **520/624-5004** for information. Early December.

Fiesta Bowl Parade, Phoenix area. Huge, nationally televised parade, featuring floats and marching bands. Phone © **800/635-5748.** December 31.

4 The Active Vacation Planner

Because Arizona is home to the Grand Canyon—the most widely known white-water-rafting spot in the world—the state is known for active, adventure-oriented vacations. For others, Arizona is synonymous with winter golf and tennis. Whichever category of active vacationer you fall into, you'll find information below to help you plan your trip.

BICYCLING With its wide range of climates, Arizona offers good biking somewhere in the state every month of the year. In winter, there's good road biking around Phoenix and Tucson, while from spring through fall, the southeastern corner of the state offers good routes. In summer, the White Mountains (in the eastern part of the state) and Kaibab National Forest (between Flagstaff and Grand Canyon National Park) offer good mountain biking. There's also excellent mountain biking at several Phoenix parks, and Tucson is one of the most bicycle-friendly cities in the country. **Backroads,** 801 Cedar St., Berkeley, CA 94710-1800 (© **800/462-2848** or 510/527-1555; www.backroads.com), offers a 6-day, inn-to-inn mountain-bike trip through the red-rock country of central Arizona. **Western Spirit Cycling,** 478 Mill Creek Dr., Moab, UT 84532 (© **800/845-2453** or 435-259-8732; www.westernspirit. com), offers a number of interesting mountain-bike tours, including trips to both the North and South rims of the Grand Canyon and through the desert south of Tucson.

For information on mountain-bike tours and recommended rides in Phoenix and Tucson, see "Outdoor Pursuits" in chapter 4, "Phoenix, Scottsdale & the Valley of the Sun," and chapter 9, "Tucson." You'll also find recommended rides in the Sedona and Prescott sections of chapter 5, "Central Arizona." If you plan to do much mountain-biking around the state, pick up a copy of *Fat Tire Tales and Trails,* by Cosmic Ray. This little book of great rides is both fun to read and fun to use; it's available in bike shops around the state.

BIRD-WATCHING Arizona is a birder's bonanza. Down in the southeastern corner of the state, many species found primarily south of the border reach the northern limits of their territories. Combine this with several mountains that rise like islands from the desert and provide an appropriate habitat for hundreds of species, and you have some of the best bird-watching in the country. Birding hot spots include Ramsey Canyon Preserve (known for its many species of hummingbirds), Cave Creek Canyon (nesting site for elegant trogons), Patagonia-Sonoita Creek Sanctuary (home to 22 species of fly-catchers, kingbirds, and phoebes, as well as Montezuma quails), Madera Canyon (another "mountain island" that attracts many of the same species seen at Ramsey Canyon and Sonoita Creek), Buenos Aires National Wildlife Refuge (home to masked bobwhite quail and gray hawks), and the sewage ponds outside the town of Willcox (known for its avocets and sandhill cranes). For further information on these birding spots, see chapter 10, "Southern Arizona." To find out which birds have been spotted lately, call the **Tucson Audubon Society's Bird Report** (© 520/798-1005).

Serious birders who want to be sure of adding lots of rare birds to their life lists may want to visit southeastern Arizona on a guided tour. These are available through **High Lonesome Ecotours** (© 800/743-2668; www. hilonesome.com), which charges about $1,200 per person for a 5-day trip.

CANOEING/KAYAKING Okay, so maybe these sports don't jump to mind when you think of the desert, but there are indeed rivers and lakes in the desert (and they happen to be some of the best places to see wildlife). By far the most memorable place for a flat-water kayak tour is on Lake Powell. **Wilderness Inquiry,** 808 14th Ave. SE, Minneapolis, MN 55414-1516 (© 800/728-0719 or 612/676-9400; www.wildernessinquiry.org), offers several 6-day trips on the lake each year in spring and fall. **Permagrin River Adventures,** 6331 S. College St., Tempe, AZ 85283 (© 480/755-1924; www.go-permagrin.com), also offers various canoeing and kayaking courses.

There are also a couple of companies that rent canoes and offer trips on the Colorado River south of Lake Mead. See chapter 11, "Western Arizona," for details.

FISHING The fishing scene in Arizona is as diverse as the landscape. Large and small lakes around the state offer excellent fishing for warm-water game fish such as largemouth, smallmouth, and striped bass. Good trout fishing can be found up on the Mogollon Rim and in the White Mountains there, as well as in the Grand Canyon, and the more easily accessible sections of the free-running Colorado River between Glen Canyon Dam and Lees Ferry.

Fishing licenses for nonresidents are available for 1 day, 5 days, 4 months, and 1 year. Various special stamps and licenses may also apply. Nonresident fishing-license fees range from $12.50 for a 1-day license (valid for trout) to $51.50 for a 1-year license ($49.50 additional for a trout stamp). Also keep in mind that if you're heading for an Indian reservation, you'll have to get a special permit for that reservation. For information, contact the **Arizona Game and Fish Department,** 2222 W. Greenway Rd., Phoenix, AZ 85021 (© 602/942-3000; www.azgfd.com).

GOLF For many of Arizona's winter visitors, golf is the main attraction. The state's hundreds of golf courses range from easy public courses to PGA championship links that have challenged the best.

In Phoenix and Tucson, greens fees, like room rates, are seasonal. In the popular winter months, fees at resort courses range from about $80 to $175 for 18 holes, although this usually includes a mandatory golf-cart rental. In summer, fees often drop to less than half this amount. Almost all resorts also offer special golf packages as well.

For information on some of the state's top courses, see "Hot Links," below. For more information on golfing in Arizona, contact the **Arizona Golf Association,** 7226 N. 16th St., Suite 200, Phoenix, AZ 85020 (© 800/458-8484 in Arizona, or 602/944-3035; www.azgolf.org), which publishes a directory ($5) listing all the courses in the state. *Golf Arizona,* 16508 Laser Dr., Suite 104A., Fountain Hills, AZ 85268 (© 800/942-5444; www.golf-arizona.com), also publishes a guide on where to golf in Arizona. You can also pick up a copy of the *Tucson and Southern Arizona Golf*

Guide or *Greater Phoenix Golf Guide* at visitor bureaus, golf courses, and many hotels and resorts.

HIKING/BACKPACKING Despite its reputation as a desert state, a large percentage of Arizona is forestland, and within these forests are wilderness areas and countless miles of hiking trails. In northern Arizona, there are good day hikes in Grand Canyon National Park, in the San Francisco Peaks north of Flagstaff, near Page and Lake Powell, and in Navajo National Monument. In the Phoenix area, popular day hikes include the trails up Camelback Mountain and Squaw Peak and the many trails in South Mountain Park. In the Tucson area, there are good hikes on Mount Lemmon and in Saguaro National Park, Sabino Canyon, and Catalina State Park. In the southern part of the state, there are good day hikes in Chiricahua National Monument, Coronado National Forest, in the Nature Conservancy's Ramsey Canyon Preserve and Patagonia-Sonoita Creek Sanctuary, in Cochise Stronghold, and in Organ Pipe National Monument.

The state's two most popular overnight backpack trips are the hike down to Phantom Ranch at the bottom of the Grand Canyon and the hike into Havasu Canyon, a side canyon of the Grand Canyon. Another popular multiday backpack trip is through Paria Canyon, beginning in Utah and ending in Arizona at Lees Ferry. There are also overnight backpacking opportunities in the San Francisco Peaks north of Flagstaff and in the White Mountains of eastern Arizona.

Guided backpacking trips of different durations and levels of difficulty are offered by the **Grand Canyon Field Institute,** P.O. Box 399, Grand Canyon, AZ 86023 (*©*520/ 638-2485; www.grandcanyon.org/ fieldinstitute); and **Grand Canyon Trail Guides,** P.O. Box 87, Grand Canyon, AZ 86023 (*©* **888/283-3194** or 520/638-3194; http:// grandcanyontrailguides.com). **Backroads,** 801 Cedar St., Berkeley, CA 94710-1800 (*©* **800/462-2848** or 510/527-1555; www.backroads.com), better known for its bike trips, also offers an 8-day walking/hiking trip to Grand Canyon, Brice, and Zion national parks.

HORSEBACK RIDING/WESTERN ADVENTURES All over Arizona, there are stables where you can saddle up for short rides. Among the more scenic spots for riding are the Grand Canyon, Monument Valley Navajo Tribal Park, Canyon de Chelly National Monument, the red-rock country around Sedona, Phoenix's South Mountain Park, at the foot of the Superstition Mountains east of Phoenix, and at the foot of the Santa Catalina Mountains outside Tucson. See the individual chapters that follow for listings of riding stables; see below for information on overnight guided horseback rides.

Among the most popular guided adventures in Arizona are the mule rides down into the Grand Canyon. These trips vary in length from 1 to 2 days; for reservations and more information, call **Amfac Parks & Resorts** (*©* **303/297-2757**). Be advised, however, that you'll need to make mule-ride reservations many months in advance. If at the last minute (5 days or fewer from the day you want to ride) you decide you want to go on a mule trip into the Grand Canyon, contact the **Bright Angel Transportation Desk,** at Grand Canyon (*©* **520/ 638-3283**), on the chance there might be space available.

It's also possible to do overnight horseback rides and cattle drives. For information, contact **Don Donnelly Stables,** 6010 S. Kings Ranch Rd., Gold Canyon (*©* **800/346-4403** or 480/ 982-7822; www.dondonnelly.com),

Hot Links

You don't have to be a hotshot golfer to get all heated up over the prospect of a few rounds of golf in Arizona. Combine near-perfect golf weather most of the year with great views and some very unique challenges, and you've got all the makings of a great game. Phoenix and Tucson are well known as winter golf destinations, but the state also offers golf throughout the year at higher-altitude courses in such places as Prescott, Flagstaff, and the White Mountains.

State legislation aimed at conserving water limits the acreage that Arizona golf courses can irrigate, which has given the state some of the most distinctive and difficult courses in the country. These desert or "target" courses are characterized by minimal fairways surrounded by natural desert landscapes. You might find yourself teeing off over the tops of cacti or searching for your ball amid boulders and mesquite. If your ball comes to rest in the desert, you can play the ball where it lies or, with a one-stroke penalty, drop it within two club lengths of the nearest point of grass (but no nearer the hole).

Keep in mind that resort courses and daily fee public courses are not cheap. For most of the year, greens fees, which include cart rentals, range from around $80 to $175 or more. Municipal courses usually have greens fees of less than $40 for 18 holes, with cart rental costing extra (usually about $20).

It might not seem so initially, but summer is really a good time to visit many of Arizona's golf resorts. No, they don't have air-conditioned golf carts or indoor courses, but in summer, greens fees can be less than half what they are in winter. How does $37 for a round on the famous Gold Course at the Wigwam Golf and Country Club sound?

The Phoenix/Scottsdale area, known as the Valley of the Sun, has the greatest concentration of golf courses in the state. Whether you're looking to play one of the area's challenging top-rated resort courses or an economical-but-fun municipal course, you'll find plenty of choices.

For spectacular scenery at a resort course, it's just plain impossible to beat the **Boulders** (© 480/488-9028), located north of Scottsdale in the town of Carefree. Elevated tee boxes beside giant balanced boulders are enough to distract anyone's concentration. Way over on the east side of the valley in Apache Junction, the **Gold Canyon Golf Resort** (© 480/982-9449) has what have been rated as three of the best holes in the state: the second, third, and fourth holes on the Dinosaur Mountain course. Jumping over to Litchfield Park, on the far west side of the valley, you'll find the **Wigwam Golf and Country Club** (© 623/935-3811) and its three 18-hole courses; the Gold Course here is legendary. Other noteworthy resort courses in the area include the links at the **Phoenician** (© 480/423-2449), which mix traditional and desert-style holes. The **Gainey Ranch Golf Club,** at the Hyatt Regency Scottsdale Resort at

which does overnight horseback trips in Monument Valley, the White Mountains, and the Superstition Mountains, among other places; or **Arizona Trail Tours** (© 800/477-0615 or 520/281-4122; www.aztrailtours.com),

Gainey Ranch (✆ **480/951-0022**), offers three decidedly different 9-hole courses: the Dunes, the Arroyo, and the Lakes courses, each with its own set of challenges; however, you must be a guest of the resort to play here. The semiprivate **Troon North Golf Club** (✆ **480/585-5300**), a course that seems only barely carved out of raw desert, garners the most local accolades (and charges some of the highest greens fees in the state). If you want to swing where the pros do, beg, borrow, or steal a tee time on the Stadium Course at the **Tournament Players Club (TPC) of Scottsdale** (✆ **480/585-3600**). The area's favorite municipal course is the **Papago Golf Course** (✆ **602/275-8428**), which has a killer 17th hole.

In recent years, Tucson has been giving the Valley of the Sun plenty of competition when it comes to great golf. Among the city's resort courses, the Mountain Course at the **Ventana Canyon Golf and Racquet Club** (✆ **520/577-1400**) is legendary, especially the spectacular 107-yard, par-3 third hole. Likewise, the eighth hole on the Sunrise Course at **El Conquistador Country Club** (✆ **520/544-1800**) is among the most memorable par-3 holes in Tucson. If you want to play where the pros do, book a room at the **Omni Tucson National Golf Resort and Spa** (✆ **520/297-2271**), home of the Tucson Open. **Randolph North** (✆ **520/ 791-4161**), Tucson's best municipal course, is the site of the city's annual LPGA tournament. The **Silverbell Municipal Course** (✆ **520/791-5235**) boasts a bear of a par-5 17th hole.

Courses worth trying in other parts of the state include the 18-hole course at **Rancho de los Caballeros** (✆ **520/684-2704**), a luxury ranch resort outside Wickenburg. *Golf Digest* has rated its course one of Arizona's top 10. For concentration-taxing scenery, few courses compare with the **Sedona Golf Resort** (✆ **520/284-9355**), which has good views of the red rocks; try it at sunset. In mile-high Prescott, the **Antelope Hills Golf Club** (✆ **520/776-7888**) offers two 18-hole courses that provide a respite from the summer heat in the lowlands. Even higher and cooler in summer, the **Alpine Country Club** (✆ **520/339-4944**), in the White Mountains, is one of the highest-elevation golf courses in the country. South of Tucson near Nogales, the **Rio Rico Resort and Country Club** (✆ **520/281-8567**) offers a challenging back nine. Over along the Colorado River, there are a couple of memorable courses. Lake Havasu City's **London Bridge Golf Club** (✆ **520/855-2719**) offers a view of, you guessed it, the London Bridge. For more dramatic views, check out the **Emerald Canyon Golf Course** (✆ **520/667-3366**), a municipal course in Parker that plays up and down small canyons and offers the sort of scenery usually associated only with the most expensive desert resort courses.

One last tip: If your ball should happen to land in the coils of a rattlesnake, consider it lost and take your penalty. Rattlesnakes make lousy tees.

which offers a 4-day trip through Coronado National Forest in southern Arizona.

HOT-AIR BALLOONING For much of the year, the desert has the perfect environment for hot-air ballooning—cool, still air and wide-open spaces. Consequently, there are dozens of hot-air balloon companies operating across the state. Most are in Phoenix (see p. 114) and Tucson (see p. 344), but several others operate near Sedona (see p. 172), which is by far the most picturesque spot in the state for a balloon ride. See the individual chapters for specific information.

HOUSEBOATING With the Colorado River turned into a long string of lakes, houseboat vacations are a natural in Arizona. Although this doesn't have to be an active vacation, fishing, hiking, and swimming are usually part of a houseboat stay. Rentals are available on Lake Powell, Lake Mead, Lake Mohave, and Lake Havasu. However, the canyon-lands scenery of Lake Powell makes it the hands-down best spot for a houseboat vacation—reserve well in advance for a summer trip. No prior experience (or license) is necessary, and plenty of hands-on instruction is provided before you leave the marina. See chapter 7, "The Four Corners Region," and chapter 11, "Western Arizona," for more information on houseboat rentals.

In 2001, certain houseboats were linked to numerous deaths due to carbon monoxide poisoning. Due to design flaws, some boats trapped carbon monoxide from the boat exhaust in an area at the back of the boat where swimmers and sunbathers often gather. Once the design flaw was recognized, actions were taken to prevent such accidental deaths from happening in the future. However, you should be sure to ask about the safety of any boat you rent.

SKIING Although Arizona is better known as a desert state, it does have plenty of mountains and even a few ski areas. The two biggest and best ski areas are **Arizona Snowbowl** (© 520/779-1951; www.arizonasnowbowl.com), outside Flagstaff, and **Sunrise Park** (© 800/772-7669 or 520/735-7669; www.sunriseskipark.com), on the Apache Reservation outside the town of McNary in the White Mountains. Snowbowl is more popular because of the ease of the drive from Phoenix and its proximity to good lodging and dining options in Flagstaff. Although Snowbowl has more vertical feet of skiing, Sunrise is our favorite Arizona ski area because it offers almost twice as many runs and the same snow conditions. Both ski areas offer rentals and lessons. When it's a good snow year, Tucsonians head up to **Mount Lemmon Ski Valley** (© 520/576-1321, or 520/576-1400 for snow report), the southernmost ski area in the United States. Snows here aren't as reliable as they are farther north.

In a good snow year, cross-country skiers can find plenty of snow-covered forest roads outside Flagstaff (there's also a Nordic center at Arizona Snowbowl), at Sunrise Park outside the town of McNary, at the South Rim of the Grand Canyon, in the White Mountains around Greer and Alpine, outside Payson on the Mogollon Rim, and on Mount Lemmon outside Flagstaff.

TENNIS Resorts all over Arizona have tennis courts; after golf, this is the most popular winter sport in the desert. Many resorts require you to wear traditional tennis attire and don't include court time in the room rates. Although there may be better courts in the state, none can match the views you'll have from those at Enchantment Resort, outside Sedona. Just don't let the scenery ruin your game. Other noteworthy tennis-oriented resorts include, in the Phoenix/Scottsdale area, the Phoenician, the Radisson

The Arizona Trail

While it sounds as though it could have been a movie starring John Wayne, the Arizona Trail is actually an ambitious plan to build a border-to-border trail across the state of Arizona from Utah to Mexico. The trail, which will be 750 miles long and link many existing trails, will be open for nonmotorized travel only. Hikers, mountain bikers, horseback riders, and cross-country skiers will all be able to enjoy various sections of the trail, which will at times cross through designated wilderness areas (closed to mountain bikes).

Connecting alpine meadows and desert arroyos, free-flowing rivers and man-made reservoirs, ponderosa pine forests and stands of saguaros, the trail will cross through the seven life zones and many landscapes that make up Arizona. As it meanders across the state, the trail takes in some of the most spectacular scenery in the Southwest, including the Grand Canyon, the San Francisco Peaks, the Mogollon Rim, and the Santa Catalina Mountains. For more information, contact the **Arizona Trail Association,** P.O. Box 36736, Phoenix, AZ 85067-6736 (© **602/252-4794;** www.aztrail.org).

Resort Scottsdale, Copperwynd Country Club & Inn, the Fairmont Scottsdale Princess, the Pointe South Mountain Resort, and the Pointe Hilton Tapatio Cliffs Resort, and, in Tucson, the Lodge at Ventana Canyon, the Sheraton El Conquistador Resort & Country Club, the Westin La Paloma, the Westward Look Resort, and the Omni Tucson National Golf Resort & Spa.

WHITE-WATER RAFTING The desert doesn't support a lot of roaring rivers, but with the white water in the Grand Canyon you don't need too many other choices. Rafting the Grand Canyon is the dream of nearly every white-water enthusiast—if it's one of your dreams, plan well ahead. Companies and trips are limited, and they tend to fill up early. For a discussion and list of companies that run trips

down the canyon, see chapter 6, "The Grand Canyon & Northern Arizona."

For 1-day rafting trips on the Colorado below the Grand Canyon, contact **Hualapai River Runners** (© **800/622-4409** or 520/769-2219; www.hualapaitours.com). For a half- or full-day float on the Colorado above the Grand Canyon, contact **Wilderness River Adventures** (© **800/ 528-6154** or 520/645-3279), which runs trips from the Glen Canyon Dam to Lees Ferry.

Daylong and multiday rafting trips are also available on the upper Salt River east of Phoenix. **Far Flung Adventures** (© **800/231-7238** or 520/425-7272; www.farflung.com), **Sun Country Rafting** (© **800/272-3353** or 602/ 493-9011), and **Mild to Wild Rafting** (© **800/567-6745**) all run trips of varying lengths down this river (conditions permitting).

5 Educational & Volunteer Vacations

Arizona has a number of opportunities for those wanting to combine a vacation with an educational or volunteer experience.

If you'd like to turn a trip to the Grand Canyon into an educational experience, contact the **Grand Canyon Field Institute,** P.O. Box 399, Grand Canyon, AZ 86023 (✆ **520/638-2485;** www.grandcanyon.org/field institute), which offers a variety of programs from early spring to late fall. Offerings include rim-based day hikes, photography and painting classes, backpacking trips for women, llama treks, archaeology trips, and plenty of guided hikes and backpacking trips with a natural-history or ecological slant.

Learning Expeditions, a program run by the **Arizona State Museum,** occasionally offers scholar-led archaeological tours, including a trip to Navajo and Hopi country. For information, contact the marketing department at the Arizona State Museum, P.O. Box 210026, Tucson, AZ 85721 (✆ **520/626-8381;** www.statemuseum.arizona.edu). The **Museum of Northern Arizona**, 3101 N. Fort Valley Rd., Flagstaff, AZ 86001 (✆ **520/774-5211,** ext. 220; www.musnaz.org), offers educational backpacking, river-rafting, and van tours primarily in the Colorado Plateau in northern Arizona in a program called Ventures. Trips range from several days to more than a week.

The **Nature Conservancy,** 1510 E. Ft. Lowell Rd., Tucson, AZ 85719 (✆ **520/622-3861;** www.tnc.org), is a nonprofit organization dedicated to the global preservation of natural diversity. The Conservancy accomplishes this goal by identifying and purchasing land that is home to rare plants, animals, and natural communities. The organization has several preserves in Arizona, seven of which are open to the public for hiking, bird-watching, and nature study and to which it operates educational field trips of 1 to 4 days. Information on overnight accommodations, trips, and membership is available by phone or online.

If you enjoy the wilderness and want to get more involved in its preservation, consider a Sierra Club Service Trip. These trips are for the purpose of building, restoring, and maintaining hiking trails in wilderness areas. It's a lot of work, but a lot of fun as well. For more information, contact the **Sierra Club Outing Department,** 85 Second St., 2nd Floor, San Francisco, CA 94105 (✆ **415/977-5500;** www.sierraclub.org). The Sierra Club also offers hiking, camping, and other sorts of adventure trips to various destinations in Arizona.

You can also join a work crew organized by the **Arizona Trail Association** (✆ **602/252-4794;** www.aztrail.org). These crews spend 1 to 2 days building and maintaining various portions of the Arizona Trail, which will eventually stretch from the Utah state line to the Mexico border.

Another sort of service trip is being offered by the National Park Service. It accepts volunteers to pick up garbage left by thoughtless visitors to Glen Canyon National Recreation Area. In exchange for picking up trash, you'll get to spend 5 days on a houseboat called the Trash Tracker, cruising through the gorgeous canyon lands of Lake Powell. Volunteers must be at least 18 years old and must provide their own food, sleeping bag, and transportation to the marina. For information, contact **Glen Canyon National Recreation Area,** P.O. Box 1507, Page, AZ 86040 (✆ **520/608-6404**).

If you'd like to lend a hand at an archaeological dig, contact the **White Mountain Archaeological Center and Raven Site Ruin,** H.C. 30, St. Johns, AZ 85936 (✆ **520/333-5857;** www.ravensite.com), which is near Springerville on the edge of the White Mountains.

Finally, if you're interested in architecture or the ecology of urban design, you may be interested in helping out on the continued construction of **Arcosanti,** the slow realization of architect Paolo Soleri's dream of a city that merges architecture and ecology.

Located 70 miles north of Phoenix, Arcosanti offers 5-week learning-by-doing workshops. For an application, contact Arcosanti, Attn: Workshop Coordinator, H.C. 74, Box 4136, Mayer, AZ 86333 (© **520/632-7135;** www.arcosanti.org).

6 Health & Insurance

STAYING HEALTHY If you've never been to the desert before, you should be sure to prepare yourself for this harsh environment. No matter what time of year it is, the desert sun is strong and bright. Use sunscreen when you're outdoors—particularly if you're up in the mountains, where the altitude makes sunburn more likely. The bright sun also makes sunglasses a necessity.

Even if you don't feel hot in the desert, the dry air steals moisture from your body, so drink plenty of fluids. You may want to use a body lotion as well. Skin dries out quickly in the desert air.

It's not only the sun that makes the desert a harsh environment. There are poisonous creatures out here, too, but with a little common sense and some precautions you can avoid them. Rattlesnakes are very common in the desert, but your chances of meeting one are slight (except during the mating season in Apr–May)—they tend not to come out in the heat of the day. However, never stick your hand into holes among the rocks in the desert, and look to see where you're going to step before putting your foot down.

Arizona is also home to a large poisonous lizard called the Gila monster. These black-and-orange lizards are far less common than rattlesnakes, and your chances of meeting one are slight.

Although the tarantula has developed a nasty reputation, the tiny black widow is more likely to cause illness. Scorpions are another danger of the desert. Be extra careful when turning over rocks or logs that might harbor either black widows or scorpions.

INSURANCE Before going out and spending money on various sorts of travel insurance, check your existing policies to see if they'll cover you while you're traveling. Make sure your health insurance covers you when you're away from home. Some credit and charge cards offer automatic flight insurance when you buy an airline ticket with that card. These policies insure against death or dismemberment in the case of an airplane crash. Also, check your cards to see if any of them pick up the loss-damage waiver (LDW) when you rent a car. The LDW can run as much as $20 a day and can add 50% or more to the cost of renting a car. Check your automobile insurance policy; it, too, may cover the LDW. If you own a home or have renter's insurance, see if that policy covers off-premises theft and loss. If you're traveling on a tour or have prepaid a large chunk of your travel expenses, you might want to ask your travel agent about trip-cancellation insurance.

If, after checking all your existing insurance policies, you decide that you need additional insurance, reputable issuers of travel insurance include **Travel Guard International,** 1145 Clark St., Stevens Point, WI 54481 (© **800/826-1300** or 877/216-4885; www.travelguard.com), and **Travelex Insurance Services,** 11717 Burt St., Omaha NE 68154 (© **800/228-9792;** www.travelex-insurance.com).

Both companies offer medical, baggage, trip-cancellation or interruption insurance (which includes such circumstances as unforeseen financial defaults of a tour operator or personal sickness), accidental death or dismemberment insurance, and flight accident insurance.

7 Tips for Travelers with Special Needs

FOR TRAVELERS WITH DISABILITIES When making airline reservations, always mention your disability. Airline policies differ regarding wheelchairs and guide dogs. Most hotels now offer wheelchair-accessible accommodations, and some of the larger and more expensive resorts also offer TDD telephones and other amenities for the hearing- and sight-impaired.

A World of Options, a book of resources for travelers with disabilities, covers everything from biking trips to scuba outfitters. It costs $35 ($31.50 for members) and is available from **Mobility International USA,** P.O. Box 10767, Eugene, OR, 97440 (© **541/343-1284,** voice and TDD; www.miusa.org). Annual membership is $35, which includes its biannual newsletter, *Over the Rainbow.*

Travelin' Talk Network, P.O. Box 1796, Wheat Ridge, CO 80034 (© **303/232-2979;** www.travelintalk. net), operates a website for travelers with disabilities, and each month e-mails a newsletter to members ($19.95 for a lifetime membership) with information about discounts, accessible hotels, trip companions, and other traveling tips. Those without Internet access can subscribe and receive two newsletters by mail every other month. Another online newsletter and database, **www.access-able. com,** is operated by the same company and supplies information on trip planning and travel agents that specialize in trips for people with disabilities.

Many of the major car-rental companies now offer hand-controlled cars for drivers with disabilities. Avis can provide such a vehicle at any of its airport locations in the United States with 72-hour advance notice; Hertz requires between 24 and 48 hours of advance notice at most of its locations. **Wheelchair Getaways** (© **800/642-2042;** www.wheelchair-getaways.com) rents specialized vans with wheelchair lifts and other features for travelers with disabilities in about 40 cities across the United States.

Travelers with disabilities might also want to consider joining a tour that caters specifically to them. **Accessible Journeys** (© **800/ TINGLES** or 610/521-0339; www. accessiblejourneys.com), for slow walkers and wheelchair travelers, offers excursions to the Tucson and Phoenix areas. **Wilderness Inquiry** (© **800/728-0719** or 612/676-9400; www.wildernessinquiry.org) offers trips to the Grand Canyon for persons of all abilities.

If you plan to visit many of Arizona's national parks or monuments, take advantage of the **Golden Access Passport,** available at any national park or monument that charges admission. This lifetime pass permits free entry into most national parks and monuments, and is issued free to any U.S. citizen or permanent resident who has been medically certified as disabled or blind. In addition, the pass provides discounts on certain camping and other fees.

FOR GAYS & LESBIANS To get in touch with the Phoenix gay community, contact the **Gay and Lesbian Community Center,** at the Parkway Inn, 8617 N. Black Canyon Hwy., Suite 135 (© **602/265-7283**). At the community center and at gay bars around Phoenix, you can pick up various publications such as *Echo* and *Heat Stroke.* **Wingspan,** Tucson's lesbian, gay, and bisexual community center, is at 300 E. Sixth St. (© **520/ 624-1779**). *Observer* (© **520/622- 7176**) is a local Tucson gay newspaper available at both Wingspan and Antigone Bookstore, 411 N. Fourth Ave. (© **520/792-3715**).

FOR SENIORS When making flight reservations, always mention that you're a senior citizen—many airlines offer discounts. You should also carry some sort of photo ID (driver's license, passport) to avail yourself of senior discounts at attractions, hotels, motels, and on public transportation. One of the best deals in Arizona for seniors is the **Golden Age Passport,** which is available for $10 to U.S. citizens and permanent residents age 62 and older. This federal government pass allows lifetime entrance privileges at most national parks and monuments, and a 50% reduction on federal use fees such as camping. You can apply in person at a national park, national forest, or other location where it's honored; you must show reasonable proof of age.

If you aren't a member of the **American Association of Retired Persons (AARP),** 601 E St. NW, Washington, DC 20049 (© **800/424-3410;** www. aarp.org), you should consider joining. This association provides discounts on many lodgings, car rentals, airfares, and attractions throughout Arizona, although you can sometimes get a similar discount simply by showing your ID.

The Mature Traveler, a monthly newsletter on senior travel, is a valuable resource. It's available by subscription ($32 a year) by calling © **800/460-6676.** *The Book of Deals,* a collection of more than 1,000 senior discounts on airlines, lodging, tours, and attractions around the country; comes free with the newsletter subscription, but is available by itself for $9.95.

Grand Circle Travel, 347 Congress St., Suite 3A, Boston, MA 02210 (© **800/221-2610** or 617/350-7500; www.gct.com), is one of the literally hundreds of travel agencies specializing in vacations for seniors. *But beware:* Many of them are of the tour-bus variety, with free trips thrown in for those who organize groups of 20 or more. Seniors seeking more independent travel should probably consult a regular travel agent. **SAGA International Holidays,** 222 Berkeley St., Boston, MA 02116 (© **800/ 343-0273;** www.sagaholidays.com), offers inclusive tours and cruises for those 50 and older. SAGA also sponsors the more substantial "Road Scholar Tours," which are fun-loving but with an educational bent, and is an agent for Smithsonian Institution tours.

If you'd like to do a bit of studying on vacation in the company of like-minded older travelers, look into **Elderhostel,** 11 Avenue de Lafayette, Boston, MA 02110-1746 (© **877/ 426-8056;** www.elderhostel.org).

8 Getting There

BY PLANE

Arizona is served by many airlines flying to both Phoenix and Tucson from around the United States. Phoenix is the more centrally located of the two airports and is closer to the Grand Canyon. However, if you are planning on exploring the southern part of the state or are going to visit both Phoenix and Tucson, we recommend flying into Tucson, which is a smaller airport and charges lower taxes on its car rentals. If, however, a visit to the Grand Canyon is your only reason for visiting Arizona, you can consider flying into Las Vegas, which sometimes has lower airfares and better car-rental rates.

Phoenix and Tucson are both served by the following airlines:

Aero México	800/237-6639	www.aeromexico.com
Alaska Airlines	800/426-0333	www.alaskaair.com
American	800/433-7300	www.im.aa.com
America West	800/235-9292	www.americawest.com
Continental	800/525-0280	www.continental.com
Delta	800/221-1212	www.delta.com
Northwest/KLM	800/225-2525	www.nwa.com
Shuttle by United	800/748-8853	www.united.com
Southwest	800/435-9792	www.iflyswa.com
United	800/241-6522	www.united.com

The following airlines serve Phoenix but not Tucson:

Frontier	800/432-1359	www.flyfrontier.com
TWA	800/221-2000	www.twa.com
US Airways	800/428-4322	www.usairways.com

Consolidators, also known as bucket shops, are a good place to find low fares. Consolidators buy seats in bulk from the airlines and then sell them back to the public at prices below even the airlines' discounted rates. Their small boxed ads usually run in the Sunday travel section of newspapers. Before you pay, however, ask for a confirmation number from the consolidator and then call the airline itself to confirm your seat. Be prepared to book your ticket with a different consolidator—there are many to choose from—if the airline can't confirm your reservation. Also be aware that such tickets are usually nonrefundable or rigged with stiff cancellation penalties, often as high as 50% to 75% of the ticket price. And when an airline runs a special deal, you won't always do better with a consolidator.

For discount and last-minute bookings, contact **McCord Consumer Direct** (Air for Less) (© **800/ FLY-FACTS** or 800/FLY-ASAP; www. better1.com), which can often get you tickets at significantly less than full fare. **1-800-airfare** (www.1800airfare. com) offers some of the deepest discounts on many airlines and can sometimes provide a next-day ticket. There are also "rebators," such as **Travel Avenue** (© **800/333-3335** or 312/876-1116; www.travelavenue. com), which rebate part of their commissions to you.

BY CAR

The distance to Phoenix from Los Angeles is approximately 369 miles; from San Francisco, 778 miles; from Albuquerque, 455 miles; from Salt Lake City, 660 miles; from Las Vegas, 287 miles; and from Santa Fe, 516 miles.

If you're planning to drive through northern Arizona anytime in the winter, bring chains.

BY TRAIN

Amtrak (© **800/872-7245** in the U.S. and Canada; www.amtrak.com) provides service aboard the *Southwest Chief* between Flagstaff and Los Angeles, Albuquerque, Santa Fe, Kansas City, and Chicago. The *Sunset Limited* connects Tucson with Orlando, New Orleans, Houston, San Antonio, El Paso, and Los Angeles. At press time, the fare from Los Angeles to Flagstaff was between $64 and $114 one way and between $128 and $228 round-trip. There is no rail service to Phoenix, but Amtrak *will* sell you a ticket and then put you on a bus from either Tucson or Flagstaff to Phoenix. However, taking Amtrak from Los Angeles to Phoenix will take somewhere between 14 and 23 hours (including the shuttle bus), depending on the schedule (you might have to wait a long time for the shuttle to Phoenix at Flagstaff or Tucson). Earlier bookings secure lower fares.

PACKAGE TOURS

If you prefer to let someone else do all your travel preparations, a package tour might be for you—whether you just want to lie by the pool at a resort or see the whole state in 2 weeks. The best way to find out about package tours is to visit a travel agent, who will likely have several booklets about different tours and airfare/hotel packages offered by different airlines.

Gray Line of Phoenix, 1646 E. University Dr., Phoenix, AZ 85040 (© **800/732-0327** or 602/495-9100), offers Arizona excursions lasting from 1 to 3 days. Tours include the Grand Canyon by way of Sedona and Oak Creek Canyon.

Maupintour, 1421 Research Park Dr., Suite 300, Lawrence, KS 66049-3858 (© **800/255-4266** or 785/331-1000; maupintour.com), one of the largest tour operators in the world, offers several Arizona itineraries that cover the Grand Canyon, the Four Corners region, Phoenix, and Scottsdale.

SPECIALTY TOURS   If you have an interest in the Native American cultures of Arizona, you might want to consider doing a tour with **Discovery Passages,** 1161 Elk Trail, Box 630, Prescott, AZ 86303 (© **520/717-0519**), which has tours that visit the Hopi, Navajo, Apache, Tohono O'odham, Hualapai, Yavapai, and Havasupai reservations. **Crossing Worlds Journeys & Retreats,** P.O. Box 623, Sedona, AZ 86339 (© **800/350-2693** or 520/203-0024; www.crossingworlds.com), also offers 1-day and multiday tours throughout the Four Corners region. Tours go to the Hopi mesas, as well as to backcountry ruins on the Navajo Reservation to view cliff dwellings and rock art.

Canyon Calling Tours, 200 Carol Canyon Dr., Sedona, AZ 86336 (© **800/664-8922;** www.canyoncalling.com), offers weeklong tours of the Four Corners region for women only. These tours visit Canyon de Chelly, Lake Powell, the Grand Canyon, and Havasu Canyon. The cost is $1,595 per person.

If you'd like to add a tour into Mexico to your Arizona visit, contact **Ajo Stage Line,** 1041 Solana Rd., Ajo, AZ 85321 (© **800/942-1981** or 520/387-6467; www.ajostageline.com). Owner Will Nelson leads 1-day and multiday trips to the Gulf of California at Puerto Peñasco, to the rugged El Pinacate region of the Sonoran Desert, to the North Rim of the Grand Canyon, and to Kartchner Cavern. Prices range from about $75 to $795.

In addition to the above-mentioned specialty-tour companies, you'll find outdoor-oriented tour companies mentioned earlier in this chapter under "The Active Vacation Planner."

9 Getting Around

BY CAR

Because Phoenix and Tucson are major resort destinations, both have dozens of car-rental agencies. Prices at agencies elsewhere in the state tend to be higher, so if at all possible, try to rent your car in either Phoenix or Tucson. Because of high taxes at both airports, consider renting at a location outside the airport. If you stay at a hotel that offers a free airport shuttle, you can check in and then have an off-airport rental-car office pick you up and drive you to their office. If you have to pay for a shuttle or taxi to either your hotel or the off-airport rental-car office, you may wipe out any savings you might realize by renting away from the airport. Be sure to weigh all the costs carefully.

Major rental-car companies with offices in Arizona include:

Alamo	800/327-9633	www.alamo.com
Avis	800/331-1212	www.avis.com
Budget	800/527-0700	www.budget.com
Dollar	800/800-4000	www.dollar.com
Enterprise	800/736-8222	www.enerprise.com
Hertz	800/654-3131	www.hertz.com
National	800/227-7368	www.nationalcar.com
Payless	800/237-2804	www.paylesscarrental.com
Thrifty	800/367-2277	www.thrifty.com

Rates for rental cars vary considerably between companies and with the model you want to rent, the dates you rent, and your pickup and drop-off points. If you call the same company three times and ask about renting the same model car, you may get three different quotes, depending on current availability of vehicles. It pays to start shopping early and ask lots of questions—rental agents don't always volunteer information about how to save, so you have to experiment with all the parameters. At press time, Budget was charging $163 per week ($201 including taxes and surcharges) for a compact car with unlimited mileage in Tucson.

If you're a member of a frequent-flier program, check to see which rental-car companies participate in your program. Also, when making a reservation, be sure to mention any discount you might be eligible for, such as corporate, military, or AAA, or any specials offered. Beware of coupons offering discounts on rental-car rates—they often discount the highest rates only. It's always cheaper to rent by the week, so even if you don't need a car for 7 days, you might find that it's still more economical than renting for 4 days only.

Taxes on car rentals vary between 10% and 25% or more and are always at the high end at both the Phoenix and Tucson airports. You can save up to 11% (the airport concession fee recoupment charge) by renting your car at an office outside the airport. Be sure to ask about the tax and the loss-damage waiver (LDW) if you want to know what your total rental cost will be before making a reservation.

A right turn on a red light is permitted after a complete stop. Seat belts are required for the driver and for all passengers; children 4 years and younger, or who weigh 40 pounds or less, must be in a child's car seat. General speed limits are 25 to 35 mph in towns and cities, 15 mph in school zones, and 55 mph on two-lane highways, except rural interstate highways, where the speed limit ranges from 65 to 75 mph.

Always be sure to keep your gas tank topped off. It's not unusual to drive 60 miles without seeing a gas station in many parts of Arizona. *Note:* A breakdown in the desert can be more than just an inconvenience—it can be dangerous. Always carry drinking water with you while driving through the desert, and if you plan to head off on back roads, carry extra water for the car as well.

Currently, because the Arizona Department of Transportation no longer publishes a road map to the state, you'll have to go with whatever you can pick up at a convenience store once you arrive in the state. If you're a member of the American Automobile Association (AAA), you can get a free map of the state that will be of some use. Other maps are available from tourist information offices in Phoenix and Tucson.

BY PLANE

Arizona is a big state (the sixth largest), so if your time is short, you might want to consider flying between cities. Several airlines offer service within the state or from Las Vegas, with America West taking most of the routes.

They include:

America West	800/235-9292	www.americawest.com
Scenic Airlines	800/446-4584	www.scenic.com
Skywest	800/453-9417	www.skywest.com
United Shuttle	800/SHUTTLE	www.united.com

Cities and towns served by these airlines include Phoenix, Tucson, Flagstaff, the Grand Canyon, Kingman, Prescott, Bullhead City (Laughlin, Nevada), Lake Havasu City, and Yuma.

BY TRAIN

The train is not really a viable way of getting around much of Arizona because there is no north-south Amtrak service between Grand Canyon/Flagstaff and Phoenix or between Tucson and Phoenix. However, Amtrak will sell you a ticket to Phoenix, which includes a shuttle-bus ride from Flagstaff or Tucson. But you can get to the town of Williams, 30 miles west of Flagstaff, on Amtrak, and in Williams transfer to the Grand Canyon Railway excursion train, which runs to Grand Canyon Village at the South Rim of the Grand Canyon (see chapter 6, "The Grand Canyon & Northern Arizona," for details). Be aware, however, that the Williams stop is on the outskirts of town; you'll have to arrange to be picked up before you board the train.

ⓒ FAST FACTS: Arizona

American Express There are offices or representatives in Phoenix and Scottsdale. For information, call American Express (ⓒ **800/528-4800**).

Banks & ATM Networks ATMs in Arizona generally use the following systems: Star, Cirrus, Plus, American Express, MasterCard, and Visa.

Bed-and-Breakfasts **Advance Reservations Inn Arizona/Mi Casa-Su Casa Bed & Breakfast Reservation Service**, P.O. Box 950, Tempe, AZ 85280-0950 (ⓒ **800/456-0682** or 480/990-0682; www.azres.com), can book you into more than 65 homes in the Valley of the Sun (and a total of 280 throughout the state), as can **Arizona Trails Bed & Breakfast Reservation Service**, P.O. Box 18998, Fountain Hills, AZ 85269-8998 (ⓒ **888/799-4284** or 480/837-4284; fax 480/816-4224; www.arizonatrails.com), which also books tour and hotel reservations. For a list of some of the best B&Bs in the state, contact the **Arizona Association of Bed and Breakfast Inns**, P.O. Box 22086, Flagstaff, AZ 86002-2086 (ⓒ **800/284-2589**; www.arizona-bed-breakfast.com).

Business Hours The following are general hours; specific establishments may vary. Banks are open Monday through Friday from 9am to 5pm (some also on Saturday from 9am–noon). Stores are open Monday through Saturday from 10am to 6pm and Sunday from noon to 5pm (malls usually stay open until 9pm Mon–Sat). Bars generally open around 11am, but are legally allowed to be open Monday through Saturday from 6am to 1am and Sunday from 10am to 1am.

Camera/Film Because the sun is almost always shining in Arizona, you can use a slower film—that is, one with a lower ASA number. This will give you sharper pictures. If your camera accepts different filters, and especially if you plan to travel in the higher altitudes of the northern part of the state, you'd do well to invest in a polarizer, which reduces contrast, deepens colors, and eliminates glare. Also, be sure to protect your camera and film from heat. Never leave your camera or film in a car parked in the sun—temperatures inside the car can climb to more than 130°F, which is hot enough to damage sensitive film.

Car Rentals See "Getting Around," earlier in this chapter.

Climate See "When to Go," earlier in this chapter.

Driving Rules See "Getting Around," earlier in this chapter.

Emergencies In most places in Arizona, © 911 is the number to call in case of a fire, police, or medical emergency. A few small towns have not adopted this emergency phone number, so if 911 doesn't work, dial 0 (zero) for the operator and state the type of emergency.

Information See "Visitor Information & Money," earlier in this chapter, and individual city chapters and sections for local information offices.

Legal Aid If you're in need of legal aid, first look in the White Pages of the local telephone book under Legal Aid. You may also want to contact the Travelers Aid Society.

Liquor Laws The legal age for buying or consuming alcoholic beverages is 21. You cannot purchase any alcoholic drinks from 1 to 6am Monday through Saturday and from 1 to 10am on Sunday.

Pets If you plan to travel with a pet, it's always best to check when making hotel reservations. At Grand Canyon Village, there's a kennel where you can board your pet while you hike down into the canyon.

Police In most places in Arizona, phone © 911. A few small towns have not adopted this emergency phone number, so if 911 doesn't work, dial 0 (zero) for the operator and state your reason for calling.

Safety When driving long distances, always carry plenty of drinking water, and if you're heading off onto dirt roads, extra water for your car's radiator as well. When hiking or walking in the desert, keep an eye out for rattlesnakes; these poisonous snakes are not normally aggressive unless provoked, so give them a wide berth, and they'll leave you alone. Black widow spiders and scorpions are also desert denizens that can be dangerous; the better-known tarantula is actually much less of a threat. If you go turning over rocks or logs, you're likely to encounter one of Arizona's poisonous residents.

Taxes There's a state sales tax of 5.5% (local communities levy additional taxes), car-rental taxes ranging from around 10% to about 27%, and hotel room taxes from around 6% to around 17% (the highest room taxes are on the Navajo reservation).

Time Arizona is in the mountain time zone. However, the state does not observe daylight saving time, so time differences between Arizona and the rest of the country vary with the time of year. From the last Sunday in October until the first Sunday in April, Arizona is 1 hour later than the West Coast and 2 hours earlier than the East Coast. The rest of the year, Arizona is on the same time as the West Coast and is 3 hours earlier than the East Coast. There is an exception, however—the Navajo Reservation observes daylight saving time. However, the Hopi Reservation, which is completely surrounded by the Navajo Reservation, does not.

Weather For current weather information, call ℂ **602/265-5550.**

3

For International Visitors

The American West is well known and well loved in many countries. Arizona's images are familiar from Western novels, movies, television shows, and advertisements. And, of course, the Grand Canyon is one of the wonders of the world. However, despite this being the Wild West, you are likely to encounter typically American situations in Arizona, and this chapter should help you prepare for your trip.

1 Preparing for Your Trip

ENTRY REQUIREMENTS

Immigration law is a hot political issue in the United States these days, and the following requirements may have changed somewhat by the time you plan your trip. Check at any U.S. embassy or consulate for current information and requirements. You can also go to the **U.S. State Department** website at **www.state.gov**.

VISAS The U.S. State Department has a **Visa Waiver Pilot Program** allowing citizens of certain countries to enter the United States without a visa for stays of up to 90 days. At press time, these countries included Andorra, Argentina, Australia, Austria, Belgium, Brunei, Denmark, Finland, France, Germany, Iceland, Ireland, Italy, Japan, Liechtenstein, Luxembourg, Monaco, the Netherlands, New Zealand, Norway, San Marino, Slovenia, Spain, Sweden, Switzerland, and the United Kingdom. Citizens of these countries need only a valid passport and a round-trip air or cruise ticket in their possession upon arrival. If they first enter the United States, they may also visit Mexico, Canada, Bermuda, and/or the Caribbean islands and return to the United States without a visa. Canadian citizens may enter the United States without a visa; they need only proof of residence.

Citizens of all other countries must have (1) a valid passport that expires at least 6 months later than the scheduled end of their visit to the United States, and (2) a tourist visa, which can be obtained without charge from any U.S. consulate.

To get a visa, the traveler must submit a completed application form (either in person or by mail) with a 1½-inch-square photo, and must demonstrate binding ties to a residence abroad. Usually you can get a visa at once or within 24 hours, but it may take longer during the summer rush from June through August. If you cannot go in person, contact the nearest U.S. embassy or consulate for directions on applying by mail. Your travel agent or airline office may also be able to supply you with visa applications and instructions. The U.S. consulate or embassy that issues your visa determines whether you will be issued a multiple- or single-entry visa and any restrictions on the length of your stay.

British subjects can get up-to-date passport and visa information by calling the **U.S. Embassy Visa Information Line** (© 0891/200-290) or the **London Passport Office** (© 020/7271-3000) for recorded information.

MEDICAL REQUIREMENTS   Unless you're arriving from an area known to be suffering from an epidemic (particularly cholera or yellow fever), inoculations or vaccinations are not required for entry into the United States. If you have a disease that requires treatment with narcotics or syringe-administered medications, carry a valid signed prescription from your physician to allay any suspicions that you may be smuggling narcotics (a serious offense that carries severe penalties in the United States).

DRIVER'S LICENSES   Foreign driver's licenses are usually recognized in the United States, although you may want to get an international driver's license if your home license is not written in English.

CUSTOMS REQUIREMENTS   Every visitor over 21 years of age may bring in, free of duty, the following: (1) 1 liter of wine or hard liquor; (2) 200 cigarettes, 100 cigars (but not from Cuba), or 3 pounds of smoking tobacco; and (3) $100 worth of gifts. These exemptions are offered to travelers who spend at least 72 hours in the United States and who have not claimed them within the preceding 6 months. It is altogether forbidden to bring into the country foodstuffs (particularly fruit, cooked meats, and canned goods) and plants (vegetables, seeds, tropical plants, and the like). Foreign tourists may bring in or take out up to $10,000 in U.S. or foreign currency with no formalities; larger sums must be declared to U.S. Customs on entering or leaving, which includes filing form CM 4790. For specific information regarding U.S. Customs, call your nearest U.S. embassy or consulate, or contact the **U.S. Customs** office at $©$ **202/927-1770** or www.customs.gov/travel/travel.htm.

INSURANCE
Although it's not required of travelers, health insurance is highly recommended. Unlike many European countries, the United States does not usually offer free or low-cost medical care to its citizens or visitors. Doctors and hospitals are expensive, and in most cases require advance payment or proof of coverage before they render their services. Other policies can cover everything from the loss or theft of your baggage to trip cancellation to the guarantee of bail in case you're arrested. Good policies also cover the costs of an accident, repatriation, or death. See "Health & Insurance" in chapter 2, "Planning Your Trip to Arizona," for more information. In Europe, packages such as **Europ Assistance** are sold by automobile clubs and travel agencies at attractive rates. **Worldwide Assistance Services** ($©$ **800/821-2828**) is the agent for Europ Assistance in the United States.

Although lack of health insurance may prevent you from being admitted to a hospital in nonemergencies, don't worry about being left on a street corner to die: The American way is to fix you now and bill the living daylights out of you later.

MONEY
The U.S. monetary system has a decimal base: one American **dollar** ($1) = 100 **cents** (100¢). Bills commonly come in $1 (a "buck"), $5, $10, $20, $50, and $100 denominations (the last two are not welcome when paying for small purchases or taxi fares). Common coins include the penny (1¢), nickel (5¢), dime (10¢), and quarter (25¢). You may come across a 50¢ or $1 coin as well.

CURRENCY EXCHANGE   The foreign-exchange bureaus so common in many countries are rare in the United States, even at airports, and nonexistent outside major cities. Try to avoid having to change foreign money or traveler's checks not denominated in U.S. dollars at a small-town bank or even a branch

bank in a big city. In fact, leave any currency other than U.S. dollars at home—
it could prove more nuisance to you than it's worth.

TRAVELER'S CHECKS   Traveler's checks *denominated in U.S. dollars* are
readily accepted at most hotels, motels, restaurants, and large stores, but might
not be accepted at small stores or for small purchases. The best place to change
traveler's checks is at a bank. Do not bring traveler's checks denominated in
other currencies. The three traveler's checks that are most widely recognized are
Visa, American Express, and **Thomas Cook.**

CREDIT CARDS & ATMS   Credit cards are the most widely used form of
payment in the United States. Among the most commonly accepted are **Visa**
(BarclayCard in Britain), **MasterCard** (EuroCard in Europe, Access in Britain,
Chargex in Canada), **American Express, Diners Club, Discover,** and **Carte
Blanche.** You must have a credit or charge card to rent a car. There are, however,
a handful of stores and restaurants that do not take credit cards, so be sure to ask
in advance. Most businesses display a sticker near their entrance to let you know
which cards they accept. (*Note:* Often businesses require a minimum purchase
price, usually around $10, to use a credit card.)

It is strongly recommended that you bring at least one major credit card.
Hotels, car-rental companies, and airlines usually require a credit-card imprint
as a deposit against expenses, and in an emergency a credit card can be priceless.

You'll find automated-teller machines (ATMs) on just about every block in
larger cities. Some ATMs allow you to draw U.S. currency against your bank
and credit cards. Check with your bank before leaving home, and remember
that you need your personal identification number (PIN) to do so. Most accept
Visa, MasterCard, and American Express, as well as ATM cards from other U.S.
banks. Expect to be charged up to $3 per transaction, however. One way around
these fees is to ask for cash back at grocery stores that accept ATM cards and
don't charge usage fees. Of course, you'll have to purchase something first.

SAFETY

While tourist areas are generally safe, U.S. urban areas tend to be less safe than
those in Europe or Japan. You should always stay alert. It is wise to ask your
hotel's front desk staff if you're in doubt about which neighborhoods are safe.
Avoid deserted areas, especially at night, and don't go into public parks at night
unless there's a concert or similar occasion that will attract a crowd.

Avoid carrying valuables with you on the street, and don't display expensive
cameras or electronic equipment. If you're using a map, consult it inconspicu-
ously. Hold onto your pocketbook, and place your billfold in an inside pocket.
In public places, keep your possessions in sight.

Remember also that hotels are open to the public, and in a large hotel, security may not be able to screen everyone entering. Always lock your room door—
don't assume that once inside your hotel you are automatically safe.

DRIVING SAFETY   Safety while driving is particularly important. Ask your
rental agency about personal safety or request a brochure of traveler safety tips

Tips **In Case of Emergency**

Be sure to keep a copy of all your travel papers separate from your wallet
or purse, and leave a copy with someone at home should you need it
faxed in an emergency.

when you pick up your car. Get written directions or a map with the route marked in red from the agency to show you how to get to your destination. If possible, arrive and depart during daylight hours.

Recently more and more crime has involved cars and drivers. If you drive off a highway into a questionable neighborhood, leave the area as quickly as possible. If you have an accident, even on the highway, stay in your car with the doors locked until you assess the situation or until the police arrive. If you are bumped from behind on the street or are involved in a minor accident with no injuries, and the situation appears to be suspicious, motion to the other driver to follow you to the nearest police precinct, gas station, or open store. Never get out of your car in such situations.

Park in well-lit, well-traveled areas if possible. Always keep your car doors locked, whether the vehicle is attended or unattended. Look around you before you get out of your car and never leave any packages or valuables in sight. If someone attempts to rob you or steal your car, do *not* try to resist the thief/carjacker—report the incident to the police department immediately by calling © **911.**

Also, make sure you have enough gasoline in your tank to reach your intended destination so that you're not forced to look for a service station in an unfamiliar and possibly unsafe neighborhood—especially at night.

2 Getting to the U.S.

Airlines with direct or connecting service from London to Phoenix (along with their phone numbers in Great Britain) include: **American** (© 0345/789-789; www.im.aa.com), **British Airways** (© 0845/773-3377; www.britishairways. com), **Continental** (© 0800/776-464; www.continental.com), **Delta** (© 0800/414-767; www.delta.com), **TWA** (© 0207/439-0707; www.twa.com), **United** (© 0800/888-555; www.united.com), and **US Airways** (© 0800/777-333; www.usairways.com). American, Delta, and United fly into Tucson.

From Canada, there are flights to Phoenix from Toronto on: **Air Canada** (© 888/247-2262; www.aircanada.ca), **American** (© 800/433-7300; www.aa.com), **America West** (© 800/235-9292; www.americawest.com), **Delta** (© 800/221-1212; www.delta.com), **Northwest** (© 800/225-2525; www.nwa.com), **TWA** (© 800/221-2000; www.twa.com), **United** (© 800/241-6522; www.united.com), and **US Airways** (© 800/428-4322; www.usairways.com).

There are flights to Phoenix from Vancouver on **Alaska Airlines** (© 800/426-0333; www.alaskaair.com), **America West** (© 800/235-9292; www.americawest.com), **Air Canada** (© 888/247-2262; www.aircanada.ca), **Northwest,** and **United.**

There are flights to Tucson from Toronto on **American, Continental** (© 800/525-0280; www.continental.com), **Delta, Northwest,** and **United,** and from Vancouver on **American, America West,** and **United.**

From New Zealand and Australia, there are flights to Los Angeles on **Qantas** (© 13 13 13 in Australia; www.qantas.com.au) and **Air New Zealand** (© 0800/737-000 in Auckland; www.airnewzealand.co.nz).

Continue on to Phoenix or Tucson on a regional airline such as **America West** (© 800/235-9292; www.americawest.com) or **Southwest** (© 800/435-9792; www.iflyswa.com).

If you're heading to the Grand Canyon, it's easier to take a flight from Los Angeles to Las Vegas.

AIRLINE DISCOUNTS Travelers from overseas can take advantage of the advance-purchase excursion (APEX) fares offered by the major U.S. and European carriers. For more money-saving airline advice, see "Getting There," in chapter 2.

IMMIGRATION & CUSTOMS CLEARANCE The visitor arriving by air, no matter what the port of entry, should cultivate patience before setting foot on U.S. soil. Getting through Immigration Control might take as long as 2 hours on some days, especially summer weekends. Add the time it takes to clear Customs, and you'll see that you should make a very generous allowance for delay in planning connections between international and domestic flights—an average of 2 to 3 hours at least.

In contrast, travelers arriving by car or by rail from Canada will find border-crossing formalities streamlined practically to the vanishing point. And air travelers from Canada, Bermuda, and some places in the Caribbean can sometimes go through Customs and Immigration at the point of departure, which is much quicker.

3 Getting Around the U.S.

For specific information on traveling to and around Arizona, see "Getting There" and "Getting Around," in chapter 2.

BY PLANE Some large airlines (for example, United and Delta) offer travelers on their transatlantic or transpacific flights special discount tickets under the name **Visit USA,** allowing mostly one-way travel from one U.S. destination to another at very low prices. These discount tickets are not on sale in the United States and must be purchased abroad in conjunction with your international ticket. This system is the best, easiest, and fastest way to see the United States at low cost. You should get information well in advance from your travel agent or the office of the airline concerned, since the conditions attached to these discount tickets can be changed without advance notice.

BY CAR The United States is a car culture through and through. Driving is the most cost-effective, convenient, and comfortable way to travel through the West. The interstate highway system connects cities and towns all over the country, and in addition to these high-speed, limited-access roadways, there's an extensive network of federal, state, and local highways and roads. Driving will give you a lot of flexibility in making, and altering, your itinerary and in allowing you to see some off-the-beaten-path destinations that cannot be reached easily by public transportation. You'll also have easy access to inexpensive motels at interstate highway off-ramps.

BY TRAIN International visitors can also buy a **USA Railpass,** good for 15 or 30 days of unlimited travel on **Amtrak** (© **800/USA-RAIL;** www.amtrak. com). The pass is available through many foreign travel agents. At press time, a 15-day pass costs $295 off-peak, $440 peak; a 30-day pass costs $385 off-peak, $550 peak. (With a foreign passport, you can also buy passes at staffed Amtrak offices in the United States, including locations in San Francisco, Los Angeles, Chicago, New York, Miami, Boston, and Washington, D.C.) Reservations are generally required and should be made for each part of your trip as early as possible. Amtrak also offers an **Air/Rail Travel Plan** that allows you to travel by both train and plane; for information, call © **800/440-8202.**

BY BUS   Although bus travel is often the most economical form of public transit for short hops between U.S. cities, it can also be slow and uncomfortable—certainly not an option for everyone (particularly when Amtrak, which is far more luxurious, offers similar rates). **Greyhound/Trailways** (© **800/ 231-2222;** www.greyhound.com), the sole nationwide bus line, offers an unlimited-travel **Ameripass** for 7 days at $185, 15 days at $285, 30 days at $385, and 60 days at $509. Passes must be purchased at a Greyhound terminal. Special rates are available for senior citizens and students.

FAST FACTS: **For the International Traveler**

Automobile Organizations   Auto clubs can supply maps, suggested routes, guidebooks, accident and bail-bond insurance, and emergency road service. The **American Automobile Association (AAA)** is the major auto club in the United States. If you belong to an auto club in your home country, inquire about AAA reciprocity before you leave. You may be able to join AAA even if you're not a member of a reciprocal club; to inquire, call **AAA** (© **800/222-4357**). AAA is actually an organization of regional auto clubs; so look under "AAA Automobile Club" in the White Pages of the telephone directory. AAA has a nationwide **emergency road service** telephone number (© **800/AAA-HELP**).

Business Hours   See "Fast Facts: Arizona," in chapter 2.

Climate   See "When to Go," in chapter 2.

Currency   See "Money" under "Preparing for Your Trip," earlier in this chapter.

Currency Exchange   You'll find currency-exchange services in major international airports. There's a **Thomas Cook** office (© **800/287-7362** or 602/392-2275) at Sky Harbor Airport in Phoenix, but not at Tucson International Airport. Elsewhere, they may be quite difficult to come by. In Phoenix, **Bank of America,** 201 E. Washington St. (© **888/279-3264** or 602/523-2371), will exchange money, as will some of the bank's other branches. Also, ask at your hotel desk; some hotels might be able to change major currencies for you.

Drinking Laws   The legal age for purchase and consumption of alcoholic beverages is 21; proof of age is required and often requested at bars, nightclubs, and restaurants, so it's always a good idea to bring ID when you go out. Beer and wine can often be purchased in supermarkets, but liquor laws vary from state to state.

Do not carry open containers of alcohol in your car or any public area that isn't zoned for alcohol consumption. The police can, and probably will, fine you on the spot. And nothing will ruin your trip faster than getting a citation for DUI ("driving under the influence"), so don't even think about driving while intoxicated.

Electricity   Like Canada, the United States uses 110 to 120 volts AC (60 cycles), compared to 220 to 240 volts AC (50 cycles) in most of Europe, Australia, and New Zealand. If your small appliances use 220 to 240 volts, you'll need a 110-volt transformer and a plug adapter with two flat parallel pins to operate them here. Downward converters that change 220 to

240 volts to 110 to 120 volts are difficult to find in the United States, so bring one with you.

Embassies & Consulates All embassies are located in Washington, D.C. Some consulates are located in major U.S. cities, and most nations have a mission to the United Nations in New York City. If your country isn't listed below, call **directory information** in Washington, D.C. (✆ **202/555-1212**), for the number of your national embassy.

The embassy of **Australia** is at 1601 Massachusetts Ave. NW, Washington, D.C. 20036 (✆ **202/797-3000;** www.austemb.org). There is no consulate in Arizona; the nearest is at Century Plaza Towers, 19th Floor, 2049 Century Park East, Los Angeles, CA 90067 (✆ **310/229-4800**).

The embassy of **Canada** is at 501 Pennsylvania Ave. NW, Washington, D.C. 20001 (✆ **202/682-1740;** www.canadianembassy.org). There is no consulate in Arizona; the nearest is at 550 S. Hope St., 9th Floor, Los Angeles, CA 90071 (✆ **213/346-2700**).

The embassy of **Ireland** is at 2234 Massachusetts Ave. NW, Washington, D.C. 20008 (✆ **202/462-3939;** www.irelandemb.org). There is no consulate in Arizona; the nearest is at 44 Montgomery St., Suite 3830, San Francisco, CA 94104 (✆ **415/392-4214**).

The embassy of **New Zealand** is at 37 Observatory Circle NW, Washington, D.C. 20008 (✆ **202/328-4800;** www.nzemb.org). There is no consulate in Arizona; the nearest is at 12400 Wilshire Blvd., Suite 1150, Los Angeles, CA 90025 (✆ **310/207-1605**).

The embassy of the **United Kingdom** is at 3100 Massachusetts Ave. NW, Washington, D.C. 20008 (✆ **202/462-1340;** www.britain-info.org). There is no consulate in Arizona; the nearest is at 11766 Wilshire Blvd., Suite 400, Los Angeles, CA 90025 (✆ **310/477-3322**).

Emergencies Dial ✆ **911** to report a fire, call the police, or get an ambulance. This is a free call (no coins are required at a public telephone).

If you encounter problems, check the local telephone directory to find an office of the **Traveler's Aid Society,** a nationwide nonprofit social-service organization geared to helping travelers in difficult straits. The society's services might include reuniting families separated while traveling, providing food and/or shelter to people stranded without cash, or even emotional counseling. If you're in trouble, seek it out.

Gasoline (Petrol) Petrol is known as gasoline (or simply "gas") in the United States, and petrol stations are known as both gas stations and service stations. Gasoline costs less here than it does in Europe, and taxes are already included in the printed price. One U.S. gallon equals 3.8 liters or .85 Imperial gallons.

Holidays Banks, government offices, post offices, and many stores, restaurants, and museums are closed on the following legal national holidays: January 1 (New Year's Day), the third Monday in January (Martin Luther King Jr. Day), the third Monday in February (Presidents' Day, Washington's Birthday), the last Monday in May (Memorial Day), July 4 (Independence Day), the first Monday in September (Labor Day), the second Monday in October (Columbus Day), November 11 (Veterans' Day/Armistice Day), the fourth Thursday in November (Thanksgiving Day), and December 25 (Christmas). Also, the Tuesday following the first

Monday in November is Election Day and is a federal government holiday in presidential-election years (held every 4 years, and next in 2004).

Internet Access Checking the Yellow Pages under Internet Access may turn up a few cybercafes. Many copy shops (Kinko's is one large national chain) also provide Internet access. If you are traveling with your laptop computer, note that many hotels, especially those frequented by business travelers, have telephones with dataports and dual phone lines in guest rooms.

Legal Aid The foreign tourist will probably never become involved with the American legal system. If you are pulled over for a minor infraction (for example, of the highway code, such as speeding), never attempt to pay the fine directly to a police officer; this could be construed as attempted bribery, a much more serious crime. Pay fines by mail or directly into the hands of the clerk of the court. If accused of a more serious offense, say and do nothing before consulting a lawyer. The burden is on the state to prove a person's guilt beyond a reasonable doubt, and everyone has the right to remain silent, whether he or she is suspected of a crime or actually arrested. Once arrested, a person can make one telephone call to a party of his or her choice. Call your embassy or consulate.

Mail Generally found at intersections, mailboxes are blue with a red-and-white stripe and carry the inscription U.S. MAIL. If your mail is addressed to a U.S. destination, don't forget to add the five-digit postal code (or ZIP code), after the two-letter abbreviation of the state to which the mail is addressed.

At press time, domestic postage rates were 22¢ for a postcard and 34¢ for a letter. International mail rates vary. For example, a 1-ounce first-class letter to England costs 80¢, or 60¢ to Canada and Mexico; a first-class postcard to England costs 70¢, or 50¢ to Canada and Mexico.

Medical Emergencies To call an ambulance, dial ℂ **911** from any phone. No coins are needed.

Newspapers & Magazines National newspapers include the *New York Times, USA Today,* and the *Wall Street Journal.* National news weeklies include *Newsweek, Time,* and *U.S. News & World Report.* In large cities, most newsstands offer a small selection of the most popular foreign periodicals and newspapers, such as *The Economist, Le Monde,* and *Der Spiegel.* For information on local publications, see the "Fast Facts" sections for Phoenix and Tucson (chapter 4, "Phoenix, Scottsdale & the Valley of the Sun," and chapter 9, "Tucson").

Safety See "Safety" in "Preparing for Your Trip," earlier in this chapter.

Taxes The United States does not have a value-added tax (VAT) or other indirect tax at a national level. Every state, and each county and city in it, is allowed to levy its own local tax on purchases. Taxes are already included in the price of certain services, such as public transportation, cab fares, telephone calls, and gasoline.

In Arizona, the state sales tax is 5.5%, but communities can add local sales tax on top of this. Expect to pay around 20% tax on car rentals at the Tucson airport and more than 25% at the Phoenix airport (considerably less if you rent outside the airports). Hotel room taxes range from around

6% to 17%. Travelers on a budget should keep both car-rental and hotel-room taxes in mind when planning a trip.

Telephone & Fax The telephone system in the United States is run by private corporations, so rates, especially for long-distance service and operator-assisted calls, can vary widely. Generally, hotel surcharges on long-distance and local calls are astronomical, so you're usually better off using a **public pay telephone,** which you'll find clearly marked in most public buildings and private establishments as well as on the street. Convenience grocery stores and gas stations always have them. Many convenience stores and packaging services sell **prepaid calling cards** in denominations up to $50; these cards can be the least expensive way to call home. Many public phones at airports now accept American Express, MasterCard, and Visa credit cards. **Local calls** made from public pay phones in most locales cost either 25¢ or 35¢. Pay phones do not accept pennies, and few take anything larger than a quarter.

Most long-distance and international calls can be dialed directly from any phone. **For calls within the United States and to Canada,** dial 1 followed by the area code and the seven-digit number. **For other international calls,** dial 011 followed by the country code, city code, and telephone number of the person you are calling.

Calls to area codes **800, 888,** and **877** are toll-free. However, calls to numbers in area codes **700** and **900** (chat lines, bulletin boards, "dating" services, and so on) can be very expensive—usually 95¢ to $3 or more per minute.

For **reversed-charge or collect calls,** and for **person-to-person calls,** dial 0 (zero, not the letter *O*) followed by the area code and number you want; an operator then comes on the line, and you should specify that you are calling collect, or person-to-person, or both. If your operator-assisted call is international, ask for the overseas operator.

For **local directory assistance** ("information"), dial 411; for long-distance information, dial 1 and then the appropriate area code and 555-1212.

Most hotels have **fax machines** available for guest use (be sure to ask about the charge to use it). A less expensive way to send and receive faxes may be at stores such as Kinko's (see "Internet Access," above) or Mail Boxes Etc., a national chain of packing service shops (look in the Yellow Pages under "Packing Services").

There are two kinds of telephone directories in the United States. The **White Pages** lists private households and business subscribers in alphabetical order. The inside front cover lists emergency numbers for police, fire, ambulance, the Coast Guard, poison-control center, crime-victims hot line, and so on. The first few pages tell you how to make long-distance and international calls, complete with country codes and area codes. Government numbers are usually printed on blue paper within the White Pages. Printed on yellow paper, the **Yellow Pages** lists all local services, businesses, industries, and houses of worship according to category, with an index at the front or back. (Drugstores/pharmacies and restaurants are also listed by geographic location.) The Yellow Pages includes city plans or detailed area maps, postal ZIP codes, and public transportation routes.

Time The United States is divided into six time zones. From east to west, they are eastern standard time (EST), central standard time (CST), mountain standard time (MST), Pacific standard time (PST), Alaska standard time (AST), and Hawaii standard time (HST). Always keep the changing time zones in mind if you are traveling (or even telephoning) long distances in the United States. For example, noon in New York City (EST) is 11am in Chicago (CST), 10am in Phoenix (MST), 9am in Los Angeles (PST), 8am in Anchorage (AST), and 7am in Honolulu (HST).

Arizona is in the mountain time zone, but it does *not* observe daylight saving time. Consequently, from the first Sunday in April until the last Sunday in October, there is no time difference between Arizona and California and other states on the West Coast.

Tipping Tipping is so ingrained in the American way of life that the annual income tax of tip-earning service personnel is based on how much they should have received in light of their employers' gross revenues. Accordingly, they may have to pay tax on a tip you didn't actually give them. Here are some rules of thumb:

In hotels, tip **bellhops** at least $1 per bag ($2–$3 if you have a lot of luggage) and tip the **chamber staff** $1 to $2 per day (more if you've left a disaster area to clean up, or if you're traveling with kids and/or pets). Tip the **doorman** or **concierge** only if he or she has provided you with some specific service (for example, calling a cab for you or obtaining difficult-to-get theater tickets). Tip the **valet-parking attendant** $1 every time you get your car.

In restaurants, bars, and nightclubs, tip **service staff** 15% to 20% of the check, tip **bartenders** 10% to 15%, tip **checkroom attendants** $1 per garment, and tip **valet-parking attendants** $1 per vehicle. Tip the **doorman** only if he has provided you with some specific service (such as calling a cab for you). Tipping is not expected in cafeterias and fast-food restaurants.

Tip **cab drivers** 15% of the fare.

As for other service personnel, tip **skycaps** (luggage carriers) at airports at least $1 per bag ($2 to $3 if you have a lot of luggage) and tip **hairdressers** and **barbers** 15% to 20%.

Toilets You won't find public toilets on the streets in most U.S. cities, but they can be found in hotel lobbies, bars, restaurants, museums, department stores, railway and bus stations, or service stations. Note, however, that restaurants and bars in resorts or heavily visited areas may reserve their restrooms for the use of their patrons. Some establishments display a notice that toilets are for the use of patrons only. You can ignore this sign or, better yet, avoid arguments by paying for a cup of coffee or a soft drink, which will qualify you as a patron. Large hotels and fast-food restaurants are probably the best bet for good, clean facilities.

4

Phoenix, Scottsdale & the Valley of the Sun

Time and again, Phoenix has lived up to its name. Like the phoenix of ancient mythology, Arizona's capital city has risen from its own ashes—in this case, the ruins of an ancient Indian village—to become one of the largest metropolitan areas in the country.

Although the city has had its economic ups and downs, the Phoenix metropolitan area, often referred to as the Valley of the Sun, is currently booming. The Camelback Corridor, which leads through north-central Phoenix, has become the corporate heartland of the city, and shiny glass office towers keep pushing up toward the desert sky. This burgeoning stretch of road has also become a corridor of upscale restaurants and shopping plazas, anchored by the Biltmore Fashion Park, the city's temple of high-end consumerism, and today Phoenicians flock to this area for both work and play.

Even downtown Phoenix, long abandoned as simply a place to work, has taken on an entirely new look, positioning itself as a center for sports and other events. First came the America West Arena. Then the Arizona Diamondbacks took up residence in the Bank One Ballpark (BOB), one of the nation's only baseball stadiums with a retractable roof. On days when there are games or concerts scheduled at either of these venues, you can bet that downtown Phoenix will be a lively place.

Additionally, the downtown area offers quite a few attractions, from historic Heritage Square (downtown's only remaining historic block) to the Phoenix Museum of Art.

In Scottsdale, luxury resorts sprawl across the landscape, convertibles and SUVs clog the streets, and new golf courses and upscale shopping centers keep springing up like wildflowers after a rainstorm. Until recently, this city billed itself the West's most Western town, but Scottsdale today is more of a Beverly Hills of the desert. The city has also now sprawled all the way north to Carefree, and it is here, in north Scottsdale, that the valley's newest golf courses and resorts are to be found.

Throughout the metropolitan area, the population is growing at such a rapid pace that an alarm has been raised: Slow down before we become another Los Angeles! Why the phenomenal growth? In large part, it's due to the climate. The 300-plus days of sunshine a year are a powerful attraction, and although summers are blisteringly hot, the mountains—and cooler temperatures—are only 2 hours away. Winter, however, is when the Valley of the Sun truly shines. While most of the country is frozen solid, the valley is usually sunny and warm, making this area the resort capital of the United States. However, with stiff competition from resorts in the Caribbean, Mexico, and Hawaii,

Valley of the Sun resorts have had to do a lot of keeping up with the Joneses in recent years. Bigger and splashier pools have been added, and nearly every resort now offers a full-service health spa.

Golf, tennis, and lounging by the pool are only the tip of the iceberg (so to speak) when it comes to winter activities. With the cooler weather comes the cultural season, and between Phoenix and the neighboring cities of Scottsdale, Tempe, and Mesa, there's an impressive array of music, dance, and theater. Scottsdale is also well known as a center of the visual arts, ranking behind only New York and Santa Fe in its concentration of art galleries.

Over the years, Phoenix has both enjoyed the benefits and suffered the problems of rapid urban growth. It has gone from tiny agricultural village to sprawling metropolis in little more than a century. Along the way it has lost its past amid urban sprawl and unchecked development; at the same time, it has forged a city that's quintessentially 21st-century American. Shopping malls, the gathering places of America, are raised to an art form in Phoenix. Luxurious resorts create fantasy worlds of waterfalls and swimming pools. Perhaps it's this willingness to create a new world on top of an old one that attracts people to Phoenix. Then again, maybe it's just all that sunshine.

1 Orientation

ARRIVING

BY PLANE   Centrally located 3 miles east of downtown Phoenix, **Sky Harbor Airport** (© 602/273-3300; www.phxskyharbor.com) has three terminals, with a free 24-hour shuttle bus offering frequent service between them. For general airport information, call © **602/273-3456;** for lost and found, call © **602/273-3307.**

There are two entrances to the airport. The west entrance can be accessed from either the Squaw Peak Parkway (Ariz. 51) or 24th Street, and the east entrance can be accessed from the Hohokam Expressway (Ariz. 143), which is an extension of 44th Street. If you're headed to downtown Phoenix, leave by way of the 24th Street exit and continue west on Washington Street. If you're headed to Scottsdale, take the 44th Street exit, go north on Ariz. 143 and then east on Ariz. 202 to Ariz. 101 north. For Tempe or Mesa, take the 44th Street exit, go north on Ariz. 143, and then east on Ariz. 202.

SuperShuttle (© **800/BLUE-VAN** or 602/244-9000) offers 24-hour door-to-door van service between Sky Harbor Airport and resorts, hotels, and homes throughout the valley. Per-person fares average $7 to $10 to the downtown and Tempe area, $15 to downtown Scottsdale, and $30 to north Scottsdale.

Taxis can be found outside all three terminals and cost only slightly more than shuttle vans. You can also call **Discount Cab** (© **602/200-2000**) or **AAA Taxicab** (© **602/437-4000**). A taxi from the airport to downtown Phoenix will cost around $9; to Scottsdale, $17 to $18.

Valley Metro provides public bus service throughout the valley, with the Red Line (R) operating between the airport and downtown Phoenix, Tempe, and Mesa. The Red Line runs daily between about 5:45am and 10pm. The ride from the airport to downtown takes about 20 minutes and costs $1.25. There is no direct bus to Scottsdale, so you would first need to go to Tempe and then transfer to a northbound bus. You can pick up a copy of *The Bus Book,* a guide and route map for the Valley Metro bus system, at Central Station, at the corner of Central Avenue and Van Buren Street.

Phoenix, Scottsdale & the Valley of the Sun

ARIZONA

⊛ Phoenix

Biltmore District **11**
Black Canyon Freeway **3**
Central Avenue **4**
Downtown Phoenix **7**
Grand Avenue **2**
Hohokam Expressway **15**
Maricopa Freeway **6**
Mill Avenue, Tempe **16**
Papago Freeway **5**
Paradise Valley **10**
Pima Freeway **8**
Red Mountain Freeway **13**
Old Town Scottsdale **17**
Scottsdale Road **9**
Sky Harbor Airport **14**
Squaw Peak Parkway **12**
Superstition Freeway **18**
Turf Paradise Racetrack **1**

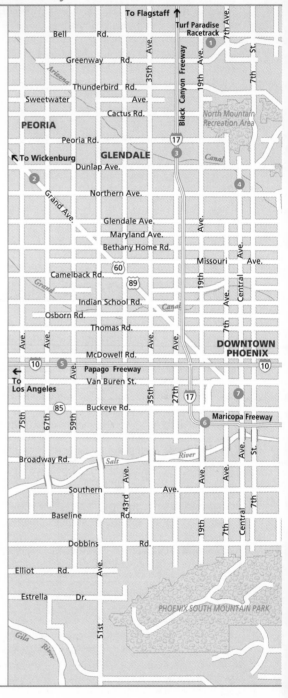

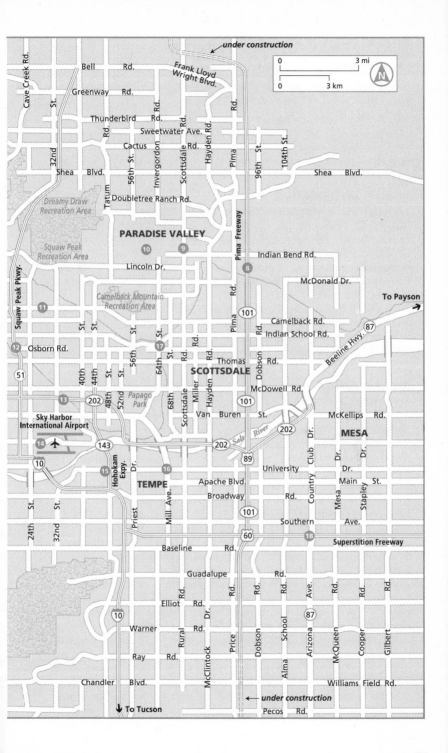

BY CAR Phoenix is connected to Los Angeles and Tucson by I-10 and to Flagstaff via I-17. If you're headed to Scottsdale, the easiest route is to take the Red Mountain Freeway (Ariz. 202) east to U.S. 101 north. U.S. 101 will eventually loop all the way around the north side of the valley. The Superstition Freeway (U.S. 60) leads to Tempe, Mesa, and Chandler.

BY TRAIN There is no passenger rail service to Phoenix. However, **Amtrak** (© **800/872-7245;** www.amtrak.com) will sell you a ticket to Phoenix, though you'll have to take a shuttle bus from either Flagstaff or Tucson. The scheduling is so horrible on these routes that you would have to be a total masochist to opt for Amtrak service to Phoenix.

VISITOR INFORMATION

You'll find **tourist information desks** in the baggage-claim areas of all three terminals at Sky Harbor Airport. However, the city's main visitor information center is the **Greater Phoenix Convention and Visitors Bureau,** 50 N. Second St. (© **877/225-5749** or 602/254-6500; www.phoenixcvb.com), on the corner of Adams Street in downtown Phoenix. The city also operates a small visitor center at the Biltmore Fashion Park shopping center at the corner of Camelback Road and 24th Street (© **602/955-1963**).

The **Visitor Information Line** (© **602/252-5588**) has recorded information about current events in Phoenix.

If you're staying in Scottsdale, you may want to drop by the **Scottsdale Chamber of Commerce and Visitors Center,** 7343 Scottsdale Mall (© **800/ 877-1117** or 480/945-8481; www.scottsdalecvb.com).

CITY LAYOUT

MAIN ARTERIES & STREETS Over the past decade, the Phoenix area has seen the construction of numerous new freeways, and it is now possible to drive from the airport to Scottsdale by freeway rather than having to deal with stoplights and local traffic. U.S. Loop 101, which currently exists only in two unconnected sections (one between Tempe and Pima Road in north Scottsdale and the other between 56th Street in north Phoenix and I-10 on the east side of the valley) will eventually form a loop around the east, north, and west sides of the valley, providing freeway access to Scottsdale from I-17 on the north side of Phoenix and from U.S. 60 in Tempe.

I-17 (Black Canyon Freeway), which connects Phoenix with Flagstaff, is the city's main north-south freeway. This freeway curves to the east just south of downtown (where it is renamed the **Maricopa Freeway** and merges with I-10). **I-10,** which connects Phoenix with Los Angeles and Tucson, is called the **Papago Freeway** on the west side of the valley and as it passes north of downtown; as it curves around to pass to the west and south of the airport, it merges with I-17 and is renamed the Maricopa Freeway. At Tempe, this freeway curves around to the south and heads out of the valley.

North of the airport, **Ariz. 202 (Red Mountain Freeway)** heads east from I-10 and passes along the north side of Tempe, providing access to downtown Tempe, Arizona State University, Mesa, and Scottsdale (via U.S. 101). On the east side of the airport, **Ariz. 143 (Hohokam Expressway)** connects Ariz. 202 with I-10.

At the interchange of I-10 and Ariz. 202, northwest of Sky Harbor Airport, **Ariz. 51 (Squaw Peak Freeway)** heads north through the center of Phoenix and is the best north-south route in the city. This freeway is currently being extended north from Bell Road and by late 2003 or early 2004 will link up with the U.S. Loop 101.

South of the airport off I-10, **U.S. 60 (Superstition Freeway)** heads east to Tempe, Chandler, Mesa, and Gilbert. **U.S. Loop 101** leads north from U.S. 60 (and Ariz. 202) toward Scottsdale. This freeway is currently being extended north from Pima Road and now provides the best route from the airport to the Scottsdale resorts. On the east side of the valley, this highway is called the Pima Freeway.

Secondary highways in the valley include the **Beeline Highway (Ariz. 87)**, which starts at the east end of Ariz. 202 (Red Mountain Freeway) in Mesa and leads to Payson, and **Grand Avenue (U.S. 60)**, which starts downtown and leads to Sun City and Wickenburg.

Phoenix and the surrounding cities of Mesa, Tempe, Scottsdale, and Chandler, and even those cities farther out in the valley, are laid out in a grid pattern with major avenues and roads about every mile. For traveling east to west across Phoenix, your best choices (other than the above-mentioned freeways) are Camelback Road, Indian School Road, and McDowell Road. For traveling north and south, 44th Street, 24th Street, and Central Avenue are good choices. Hayden Road is a north-south alternative to Scottsdale Road, which gets jammed at rush hours.

FINDING AN ADDRESS **Central Avenue,** which runs north to south through downtown Phoenix, is the starting point for all east and west street numbering. **Washington Street** is the starting point for north and south numbering. North-to-south numbered *streets* are to be found on the east side of the city, while north-to-south numbered *avenues* will be found on the west. For the most part, street numbers change by 100 with each block. Odd-numbered addresses are on the south and east sides of streets, while even-numbered addresses are on north and west sides of streets.

For example, if you're looking for 4454 East Camelback Rd., you'll find it 44 blocks east of Central Avenue between 44th and 45th streets on the north side of the street. If you're looking for 2905 North 35th Ave., you'll find it 35 blocks west of Central Avenue and 29 blocks north of Washington Street on the east side of the street. Just for general reference, Camelback marks the 5000 block north.

STREET MAPS The street maps handed out by rental-car companies may be good for general navigation around the city, but they are almost useless for finding a particular address if it is not on a major arterial, so as soon as you can, stop in at a minimart and buy a Phoenix map. Unfortunately, you'll probably also have to buy a separate Scottsdale map. Alternatively, if you are a member of AAA, you can get a good Phoenix map before you leave home. You can also get a simple map at the airport tourist information desks or at the downtown visitor information center.

NEIGHBORHOODS IN BRIEF

Because of urban sprawl, Phoenix has yielded its importance to an area known as the Valley of the Sun (or just "The Valley"), an area encompassing Phoenix and its metropolitan area of more than 20 cities. Consequently, neighborhoods per se have lost much of their significance as outlying cities have taken on regional importance. That said, there are some neighborhoods worth noting.

Downtown Phoenix Roughly bordered by Thomas Road on the north, Buckeye Road on the south, 19th Avenue on the west, and Seventh Street on the east, downtown is primarily a business, financial, and government district, where both the city hall and state capitol are located. However, downtown Phoenix has been struggling to rise from the ashes of neglect for several years now and to that end has positioned itself as the valley's prime sports, entertainment, and museum district. The Arizona Diamondbacks play big-league baseball in the **Bank One Ballpark (BOB),** while the Phoenix Suns shoot hoops at the **America West Arena.** There are three major performing-arts venues—the historic **Orpheum Theatre, Phoenix Symphony Hall,** and the **Herberger Theater Center.** At the Arizona Center shopping and entertainment plaza, there's a huge multiplex movie theater as well as several large bars. Downtown museums include the **Phoenix Museum of History** and the **Arizona Science Center,** both of which are located in Heritage and Science Park. Other area attractions include **Heritage Square** (historic homes), the **Arizona State Capitol Museum,** and the **Arizona Mining & Mineral Museum.** On the northern edge of downtown are the **Heard Museum,** the **Phoenix Central Library** (an architectural gem), and the **Phoenix Art Museum.** Currently, the core of the downtown area is being referred to as Copper Square in yet another attempt by the city to give the area an identity.

Biltmore District The Biltmore District, also known as the **Camelback Corridor,** centers along Camelback Road between 24th and 44th streets and is Phoenix's upscale shopping, residential, and business district. The area is characterized by modern office buildings and is anchored by the Arizona Biltmore Hotel and Biltmore Fashion Park shopping mall.

Scottsdale A separate city of more than 200,000 people, Scottsdale extends from Tempe in the south to Carefree in the north, a distance of more than 20 miles.

Scottsdale Road between Indian School Road and Shea Boulevard has long been known as **"Resort Row"** and is home to more than a dozen major resorts. However, as Scottsdale has sprawled ever northward, so, too, have the resorts, and now north Scottsdale is rapidly becoming the center of the resort scene. Downtown Scottsdale, which consists of Old Town, the Main Street Arts and Antiques District, the Marshall Way Contemporary Arts District, and the Fifth Avenue Shops, is filled with tourist shops, galleries, boutiques, Native American crafts stores, and restaurants.

Tempe Tempe is the home of Arizona State University and has all the trappings of a university town, which means lots of nightclubs and bars. The center of activity, both day and night, is **Mill Avenue,** which has dozens of interesting shops along a stretch of about 4 blocks. This is one of the few areas in the valley where locals actually walk the streets and hang out at sidewalk cafes (Old Town Scottsdale often has people on its streets, but few are locals).

Paradise Valley If Scottsdale is Phoenix's Beverly Hills, then Paradise Valley is its Bel-Air. The most exclusive neighborhood in the valley is almost entirely residential, but you won't see too many of the more lavish homes because they're set on large tracts of land.

Mesa This eastern suburb of Phoenix is the valley's main high-tech area. Large shopping malls, many inexpensive chain motels, and a couple of small museums attract both locals and visitors to Mesa.

Glendale Northwest of downtown Phoenix, Glendale has numerous historic buildings in its downtown. With its dozens of antiques and collectibles stores, it has become the antiques capital of the valley. The city also has several small museums, including the Bead Museum and Historic Saguaro Ranch.

Carefree & Cave Creek   Located about 20 miles north of Old Scottsdale, these two communities represent the Old West and the new West. Carefree is a planned community and home to the prestigious Boulders resort and El Pedregal shopping center. Neighboring Cave Creek, on the other hand, plays up its Western heritage in its architecture and preponderance of bars, steakhouses, and shops selling Western crafts and other gifts.

2 Getting Around

BY CAR

Phoenix and the surrounding cities that together make up the Valley of the Sun sprawl over more than 400 square miles, so if you want to make the best use of your time, it's essential to have a car. Outside downtown Phoenix, there's almost always plenty of free parking wherever you go (although finding a parking space can be time consuming in Old Scottsdale and at some of the more popular malls and shopping plazas).

RENTALS   Because Phoenix is a major tourist destination, excellent car-rental rates are often available. However, taxes on rentals at Sky Harbor Airport run around 25% to 27%, which pretty much negates any deal you might get on your rate. The best rates are those reserved at least a week in advance, but car-rental companies change rates frequently as demand goes up and down. If you book far enough in advance, you might get a compact car for less than $165 per week. See also chapter 2, "Planning Your Trip to Arizona," for general tips on car rentals.

All major rental-car companies have offices at Sky Harbor Airport as well as other locations in the Phoenix area. Among them are the following: **Alamo** (© 800/327-9633 or 602/244-0897), **Avis** (© 800/331-1212 or 602/273-3222), **Budget** (© 800/527-0700 or 602/267-1717), **Dollar** (© 800/800-4000 or 602/275-7588), **Enterprise** (© 800/736-8222 or 602/225-0588), **Hertz** (© 800/654-3131 or 602/267-8822), **National** (© 800/227-7368 or 602/275-4771), and **Thrifty** (© 800/367-2277 or 602/244-0311).

If you'd like a bit more style while you cruise from resort to golf course to nightclub to wherever, **Rent-a-Vette**, 1215 N. Scottsdale Rd., Tempe (© **480/941-3001**), can put you behind the wheel of a car that will get you a bit more respect from valet-parking attendants. A Corvette runs $199 to $249 per day. Rent-a-Vette also rents Porsche Boxters, Mustang GTs, Jaguars XKAs, and Plymouth Prowlers.

At the rugged end of the car-rental spectrum is **Arizona Jeep & Hummer** (© **602/674-8469;** www.sedonajeeprentals.com), which rents Jeep Wranglers for $99 for a half day or $129 to $149 for a full day. Rates go down the more days you rent, and special lower rates are sometimes available. Along with your rental, you can get a trail book and directions for various trails into the desert. For two or more people, this is an economical alternative to doing a Jeep tour.

If a Jeep still doesn't offer enough excitement and wind in your hair, how about a motorcycle? **Western States Motorcycle Tours** (© **602/943-9030;** www.azmcrent.com) rents Harley-Davidson, BMW, and Suzuki motorcycles for between $70 and $175 per day ($400–$750 per week). You must have a valid motorcycle driver's license. In Arizona you don't have to wear a helmet, so you really can ride with the wind in your hair.

BY PUBLIC TRANSPORTATION

Unfortunately, **Valley Metro** (© 602/253-5000; www.valleymetro.maricopa. gov), the Phoenix public bus system, is not very useful to tourists. It's primarily meant to be used by commuters. However, if you decide you want to take the bus, pick up a copy of *The Bus Book* at one of the tourist information desks in the airport (where it's sometimes available), at Central Station at the corner of Central Avenue and Van Buren Street, or any Frys supermarket. Local bus fare is $1.25, and express bus fare is $1.75. A 10-ride ticket book, all-day passes, and monthly passes are available.

Of slightly more value to visitors is the free **Downtown Area Shuttle (DASH),** which provides bus service within the downtown area. These buses operate Monday through Friday between 6:30am and 5:30pm. The buses serve regular stops every 6 to 12 minutes. This shuttle is primarily for downtown workers, but attractions along the route include the state capitol, Heritage Square, and the Arizona Center shopping mall. In Tempe, **Free Local Area Shuttle (FLASH)** buses provide a similar service on a loop around Arizona State University. The route includes Mill Avenue and Sun Devil Stadium. A separate FLASH route, called FLASH Lite, operates between Mill Avenue and Papago Park, where you'll find the Desert Botanical Garden and Phoenix Zoo. For information on both DASH and FLASH, call © **602/253-5000.**

In Scottsdale, you can ride the **Scottsdale Round Up** (© **480/312-7696**) shuttle buses between Scottsdale Fashion Square, the Fifth Avenue shops, the Main Street Arts and Antiques district, and the Old Town district. These buses operate Monday through Saturday between mid-November and late May.

BY TAXI

Because distances in Phoenix are so great, the price of an average taxi ride can be quite high. However, if you don't have your own wheels and the bus isn't running because it's late at night or the weekend, you won't have any choice but to call a cab. **Yellow Cab** (© **602/252-5252**) charges $3 for the first mile and $1.50 per mile thereafter. **Scottsdale Cab** (© **480/994-1616**) charges $2 per mile, with a $5 minimum.

Ⓒ *FAST FACTS:* **Phoenix**

American Express   There are American Express offices at 2508 E. Camel-back Rd. (© **602/468-1199**), open Monday through Saturday from 10am to 6pm, and in Scottsdale Fashion Square at 6900 E. Camelback Rd., Scottsdale (© **480/949-7000**), open Monday through Friday from 9:30am to 5:30pm and Saturday from 9:30am to 3pm.

Airport   See "Orientation," earlier in this chapter.

Baby-Sitters   If your hotel can't recommend or provide a sitter, contact the **Granny Company** (© 602/956-4040). For baby equipment rentals, such as a crib or stroller, contact **Baby Boom Rentals** (© 602/331-8881).

Car Rentals   See "Getting Around," earlier in this chapter.

Climate   See "When to Go," in chapter 2.

Dentist Call Dental Referral Service (✆ **800/510-7765**) for a referral.

Doctor Call the Maricopa County Medical Society (✆ **602/252-2844**) or the Physician Referral and Resource Line (✆ **602/230-2273**) for doctor referrals.

Emergencies For police, fire, or medical emergency, phone ✆ **911.**

Eyeglass Repair The **Nationwide Vision Center** has more than 10 locations around the valley, including 5130 N. 19th Ave. (✆ **602/242-5293**); 3202 E. Greenway, Paradise Valley (✆ **602/788-8413**); 4615 E. Thomas Rd. (✆ **602/952-8667**); and 933 E. University Dr., Tempe (✆ **480/966-4992**).

Hospitals The Good Samaritan Regional Medical Center, 1111 E. McDowell Rd. (✆ **602/239-2000**), is one of the largest hospitals in the valley.

Hot Lines The **Visitor Information Line** (✆ **602/252-5588**) has recorded tourist information on Phoenix and the Valley of the Sun. **Tell Me/Pressline** (✆ **602/271-5656**) provides access to daily news, the correct time, weather, and other topics.

Information See "Visitor Information" under "Orientation," earlier in this chapter.

Internet Access If your hotel doesn't provide Internet access, your next best bet is to visit one of the **Kinko's** in the area. There are Kinko's locations in downtown Phoenix at 201 E. Washington St., Suite 101 (✆ **602/252-4055**); off the Camelback corridor at 3801 N. Central Ave. (✆ **602/241-9440**); and in Scottsdale just off Indian School Road at 4150 N. Drinkwater Blvd. (✆ **480/946-0500**).

Lost Property If you lose something in the airport, call ✆ **602/273-3307**; on a bus, call ✆ **602/253-5000.**

Maps See "City Layout" under "Orientation," earlier in this chapter.

Newspapers & Magazines The *Arizona Republic* is Phoenix's daily newspaper. The Thursday edition has a special section ("The Rep") with schedules of the upcoming week's movie, music, and cultural performances. *New Times* is a free weekly news and arts journal with comprehensive listings of cultural events, film, and rock club and concert schedules. The best place to find *New Times* is at corner newspaper boxes in downtown Phoenix, Scottsdale, or Tempe.

Pharmacies Call ✆ **800/WALGREENS** for the Walgreens pharmacy that's nearest you; some are open 24 hours a day.

Police For police emergencies, phone ✆ **911.**

Post Office The Phoenix Main Post Office, 5252 N. Central Ave. (✆ **800/275-8777**), is open Monday through Friday from 9am to 5pm.

Safety Don't leave valuables in view in your car, especially when parking in downtown Phoenix. Put anything of value in the trunk, or under the seat if you're driving a hatchback. Take extra precautions after dark in the south-central Phoenix area and downtown. Violent acts of road rage are all too common in Phoenix, so it's a good idea to be polite when driving. Aggressive drivers should be given plenty of room.

   Many hotels now provide in-room safes, for which there's sometimes a daily charge. Others will be glad to store your valuables in a safety-deposit box at the front office.

Taxes State sales tax is 5.5% (plus variable local taxes). Hotel room taxes vary considerably by city but are mostly between 10% and 11%. However, it is in renting a car that you really get pounded. Expect to pay taxes in excess of 25% when renting a car at Sky Harbor Airport. You can save up to 11% (the airport concession fee recoupment charge) by renting your car at an office outside the airport.

Taxis See "Getting Around," earlier in this chapter.

Transit Information For Phoenix Transit System public bus information, call ℂ **602/253-5000.**

Weather For weather information, call ℂ **602/271-5656,** ext. 1010.

3 Where to Stay

Because the Phoenix area has long been popular as a winter refuge from cold and snow, it now has the greatest concentration of resorts in the continental United States. However, even with all the hotel rooms here, sunshine and spring training combine to make it hard to find a room on short notice between February and April (the busiest time of year in the valley). If you're planning to visit during these months, make your reservations as far in advance as possible. Also keep in mind that in winter, the Phoenix metro area has some of the highest rates in the country. Hotels are increasingly turning to the airline model: Rates go up and down with demand, so you never know what they might be charging on a given date. Don't forget that it's often possible to get a lower rate simply by asking. If a hotel isn't full and isn't expected to be, you should be able to get a lower rate. Unfortunately, the reverse also holds true.

With the exception of valet-parking services and parking garages at downtown convention hotels, parking is free at most Phoenix hotels. If there is a parking charge, we have noted it. You'll find that all hotels have no-smoking rooms and all but the cheapest have wheelchair-accessible rooms.

Also, keep in mind that most resorts offer a variety of weekend, golf, and tennis packages, as well as special off-season discounts and corporate rates (which you can often get just by asking). We've given only the official "rack rates," or walk-in rates, below, but it always pays to ask if there's any kind of special discount or package available. Don't forget your AAA or AARP discounts if you belong to these organizations. Remember that business hotels downtown and near the airport often lower their rates on weekends.

If you're looking to save money, consider traveling during the shoulder seasons of late spring and late summer. Temperatures are not at their midsummer peak nor are room rates at their midwinter highs. (And if you can stand the heat of summer, you can often save more than 50% on room rates.) If you'll be traveling with children, always ask whether your child will be able to stay for free in your room, and whether there's a limit to the number of children who can stay for free.

Request a room with a view of the mountains whenever possible. You can overlook a swimming pool anywhere, but some of the main selling points of Phoenix and Scottsdale hotels are the views of Mummy Mountain, Camelback Mountain, and Squaw Peak.

BED & BREAKFASTS While most people dreaming of an Arizona winter vacation have visions of luxury resorts dancing in their heads, there are also plenty of bed-and-breakfast inns around the valley. **Advance Reservations Inn Arizona/Mi Casa-Su Casa Bed & Breakfast Reservation Service,** P.O. Box 950, Tempe, AZ 85280-0950 (© **800/456-0682** or 480/990-0682; www.azres.com), can book you into more than 65 homes in the Valley of the Sun (and a total of 280 throughout the state), as can **Arizona Trails Bed & Breakfast Reservation Service,** P.O. Box 18998, Fountain Hills, AZ 85269-8998 (© **888/799-4284** or 480/837-4284; fax 480/816-4224; www. arizonatrails.com), which also books tour and hotel reservations.

SCOTTSDALE

Scottsdale is the center of the valley's resort scene, with a dozen or more resorts lined up along Scottsdale Road. Because Scottsdale is also the valley's prime shopping and dining district, this is the most convenient place to stay if you're here to eat and shop. However, traffic in Scottsdale is bad, the landscape at most resorts is flat (as compared to hillside settings in north Scottsdale), and you don't get much feel for being in the desert.

VERY EXPENSIVE

Hyatt Regency Scottsdale ★★★ *Kids* From the colonnades of palm trees to the lobby walls that slide away, this luxurious resort is designed to astonish. A 2½-acre water playground serves as the resort's focal point, and the extravagant complex of 10 swimming pools includes a water slide, a sand beach, a water-volleyball pool, waterfalls, and a huge whirlpool spa. The grounds are planted with hundreds of palm trees that frame the gorgeous views of the distant McDowell Mountains; closer at hand, original works of art have been placed throughout the resort. Guest rooms are luxurious and reflect the desert location. The top-end Golden Swan restaurant has an unusual sunken waterside terrace (see "Where to Dine," later in this chapter), while another restaurant provides after-dinner gondola rides. The resort's Hopi Learning Center, staffed by Hopi interpreters, provides a glimpse into Native American culture.

7500 E. Doubletree Ranch Rd., Scottsdale, AZ 85258. © **800/55-HYATT** or 480/991-3388. Fax 480/483-5550. www.scottsdale.hyatt.com. 493 units. Jan–late May $375–$515 double, from $555 suite and casita; late May–early Sept $195–$485 double, from $245 suite and casita; early Sept–Dec $330–$460 double, from $500 suite and casita. AE, DC, DISC, MC, V. **Amenities:** 4 restaurants (new American, Southwestern, Italian), 2 snack bars, 2 lounges, coffee bar, juice bar; 10 pools; 27-hole golf course (with lots of water hazards); 8 tennis courts; croquet court; health club and spa; Jacuzzi; children's programs; concierge; car-rental desk; business center; shopping arcade; salon; 24-hour room service; massage; baby-sitting; laundry service; dry cleaning. *In room:* A/C, TV, dataport, minibar, hair dryer, iron, safe.

Marriott's Camelback Inn ★★★ Set at the foot of Mummy Mountain and overlooking Camelback Mountain, the Camelback Inn, which opened in 1936, is one of the grande dames of the Phoenix hotel scene and abounds in traditional Southwestern character. Over the past few years, the resort has undergone $35 million worth of renovations, which have brought the Camelback Inn into the 21st century and added lots of great amenities that vacationers will appreciate. Although the two 18-hole golf courses are the main attractions for many guests, the spa is among the finest in the state, and there's also an extensive pool complex that appeals to families. The guest rooms, which are spread out over the sloping grounds, are decorated with Southwestern furnishings and art, and all have balconies or patios. The resort's top restaurant, the Chaparral, has long been a valley favorite (see "Where to Dine," later in this chapter, for details).

Phoenix, Scottsdale & the Valley of the Sun Accommodations

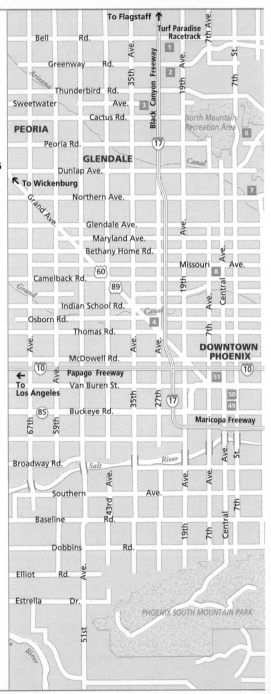

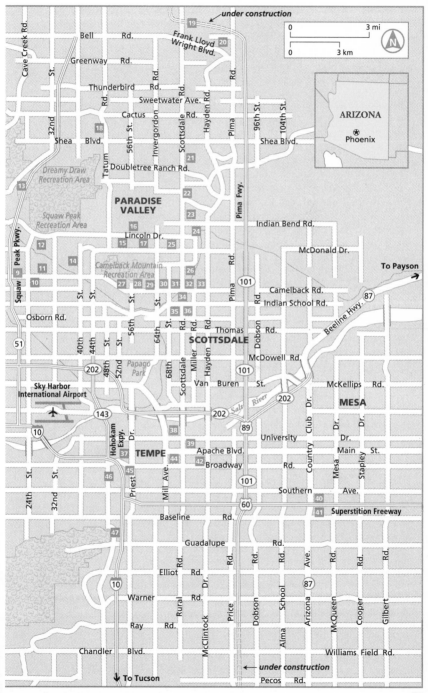

5402 E. Lincoln Dr., Scottsdale, AZ 85253. (✆ **800/24-CAMEL** or 480/948-1700. Fax 480/951-8469. www.camelbackinn.com. 453 units. Jan to early May $419–$459 double, $629–$2,050 suite; early May to early Sept $179–$349 double, $215–$1,525 suite; early Sept to Dec $349 double, $375–$1,525 suite. AE, DC, DISC, MC, V. Small pets accepted. **Amenities:** 4 restaurants (Continental, Southwestern, healthy, American), 2 snack bars/cafes, lounge; 3 pools; 2 outstanding 18-hole golf courses; pitch-and-putt green; 6 tennis courts; basketball and volleyball courts; exercise room; one of the valley's best full-service spas; 3 Jacuzzis; bike rentals; children's programs and playground; concierge; car-rental desk; business center; salon; room service; massage; baby-sitting; coin-op laundry and laundry service; dry cleaning. *In room:* A/C, TV, dataport, minibar, fridge, coffeemaker, hair dryer, iron, safe.

Millennium Resort Scottsdale McCormick Ranch ★★

If you like the heat but not the desert, this resort, with its lakefront setting, is a good bet. Surrounded by green lawns, a golf course, and the water, this relatively small resort strives to convince you that you're not in the desert. The lake (complete with sailboats for guests) is the focal point, but more traditional resort activities are available at the two 18-hole golf courses and three tennis courts. The guest rooms all have private balconies or patios, and more than half overlook the lake. If you're here with your family, consider the spacious villas. The resort's restaurant serves good Southwestern fare and has a lake view, as does the adjacent lounge.

7401 N. Scottsdale Rd., Scottsdale, AZ 85253-3548. (✆ **800/243-1332** or 480/948-5050. Fax 480/991-5572. www.millennium-hotels.com. 180 units. Feb–Apr $219–$329 double, from $395 suite or villa; May $169–$239 double, from $235 suite or villa; June–Aug $69–$139 double, from $160 suite or villa; Sept–Jan $279–$349 double, from $265 suite or villa. AE, DC, DISC, MC, V. **Amenities:** 2 restaurants (Southwestern), lounge; outdoor pool; 2 18-hole golf courses; 3 tennis courts; volleyball court; pro shop; exercise room; Jacuzzi; water sports; concierge; business center; room service; baby-sitting; laundry service; dry cleaning. *In room:* A/C, TV, dataport, minibar, coffeemaker, hair dryer, iron.

The Phoenician ★★★ (Kids)

No expense was spared in the construction of this palatial resort, which is situated on 250 acres at the foot of Camelback Mountain, and the Phoenician consistently ranks among the finest resorts in the world. Polished marble and sparkling crystal abound in the lobby, but the view of the valley through a long wall of glass is what commands most guests' attention. Service here is second to none (and can even be overbearing at times). The pool complex, which includes a water slide for the kids, is one of the finest in the state, and the resort's Centre for Well Being offers all the spa pampering anyone could ever need. There are also 27 challenging holes of golf. Mary Elaine's is Phoenix's ultimate special-occasion restaurant, while Windows on the Green is just a step behind (see "Where to Dine," later in this chapter). Guest rooms are as elaborate as the public areas and include large patios and sunken bathtubs for two. However, as luxurious as the rooms are, it's questionable whether they warrant the price tag. All rooms were scheduled for face-lifts in the summer of 2001.

6000 E. Camelback Rd., Scottsdale, AZ 85251. (✆ **800/888-8234** or 480/941-8200. Fax 480/947-4311. www.thephoenician.com. 654 units. Late Dec to mid-May $550–$675 double, $1,450–$5,500 suite; mid-May to early June $455–$515 double, $1,325–$5,500 suite; early June to mid-Sept $215–$275 double, $650–$5,300 suite; mid-Sept to late Dec $455–$515 double, $1,325–$5,500 suite. AE, DC, DISC, MC, V. Valet parking $18. Pets under 25 lb. accepted. **Amenities:** 3 restaurants (French, Southwestern, Continental/ American), 4 snack bars/cafes, lounge; 9 pools; 27-hole golf course; putting green; 12 tennis courts; health club and spa; Jacuzzi; lawn games; bike rentals; children's programs; concierge; car-rental desk; business center; shopping arcade; salon; 24-hour room service; massage; baby-sitting; laundry service; dry cleaning. *In room:* A/C, TV, dataport, minibar, hair dryer, iron, safe, CD player.

Renaissance Scottsdale Resort ★★ (Value)

Located behind the upscale Borgata shopping center (which is designed to resemble the Tuscan hill town of San Gimignano), this is an unpretentious-yet-luxurious boutique resort. Set amid shady lawns, the Renaissance Scottsdale Resort consists of spacious suites designed for those who need plenty of room and comfort. More than 100 of the suites have their own private hot tubs on private patios, and all the suites are done in Southwestern style. Several excellent restaurants are within walking distance, which makes this a good choice for gourmands who don't want to spend their vacation fighting rush-hour traffic on Scottsdale Road.

6160 N. Scottsdale Rd., Scottsdale, AZ 85253. © **800/HOTELS-1** or 480/991-1414. Fax 480/951-3350. www.renaissancehotels.com. 171 units. Early Jan to early May $219–$249 double, $269–$349 suite; early June to early Sept $89 double, $109–$129 suite; early Sept to Dec $199 double, $249–$309 suite. AE, DC, DISC, MC, V. Pets under 25 lb. accepted ($50 deposit). **Amenities:** Restaurant (Mediterranean), lounge, poolside snack bar; 2 pools; putting green; 4 tennis courts; access to nearby health club; croquet court; exercise room; two Jacuzzis; bike rentals; concierge; room service; baby-sitting; laundry service; dry cleaning. *In room:* A/C, TV, dataport, minibar, coffeemaker, hair dryer, iron, safe.

The Sunburst Resort ★★ *Value*   An exceptional location in the heart of the Scottsdale shopping district, a dramatic Southwestern styling (the focal point of the lobby is a massive sandstone fireplace), and a small but well-designed pool area are the primary appeals of this resort. Set in a lushly planted courtyard are a small lagoon-style pool, complete with sand beach and short water slide, and a second pool with flame-topped columnar waterfalls. An artificial stream and fake sandstone ruins all add up to a fun desert fantasy landscape (although not on the grand scale to be found at some area resorts). The comfortable guest rooms are decorated in new "Old West" style, with cowhide prints and peeled log furnishings; French doors open onto patios.

4925 N. Scottsdale Rd., Scottsdale, AZ 85251. © **800/528-7867** or 480/945-7666. Fax 480/946-4056. www.sunburstresort.com. 210 units. Jan to mid-Apr $235–$285 double, $635–$950 suite; mid-Apr to mid-May $215–$255 double, $575–$850 suite; late May to mid-Sept $95–$135 double, $300–$450 suite; mid-Sept to Dec $185–$225 double, $500–$750 suite. AE, DC, DISC, MC, V. **Amenities:** Restaurant (Mediterranean/Southwestern), lounge, snack bar; 2 pools; exercise room; Jacuzzi; concierge; car-rental desk; business center; room service; laundry service; dry cleaning; Fri-night wine tastings. *In room:* A/C, TV, dataport, minibar, coffeemaker, hair dryer, iron.

EXPENSIVE

Doubletree La Posada Resort ★★ *Kids*   If you prefer to spend your time by the pool rather than on the fairways, La Posada is a great choice, especially if you have the kids along. The pool here, which has a view of Camelback Mountain, covers half an acre and features its own two-story waterfall that cascades over artificial boulders. Connecting the two halves of the pool is a swim-through grotto complete with bar/cafe (and exercise room). The dining room serves pricey meals, with the exception of Sunday brunch, which is a bargain by Scottsdale standards. Mission Revival architecture prevails throughout the resort. Guest rooms are larger than average and have tiled bathrooms with double vanities.

4949 E. Lincoln Dr., Scottsdale, AZ 85253. © **800/222-TREE** or 602/952-0420. Fax 602/840-8576. www.doubletreelaposada.com. 262 units. Mid-Sept to mid-May $140–$200 double, $400–$550 suite; mid-May to mid-Sept $79–$112 double, $400–$550 suite. AE, DC, DISC, MC, V. Pets accepted. **Amenities:** Restaurant (Southwestern), snack bar, 2 lounges; 2 pools; 2 putting greens; 6 tennis courts; 2 racquetball courts; volleyball court; tennis pro shop; exercise room; spa; 4 Jacuzzis; sauna; bike rentals; concierge; car-rental desk; room service; massage; laundry service; dry cleaning. *In room:* A/C, TV, dataport, minibar, fridge, coffeemaker, hair dryer, iron.

Doubletree Paradise Valley Resort ★★   This resort gives a bow to the pioneering architectural style of Frank Lloyd Wright, and thus stands out from other comparable Scottsdale resorts. Built around several courtyards containing swimming pools, bubbling fountains, and gardens with desert landscaping, the property has much the look and feel of the nearby Hyatt Regency Scottsdale Resort (although on a less grandiose scale). Mature palm trees lend a sort of Moorish feel to the grounds and cast fanciful shadows in the gardens. Accommodations have a very contemporary feel, with lots of blond wood and, in some cases, high ceilings that make the rooms feel particularly spacious.

5401 N. Scottsdale Rd., Scottsdale, AZ 85250. ✆ **800/222-TREE** or 480/947-5400. Fax 480/481-0209. www.doubletreehotels.com. 387 units. Jan–Mar $205–$259 double, from $305 suite; Apr and Sept–Dec $99–$155 double, from $235 suite; May–Aug $65–$119 double, from $189 suite. AE, DC, DISC, MC, V. **Amenities:** 2 restaurants (Southwestern, steakhouse), lounge with live music, snack bar; 2 outdoor pools; putting green; 2 tennis courts; 5 racquetball courts; exercise room; 2 Jacuzzis; saunas; concierge; car-rental desk; business center; room service; massage; baby-sitting; laundry service; dry cleaning. *In room:* A/C, TV, dataport, minibar, coffeemaker, hair dryer, iron.

Embassy Suites Phoenix/Scottsdale ✷

While cities from New York to San Francisco are busy opening chic and stylishly contemporary hotels as fast as they can, the Valley of the Sun has nearly missed the boat completely. This hotel, however, is the exception and appeals to young, hip travelers. As soon as you see the dyed concrete floor and unusual wall sculpture in the lobby, you'll know that this is not your standard business hotel. However, it might be difficult to take your eyes off the views across Stonecreek Golf Course to Camelback Mountain, Mummy Mountain, and Squaw Peak, and those views just get better the higher up you go (be sure to ask for a room on the south side of an upper floor). Keep in mind that this is an all-suite property; the two-room accommodations are very spacious and come complete with galley kitchens.

4415 E. Paradise Village Pkwy. S., Paradise Valley, AZ 85032. ✆ **800/EMBASSY** or 602/765-5800. Fax 602/765-5890. www.embassysuitesaz.com. 270 units. Jan–Mar $189 double; Mar to late May $169 double; late May to mid-Sept $109 double; mid-Sept to Dec $159 double. Rates include full breakfast. AE, DC, DISC, MC, V. **Amenities:** Restaurant (Continental), lounge, complimentary cocktail reception; small outdoor pool; exercise room; access to nearby health club; Jacuzzi; concierge; business center; room service; massage; baby-sitting; coin-op laundry; laundry service; dry cleaning. *In room:* A/C, TV, dataport, kitchenette, minibar, coffeemaker, hair dryer, iron, safe.

Holiday Inn SunSpree Resort ✷✷ *Kids*

Long one of the valley's best resort deals, the SunSpree has been upgrading over the past few years—and its rates seem to be creeping up. Still, compared to other area resorts, it is relatively economical. Situated on 16 acres amid wide expanses of lawn, the SunSpree may not be as luxurious as other area resorts, but it is a good choice for families (the adjacent McCormick-Stillman Railroad Park is a big hit with kids). Guests can golf at the new Scottsdale Silverado Golf Club, located immediately adjacent to the resort, while nongolfers can avail themselves of many other recreational options. Guest rooms have a plush feel that belies the reasonable rates. Ask for a room with mountain view or a lakeside unit with patio. At press time, there were plans to add a second pool, complete with a sand beach.

7601 E. Indian Bend Rd., Scottsdale, AZ 85250. ✆ **800/852-5205** or 480/991-2400. Fax 480/998-2261. www.arizonaguide.com/sunspree. 200 units. Jan to early Apr $189–$209 double; early Sept to Dec and mid-Apr to late May $165–$185 double; late May to early Sept $105–$125 double. AE, DC, DISC, MC, V. **Amenities:** Restaurant (new American), lounge, snack bar; 2 pools; 18-hole golf course; 2 tennis courts; volleyball court; lawn games; exercise room; Jacuzzi; bike rentals; room service; coin-op laundry; dry cleaning. *In room:* A/C, TV, dataport, fridge, coffeemaker, hair dryer, iron, safe.

Marriott's Mountain Shadows Resort & Golf Club ✷✷ *Value*

Located across the road from Marriott's Camelback Inn, Mountain Shadows has a much more casual atmosphere than its sister property. Built in the late 1950s and somewhat dated architecturally, this resort is well maintained and will appeal to anyone looking for a good value and an informal setting. While an 18-hole executive course keeps most guests happy, guests also have access to the Camelback Inn's two golf courses, as well as that resort's superb spa. Standard rooms have high ceilings, wet bars, king-size beds, and balconies; the units in the Palm section offer the best views of the mountain. The rooms around the main pool, although large, can be a bit noisy during spring break and other times of year that attract families.

5641 E. Lincoln Dr., Scottsdale, AZ 85253. ⓒ 800/228-9290 or 480/948-7111. Fax 480/951-5430. 337 units. Early Jan to early June $219–$249 double, $269–$709 suite; early June to early Sept $99 double, $125–$350 suite; early Sept to Dec $199 double, $269–$669 suite. AE, DC, DISC, MC, V. Small pets accepted. **Amenities:** 4 restaurants (seafood, Southwestern, American), snack bar, lounge; 3 pools (1 is quite large); 18-hole executive golf course; 8 tennis courts; volleyball court; exercise room; spa; 2 Jacuzzis; bike rentals; seasonal children's programs; concierge; car-rental desk; business center; pro shops; room service; massage; baby-sitting; coin-op laundry; dry cleaning. In room: A/C, TV, dataport, minibar, coffeemaker, hair dryer, iron, safe.

Radisson Resort Scottsdale 🟌🟌 With all its green lawns, orange trees, and oleanders, this resort doesn't exactly feel Southwestern, despite the attractive new flagstone façade on the front of the main building. However, if a lush landscape and a conservative atmosphere are what you're looking for, this is a good bet. Most guests are attracted by the resort's 21 tennis courts or the two traditional 18-hole golf courses at the adjacent McCormick Ranch Golf Club (which, however, are not among the valley's top courses). Also featured on the property are a large Japanese-style health spa and a pool that's twice normal Olympic size (although the poolside patio seems designed more for conventioneers than for vacationers). Most bedrooms are large and have private patios; the golf-course rooms, with views of the McDowell Mountains, are our favorites.

7171 N. Scottsdale Rd., Scottsdale, AZ 85253. ⓒ 800/333-3333 or 480/991-3800. Fax 480/948-1381. www.radisson.com/scottsdaleaz. 318 units. Early Jan to mid-Apr $169–$279 double, $219–$1,500 suite; mid-Apr to early June $109–$219 double, $159–$1,500 suite; early June to early Sept $59–$139 double, $109–$1,500 suite; early Sept to early Jan $109–$219 double, $159–$1,500 suite. AE, DC, DISC, MC, V. **Amenities:** 2 restaurants (new American, Asian), lounge, snack bar, patisserie; 3 pools, including a large central pool; 2 18-hole golf courses; 21 tennis courts; health club and spa; Jacuzzi; concierge; car-rental desk; business center; pro shop; salon; room service; massage; coin-op laundry; laundry service; dry cleaning. In room: A/C, TV, dataport, minibar, coffeemaker, hair dryer, iron.

MODERATE

Hacienda Resort (Finds) Don't be taken in by the name; this little place is hardly a resort, but it is a well-placed and well-priced getaway spot with the look and feel of an updated 1960s apartment court. Funky and hip are the watchwords here, although the hipness is mostly in the tiny lobby. The inn's grassy little courtyard, which has a small pool and a hot tub, is set off from busy Camelback Road by a brick wall that gives the complex a private, residential feel. Rooms are fairly well maintained and range from big to huge. Although the bathrooms are small, most guest rooms have full kitchens. Within just a few blocks are lots of nightclubs, great restaurants, and excellent shopping. A good choice for younger travelers.

7320 E. Camelback Rd., Scottsdale, AZ 85251. ⓒ 480/994-4170. www.haciendaresort.com. 22 units. Mid-Nov to late May $99–$149 double, $159–$979 suite; mid-May to Dec 31 $79–$89 double, $109–$179 suite. AE, MC, V. Pets accepted ($15 per night). **Amenities:** Small outdoor pool; Jacuzzi; coin-op laundry. In room: A/C, TV, dataport, kitchenette, coffeemaker, hair dryer.

Holiday Inn Old Town Scottsdale 🟌 Guest rooms at this low-rise hotel are fairly small (as are the bathrooms), but the location—right on the beautifully landscaped Scottsdale Civic Center Mall (a park, not a shopping center)—is very appealing. The Scottsdale Center for the Arts is just across the mall, and you're only a block away from Old Town Scottsdale and 2 blocks from the art-gallery district. The best units are those opening onto the mall—be sure to ask for one. The hotel's dining room is a very economical steakhouse overlooking the green lawns of the mall.

7353 E. Indian School Rd., Scottsdale, AZ 85251. ℂ 800/695-6995 or 480/994-9203. Fax 480/941-2567. www.holidayinnscottsdale.com. 206 units. Jan–Apr $135–$160 double; May $109–$159 double; June to mid-Sept $59–$119 double; mid-Sept to Dec 31 $109–$160 double. AE, DC, DISC, MC, V. Pets accepted. **Amenities:** Restaurant (steakhouse), lounge; small outdoor pool; putting green; tennis court; Jacuzzi; bike rentals; concierge; courtesy shopping shuttle; room service; baby-sitting; laundry service; dry cleaning. *In room:* A/C, TV, dataport, coffeemaker, hair dryer, iron.

INEXPENSIVE

Despite the high-priced real estate, Scottsdale does have a few relatively inexpensive chain motels, although during the winter season, prices are higher than you'd expect. The rates given here are for the high season. The **Days Inn—Scottsdale/Fashion Square Resort,** 4710 N. Scottsdale Rd. (ℂ **480/947-5411**), charges $79 to $135 for a double. **Motel 6—Scottsdale,** 6848 E. Camelback Rd. (ℂ **480/946-2280**), offers doubles for $66. **Rodeway Inn—Phoenix/Scottsdale,** 7110 E. Indian School Rd. (ℂ **480/946-3456**), has rates of $113 to $156 double.

Econo Lodge—Scottsdale Riverwalk   For convenience and price, this motel can't be beat (at least not in Scottsdale). Located at the west end of the Fifth Avenue shopping district, this motel is within walking distance of some of the best shopping and dining in Scottsdale. The guest rooms are large and have been fairly recently renovated. The three-story building is arranged around a central courtyard, where you'll find the small pool.

6935 Fifth Ave., Scottsdale, AZ 85251. ℂ 800/528-7396 or 480/994-9461. Fax 480/947-1695. www.econolodge.com. 92 units. Jan to mid-Apr $69–$109 double; mid-Apr to June 30 $49–$79 double; July 1–Dec 31 $59–$89 double. Rates include continental breakfast. AE, DC, DISC, MC, V. **Amenities:** Restaurant; small outdoor pool; Jacuzzi; exercise room; coin-op laundry; laundry service; dry cleaning. *In room:* A/C, TV, fridge, coffeemaker, hair dryer, iron.

NORTH SCOTTSDALE, CAREFREE & CAVE CREEK

North Scottsdale is the brave new world for Valley of the Sun resorts. Situated at least a 30-minute drive from downtown Scottsdale, this area may be too far out of the mainstream for many visitors. However, if you're willing to stay this far north of all the action, what you'll get is the newest resorts and the most spectacular hillside settings in the valley. North Scottsdale is also home to the area's most highly regarded golf courses.

VERY EXPENSIVE

The Boulders ★★★   Set amid a jumble of giant boulders 45 minutes north of Scottsdale, this prestigious golf resort, more than any other in the Phoenix area, epitomizes the Southwest aesthetic. Adobe buildings blend unobtrusively into the desert, as do the two acclaimed golf courses. If you can tear yourself away from the fairways, you can relax around the pool, play tennis, take advantage of the new Golden Door Spa (which was scheduled to open in September 2001), or even try your hand at rock climbing. The lobby is in an adobe-style building with tree-trunk pillars and a flagstone floor, and the guest rooms continue the adobe styling with stucco walls, beehive fireplaces, and beamed ceilings. The best views are from the second-floor rooms. Bathrooms are large and luxuriously appointed, with tubs for two and separate showers. In addition to the upscale on-site restaurants, there are several other dining options at the adjacent El Pedregal Festival Marketplace.

34631 N. Tom Darlington Dr. (P.O. Box 2090), Carefree, AZ 85377. © 800/553-1717, 800/WYNDHAM, or 480/488-9009. Fax 480/488-4118. www.wyndham.com/luxury. 160 casitas. Mid-Jan to late Apr $595–$625 double, from $805 villa; early to mid-Jan, late Apr to late May, and early Sept to early Dec $475–$505 double, from $655 villa; late May to early June and mid-Dec $275–$305 double, from $435 villa; mid-June to early Sept $195–$225 double, from $435 villa (plus nightly service charge of $22 to $26, year-round). AE, DC, DISC, MC, V. Pets accepted ($100 nonrefundable deposit). **Amenities:** 7 restaurants (new American, Southwestern, American), lounge; 4 pools; 2 18-hole golf courses; pro shop; 8 tennis courts; exercise room; spa; 3 Jacuzzis; bike rentals; children's programs; concierge; business center; shopping arcade; salon; room service; massage; baby-sitting; laundry service; dry cleaning. *In room:* A/C, TV, dataport, minibar, coffeemaker, hair dryer, iron, safe.

The Fairmont Scottsdale Princess ✦✦✦   With its royal palms, tiled fountains, and waterfalls, the Princess is a modern rendition of a Moorish palace and offers an exotic atmosphere unmatched by any other valley resort. It's also home to the Phoenix Open golf tournament and the city's top tennis tournament, which means the two golf courses here are superb and the courts are top-notch. There's also a water playground complete with the two longest resort water slides in Arizona, and a new spa was scheduled to open in December 2001. This resort, which is located a 20-minute drive north of Old Town Scottsdale, will delight anyone in search of a romantic hideaway, while families will enjoy both the water playground and the pond where kids can go fishing. The decor of the guest rooms is elegant Southwestern, and all units have private balconies. The spacious bathrooms have double vanities and separate showers and tubs. The Marquesa serves superb Spanish cuisine, while upscale Mexican food and mariachis are the specialties at La Hacienda. (See "Where to Dine," later in this chapter).

7575 E. Princess Dr., Scottsdale, AZ 85255. © 800/344-4758 or 480/585-4848. Fax 480/585-0086. www.fairmont.com. 650 units. Jan to late Apr $359–$569 double, $569–$3,700 suite; late Apr to May and early Sept to Dec $229–$409 double, $439–$3,700 suite; June to early Sept $159–$319 double, $369–$3,700 suite. AE, DC, DISC, MC, V. **Amenities:** 4 restaurants (Spanish, Mexican, steakhouse, American), 3 lounges; 3 pools; 2 18-hole golf courses; 7 tennis courts; racquet, squash, and basketball courts; health club and spa; Jacuzzi; concierge; car-rental desk; courtesy shopping shuttle; business center; golf and tennis pro shops; shopping arcade; salon; 24-hour room service; massage; baby-sitting; laundry service; dry cleaning. *In room:* A/C, TV, dataport, minibar, coffeemaker, hair dryer, iron, safe.

Four Seasons Resort Scottsdale at Troon North ✦✦✦   Located in the foothills of north Scottsdale adjacent to and with privileges at the Troon North golf course (one of the state's most highly acclaimed courses), the Four Seasons has been working hard to knock the Boulders resort from its pinnacle. With casita accommodations scattered across a boulder-strewn hillside, the Four Seasons can certainly boast one of the most dramatic settings in the valley. Likewise, the guest rooms and suites are among the most spacious and luxurious you'll find in Arizona. If you can afford it, opt for one with a private plunge pool and an outdoor shower—a luxury usually found only in tropical resorts. With three restaurants on the premises, it's easy to forget how far out of the Scottsdale mainstream this place is.

10600 E. Crescent Moon Dr., Scottsdale, AZ 85255. © 800/332-3442 or 480/515-5700. Fax 480/515-5599. www.fourseasons.com. 210 units. Jan to mid-May $500–$650 double, $900–$4,000 suite; mid-May to mid-June and early Sept to late Dec $415–$515 double, $900–$4,000 suite; mid-June to early Sept $175–275 double, $495–$4,000 suite. AE, DC, DISC, MC, V. Pets accepted. **Amenities:** 3 restaurants (Italian, new American, Mexican), lounge; large 2-level pool plus children's pool; 2 18-hole golf courses; 4 tennis courts; large exercise room; spa; Jacuzzi; children's programs; concierge; car-rental desk; business center; salon; 24-hour room service; massage; baby-sitting; laundry service; dry cleaning. *In room:* A/C, TV/VCR, dataport, minibar, coffeemaker, hair dryer, iron, safe.

EXPENSIVE

Copperwynd Country Club & Inn ★★ *Value*   Although it's a long way out, this boutique hotel, high on a ridge top overlooking the town of Fountain Hills, is one of the most luxurious in the area. The property, part of an exclusive country-club community, is surrounded by a rugged desert landscape, which is one of the reasons we like this place so much: You know you're in the desert when you stay here. Although there's no golf course on the premises, there are several nearby, and the resort does have an impressive health club and small spa. The views are among the finest you'll find in the valley, and the Jacuzzi by the main pool is tucked into a rocky hillside and is as romantic as they come. All guest rooms have great views and feature a sort of European deluxe decor. Balconies provide plenty of room for lounging and taking in the vista.

13225 N. Eagle Ridge Dr., Fountain Hills, AZ 85268. © 877/707-7760 or 480/333-1900. www. copperwynd.com. 40 units. Late Dec to late Apr $249–$425 double, $1,000–$1,600 villa; late Apr to late May and late Sept to late Dec $179–$249 double, $800–$1,000 villa; late May to late Sept $99–$129 double, $400–$500 villa. AE, DC, DISC, MC, V. **Amenities:** 2 restaurants (new American, American) lounge, juice bar; 2 pools; 9 tennis courts; health club and spa; Jacuzzi; bike rentals; children's programs; concierge; business center; pro shop; salon; room service; massage; baby-sitting; laundry service; dry cleaning. *In room:* A/C, TV, dataport, fridge, coffeemaker, hair dryer, iron, safe.

Scottsdale Marriott at McDowell Mountains ★   This all-suite hotel, not far from the Scottsdale Princess, overlooks the Tournament Players Club (TPC) Desert Course, and while this may not be the TPC's main course, it still manages to give this hotel a very resortlike feel. Suites provide lots of space and feature luxurious bathrooms done in marble and granite; some have balconies as well. Those units overlooking the golf course are worth requesting, although there are also good views of the McDowell Mountains from some rooms.

16770 N. Perimeter Dr., Scottsdale, AZ 85260. © 800/228-9290 or 480/502-3836. Fax 480/502-0653. www.marriottscottsdale.com. 270 units. Jan to mid-May $229–$289 double; mid-May to mid-Sept $99–$119 double; mid-Sept to Dec $189–$219 double. AE, DC, DISC, MC, V. **Amenities:** Restaurant (Mediterranean), lounge, poolside snack bar; pool; adjacent 18-hole golf course; exercise room; Jacuzzi; saunas; concierge; car-rental desk; business center; room service; coin-op laundry; dry cleaning. *In room:* A/C, TV, dataport, fridge, coffeemaker, hair dryer, iron.

CENTRAL PHOENIX & THE CAMELBACK CORRIDOR

This area is the heart of the upscale Phoenix shopping and restaurant scene and is home to the Arizona Biltmore, one of the most prestigious resorts in the city. Old money and new money rub shoulders along the avenues here, and valet parking is de rigueur. Located roughly midway between downtown Scottsdale and downtown Phoenix, this area is a good bet for anyone intending to split his time between the downtown Phoenix cultural and sports district and the world-class shopping and dining in Scottsdale. The area has only one golf resort, but boasts a couple of smaller boutique hotels with loads of Arizona character.

VERY EXPENSIVE

Arizona Biltmore Resort & Spa ★★★   For timeless elegance, a prime location, and historic character, no other resort in the valley can touch the Arizona Biltmore. For decades this has been the favored Phoenix address of celebrities and politicians, and the distinctive cast-cement blocks designed by Frank Lloyd Wright make it one of the valley's architectural gems. While the two golf courses and expansive spa are the main draws for many guests, the children's activities center also makes this a popular choice for families. Of the several different styles of accommodations, the "resort rooms" are large and quite comfortable, and come with balconies or patios. Those rooms in the Arizona Wing are also good choices. The villa suites are the most spacious and luxurious of all. Afternoon tea, a Phoenix institution, is served in the lobby. In the main dining room, Wright's, guests dine amid the handiwork of Frank Lloyd Wright.

24th St. and Missouri Ave., Phoenix, AZ 85016. © 800/950-0086 or 602/955-6600. Fax 602/954-2548. www.arizonabiltmore.com. 730 units. Jan to early May $340–$510 double, from $650 suite; early May to late May and early Sept to Dec $300–$435 double, from $550 suite; late May to early Sept $170–$255 double, from $340 suite (plus daily service fee of $12, year-round). AE, DC, DISC, MC, V. Pets under 15 lb. accepted in cottage rooms with $200 deposit, $50 nonrefundable. **Amenities:** 3 restaurants (new American, Southwestern, American), snack bar, lounge; 8 pools (including 1 with a water slide and 1 with rental cabanas); 2 18-hole golf courses plus 18-hole putting course; 7 tennis courts; lawn games; health club and spa; 2 Jacuzzis; bike rentals; children's programs; concierge; car-rental desk; courtesy shopping shuttle; business center; shopping arcade; room service; massage; laundry service; dry cleaning. *In room:* A/C, TV, dataport, minibar, hair dryer, iron, safe.

Hermosa Inn ⭐⭐ *(Finds)*   This luxurious boutique hotel, once a guest ranch, is now one of the only hotels in the Phoenix area to offer a bit of Old Arizona atmosphere. Originally built in 1930 as the home of Western artist Lon Megargee, the inn is situated in a quiet residential neighborhood on more than 6 acres of neatly landscaped gardens. If you don't like the crowds of big resorts, but do enjoy the luxury, this is the spot for you. Rooms here vary from cozy to spacious and are individually decorated in tastefully contemporary Western decor. The largest suites, which have more Southwestern flavor than just about any other rooms in the area, incorporate a mixture of contemporary and antique furnishings and accents. The dining room, located in the original adobe home, serves excellent new American and Southwestern cuisine in a rustic, upscale setting (see "Where to Dine," later in this chapter).

5532 N. Palo Cristi Rd., Paradise Valley, AZ 85253. © 800/241-1210 or 602/955-8614. Fax 602/955-8299. www.hermosainn.com. 35 units. Early Jan to early May $265–$340 double, $450–$665 suite; early May to late May $170–$210 double, $330–$520 suite; late May to mid-Sept $95–$140 double, $300–$450 suite; early Sept to early Jan $220–$275 double, $400–$550 suite. Rates include continental breakfast. AE, DC, DISC, MC, V. Take 32nd St. north from Camelback Rd., turn right on Stanford Rd., and turn left on N. Palo Cristi Rd. From Lincoln Dr., turn south on N. Palo Christi Rd. (east of 32nd St.). Pets under 20 lb. accepted with $250 deposit, $50 nonrefundable. **Amenities:** Restaurant, lounge; small outdoor pool; 2 Jacuzzis; 3 tennis courts; access to nearby health club; concierge; laundry service; dry cleaning. *In room:* A/C. TV, dataport, minibar, hair dryer, iron.

The Ritz-Carlton Phoenix ⭐⭐   Located directly across the street from the Biltmore Fashion Park shopping center in the heart of the Camelback Corridor business and shopping district, the Ritz-Carlton is the city's finest nonresort hotel and is known for providing impeccable service. The public areas are filled with European antiques, and although this decor might seem a bit out of place in Phoenix, it's still utterly sophisticated. In the guest rooms, you'll find reproductions of antique furniture and marble bathrooms with ornate fixtures. There's a lively French bistro, an elegant lobby lounge that serves afternoon tea as well as cocktails, and a clublike lounge offering fine cigars and premium spirits.

2401 E. Camelback Rd., Phoenix, AZ 85016. © 800/241-3333 or 602/468-0700. Fax 602/468-9883. 281 units. Early Sept to Apr $335–$399 double, $450 suite; May $275–$325 double, $375 suite; June to early Sept $199–$249 double, $299 suite. AE, DC, DISC, MC, V. Valet parking $18. **Amenities:** Restaurant, 2 lounges; small outdoor pool; tennis court; health club; saunas; bike rentals; concierge; car-rental desk; business center; 24-hour room service; massage; baby-sitting; laundry service; dry cleaning. *In room:* A/C, TV, dataport, minibar, hair dryer, iron, safe.

Royal Palms Hotel and Casitas ⭐⭐   Midway between Scottsdale and Biltmore Fashion Park, this is one of the finest, most romantic resorts in the valley. The main building, constructed more than 50 years ago, was built by Cunard Steamship executive Delos Cooke in the Spanish Mission style and is filled with

European antiques that once belonged to Cooke. Surrounding the building, and giving the property the tranquil feel of a Mediterranean monastery cloister, are lush walled gardens where antique water fountains splash. The most memorable guest rooms are the deluxe casitas, each with a distinctive decor (ranging from opulent contemporary to classic European), private back patios, and front patios that can be enclosed by heavy curtains. Other rooms are luxuriously appointed, although not quite so opulent. The antique-filled dining room, T. Cook's, serves Mediterranean cuisine and is one of the city's most romantic restaurants (see "Where to Dine," later in this chapter). An adjacent bar/lounge conjures up a Spanish villa setting.

5200 E. Camelback Rd., Phoenix, AZ 85018. (€) **800/672-6011** or 602/840-3610. Fax 602/840-6927. www.royalpalmshotel.com. 116 units. Jan–May $375–$515 double, $415–$3,500 suite; June to early Sept $159–$219 double, $179–$2,500 suite; early Sept to Dec $355–$445 double, $375–$3,500 suite (plus daily service fee of $16, year-round). AE, DC, DISC, MC, V. **Amenities:** Restaurant (Mediterranean), snack bar, lounge; outdoor pool with cabanas; tennis court; large exercise room; access to nearby health club; Jacuzzi; concierge; car-rental desk; business center; room service; massage; laundry service; dry cleaning. *In room:* A/C, TV, dataport, minibar, coffeemaker, hair dryer, iron, safe.

EXPENSIVE

Embassy Suites Biltmore ★★ Located across the parking lot from the Biltmore Fashion Park (Phoenix's most upscale shopping center), this atrium hotel makes a great base if you want to be within walking distance of half a dozen good restaurants. The huge atrium is filled with interesting tile work and other artistic Southwestern touches, as well as tropical greenery, waterfalls, and ponds filled with koi. The hotel's atrium also houses the breakfast area and a romantic lounge with huge banquettes shaded by palm trees. Unfortunately, the rooms, all suites, are dated and a bit of a letdown, but they're certainly large. All in all, this hotel is a good value when you consider that rates include both breakfast and afternoon drinks.

2630 E. Camelback Rd., Phoenix, AZ 85016-4206. (€) **800/EMBASSY** or 602/955-3992. Fax 602/955-6479. www.embassy-suites.com. 232 units. Jan to late May $249–$269 double; late May to early Sept $129–$149 double; early Sept to Dec $219–$239 double. Rates include full breakfast and afternoon drinks. AE, DC, DISC, MC, V. Pets accepted, $25. **Amenities:** Restaurant (high-end steakhouse), lounge; cocktail hour; large outdoor pool; Jacuzzi; exercise room; concierge; courtesy car; business center; room service; laundry service; coin-op laundry; dry cleaning. *In room:* A/C, TV, dataport, fridge, coffeemaker, microwave, hair dryer, iron.

MODERATE

Hacienda Alta *(Finds)* Located adjacent to the Phoenician, yet very much in its own separate world surrounded by a desert landscape, this home offers a very convenient location, reasonable rates, and a chance to feel away from it all in the middle of the city. Don't expect the fussiness of most other B&Bs; owners Margaret and Ed Newhall make this casual, eclectic place a fun home away from home. The inn is housed in a 1920s territorial-style adobe home, and in the old gardens are orange and grapefruit trees that often provide the juice for breakfast. There's also a large suite with a sleeping loft, whirlpool tub, fireplace, and balcony overlooking the Phoenician's golf course.

5750 E. Camelback Rd., Phoenix, AZ 85018. (€) **480/945-8525.** 3 units. $100–$125 double; $150 suite. Rates include full breakfast. No credit cards. **Amenities:** Access to nearby health club; concierge; baby-sitting; laundry service. *In room:* A/C, TV, fridge, hair dryer.

Maricopa Manor Centrally located between downtown Phoenix and Scottsdale, this bed-and-breakfast is just a block off busy Camelback Road, and for many years was one of Phoenix's only official B&Bs. The inn's main building, designed to resemble a Spanish manor house, was built in 1928. The orange

Kids Family-Friendly Hotels

Doubletree La Posada Resort *(see p. 69)*   If you're a kid, it's hard to imagine a cooler pool than the one here. It's got a two-story waterfall, a swim-through cave, and big artificial boulders. There are also horse-shoe pits, a volleyball court, and a pitch-and-putt green.

Holiday Inn SunSpree Resort *(see p. 70)*   Reasonable rates, a good Scottsdale location adjacent to the McCormick-Stillman Railroad Park, lots of grass for running around on, and free meals for kids under 12 make this one of the valley's best choices for families on a budget.

Hyatt Regency Scottsdale *(see p. 65)*   Not only is there a totally awe-some water playground complete with sand beach and water slide, but the Kamp Hyatt Kachina program provides supervised, structured activities.

The Phoenician *(see p. 68)*   Kids absolutely love the water slide here, and both parents and children appreciate the Funicians Club, a super-vised activities program for those ages 5 to 12. A putting green and croquet court offer further diversions.

Pointe Hilton Squaw Peak Resort *(see p. 78)*   A water slide, a tubing river, a waterfall, water volleyball, a miniature golf course, a game room, and a children's program guarantee that your kids will be exhausted by the end of the day.

trees, palms, and large yard all lend an Old Phoenix atmosphere. All the guest rooms are large suites, and although the furnishings are a bit dated, the accom-modations are quite comfortable. One suite has a sunroom and kitchen, while another has two separate sleeping areas. There are tables in the garden where you can eat your breakfast, which is delivered to your door.

15 W. Pasadena Ave., Phoenix, AZ 85013. ✆ **800/292-6403** or 602/274-6302. Fax 602/266-3904. www.maricopamanor.com. 7 suites. Sept–May $179–$249 double; June–Aug $89–$129 double. Rates include continental breakfast. AE, DC, DISC, MC, V. **Amenities:** Pool; Jacuzzi. *In room:* A/C, TV, dataport, fridge, coffeemaker, hair dryer.

Sierra Suites   Billing itself as a temporary residence and offering discounts for stays of 5 days or more, this hotel consists of studio-style apartments and is located just north of Camelback Road and not far from Biltmore Fashion Park. Although designed primarily for corporate business travelers on temporary assignment in the area, this hotel makes a good choice for families as well. All rooms have full kitchens, big closets and bathrooms, and separate sitting areas.

5235 N. 16th St., Phoenix, AZ 85016. ✆ **800/4-SIERRA** or 602/265-6800. Fax 602/265-1114. 113 units. Oct–Apr $125–$164; May–Sept $69–$89. AE, DISC, MC, V. **Amenities:** Small outdoor pool; exercise room; Jacuzzi; coin-op laundry; dry cleaning. *In room:* A/C, TV, dataport, kitchen, coffeemaker, hair dryer, iron.

NORTH PHOENIX

Some of the valley's best scenery is to be found in north Phoenix, where several small mountains have been preserved as parks and preserves; the two Pointe Hilton resorts claim great locations close to these parks. However, the valley's best shopping and dining, as well as most major attractions, are all at least a 30-minute drive away (through generally unattractive parts of the city).

VERY EXPENSIVE

Pointe Hilton Squaw Peak Resort ★★★ (Kids)   Located at the foot of Squaw Peak, this lushly landscaped resort makes a big splash with its Hole-in-the-Wall River Ranch, a 9-acre aquatic playground that features a tubing "river," water slide, waterfall, sports pool, and lagoon pool. An 18-hole putting course, game room, and children's activity center also help make it a great family vacation spot. The resort is done in the Spanish villa style, and most of the guest rooms are large, two-room suites outfitted with a mix of contemporary and Spanish colonial–style furnishings. Suites are currently undergoing renovations that will give them bigger bathrooms, so be sure to ask for one of the updated units. The resort's Mexican restaurant is located in an 1880 adobe building.

7677 N. 16th St., Phoenix, AZ 85020-9832. ℂ 800/876-4683 or 602/997-2626. Fax 602/997-2391. www.pointehilton.com. 564 units. Jan to late Apr $239–$329 double, $950 grande suite; late Apr to late May and early Sept to Dec $109–$249 double, $659 grande suite; late May to early Sept $99–$159 double, $659 grande suite (plus daily resort fee of $8, year-round). AE, DC, DISC, MC, V. **Amenities:** 3 restaurants (American/Southwestern, Mexican, steakhouse), 2 snack bars, 5 lounges; 7 pools; 18-hole golf course (4 miles away by shuttle); 4 tennis courts; health club and small spa; 6 Jacuzzis; saunas; bike rentals; children's programs; concierge; car-rental desk; business center; room service; massage; baby-sitting; laundry service; coin-op laundry; dry cleaning. *In room:* A/C, TV, dataport, minibar, coffeemaker, hair dryer, iron.

Pointe Hilton Tapatio Cliffs Resort ★★★   If you love to lounge by the pool, then this resort is a great choice. The Falls, a 3-acre water playground, includes two lagoon pools, a 138-foot water slide, 40-foot-high cascades, a whirlpool tucked into an artificial grotto, and poolside rental cabanas for that extra dash of luxury. Hikers will enjoy the easy access to trails in the adjacent North Mountain Recreation Area, while golfers can avail themselves of the resort's course. There's also a small full-service health spa. All rooms are spacious suites with Southwestern furnishings; the corner units are particularly bright. Situated on the shoulder of North Mountain, this resort has steep roads and walkways (get your heart and brakes checked); at the very top of the property is Different Pointe of View, a pricey restaurant with one of the finest views in the city (see "Where to Dine," below).

11111 N. Seventh St., Phoenix, AZ 85020. ℂ 800/876-4683 or 602/866-7500. Fax 602/993-0276. www.pointhilton.com. 585 units. Jan to late Apr $199–$299 double, $899 grande suite; late Apr to late May and early Sept to Dec $109–$249 double, $749 grande suite; late May to early Sept $89–$159 double, $559 grande suite (plus daily resort fee of $9, year-round). AE, DC, DISC, MC, V. **Amenities:** 3 restaurants, 2 poolside cafes, 4 lounges; 7 pools; golf course; 12 tennis courts; fitness center; spa; 8 Jacuzzis; sauna; steam room; bike rentals; horseback riding; children's programs; concierge; car-rental desk; free shuttle between Pointe Hilton properties; business center; pro shop; room service; massage; baby-sitting; laundry service; dry cleaning. *In room:* A/C, TV, dataport, minibar, coffeemaker, hair dryer, iron.

EXPENSIVE

Embassy Suites—Phoenix North ★★ (Value)   This resortlike hotel in north Phoenix is right off I-17, a 30- to 45-minute drive from the rest of the valley's resorts (and good restaurants)—but if you happen to have relatives in Sun City or are planning a trip north to Sedona or the Grand Canyon, it's a good choice. The lobby of the Mission-style, all-suite hotel has the feel of a Spanish church interior, but instead of a cloister off the lobby, there's a garden courtyard with a huge swimming pool and lots of palm trees. The guest rooms are all suites, although furnishings are fairly basic and bathrooms small.

2577 W. Greenway Rd., Phoenix, AZ 85023-4222. ℂ 800/EMBASSY or 602/375-1777. Fax 602/375-4012. www.embassy-suites.com. 314 units. Jan–Apr $99–$159 double; May–Dec $65–$79 double. Rates include full breakfast. AE, DC, DISC, MC, V. **Amenities:** Restaurant, lounge, snack bar, complimentary cocktail reception; large pool and children's pool; 2 tennis courts; volleyball court; exercise room; Jacuzzi; sauna; car-rental desk; room service; laundry service; dry cleaning. *In room:* A/C, TV, dataport, fridge, coffeemaker, microwave, iron.

MODERATE/INEXPENSIVE

Among the better moderately priced chain motels in north Phoenix are the **Best Western Inn Suites Hotel Phoenix,** 1615 E. Northern Ave. at 16th Street (© **800/752-2204** or 602/997-6285), charging high-season rates of $99 to $129 double; and the **Best Western Bell Hotel,** 17211 N. Black Canyon Hwy. (© **800/528-1234** or 602/993-8300), charging $89 to $119 double.

Among the better budget chain motels in the area are the **Motel 6—Sweetwater,** 2735 W. Sweetwater Ave. (© **800/4-MOTEL-6** or 602/942-5030), charging $46 to $54 double; and **Super 8—Phoenix Metro/Central,** 4021 N. 27th Ave. (© **800/800-8000** or 602/248-8880), charging $50 to $56 double.

DOWNTOWN PHOENIX

Unless you're a sports fan or are in town for a convention, there's not much to recommend in downtown Phoenix. There are lots of sports bars, and you can walk to the Bank One Ballpark and America West Arena, but downtown is pretty much a 9-to-5 kind of place that can feel like a modern ghost town when there's no big convention in town.

VERY EXPENSIVE

Crowne Plaza—Phoenix Downtown ⊛ This 19-story business and convention hotel is one of your best choices in downtown, although with the crowds of conventioneers, individual travelers are likely to feel overlooked. A Mediterranean villa theme has been adopted throughout the public areas, with slate flooring and walls painted to resemble cracked stucco. Guest rooms continue the Mediterranean feel and are designed with the business traveler in mind.

100 N. First St., Phoenix, AZ 85004. © **800/2-CROWNE** or 602/333-0000. Fax 602/333-5181. www.phxcrowneplaza.com. 532 units. Mid-Sept to late May $250–$290 double, $300–$1,300 suite; late May to mid-Sept $150–$190 double, $200–$900 suite. AE, DC, DISC, MC, V. Valet parking $10. **Amenities:** Restaurant (American), 2 cafes, lounge; pool; exercise room; access to nearby health club; Jacuzzi; concierge; car-rental desk; business center; salon; room service; laundry service; dry cleaning. *In room:* A/C, TV, dataport, coffeemaker, hair dryer, iron.

EXPENSIVE

Hyatt Regency Phoenix ⊛⊛ Located directly across the street from the Phoenix Civic Plaza, this high-rise Hyatt is almost always packed with conventioneers. Whether full or empty, the hotel seems somewhat understaffed, so don't expect top-notch service if you're stuck here on a convention. The guest rooms are fairly standard, though comfortably furnished. Ask for one above the eighth floor to take advantage of the views from the glass elevators. The hotel's rotating rooftop restaurant serves Southwestern dishes; if you're more interested in views than in haute cuisine, give it a try.

122 N. Second St., Phoenix, AZ 85004. © **800/233-1234** or 602/252-1234. Fax 602/254-9472. www.phoenix.hyatt.com. 712 units. $119–$299 double; $450–$1,550 suite. AE, DC, DISC, MC, V. Valet parking $18; self-parking $14. **Amenities:** 3 restaurants (Southwestern, American), 2 lounges; small outdoor pool; exercise room; access to nearby health club; Jacuzzi; concierge; car-rental desk; business center; shopping arcade; room service; baby-sitting; laundry service; dry cleaning. *In room:* A/C, TV, dataport, coffeemaker, hair dryer.

MODERATE

Hotel San Carlos ⭐ If you don't mind staying in downtown Phoenix with the convention crowds, you'll get a good value at this historic hotel. Built in 1928 and listed on the National Register of Historic Places, the San Carlos is a small hotel that provides that touch of elegance and charm missing from the other downtown hotels. Unfortunately, bedrooms are rather small by today's standards, and the decor needs updating.

202 N. Central Ave., Phoenix, AZ 85004. ⓒ **602/253-4121.** Fax 602/254-9965. www.hotelsancarlos.com. 133 units. Jan–Apr $149 double, $209 suite; May–Sept $99 double, $145 suite; Oct–Dec $125 double, $199 suite. Rates include continental breakfast. AE, DC, DISC, MC, V. Valet and self-parking $15. Pets allowed, $25. **Amenities:** 2 restaurants (Irish pub, espresso bar); rooftop pool; concierge; laundry service; dry cleaning. *In room:* A/C, TV, dataport, coffeemaker, iron.

TEMPE, MESA, SOUTH PHOENIX & THE AIRPORT AREA

For the most part, south Phoenix is one of the poorest parts of the city. However, it does have a couple of exceptional resorts, and Phoenix South Mountain Park is one of the best places in the city to experience the desert. Tempe, which lies just a few miles east of the airport, is home to Arizona State University, and consequently supports a lively nightlife scene. Along Tempe's Mill Avenue, you'll find one of the only neighborhoods in the valley where locals actually get out of their cars and walk the streets. Tempe is also convenient to Papago Park, which is home to the Phoenix Zoo, the Desert Botanical Garden, the Arizona Historical Society Museum, a municipal golf course, and hiking and mountain-biking trails.

VERY EXPENSIVE

The Buttes, A Wyndham Resort ⭐⭐ This spectacular resort, only 3 miles from Sky Harbor Airport, makes the most of its craggy hilltop location. Although some people complain that the freeway in the foreground ruins the view, the rocky setting and desert landscaping leave no doubt you're in the Southwest. From the cactus garden, stream, waterfall, and fish pond *inside* the lobby to the circular restaurant and free-form swimming pools, every inch of this resort is calculated to take your breath away. The pools (complete with waterfalls) and four whirlpools (one of which is the most romantic in the valley) are the best reasons to stay here. Guest rooms are stylishly elegant, and many have views across the valley. The valley/highway-view rooms are a bit larger than the pool-view rooms, but second floor pool-view rooms have patios. Unfortunately for fans of long soaks, most bathrooms have only three-quarter-size tubs. The Top of the Rock restaurant snags the best view around, and sunset dinners are memorable (see "Where to Dine," below).

2000 Westcourt Way, Tempe, AZ 85282. ⓒ **800/WYNDHAM** or 602/225-9000. Fax 602/438-8622. www.wyndham.com. 353 units. Jan–Apr $239–$289 double, $475–$575 suite; May and early Sept to Dec $139–$189 double, from $475 suite; June to early Sept $109–$169 double, from $375 suite. AE, DC, DISC, MC, V. **Amenities:** 2 restaurants (new American/Southwestern, American), 3 lounges, snack bar; 2 pools; 4 tennis courts; volleyball courts; exercise room; spa services; 4 Jacuzzis; concierge; business center; room service; massage; laundry service; dry cleaning. *In room:* A/C, TV, dataport, minibar, coffeemaker, hair dryer, iron.

Pointe South Mountain Resort ⭐⭐⭐ Located on the south side of the valley, this sprawling resort abuts the 17,000-acre South Mountain Park, and although the property's grand scale seems designed primarily to accommodate convention crowds, individual travelers, especially active ones, will find plenty to keep them busy here. Golfers get great views from the greens, urban cowboys can ride right into the sunset on South Mountain, and if it's abs and pecs you want to work on, the 40,000-square-foot health club should keep you pumped up. By early 2002, there should be a new water-park-style pool area. The guest rooms are all suites and feature contemporary Southwestern furnishings. Mountainside units offer the best views of the golf course and South Mountain. A wide variety of restaurant choices makes this a good bet for anyone who wants a true resort-style vacation. Rustler's Rooste, a cowboy steakhouse, even serves rattlesnake appetizers (see "Where to Dine," below).

7777 S. Pointe Pkwy., Phoenix, AZ 85044. © **877/800-4888** or 602/438-9000. Fax 602/431-6425. www.pointesouthmtn.com. 640 units. Jan to mid-Apr $259–$309 double, $569 grande suite, $1,500 presidential suite; mid-Apr to late May and early Sept to Dec $229–$279 double, $569 grande suite, $15,000 presidential suite; late May to early Sept $159–$209 double, $539 grande suite, $900 presidential suite (plus daily resort fee of $10, year-round). AE, DC, DISC, MC, V. **Amenities:** 4 restaurants (Mediterranean/ Continental, steakhouse, Mexican, Southwestern), 2 snack bars, 3 lounges; 6 outdoor pools; 18-hole golf course; 10 tennis courts; volleyball courts; racquetball courts; pro shop; health club; 3 Jacuzzis; horseback riding; concierge; car-rental desk; business center; room service; massage; baby-sitting; laundry service; coin-op laundry; dry cleaning. In room: A/C, TV, dataport, minibar, coffeemaker, hair dryer, iron.

EXPENSIVE

Fiesta Inn ♠ (Value) Reasonable rates, green lawns, palm- and eucalyptus-shaded grounds, extensive recreational facilities, and a location close to the airport, ASU, and Tempe's Mill Avenue make this older, casual resort one of the best deals in the valley. Okay, so it isn't as fancy as the resorts in Scottsdale, but you can't argue with the rates. The large guest rooms were all renovated in 2000, and though a bit dark, they have an appealing retro Mission styling. You may not feel like you're in the desert when you stay here (due to the lawns and shade trees), but you'll certainly get a lot more for your money than at other area hotels in this price range.

2100 S. Priest Dr., Tempe, AZ 85282. © **800/528-6481** or 480/967-1441. Fax 480/967-0224. www. fiestainnresort.com. 270 units. Jan 1 to late Apr $171 double; late Apr to May $135 double; June–Sept $89 double; Oct–Dec $155 double. AE, DC, DISC, MC, V. Pets accepted. **Amenities:** Restaurant (American), lounge; pool; putting green and driving range; 3 tennis courts; exercise room; Jacuzzi; bike rentals; concierge; car-rental desk; courtesy airport shuttle; business center; room service; baby-sitting; laundry service; dry cleaning. In room: A/C, TV, dataport, fridge, coffeemaker, hair dryer, iron.

Tempe Mission Palms Hotel ♠ College students, their families, and anyone else who wants to be close to Tempe's nightlife will find this an ideal, although somewhat overpriced, location right in the heart of the Mill Avenue shopping, restaurant, and nightlife district. When you've had enough of the hustle and bustle, you can retreat to the hotel's rooftop pool. For the most part, guest rooms are quite comfortable and boast lots of wood, marble, and granite.

60 E. Fifth St., Tempe, AZ 85281. © **800/547-8705** or 480/894-1400. Fax 480/968-7677. www.mission-palms.com. 303 units. Sept–Mar $149–$199 double, from $399 suite; Apr–May $119–$199 double, from $399 suite; June–Aug $79–$99 double, from $299 suite. AE, DC, DISC, MC, V. Pets accepted, $100 deposit ($25 nonrefundable). **Amenities:** Restaurant (Southwestern), lounge; medium-size outdoor pool; tennis court; exercise room; access to nearby health club; 2 Jacuzzis; sauna; bike rentals; concierge; car-rental desk; courtesy airport shuttle; business center; room service; laundry service; dry cleaning. In room: A/C, TV, dataport, coffeemaker, hair dryer, iron.

Twin Palms Hotel ♠ Although the rooms at this midrise hotel, located right off the ASU campus, are just standard, the Twin Palms is a great choice for fitness fanatics. Hotel guests have full access to the nearby ASU Student Recreation Complex, which covers 135,000 square feet and includes a huge weight-training room; Olympic pool; and racquetball, tennis, and basketball courts. The hotel is also close to Sun Devil Stadium, the ASU-Karsten Golf Course, and busy Mill Avenue.

225 E. Apache Blvd., Tempe, AZ 85281. ℂ **800/367-0835** or 480/967-9431. Fax 480/968-1877. www. twinpalmshotel.com. 140 units. Jan–Apr $169 double; May–Sept $89 double; Oct–Dec $139 double. AE, DC, DISC, MC, V. **Amenities:** Lounge; outdoor pool; access to nearby health club; car-rental desk; courtesy airport shuttle; business center; 24-hour room service; coin-op laundry; laundry service; dry cleaning. *In room:* A/C, TV, dataport, coffeemaker, hair dryer.

MODERATE/INEXPENSIVE

Apache Boulevard in Tempe becomes Main Street in Mesa, and along this stretch of road there are numerous old motels charging some of the lowest rates in the valley. However, these motels are very hit-or-miss. If you're used to staying at nonchain motels, you might want to cruise this strip and check out a few places. Otherwise, try the chain motels mentioned below (which tend to charge $20 to $40 more per night than nonchain motels).

Chain options in the Tempe area include the **Days Inn—Tempe,** 1221 E. Apache Blvd. (ℂ **480/968-7793**), charging $69 to $159 double; and **Super 8—Tempe/Scottsdale,** 1020 E. Apache Blvd. (ℂ **480/967-8891**), charging $60 to $90 double.

Chain options in the Mesa area include the **Days Inn—Mesa,** 333 W. Juanita Ave. (ℂ **480/844-8900**), charging $69 to $99 double; **Motel 6—Mesa North,** 336 W. Hampton Ave. (ℂ **480/844-8899**), charging $52 double; and **Super 8—Mesa,** 6733 E. Main St. (ℂ **480/981-6181**), charging $69 to $84 double.

Chain motels in the airport area include the **Best Western Airport Inn,** 2425 S. 24th St. (ℂ **602/273-7251**), charging $69 to $120 double; and **Rodeway Inn—Airport East,** 1550 S. 52nd St. (ℂ **480/967-3000**), charging $100 to $110 double. All rates are for high season.

OUTLYING RESORTS

Gold Canyon Golf Resort ★★ *Value*   Located way out on the east side of the valley near Apache Junction (at least a 30- to 45-min. drive from the airport), Gold Canyon is a favorite of devoted golfers who come to play some of the most scenic holes in the state (the Superstition Mountains provide the backdrop). Although nongolfers will appreciate the scenery, the small pool makes it clear that golfers, not swimmers, take the fore here. The guest rooms, housed in blindingly white pueblo-inspired buildings, are spacious; some have fireplaces while others have whirlpools.

6100 S. Kings Ranch Rd., Gold Canyon, AZ 85219. ℂ **800/624-6445** or 480/982-9090. Fax 480/983-9554. www.gcgr.com. 101 units. Mid-Jan to mid-Apr $200–$250 double; mid-Apr to Sept $125–$175 double; Oct to mid-Jan $175–$225 double. AE, DC, DISC, MC, V. Pets accepted, $50. **Amenities:** 2 restaurants (Southwestern, American), lounge; pool; 2 gorgeous and highly regarded 18-hole golf courses; 2 tennis courts; Jacuzzi; bike rentals; horseback riding; concierge; room service; baby-sitting; laundry service; dry cleaning. *In room:* A/C, TV, dataport, fridge, coffeemaker, hair dryer, iron.

The Wigwam Resort ★★   Located 20 minutes west of downtown Phoenix and more than twice as far from Scottsdale, this property opened its doors to the public in 1929 and remains one of the nation's premier golf resorts. Three challenging golf courses and superb service are the reasons most people choose this resort, which, although elegant, is set amid flatland that lacks the stunning desert scenery of the Scottsdale area. The Wigwam has a very traditional feel about it, right down to the skeet and trap shooting range. Most of the guest rooms are in Santa Fe–style buildings, surrounded by green lawns and colorful gardens, and all the spacious units feature contemporary Southwestern furniture. Some rooms have fireplaces, but most popular are those units along the golf course. The resort is in the midst of a $10 million makeover, so look for updated rooms and a new look for the main pool. There are also plans to add a full-service spa.

300 Wigwam Blvd., Litchfield Park, AZ 85340. © 800/327-0396 or 623/935-3811. Fax 623/935-3737. www.wigwamresort.com. 331 units. Early Jan to late May $350–$410 double, $410–$545 suite; late May to early Sept $165–$205 double, $205–$295 suite; early Sept to early Jan $265–$315 double, $315–$450 suite (plus daily resort fee of $12, year-round). AE, DC, DISC, MC, V. Pets under 20 lb. accepted ($50 deposit, $25 nonrefundable). **Amenities:** 3 restaurants (Continental, Southwestern, American), 2 lounges, afternoon tea, snack bar; 2 pools; 3 18-hole golf courses; putting green; 9 tennis courts; volleyball court; croquet court; exercise room; spa services; Jacuzzi; sauna; bike rentals; children's programs; concierge; car-rental desk; golf and tennis pro shops; room service; massage; laundry service; dry cleaning. *In room:* A/C, TV, dataport, minibar, coffeemaker, hair dryer, iron.

4 Where to Dine

The Valley of the Sun boasts some excellent restaurants, with most of the best dining options concentrated in the Scottsdale and Biltmore Corridor areas. If you want to splurge on only one expensive meal while you're here, consider a resort restaurant that offers a view of the city lights. Other meals not to be missed are the cowboy dinners served amid Wild West decor at such places as Pinnacle Peak and Rustler's Rooste.

Phoenix also has plenty of those big and familiar chains that you've heard so much about. There's a **Hard Rock Cafe,** 2621 E. Camelback Rd. (© **602/956-3669**), where you can toss down a burger and then buy that all-important T-shirt to prove you were here. As Arizona's version of L.A., Phoenix also has a **California Pizza Kitchen,** 2400 E. Camelback Rd. (© **602/553-8382**), located in Biltmore Fashion Park; there's one in Scottsdale at 10100 Scottsdale Rd., at Gold Dust Avenue (© **480/596-8300**).

The big chain steakhouses are also duking it out here. You'll find two **Ruth's Chris** steakhouses: in the Biltmore district at 2201 E. Camelback Rd. (© **602/957-9600**), and in the Scottsdale Seville shopping plaza, 7001 N. Scottsdale Rd. (© **480/991-5988**). You'll find **Morton's Steakhouses** in the Biltmore district at 2501 E. Camelback Rd. (© **602/955-9577**), and in north Scottsdale across from the Scottsdale airport, 15233 N. Kierland Blvd. (© **480/951-4440**).

Good places to go trolling for a place to eat include the trendy Biltmore Fashion Park and Old Town Scottsdale. At the former, which by the way is a shopping mall, not a park, you'll find the chain restaurant California Pizza Kitchen (mentioned above) as well as nearly a dozen other excellent restaurants. In downtown Scottsdale, within an area of roughly 4 square blocks, you'll find about a dozen good restaurants. A few of our favorites in both places are listed in the following pages.

Phoenix is a sprawling city, and it can be a real pain to have to drive around in search of a good lunch spot. If you happen to be visiting the Phoenix Art Museum, the Heard Museum, or the Desert Botanical Garden anytime around lunch, stay put for your noon meal. All three of these attractions have cafes serving decent, if limited, menus.

SCOTTSDALE
EXPENSIVE

The Chaparral ★★ CONTINENTAL   Management changed the decor and the menu at this Scottsdale landmark a couple of years back, and then seemed to have second thoughts. The menu has now gone back to basics—escargots, chateaubriand, steaks, lobster tails. You get the picture. This classic Continental

Phoenix, Scottsdale & the Valley of the Sun Dining

To Flagstaff ↑

Turf Paradise
Racetrack

Bell   Rd.

Arizona

Greenway   Rd.

35th   Ave.

Black Canyon Freeway

19th   Ave.

7th   St.

7th   St.

Thunderbird Rd.

Sweetwater   Ave.

Cactus Rd.

North Mountain
Recreation Area 1

PEORIA

Peoria Rd.

GLENDALE

Dunlap Ave.

Canal

↖ To Wickenburg

Northern Ave.

Grand Ave.

Glendale Ave.

Maryland Ave.

Bethany Home Rd.

Missouri   Ave.

Grand

Camelback Rd. 60

89

19th   Ave.

Central   Ave.

3   2

Indian School Rd.

Canal

Osborn Rd.

Thomas Rd.

7th   Ave.

Ave.

Ave.

8   4

Lon's 15

L'Ecole/Scottsdale Culinary Institute 35

**DOWNTOWN
PHOENIX**

McDowell Rd.

10

Ave.   Papago Freeway

←
To
Los Angeles

Van Buren St.

35th   Ave.

27th   Ave.

17

10

5

85   Buckeye Rd.

Maricopa Freeway

67th   Ave.

59th   Ave.

6

7

Broadway Rd.

Salt

River

Ave.

St.

Southern   Ave.

43rd   Ave.

Ave.

Ave.

Baseline   Rd.

19th   Ave.

7th   Ave.

Central   Ave.

Dobbins   Rd.

7th   St.

Elliot   Rd.

Ave.

Estrella   Dr.

51st   Ave.

PHOENIX SOUTH MOUNTAIN PARK

River

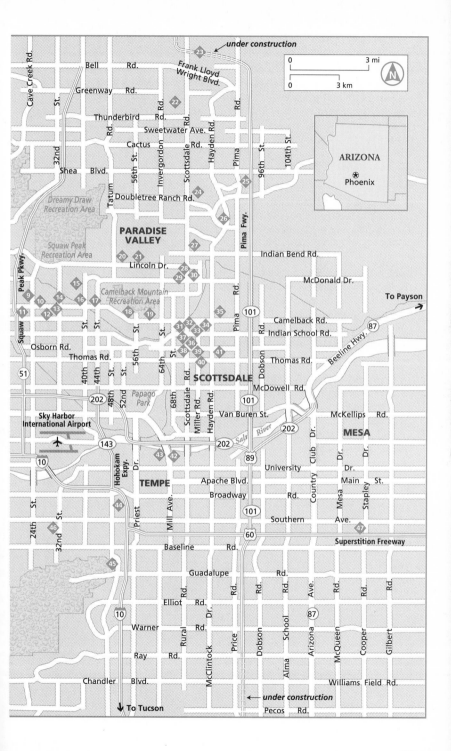

fare just seems to be what the Camelback Inn's guests prefer. Rest assured that through all this change, the view of Camelback Mountain out the restaurant's picture windows remains the same (give or take a few new mansions on the mountain's slopes). Also unchanged is the decadently rich lobster bisque, which is covered with puff pastry and served with a spoonful of caviar crème fraîche; this soup is an elegant experience not to be missed. Service is as attentive as you would expect. The restaurant is now also a wine bar, which means you can choose from an astonishing number of wines by the glass if you're so inclined.

At Marriott's Camelback Inn, 5402 E. Lincoln Dr. ✆ **480/948-1700**, ext. 7888. Reservations recommended. Main courses $20–$56. AE, DC, DISC, MC, V. Daily 5:30–9:30pm.

El Chorro Lodge ✪ CONTINENTAL   Built in 1934 as a school for girls and converted to a lodge and restaurant 3 years later, El Chorro Lodge is a valley landmark and one of the area's last old traditional establishments. At night, lights twinkle on the saguaro cactus and the restaurant takes on a timeless tranquility, even if the interior is a little dowdy. The adobe building houses several dining rooms, but the patio is the place to sit, either in the daytime or on a chilly night near the crackling fireplace. Both old-timers and families like the traditional decor and menu, which features such classic dishes as chateaubriand and rack of lamb. In addition to the favorites, there are several dishes low in salt and fat, as well as seafood options. Save room for the legendary sticky buns.

5550 E. Lincoln Dr. ✆ **480/948-5170**. Reservations recommended. Lunch $8–$17; full dinner $12–$63. AE, DC, DISC, MC, V. Mon–Fri 11am–3pm and 5:30–11pm; Sat 5:30–11pm; Sun 10am–2pm and 5–10pm.

Golden Swan ✪✪✪ REGIONAL AMERICAN   At this restaurant within the Hyatt Regency Scottsdale Resort, the combination of cuisine and setting makes for a very special meal. Dramatically spotlit royal palms, geometric architecture, and the sound of fountains and waterfalls set the tone, while the food is just as pleasurable, beautifully presented with plenty of attention paid to detail. Artistically arranged entrees range from orange-honey barbecued salmon to a grilled lamb chop with jalapeño-honey mustard crusted with toasted pistachios. End your meal with one of the Golden Swan's decadent desserts—perhaps a silky chocolate mousse cake with fresh berries soaked in zinfandel sauce. Before or after dinner, the open-air lounge at the resort is a romantic place to have a drink and listen to live music. There are also regularly scheduled winemaker dinners.

At the Hyatt Regency Scottsdale Resort, 7500 E. Doubletree Ranch Rd. ✆ **480/991-3388**. Reservations recommended. Main courses $28–$37; Sun brunch $42. AE, DC, DISC, MC, V. Daily 6–10pm; Sun brunch 9:30am–2pm.

Mancuso's ✪✪ NORTHERN ITALIAN/CONTINENTAL   With its ramparts, towers, stone walls, and narrow, uneven alleyways, the Borgata shopping plaza is modeled after the Tuscan village of San Gimignano, so it seems only fitting that Mancuso's would affect the look of a castle banquet hall. A cathedral ceiling, arched windows, and huge roof beams set the stage for the gourmet cuisine; a pianist playing soft jazz sets the mood. If you lack the means to start your meal with the beluga caviar, perhaps *carpaccio di manzo*—sliced raw beef with mustard sauce and capers—will do. Veal is a specialty (with *osso buco* a long-time favorite), but it's always difficult just to get past the pasta offerings. Fish and daily seafood specials round out the menu. The professional service will have you feeling like royalty by the time you finish your dessert and coffee.

At the Borgata, 6166 N. Scottsdale Rd. ✆ **480/948-9988**. Reservations recommended. Main courses $18–$29; pastas $17–$24. AE, DC, DISC, MC, V. Daily 5–10pm.

Mary Elaine's ★★★ FRENCH   In the Phoenix area, this restaurant is the very height of elegance and sophistication, and we say this not just because the restaurant is located on the top floor of the prestigious Phoenician resort's main building and boasts one of the best views in the valley. No, Mary Elaine's represents the pinnacle of Arizona dining for its haute cuisine, its exemplary service, and its superb table settings (Austrian crystal, French silver, and Wedgwood china). The chef focuses on the flavors of the modern French kitchen, which are usually dictated by the changing seasons. However, you're almost certain to encounter the signature pan-seared John Dory with fennel, artichokes, and pearl onions. Wild game, such as red currant–glazed rack of venison, also shows up regularly, and be sure to keep an eye out for the seared foie gras with 100-year-old balsamic vinegar. The very extensive wine list has won numerous awards.

At the Phoenician, 6000 E. Camelback Rd. ✆ **480/423-2530.** Reservations highly recommended. Jackets required for men. Main courses $38–$45; 6-course seasonal tasting menu $110 (matched wines are an additional $55). AE, DC, DISC, MC, V. Mon–Thurs 6–10pm; Fri–Sat 6–11pm.

Medizona ★★ MEDITERRANEAN/SOUTHWESTERN   Foodies, take note. This downtown Scottsdale restaurant, though tucked away on an otherwise unremarkable street, is one of the most talked about establishments in town these days. Chef Lenard Rubin has worked his way through the area's top resort restaurants, including Windows on the Green at the Phoenician and the Palo Verde Room at the Boulders. As the restaurant's name implies, the menu here is a masterful blend of both the bold flavors of the Southwest and the more subtle flavors of the Mediterranean. Though it sounds a bit odd, the rabbit, fig, and pine-nut baklava is an excellent way to start a meal before moving on to achiote-rubbed salmon with crawfish-corn risotto. For dessert, how can you resist prickly pear tiramisu with Turkish coffee-pistachio sauce?

7217 E. Fourth Ave. ✆ **480/947-9500.** Reservations highly recommended. Main courses $21–$27. AE, DISC, MC, V. Tues–Sat 6–10pm.

Windows on the Green ★★ SOUTHWESTERN   Slightly more casual than Mary Elaine's, the Phoenician's premier restaurant, but no less elegant, Windows on the Green has a sweeping view of the resort's golf course. With its innovative Southwestern cuisine, this place is best appreciated by those with a taste for unusual flavor combinations such as chipotle pepper–braised wild boar tortellini, ancho chile–fennel-glazed sea bass, or jalapeño-and-cumin gnocchi. While the flavors on the menu are predominantly Southwestern, not every dish is doused with chile peppers; diners with sensitive palates will find plenty to choose from. The wine list is chosen to complement these regional flavors. All in all, a good but somewhat pricey introduction to Southwestern cuisine.

At the Phoenician, 6000 E. Camelback Rd. ✆ **480/423-2530.** Reservations recommended. Main courses $18.50–$42; regional tasting menu $59. AE, DC, DISC, MC, V. Wed–Mon 6–10pm.

MODERATE

Sam's Cafe, North Scottsdale Road and Shea Boulevard (✆ **480/368-2800**), which has other branches around the valley, is another area restaurant worth trying. For more information, see the section on Downtown Phoenix, later in this chapter.

Café Terra Cotta ★★ *Value* SOUTHWESTERN   Café Terra Cotta started out in Tucson, where it pioneered trendy Southwestern foods. The list of choices at this casually sophisticated yet low-key restaurant includes wood-oven pizzas, sandwiches, and smaller meals as well as full-size main courses. Imaginative combinations are the rule, so you'll want to take your time with the menu before ordering. For example, roll this over your imaginary taste buds: chile-roasted duck breast with chipotle sauce on a potato-horseradish pancake and carrot-jicama salad. Don't miss the garlic custard with warm salsa vinaigrette, which goes great with a glass of wine chosen from the well-rounded wine list.

At the Borgata, 6166 N. Scottsdale Rd., Suite 100. © 480/948-8100. www.cafeterracotta.com. Reservations recommended for dinner. Main courses $8–$23. AE, DC, DISC, MC, V. Daily 11:30am–9:30pm.

Cowboy Ciao Wine Bar & Grill ✦ SOUTHWESTERN/FUSION   Delicious food and a fun, trendy atmosphere furnished in "cowboy chic" make this a great place for a meal. Located in fashionable downtown Scottsdale, it attracts a diverse group of people who like to dive into the likes of pesto-crusted elk loin or pan-seared lavender–green tea tuna. However, it's the soup and the mushroom pan-fry that really shouldn't be missed. Cowboy Ciao is also notable for its wine list and bar, where customers can order a flight (tasting assortment) of wines. If you're feeling adventurous when it comes time for dessert, opt for the Mexican chocolate pot de crème with chipotle cream. Unfortunately, service here can be uneven.

7133 E. Stetson Dr. (corner Sixth Ave.). © 480/WINE-111. www.cowboyciao.com. Reservations recommended. Main courses $7–$11 lunch, $16–$32 dinner. AE, DC, DISC, MC, V. Tues–Sat 11:30am–2:30pm and 5–10pm; Sun–Mon 5–10pm.

L'Ecole ✦ _Value_ FRENCH/MEDITERANNEAN   This culinary opportunity is a well-kept local secret—there aren't many places where you can get a three-course lunch for under $10 or a five-course dinner for $25. Although you don't have to bring a lot of money here, you do have to have a lot of patience—the cooking and serving is done by students, and it's all a learning experience for them. The menu changes frequently, but you can expect a good mix of classic and contemporary dishes. There's a respectable selection of wines and liquors to accompany the meal.

At the Scottsdale Culinary Institute, 8100 E. Camelback Rd. (just east of Hayden Rd.). © 480/990-7639. Reservations highly recommended several days in advance. Three-course lunch $9.25–$13; 5-course dinner $25–$30. DISC, MC, V. Mon–Fri 11:30am–1pm and 6–7:30pm. Closed every 3rd Mon.

Pepin ✦ SPANISH   For traditional Spanish fare and plenty of lively entertainment, you won't do better than Pepin. Located on the Scottsdale Mall, this small restaurant offers such a wide selection of tapas that you can easily have dinner without ever glancing at the main-course list. There are also several styles of paella, most of which are seafood extravaganzas. Thursday through Saturday evenings bring live flamenco performances, along with salsa dancing on Friday and Saturdays. Call for times.

7363 Scottsdale Mall. © 480/990-9026. Reservations recommended. Main courses $13–$25; tapas $5–$9. AE, DC, DISC, MC, V. Tues–Sat 11:30am–3pm and 4:30–10pm; Sun 4:30–10pm. Happy hour Tues–Fri 4:30–6:30pm.

Rancho Pinot ✦✦ NEW AMERICAN   Rancho Pinot, in a shopping center adjacent to the Borgata, combines a homey cowboy-chic decor with nonthreatening contemporary American cuisine; it has long been a favorite with Scottsdale and Phoenix residents. Look elsewhere if you're craving wildly creative flavor combinations, but if you like simple, well-prepared food, Rancho Pinot may be the place. Our favorite starter is the grilled squid salad with preserved lemon; for an entree, you can always count on the handmade pasta or Nonni's chicken, braised with white wine, mushrooms, and herbs. There's a short but well-chosen list of beers and wines by the glass. The staff is friendly and tends to treat you as though you're a regular, even if it's your first visit.

6208 N. Scottsdale Rd. (southwest corner of Scottsdale Rd. and Lincoln Dr.). $\textcircled{C}$ 480/367-8030. Reservations recommended. Main courses $17.50–$29. AE, DISC, MC, V. Tues–Sat 5:30–10pm. Summer hours subject to change.

Restaurant Hapa ★★ PAN-ASIAN   Even this far from the Pacific, Pan-Asian cuisine can cause a stir, and for several years now, this has been one of the hottest restaurants in Scottsdale. Small and somewhat intimate, Hapa attracts a wide range of diners. Most come because the restaurant just seems to have a way with the grill and can really bring out the flavor of shrimp, fish, and vegetables. The wood-burning oven also produces its share of outstanding dishes, including deftly prepared fish with roasted vegetables. We're particularly partial to the strong flavor combinations to be found on the appetizer list: Dungeness crab cakes with wasabi aioli; shrimp, quail, and chicken satay with three sauces; and pork and ginger pot stickers with curried mustard sauce. An adjoining sushi lounge specializes in pairing sushi with wine. To round out this Asian-American eating experience, try the delicious chocolate cake made with Chinese five-spice powder for an unusual mélange of contrasting flavors.

6204 N. Scottsdale Rd. (southwest corner of Scottsdale Rd. and Lincoln Dr.). $\textcircled{C}$ 480/998-8220. www. restauranthapa.com. Reservations recommended. Main courses $16–$34; sushi $10. AE, DC, MC, V. Mon–Sat 5:30–10pm.

Roaring Fork ★★ SOUTHWESTERN   This trendy Southwestern restaurant is the creation of chef Robert McGrath, who once was the chef at the Phoenician's Windows on the Green. With its stone walls, mélange of Mexican-hacienda and Italian-villa architectural styles, and impeccably upscale Southwestern interior, Roaring Fork is a much more casual space than Windows on the Green, yet the cuisine is just as creative. The bread basket alone, filled with herb-infused rolls and corn muffins accompanied by honey-chile butter, is enough to make you weep with joy. Be sure you try the sugar-and-chile-cured duck breast with green chile macaroni, a house specialty. If you can't get a table, dine at the bar, where you'll see bowls of interesting bar munchies such as pieces of spicy jerky. Don't miss the huckleberry margaritas.

7243 E. Camelback Rd. (near Scottsdale Rd.). $\textcircled{C}$ 480/947-0795. www.roaringfork.com. Reservations highly recommended. Main courses $15–$29. AE, DISC, MC, V. Mon–Sat 5:30–10pm.

Roy's of Scottsdale ★★ _Value_ EURO-ASIAN   So you decided to go to Arizona instead of Hawaii this year, but you really prefer Asian flavors to those of the Southwest. Don't worry—even in Scottsdale you can now get Hawaiian chef Roy Yamaguchi's patented Pan-Asian cuisine. Brilliant combinations and flamboyant presentations are the hallmarks, and despite the lively atmosphere, service usually runs like clockwork. The menu includes nightly specials such as wood-fired tiger shrimp and bacon pizza, as well as such signature dishes as blackened ahi tuna with a hot soy-mustard sauce. If you can't get a reservation, try for a seat at the counter, which provides a great floor show of cooks preparing food at lightning speed.

There's another Roy's at 2501 E. Camelback Rd., in the Camelback Esplanade ($\textcircled{C}$ 602/381-1155).

7001 N. Scottsdale Rd., at the Scottsdale Seville. $\textcircled{C}$ 480/905-1155. Reservations recommended. Main courses $16.50–$28; smaller plates $7–$11. AE, MC, V. Sun–Thurs 5–10pm; Fri–Sat 5–11pm.

6th Avenue Bistrot ⊀ CLASSIC FRENCH   Who says French has to be fussy? This little bistro less than a block off Scottsdale Road is, at lunch, as casual as a French restaurant gets (although it's a bit more formal in the evening). The draw here is a simple menu of reliable dishes at fairly reasonable prices: a bit of country pâté, tenderloin of pork with port-wine sauce, a hearty Beaujolais, all topped off with *mousse au chocolat,* and you have a perfect French dinner. Lunch is a great deal, and wines by the glass are reasonably priced.

7150 E. Sixth Ave. ℂ 480/947-6022. Reservations recommended. Main courses $7.25–$14.25 lunch, $18.75–$22.50 dinner. AE, MC, V. Sun–Mon 5–9pm; Tues 11am–2pm and 5–9pm; Wed–Fri 11am–2pm and 5–10pm; Sat 5–10pm.

Sushi Ko ⊀ *Finds* JAPANESE   Recommended by those who know good sushi and popular with the Japanese community, Sushi Ko is a little restaurant in a shopping plaza not far from both the Fairmont Scottsdale Princess and the Hyatt Regency Scottsdale Resort. What makes this place stand out, in addition to the fresh and well-prepared sushi, are the unusual items that sometimes appear on the sushi menu—fresh sardine sushi, monkfish pâté, edamame (steamed and salted soybeans that you pop from the shell and eat), and dynamite green mussels (mussels baked with mushrooms and mayonnaise—sounds strange, but tastes great). Table-side cooking is a specialty here, and you can get shabu-shabu, a hot-pot dish of thinly sliced beef and vegetables served with ponzu sauce.

9301 E. Shea Blvd. #126 (in the Mercado del Rancho shopping plaza). ℂ 480/860-2960. Reservations recommended for dinner. Main courses $4.50–$12 lunch, $10–$20 dinner. AE, DC, DISC, MC, V. Mon–Thurs 11:30am–2pm and 5:30–10pm; Fri 11:30am–2pm and 5:30–10:30pm; Sat 5:30–10:30pm; Sun 5:30–9:30pm.

Tortilla Factory ⊀ MEXICAN   Moderately priced Mexican restaurants abound in Phoenix and Scottsdale, but this is one of the most enjoyable. Located in an old house surrounded by attractive patios and citrus trees that bloom in winter and spring, this place stays busy both for its creative Mexican fare and for its lively bar scene (more than 100 premium tequilas are available). As you enter the restaurant grounds, you might see someone making the tortillas of the day (potato tortillas last time we were here), which will arrive at your table accompanied by spicy chile-flavored butter. The rich and spicy tortilla soup or the tequila-lime salad make good starters; among the entrees, we're big fans of the orange-tequila-glazed swordfish with cilantro sauce.

6910 E. Main St. ℂ 480/945-4567. Reservations recommended. Main courses $10–$21. AE, DC, DISC, MC, V. Sun–Thurs 5–9pm; Fri–Sat 5–10:30pm.

Veneto Trattoria Italiana ⊀ VENETIAN ITALIAN   This pleasantly low-key bistro, specializing in the cuisine of Venice, serves simple and satisfying "peasant food" (surprising, since the owner formerly ran the restaurant at the Giorgio Armani boutique in Beverly Hills). *Baccala mantecato* (creamy fish mousse on grilled polenta, made with dried salt cod soaked in milk overnight) may sound unusual, but it's heavenly—for this alone we would recommend the restaurant. Other good bets include the salad of thinly sliced smoked beef, shaved Parmesan, and arugula greens. For a finale, the *semifreddo con frutta secca,* a partially frozen meringue with dry fruits in a pool of raspberry sauce, has an intoxicating texture. There's outdoor seating on the patio (where you almost forget you're in a shopping mall) and a welcoming bistro ambience inside.

6137 N. Scottsdale Rd. (in Hilton Village). ℂ 480/948-9928. www.venetotrattoria.com. Reservations recommended. Main courses $8–$22. AE, DC, DISC, MC, V. Mon–Sat 11:30am–2:30pm and 5–10pm.

INEXPENSIVE

Bandera ⭐ *Value* AMERICAN   Frugal travelers will want to know about this place, as will those who've been craving barbecue or grilled chicken after smelling the wood-roasted chickens turning on the rotisseries in Bandera's back-of-the-building, open-air stone oven. What an aroma! The succulent spit-roasted chicken is served with the ultimate comfort food, a mountain of creamy mashed potatoes flecked with green onion and black pepper. Sure, you could order prime rib or clams, but you'd be a fool if you did. Stick with the chicken or maybe the honey-barbecued ribs, and you won't go wrong. The succulent smoked-salmon appetizer is also a hit.

3821 N. Scottsdale Rd., Scottsdale. ✆ 480/994-3524. Reservations not accepted. Main courses $9–$24. AE, DISC, MC, V. Sun–Thurs 4:30–10pm; Fri–Sat 4:30–11pm.

Carlsbad Tavern ⭐ NEW MEXICAN   Carlsbad Tavern blends the fiery tastes of New Mexican cuisine with a hip and humorous bat-theme atmosphere (a reference to Carlsbad Caverns). The menu lists traditional New Mexican dishes, such as *carne adovada,* pork simmered in a fiery red chile sauce, as well as nouvelle Southwestern specialties like grilled chicken, andouille sausage, and pine nuts tossed with pasta in a spicy peppercorn-cream sauce. Cool off your taste buds with a margarita made with fresh-squeezed juice. A lagoon makes this place feel like a beach bar, while the big patio fireplace is cozy on a cold night.

3313 N. Hayden Rd., Scottsdale (south of Osborn). ✆ 480/970-8164. Reservations recommended for dinner. Main courses $6.25–$19. AE, DC, DISC, MC, V. Mon–Sat 11am–1am; Sun 1pm–1am; limited menu from 10 or 11pm–1am.

El Guapo's Taco Shop & Salsa Bar *Finds* MEXICAN   *El Guapo* means "handsome," which certainly doesn't refer to this nondescript little hole-in-the-wall taco shop, but might be referring to Danny, the proprietor. The tacos—among them mahimahi, *carne asada,* and marinated pork—are prepared without the standard lettuce and tomatoes, so you can build your own by liberally dousing your order with salsa and vegetable toppings from the salsa cart. El Guapo also serves cheese crisps, burritos, and nachos. Try the armadillo eggs—jalapeño peppers stuffed with cheese and deep-fried. There are about half a dozen tables packed into the little space, but if you can squeeze your way up to the order counter, you'll be glad you found this place.

3015 N. Scottsdale Rd. (in Plaza 777), Scottsdale. ✆ 480/423-8385. Main dishes $2–$8. AE, MC, V. Mon–Sat 10:30am–8pm.

El Paso Barbeque Company ⭐ BARBECUE   This is barbecue Scottsdale style, with an upscale cowboy decor and a bar with two noisy TVs that can make for difficult conversation. But hey, if you're not in a romantic mood, this place is worth the trip for some lip-smacking barbecue, which runs the gamut from ribs to smoked chicken to more uptown dishes such as barbecued salmon and prime rib. The pulled pork with a smoky sauce and fresh coleslaw is scrumptious. There's also a wide variety of sandwiches, which makes this a good lunch spot or place to get carryout. Want to dine on the lighter side? Order the smoked-salmon salad.

8220 N. Hayden Rd. ✆ 480/998-2626. Reservations accepted for parties of 8 or more. Main courses $6–$17. AE, DISC, MC, V. Sun–Thurs 11am–10pm; Fri–Sat 11am–11pm.

Garlic's Pasta and Bread Company AMERICAN/ITALIAN   Tucked into the back of the same shopping center that houses the more upscale Roy's is this popular lunch spot. Although Garlic's does serve dinner a couple of nights a week, this is first and foremost a great spot to grab a quick lunch if you happen to be cruising Scottsdale Road at midday. Creative sandwiches are the big attraction, but there are also pasta salads and even brick-oven pizzas.

In Scottsdale Seville shopping center, 7001 N. Scottsdale Rd. © 480/368-9699. Reservations not accepted. Main courses $7 lunch, $11–$14 dinner. AE, MC, V. Mon–Tues 9am–6pm; Wed–Sat 9am–9pm.

Oregano's Pizza Bistro PIZZA/PASTA   With very reasonable prices and a location convenient to the many shops and galleries of downtown Scottsdale, this sprawling pizza joint (two buildings and the courtyard/parking lot between) is a big hit with the area's young crowd. Both the thin-crust pizzas—topped with the likes of barbecued chicken and feta cheese—and the Chicago stuffed pizza are all the good things pizza should be. The menu also offers artichoke lasagna, barbecued chicken wings, a variety of salads, and even a pizza cookie for dessert. Because this is such a popular spot, expect a wait at dinner.

Other locations are in Phoenix at 130 E. Washington St. (© **602/253-9577**), and in Tempe at 523 W. University Dr. (© **480/858-0501**).

3622 N. Scottsdale Rd. (south of Indian School Rd.). © 480/970-1860. Reservations not accepted. Main courses $5–$17. AE, DISC, MC, V. Mon–Thurs 11am–10pm; Fri–Sat 11am–11pm; Sun noon–10pm.

NORTH SCOTTSDALE, CAREFREE & CAVE CREEK
EXPENSIVE

La Hacienda ★★ GOURMET MEXICAN   As you may guess from the price range below, this is not your average taco joint. La Hacienda serves gourmet Mexican cuisine in an upscale, glamorous-but-rustic setting reminiscent of an early 1900s hacienda (stone tiled floor, Mexican glassware and crockery, a bee-hive fireplace). Here, a relleno might mean an artichoke bottom stuffed with crabmeat, and an appetizer of sautéed mushrooms might include *huitlacoche,* an unusual fungus popular in Mexico. Suckling pig stuffed with chorizo is the restaurant's signature dish, but you might also encounter grilled venison chops or rack of lamb crusted with pumpkin seeds. Live music adds to the lively atmosphere.

At the Fairmont Scottsdale Princess resort, 7575 E. Princess Dr. (about 12 miles north of downtown Scottsdale). © 480/585-4848. Reservations recommended. Main courses $22–$30. AE, DC, DISC, MC, V. Daily 6–10pm.

Marquesa ★★★ MEDITERRANEAN/CATALAN   Simply put, the Marquesa, with ambience reminiscent of an 18th-century Spanish villa, is as romantic a restaurant as you're likely to find in the valley. The menu is a contemporary interpretation of Catalonian (regional Spanish) with other Mediterranean influences, and though the prices are high, we can think of few better places for a very special dinner. The menu changes with the seasons, but expect it to be ripe with exotic ingredients imported from around the world, and count on almost every dish being an intensive labor of love. Because Catalonian food is unfamiliar to most people, you'll need to be something of a culinary adventurer to try such dishes as lobster-and-salt-cod cakes with oxtail fondue of wild mushrooms or arborio-crusted sweetbreads. *Paella Valenciana,* the signature dish, includes such ingredients as lobster, frog legs, mussels, shrimp, and cockles, and should not be missed. The Sunday "market-style" brunch is one of the best in the valley.

At the Fairmont Scottsdale Princess resort, 7575 E. Princess Dr. (about 12 miles north of downtown Scottsdale). © 480/585-4848. Reservations recommended. Main courses $29–$43; champagne brunch $49. AE, DC, DISC, MC, V. Tues–Sat 6–10pm; Sun 10:30am–2:30pm.

Michael's ★★ NEW AMERICAN/INTERNATIONAL   Located in the Citadel shopping/business plaza in north Scottsdale, Michael's was once a remote culinary outpost. But as Scottsdale's upscale suburbs have marched ever northward, the city has bulldozed its way to Michael's doorstep. Push through the restaurant's front door, and you'll find out exactly why foodies are willing to make the drive out here. The setting is simple yet elegant, which allows the drama of food presentation to take the fore. To start things off, do not miss the "silver spoons" hors d'oeuvres—tablespoons each containing three or four ingredients that burst with flavors. From there it's on to such main courses as maple-glazed duck and foie gras on bean mash and cippollini onions. Throughout the year, chef Michael DeMaria partners with other local chefs to present special themed lunches and dinners. Call ☎ **480/515-3550** for information.

8700 E. Pinnacle Peak Rd. ☎ **480/515-2575**. www.michaelsrestaurant.com. Reservations recommended. Main courses $18–$27. AE, DC, MC, V. Mon–Sat 11am–2pm and 6–10pm; Sun 10am–3pm (brunch) and 6–10pm.

Restaurant Oceana ★★ SEAFOOD   North Scottsdale is where the action is these days when it comes to new resorts, golf courses, posh suburbs, and restaurants. Among the best of the latter is a rather small seafood restaurant in an attractive shopping center that has no fewer than four upscale restaurants. As the name implies, Oceana specializes in all things finny, plus plenty of crustaceans, and everything is as fresh as it can be here in the middle of the desert. A wood oven and a sushi bar guarantee that the restaurant will appeal to a wide variety of palates. Standouts well worth trying include the wood-oven-baked mussels, the grilled rare ahi tuna, and the Dungeness crab cakes. When it comes time for dessert, be sure to order a sampler plate.

8900 E. Pinnacle Peak Rd. (at Pima Rd.), La Mirada shopping center. ☎ **480/515-2277**. www.restaurantoceana. com. Reservations recommended. Main courses $19–$39. AE, DC, DISC, MC, V. Sun–Thurs 5:30–9pm; Fri–Sat 5:30–10pm. Closed Sun–Mon in summer.

INEXPENSIVE

The Original Crazy Ed's Satisfied Frog Saloon & Restaurant *Finds* AMERICAN/BARBECUE   Cave Creek is the Phoenix area's favorite cow-town hangout and is filled with Wild West–theme saloons and restaurants. Crazy Ed's, affiliated with the Black Mountain Brewing Company, which produces Cave Creek Chili Beer, is our favorite. You'll find Crazy Ed's in Frontier Town, a tourist-trap cow town, but don't let the location put you off. This place is just plain fun, with big covered porches and sawdust on the floor. Although the restaurant offers dishes "from the pond" and "from the chicken coop," you should stick to steaks and barbecue.

In Frontier Town, 6245 E. Cave Creek Rd., Cave Creek. ☎ **480/488-3317**. www.satisfiedfrog.com. Reservations not accepted. Main courses $7–$11 lunch, $9.50–$21 dinner. AE, DISC, MC, V. Sun–Thurs 11am–9 or 10pm; Fri–Sat 11am–11pm.

CENTRAL PHOENIX & THE CAMELBACK CORRIDOR
EXPENSIVE

Harris' ★★ STEAKHOUSE   Enormous slabs of steak, perfectly cooked and allowed to express their inner beefiness unsullied by silly sauces, are de rigueur from Manhattan to Marin County these days, and no longer is it necessary to visit some steakhouse that has aged longer than the meat it serves. Harris', smack in the middle of the bustling big-money Camelback Corridor, is one of Phoenix's biggest contemporary steakhouses and is popular with wealthy retirees. With a Southwestern pueblo-modern styling, valet-parking attendants, and prime rib a specialty of the house, this impressive restaurant leaves no doubt that this is where the beef is. At lunch (when prices are lower), the New York steak salad with blue cheese and candied pecans fairly snaps with flavor—ask for it if you don't see it on the menu.

3101 E. Camelback Rd. © **602/508-8888.** Reservations highly recommended. Main courses $8–$18.50 lunch, $13–$32 dinner. AE, DC, DISC, MC, V. Mon–Fri 11:30am–2pm and 5:30–10pm; Sat 5:30–10pm.

Lon's ★★ AMERICAN REGIONAL   Located in an old adobe hacienda built by cowboy artist Lon Megargee and surrounded by colorful gardens, this restaurant is one of the most "Arizonan" places in the Phoenix area, and the patio, with its views of Camelback Mountain, is so tranquil that you'll likely want to start shopping for a house in the neighborhood. At midday this place is popular with both retirees and the power-lunch set, while at dinner it bustles with a wide mix of people. Don't miss the fried sweet potatoes and red onion rings at lunch—they're deliciously salty-sweet and crispy. Dinner entrees are beautifully presented works of art, blending subtle flavors such as grilled salmon with fennel and leeks or pan-seared tiger prawns with watercress sauce. There's a good selection of wines by the glass, though they're a little on the pricey side. The bar is cozy and romantic.

At the Hermosa Inn, 5532 N. Palo Cristi Rd. © **602/955-7878.** www.lons.com. Reservations recommended. Main courses $10–$16 lunch, $18.50–$29 dinner. AE, DC, MC, V. Mon–Fri 11:30am–2pm and 6–10pm; Sat 6–10pm; Sun 10am–2pm (brunch) and 6–10pm.

T. Cook's ★★★ MEDITERRANEAN   Simply put, there is no restaurant in the Valley of the Sun more romantic than T. Cook's. Located within the walls of the Mediterranean-inspired Royal Palms resort, it's surrounded by decades-old gardens and even has palm trees growing right through the roof of the dining room. The focal point of the open kitchen is a wood-fired oven that produces dishes such as pork loin and spit-roasted chicken. Dishes that don't originate in the wood oven, such as the sautéed lobster with fresh tortellini and asparagus, are also worth considering. T. Cook's continues to make big impressions right through to the dessert course. Although this is one of the most popular upper-end restaurants in Phoenix, it manages to avoid pretentiousness.

In the Royal Palms resort, 5200 E. Camelback Rd. © **602/808-0766.** www.royalpalmshotel.com. Reservations highly recommended. Main courses $12–$16 lunch, $21–$31 dinner. AE, DC, DISC, MC, V. Mon–Sat 6–10am, 11am–2pm, and 5:30–10pm; Sun 10am–2pm (brunch) and 5:30–10pm.

MODERATE

Altos Bistro-N-Loft Bar ★ *(Finds* SPANISH   Well hidden in the back of a Camelback Road shopping plaza, Altos is a little difficult to find, but it's definitely worth searching out. It's a casually chic place to enjoy a light meal of tapas and sangria, though more substantial dishes are also quite good. Contemporary and classic treatments of Spanish food are the specialty here, including tapas such as mussels in sherry sauce or sautéed shrimp with almonds. Paella with seafood, chicken, Basque sausage, pork, and saffron rice is a complex melding of flavors. Brandy bread pudding or espresso crème brûlée round out the experience, along with live flamenco-fusion guitar on weekends.

5029 N. 44th St. (at the northeast corner of 44th St. and Camelback). © **602/808-0890.** Reservations recommended. Main courses $19–$23; tapas $9–$12. AE, MC, V. Sun 5:30–9pm; Mon–Thurs 5:30–10pm; Fri–Sat 5:30–11pm.

Christopher's Fermier Brasserie and Paola's Wine Bar ✦ RUSTIC FRENCH   Local celeb chef Christopher Gross's current venue in Biltmore Fashion Park covers many bases. There's a wine bar, a brewery, a cigar room, oh yeah, and even a restaurant, which all add up to the uneasy feeling that style, not substance, is what's really important in this see-and-be-seen establishment. Although there are some tasty standouts, such as the house-smoked salmon and a velvety roasted red bell pepper soup with truffle essence (both long-time Gross standards), the menu can be very hit-or-miss. The brewery produces a wide range of beer styles; we prefer the darker ones, but you can give them all a try by ordering a flight. A wine bar menu is served from 3 to 5pm, when you can nibble on such things as smoked-chicken pizza or French cheeses.

2584 E. Camelback Rd. (in Biltmore Fashion Park). ℂ 602/522-2344. Reservations recommended. Main courses $9–$15 lunch, $17–$30 dinner. AE, DISC, MC, V. Mon–Thurs 11am–3pm and 5–10pm; Fri 11am–3pm and 5–11pm; Sat noon–3pm and 5–11pm; Sun noon–3pm and 5–10pm.

Coup des Tartes ✦ *Finds* COUNTRY FRENCH   Chain restaurants, theme restaurants, restaurants that are all style and little substance: Sometimes in Phoenix it seems impossible to find a genuinely homey little hole-in-the-wall restaurant that serves good food. Coupe des Tartes is just such a place. With barely a dozen tables and no liquor license (bring your own wine), it's about as removed from the standard Phoenix glitz as you can get without boarding a plane and leaving town. Start your meal with pâté de campagne or brie brûlée, which is covered with caramelized apples. The entree menu is always quite short, but you might opt for Moroccan lamb shanks with couscous or filet mignon with the sauce of the moment.

4626 N. 16th St. (2 blocks off Camelback Rd.). ℂ **602/212-1082**. Reservations recommended. Main courses $12–$25. AE, MC, V. Tues–Sat 5:30–9:30pm.

Eddie Matney's ✦✦ NEW AMERICAN   Eddie Matney has been on the Phoenix restaurant scene for quite a few years now, and continues to keep local diners happy with his mix of creativity and comfort. This upscale bistro is in a glass office tower at Camelback Road's most upscale corner, which means it's a popular power-lunch and business-dinner spot, but it also works well for a romantic evening out. The menu ranges far and wide for inspiration and features everything from Eddie's famous meatloaf to sesame-seared ahi tuna.

2398 E. Camelback Rd. ℂ **602/957-3214**. www.eddiematneys.com. Reservations recommended. Main courses $9–$15 lunch, $16–$25 dinner. AE, DISC, MC, V. Mon–Thurs 11:30am–2:30pm and 5–10:30pm; Fri 11:30am–2:30pm and 5–11:30pm; Sat 5–11:30pm; Sun 5–10:30pm.

Roxsand ✦ NEW AMERICAN/FUSION   Located on the second floor of the exclusive Biltmore Fashion Park mall, Roxsand is a place of urban sophistication, a restaurant at which to see and be seen. The menu is a mélange of flavors fused from around the world, which can leave you agonizing over whether to have the Moroccan *b'stilla* (braised chicken in phyllo with roasted-eggplant puree), the African spicy shrimp salad, or the curried-lamb tamale (and those are just the appetizers). Sauces sometimes lack complexity, but we do recommend the air-dried duck with pistachio onion marmalade, buckwheat crepes, and three sauces—Szechwan black-bean sauce, evil jungle prince sauce, and plum sauce. After dinner, amble over to the awesome dessert case; your choice will be served on a dinner plate adorned with additional cookies and perhaps a dollop of sorbet.

2594 E. Camelback Rd. ℂ 602/381-0444. Reservations recommended. Main courses $10–$13 lunch, $11–$34 dinner. AE, DC, DISC, MC, V. Mon–Thurs 11am–3pm and 5–10pm; Fri–Sat 11am–3pm and 5–11pm; Sun noon–3pm and 5–9pm.

Vincent Guerithault on Camelback ★★★ ⓥ𝘢𝘭𝘶𝘦 SOUTHWESTERN
With its well-balanced blend of Southwestern and European flavors and great
lunch values, this just might be our favorite Phoenix restaurant. Our only complaint is the mandatory valet parking (we're perfectly capable of parking our own
car). Although this place has an unpretentious French-country atmosphere, the
cuisine is as much Southwestern as French (think sweetbreads with blue cornmeal or tequila soufflé). Grilled meats and seafood are the specialty, and might
come accompanied by cilantro salsa or habanero pasta. The extensive wine list
has selections from both California and France.

3930 E. Camelback Rd. ⓒ 602/224-0225. Reservations highly recommended. Main courses $12–$16 lunch,
$16–$29 dinner. AE, DC, MC, V. Mon–Fri 11:30am–2:30pm and 6–10:30pm; Sat 5:30–10:30pm.

INEXPENSIVE

Blue Burrito Grille ★ MEXICAN   This is a great place for fast, cheap,
healthy food smack in the middle of the Camelback Corridor shopping district.
Located in a plaza that also houses the most expensive jewelry store in the valley, it's obviously not your usual greasy-tortilla Mexican joint. Catering to a
health-conscious and affluent community, the Blue Burrito specializes in healthful Mexican food (with no lard and plenty of vegetarian offerings). Okay, so the
deep-fried chimichanga isn't good for you, but the fish tacos, enchiladas
rancheras, and tamales Mexicanos certainly are. Wash it all down with a mango
margarita.

Other locations are in Phoenix at 3815 N. Central Ave. (ⓒ **602/234-3293**),
and in Scottsdale at 7318 E. Shea Blvd. (ⓒ **480/951-3151**).

In the Biltmore Plaza, 3118 E. Camelback Rd. ⓒ 602/955-9596. Reservations not accepted. Main courses
$4.50–$7. AE, DC, MC, V. Mon–Sat 11am–10pm; Sun 11am–9pm.

Ed Debevic's Short Orders Deluxe 𝘒𝘪𝘥𝘴 AMERICAN   Hidden away
behind the Town and Country Shopping Center, Ed's is a classic 1950s diner
right down to the little jukeboxes in the booths. Not only does it make its own
burgers, chili, and bread, but Ed's also serves the best malteds in Phoenix. The
sign in the front window that reads WAITRESSES WANTED, PEOPLE SKILLS NOT
NECESSARY should give you a clue that service here is unique. The place stays
busy, and the waitresses are overworked (although they do break into song now
and again), so don't be surprised if your waitress sits down in the booth with you
to wait for your order. That's just the kind of place Ed runs, and as he says, "If
you don't like the way I do things—buy me out."

2102 E. Highland Ave. ⓒ 602/956-2760. Reservations not accepted. Sandwiches and blue-plate specials
$4–$9. AE, DC, DISC, MC, V. Sun–Thurs 11am–9pm; Fri–Sat 11am–10pm.

5 & Diner AMERICAN   If it's 2am and you just have to have a big burger and
a side of fries after a night of dancing, head for the 24-hour 5 & Diner. You can't
miss it—it's the classic streamliner diner that looks as though it just materialized
from New Jersey.

Other locations are in Paradise Valley at 12802 N. Tatum Blvd. (ⓒ **602/
996-0033**) and in Scottsdale at Scottsdale Pavilions, 9069 E. Indian Bend Rd.
(ⓒ **480/949-1957**).

5220 N. 16th St. ⓒ 602/264-5220. Sandwiches/plates $4.50–$12. AE, MC, V. Daily 24 hours.

Vintage Market 𝘍𝘪𝘯𝘥𝘴 UPSCALE DELI/WINE BAR   This is a prime people-
watching spot and a great place for European-style sandwiches, accompanied by
a latte or a glass of wine chosen from a long list. Prices here are lower than at

Kids Family-Friendly Restaurants

Ed Debevic's Short Orders Deluxe *(see p. 96)* This classic 1950s diner is full of cool stuff, including little jukeboxes in the booths. You can tell your kids about hanging out in places like this when you were a teenager.

Organ Stop Pizza *(see p. 99)* A mighty Wurlitzer organ, with all the bells and whistles, entertains families while they chow down on pizza at long, communal tables. Nobody cares if the kids run around, and there are enough theatrics to keep them interested even if they can't relate to the music.

Pinnacle Peak Patio *(see p. 100)* Way out in north Scottsdale, this restaurant is a Wild West steakhouse complete with cowboys, shootouts, hayrides, and live western music nightly.

Rawhide Western Town *(see p. 111)* This place, once just a cowboy steakhouse, has become such an attraction that we've had to move it to the "Seeing the Sights" section of this book under "Wild West Theme Towns," but it's still a great place to bring the kids for dinner and lots of entertainment.

Rustler's Rooste *(see p. 101)* Similar to Pinnacle Peak but closer to the city center, Rustler's Rooste has a slide from the lounge to the main dining room, a big patio, and live cowboy bands nightly. See if you can get your kids to try the rattlesnake appetizer—it tastes like chicken.

practically any other place in Biltmore Fashion Park, and you can get the likes of Mediterranean focaccia or Asian vegetable and shrimp salad.

Another location is in Scottsdale at the Borgata, 6166 N. Scottsdale Rd. (© **480/315-8199**).

24th St. and Camelback Rd. (Biltmore Fashion Park). © **602/955-4444.** Reservations not necessary. Salads/sandwiches $8–$10.50. AE, DC, MC, V. Mon–Wed 10am–7pm; Thurs–Sat 10am–9pm; Sun 11am–5pm.

DOWNTOWN PHOENIX
MODERATE

Sam's Café ★★ *Value* SOUTHWESTERN Sam's Cafe, one of only a handful of decent downtown restaurants, offers food that's every bit as imaginative, but not nearly as expensive, as that served at other (often overrated) Southwestern restaurants in Phoenix. Breadsticks with picante-flavored cream cheese, grilled vegetable tacos, and angel-hair pasta in a spicy jalapeño sauce with shrimp and mushrooms all have a nice balance of flavors and are just spicy enough. Salads and dipping sauces are complex and interesting. The downtown Sam's has a large patio that overlooks a fountain and palm garden; it stays packed with the lunchtime, after-work, and convention crowds.

Other Sam's are located in the Biltmore Fashion Park, 2566 E. Camelback Rd. (© **602/954-7100**), and in Scottsdale at 10010 N. Scottsdale Rd., at Shea Boulevard (© **480/368-2800**).

In the Arizona Center, 455 N. Third St. © **602/252-3545.** Reservations recommended. Main courses $8–$22. AE, DISC, MC, V. Mon–Thurs 11am–10pm; Fri–Sat 11am–11pm; Sun 11am–9pm.

INEXPENSIVE

Alice Cooper'stown ★ BARBECUE   Owned by Alice Cooper himself, this sports-and-rock theme restaurant/bar located between the Bank One Ballpark and America West Arena is downtown's premier eat-o-tainment center. Sixteen video screens (most likely showing sports) are the centerpiece of the restaurant, but there's also an abundance of memorabilia on the walls, from Alice Cooper's platinum records to guitars from Fleetwood Mac and Eric Clapton to plenty of celebrity photographs. The wait staff even wears Alice Cooper makeup. Barbecue is served in various permutations, from a huge and moderately tasty sandwich to a BBQ Feast platter. Other choices include a 2-foot-long hot dog, ribs, and "Megadeth" meatloaf. If you were a fan, this place is a must; if you weren't, it's a miss.

101 E. Jackson St. ⓒ 602/253-7337. www.alicecooperstown.com. Reservations not accepted. Sandwiches/barbecue $6–$19. AE, DC, MC, V. Sun–Thurs 10am–9pm; Fri–Sat 10am–10pm.

Honey Bear's BBQ *Finds* BARBECUE   We can definitely say that Honey Bear's has a dud-free menu, and it couldn't be simpler—pork barbecue, beef barbecue, and chicken barbecue. Accompanied, maybe, by some coleslaw, with sweet potato pie for dessert.

This fast-food joint has another location at 5012 E. Van Buren St. (ⓒ **602/ 273-9148**).

2824 N. Central Ave. ⓒ **602/279-7911**. Sandwiches and dinners $3.70–$12.50. AE, DC, MC, V. Mon–Sat 10am–10pm; Sun 10am–9:30pm.

MacAlpine's Nostalgic Soda Fountain & Coffee Shoppe *Finds* AMERICAN   Fans of old-time diners and soda fountains will not want to miss this place. It's the real thing, and it hasn't changed much since its opening in 1928. In fact, it's the oldest operating soda fountain in the Southwest. The atmosphere is laid-back, and wooden booths and worn countertops show the patina of time. Order a breakfast egg on a bagel or a big hamburger or tuna sandwich. Wash it down with a lemon phosphate, chocolate malted, or egg cream.

2303 N. Seventh St. ⓒ **602/252-3039**. Sandwiches/specials $3.25–$6. AE, MC, V. Mon–Fri 7am–4pm; Sat 7am–2pm.

Pizzeria Bianco ★ ITALIAN   Even though this historic brick building is located smack dab in the center of downtown Phoenix, the atmosphere is so friendly and cozy it feels like your neighborhood local. The wood-burning oven turns out deliciously rustic pizzas with chewy-crunchy crusts. One of our favorites is made with red onion, Parmesan, rosemary, and crushed pistachios. Don't miss the fresh mozzarella, either. Pizzeria Bianco makes its own, and it can be ordered as an appetizer or on a pizza.

In Heritage Square, 623 E. Adams St. ⓒ **602/258-8300**. Reservations accepted for parties of 6 or more. Pizzas $8–$12. MC, V. Tues–Sat 5–10pm; Sun 5–9pm.

TEMPE, MESA, SOUTH PHOENIX & THE AIRPORT AREA
MODERATE

House of Tricks ★★ NEW AMERICAN   House of Tricks is housed in a pair of old Craftsman bungalows surrounded by an attractive garden of shady trees, and consequently, the restaurant has a completely different feel from modern Mill Avenue, Tempe's main drag, which is only 2 blocks away. This is where Arizona State University students take their parents when they come to visit, but it's also a nice spot for a romantic evening and a good place to try innovative cuisine without blowing your vacation budget. The grape arbor–covered patio, where there's also a shady bar, is the preferred seating area. The dinner menu changes regularly and consists of a single page of tempting salads, appetizers, and main dishes. The garlic-inspired Caesar salad and the house-smoked salmon with avocado, capers, and lemon cream are good bets for starters. Among the entrees, look for the pork rack with jalapeño marmalade.

114 E. Seventh St., Tempe. ✆ **480/968-1114.** Reservations recommended. Main courses $16.25–$22.50. AE, DC, DISC, MC, V. Mon–Sat 11am–10pm. Closed first 2 weeks of Aug.

Monti's La Casa Vieja ✿ AMERICAN   If you're tired of the glitz and glamour of the Valley of the Sun and are looking for Old Arizona, head to Tempe and Monti's La Casa Vieja. The adobe building was constructed in 1873 (*casa vieja* means "old house" in Spanish) on the site of the Salt River ferry, which operated in the days when the river flowed year-round and Tempe was nothing more than a ferry crossing. Today, local families who have been in Phoenix for generations know Monti's well, and rely on the restaurant for solid meals and low prices— you can get a filet mignon for under $12. The dining rooms are dark and filled with memorabilia of the Old West.

1 W. Rio Salado Pkwy. (at the corner of Mill Ave.), Tempe. ✆ **480/967-7594.** www.monti.com. Reservations recommended for dinner. Main courses $5–$27. AE, DC, DISC, MC, V. Sun–Thurs 11am–10pm; Fri–Sat 11am–11pm.

INEXPENSIVE

The Farm at South Mountain ✿ *Finds* SANDWICHES/SALADS   If being in the desert has you dreaming of shady trees and green grass, you'll enjoy this little oasis reminiscent of a New England orchard or Midwestern farm. A rustic outbuilding surrounded by potted flowers has been converted to a stand-in-line restaurant where you can order a mesquite grilled eggplant sandwich or one of the fresh salads, such as a pecan turkey Waldorf with sour cream and dried apricot dressing. Breakfast choices are baked goods such as muffins and scones, teas, and juices. The grassy lawn is ideal for a picnic on a blanket under the pecan trees.

On a couple of Friday nights each month during the cooler season, five-course gourmet dinners ($55) using garden produce are served. Sunday brunches ($35–$50) are also sometimes scheduled. Reservations made far in advance are a necessity. For information, call **Quiessence** (✆ **602/243-9081**).

6106 S. 32nd St. ✆ **602/276-6360.** Sandwiches and salads $8.50. AE, DC, MC, V. Daily 8am–3pm (if weather is inclement, call to be sure it's open). Take exit 151A off I-10 and go south on 32nd St.

Organ Stop Pizza ✿ *Kids* PIZZA   The pizza here may not be the best in town, but the Mighty Würlitzer theater organ, the largest in the world, sure is memorable. The massive instrument, which contains more than 5,500 pipes, has four turbine blowers to provide the wind to create the sound, and with 40-foot ceilings in the restaurant, the acoustics are great. As you marvel at the skill of the organist, who performs songs ranging from the latest pop tunes to "The Phantom of the Opera," you can enjoy simple pizzas, pastas, or snack foods such as nachos or onion rings.

1149 E. Southern Ave. (southwest corner of Southern Ave. and Stapley Dr.), Mesa. ✆ **480/813-5700.** www.organstoppizza.com. Pizzas and pastas $4.50–$14.50. Credit cards not accepted. Thanksgiving to mid-Apr Sun–Thurs 4–9pm, Fri–Sat 4–10pm; mid-Apr to Thanksgiving Sun–Thurs 5–9pm, Fri–Sat 5–10pm.

DINING WITH A VIEW

Different Pointe of View ★★ CLASSIC FRENCH/REGIONAL
AMERICAN   If you're staying anywhere on the north side of Phoenix or
Scottsdale and crave a dining room with a view, then put the SUV in low and
drive to the top of the hill at the Pointe Hilton Tapatio Cliffs Resort. Built into
a mountaintop, this restaurant takes in dramatic, sweeping vistas of the city,
mountains, and desert through its curving walls of glass. Come early, and you
can enjoy views to the north from the lounge before heading into the south-
facing dining room. The menu changes regularly but tends to emphasize the
classic ingredients of French haute cuisine and American fine dining: foie gras
(here served with tangerine-scented figs and 100-year-old balsamic vinegar),
escargot, lobster—you get the picture. Despite the excellent food, award-
winning wine list, and live jazz Wednesday through Saturday, the view steals
the show.

At the Pointe Hilton Tapatio Cliffs Resort, 11111 N. Seventh St. ✆ 602/863-0912. Reservations highly recommended. Main courses $29–$40. AE, DC, DISC, MC, V. Sun–Thurs 6–9:30pm; Fri–Sat 5:30–10pm (lounge
open later).

Top of the Rock ★★ NEW AMERICAN/SOUTHWESTERN   Almost all
of the best views in Phoenix are from expensive resort restaurants, so if you want
to dine with a view of the valley, you're going to have to pay the price. For desert
drama, no other view restaurant can compare with Top of the Rock, which,
quite literally, is built into the top of a rocky hill looking north across the valley.
Luckily, quality accompanies the high prices, and in addition to the romantic
setting, you can enjoy some very creative cuisine. Ostrich ranching has long
been popular in Arizona, and on the appetizer menu you'll find perfectly done
ostrich medallions that should not be missed. Surprisingly, the Dungeness crab
cakes are also excellent. Be forewarned that chile peppers play an important role
in many entrees, such as the excellent seared beef tenderloin with chipotle-
pepper demi-glace. The ambience is a little on the formal side, but you don't
necessarily have to get dressed up.

At Wyndham Buttes Resort, 2000 Westcourt Way, Tempe. ✆ 602/225-9000. Reservations recommended.
Main courses $24–$30; Sun brunch $35. AE, DC, DISC, MC, V. Sun–Thurs 5–10pm; Fri–Sat 5–11pm; Sun
10am–2pm and 5–10pm.

COWBOY STEAKHOUSES

These family restaurants generally provide big portions of grilled steaks and barbecued ribs, outdoor and "saloon" dining, live country music, and various other
sorts of entertainment. The biggest of these is **Rawhide Western Town,** a Wild
West theme park with a big steakhouse, stagecoach rides, and shootouts in the
street. See p. 111 for details.

Pinnacle Peak Patio ★ (Kids) STEAKHOUSE   Once located miles out in the
desert, this "Hollywood western" steakhouse is now surrounded by some of the
valley's poshest suburbs. Despite the million-dollar homes, this joint still knows
how to keep 'em comin' back for more. Although you can indulge in mesquite-
broiled steaks (and even a 2-lb. porterhouse monster) with all the traditional
trimmings, a meal here is more an event than just an opportunity to put on the
feed bag. The real draw is all the free Wild West entertainment—gunfights,
cowboy bands, two-stepping, and cookouts. Also of interest are the museum-like
displays of interesting collections such as can openers, police badges, and license
plates. Businessmen, beware! Wear a tie into this place, and you'll have it cut off
and hung from the rafters along with the quarter million other ties up there.

10426 E. Jomax Rd., Scottsdale. © 480/585-1599. Reservations accepted for parties of 8 or more. Main courses $12.50–$29; children's menu $2.50–$6.50. AE, DC, DISC, MC, V. Mon–Thurs 4–10pm; Fri–Sat 4–11pm; Sun noon–10pm. Take Scottsdale Rd. north to Pinnacle Peak Rd., turn right and continue to Pima Rd., turn left and follow the signs.

Rustler's Rooste ★ *Kids* STEAKHOUSE   This location, in the middle of a sprawling golf resort, doesn't exactly seem like cowboy country. But up at the top of the hill, you'll find a fun Western-theme restaurant where you can start your meal by going down a big slide from the bar to the main dining room. While the view north across Phoenix is entertainment enough for most people, there are also Western bands playing for those who like to kick up their heels. If you've ever been bitten by a snake, you can exact your revenge here by ordering the rattlesnake appetizer. Follow that (if you've got the appetite of a hardworking cowpoke) with the enormous cowboy "stuff" platter consisting of, among other things, broiled steak, barbecued ribs, cowboy beans, fried shrimp, barbecued chicken, and skewered swordfish.

At the Pointe Hilton on South Mountain, 7777 S. Pointe Hwy., Phoenix. © 602/431-6474. Reservations recommended. Main courses $13–$32. AE, DC, DISC, MC, V. Daily 5–10pm.

BREAKFAST, BRUNCH & QUICK BITES

Most of Phoenix's best Sunday brunches are to be had at restaurants in major hotels and resorts. Among the finest are those served at **Marquesa** (in the Scottsdale Princess), the **Golden Swan** (in the Hyatt Regency Scottsdale Resort), **Wright's** (in the Arizona Biltmore Resort & Spa), and the **Terrace Dining Room** (in the Phoenician). For information on the two former restaurants, see the Scottsdale section of "Where to Dine." For information on the latter two restaurants, see "Where to Stay."

The **Desert Botanical Garden,** 1201 N. Galvin Pkwy., in Papago Park (© 480/941-1225; www.dbg.org), serves brunch with its Music in the Garden concerts held on Sundays between September and March. Tickets are $13.50 and include admission to the gardens, but meals cost extra.

If your idea of the perfect breakfast is a French pastry and a good cup of coffee, try **Pierre's Pastry Café,** 7119 E. Shea Blvd., Scottsdale (© 480/443-2510), where the croissants and brioche have a luxurious, buttery texture (desserts here are also irresistible). Along Camelback Road, in the Biltmore Plaza shopping center, try **La Madeleine,** 3102 E. Camelback Rd. (© 602/952-0349), *the* place for a luscious and leisurely French breakfast amid antique farm implements. Other branches are at Fashion Square Mall, 7014 E. Camelback Rd., Scottsdale (© 480/945-1663), and at Tatum and Shea boulevards in Paradise Valley (© 480/483-0730).

For fruit smoothies, muffins, and healthy things, try **Wild Oats Community Market,** which has stores at 3933 E. Camelback Rd. (© 602/954-0584), in North Phoenix at 13823 N. Tatum Blvd. (© 602/953-7546), and in Scottsdale at Shea Boulevard and Scottsdale Road (© 480/905-1441).

5 Seeing the Sights

THE DESERT & ITS NATIVE CULTURES

Heard Museum ★★★   The Heard Museum is one of the nation's finest museums dealing exclusively with Native American cultures and is an ideal introduction to the indigenous peoples of Arizona. The extensive exhibit *Native Peoples of the Southwest* examines the culture of each of the major tribes of the region and includes a Navajo hogan, an Apache wickiup, and a Hopi

Phoenix, Scottsdale & the Valley of the Sun Attractions

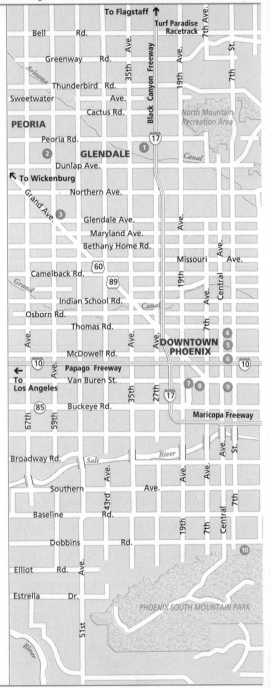

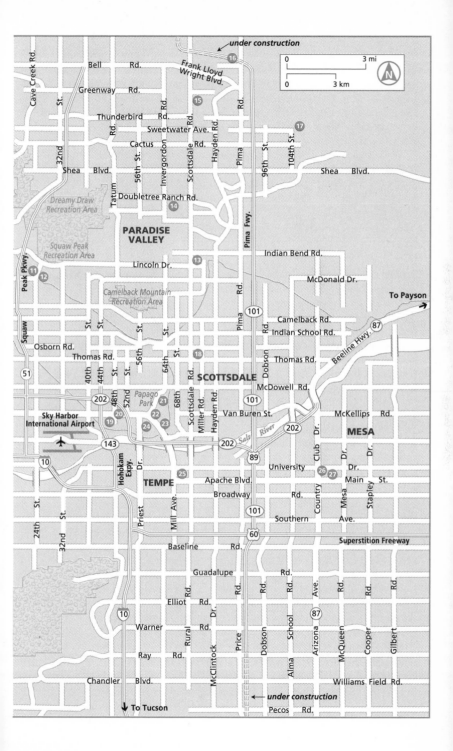

corn-grinding display. In the large Katsina Doll Gallery, you'll get an idea of the number of different kachina spirits that populate the Hopi and Zuni religions, while the Crossroads Gallery offers a fascinating look at contemporary Native American art. On many weekends, there are performances by Native American singers and dancers, and throughout the week, artists demonstrate their work. Guided tours are offered daily. The annual **Indian Fair and Market,** held on the first weekend in March, includes traditional dances and arts and crafts demonstrations and sales.

The museum also operates **Heard Museum North,** El Pedregal Festival Marketplace, 34505 N. Scottsdale Rd. (② **480/488-9817**), in Carefree. This gallery features changing exhibits and is open Monday through Saturday from 10am to 5:30pm and Sunday from noon to 5pm. Admission is $2 for adults and $1 for children 4 to 12.

2301 N. Central Ave. ② **602/252-8848.** www.heard.org. Admission $7 adults, $6 seniors, $3 children 4–12. Daily 9:30am–5pm. Closed major holidays. Bus: Blue (B), Red (R), O.

Desert Botanical Garden ★★★   Located adjacent to the Phoenix Zoo and devoted exclusively to cacti and other desert plants, this botanic garden displays more than 20,000 plants from all over the world. The Plants and People of the Sonoran Desert trail is the state's best introduction to ethnobotany (human use of plants) in the Southwest. Along the trail are interactive displays that demonstrate how Native Americans once used wild and cultivated plants. You can make a yucca-fiber brush and practice grinding corn and mesquite beans. At the garden's Center for Desert Living, there are demonstration gardens and an energy- and water-conservation research house. If you come late in the day, you can stay until after dark and see night-blooming flowers and dramatically lit cacti. A cafe on the grounds serves surprisingly good food. In spring and fall, there are also concerts in the garden. The Christmas season sees the gardens illuminated by *luminárias* (candles inside small bags) at night. The new Harriet K. Maxwell Desert Wildflower Trail is the latest addition to the garden and features an ever-changing palette of colorful wildflowers throughout much of the year.

Papago Park, 1201 N. Galvin Pkwy. ② **480/941-1225.** www.dbg.org. Admission $7.50 adults, $6.50 seniors, $4 students 13–18, $1.50 children 5–12. Oct–Apr daily 8am–8pm; May–Sept daily 7am–8pm. Closed Christmas. Bus: 3.

Deer Valley Rock Art Center ★   Located in the Hedgepeth Hills in the northwest corner of the Valley of the Sun, the Deer Valley Rock Art Center preserves an amazing concentration of Native American petroglyphs, some of which date back 5,000 years. Although these petroglyphs may not at first seem as impressive as more famous images that have been reproduced ad nauseam in recent years, the sheer numbers make this a fascinating spot. The drawings, which range from simple spirals to much more complex renderings of herds of deer, are on volcanic boulders along a quarter-mile trail. An interpretive center provides background information on this site and on rock art in general.

3711 W. Deer Valley Rd. ② **623/582-8007.** Admission $4 adults, $2 seniors, $1 children 6–12. Oct–Apr Tues–Sat 9am–5pm, Sun noon–5pm; May–Sept Tues–Fri 8am–2pm, Sat 9am–5pm, Sun noon–5pm. Closed major holidays. Take Deer Valley Rd. exit off I-17 on the north side of Phoenix and go west to just past 35th Ave.

Pueblo Grande Museum and Archaeological Park   Located near Sky Harbor Airport and downtown Phoenix, the Pueblo Grande Museum and Archaeological Park houses the ruins of an ancient Hohokam village that was one of several villages along the Salt River between A.D. 300 and 1400.

Sometime around 1450, this and other villages were mysteriously abandoned. Some speculate that drought and a buildup of salts from irrigation water reduced the fertility of the soil and forced the people to leave their homes and seek more fertile lands. Before touring the grounds to view the partially excavated ruins, you can walk through the small museum, which displays many of the artifacts that have been dug up on the site; it's actually more interesting than the ruins themselves. The latest addition is a display of reconstructed and furnished Hohokam-style houses. The museum also sponsors interesting workshops (some just for kids), demonstrations, and tours (including petroglyph hikes) throughout the year.

4619 E. Washington St. (between 44th and 48th sts.). © 877/706-4408 or 602/495-0901. www. pueblogrande.com. Admission $2 adults, $1.50 seniors, $1 children 6–17; free on Sun. Mon–Sat 9am–4:45pm; Sun 1–4:45pm. Closed major holidays. Bus: Yellow (Y).

ART MUSEUMS

Phoenix Art Museum ★★   This is the largest art museum in the Southwest, and within the museum's labyrinth of halls and galleries is a very respectable collection that spans the major artistic movements from the Renaissance to the present. The collection of modern and contemporary art is particularly good, with works by Diego Rivera, Frida Kahlo, Pablo Picasso, Alexander Calder, Henry Moore, Georgia O'Keeffe, Henri Rousseau, and Auguste Rodin. Exhibits cover decorative arts, historic fashions, Asian art, Spanish-colonial furnishings and religious art, and, of course, works by members of the Cowboy Artists of America. The first-floor gallery is used for special exhibits including major touring retrospectives. Until April 7, 2002, you can marvel at the *Secret World of the Forbidden City: Splendors from China's Imperial Palace.* There will also be Dale Chihuly installations in place until June 23, 2002. The Thorne Miniature Collection is one of the museum's most popular exhibits and consists of tiny rooms on a scale of 1 inch to 1 foot.

1625 N. Central Ave. (at the northeast corner of McDowell Rd.). © 602/257-1222. www.phxart.org. Admission $7 adults, $5 seniors and students, $2 children 6–18; free on Thurs. Tues–Wed and Fri–Sun 10am–5pm; Thurs 10am–9pm. Closed major holidays. Bus: Blue (B), Red (R), O.

Scottsdale Museum of Contemporary Art ★★   Scottsdale may be obsessed with art featuring lonesome cowboys and solemn Indians, but this boldly designed museum makes it clear that patrons of contemporary art are also welcome here. Cutting-edge art, from the abstract to the absurd, fills the galleries, with exhibits rotating every few months. In addition to the main museum building, there are several galleries in the adjacent Scottsdale Center for the Arts, which also has a pair of Dale Chihuly art-glass installations. The museum shop is excellent.

7374 E. Second St., Scottsdale. © 480/994-ARTS. www.scottsdalearts.org. Admission $5 adults, $3 students, free for children under 15; free on Thurs. Tues–Wed 10am–5pm; Thurs–Sat 10am–8pm; Sun noon–5pm. Bus: 41, 50, 72. Also accessible on Scottsdale Round Up shuttle bus.

Arizona State University Art Museum ★   Although it isn't very large, this museum is memorable for its innovative architecture and excellent temporary exhibitions. With its purplish-gray stucco façade and pyramidal shape, the stark and angular building conjures up images of sunsets on desert mountains. The entrance is down a flight of stairs that leads to a cool underground garden area. Inside are galleries for crafts, prints, contemporary art, Latin American art, and temporary exhibits, along with two outdoor sculpture courts and a gift shop. The collection of American art includes works by Georgia O'Keeffe, Edward Hopper, and Frederic Remington. Definitely a must for art and architecture fans.

In the Nelson Fine Arts Center, 10th St. and Mill Ave., Tempe. (C) **480/965-2787**, http://asuam.fa.asu.edu. Free admission. Tues 10am–9pm; Wed–Sat 10am–5pm; Sun 1–5pm. Closed major holidays. Bus: Red (R), Yellow (Y), 66, or 72.

Fleischer Museum This museum, located in an office park in north Scottsdale, was the first gallery in the country to focus on what is now known as the California School of American Impressionism, which drew extensively on French Impressionist styles and holds a quiet place in American art history. Unless you're a serious student of art (or a big fan of Impressionism), you probably won't want to make a special drive out here. If you're out this way anyway (perhaps to do a tour at nearby Taliesin West), you may want to stop by.

17207 N. Perimeter Dr., Scottsdale. (C) **480/585-3108**. www.fleischer.org. Free admission. Daily 10am–4pm. Closed major holidays. Located just north of Frank Lloyd Wright Blvd. and east of Greenway-Hayden Loop.

HISTORY MUSEUMS & HISTORIC LANDMARKS

Arizona Historical Society Museum in Papago Park ⊛ This museum, at the headquarters of the Arizona Historical Society, focuses its modern, well-designed exhibits on the history of central Arizona over the past century. Temporary exhibits on the lives and works of the people who helped shape this region are always highlights of a visit. One of the more interesting permanent exhibits features life-size statues of everyday people from Arizona's past (a Mexican miner, a Chinese laborer, and so on). Quotes relate their individual stories, while props reveal what items they might have traveled with during their days in the desert.

1300 N. College Ave. (just off Curry Rd.), Tempe. (C) **480/929-0292**. www.tempe.gov/ahs. Free admission. Mon–Sat 10am–4pm; Sun noon–4pm. Bus: 66.

Phoenix Museum of History ⊛ Located adjacent to Heritage Square in downtown Phoenix, this state-of-the-art museum is one of the anchors of the city's downtown revitalization plan. It presents an interesting look at the history of a city that, to the casual visitor, might not seem to *have* any history. Interactive and unusual exhibits make this place much more interesting than your average local history museum. A beer-bottle sidewalk shows how one saloonkeeper solved the problem of the muddy streets that once plagued the city; another exhibit explores how "lungers" (tuberculosis sufferers) inadvertently helped originate the tourism industry in Arizona.

105 N. Fifth St. (C) **602/253-2734**. Admission $5 adults, $3.50 seniors and students, $2.50 children 6–12. Mon–Sat 10am–5pm; Sun noon–5pm. Closed major holidays. Bus: Red (R) or Yellow (Y).

Pioneer Arizona Living History Museum ⊛ This museum 20 miles north of downtown Phoenix includes nearly 30 original and reconstructed buildings, as well as costumed interpreters practicing traditional frontier activities. Among the buildings are a carpentry shop, blacksmith shop, miner's cabin, stagecoach station, one-room schoolhouse, opera house, church, farmhouses, and Victorian mansion. Melodramas and gunfights are staged daily.

3901 W. Pioneer Rd. (take exit 225 off I-17). (C) **623/465-1052**. Oct–May Wed–Sun 9am–5pm; June–Sept Fri–Sun 5–9pm. Admission $5.75 adults, $5.25 seniors and students, $5 children 6–12.

Arizona Capitol Museum In the years before Arizona became a state, the territorial capital moved from Prescott to Tucson, then back to Prescott, before finally settling in Phoenix. In 1898, a stately territorial capitol building was erected (with a copper roof to remind the local citizenry of the importance of that metal in the Arizona economy). Atop this copper roof was placed the statue *Winged Victory,* which still graces the old capitol building today. This building no longer serves as the actual state capitol, but has been restored to the way it appeared in 1912, the year Arizona became a state. Among the rooms on view are the senate and house chambers, as well as the governor's office. Excellent historical exhibits provide interesting perspectives on early Arizona events and lifestyles.

1700 W. Washington St. (C) **602/542-4575.** Free admission. June–Dec Mon–Fri 8am–5pm; Jan–May Mon–Wed and Fri 8am–5pm, Thurs 8am–8pm, Sat 10am–3pm. Closed state holidays. Bus: Yellow (Y).

Historic Heritage Square   Although the city of Phoenix was founded as recently as 1870, much of its history has been obliterated. If you have an appreciation for old homes and want a glimpse of how Phoenix once looked, stroll around this collection of some of the few remaining 19th-century houses and the original town site. All the buildings are listed on the National Register of Historic Places, and most display Victorian architectural styles popular just before the turn of the last century. Today they house museums, restaurants, and gift shops. The Eastlake Victorian Rosson House, furnished with period antiques, is open for tours. The Silva House contains historical exhibits on life back then. The Stevens-Haustgen House offers a gift shop, while the Stevens House features the Arizona Doll and Toy Museum. The Burgess Carriage House has a gift shop and ticket window for the Rosson House tours. The Teeter House, an 1899 bungalow, now serves as a Victorian tearoom, and the old Baird Machine Shop contains Pizzeria Bianco.

115 N. Sixth St., at Monroe. (C) **602/262-5029** or 602/262-5071. Rosson House tours $4 adults, $3 seniors, $1 children 6–12. Hours vary for each building; call for information. Bus: Red (R), Yellow (Y), 0.

Historic Saguaro Ranch   Phoenix and neighboring valley communities started out as farming communities, but today there's little sign of this early agricultural heritage. This historic ranch in Glendale is one noteworthy exception. With its tall date palms, resident peacocks, and restored farmhouse, Saguaro Ranch is a great introduction to what life was like here in the valley in the late 19th and early 20th century. The old fruit-packing shed now serves as a gallery hosting temporary exhibits; tours of the main house are offered.

9802 N. 59th Ave. (at Mountain View Rd.), Glendale. (C) **623/939-5782.** Admission $3, free for children 12 and under. Wed–Fri 10am–2pm; Sat 10am–4pm; Sun noon–4pm. Bus: 59.

SCIENCE & INDUSTRY MUSEUMS

Arizona Science Center ⭐ *Kids*   Aimed primarily at children but also loads of fun for adults, this hands-on facility is one of the anchors of Phoenix's ongoing downtown renewal. You'll find more than 300 state-of-the-art interactive exhibits covering a variety of topics, from the human body to coping with life in the desert. There's a huge ant farm, a virtual-reality game that puts you inside a video game, a massive truck tire weighing almost 4 tons, a flight simulator, and a cloud maker. Up on the roof is a terrace for occasional stargazing events. In addition to the many exhibits, the science center includes a planetarium (night sky and laser shows) and a large-screen theater, both of which carry additional charges.

600 E. Washington St. (C) **602/716-2000.** www.azscience.org. Admission $8 adults, $6 seniors and children 4–12. Planetarium and film combination tickets also available. Daily 10am–5pm. Closed Thanksgiving and Christmas. Bus: Red (R), Yellow (Y), 0.

Mesa Southwest Museum *Kids* Recently expanded and updated, this downtown Mesa museum is now one of the best museums in the valley, and with its wide variety of exhibits will appeal to people with a range of interests. For the kids, there are animated dinosaurs on an indoor "cliff" with a roaring waterfall, plus plenty of dinosaur skeletons. Other interesting exhibits include a walk-through mine mock-up with exhibits on the Lost Dutchman Mine, movies that have been filmed in the state, Arizona mammoth kill sites, and some old jail cells. There's also a mock-up of a pre-Columbian temple and an artificial cave filled with beautiful mineral specimens.

53 N. MacDonald St. (at the corner of First St.), Mesa. ✆ 480/644-2230. www.ci.mesa.az.us. Admission $6 adults, $5 seniors, $3 children 3–12. Tues–Sat 10am–5pm; Sun 1–5pm. Closed major holidays. Bus: Red (R).

A MUSEUM MISCELLANY: PLANES, FLAMES & MORE

Arizona Mining & Mineral Museum Arizonans have been romancing the stones for more than a century at colorfully named mines, such as the Copper Queen, Sleeping Beauty, No-Name Creek, Lucky Boy, and Bluebird. Out of such mines have come countless tons of copper, silver, and gold, as well as beautiful minerals with tongue-twisting names. Azurite, chalcanthite, chalcoalumi-nate, malachite, and chrysocolla are just some of the richly colored and fascinatingly textured minerals on display at this small downtown museum dedicated to the state's mining industry. Rather than playing up the historical or profit-making side of the industry, exhibits focus on the amazing variety and beauty of Arizona minerals. Displays have a dated feel, but the beauty of the minerals makes this an interesting stop for aspiring rockhounds.

1502 W. Washington St. ✆ 602/255-3795. www.admmr.state.az.us. Free admission. Mon–Fri 8am–5pm; Sat 11am–4pm. Closed state holidays. Bus: Yellow (Y).

The Bead Museum Beads and body adornments from around the world are displayed at this interesting little museum in the Glendale antiques district. Beads both ancient and modern are on display, and exhibits often focus on such subjects as beaded bags, prayer beads, or natural beads.

5754 Glenn Dr., Glendale. ✆ 623/931-2737. www.thebeadmuseum.com. Admission $3. Mon–Sat 10am–5pm (Thurs until 8pm); Sun 11am–4pm.

Champlin Fighter Aircraft Museum This aeronautical museum, dedicated exclusively to fighter planes and the fighter aces who flew them, houses aircraft from World Wars I and II, the Korean War, and the Vietnam War, with a strong emphasis on the wood-and-fabric biplanes and triplanes of World War I (several Sopwiths and Fokkers). Jet fighters from more recent battles include a MiG-15, a MiG-17, and an F4 Phantom. In total, there are 33 flyable fighters here. Also here at Falcon Field is the **Arizona Wing,** 2017 N. Greenfield Rd. (✆ **480/ 924-1940**), which showcases the restored *Sentimental Journey,* a 1944 B-17 bomber.

4636 Fighter Aces Dr. (at Falcon Field Airport off McKellips Rd.), Mesa. ✆ 480/830-4540. Admission $6.50 adults, $3 children 5–12. Daily 10am–5pm. Take Ariz. 202 (Red Mountain Fwy.) east to the McKellips Rd. exit; continue slightly more than 6 miles east on McKellips Rd.

Hall of Flame Firefighting Museum *Kids* The world's largest firefighting museum houses a fascinating collection of vintage firetrucks. The displays date from a 1725 English hand pumper to several classic fire engines from the 20th century. All are beautifully restored and, of course, fire-engine red (mostly). In all, there are more than 90 vehicles on display.

C **Frommer's Favorite Phoenix Experiences**

Hiking up Camelback Mountain or Squaw Peak. Hiking the trails up these two mountains is a favorite activity among the city's more active residents. Both trails are steep climbs, but the views from up top are superb. Bring water and start early in the morning if it's going to be a hot day.

Strolling through the Desert Botanical Garden after Dark. This cactus-filled garden is beautiful any time of day, but is particularly enjoyable after dark, when the crowds are gone and hidden lights illuminate the cacti.

Lounging by the Pool at the Hyatt Regency Scottsdale. Phoenix and Scottsdale have plenty of great pools, but the collection of large and small pools at the Hyatt is our favorite. Try swimming laps through all the different pools!

Taking the Scottsdale Art Walk. Thursday evenings from October to May, both dilettantes and connoisseurs turn out to visit the nearly 60 galleries in downtown Scottsdale, many of which have artists on hand and provide complimentary refreshments.

Attending a Spring-Training Baseball Game. Get a head start on all your fellow baseball fans by going to a spring-training game while you're in Phoenix. Just be sure to book your hotel well in advance; these games are the biggest thing going in the valley each spring.

Mountain Biking in South Mountain or Papago Park. The trails of these two desert parks are ideal for mountain biking, and whether you're a novice making your first foray onto the dirt or a budding downhill racer, you'll find miles of riding that are just your speed.

Spending the Day at a Spa. When it comes to stress relief, there's nothing like a massage or an herbal wrap. The chance to lie back and do nothing at all is something few of us take the time for anymore. For the price of a single 1-hour treatment, you can usually spend the whole day at a spa.

Papago Park, 6101 E. Van Buren St. (C) **602/275-3473.** www.hallofflame.org. Admission $5 adults, $4 seniors, $3 students 6–17, $1.50 children under 6. Mon–Sat 9am–5pm; Sun noon–4pm. Closed Thanksgiving, Christmas, and New Year's Day. Bus: 3.

ARCHITECTURAL HIGHLIGHTS

Taliesin West ★★★ Frank Lloyd Wright fell in love with the Arizona desert and, in 1937, built Taliesin West as a winter camp that served as his office and school. Today the buildings of Taliesin West are the headquarters of the Frank Lloyd Wright Foundation and School of Architecture.

Tours explain the campus buildings and include a general introduction to Wright and his theories of architecture. Wright believed in using local materials in his designs, and this is in evidence at Taliesin West where local stone was used for building foundations. He developed a number of innovative methods for dealing with the extremes of the desert climate, such as sliding wall panels to let in varying amounts of air and light.

Architecture students, and anyone interested in the work of Wright, will enjoy browsing through the excellent books in the gift shop. Expanded Insight Tours ($16–$20), behind-the-scenes tours ($35), guided desert walks ($20), and night hikes ($25) are also available at certain times of year. Call ahead to be sure you can get the tour you want at the time you want.

12621 Frank Lloyd Wright Blvd. (at 114th St.), Scottsdale. ✆ 480/860-2700, ext. 494 or 495. www. franklloydwright.org. Basic tours: Oct 1–May 31 $14.50 adults, $12 seniors and students, $3 children 4–12; June 1–Sept 30 $12 adults, $10 students and seniors, $3 children 4–12. Oct 1–May 31 daily 10am–4pm; June 1–Sept 30 daily 9am–4pm. Closed Tues–Wed in July and Aug, Easter, Thanksgiving, Christmas, New Year's Day, and occasional special events. From Scottsdale Rd., go east on Shea Blvd. to 114th St., then north 1 mile to the entrance road.

Arizona Biltmore   This resort hotel, although not designed by Frank Lloyd Wright, shows the famed architect's hand in its distinctive cast-cement blocks. It also displays sculptures, furniture, and stained glass designed by Wright. The best way to soak up the ambience of this exclusive resort (if you aren't staying here) is over dinner, a cocktail, or tea. If you'd like to spend the day by the pool, you can even rent a cabana.

24th St. and Missouri Ave. ✆ 602/955-6600. Free admission. Open 24 hr., but best visited during regular business hours.

Burton Barr Library   This library is among the most daring pieces of public architecture in the city, and no fan of futuristic art or science fiction should miss it. The five-story cube is partially clad in enough ribbed copper sheeting to produce roughly 17,500,000 pennies (it took a lot of overdue books to pay for that feature). The building's design makes use of the desert's plentiful sunshine to provide light for reading, but also incorporates computer-controlled louvers and shade sails to reduce heat and glare.

1221 N. Central Ave. ✆ 602/262-4636. Free admission. Mon–Thurs 9am–9pm; Fri–Sat 9am–6pm; Sun noon–9pm.

Cosanti   This complex of cast-concrete structures served as a prototype and learning project for architect Paolo Soleri's much grander Arcosanti project, currently under construction north of Phoenix (see "En Route to Northern Arizona," below). It's here at Cosanti that Soleri's famous bells are cast, and most weekday mornings you can see the foundry in action.

6433 Doubletree Ranch Rd., Scottsdale. ✆ 480/948-6145. www.cosanti.com. Suggested donation $1. Daily 9am–5pm. Closed major holidays. Drive 1 mile west of Scottsdale Rd. on Doubletree Ranch Rd.

Mystery Castle ★ *Finds*   Built for a daughter who longed for a castle more permanent than those built in sand at the beach, Mystery Castle is a wondrous work of folk-art architecture. Boyce Luther Gulley, who had come to Arizona in hopes of curing his tuberculosis, constructed the castle during the 1930s and early 1940s using stones from the property. The resulting 18-room fantasy has 13 fireplaces, a wedding chapel, parapets, and many other unusual touches. This castle is a must for fans of folk-art constructions. Tours are usually led by the daughter for whom the castle was built.

800 E. Mineral Rd. ✆ 602/268-1581. Admission $5 adults, $4 seniors, $2 children 5–14. Thurs–Sun 11am–4pm. Closed July–Sept. Take Central Ave. south to Mineral Rd. (2 miles south of Baseline Rd.) and turn east.

Tovrea Castle   Another architectural confection of the Phoenix landscape, Tovrea Castle has been likened to a giant wedding cake and is currently under renovation. Although the gardens should be open to the public by the time you read this, work on the building itself is still at least a couple of years from completion. Call for updates.

5041 E. Van Buren St. ℂ 602/262-6412. Call for hours and admission information.

Wrigley Mansion   Situated on a hilltop adjacent to the Arizona Biltmore, this classically elegant mansion was built by chewing-gum magnate William Wrigley Jr. between 1929 and 1931 as a present for his wife, Ada. Designed with Italianate styling, the many levels and red-tile roofs make it seem like an entire village. The mansion is now a National Historic Landmark, with the interior restored to its original elegance. Although this is currently a private club, membership is only $10 and basically gives you dining privileges, although you can eat here once without having a membership.

2501 E. Telawa Trail. ℂ 602/955-4079. Admission $10.75. Tours ($10) Tues–Thurs 10am and 3pm.

WILD WEST THEME TOWNS

Despite a population running to the millions, Phoenix and Scottsdale still occasionally like to present themselves as grown up Wild West cow towns. But since there are more Ford Mustangs than wild mustangs around these parts, you'll have to get out of town if you want a taste of the Old West. Scattered around the valley are a handful of Hollywood-style cow towns that are basically just tourist traps, but, hey, if you've got the kids along, you owe it to them to visit at least one of these places.

Cave Creek, founded as a gold-mining camp in the 1870s, is the last of the valley towns that still has some semblance of Wild West character, but this is rapidly fading as real-estate prices in the area skyrocket and Scottsdale's population center moves ever northward. Still, you'll see several steakhouses, saloons, and shops selling Western and Native American crafts and antiques. The main family attraction is a place called **Frontier Town,** which is right on Cave Creek Road in the center of town. It's a sort of mock-up cow town that is home to the Black Mountain Brewing Company, which brews Cave Creek Chili Beer. You can try this fiery beer at **Crazy Ed's Satisfied Frog Restaurant and Saloon,** located here in Frontier Town (see "Where to Dine," earlier in this chapter, for details). To learn more about the history of this area, stop in at the **Cave Creek Museum,** at the corner of Skyline Drive and Basin Road (ℂ **480/488-2764**). It's open from October to May, Wednesday through Sunday from 1 to 4:30pm; admission is by donation.

Rawhide Western Town ★ (Kids   Sure, it's a tourist trap, but Rawhide is so much fun and such a quintessentially Phoenician experience that no family should get out of town before or after sundown without first moseying down the dusty streets of this fake cow town. Those streets are lined with lots of tourist shops and plenty of places for refreshments, including a steakhouse that was the original reason for Rawhide's existence. The basic admission gets you into all the Rawhide shows (six-gun stunt shows, "high noon" gunfights, Native American dance performances, and others), while the premium admission gets you the shows plus tickets to the various theme-park rides (including a mechanical bull) as well as the stagecoach and train. Half-hour horseback rides are an additional $12. If you want to come for just a meal, your basic admission is good for $3 off ($2 for kids).

23023 N. Scottsdale Rd. (4 miles north of Bell Rd.), Scottsdale. ℂ 480/502-1880. www.rawhide.com. Admission $8–$20 adults, $5–$16 children 4–11. Hours vary; call for details.

Carefree Living

Carefree, a planned community established in the 1950s and popular with retirees, is much more subdued than its neighbor Cave Creek, which effects a sort of Wild West character. Ho Hum Road and Easy Street are just two local street names that reflect the sedate nature of Carefree, which is home to the exclusive **Boulders** resort. Boasting one of the most spectacular settings of any resort in Arizona, the Boulders also has a couple of excellent restaurants.

On Easy Street, in what passes for Carefree's downtown, you'll find one of the world's largest sundials. The dial is 90 feet across, and the gnomon (the part that casts the shadow) is 35 feet tall. From the gnomon hangs a colored-glass star, and in the middle of the dial is a pool of water and a fountain. Also downtown is a sort of reproduction Spanish-village shopping area, and just south of town, adjacent to the Boulders, is the upscale **El Pedregal Festival Marketplace** shopping center, with interesting boutiques, galleries, and a few restaurants.

Goldfield Ghost Town *Kids*   Over on the east side of the valley, just 4 miles northeast of Apache Junction, you'll find a reconstructed 1890s gold-mining town. Although it's a bit of a tourist trap—gift shops, an ice-cream parlor, and the like—it's also home to the **Superstition Mountain/Lost Dutchman Museum** (© 480/983-4888), which has interesting exhibits on the history of the area. Of particular note is the exhibit on the Lost Dutchman gold mine, perhaps the most famous mine in the country despite the fact its location is unknown. Goldfield Ghost Town and Mine Tours provides guided tours of the gold mine beneath the town. The **Superstition Scenic Railroad,** a narrow-gauge railroad, circles the town, and the **Goldfield Livery** (© 480/982-0133) offers horseback riding and carriage rides. If you're here at lunchtime, you can get a meal at the steakhouse/saloon.

Ariz. 88 (4 miles northeast of Apache Junction). © 480/983-0333. www.goldfieldghosttown.com. Museum admission $2 adults, $1.50 seniors, and 75¢ children; train rides $4 adults, $3.50 seniors, $2 children 5–12; mine tours $5 adults, $3 children 6–12; 1-hr. horseback rides $20.

ZOOS & PARKS

The newest and perhaps most unusual park in the Phoenix metro area centers on **Tempe Town Lake** (© 480/350-8625; www.tempe.gov/rio), which was created in 1999 by damming the Salt River with inflatable dams. With its construction, Tempe now has a 2-mile-long lake for boating, and lining the north and south shores are bike paths and parks. The best lake access is at Tempe Town Beach, at the foot of the Mill Avenue Bridge. Here you can rent kayaks ($10–$12 per hr.) and other small boats, and even take a brief excursion ($6 for adults, $5 for seniors and children 6–12, $4 for children 5 and under) with **Rio Lago Cruise** (© 480/517-4050). Tempe Town Lake is the focus of a grand development plan known as the Rio Salado Project, which will eventually include a hotel and other commercial facilities. Until then, most of the south shore of the lake is a barren wasteland waiting to be developed.

Among the city's most popular parks are its natural areas and preserves. These include Phoenix South Mountain Park, Papago Park, Phoenix Mountains Preserve (site of Squaw Peak), North Mountain Preserve, North Mountain Recreation Area, and Camelback Mountain–Echo Canyon Recreation Area. For more information on these parks, see "Hiking," "Bicycling," and "Horseback Riding" under "Outdoor Pursuits," later in this chapter.

Out of Africa Wildlife Park *(Kids)*   At this small wildlife park northeast of Scottsdale, animals put on shows for you rather than just lazing in the shade as they do at most zoos. The most popular performances are those in the park's swimming pool. You've probably never seen tigers, wolves, and bears having so much fun in the water. Call for a schedule of daily animal shows.

Fort McDowell Rd., Fountain Springs. © 480/837-7779. Admission $13.95 adults, $12.95 seniors, $4.95 children 3–12. Oct–May Tues–Sun 9:30am–5pm; June–Sept Wed–Fri 4–9:30pm, Sat 9:30am–9:30pm, Sun 9:30am–5pm. Take Ariz. 87 northeast from Mesa and 2 miles past Shea Blvd.; turn right on Fort McDowell Rd.

The Phoenix Zoo *(Kids)*   Forget about polar bears and other cold-climate creatures; this zoo focuses its attentions primarily on animals that come from climates similar to that of the Phoenix area (although the rain-forest exhibit is a definite exception). Most impressive of the displays are the 4-acre, mixed-species African savanna exhibit and the baboon colony. The Southwestern exhibits are also of particular interest, as are the giant Galapagos tortoises. All animals are kept in naturalistic enclosures, and what with all the palm trees and tropical vegetation, the zoo sometimes manages to make you forget that this really is the desert. Young kids will enjoy Harmony Farm, a hands-on area.

Papago Park, 455 N. Galvin Pkwy. © 602/273-1341. www.phoenixzoo.org. Admission $10 adults, $9 seniors, $5 children 3–12. Labor Day to Apr daily 9am–5pm; May 1 to Labor Day daily 7:30am–4pm. Closed Christmas. Bus: 3, FLASH Lite.

ESPECIALLY FOR KIDS

In addition to the following suggestions, kids are likely to enjoy the Arizona Science Center, the Mesa Southwest Museum, the Hall of Flame Firefighting Museum, the Phoenix Zoo, and Out of Africa Wildlife Park—all described in detail above.

Arizona Doll & Toy Museum   This small museum is located in the historic Stevens House on Heritage Square in downtown Phoenix. The miniature classroom peopled by doll students is one of the favorite exhibits. With dolls dating from the 19th century, this is a definite must for doll collectors.

In Heritage Square, southwest corner of Seventh and Monroe sts. © 602/253-9337. Admission $2.50 adults, $1 children. Tues–Sat 10am–4pm; Sun noon–4pm. Closed Aug. Bus: Red (R), Yellow (Y), 0.

Arizona Museum for Youth   Using both traditional displays and participatory activities, this museum allows children to explore the fine arts and their own creativity. It's housed in a refurbished grocery store, which for past exhibits has been transformed into a zoo, a ranch, and a foreign country. Exhibits are geared mainly to toddlers through 12-year-olds, but all ages can work together to experience the activities.

35 N. Robson St. (between Main and First sts.), Mesa. © 480/644-2467. www.ci.mesa.az.us/amfy. Admission $2.50, free for children under 2. Fall–spring Sun and Tues–Fri 1–5pm, Sat 10am–5pm; summer Tues–Sat 9am–5pm, Sun 1–5pm. Closed for 2 weeks between exhibits. Bus: R.

Castles & Coasters   Located adjacent to Metrocenter, one of Arizona's largest shopping malls, this small amusement park boasts a very impressive double-loop roller coaster, plenty of tamer rides, four 18-hole miniature-golf courses, and a huge pavilion full of video games.

9445 N. Metro Pkwy. E. ✆ 602/997-7575. Ride and game prices vary; $6 minimum; all-day pass $18. Open daily (hours change seasonally; call ahead). Bus: Red (R) or 27.

CrackerJax Family Fun & Sports Park Three miniature-golf courses are the main attraction here, but you'll also find a bilevel driving range, batting cages, go-kart tracks, sand volleyball courts, and a video-game arcade.

16001 N. Scottsdale Rd. (¼ mile south of Bell Rd.), Scottsdale. ✆ 480/998-2800. Activity prices vary. Open daily (hours change seasonally; call ahead). Bus: 72.

McCormick-Stillman Railroad Park If you or your kids happen to like trains, you won't want to miss this Scottsdale park dedicated to railroading. On the grounds are a ⁵/₁₂-scale model railroad that takes visitors around the park, restored cars and engines, two old railway depots, and model railroad layouts operated by a local club. There's also a 1929 carousel and a general store.

7301 E. Indian Bend Rd. (at Scottsdale Rd.), Scottsdale. ✆ 480/312-2312. www.therailroadpark.com. Train and carousel rides $1; train museum $1 ages 13 and up. Hours vary with the season; call for schedule. Bus: 72.

6 Organized Tours & Excursions

The Valley of the Sun is a sprawling, often congested place, and if you are unfamiliar with the area, you may be surprised at how great the distances are. If map reading and urban navigation are not your strong points, consider taking a guided tour. There are numerous companies offering tours of both the Valley of the Sun and the rest of Arizona. However, tours of the valley tend to include only brief stops at highlights.

BUS TOURS **Gray Line of Phoenix** (✆ 800/732-0327 or 602/495-9100; www.graylinearizona.com) is one of the largest tour companies in the valley. It offers a 3½-hour tour of Phoenix and the Valley of the Sun for $30 to $37; advance reservations are necessary. The tour points out such local landmarks as the state capitol, Heritage Square, Arizona State University, and Old Town Scottsdale.

GLIDER RIDES The thermals that form above the mountains in the Phoenix area are ideal for sailplane (glider) soaring. On the south side of the valley in Maricopa, **Arizona Soaring** (✆ 800/861-2318 in Arizona, or 520/568-2318; 480/821-2903 for information), offers sailplane rides as well as instruction. A basic 20-minute flight is $74.95; for $119.95, you can take an aerobatic flight with loops, rolls, and inverted flying. To reach the airstrip, take I-10 east to exit 164 (Maricopa Road), go 15 miles, turn west on Ariz. 238, and continue 6½ miles. On the north side of the valley, there's **Turf Soaring School,** 8700 W. Carefree Hwy., Peoria (✆ 602/439-3621), which charges $85 for a basic flight and $125 for an aerobatic flight. This outfitter also offers flights for two people ($150), although your combined weight can't exceed 300 pounds. Reservations are a good idea at either place.

HOT-AIR BALLOON RIDES The still morning air of the Valley of the Sun is perfect for hot-air ballooning, and because of the stiff competition, prices are among the lowest in the country—between $110 and $140 per person for a 1- to 1½-hour ride. Companies to try include **A Aerozona Adventure** (✆ 888/ 991-4260 or 480/991-4260), **Adventures Out West** (✆ 800/755-0935 or

602/996-6100; www.adventuresoutwest.com), and **Unicorn Balloon Company** (© **800/468-2478** or 480/991-3666; www.unicornballoon.com).

JEEP TOURS   After spending a few days in Scottsdale, you'll likely start wondering where the desert is. Well, it's out there, and the easiest way to explore it is to book a Jeep tour. Most hotels and resorts have particular companies they work with, so start by asking your concierge. Alternatively, you can contact one of the following companies. Most will pick you up at your hotel, take you off through the desert, give you lots of information on this corner of the West, and maybe even let you try panning for gold or shooting a six-gun. Rates are around $65 to $75 for a 4-hour tour. Companies include **Western Events** (© **800/ 567-3619** or 480/860-1777), **Arizona Bound Tours** (© **480/994-0580;** www.arizonabound.com), and **Rawhide Jeep Adventures** (© **480/488-0023**). The latter operates out of the popular Rawhide Wild West theme town.

Jeep tours are available all over Arizona, so if you want to really impress your friends when you get home, you'll need to try something a little different. How about a Hummer tour? Sure, a Hummer is nothing but a Jeep on steroids, but these military-issue off-road vehicles still turn heads. **Extreme Hummer Adventures** (© **602/402-0584;** www.stellaradventures.com) will take you out into the desert northeast of Scottsdale and show you what these things can really do. **Desert Storm Hummer Tours** (© **480/922-0020;** www.dshummer.com) offers similar tours. Expect to pay $100 to $110 for a 4-hour tour.

SCENIC FLIGHTS   If you're short on time but want to at least see the Grand Canyon, book an air tour in a small plane. **Westwind Tours** (© **888/869-0866** or 480/991-5557) charges $270 to $325 for its Grand Canyon tours and $390 to $445 for its Monument Valley tours. This company flies out of the Deer Valley Airport in the northwest part of the valley.

7 Outdoor Pursuits

BICYCLING   Although the Valley of the Sun is a sprawling place, it's mostly flat and has numerous paved bike paths, which makes bicycling a breeze as long as it isn't windy or in the heat of summer. **Wheels 'n Gear,** 7607 E. McDowell Rd., Scottsdale (© **480/945-2881**), in the Plaza Del Rio Shopping Center, rents cruisers for $20 per day and mountain bikes for between $25 and $50 per day. Mountain-biking trail maps are also available. Among the best mountain-biking spots in the city are Papago Park (at Van Buren Street and Galvin Parkway), Phoenix South Mountain Park (use the entrance off Baseline road on 48th Street), and North Mountain Recreation Area (off Seventh Street between Dunlap Avenue and Thunderbird Road). With its rolling topography and wide dirt trails, Papago Park is the best place for novice mountain-bikers to get in some desert riding (and the scenery here is great). For hard-core pedalers, Phoenix South Mountain Park is the place to go. The National Trail is the ultimate death-defying ride here, but there are lots of trails for intermediate riders, including the Desert Classic Trail and the short loop trails just north of the parking area at the 48th Street entrance parking area. North Mountain is another good place for intermediate riders. In north Scottsdale, on the edge of Carefree, are some great easy-to-moderate trails beginning at the intersection of Pima and Dynamite roads.

There's also plenty of good mountain biking up in the Cave Creek area, where you can rent a bike for $35 to $45 a day at **Cave Creek Bikes,** 6149 Cave Creek

Rd. (© **480/488-5261**). Ask for a map of the nearby trails at the intersection of Pima and Dynamite roads. This shop also offers guided mountain-bike tours for $65. If you'd like a guide for some of the best biking in the desert, contact **Desert Biking Adventures** (© **888/249-BIKE** or 602/320-4602), which leads 2-, 3-, and 4-hour mountain-bike tours (and specializes in downhill rides). Prices range from $55 to $85.

If you'd rather confine your cycling to a paved surface, there's no better route than Scottsdale's **Indian Bend Wash greenbelt,** a paved multiuse path that extends for more than 15 miles along Hayden Road (from north of Shea Boulevard to Tempe). The Indian Bend Wash pathway can be accessed at many points along Hayden Road. At the south end, the path connects to paved paths on the shores of Tempe Town Lake and provides easy access to Tempe's Mill Avenue shopping district.

GOLF   With nearly 200 courses in the Valley of the Sun, golf is just about the most popular sport in Phoenix and one of the main reasons people flock here in winter. Sunshine, spectacular views, and the company of coyotes, quail, and doves make playing a round of golf here a truly memorable experience.

Despite the number of courses, it can still be difficult to get a tee time on any of the more popular courses (especially during the busy months of February, March, and April). If you're staying at a resort with a course, be sure to make your tee-time reservations at the same time you make your room reservations. If you aren't staying at a resort, you might still be able to play a round on a resort course if you can get a last-minute tee time. Try one of the tee-time reservations services below.

The only thing harder than getting a winter or spring tee time in the valley is facing the bill at the end of your 18 holes. Greens fees at most public and resort courses range from around $90 to $170, with the top courses at the most expensive resorts often charging $200 or more. Municipal courses, on the other hand, charge under $40. You can save money on many courses by opting for twilight play, which usually begins at 1, 2, or 3pm. We've listed high- and low-season greens fees below; you'll find that spring and autumn fees fall somewhere in between.

You can get more information on Valley of the Sun golf courses from the **Greater Phoenix Convention & Visitors Bureau,** 50 N. Second St. (© **877/225-5749** or 602/254-6500; www.phoenixcvb.com). You can also pick up a copy of the *Greater Phoenix Golf Guide* at golf courses and many hotels and resorts.

It's a good idea to make reservations well in advance. You can avoid the hassle of booking tee times yourself by contacting, **Golf Xpress** (© **800/878-8580** or 602/404-GOLF; www.azgolfxpress.com), which can make reservations farther in advance than you could if you called the golf course directly, and can sometimes get you lower greens fees as well. This company also makes hotel reservations, rents golf clubs, and provides other assistance to golfers visiting the valley. For last-minute reservations, call **Stand-by Golf** (© **480/874-3133**).

The many resort courses are, of course, the favored fairways of valley visitors. For spectacular scenery, the two Jay Morrish–designed 18-hole courses at **The Boulders,** N. Scottsdale Road and Carefree Highway, Carefree (© **800/553-1717** or 480/488-9028), just can't be beat. Given the option, play the South Course, and watch out as you approach the tee box on the seventh hole— it's a real heart-stopper. Tee times for nonresort guests are very limited in winter and spring, and you'll pay $240 for a round. In summer, you can play for as little as $75 (just be sure you get the earliest possible tee time and bring plenty of water).

Jumping over to Litchfield Park, on the far west side of the valley, is the **Wigwam Golf and Country Club,** 300 Wigwam Blvd. (© **623/935-3811**), and, count 'em, three championship 18-hole courses. The **Gold Course** is legendary, but even the Blue and Red courses are worth playing. These are traditional courses for purists who want vast expanses of green rather than cactus and boulders. In high season, greens fees are $120 for any of the three courses ($60 for twilight play on the Blue or Red course; $24–$37 in summer). High-season reservations for nonguests can be made no more than 5 days in advance.

Way over on the east side of the valley at the foot of the Superstition Mountains is the **Gold Canyon Golf Resort,** 6100 S. Kings Ranch Rd., Gold Canyon (© **800/624-6445** or 480/982-9449; www.gcgr.com), which has been rated one of the best public courses in the state and has what have been rated as three of the best holes in the state—the second, third, and fourth on the a visually breathtaking, desert-style Dinosaur Mountain course. Greens fees on this course range from $135 to $165 in winter and from $50 to $65 in summer. The Sidewinder course is more traditional and less dramatic, but much more economical. Greens fees range from $60 to $75 in winter and from $35 to $45 in summer. Make reservations a week in advance. It's well worth the drive.

If you want to swing where the pros do, beg, borrow, or steal a tee time on the Tom Weiskopf and Jay Morrish–designed Stadium Course at the **Tournament Players Club (TPC) of Scottsdale** ✶✶, 17020 N. Hayden Rd. (© **888/400-4001** or 480/585-4334; www.playatpc.com), which hosts the Phoenix Open. The 18th hole has standing room for 40,000 spectators, but it is hoped there won't be that many around (or any TV cameras) the day you double bogey on this hole. The TPC's second 18, the Desert Course, is actually a municipal course, thanks to an agreement with the landowner, the Bureau of Land Management. Stadium course fees are $203 in winter and spring, $90 in summer. Desert Course fees range from $40 to $50.

At the **Gainey Ranch Golf Club,** at the Hyatt Regency Scottsdale Resort at Gainey Ranch, 7600 E. Gainey Club Dr. (© **480/951-0022**), you'll find three decidedly different nine-hole courses (the Dunes, the Arroyo, and the Lakes courses), each with its own set of challenges. These courses are open only to resort guests.

If you want a traditional course that has been played by presidents and celebrities alike, try to get a tee time at one of the two 18-hole courses at the **Arizona Biltmore Country Club,** 24th Street and Missouri Avenue (© **602/955-9655**). The courses here are more relaxing than challenging, good to play if you're not yet up to par. Greens fees are $165 in the winter and spring, $48 in summer. Reservations can be made 7 days in advance. There's also a championship 18-hole putting course.

Of the two courses at the **Camelback Golf Club,** 7847 N. Mockingbird Lane (© **800/24-CAMEL** or 480/596-7050), the Resort Course has recently undergone a $16 million redesign, with new water features and bunkers. The Club Course is a links-style course with great mountain views and lots of water hazards. Resort Course greens fees are $140 to $155 in winter and $40 to $50 in summer; Club Course fees are $90 to $105 in winter and $30 to $40 in summer. Reservations can be made up to 30 days in advance.

Set at the base of Camelback Mountain, **The Phoenician Golf Club,** 6000 E. Camelback Rd. (© **800/888-8234** or 480/423-2449), at the valley's most glamorous resort, has 27 holes that mix traditional and desert styles. Greens fees for nonresort guests are $170 in winter and spring, $95 in summer.

Of the valley's many daily fee courses, it's the two 18-hole courses at **Troon North Golf Club,** 10320 E. Dynamite Blvd., Scottsdale (© **888/TROON-US** or 480/585-5300; www.troongolf.com), seemingly just barely carved out of raw desert, that garner the most local accolades. Greens fees are $240 in winter and spring, $75 to $90 in summer. Reservations are taken up to 30 days in advance (and fill up quickly in winter).

The Pete Dye–designed **ASU-Karsten Golf Course,** 1125 E. Rio Salado Pkwy., Tempe (© **480/921-8070**), part of Arizona State University, is also highly praised and a very challenging training ground for top collegiate golfers. Greens fees are $65 to $88 in winter and $25 to $35 in summer. Make reservations up to 14 days in advance in winter.

If you haven't yet gotten your handicap down, but want to try a desert-style course, head to **Tatum Ranch Golf Club,** 29888 N. Tatum Ranch Dr., Cave Creek (© **480/585-2399;** www.tatumranchgc.com), which is regarded as a forgiving course with a desert sensibility. Note that this course is in the process of going private and may no longer be accepting outside play by the time you read this. Greens fees are $70 to $150 in winter and around $40 to $80 in summer.

Other worthwhile resort and daily fee courses include **Kokopelli Golf Resort,** 1800 W. Guadalupe Rd., Gilbert (© **800/VIP-GOLF,** 480/926-3589, or 480/962-GOLF), with greens fees of $59 to $79 in winter and $39 to $59 in summer, and **The Legend at Arrowhead,** 21027 N. 67th Ave., Glendale (© **800/VIP-GOLF,** 623/561-1902, or 480/962-GOLF), with greens fees of $75 to $95 in winter and $44 to $59 in summer. The **Kierland Golf Club,** 15636 Clubgate Dr., Scottsdale (© **888/TROON-US** or 480/922-9283; www.troongolf.com), which was designed by Scott Miller and consists of three nine-hole courses that can be played in combination, is another much-talked-about local daily fee course. Greens fees are $130 to $155 in winter and $55 to $65 in summer. Book up to 60 days in advance.

Of the municipal courses in Phoenix, **Papago Golf Course,** 5595 E. Moreland St. (© **602/275-8428**), at the foot of the red-sandstone Papago Buttes, offers fine views, economical rates ($35 in winter), and a killer 17th hole. **Encanto Golf Course,** 2775 N. 15th Ave. (© **602/253-3963**), is equally inexpensive for a round of golf ($35 in winter). Keep in mind that these rates don't include a golf cart, which is another $20 in winter.

HIKING   Several mountains around Phoenix, including Camelback Mountain and Squaw Peak, have been set aside as parks and nature preserves, and these natural areas are among the city's most popular hiking spots. The city's largest nature preserve, **Phoenix South Mountain Park** (© **602/495-0222**), said to be the largest city park in the world, contains miles of hiking, mountain-biking, and horseback-riding trails, and the views of Phoenix (whether from along the National Trail or from the parking lot at the Buena Vista Overlook) are spectacular, especially at sunset. To reach the park's main entrance, drive south on Central Avenue, which leads right into the park. Once inside the park, turn left on Summit Road and follow it to the Buena Vista Lookout, which provides a great view of the city and is the trailhead for the National Trail. If you hike east on this trail for 2 miles, you'll come to an unusual little tunnel that makes a good

Jugglers, dancers and an assortment of acrobats fill the street.
She shoots you a wide-eyed look as a seven-foot cartoon character approaches.
What brought you here was wanting the kids
to see something magical while they still believed in magic.
Travelocity® and Travelocity.com are trademarks of Travelocity.com LP and Sabre® is a trademark of an affiliate of Sabre Inc. © 2001 Travelocity.com LP. All rights reserved.
America Online Keyword: Travel
With 700 airlines, 50,000 hotels and over 5,000 cruise and vacation getaways, you can now go places you've always dreamed of.
Travelocity.com™
A Sabre Company
Go Virtually Anywhere.
"WORLD'S LEADING TRAVEL WEB SITE, 5 YEARS IN A ROW." WORLD TRAVEL AWARDS

turn-around point. Another stretch of the National Trail can be accessed from the 48th Street park entrance, which is accessed by driving through the property of the Point South Mount Resort.

Another good place to get in some relatively easy and convenient hiking is at **Papago Park** (© 602/262-4837), home to the Desert Botanical Garden, the Phoenix Zoo, and the fascinating Hole in the Rock (a red-rock butte with a large opening in it). There are both paved and dirt trails within the park; the most popular hikes are around the Papago Buttes (park on West Park Drive) and up onto the rocks at Hole in the Rock (park past the zoo at the information center).

Perhaps the most popular hike in the city is the trail to the top of **Camelback Mountain** (© 602/256-3220), near the boundary between Phoenix and Scottsdale. This is the highest mountain in Phoenix, and the 1.2-mile Summit Trail to the top is very steep, yet on any given day there will be ironmen and -women nonchalantly jogging up and down to stay fit. At times, if almost feels like a health-club singles scene. The views are the finest in the city. To reach the trailhead, drive up 44th Street until it becomes McDonald Drive, then turn right on East Echo Canyon Drive, and continue up the hill until the road ends at a large parking lot, which is often full. Don't attempt this one in the heat of the day, and bring at least a quart of water.

At the east end of Camelback Mountain is the Cholla Trail, which, at 1¾ miles in length, isn't as steep as the Summit Trail (at least not until you get close to the summit, where the route gets steep, rocky, and quite difficult). The only parking for this trail is along Invergordon Road at Chaparral Road, just north of Camelback Road (along the east boundary of the Phoenician resort). Be sure to park in a legal parking space and watch the hours that parking is allowed. There's a good turn-around point about 1½ miles up the trail, and great views down onto the fairways of the golf course at the Phoenician.

Squaw Peak in the **Phoenix Mountains Preserve** (© 602/262-7901) offers another aerobic workout of a hike and has views almost as spectacular as those from Camelback Mountain. The round-trip to the summit is 2.4 miles. Squaw Peak is reached from Squaw Peak Drive off Lincoln Drive between 22nd and 23rd streets.

For much less vigorous hiking, try the **North Mountain Recreation Area** (© 602/262-7901) in North Mountain Preserve. This natural area, located on either side of Seventh Street between Dunlap Avenue and Thunderbird Road, has more flat hiking than Camelback Mountain or Squaw Peak.

HORSEBACK RIDING   Even in the urban confines of the Phoenix metro area, people like to play at being cowboys. If you get the urge to saddle up, there are plenty of places around the valley to go for a horseback ride. Keep in mind that most stables require or prefer reservations. Since any guided ride is going to lead you through interesting desert scenery, your best bet is to pick a stable close to where you're staying. Two area resorts—Pointe Hilton Tapatio Cliffs Resort and Pointe South Mountain Resort—have on-site riding stables.

On the south side of the city, try **Ponderosa Stables,** 10215 S. Central Ave. (© 602/268-1261), or **South Mountain Stables,** 10005 S. Central Ave. (© 602/276-8131), both of which lead rides into South Mountain Park and charge $18 per hour. In the Scottsdale area, **MacDonald's Ranch,** 26540 N. Scottsdale Rd. (© 480/585-0239; www.macdonaldsranch.com), charges $24 for a 1-hour ride and $30 for a 1½-hour ride.

On the north side of the valley, in the Cave Creek area, **Cave Creek Outfitters,** off Dynamite Boulevard on 144th Street (𝄐 **480/471-4635**), offers 2-hour rides for $55. **Trail Horse Adventures,** Spur Cross Road, Cave Creek (𝄐 **800/723-3538;** www.trailhorseadventures.com), does everything from 1-hour rides ($30) to full-day rides ($135) to overnight trips ($250).

On the east side of the valley are several riding stables in the foothills of the Superstition Mountains. In Apache Junction, **Trail Horse Adventures** (𝄐 **800/723-3538;** www.trailhorseadventures.com) offers half-day to overnight rides ($90–$250). Over in Gold Canyon, on the southern slopes of the Superstitions, is one of the most famous names in Arizona horseback riding. **Don Donnelly Stables,** 6010 S. Kings Ranch Rd., Gold Canyon (𝄐 **800/346-4403** or 480/982-7822), does 2-hour sunset rides for $38.50. These stables are best known for their overnight horseback trips, but they also conduct cookouts and hayrides.

IN-LINE SKATING   In the Scottsdale area, you can rent in-line skates, including all protective equipment, at **Wheels 'n Gear,** 7607 E. McDowell Rd. (𝄐 **480/945-2881**), in the Plaza Del Rio Shopping Center. Rates are $6 for 2 hours or $12 per day. Its staff members can point you toward nearby spots that are good for skating. Adjacent to the shop is one of the best places, the **Indian Bend Wash greenbelt,** a paved multiuse path that extends for around 15 miles. It runs parallel to Hayden Road in Scottsdale from north of Shea Boulevard to Washington Street. The Indian Bend Wash pathway can be accessed at many points along Hayden Road.

TENNIS   Most major hotels in the area have one or more tennis courts, and there are several tennis resorts around the valley. If you're staying someplace without a court, try the **Scottsdale Ranch Park,** 10400 E. Via Linda, Scottsdale (𝄐 **480/312-7774**). Court fees range from $3 to $6 per hour.

WATER PARKS   At **Waterworld Safari Water Park,** 4243 W. Pinnacle Peak Rd., Phoenix (𝄐 **623/581-1947**), you can free-fall 6½ stories down the Avalanche speed water slide or catch a gnarly wave in the wave pool. Other water slides offer tamer times. **Mesa Golfland-Sunsplash,** 155 W. Hampton Ave., Mesa (𝄐 **480/834-8319**), has a wave pool and a tunnel called the Black Hole. **Big Surf,** 1500 N. McClintock Rd. (𝄐 **480/947-7873**), has a wave pool, underground tube slides, and more.

All three of these parks charge about $17 for adults and $14 for children 4 to 11 (prices tend to go down after 3 or 4pm). Waterworld Safari Water Park and Mesa Golfland-Sunsplash are open from approximately Memorial Day to Labor Day, Monday through Thursday from 10am to 8pm, Friday and Saturday from 10am to 9pm, and Sunday from 11am to 7pm; Big Surf is open Monday through Saturday from 10am to 6pm and Sunday from 11am to 7pm.

WHITE-WATER RAFTING & TUBING ON THE SALT RIVER   The desert may not seem like the place for white-water rafting, but up in the mountains to the northeast of Phoenix, the **Upper Salt River** still flows wild and free and offers some exciting rafting. Most years from about late February to late May, snowmelt from the White Mountains turns the river into a Class III and IV river filled with exciting rapids (some years, there just isn't enough water). Companies operating full-day, overnight, and multiday rafting trips on the Upper Salt River (conditions permitting) include **Far Flung Adventures** (𝄐 **800/231-7238** or 520/425-7272; www.farflung.com), **Sun Country**

Rafting (© **800/272-3353** or 602/493-9011), and **Mild to Wild Rafting** (© **800/567-6745**). Prices range from $80 to $100 for a day trip.

Tamer river trips can be had from **Salt River Recreation** (© **480/984-3305;** www.saltrivertubing.com), which has its headquarters 20 miles northeast of Phoenix on the Power Road at the intersection of Usery Pass Road in the Tonto National Forest. For $10, the company will rent you a large inner tube and shuttle you by bus upriver for the float down. The inner-tubing season runs May through September.

8 Spectator Sports

Phoenix has gone nuts over pro sports and is now one of the few cities in the country with all four of the major sports teams (baseball, basketball, football, and hockey). Add to this baseball's spring training, professional women's basketball, three major golf tournaments, tennis tournaments, the annual Fiesta Bowl college football classic, and ASU football, basketball, and baseball, and you have enough action to keep even the most rabid sports fans happy. The all-around best month to visit is March, when you could feasibly catch baseball's spring training, the Suns, the Coyotes, and ASU basketball and baseball, as well as the Franklin Templeton Tennis Classic and the Standard Register PING LPGA Tournament.

Call **TicketMaster** (© **480/784-4444;** www.ticketmaster.com) for tickets to most of the events below. For sold-out events, try **Tickets Unlimited** (© **800/ 289-8497** or 602/840-2340; www.ticketsunlimited.com) or **Ticket Exchange** (© **800/800-9811** or 602/254-4444).

AUTO RACING   At the **Phoenix International Raceway,** South 115th Avenue and Baseline Road, Avondale (© **602/252-2227;** www.phoenixinternationalraceway.com), there's NASCAR and Indy car racing on the world's fastest 1-mile oval. Ticket prices range from $10 to $40.

BASEBALL   The **Arizona Diamondbacks** (© **602/514-8400;** www. azdiamondbacks.com) play in downtown Phoenix at the Bank One Ballpark (BOB), a state-of-the-art stadium with a retractable roof that allows for comfortable play during Phoenix's blistering summers. The retractable roof makes this one of the only enclosed baseball stadiums with natural grass. If you're fascinated, take one of the **Bank One Ballpark Tours** (© **602/462-6799**), which cost $6 for adults, $4 for children 7 to 12, and $2 for children 4 to 6. Tickets to ballgames are available through the Bank One Ballpark ticket office and cost between $1 and $70.

For decades, it has been **spring training** that gives Phoenix its annual shot of baseball, and don't think that the Cactus League's preseason exhibition games will be any less popular just because the Diamondbacks are around all summer. Spring-training games may rank second only to golf in popularity with winter visitors to the valley. Seven major league baseball teams have spring-training camps around the valley during March and April, and exhibition games are scheduled at six different stadiums. Ticket prices range from $3 to $19. Get a schedule from a visitor center, check the *Arizona Republic* while you're in town, or go to www.Cactus-League.com. Games often sell out, especially on weekends, so be sure to order tickets in advance. The spring-training schedule for 2002 should be out in December 2001.

Teams training in the valley include the **San Francisco Giants,** Scottsdale Stadium, 7408 E. Osborn Rd., Scottsdale (© 800/225-2277 or 480/312-2580); the **Oakland A's,** Phoenix Municipal Stadium, 5999 E. Van Buren St., Phoenix

(© 800/225-2277); the **Anaheim Angels,** Tempe Diablo Stadium, 2200 W. Alameda Dr. (48th Street and Broadway Road), Tempe (© 888/796-HALO or 480/784-4444); the **Chicago Cubs,** HoHoKam Park, 1235 N. Center St., Mesa (© 800/905-3315 or 480/964-4467); the **San Diego Padres,** Peoria Sports Complex, 15999 N. 81st Ave., Peoria (© 800/409-1511 or 623/878-4337); the **Seattle Mariners,** Peoria Sports Complex, 16101 N. 83rd Ave., Peoria (© 800/409-1511 or 623/878-4337); and the **Milwaukee Brewers,** Maryvale Baseball Park, 3508 N. 53rd Ave., Phoenix (© 800/905-3315 or 623/245-5500).

BASKETBALL   The NBA's **Phoenix Suns** play at the America West Arena, 201 E. Jefferson St. (© **602/379-SUNS;** www.suns.com). Tickets cost $10 to $85 and are available at the America West Arena box office and through TicketMaster (see above). Suns tickets are hard to come by. If you want good seats, you really have to buy your tickets the day they go on sale (usually around mid-October). If you haven't planned ahead, try contacting the box office the day before or the day of a game to see if tickets have been returned. Otherwise, you'll have to try a ticket agency and pay a premium.

Phoenix also has a WNBA (Women's National Basketball Association) team, the **Phoenix Mercury** (© **602/252-WNBA** or 602/379-7800; www.wnba. com/mercury), which plays at the America West Arena between late May and mid-August. Ticket prices range from $8 to $38.

FOOTBALL   Although the **Arizona Cardinals** (© **800/999-1402** or 602/379-0102; www.azcardinals.com) are in the process of building a new stadium, it won't be ready until the 2004 season. Until then, the team will continue to play at Arizona State University's Sun Devil Stadium, which is also home to the Fiesta Bowl Football Classic. Tickets cost $35 to $135. Except for a few specific games each season, it is generally possible to get Cardinals tickets.

While the Cardinals get to use Sun Devil Stadium, this field really belongs to Arizona State University's **Sun Devils** (© **480/965-2381**). Ticket prices range from $22 to $26.

Despite the desert heat and presence of a baseball team, Phoenicians don't give up football just because it's summer. The **Arizona Rattlers** arena football team (© **602/514-8383;** www.azrattlers.com) plays 50-yard indoor football at the America West Arena, 201 E. Jefferson St. Tickets are $9 to $23 and are available at the America West Arena box office and through TicketMaster (see above).

GOLF TOURNAMENTS   It's not surprising that, with nearly 200 golf courses and ideal golfing weather throughout the fall, winter, and spring, the Valley of the Sun hosts three major PGA tournaments each year. Tickets for all three are available through TicketMaster outlets (see above).

January's **Phoenix Open Golf Tournament** (© **602/870-4431;** www.phoenixopen.com) is the largest. Held at the Tournament Players Club (TPC) of Scottsdale, it attracts more spectators than any other golf tournament in the world (more than 400,000 each year). The 18th hole has standing room for 40,000. Tickets usually go on sale in June (but are always available the week of the tournament), with prices starting at $20.

Each March, the **Standard Register PING LPGA Tournament** (© **602/ 495-4653;** www.standardregisterping.com), held in the year 2001 at the Moon Valley Country Club, lures nearly 150 of the top women golfers from around the world. Daily ticket prices are $15; weekly tickets are $50.

The Tradition (© 480/595-4070; www.countrywidetradition.com), a Senior PGA Tour event held each April at the Desert Mountain course, has a loyal following of fans who would rather watch the likes of Jack Nicklaus and Chi Chi Rodriguez than see Tiger Woods win yet another tournament. Daily tickets are $40, and usually go on sale in March.

Now even amateurs can get in on some tournament action at the **Phoenix Amateur Golf Championship** (© 877/990-GOLF; www.phxamateur.com), held in mid-July (partly to prove that it's possible to play golf in the summer in Phoenix).

HOCKEY   Ice hockey in the desert? It may not make sense, but even Phoenicians are crazy about ice hockey (maybe it's all those northern transplants). The NHL's **Phoenix Coyotes** (© 888/255-PUCK or 480/563-PUCK; www.phoenixcoyotes.com) play at America West Arena, 201 E. Jefferson St. Tickets range from $11 to $125 and are sold through the America West Arena box office and TicketMaster (see above).

HORSE/GREYHOUND RACING   The **Phoenix Greyhound Park,** 3801 E. Washington St. (© 602/273-7181; www.phoenixgreyhoundpark.com), is a large, fully enclosed, and air-conditioned facility offering seating in various grandstands, lounges, and restaurants. There's racing throughout the year; tickets are $1.50 to $3.

Turf Paradise, 1501 W. Bell Rd. (© 602/942-1101; www.turfparadise.com), is Phoenix's horse-racing track. The season runs from October to May, with post time at 12:30pm Friday through Tuesday. Admission ranges from $2 to $5.

RODEOS, POLO & HORSE SHOWS   Cowboys, cowgirls, and other horsey types will find plenty of the four-legged critters going through their paces most weeks at **Westworld Equestrian Center,** 16601 N. Pima Rd., Scottsdale (© 480/312-6802). With its 500 stables, 11 equestrian arenas, and a polo field, this 400-acre complex provides an amazing variety of entertainment and sporting events. There are rodeos, polo matches, an Arabian-horse show, horse rentals, and horseback-riding instruction.

TENNIS TOURNAMENTS   Each March, top international men's tennis players compete at the **Franklin Templeton Tennis Classic** (© 480/922-0222; www.scottsdaletennis.com), at the Fairmont Scottsdale Princess resort, 7575 E. Princess Dr., Scottsdale. Tickets run from $12 to $60 (tickets to later rounds are more expensive) and are available through TicketMaster outlets (see above).

In late February, women's tennis players compete in the **State Farm Women's Tennis Classic** (© 480/778-9799; www.scottsdaletennis.com), also held at the Fairmont Scottsdale Princess resort. Ticket prices range from $12 to $60 and are available through TicketMaster (see above).

9 Day Spas

Ever since the first "lungers" showed up in the Phoenix area hoping to cure their tuberculosis, the desert has been a magnet for those looking to get healthy. In the first half of the 20th century, health spas were all the rage in Phoenix, and with the health-and-fitness trend continuing to gather steam, it comes as no surprise that spas are now immensely popular in the Valley of the Sun. In the past few years, several of the area's top resorts have added new full-service spas or expanded existing ones to cater to guests' increasing requests for services such as massages, body wraps, mud masks, and salt glows.

If you can't or don't want to spend the money to stay at a top resort and avail yourself of the spa, you may still be able to indulge. Most resorts open their spas to the public, and, for the cost of a body treatment or massage, you can spend the day at the spa, taking classes, working out in an exercise room, lounging by the pool, and otherwise living the life of the rich and famous. Barring this indulgence, you can slip into a day spa, of which there are many scattered around the valley, and take a stress-reduction break the way other people take a latte break.

The **Spa at Gainey Village,** 7477 E. Doubletree Ranch Rd., Scottsdale (© **480/609-6980;** www.thespaatgainey.com), is a state-of-the-art spa and exercise facility near the Hyatt Regency Scottsdale resort. Specialized treatments include massage in a hydrotherapy tub or with water pressure, a couples massage (complete with champagne and chocolate truffles) in a VIP room with a waterfall shower, and just about anything else you can think of, from mineral skin glows to pumpkin peels to purifying facials. With any hour-long treatment (average price $75 to $85), you can use the extensive exercise facilities or take a class. Multiple-treatment packages range in price from $130 to $290.

Located high on the flanks of Mummy Mountain with a nice view over the valley, the **Spa at Camelback Inn,** 5402 E. Lincoln Dr., Scottsdale (© **480/ 596-7040**), is a great place to spend the day being pampered. For the cost of a single 1-hour treatment—between $95 and $115—you can use all the facilities. Among the treatments available are a para-joba body moisturizer that will leave your skin feeling like silk. Multiple-treatment packages run $150 to $275.

The **Centre for Well Being,** at the Phoenician, 6000 E. Camelback Rd., Scottsdale (© **800/843-2392** or 480/423-2452), is the valley's most prestigious day spa, the place to head if you want to be pampered with the rich and famous. For as little as $105, you can spend the day receiving one or more treatments and using the many facilities. Multiple-treatment packages range from $215 to $485.

If you want a truly spectacular setting, head north to Carefree and the **Golden Door Spa at the Boulders,** 34631 N. Tom Darlington Dr. (© **480/488-9009**), which is scheduled to open in September 2001. With the cachet that the Golden Door name brings, this 33,000-square-foot facility with 25 treatment spaces will likely be the valley's premier full-service spa.

The historic setting and convenient location of the **Arizona Biltmore Spa,** 24th Street and Missouri Avenue (© **602/381-7632** or 602/381-7683; www.arizonabiltmore.com), make this 22,000-square-foot facility an excellent choice if you're spending time along the Camelback Corridor. The spa menu includes 80 different treatments, such as hot-rock therapy, mud purification, and a cactus-flower wrap. If you aren't staying at the resort, you can use the facilities for $25; body and beauty treatments range from $65 to $175. Use of the facilities is free with a 50-minute treatment. Multiple-treatment packages cost between $240 and $405.

The **Mist Spa,** at the Radisson Resort & Spa Scottsdale, 7171 N. Scottsdale Rd., Scottsdale (© **877/MIST-SPA** or 480/905-2882; www.themistspa.com), allows nonresort guests use of the facilities for $25 per day (fee is waived with purchase of a 50-min. spa treatment). The 20,000-square-foot spa has a Japanese design, complete with Japanese-style massage rooms and a tranquil rock garden in a central covered courtyard. Treatments, which include the likes of collagen facials, Dead Sea mud wraps, and green-tea detoxifying wraps, cost between $85 and $115. Multiple-treatment packages range in price from $123 to $375.

10 Shopping

For the most part, shopping in the valley means malls. They're everywhere, and they're air-conditioned, which, we're sure you'll agree, makes shopping in the desert far more enjoyable when it's 110°F outside.

Scottsdale and the Biltmore District of Phoenix (along Camelback Road) are the valley's main upscale shopping areas, with several high-end centers and malls. The various distinct shopping districts of downtown Scottsdale are among the few outdoor shopping areas in the valley and are home to hundreds of boutiques, galleries, jewelry stores, Native American crafts stores, and souvenir shops. The Western atmosphere of Old Town Scottsdale is partly real and partly a figment of the local merchants' imaginations, but nevertheless it's the most popular tourist shopping area in the valley. With dozens of galleries in the Main Street Arts and Antiques District and the nearby Marshall Way Contemporary Arts District, it also happens to be the heart of the valley's art market.

Shopping hours are usually Monday through Saturday from 10am to 6pm and Sunday from noon to 5pm; malls usually stay open until 9pm Monday through Saturday.

ANTIQUES

With more than 80 antiques shops and specialty stores, downtown Glendale (northwest of downtown Phoenix) is the valley's main antiques district. You'll find the greatest concentration of antiques stores just off Grand Avenue between 56th and 59th avenues. Four times a year, the **Phoenix Antique Market** (© **800/678-9987** or 602/943-1766; www.jackblack.com), Arizona's largest collectors' show, is held at the Arizona State Fairgrounds, 19th Avenue and McDowell Road. Shows are usually in January, May, September, and November.

Antiques Super-Mall   If you love browsing through packed antiques malls searching for your favorite collectibles, then this should be your first stop in the valley. It's one of the biggest antiques malls in the area, and within a block are two others: the **Antique Centre,** 2012 N. Scottsdale Rd. (© **480/675-9500**), and the **Antique Trove,** 2020 N. Scottsdale Rd. (© **480/947-6074**). 1900 N. Scottsdale Rd., Scottsdale. © **480/874-2900**.

Arizona West Galleries   Nowhere else in Scottsdale will you find such an amazing collection of cowboy collectibles and Western antiques. There are antique saddles and chaps, old rifles and six-shooters, sheriffs' badges, spurs, and the like. 7149 E. Main St., Scottsdale. © **480/994-3752**.

Bishop Gallery for Art & Antiques   This cramped shop is wonderfully eclectic, featuring everything from Asian antiques to unusual original art. Definitely worth a browse. 7164 Main St., Scottsdale. © **480/949-9062**. www.Bishop-Gallery.com.

ART

In the Southwest, only Santa Fe is a more important art market than Scottsdale, and along the streets of Scottsdale's Main Street Arts and Antiques District and the Marshall Way Contemporary Arts District, you'll see dozens of galleries selling everything from monumental bronzes to contemporary art created from found objects. On Main Street, you'll find primarily cowboy art, both traditional and contemporary, while on North Marshall Way, you'll discover much more imaginative and daring contemporary art.

In addition to the galleries listed here, you'll usually find a huge tent full of art along Scottsdale Road in north Scottsdale. The annual **Celebration of Fine**

Art (© **480/443-7695;** www.celebrateart.com) takes place each year between mid-January and late March. Not only will you get to see the work of 100 artists, but on any given day, you'll also find dozens of the artists at work on the premises. Admission is $6.50 for adults and $5.50 for seniors. Call for this year's location and hours of operation.

Art One   If you want to see the possible directions that area artists will be heading in the next few years, stop in at this Marshall Way gallery that specializes in works by art students and other area cutting-edge artists. The works here can be surprisingly good, and prices are very reasonable. 4120 N. Marshall Way, Scottsdale. © **480/946-5076.**

gallerymateria   It's difficult to classify this fascinating boutique, which answers the question, "Is it useful, or is it art?" with clothing and household items that could double as art (with prices to match). You'll also find jewelry that looks like miniature sculptures, plus crafts at the cutting edge of style. There are two parts to the boutique, and in between is a sculpture courtyard. 4222 N. Marshall Way, Scottsdale. © **480/949-1262.** www.gallerymateria.com.

Hollywood Cowboy   If you believe that nothing says *cowboy* like an old Western movie, then be sure to check out the old movie posters at this Scottsdale poster gallery. Old B Westerns are the specialty here, but there are also non-Western posters, as well as posters in French and Spanish. 7077 E. Main St., Scottsdale. © **480/949-5646.** wwwhollywoodcowboy.com.

Lisa Sette Gallery   If you aren't a fan of cowboy or Native American art, you may feel left out of the Scottsdale art scene. Don't despair. Instead, drop by this gallery, which represents international, national, and local artists working in a wide mix of media. 4142 N. Marshall Way, Scottsdale. © **480/990-7342.** www.lisasette.com.

Meyer Gallery   This gallery is notable for its selection of Old West, landscape, and mood paintings by living Impressionists. Most interesting of all are the original paintings for the covers of Western pulp-fiction novels. 7173 E. Main St., Scottsdale. © **480/947-6372.**

Overland Gallery   Traditional Western paintings and a collection of Russian Impressionist paintings form the backbone of this gallery's fine collection. These are museum-quality works (prices sometimes approach $100,000) and definitely worth a look. 7155 Main St., Scottsdale. © **480/947-1934.**

Roberts Gallery   The feathered masks and sculptures of Virgil Walker are the highlights here, and if you have an appreciation for fine detail work, you'll likely be fascinated by these pieces. Walker creates fantasy figures, every inch of which are covered with feathers; his annual show is held on Thanksgiving weekend. El Pedregal Festival Marketplace, 34505 N. Scottsdale Rd., Carefree. © **480/488-1088.**

Wilde Meyer Gallery   Brightly colored and playful are the norm at this gallery, which represents Linda Carter-Holman, a Southwestern favorite who does colorful cowgirl-inspired paintings. There are also Wilde Meyer galleries at 7100 Main St., Scottsdale (© **480/947-1489**), and in El Pedregal Festival Marketplace, Carefree (© **480/488-3200**). 4142 N. Marshall Way, Scottsdale. © **480/945-2323.**

BOOKS

Major chain bookstores in the Phoenix and Scottsdale area include **Borders,** at 2402 E. Camelback Rd., Phoenix (© **602/957-6660**), and 4555 E. Cactus Rd., Phoenix (© **602/953-9699**); and **Barnes & Noble,** at 10235 N. Metro

Parkway East, Phoenix (© **602/678-0088**), 4847 E. Ray Rd., Phoenix (© **480/ 940-7136**), and 10500 N. 90th St., Scottsdale (© **480/391-0048**).

T. A. Swinford Rare and out-of-print books about the American West are the specialty. If you're looking for the likes of *Triggernometry, A Gallery of Gunfighters* (1934) or *Range Murder: How the Red-Sash Gang Dry-Gulched Deputy United States Marshal George Wellman* (1955), you'll find it here. 7134 W. Main St., Scottsdale. © 480/946-0022.

The Poisoned Pen The store name and the police-style outline of a body on the floor just inside the door should give you a clue as to what sort of bookstore this is. If you still haven't figured out that it specializes in mysteries, then maybe you should stick to other genres. 4014 N. Goldwater Blvd., Suite 101, Scottsdale. © 888/560-9919 or 480/947-2974. www.poisonedpen.com.

FASHION
In addition to the options mentioned below, there are many excellent shops in malls all over the city. Favorite spots for upscale fashions include Biltmore Fashion Park, the Borgata of Scottsdale, El Pedregal Festival Marketplace, and Scottsdale Fashion Square. See "Malls & Shopping Centers," below, for details.

For cowboy and cowgirl attire, see "Western Wear," below.

Carol Dolighan The hand-painted, hand-woven, and handmade dresses, skirts, and blouses here abound in rich colors. Each is unique. There's another Carol Dolighan store in El Pedregal Festival Marketplace, 34505 N. Scottsdale Rd., Carefree (© **480/488-4505**). At the Borgata, 6166 N. Scottsdale Rd., Scottsdale. © 480/922-0616.

Objects This eclectic shop carries hand-painted, wearable art both casual and dressy, along with unique artist-made jewelry, African masks and Indian art, books, and all kinds of delightful and unusual things. 8787 N. Scottsdale Rd., Scottsdale. © 480/994-4720. www.objectsgallery.com.

Uh Oh Uh Oh carries simple, tasteful, and oh-so-elegant (as well as Scottsdale hip) fashions, footwear, jewelry, and accessories. The Southwestern contemporary styling makes this a great place to pick up something to be seen in. There are also stores in Kierland Commons shopping center, 15210 N. Scottsdale Rd., Scottsdale; and La Mirada shopping plaza, 8900 E. Pinnacle Peak Rd., Scottsdale. The phone number below works for all three stores. In Hilton Village, 6137 N. Scottsdale Rd., Scottsdale. © 480/991-1618. www.uhohclothing.com.

GIFTS & SOUVENIRS
One of the best places to shop for souvenirs is the Arizona Center mall in downtown Phoenix. See "Malls & Shopping Centers," below, for details.

Bischoff's Shades of the West This is one-stop shopping for all things Southwestern. From T-shirts to regional foodstuffs, this sprawling store has it all. It has good selections of candles, chile garlands (*ristras*), wrought-iron cabinet hardware that can give your kitchen a Western look, and Mexican crafts. There's even a room full of African carvings. 7247 Main St., Scottsdale. © 480/945-3289. www.shadesofthewest.com.

A GOLF SHOP
In Celebration of Golf Sort of a supermarket for golfers (with a touch of Disneyland thrown in), this amazing store sells everything from clubs and golf shoes to golf art and golf antiques. There are even unique golf cars on display in

case you want to take to the greens in a custom car. A golf simulation room allows you to test out new clubs and get in a bit of video golfing at the same time. An old club-maker's workbench, complete with talking mannequin, makes a visit to this shop educational as well as a lot of fun. 7001 N. Scottsdale Rd., Suite 172, Scottsdale. ✆ 480/951-4444. www.celebrategolf.com.

JEWELRY

Cornelis Hollander   Although this shop is much smaller and not nearly so dramatic as that of the nearby Jewelry by Gauthier store, the designs are just as cutting edge. The mix-and-match collection, which melds gold, silver, and precious stones into fascinating designs, is a highlight. 4151 N. Marshall Way, Scottsdale. ✆ 480/423-5000. www.cornelisHollander.com.

Jewelry by Gauthier   This store sells the designs of the phenomenally talented jewelry designer Scott Gauthier. Very stylish, modern pieces using precious stones are miniature works of art. The elegant shop features a lit-from-below green onyx floor. 4211 N. Marshall Way, Scottsdale. ✆ 888/411-3232 or 480/941-1707. www.jewelrybygauthier.com.

Molina Fine Jewelers   If you can spend as much on a necklace as you can on a Mercedes, then this is *the* place to shop for your baubles. Although you don't have to have an appointment to get into this very exclusive jewelry store, it's highly recommended. You'll then get personalized service as you peruse the Tiffany exclusives and high-end European jewelry. 3134 E. Camelback Rd. ✆ 800/ 257-2695 or 602/955-2055.

MALLS & SHOPPING CENTERS

Arizona Center   With its gardens and fountains, this modern downtown shopping center is both a peaceful oasis amid downtown's asphalt and a good place to shop for Arizona souvenirs. It's also home to several nightclubs and Sam's Cafe, which serves Southwestern-style meals. Van Buren St. and Third St. ✆ 602/949-4FUN. www.arizonacenter.com.

Biltmore Fashion Park   This open-air shopping plaza with garden court-yards and upscale boutiques is *the* place to be if shopping is your obsession and you keep your wallet full of platinum cards. Storefronts bear the names of international designers and exclusive boutiques such as Gucci, Cartier, and Cole-Haan. Saks Fifth Avenue and Macy's are the two anchors. There are also more than a dozen moderately priced restaurants here. Valet parking is available. E. Camelback Rd. and 24th St. ✆ 602/955-8400. www.shopbiltmore.com.

The Borgata of Scottsdale   Designed to resemble a medieval Italian village complete with turrets, stone walls, and ramparts, the Borgata is far and away the most architecturally interesting mall in the valley. It contains about 50 upscale boutiques, galleries, and restaurants. 6166 N. Scottsdale Rd. ✆ 480/998-1822. www. borgata.com.

El Pedregal Festival Marketplace   Located adjacent to the Boulders resort 30 minutes north of Old Scottsdale, El Pedregal is the most self-consciously Southwestern shopping center in the valley, and it's worth the long drive out just to see the neo–Santa Fe architecture and colorful accents. The shops offer high-end merchandise, fashions, and art. The Heard Museum also has a branch here. 34505 N. Scottsdale Rd., Carefree. ✆ 480/488-1072. www.elpedregal.com.

Scottsdale Fashion Square   Scottsdale has long been the valley's shopping mecca, and for years this huge mall has been the reason why. It now houses five major department stores—Nordstrom, Dillard's, Neiman Marcus, Robinsons-May, and Sears—and smaller stores such as Eddie Bauer, J. Crew, and Louis Vuitton. 7014–590 E. Camelback Rd. (at Scottsdale Rd.), Scottsdale. ☎ **480/941-2140**. www. westcor.com.

NATIVE AMERICAN ARTS, CRAFTS & JEWELRY

Bischoff's Shades of the West   This museum-like store and gallery is affiliated with another Bischoff's right across the street (see above under "Gifts & Souvenirs"). This outpost carries higher-end jewelry, Western-style home furnishings and clothing, ceramics, sculptures, books and music with a regional theme, and contemporary paintings. 3925 N. Brown Ave., Scottsdale. ☎ **480/946-6155**. www.shadesofthewest.com.

Faust Gallery Fine American Indian Art   Old Native American baskets and pottery, as well as old and new Navajo rugs, are the specialties at this interesting shop. It also sells Native American and Southwest art, including ceramics, paintings, bronzes, home furnishings, and unusual sculptures. 7103 E. Main St., Scottsdale. ☎ **480/946-6345**. www.faustgallery.com.

Gilbert Ortega Museum Gallery   You'll find Gilbert Ortega shops all over the valley, but this is the biggest and best. As the name implies, there are museum displays throughout the store. Cases full of jewelry are the main attraction, but there are also baskets, sculptures, pottery, rugs, paintings, and kachinas. There's another Gilbert Ortega store nearby at 7237 E. Main St., Scottsdale (☎ **480/481-0788**). 3925 N. Scottsdale Rd. ☎ **480/990-1808**.

Heard Museum Gift Shop   The Heard Museum (see "Seeing the Sights," earlier in this chapter) has an awesome collection of extremely well-crafted and very expensive Native American jewelry, art, and crafts of all kinds. Because the store doesn't have to charge sales tax, you'll save a bit of money. This is the best place in the valley to shop for Native American arts and crafts; you can be absolutely assured of the quality. In the Heard Museum, 2301 N. Central Ave. ☎ **602/252-8344**. www.heard.org.

John C. Hill Antique Indian Art   While shops selling Native American art and artifacts abound in Scottsdale, few offer the high quality available in this tiny shop. Not only does the store have one of the finest selections of Navajo rugs in the valley, including quite a few older rugs, but there are also kachinas, superb Navajo and Zuni silver-and-turquoise jewelry, baskets, and pottery. 6962 E. First Ave., Scottsdale. ☎ **480/946-2910**.

Old Territorial Shop   This is the oldest Indian arts-and-crafts store on Main Street and offers good values on a large selection of jewelry, sand paintings, concha belts, kachinas, fetishes, pottery, and Navajo rugs. 7220 E. Main St., Scottsdale. ☎ **480/945-5432**. www.oldterritorialshop.com.

OUTLET MALLS & DISCOUNT SHOPPING

Arizona Mills   This huge mall in Tempe is on the cutting edge when it comes to shop-o-tainment. You'll find not only lots of name-brand outlets, but also a video arcade, multiplex theater, and IMAX theater. With nearly three-quarters of a mile of sensory bombardment, it might be a good idea to bring earplugs and walking shoes. 5000 Arizona Mills Circle, Tempe. ☎ **480/491-9700**. www.arizonamills.com. From I-10, take the Baseline Rd. east exit. From Ariz. 60, exit Priest Dr. south.

My Sister's Closet   This is where the crème de la crème of Scottsdale's used clothing comes to be resold. You'll find such labels as Armani, Donna Karan, and Calvin Klein. Prices are pretty reasonable, too. Also at **Town & Country** shopping plaza at 20th Street and Camelback Road, Phoenix (© **602/ 954-6080**). In Lincoln Village, 6206 N. Scottsdale Rd. (near Trader Joe's), Scottsdale. © 480/ 443-4575. www.mysisterscloset.com.

WESTERN WEAR

Az-Tex Hat Company If you're looking to bring home a cowboy hat, this is a good place to get it. The small shop in Old Scottsdale offers custom shaping and fitting of both felt and woven hats. There's a second store at 15044 N. Cave Creek Rd., Phoenix (© **602/971-9090**). 3903 N. Scottsdale Rd., Scottsdale. © 800/ 972-2116 or 480/481-9900. www.aztexhats.com.

Out West If the revival of 1950s cowboy fashions and interior decor has hit your nostalgia button, then you'll want to high-tail it up to this eclectic shop. All things Western are available, and the fashions are both beautiful and fun (although fancy and pricey). In El Pedregal Festival Marketplace, 34505 N. Scottsdale Rd., Carefree. © **888/454-WEST** or 480/488-0180. www.outwestscottsdale.com.

Saba's Western Stores Since 1927, this store has been outfitting Scottsdale's cowboys and cowgirls, visiting dude ranchers, and anyone else who wants to adopt the look of the Wild West. Call for other locations around Phoenix. 7254 Main St., Scottsdale. © 480/949-7404. www.sabaswesternwear.com.

Sheplers Western Wear Although it isn't the largest Western-wear store in the valley, Sheplers is still sort of a department store of cowboy duds. If you can't find it here, it just ain't available in these parts. Other locations include 8979 E. Indian Bend Rd., Scottsdale (© **480/948-1933**); 2643 E. Broadway Rd., Mesa (© **480/827-8244**); and 2700 W. Baseline Rd., Tempe (© **602/438-7400**). 9201 N. 29th Ave. © 602/870-8085. www.sheplers.com.

Stockman's Cowboy & Southwestern Wear This is one of the oldest Western-wear businesses in the valley, although the store is now housed in a modern shopping plaza. You'll find swirly skirts for cowboy dancing, denim jackets, suede coats, and flashy cowboy shirts. Prices are reasonable and quality is high. 23587 N. Scottsdale Rd. (at the corner of Pinnacle Peak Rd.), Scottsdale. © 480/ 585-6142.

11 Phoenix After Dark

If you're looking for nightlife in the Valley of the Sun, you won't have to look hard, but you may have to drive quite a ways. Although much of the nightlife scene is centered on Old Scottsdale, Tempe's Mill Avenue, and downtown Phoenix, you'll find things going on all over.

The weekly *Phoenix New Times* tends to have the most comprehensive listings for clubs and concert halls. *The Rep Entertainment Guide,* in the Thursday edition of the *Arizona Republic* (and also distributed free of charge from designated newspaper boxes on sidewalks around the valley) is another good place to look for listings of upcoming events and performances, although you won't find as many club listings as in the *New Times. Get Out,* published by the *Tribune,* is another similar tabloid-format arts-and-entertainment publication that is available free around Scottsdale and Tempe. Other publications to check for abbreviated listings are *Valley Guide Quarterly, Key to the Valley, Where Phoenix/Scottsdale,* and *Quick Guide Arizona,* all of which are free and can usually be found at hotels and resorts.

Tickets to many concerts, theater performances, and sporting events are available through **TicketMaster** (© 480/784-4444; www.ticketmaster.com), which has outlets at Wherehouse Records, Tower Records, and Robinsons-May department stores.

THE CLUB & MUSIC SCENE

This region has a very diverse club and music scene that's spread out across the length and breadth of the valley. However, there are a few concentrations of clubs and bars, in downtown Phoenix, Tempe's Mill Avenue, and downtown Scottsdale.

With at least three sports bars, as many regular bars, a massive multiplex movie theater, and half a dozen restaurants, downtown Phoenix's **Arizona Center** is a veritable entertainment mecca. Within a few blocks of this complex, you'll find Phoenix Symphony Hall, the Herberger Theater Center, and several sports bars. However, much of the action revolves around games and concerts at the America West Arena and Bank One Ballpark (BOB).

Another place to wander around until you hear your favorite type of music is **Mill Avenue** in Tempe. Because Tempe is a college town, there are plenty of clubs and bars on this short stretch of road.

In **Scottsdale,** you'll find an eclectic array of clubs in the neighborhoods surrounding the corner of Camelback Road and Scottsdale Road (especially along Stetson Drive, which is divided into two sections east and west of Scottsdale Road). This is where the wealthy (and the wannabes) come to party, and you'll see lots of limos pulling up in front of the hot spot of the moment (currently Axis/Radius).

As we're sure you know if you're a denizen of any urban nightlife scene, clubs come and go. To find out what's hot, get a copy of the *New Times.* Many dance clubs in the Phoenix area are open only on weekends, so be sure to check what night the doors will be open. Bars and clubs are allowed to serve alcohol until 1am.

COUNTRY

Handlebar-J We're not saying that this Scottsdale landmark is a genuine cowboy bar, but cowpokes do make this one of their stops when they come in from the ranch. You'll hear live git-down two-steppin' 7 nights a week; free dance lessons are given Wednesday, Thursday, and Sunday. 7116 E. Becker Lane, Scottsdale. © 480/948-0110. No cover to $4.

Rusty Spur Saloon A small, rowdy, drinkin' and dancin' place frequented by tourists, this bar is a lot of fun, with peanut shells all over the floor, dollar bills stapled to the walls, and the occasional live act in the afternoon or evening. 7245 E. Main St., Old Scottsdale. © 480/941-2628.

ROCK & R&B

The Bash on Ash If it appeals to college students, you'll hear it on stage at Tempe's top live-music club. Currently hip hop, salsa, and swing all get their own night of the week, while heavy metal, reggae, and alternative get equal time, too. 230 W. Fifth St., Tempe. © 480/966-8200. www.bashonash.com. Cover $5–$15.

Cajun House The interior of this cavernous dance club is done up as a New Orleans street scene, with doors opening into various bars, dining rooms, and lounges. Fun and worth checking out. 7117 E. Third Ave., Scottsdale. © 480/945-5150. www.cajunhouse.com. Cover $5 and up.

BLUES

Char's Has the Blues   Yes, indeed, Char's does have those mean-and-dirty, lowdown blues, and if you want them, too, this is where you head in Phoenix. All the best blues brothers and sisters from around the city and around the country make the scene. 4631 N. Seventh Ave., 4 blocks south of Camelback Rd. ✆ 602/230-0205. www.charshastheblues.com. No cover to $8.

The Rhythm Room   This blues club, long the valley's most popular, books quite a few national acts as well as the best of the local scene, and has a dance floor if you want to move to the beat. 1019 E. Indian School Rd. ✆ 602/265-4842. www.rhythmroom.com. No cover to $15.

JAZZ

The Famous Door   Named for the New York jazz club, this bar is even down a few steps from the sidewalk, as all good New York jazz clubs should be. Martinis and cigars are de rigueur with the young and affluent 20- and 30-something crowd. With a jazz combo wedged into the corner and a pall of smoke hanging in the air, this place manages to pull it all off. 7419 Indian Plaza, Scottsdale. ✆ 480/970-1945. www.thefamousdoor.com.

Orbit Restaurant & Jazz Club   Big and trendy, this space has a very urban feel to it, which is surprising considering its shopping-plaza location. Orbit is one of the most popular jazz clubs in the valley, though the music line-up sometimes includes blues and Motown. In Uptown Plaza, Central Ave. and Camelback Rd. ✆ 602/265-2354. No cover (2-drink minimum if you're not having dinner).

Velvet Room Supper Club   Here's another Scottsdale nightclub affecting a retro New York character: that of a classic supper club. Although this place is small, it's got loads of atmosphere. There are two shows nightly, with two bands usually performing Thursday through Sunday. 7111 E. Fifth Ave., Scottsdale. ✆ 480/941-6000. www.thevelvetroom.com. No cover.

DANCE CLUBS & DISCOS

Axis/Radius   If you're looking to do a bit of celebrity spotting, Axis is the place. Currently Scottsdale's hottest dance club and liveliest singles scene, this two-story glass box is a boldly contemporary space with an awesome sound system. 7340 E. Indian Plaza (2 blocks east of Scottsdale Rd. and 1 block south of Camelback Rd.), Scottsdale. ✆ 480/970-1112. Cover $5–$10.

Buzz Original Funbar   In Scottsdale, folks like to think big. The resorts are big, the houses are big, the cars are big, the restaurants are big, and the nightclubs are big. Buzz is no exception, boasting three different theme areas including the Rat Pack Lounge, the Rhino Room (with a zebra-striped dance floor), and a patio up on the roof. Clientele is primarily of the barely legal persuasion. 10345 N. Scottsdale Rd. (at the southeast corner of Scottsdale Rd. and Shea Blvd.). ✆ 480/991-FUNN. No cover to $10.

Club Rio   Popular primarily with students from ASU, which is just across the Tempe Town Lake, this club has a dance floor big enough for football practice. Music is primarily Top 40, alternative, and retro music, and there are also plenty of live shows. 430 N. Scottsdale Rd., Tempe. ✆ 480/894-0533. www.clubrio.com. Cover $1–$7.

Pepin   A DJ plays Latin dance music from 10pm on Friday and Saturday at this small Spanish restaurant located on the Scottsdale Mall. Thursday through Saturday evenings, there are also live flamenco performances. 7363 Scottsdale Mall, Scottsdale. ✆ 480/990-9026. Cover $8.

Phoenix Live! at Arizona Center   Located on the second floor of the Arizona Center shopping center in downtown Phoenix, this trio of clubs (a piano bar, a dance club, and a sports bar) provides enough options to keep almost any group of bar-hoppers happy. Also in Arizona Center is **Moondoggie's,** a beach-theme bar. 455 N. Third St. ✆ **602/252-2502.** No cover to $5.

Sanctuary   Sanctuary, one of the hottest clubs in downtown Scottsdale, has raised the bar for high-end dance clubs. As with other area megaclubs, there are different theme rooms, including a Moroccan room. Great martinis. This club is open Wednesday, Friday, and Saturday nights only. 7340 E. Shoeman Lane, Scottsdale. ✆ **480/970-5000.** Cover $7 for women, $10 for men.

COMEDY & CABARET

The Tempe Improv   With the best of the national comedy circuit harassing the crowds and rattling off one-liners, the Improv is the valley's most popular comedy club. Dinner is served and reservations are advised. 930 E. University Dr., Tempe. ✆ **480/921-9877.** www.improvclubs.com. Cover $12–$15 plus 2-item minimum.

THE BAR, LOUNGE & PUB SCENE

AZ88   Across the park from the Scottsdale Center for the Arts, this sophisticated bar/restaurant has a cool ambience that's just right for a cocktail before or after a performance. There's also a great patio area. 7353 Scottsdale Mall, Scottsdale. ✆ **480/994-5576.**

Bandersnatch Brew Pub   With good house brews and a big patio in back, Bandersnatch is a favorite of those unusual ASU students who prefer quality to quantity when it's beer-drinking time. There's live music Irish music on Wednesdays. 125 E. Fifth St., Tempe. ✆ **480/966-4438.** www.bandersnatchpub.com.

Durant's   In business for decades, Durant's has long been downtown Phoenix's favorite after-work watering hole with the old guard and has caught on with the young martini-drinking crowd. Through wine coolers, light beers, and microbrews, Durant's has remained true to the martini and other classic cocktails. 2611 N. Central Ave. ✆ **602/264-5967.**

Four Peaks Brewing Company   Consistently voted the best brewpub in Phoenix, this Tempe establishment, housed in a former creamery building, brews good beers, including the memorable Kiltlifter Scottish ale, and serves decent pub grub. A favorite of ASU students. 1340 E. Eighth St., Tempe. ✆ **480/303-9967.**

Hyatt Regency Scottsdale Lobby Bar   The open-air lounge just below the main lobby of this posh Scottsdale resort sets a romantic stage for nightly live music (often Spanish-influenced guitar or flamenco music). Wood fires burn in patio fire pits, and the terraced gardens offer plenty of dark spots for a bit of romance. 7500 E. Doubletree Ranch Rd., Scottsdale. ✆ **480/991-3388.**

Kazimierz World Wine Bar   Sort of a spacious speakeasy crossed with a wine bar, this unmarked place, associated with the nearby Cowboy Ciao restaurant, offers the same wide selection of wines available at the restaurant. 7137 E. Stetson Dr., Scottsdale. ✆ **480/946-3004.**

The Squaw Peak Bar   Even if you can't afford the lap of luxury, at least you can pull up a comfortable chair. For the cost of a couple of drinks, you can sink into a seat here at the Biltmore's main lounge and watch the sunset test its color palate on Squaw Peak. Alternatively, you can slide into a seat near the piano and let the waves of mellow jazz wash over you. In the Arizona Biltmore Resort & Spa, 24th St. and Missouri Ave. (✆ 602/955-6600.

T. Cook's   If you aren't planning on having dinner at this opulent Mediterranean restaurant, you'll at least enjoy lounging in the bar. With its mix of Spanish-colonial and 1950s tropical furnishings, this is as romantic a lounge as you'll find anywhere in the valley. You can snuggle up out on the patio by the fireplace 5200 E. Camelback Rd. (✆ 602/808-0766.

Thirsty Camel   Whether you've made your millions or are still working your way up the corporate ladder, you owe it to yourself to spend a little time in the lap of luxury. You may never drink in more ostentatious surroundings than here at Charles Keating's Xanadu. The view's pretty good, too. At the Phoenician, 6000 E. Camelback Rd. (✆ 480/423-2530.

Vinterra   Associated with Altos, a popular Spanish restaurant, this tiny wine bar/wine shop not only serves a wide variety of interesting wines, but also offers flights, live music, and tapas from the restaurant. 5029 N. 44th St. (at the northeast corner of 44th St. and Camelback Rd.). (✆ 602/954-4040.

COCKTAILS WITH A VIEW

The Valley of the Sun has more than its fair share of spectacular views. Unfortunately, most of them are from expensive restaurants. All these restaurants have lounges, though, where for the price of a drink (and perhaps valet parking) you can sit back and ogle a crimson sunset and the purple mountains' majesty. Choices include **Different Pointe of View,** at the Pointe Hilton Tapatio Cliffs Resort; **Rustler's Rooste,** at the Pointe Hilton on South Mountain; and **Top of the Rock,** at the Buttes. All these restaurants can be found in the "Where to Dine" section of this chapter.

SPORTS BARS

Alice Cooper'stown   Sports and rock mix it up at this downtown restaurant/bar run by, you guessed it, Alice Cooper. Lots of TVs and lots of signed memorabilia. The Bank One Ballpark is only a block away. See p. 121 for more information. 101 E. Jackson St. (✆ 602/253-7337. Most nights no cover; special shows up to $25.

Phoenix Live/America's Original Sports Bar   Located in the Arizona Center, this huge sports bar (nearly an acre) is a sort of fun center for grown-ups. There's a huge back deck, innumerable TVs, and even a Phoenix Sports Hall of Fame. 455 N. Third St. (✆ 602/252-2502. No cover to $5.

Majerle's Sports Grill   If you're a Phoenix Suns fan, you won't want to miss this sports bar located only a couple of blocks from the America West Arena, where the Suns play. Suns memorabilia covers the walls. 24 N. Second St. (✆ 602/253-9004.

McDuffy's   With 70 TVs and two dozen beers on tap, this is a favorite of Sun Devils fans. 230 W. Fifth St. (a block off Mill Ave.), Tempe. (✆ 480/966-5600.

GAY & LESBIAN BARS & DANCE CLUBS

Ain't Nobody's Bizness   Located in a small shopping plaza, this is the city's most popular lesbian bar, with pool tables and a smoke-free lounge. On weekends, the dance floor is usually packed. 3031 E. Indian School Rd. (✆ 602/224-9977.

Amsterdam   Just a few doors away from Crowbar, Amsterdam draws a crowd that prefers sipping martinis to tossing down beers. There's no sign outside—

just look carefully for the number. 718 N. Central Ave. ℂ **602/258-6122.** www. amsterdambar.com.

Crowbar   Okay, so it may be a long way to drive if you happen to be staying in Scottsdale, but this downtown Phoenix club stays packed with sweaty bodies on weekends. The after-hours scene pulls in the underagers and goes on until 4am. Open Friday and Saturday only. 710 N. Central Ave. ℂ **602/258-8343.** Cover $6–$8.

THE PERFORMING ARTS

Although downtown Phoenix claims the valley's greatest concentration of performance halls, including the Phoenix Symphony Hall, the Orpheum Theatre, and the Herberger Theater Center, there are major performing-arts venues scattered across the valley. No matter where you happen to be staying, you're likely to find performances being held somewhere nearby.

Calling these many valley venues home are such major companies as the Phoenix Symphony, Scottsdale Symphony Orchestra, Arizona Opera Company, Ballet Arizona, Center Dance Ensemble, Actors Theatre of Phoenix, and Arizona Theatre Company. Adding to the performances held by these companies are the wide variety of touring companies that make stops here throughout the year. These national and international acts give the valley just the diversity of performers you would expect to find in a city of this size.

While you'll find box-office phone numbers listed below, you can also purchase most performing-arts tickets through **TicketMaster** (ℂ **480/784-4444**). For sold-out shows, check with your hotel concierge, or try **Western States Ticket Service** (ℂ **602/254-3300;** www.wstickets.com) or **Tickets Unlimited** (ℂ **800/289-8497** or 602/840-2340; www.ticketsunlimited.com).

MAJOR PERFORMING-ARTS CENTERS

Phoenix's premier performance venue is the **Phoenix Symphony Hall,** 225 E. Adams St. (ℂ **602/262-7272**), home to the Phoenix Symphony and the Arizona Opera Company. It also hosts other classical music performances, Broadway touring shows, and various other concerts and theatrical productions.

The **Orpheum Theatre,** 203 W. Adams St. (ℂ **602/262-7272**), a historic Spanish-colonial baroque theater, was built in 1929 and at the time was considered the most luxurious theater west of the Mississippi. Today, its ornately carved sandstone façade stands in striking contrast to the glass-and-steel City Hall building, with which the theater shares a common wall. The Orpheum is the most elegant hall in the valley.

The Frank Lloyd Wright–designed **Grady Gammage Memorial Auditorium,** Mill Avenue and Apache Boulevard, Tempe (ℂ **480/965-3434**), on the Arizona State University campus, is at once massive and graceful. This 3,000-seat hall hosts everything from barbershop quartets to touring Broadway shows.

The **Scottsdale Center for the Arts,** 7380 E. Second St., Scottsdale (ℂ **480/ 994-ARTS;** www.scottsdalearts.org), hosts a wide variety of performances and series ranging from alternative dance to classical music. This center seems to get the best of the touring performers who come through the valley.

In Scottsdale, near the Borgata shopping center, you'll find **ASU's Kerr Cultural Center,** 6110 N. Scottsdale Rd. (ℂ **480/965-5377;** www.asukerr.com), a tiny venue in a historic home. It offers up an eclectic season that includes music from around the world.

OUTDOOR VENUES & SERIES

Given the weather, it should come as no surprise that Phoenicians like to attend performances under the stars.

The city's top outdoor venue is the **Blockbuster Desert Sky Pavilion,** a half mile north of I-10 between 79th and 83rd avenues (© **602/254-7200** or 602/254-7599). This 20,000-seat amphitheater is open year-round and hosts everything from Broadway musicals to rock concerts.

The **Mesa Amphitheater,** at the corner of University Drive and Center Road, Mesa (© **480/644-2567**), is a much smaller amphitheater that holds a wide variety of concerts in spring and summer, and occasionally other times of year as well.

Throughout the year, the **Scottsdale Center for the Arts** (© **480/994-ARTS;** www.scottsdalearts.org) stages outdoor performances in the adjacent Scottsdale Amphitheater on the Scottsdale Civic Center Mall. The Sunday A'fair series runs October through April, with free concerts from noon to 4:30pm on selected Sundays of each month. Performances range from acoustic blues to zydeco.

Two perennial favorites of valley residents take place in particularly attractive surroundings. The Music in the Garden concerts at the **Desert Botanical Garden,** 1201 N. Galvin Pkwy., in Papago Park (© **480/941-1225;** www.dbg.org), are held on Sundays between September and March. The season always includes an eclectic array of musical styles. Tickets are $13.50 and include admission to the gardens. Sunday brunch is served for an additional charge. Up on the north side of the valley, in Carefree, **El Pedregal Festival Marketplace** (© **480/488-1072;** www.elpedregal.com) stages jazz, blues, and rock concerts on Thursday evenings in May, June, and September. Tickets are $10.

Outdoor concerts are also held at various parks and plazas around the valley during the warmer months. Check local papers for listings.

CLASSICAL MUSIC, OPERA & DANCE

The **Phoenix Symphony** (© **800/776-9080** or 602/495-1999; www.phoenixsymphony.org.), the Southwest's leading symphony orchestra, performs at the Phoenix Symphony Hall (tickets run $18–$45), while the **Scottsdale Symphony Orchestra** (© **480/945-8071;** www.scotsymph.org) performs at the Scottsdale Center for the Arts (tickets go for $15–$18).

Opera buffs may want to see what the **Arizona Opera Company** (© **602/266-7464;** www.azopera.com) has scheduled. This company stages up to five operas, both familiar and more obscure, and splits its time between Phoenix and Tucson. Tickets cost $21 to $72. Performances are held in Phoenix Symphony Hall.

Ballet Arizona (© **602/381-1096;** www.balletarizona.org) performs at Symphony Hall and the Orpheum and stages both classical and contemporary ballets; tickets run $16 to $38. The **Center Dance Ensemble** (© **602/252-8497;** www.centerdance.com), the city's contemporary dance company, stages several productions a year (including one during the Christmas holidays) at the Herberger Theater Center. Tickets go for $18. Between September and March, **Southwest Arts & Entertainment** (© **602/482-6410**) brings acclaimed dance companies and music acts from around the world to Phoenix, with performances staged primarily at the Orpheum. Ticket prices range from $28 to $45.

THEATER

With nearly a dozen professional companies and the same number of nonprofessional companies taking to the boards throughout the year, there is always some play being staged somewhere in the valley.

The **Herberger Theater Center,** 222 E. Monroe St. (✆ **602/252-8497;** www.herbergertheater.org), which is located downtown and vaguely resembles a Spanish colonial church, is the city's main venue for live theater. Its two Broadway-style theaters together host hundreds of performances each year, including productions by the **Actors Theatre of Phoenix (ATP)** and the **Arizona Theatre Company (ATC).** ATP (✆ **602/253-6701**) tends to stage smaller, lesser-known off-Broadway–type works, with musicals, dramas, and comedies equally represented; tickets go for $23 to $34. ATC (✆ **602/256-6899**) is the state theater company of Arizona and splits its performances between Phoenix and Tucson. Founded in 1967, it's the major force on the Arizona thespian scene. Productions range from world premieres to recent Tony award-winners to classics. Tickets run $23 to $48.

The **Phoenix Theatre,** 100 E. McDowell Rd. (✆ **602/254-2151**), has been around for almost 80 years and stages a wide variety of productions; tickets are $26 to $28. If your interest lies in Broadway plays, see what the **Valley Broadway Series** (✆ **480/965-3434;** www.broadwayseries.com/tempe) has scheduled. The series, focusing mostly on comedies and musicals, is held at the Gammage Auditorium in Tempe; tickets cost about $22 to $56. The **Theater League** (✆ **602/952-2881;** www.theaterleague.com) is another series that brings in Broadway musicals. Performances are held in the Orpheum Theatre, and tickets range from $33.50 to $39.50. Scottsdale's small **Stagebrush Theatre,** 7020 E. Second St. (✆ **480/990-7405**), is a community theater that features tried-and-true comedies and musicals (and children's theater), with the occasional drama thrown in. Tickets are about $10 to $17. For more daring new works and children's theater, check the schedule at **PlayWright's Theatre,** 1121 N. First St. (✆ **602/253-5151**). Tickets cost about $15. The **Arizona Jewish Theatre Co.** (✆ **602/264-0402**), which stages plays by Jewish playwrights and with Jewish themes, performs at Playhouse on the Park, in the Viad Corporate Center, 1850 N. Central Ave. (at Palm Lane). Tickets range from $25 to $27.

CASINOS

Casino Arizona These two casinos are the newest and most conveniently located casinos in the area. They are both just off U.S. 101 on the east side of Scottsdale and offer plenty of slot machines, cards, and other games of chance. They're not as grand and impressive as the advertising campaign would have you believe, but do stay packed. U.S. 101 and Indian Bend Rd., and U.S. 101 and McKellips Rd. ✆ 480/850-7777.

Fort McDowell Casino Located about 45 minutes northeast of Scottsdale, this Indian casino is the oldest in the state, offering slot machines, video-poker games, and free shuttles from locations around the valley. On Fort McDowell Rd. off Ariz. 87, 2 miles northeast of Shea Blvd., Fountain Hills. ✆ 800/THE-FORT.

Harrah's Phoenix Ak-Chin Casino This establishment on the Ak-Chin Indian Reservation, 25 miles south of Phoenix, recently added a hotel in hopes of competing with the ever-growing number of casinos around the Phoenix metro area. It features lots of slot machines, video poker, a card room, keno, and bingo. 15406 Maricopa Rd., Maricopa. ✆ 800/427-7247. Take exit 164 (Queen Creek Rd.) off I-10, turn right, and drive 17 miles to the town of Maricopa.

12 A Side Trip from Phoenix: The Apache Trail ✸✸

There isn't a whole lot of desert or history left in Phoenix, but only an hour's drive to the east you'll find quite a bit of both. The **Apache Trail,** a winding, partially gravel road that snakes its way around the north side of the Superstition Mountains, offers some of the most scenic desert driving in central Arizona. Along the way are ghost towns and legends, saguaros and century plants, ancient ruins and artificial lakes. You could easily spend a couple days traveling this route, though most people make it a day trip. Pick and choose the stops that appeal to you, and be sure to get an early start.

This trip travels a narrow, winding gravel road, and if you'd rather leave the driving to someone else, consider contacting **Apache Trail Tours** (✆ 480/982-7661; www.apachetrailtours.com), which offers four-wheel-drive tours of different lengths ($65–$125), as well as hiking tours into the Superstition Mountains.

To start this drive, head east on U.S. 60 to the town of Apache Junction, and then head north on Ariz. 88. About 4 miles out of town, you'll come to **Goldfield Ghost Town,** a reconstructed gold-mining town (see "Wild West Theme Towns" under "Seeing the Sights," earlier in this chapter). Leave yourself plenty of time if you plan to stop here.

Not far from Goldfield is **Lost Dutchman State Park** (✆ 480/982-4485), where you can hike into the rugged Superstition Mountains and see what the region's gold seekers were up against. Park admission is $5 per vehicle; there's a campground that charges $10 per site.

Continuing northeast, you'll reach **Canyon Lake,** set in a deep canyon flanked by colorful cliffs and rugged rock formations. It's the first of three reservoirs you'll pass on this drive. The three lakes provide much of Phoenix's drinking water, without which the city would never have been able to grow as large as it is today. Here at Canyon Lake you can go for a swim at the Acacia Picnic Area or the nearby Boulder Picnic Area, which is on a pretty side cove. You can also take a cruise on the *Dolly* steamboat (✆ 480/827-9144). A 90-minute jaunt on this reproduction paddle-wheeler costs $14 for adults and $8 for children 6 to 12. Dinner cruises are also available, and there's a lakeside restaurant at the boat landing. However, if you're at all hungry, try to hold out for nearby **Tortilla Flat** (✆ 480/984-1776; www.tortillaflataz.com), an old stagecoach stop with a restaurant, saloon, and general store, all of which are papered with business cards and more than $25,000 worth of dollar bills left by travelers who have stopped by. If it's a hot day, don't miss the prickly-pear ice cream (guaranteed spineless).

A few miles past Tortilla Flat, the pavement ends and the truly spectacular desert scenery begins. Among the rocky ridges, arroyos, and canyons of this stretch of road, you'll see saguaro cacti and century plants (a type of agave that dies after sending up its 15-foot-tall flower stalk). Next you'll come to **Apache Lake,** which is not nearly as spectacular a setting as Canyon Lake. However, this lake does have the **Apache Lake Marina and Resort** (✆ 520/467-2511; www.apachelake.com), where you'll find a motel, restaurant, general store, and campground. If you're inclined to turn this drive into an overnight trip, this would be a good place to spend the night. Room rates are $70 to $85; boat rentals are available.

Shortly before reaching pavement again, you'll see **Theodore Roosevelt Dam.** This dam, built in 1911, forms Roosevelt Lake and is the largest masonry dam in the world.

Continuing on Ariz. 88, you'll next come to **Tonto National Monument** (© 520/467-2241; www.nps.gov/tont), which preserves some of the southern-most cliff dwellings in Arizona. These pueblos were occupied between about 1300 and 1450 by the Salado people and are some of the few remaining traces of this tribe, which once cultivated lands now flooded by Roosevelt Lake. The lower ruins are a half mile up a steep trail from the visitor center, while getting to the upper ruins requires a 3-mile round-trip hike. The lower ruins are open daily year-round except Christmas; the upper ruins are open November through April by reservation (reserve at least 2 weeks in advance). The park is open daily from 8am to 5pm (you must begin the lower ruin trail by 4pm); admission is $3.

Keep going on Ariz. 88 to the copper-mining town of **Globe.** The mines here are open pits, and although you can't see the mines themselves, the tailings (remains of rock removed from the copper ore) can be seen piled high all around the town. Be sure to visit **Besh-Ba-Gowah Archaeological Park** ✿ (© 520/425-0320), on the eastern outskirts of town. This Salado Indian pueblo site has been partially reconstructed, and several rooms are set up to reflect the way they might have looked when they were first occupied about 700 years ago. For this reason, they're among the most fascinating ruins in the state. Open daily from 9am to 5pm; admission is $3 for adults, $2 for seniors, and free for children 12 and under. To get here, head out of Globe on South Broad Street to Jesse Hayes Road.

From Globe, head west on U.S. 60. On the west side of Superior is **Boyce Thompson Southwestern Arboretum** ✿✿, 37615 U.S. 60 (© 520/689-2811; http://arboretum.ag.arizona.edu), dedicated to researching and propagating desert plants and instilling in the public an appreciation for them. This was the nation's first botanical garden established in the desert, and the cactus gardens are impressive. The setting in Queen Creek and Anett canyons is quite dramatic, with cliffs for a backdrop and a stream running through the gardens. As you hike the miles of nature trails, watch for the two bizarre boojum trees. The arboretum is open daily, except Christmas, from 8am to 5pm; admission is $5 for adults and $2 for children 5 to 12.

If after a long day on the road you're looking for a place to eat, stop in at **Gold Canyon Golf Resort,** 6100 S. Kings Ranch Rd., Gold Canyon (© 480/982-9090), which has a good formal dining room and a more casual bar and grill.

13 En Route to Tucson

Driving southeast from Phoenix for about 60 miles will bring you to the Florence and Casa Grande area, where you can learn about Indian cultures both past and present and view the greatest concentration of historic adobe buildings in Arizona. To reach Florence, drive south on I-10 to exit 185 (Ariz. 387) and head east. If you're continuing south toward Tucson from Florence, we suggest taking the scenic **Pinal Pioneer Parkway** (Ariz. 79), which was the old highway between Phoenix and Tucson. Along the way, you'll see signs identifying desert plants and a memorial to silent-film star Tom Mix, who died in a car crash here in October 1940.

WHAT TO SEE & DO IN FLORENCE

Florence, which also happens to be home to a large state prison, may at first glance seem to have little to recommend it, but closer inspection turns up nearly 140 buildings on the National Register of Historic Places. The majority of these buildings were constructed of adobe and originally built in the Sonoran style, a style influenced by Spanish architectural ideas. Most buildings were altered over the years and now display aspects of various architectural styles popular during territorial days in Arizona. The current county courthouse, built in 1891, displays one of the oddest mixes of styles. The annual **Florence Historic Tour** (© **800/437-9433** or 520/868-4496), which takes place in early February, includes 16 historic buildings. Tickets are $8 to $10 for adults and $3 to $5 for children. To find out more about the buildings of Florence, stop in at the **Florence Visitor Center,** 291 N. Bailey St. (© **800/437-9433** or 520/868-9433; http://florenceaz.org), in a historic 1891 bakery in the center of town.

McFarland State Historic Park   This historic park consists of the former Pinal County Courthouse, built in 1878. Inside the old adobe building, you'll see some rooms that recreate the days when this was the courthouse, other rooms furnished from the days when this was a hospital.

Main and Ruggles sts. © **520/868-5216.** www.pr.state.az.us. Admission $2 adults, $1 children 12–18. Thurs–Mon 8am–5pm.

Pinal County Historical Society Museum   Before touring the town, stop in at this small museum to orient yourself and learn more about the history of the area.

715 S. Main St. © **520/868-4382.** Admission by donation. Tues–Sat 11am–4pm; Sun noon–4pm. Closed mid-July to Aug.

ATTRACTIONS ALONG THE WAY

There are a couple of **factory-outlet shopping malls** in the town of Casa Grande, at exits 194 and 198 off I-10. They are only a short distance out of your way to the south if you're headed back to Phoenix.

Casa Grande Ruins National Monument 🎯🎯   Before reaching Florence, near the town of Coolidge, you'll come to this national monument. In Spanish, *Casa Grande* means "Big House," and that's exactly what you'll find. In this instance, the big house is the ruin of an earth-walled structure built 650 years ago by the Hohokam people. It is speculated that the building was once some sort of astronomical observatory, but this is not known for certain. Whatever the original purpose of the building, today it provides a glimpse of a style of ancient architecture rarely seen. Instead of using adobe bricks or stones, the people who built this structure used layers of hard-packed soil that have survived the ravages of the weather. The Hohokam people who once occupied this site began farming the valleys of the Gila and Salt rivers about 1,500 years ago, and eventually built an extensive network of irrigation canals for watering their fields. By the middle of the 15th century, the Hohokam had abandoned both their canals and their villages and disappeared without a trace.

Ariz. 87, 1 mile north of Coolidge. © **520/723-3172.** www.nps.gov/cagr. Admission $3. Daily 8am–5pm. Closed Christmas.

Picacho Peak State Park 🎯🎯   Alternatively, if you're heading to Tucson by way of I-10, and it isn't too hot outside, consider a stop at this state park, 20 miles south of Casa Grande at exit 219. Picacho Peak, a wizard's cap of rock rising 1,500 feet above the desert, is a visual landmark for miles around. Hiking trails lead around the lower slopes of the peak and up to the summit; these trails are especially popular in spring, when the wildflowers bloom (the park is well known as one of the best places in Arizona to see wildflowers). In addition to its natural beauty, Picacho Peak was the site of the only Civil War battle to take place in the state. Each year in March, Civil War reenactments are staged here. Campsites in the park cost $10 to $15.

Exit 219 off I-10. (Ⓒ 520/466-3183. www.pr.state.az.us. Admission $5 per car.

14 En Route to Northern Arizona

If your idea of a great afternoon is searching out deals at factory-outlet stores, then you'll be in heaven at **Prime Outlets at New River,** 4250 W. Honda Bow Rd. (Ⓒ **888/4-VALUE-4U** or 623/465-9500). Among the offerings are Ann Taylor, Bugle Boy, the Gap, Geoffrey Beene, and Levi's. Take exit 229 (Desert Hills Road) off I-17.

Some 13 miles farther north is the town of Rock Springs, which is barely a wide spot in the road and is easily missed by drivers roaring up and down I-17. However, if you're a fan of pies, then do *not* miss exit 242. Here you'll find the **Rock Springs Cafe** (Ⓒ **623/374-5794**), in business since 1920. Although this aging, nondescript building looks like the sort of place that would best be avoided, the packed parking lot says different. Why so popular? It's not the coffee or the "hogs in heat" barbecue or even the Bradshaw Mountain oysters. No, what keeps this place packed are Penny's pies, the most famous in Arizona (37,748 sold in 2000). No matter what your favorite kind, you'll likely find it in the pie case. If one slice isn't enough, order a whole pie to go. As the menu says, this place is "worth the drive from anywhere."

If you appreciate innovative architecture, don't miss the Cordes Junction exit (exit 262) off I-17. Here you'll find **Arcosanti** (Ⓒ **520/632-7135** or 602/254-5309; www.arcosanti.org), Italian architect Paolo Soleri's vision of the future—a "city" that merges architecture and ecology. Soleri, who came to Arizona to study with Frank Lloyd Wright at Taliesin West, envisions a compact, energy-efficient city that disturbs the natural landscape as little as possible—and that's just what's rising out of the desert here at Arcosanti. The organic design built of cast concrete will fascinate both students of architecture and those with only a passing interest in the discipline. Arcosanti has been built primarily with the help of students and volunteers who live here for various lengths of time. To help finance the construction, Soleri designs and sells wind bells cast in bronze or made of ceramic. These distinctive bells are available at the gift shop.

If you'd like to stay overnight, there are basic accommodations ($30–$75 double) available by reservation. You'll also find a bakery and cafe on the premises. Arcosanti is open daily from 9am to 5pm, and tours are held hourly between 10am and 4pm ($6 suggested donation).

In early 2000, some 71,000 acres of land east of I-17 between Black Canyon City and Cordes Junction was designated the **Agua Fria National Monument,** which is administered by the Bureau of Land Management, Phoenix Field Office, 21605 N. Seventh Ave., Phoenix (Ⓒ **623/580-5500**). The monument was created to protect the region's numerous prehistoric Native American ruin sites, which date from between A.D. 1250 and 1450 (at least 450 prehistoric sites are known to exist in this area). There is very limited access to the monument and no facilities for visitors. The only roads within the monument are rugged dirt roads, many of which require four-wheel-drive, high-clearance vehicles. However, if you'd like to assist with the mapping and recording of archaeological sites in the vicinity of the national monument, contact **Archaeological Adventures** (Ⓒ **623/465-1981;** www.ArchaeologicAdventures.com), which charges $200 per person for a day of documenting unexplored prehistoric sites in the area.

5

Central Arizona

Let's say you're planning a trip to Arizona. You're going to fly in to Phoenix, rent a car, and head north to the Grand Canyon. Glancing at a map of the state, you might easily imagine that there is nothing to see or do between Phoenix and the Grand Canyon. This is the desert, right? Miles of desolate wasteland, that sort of thing. Wrong!

Between Phoenix and the Grand Canyon lies one of the most beautiful landscapes on earth, the red-rock country of Sedona—but don't get the idea that Sedona is some sort of wilderness waiting to be discovered. Decades ago Hollywood came to Sedona to shoot Westerns; then came the artists and the retirees and the New Agers. Now it seems Hollywood is back, but this time the stars are building huge homes in the hills. There's even talk of Sedona becoming the next Aspen, albeit without a ski slope (although there is a ski area not too far away on the other side of Flagstaff).

Central Arizona isn't just red rock and retirees, though. It also has the former territorial capital of Prescott, historic sites, ancient Indian ruins, old mining towns turned artists' communities, even a few good old-fashioned dude ranches out Wickenburg way. There are, of course, thousands of acres of cactus-studded desert, but there are also high mountains, cool pine forests, and a fertile river valley, appropriately named the Verde (Green) Valley. And heading up from Sedona's red rocks is Oak Creek Canyon, one of the most beautiful scenic drives in the state.

If you should fall in love with this country, don't be too surprised. People have been drawn to this region for hundreds of years. The Hohokam people farmed the fertile Verde Valley as long ago as A.D. 600, followed by the Sinagua and then the first white settlers. Although the early tribes had disappeared by the time the first white settlers arrived in the 1860s, Apache and Yavapai tribes inhabited the area. It was to protect settlers from these hostile tribes that the U.S. Army established Fort Verde here in 1871.

When Arizona became a U.S. territory in 1863, Prescott was chosen as its capital, due to its central location. Although the town would eventually lose that title to Tucson and then to Phoenix, it was the most important city in Arizona for part of the late 19th century. Wealthy merchants and legislators rapidly transformed this pioneer outpost into a beautiful town filled with stately Victorian homes surrounding an imposing county courthouse.

Settlers were lured to this region not only by fertile land but also by the mineral wealth that lay hidden in the ground. Miners founded a number of communities in central Arizona, among them Jerome. When the mines shut down, Jerome was almost completely abandoned, but now artists and craftspeople have moved in to reclaim and revitalize the old mining town.

Once called the dude ranch capital of the world, Wickenburg still clings to its Western roots and has restored much of its downtown to its 1880s appearance. It is here you find most of the region's few remaining dude ranches—now called "guest ranches."

1 Wickenburg

53 miles NW of Phoenix; 61 miles S of Prescott; 128 miles SE of Kingman

Once known as the Dude Ranch Capital of the World, the town of Wickenburg, located in the desert northwest of Phoenix, attracted celebrities and families from all over the country. Those were the days when the West had only just stopped being wild, and spending the winter in Arizona was an adventure, not just a chance to escape winter weather. Today, although the area has only a handful of dude (or guest) ranches still in business, Wickenburg clings to its Wild West image. The dude ranches that remain range from rustic to luxurious, but a chance to ride the range is still the area's main attraction.

Wickenburg lies at the northern edge of the Sonoran Desert on the banks of the Hassayampa River, one of the last free-flowing rivers in the Arizona desert. The town was founded in 1863 by Prussian gold prospector Henry Wickenburg, who discovered what would eventually become the most profitable gold and silver mine in Arizona: the Vulture Mine. The mine closed in 1942 and is now operated as a tourist attraction.

When the dude ranches flourished back in the 1920s and 1930s, Wickenburg realized that visitors wanted a taste of the Wild West, so the town gave the tenderfoots what they wanted—trail rides, hayrides, cookouts, the works. Wickenburg has even preserved one of its downtown streets much as it may have looked in 1900. If you've come to Arizona searching for the West the way it used to be, Wickenburg is a good place to look. Just don't expect staged shootouts in the streets; this ain't Tombstone.

ESSENTIALS

GETTING THERE   From Phoenix, take U.S. 60, which heads northwest and becomes U.S. 93/Ariz. 89. Ariz. 89 also comes down from Prescott in the north, while U.S. 60 comes in from I-10 in western Arizona. U.S. 93 comes down from I-40 in northwestern Arizona. **Airport Express of Wickenburg** (© 888/684-8667 or 520/684-0925) offers a shuttle from the Phoenix Sky Harbor Airport for $75 for two people. Call ahead for a reservation.

VISITOR INFORMATION   Contact the **Wickenburg Chamber of Commerce,** 216 N. Frontier St. (© 800/942-5242 or 520/684-5479; www.wickenburgchamber.com).

SPECIAL EVENTS   **Gold Rush Days,** held on the second full weekend in February, is the biggest festival of the year in Wickenburg. Events include gold panning, a rodeo, and shootouts in the streets. On the second full weekend in November, the **Bluegrass Festival** features contests for fiddle and banjo. On the first weekend in December, Wickenburg holds its annual **Cowboy Poetry Gathering,** with lots of poetry and music.

WHAT TO SEE & DO
A WALK AROUND TOWN

While Wickenburg's main attraction remains the several guest ranches outside town, a stroll around downtown provides a glimpse of the Old West. Most of the buildings were built between 1890 and the 1920s (although a few are older), and although not all of these old buildings look their age, there is just enough Western character to make a walk around on foot worthwhile (if the heat isn't too bad).

The old **Santa Fe train station** is now the Wickenburg Chamber of Commerce, which should be your first stop in town. You can pick up a map that tells a bit about the history of the older buildings. The brick **post office,** almost across the street from the train station, once had a ride-up window providing service to people on horseback. **Frontier Street** is preserved as it looked in the early 1900s. The covered sidewalks and false fronts are characteristic of frontier architecture; the false fronts often disguised older adobe buildings that were considered "uncivilized" by settlers from back east. The oldest building in town is the **Etter General Store,** adjacent to the Homestead Restaurant. The adobe-walled store was built in 1864 and has long since been disguised with a false wooden front.

Two of the town's most unusual attractions aren't buildings at all. The **Jail Tree,** behind the Circle K store at the corner of Wickenburg Way and Tegner Street, is an old mesquite tree that served as the local hoosegow. Outlaws were simply chained to the tree. Their families would often come to visit and have a picnic in the shade of the tree. The second, equally curious, town attraction is the **Wishing Well,** which stands beside the bridge over the Hassayampa. Legend has it that anyone who drinks from the Hassayampa River will never tell the truth again. How it became a wishing well is unclear.

MUSEUMS & MINES

Desert Caballeros Western Museum ✦ Wickenburg thrives on its Western heritage, and inside this museum you'll find Western art depicting life on the range in the days of "cowboys and Indians." Although it's not too large, the museum manages to convey a great deal about the history of this part of Arizona. There's an excellent display of colorful minerals and a small collection of Indian artifacts. On the main floor, dioramas depict important scenes from the history of the region. Downstairs, a 1900 street scene from a Western town is recreated, complete with saloon and general store. There are also regularly scheduled special exhibits and an art collection containing work by Remington, Russell, and members of the Cowboy Artists of America.

21 N. Frontier St. ℂ **520/684-2272.** www.westernmuseum.org. Admission $5 adults, $4 seniors, $1 children 6–16. Mon–Sat 10am–5pm; Sun noon–4pm. Closed major holidays.

Robson's Arizona Mining World Boasting the world's largest collection of antique mining equipment, this private museum is a must for anyone who is fascinated by Arizona's rich mining history. Located on the site of an old mining camp, it consists of 26 buildings filled with antiques. More like a ghost town than a museum, Robson's buildings contain displays pertaining to life in a mining camp. In addition to touring the museum, you can pan for gold or hike to see Native American petroglyphs. A three-story hotel (charging $75–$85 double; no credit cards accepted) and a restaurant are also on the premises.

Ariz. 71, 28 miles west of Wickenburg. ℂ **520/685-2609.** Admission $5 adults, $4.50 seniors, free for children 10 and under. Mon–Fri 10am–4pm; Sat–Sun 8am–6pm. Closed May 1–Oct 15. Head west out of Wickenburg on U.S. 60 and, after 24 miles, turn north on Ariz. 71.

The Vulture Mine *Kids* Lying at the base of Vulture Peak (the most visible landmark in the Wickenburg area), the Vulture Mine was first staked by Henry

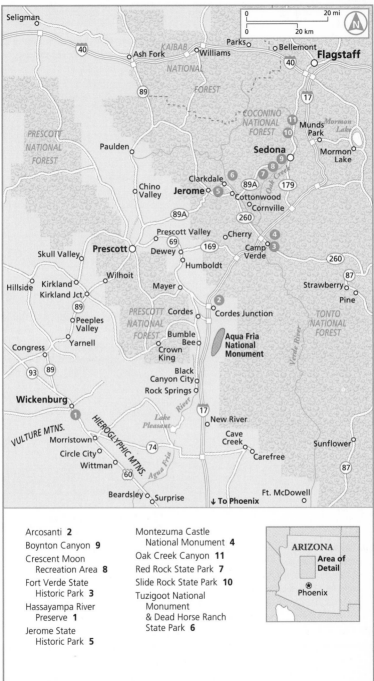

Arcosanti **2**

Boynton Canyon **9**

Crescent Moon
Recreation Area **8**

Fort Verde State
Historic Park **3**

Hassayampa River
Preserve **1**

Jerome State
Historic Park **5**

Montezuma Castle
National Monument **4**

Oak Creek Canyon **11**

Red Rock State Park **7**

Slide Rock State Park **10**

Tuzigoot National
Monument
& Dead Horse Ranch
State Park **6**

ARIZONA

Area of
Detail

⊛
Phoenix

Wickenburg in 1863. This mine fueled the small gold rush that helped popu-late this section of the Arizona desert. Today the Vulture Mine has the feel of a ghost town, and though you can't go down into the old mine itself, you can wan-der around among the aboveground shacks and mine structures on either a self-guided or guided tour (by prior arrangement). Mildly interesting for those who appreciate old mines, and fun for kids.

Vulture Mine Rd. © **602/859-2743.** Admission $6 adults, $5 children 6–12. Sept–Mar daily 8am[nd4pm; Apr Fri–Tues 8am–4pm; May Fri–Mon 8am–4pm; June–July Sat–Sun 8am–4pm; closed Aug. Take U.S. 60 west out of town, turn left on Vulture Mine Rd., and drive 12 miles south.

A BIRDER'S PARADISE

Hassayampa River Preserve ✿   At one time the Arizona desert was laced with rivers that flowed for most, if not all, of the year. In the past 100 years, however, these rivers, and the riparian habitats they once supported, have disap-peared at an alarming rate due to the damming of rivers and the lowering water tables caused by the large number of wells drilled throughout the state. Ripar-ian areas support trees and plants that require more water than is usually avail-able in the desert, and this lush growth provides food and shelter for hundreds of species of birds, mammals, and reptiles. Today the riparian cottonwood-willow forests of the desert Southwest are considered the country's most endan-gered forest type.

The Nature Conservancy, a nonprofit organization dedicated to purchasing and preserving threatened habitats, owns and manages the Hassayampa River Preserve, which is now one of the state's most important bird-watching sites (more than 230 species of birds have been spotted here). Nature trails lead along the river beneath cottonwoods and willows and past the spring-fed Palm Lake. On site are a visitor center and bookshop. Free naturalist-guided walks are offered (reservations required).

49614 U.S. 60 (3 miles south of Wickenburg on U.S. 60). © **520/684-2772.** www.tncarizona.org. Suggested donation $5 (free for Nature Conservancy members). Mid-Sept to mid-May Wed–Sun 8am–5pm; mid-May to mid-Sept Fri–Sun 8am–5pm. Closed major holidays.

OUTDOOR PURSUITS

If you're in the area for more than a day or just can't spend another minute in the saddle, you can get out on a Jeep tour and explore the desert backcountry, visit Vulture Peak, see some petroglyphs, or check out old mines. **B.C. Jeep Tours** (© **520/684-3883**) charges around $50 for adults. However, if you've got time for only one Jeep tour on your Arizona vacation, make it in Sedona.

Los Caballeros Golf Club, 1551 S. Vulture Mine Rd. (© **520/684-2704**), has been rated one of the best courses in the state. Greens fees are about $120 in peak season and $49 in summer.

If you'd rather do some hiking, there are a couple of interesting options. Southwest of town at the end of Vulture Mine Road (off U.S. 60), you can climb **Vulture Peak,** a steep climb best done in the cooler months. However, the views from up top (or even just the saddle near the top) are well worth the effort. For an easier hike, stop by the Wickenburg Chamber of Commerce and get its map of **Box Canyon,** a scenic stretch of the Hassayampa River.

WHERE TO STAY
GUEST RANCHES

Flying E Ranch ✿ *Kids*   Of the handful of guest ranches still operating in Wickenburg, this is the only real working cattle ranch, with 20,000 high, wide, and handsome acres for you and the cattle to roam. Family owned since 1952, the Flying E attracts plenty of repeat business, with families finding it a particularly appealing and down-home kind of place. The main lodge features a spacious lounge where guests like to gather by the fireplace. The accommodations vary in size, but all have Western-style furnishings and either twin or king beds. Three family style meals are served in the wood-paneled dining room, but there's no bar, so you'll need to bring your own liquor. Also on offer are breakfast cookouts, lunch rides, and evening chuck-wagon dinners.

2801 W. Wickenburg Way, Wickenburg, AZ 85390. (C) **888/684-2650** or 520/684-2690. Fax 520/684-5304. www.flyingeranch.com. 17 units. $230–$295 double. Rates include all meals. 2- to 4-night minimum. No credit cards. Closed May–Oct. Drive 4 miles west of town on U.S. 60. **Amenities:** Dining room; small outdoor pool; tennis court; exercise room; Jacuzzi; sauna; horseback riding ($30–$40 per day additional); horseshoes; hayrides; guest rodeos. *In room:* A/C, TV, fridge.

Kay El Bar Guest Ranch ⭐ This is the smallest and oldest of the Wickenburg guest ranches, and its adobe buildings, built between 1914 and 1925, are listed on the National Register of Historic Places. The well-maintained ranch is quintessentially Wild West in style (telegraph poles hold up the ceiling of the main lodge, where there's a large stone fireplace). The setting, on the bank of the (usually dry) Hassayampa River, lends the ranch a surprisingly lush feel compared with the arid surrounding landscape. While the cottage and the new Casa Grande room are the most spacious, the smaller rooms in the adobe main lodge have original Monterey-style furnishings and other classic 1950s dude-ranch decor. The ranch has only 60 acres, but it abuts thousands of acres of public lands where guests can ride or hike. A tile floor and beehive fireplace in the dining room provide an authentic Southwestern feel. The meals vary from Chinese to prime rib, and are served in heaping portions.

Rincon Rd. (off U.S. 93; P.O. Box 2480), Wickenburg, AZ 85358. (C) **800/684-7583** or 520/684-7593. Fax 520/684-4497. www.kayelbar.com. 11 units. $300–$330 double; $660 cottage for 4. Rates include all meals and horseback riding. Minimum stay may apply. MC, V. Closed May 1 to mid-Oct. **Amenities:** Dining room, lounge; small outdoor pool; Jacuzzi; horseback riding. *In room:* No phone.

Rancho de los Caballeros ⭐⭐ Located on 20,000 acres 2 miles west of Wickenburg, Rancho de los Caballeros is part of an exclusive country club–resort community and as such feels more like an exclusive resort than a guest ranch. However, the main lodge building itself, with its flagstone floor, copper fireplace, and colorfully painted furniture, has a very Southwestern feel. Peace and quiet are the keynotes of a visit here, and most guests focus on golf (the golf course is one of the best in the state) and horseback riding. In addition, the ranch offers skeet and trap shooting, stargazing, and guided nature walks. Bedrooms are filled with handcrafted Southwestern-style furnishings, exposed-beam ceilings, Indian rugs, and, in some, tile floors and fireplaces. While breakfast and lunch are quite casual, dinner is a rather formal affair, with proper attire required. After dinner, you can catch a little cowboy music or an old Western movie in the ranch's "saloon."

1551 S. Vulture Mine Rd. (off U.S. 60 west of town), Wickenburg, AZ 85390. (C) **800/684-5030** or 520/684-5484. Fax 520/684-2267. www.SunC.com. 79 units. Oct–Jan and May $309–$359 double, $399 suite; Feb–Apr $359–$419 double, $499 suite (plus 15% gratuity, year-round). Rates include all meals. Riding and golf packages available. No credit cards. Closed mid-May to mid-Oct. **Amenities:** Dining room, lounge; small outdoor pool; 18-hole golf course; 4 tennis courts; horseback riding ($30–$38 per ride); bike rentals; children's programs; courtesy shuttle; pro shop; massage; baby-sitting; laundry service. *In room:* A/C, TV, dataport, hair dryer, iron.

OTHER ACCOMMODATIONS

Best Western Rancho Grande   Located right in the heart of downtown Wickenburg, this place is built in Spanish colonial style, with tile roofs, stucco walls, arched colonnades, and tile murals. There's a wide range of room types— the more you pay, the bigger things get (larger room, larger bathroom). The property is within walking distance of good restaurants and the town's historic sites.

293 E. Wickenburg Way, Wickenburg, AZ 85390. ℂ **800/854-7235** or 520/684-5445. Fax 520/684-7380. www.bwranchogrande.com. 80 units. May–Sept $65–$99 double; Oct–Apr $69–$113 double. AE, DC, DISC, MC, V. Pets accepted. **Amenities:** Outdoor pool; Jacuzzi; tennis court. *In room:* A/C, TV, coffeemaker.

WHERE TO DINE

Get a quick salad or sandwich right in the center of downtown at the friendly **Pony Espresso Café,** 233 E. Wickenburg Way (ℂ **520/684-0208**).

House Berlin GERMAN/CONTINENTAL   Wickenburg may seem like an unusual place to find an authentic German restaurant, but that's exactly what you'll find right downtown. The place is small and casual and serves a mix of German and other Continental dishes. Local favorites include the jaeger schnitzel, Wiener schnitzel, and sauerbraten.

169 E. Wickenburg Way. ℂ **520/684-5044.** Main courses lunch $6–$11, dinner $10–$14. MC, V. Wed–Sun 11:30am–2pm; Tues–Sun 5–9pm.

Rancho de los Caballeros ★★ CONTINENTAL/SOUTHWESTERN Wickenburg's most exclusive guest ranch also opens its restaurant to the public. The formerly conservative menu has been updated with contemporary South-western dishes, and although it changes daily, you always have a choice of several soups and salads, main courses, and desserts. You might start with *albondigas,* a Spanish-style meatball soup, or black-bean soup with goat cheese, and then move on to chile-accented salmon with a cilantro and basil sauce or steak au poivre with a spinach soufflé. For dessert, choose crème brûlée or chocolate mousse pie. Men are required to wear a sports jacket or Western vest, and women must also dress appropriately.

1551 S. Vulture Mine Rd. ℂ **520/684-5484.** Reservations required. Jackets required for men. Lunch $11–$14, complete dinner $26. No credit cards. Mon–Sat 12:30–1:30pm and 6:30–8:30pm; Sun noon–2pm (buffet lunch) and 6:30–8:30pm. Closed mid-May to mid-Oct.

EN ROUTE TO PRESCOTT

Between Wickenburg and Prescott, Ariz. 89 climbs up out of the desert at the town of **Yarnell,** which lies at the top of a steep stretch of road. The landscape around Yarnell is a jumble of weather-worn granite boulders that give the town a unique appearance. Several little crafts and antiques shops here are worth a stop, but the town's main claim to fame is the **Shrine of St. Joseph of the Mountains,** which is known for its carved stone stations of the cross.

2 Prescott

100 miles N of Phoenix; 60 miles SW of Sedona; 87 miles SW of Flagstaff

Prescott is an Arizona anomaly. What attracts many people to this town, the for-mer territorial capital of Arizona, is that it doesn't seem like Arizona at all. With its stately courthouse on a tree-shaded square, its well-preserved historic down-town business district, and its old Victorian homes, Prescott wears the air of the quintessential American small town, the sort of place where the Broadway show

The Music Man might have been staged. Prescott has just about everything a small town should have: a burger shop (Kendall's), an 1890s saloon (The Palace), an old cattlemen's hotel (Hassayampa Inn), a brew pub (Prescott Brewing Company), and a European-style cafe (Café St. Michaels). Add to this several small museums, a couple of other historic hotels, the strange landscape of the Granite Dells, and the nearby Prescott National Forest, and you have a town that appeals to visitors with a diverse range of interests.

The town's Anglo history dates from 1863, when the Walker party discovered gold in the mountains of central Arizona. Soon miners were flocking to the area to seek their own fortunes. A year later, Arizona became a U.S. territory, and the new town of Prescott, located right in the center of Arizona, was made the territorial capital. Prescott later lost its statewide influence when the capital moved to Phoenix, but because of the importance of ranching and mining in central Arizona, Prescott continued to be a major regional town. Today Prescott has become an upscale retirement community, as much for its historic heritage as for its mild year-round climate. In summer, Prescott is also a popular weekend getaway for Phoenicians, since it is usually 20° cooler here than it is in Phoenix.

ESSENTIALS

GETTING THERE   Prescott is at the junction of Ariz. 89, Ariz. 89A, and Ariz. 69. If you're coming from Phoenix, take the Cordes Junction exit (exit 262) from I-17. From Flagstaff, the most direct route is I-17 to Ariz. 169 to Ariz. 69. From Sedona, just take Ariz. 89A all the way.

There is regularly scheduled service between Prescott's Ernest A. Love Airport, on U.S. 89, and the Phoenix Sky Harbor Airport on **America West** (② **800/ 235-9292**). Shuttle "U" provides service between Prescott and the Phoenix Sky Harbor Airport. The fare is $24 one way and $42 round-trip. Phone ② **800/ 304-6114** (outside of Prescott) or 520/772-6114 for schedule information.

ORIENTATION   Ariz. 89 comes into Prescott on the northeast side of town, where it joins with Ariz. 69 coming in from the east. Five miles north of town, Ariz. 89A from Sedona also merges with Ariz. 89. The main street into town is **Gurley Street,** which forms the north side of Courthouse Plaza. **Montezuma Street,** also known as Whiskey Row, forms the west side of the plaza. If you continue south on Montezuma Street, you'll be on Ariz. 89 heading toward Wickenburg.

VISITOR INFORMATION   The **Prescott Chamber of Commerce** is at 117 W. Goodwin St. (② **800/266-7534** or 520/445-2000; www.prescott.org).

GETTING AROUND   If you need to rent a car, contact **Budget** (② **800/ 527-0700** or 520/778-3806) or **Enterprise** (② **800/RENT-A-CAR** or 520/778-6506). If you need a taxi, call **Ace City Cab** (② **520/445-1616**).

SPECIAL EVENTS   The **World's Oldest Rodeo** is held in early July as part of the city's Prescott Frontier Days celebration. Also included in this celebration are a Western-art show, golf tournament, carnival, and parade. **Territorial Days,** held in early to mid-June, is another big festival with special art exhibits, performances, tournaments, races, and lots of food and free entertainment. In mid-July, the Sharlot Hall Museum hosts the **Prescott Indian Art Market,** and on the third weekend in August, the **Arizona Cowboy Poets Gathering** takes place there as well. Prescott is also officially recognized as Arizona's **Christmas City**. In December, the city is decked out with lights, and there are numerous holiday events.

EXPLORING THE TOWN

A walk around **Courthouse Plaza** should be your introduction to Prescott. The stately old courthouse in the middle of the tree-shaded plaza sets the tone for the whole town. The building, far too large for a small regional town such as this, dates from the days when Prescott was the capital of the Arizona Territory. Under the big shade trees, you'll find several large bronze statues of cowboys and soldiers.

Surrounding the courthouse and extending north for a block is Prescott's **historic business district.** Stroll around admiring the brick buildings, and you'll realize that Prescott was once a very important place. Duck into an old saloon or the lobby of one of the historic hotels, and you'll understand that the town was also part of the Wild West. After you've gotten a taste of Prescott, there are several museums, listed below, you might like to visit.

To learn more about the history of Prescott, contact Melissa Ruffner at **Prescott Historical Tours** (✆ 520/445-4567), which offers both a historical tour ($40 per couple) and a Victorian tea tour ($50 per couple).

Phippen Museum ☆ If you're a fan of classic Western art, you won't want to miss this small museum. Located on a hill a few miles north of town, the Phippen exhibits works by both established Western artists and newcomers and is named after the first president of the prestigious Cowboy Artists of America organization. The museum also displays historic artifacts and photos that help place the artwork in the context of the history of the region. Each year on Memorial Day weekend, the museum sponsors the **Phippen Western Art Show.** More than 100 Arizona artists are represented in the museum store.

4701 U.S. 89N. ✆ 520/778-1385. www.phippenmuseum.org. Admission $3 adults, $2 seniors and students, free for children 12 and under. Mon and Wed–Sat 10am–4pm; Sun 1–4pm.

Sharlot Hall Museum ☆ In 1882, at the age of 12, Sharlot Hall traveled to the Arizona territory with her parents. As an adult, she began collecting artifacts from Arizona's pioneer days. From 1909 to 1911, she was the territorial historian, and in 1928, she opened this museum in Prescott's **Old Governor's Mansion,** a log home built in 1864. In addition to the mansion, which is furnished much as it might have been when it was built, there are several other interesting buildings that can be toured. The **Frémont House** was built in 1875 for the fifth territorial governor. Its traditional wood-frame construction shows how quickly Prescott grew from a remote logging and mining camp into a civilized little town. The 1877 **Bashford House** reflects the Victorian architecture that was popular throughout the country around the turn of the century. The **Sharlot Hall Building** houses exhibits on Native American cultures and territorial Arizona. The museum's rose garden honors famous women of Arizona. Every year in early summer, artisans, craftspeople, and costumed exhibitors participate in the **Folk Arts Fair.**

415 W. Gurley St. ✆ 520/445-3122. www.sharlot.org. Suggested donation $4 adults, $3 seniors, $5 families. Apr 1–Oct 31 Mon–Sat 10am–5pm, Sun 1–5pm; Nov 1–Mar 31 Mon–Sat 10am–4pm, Sun 1–5pm. Closed Thanksgiving, Christmas, and New Year's Day.

The Smoki Museum This interesting little museum, which houses a collection of Native American artifacts in a historic stone building, is named for the fictitious Smoki tribe. The tribe was dreamed up in 1921 by a group of non-Indians who wanted to inject some new life into Prescott's July 4th celebrations. Despite its phony origins, the museum contains genuine artifacts and basketry from many different tribes, mainly Southwestern.

147 N. Arizona St. ✆ 520/445-1230. www.smoki.com. Admission $4 adults, $3 seniors, $2 students. Apr 15–Oct 31 Mon–Sat 10am–4pm, Sun 1–4pm The rest of the year, call for possible openings on weekends.

OUTDOOR PURSUITS

Prescott is situated on the edge of a wide expanse of high plains with the pine forests of **Prescott National Forest** at its back. There are hiking and mountain-biking trails, several lakes, and campgrounds within the national forest. Our favorite hiking and biking areas are Thumb Butte (west of town) and the Granite Mountain Wilderness (northwest of town).

Thumb Butte, a rocky outcropping that towers over the forest just west of town, is Prescott's most readily recognizable natural landmark. A 1.2-mile trail leads nearly to the top of this butte, and from the saddle near the top, there's a panoramic vista of the entire region. The trail itself is very steep, but paved much of the way. The summit of the butte is a popular rock-climbing spot. An alternative return trail makes a loop hike possible. To reach the trailhead, drive west out of town on Gurley Street, which becomes Thumb Butte Road. Follow the road until you see the National Forest signs, after which there's a parking lot, picnic area, and trailhead. Parking is $2 (free on Wednesdays).

The Granite Basin area, which provides access to the **Granite Mountain Wilderness,** is another of our favorite area hiking spots. Trails lead beneath the cliffs of Granite Mountain, where you might spot peregrine falcons. For the best views, hike 1½ miles to Blair Pass and then on up the Granite Mountain trail as far as you feel like going. To reach this area, take Gurley Street west from downtown, turn right on Grove Avenue, and follow it around to Iron Springs Road, which will take you northwest out of town to the signed road for the Granite Basin Recreation Area (less than 8 miles from downtown).

Both of the above areas also offer mountain-biking trails. Although the scenery isn't as spectacular as in Sedona, the trails are great. You can rent a bike and get maps and specific trail recommendations at **Mountain Sports,** 142 N. Cortez St. (© 520/445-8310), which charges $25 for bike rentals.

For maps and information on these and other hikes and bike rides in the area, stop by the **Bradshaw Ranger Station,** 344 S. Cortez St. (© 520/771-4700), where you can also get a $5 seasonal parking pass.

North of town 5 miles on Ariz. 89 is an unusual and scenic area known as the **Granite Dells.** Jumbled hills of rounded granite suddenly jut up from the landscape, creating a maze of huge boulders and smooth rock. In the middle of this dramatic landscape lies Watson Lake, the waters of which push their way in among the boulders to create one of the prettiest lakes in the state. On the highway side of the lake, you'll find Watson Lake Park, which has picnic tables and great views. However, if you turn east onto Sun Dog Ranch Road, which is between Prescott and the Granite Dells, and follow it for about 1½ miles, you'll find a trailhead parking area for the Peavine Trail, a multiuse rails-to-trails path that extends for several miles through the middle of the Granite Dells. This trail is the best way to see the Dells. Also accessible from this same trailhead is the Watson Woods Riparian Preserve, which has some short trails through the wetlands and riparian zone along Granite Creek. We love biking this trail, but it's equally enjoyable to hike. For information, contact **Prescott Parks & Recreation** (© 520/445-5880).

If you want to explore the area on horseback, there are several options. **Rafter 6 Outdoor Adventures** (© 520/636-5007; www.rafter6.com) does everything from 1½-hour rides ($30) to overnight cowboy campouts ($160 per day) to chuck-wagon rides ($65). **Prescott Ranch** (© 800/684-7433 or 520/636-9737), about 25 minutes north of Prescott off Ariz. 89 near the town of Paulden, offers guided trail rides in the Prescott National Forest. A 2-hour ride is $35. Also in the Paulden area, the **Double D Ranch** (℧ **520/636-0418**), which operates a small guest ranch, leads all-day rides into the Prescott National Forest. These rides visit ancient Indian ruins and even include a bit of six-gun and Winchester practice. Rides run $30 per hour and are offered between October and March.

Reasonably priced golf is available at the **Antelope Hills Golf Courses,** 1 Perkins Dr. (℧ **800/972-6818** in Arizona, or 520/776-7888).

SHOPPING

Downtown Prescott is filled with antiques stores, especially along North Cortez Street. In the Hotel St. Michael's shopping arcade, check out **Hotel Trading,** 110 S. Montezuma St. (℧ **520/778-7276**), which carries some genuine Native American artifacts at reasonable prices. Also in this same block is the **Arts Prescott Cooperative Gallery,** 134 S. Montezuma St. (℧ **520/776-7717**), a cooperative of local artists.

WHERE TO STAY
EXPENSIVE

Double D Guest Ranch ⋆ *Finds*   Located out in the ranch country north of Prescott, this guest ranch is unusual in that owners Doug and Denise Dipietro (the Double Ds of the name) accept only one party of guests at a time, so if you book a stay here, you'll have the rammed-earth ranch house all to yourself. With its flagstone floors and contemporary decor, the house is much more 1990s than 1890s. An interesting variety of excursions, from Jeep tours to train trips to the Grand Canyon, are offered, though most guests spend their days horseback riding. At the end of a day in the saddle, you can soak your sore muscles in the inn's unique "cowboy hot tub," which is made from a horse watering trough!

P.O. Box 334, Paulden, AZ 86334. ℧ 520/636-0418. www.virtualcities.com or www.ranchweb.com. 2 units (only 1 party of guests at a time). $139–$179 per person per night. Rates include all meals and various activities based on length of stay. 3-night minimum. AE, DISC, MC, V. **Amenities:** Hot tub; horseback riding; laundry service. *In room:* A/C, TV, fridge, hair dryer.

Hassayampa Inn ⋆   Built as a luxury hotel in 1927, the Hassayampa Inn, which is listed on the National Register of Historic Places, evokes the time when Prescott was the bustling capital of the Arizona Territory. In the lobby, stenciled exposed ceiling beams, wrought-iron chandeliers, and arched doorways all reflect the place's Southwestern heritage. Each guest room is unique and features either original furnishings or antiques. One room is said to be haunted, and any hotel employee will be happy to tell you the story of the ill-fated honeymooners whose ghosts are said to reside here. New owners have plans for renovations and upgrading in late 2001.

122 E. Gurley St., Prescott, AZ 86301. ℧ 800/322-1927 or 520/778-9434. Fax 520/445-8590. www. hassayampainn.com. 68 units. Apr–Oct $109–$149 double, $159–$199 suite; Nov–Mar $99–$129 double, $159–$199 suite. Rates include full breakfast. AE, DC, DISC, MC, V. **Amenities:** Restaurant; lounge; access to nearby health club; room service; laundry service; dry cleaning. *In room:* A/C, TV, hair dryer.

Prescott Resort, Conference Center, and Casino ⋆   This is Prescott's only full-service resort hotel, and it focus its attentions on conferences and some of the business that once went to Laughlin or Las Vegas. Built high on a hill overlooking the city and the surrounding valley and mountains, the resort has the best view of any lodging in Prescott. However, the town's Western heritage is played up only in the overabundance of Western art that covers the walls leading out from the lobby. Public rooms aside, the guest rooms are spacious and comfortable, and each has its own balcony overlooking the valley. The dining room offers a great panorama to accompany the meals. The 24-hour casino is the resort's biggest draw for most guests.

1500 Hwy. 69, Prescott, AZ 86301. ℂ **800/967-4637** or 520/776-1666. Fax 520/776-8544. www. prescottresort.com. 160 units. $135–$165 double; $155–$185 suite. AE, DC, DISC, MC, V. **Amenities:** Restaurant, lounge; outdoor pool; 2 tennis courts; racquetball court; health club; Jacuzzi; sauna; salon; room service; massage; laundry service; dry cleaning. *In room:* A/C, TV, dataport, fridge, coffeemaker, hair dryer, iron.

MODERATE

Hotel Vendome   Not quite as luxurious as the Hassayampa, yet not as basic as the St. Michael, the Vendome offers a good middle-price choice for those who want to stay in a historic hotel. Built in 1917 as a lodging house, the restored two-story brick building is only 2 blocks from the action of Whiskey Row, but far enough away that you can get a good night's sleep. The guest rooms are outfitted with new furnishings, but some of the bathrooms still contain original claw-foot tubs. Naturally, this hotel, like so many others in town, has its own resident ghost.

230 S. Cortez St., Prescott, AZ 86303. ℂ **888/468-3583** or 520/776-0900. Fax 520/771-0395. www. vendomehotel.com. 21 units. $79–$169 double; $119–$189 suite. Rates include continental breakfast. AE, DC, DISC, MC, V. *In room:* A/C, TV, dataport.

The Marks House Victorian Bed & Breakfast   Located high on a hill only a block from the courthouse, this large Victorian inn has the best views of any bed-and-breakfast in town. While not as immaculate as some of the other local B&Bs, the Marks House has the most authentic atmosphere and some of the most interesting rooms. The Princess Victoria features an unusual copper bathhouse-style tub, while in the Queen Anne room, you'll find a claw-foot tub in one corner and a small turret sitting area in another. The evening social hour is a good time to get to know the innkeepers. So many B&Bs claim to be just like Grandma's house, but this one really is.

203 E. Union St., Prescott, AZ 86303. ℂ **800/370-6275** or 520/778-4632. www.virtualcities.com/ons/ az/r/azr2602.htm. 4 units. $85–$135 double. Rates include full breakfast. DISC, MC, V. *In room:* No phone.

Rocamadour Bed & Breakfast for (Rock) Lovers ★★   The Granite Dells, just north of Prescott, is the area's most fantastic feature. Should you wish to stay amid these jumbled boulders, there is no better choice than Rocamadour. Mike and Twila Coffey honed their innkeeping skills as owners of a 40-room château in France, and antique furnishings from that château can now be found throughout this inn. The most elegant pieces are in the Chambre Trucy, which also boasts an amazing underlit whirlpool tub. One cottage is built into the boulders and has a large whirlpool tub on its deck. The unique setting, engaging innkeepers, and thoughtful details everywhere you turn make this one of the state's must-stay inns.

3386 N. Hwy. 89, Prescott, AZ 86301. ℂ **888/771-1933** or 520/771-1933. 4 units. $99–$139 double; $189 suite. Rates include full breakfast. *In room:* A/C, TV/VCR.

INEXPENSIVE

In addition to the following hotel, Prescott has several budget chain motels. Try the **Super 8,** 1105 E. Sheldon St. (ℂ **520/776-1282**), charging $53 to $63 double, or **Motel 6,** 1111 E. Sheldon St. (ℂ **520/776-0160**), charging $42 to $54.

Hotel St. Michael *Value* Located right on Whiskey Row, this restored hotel, complete with resident ghost and the oldest elevator in Prescott, offers a historic setting at budget prices (don't expect the best of mattresses or most stylish furnishings). All rooms are different; some have bathtubs but no showers. The casual Café St. Michael, where breakfast is served, overlooks Courthouse Plaza.

205 W. Gurley St., Prescott, AZ 86301. ☏ 800/678-3757 or 520/776-1999. Fax 520/776-7318. 72 units. $49–$79 double; $89–$99 suite. Rates include continental breakfast. AE, MC, V. **Amenities:** Cafe; shopping arcade. *In room:* A/C, TV, hair dryer.

WHERE TO DINE

The best place in town to savor a mocha and pastry while watching the world go by is at the **Café St. Michael,** 205 W. Gurley St. (☏ **520/776-1999**), at the historic hotel of the same name (see "Where to Stay," above). With its pressed-tin ceiling, brick walls, and battered wood floor, this place has the feel of an old saloon. For tasty crepes, try **Courthouse Coffee Company** (☏ **520/445-2325**), a little espresso bar at 108 W. Gurley St. Grab picnic fare at **New Frontiers Natural Foods,** 1112 Iron Springs Rd. (☏ **520/445-7370**).

MODERATE

Murphy's ✵ AMERICAN Murphy's, housed in the oldest mercantile building in the Southwest, has long been Prescott's favorite special-occasion restaurant and is best known for its mesquite-broiled meats and excellent seafood dishes. The building, which is on the National Register of Historic Places, was constructed in 1890, and many of the shop's original shelves can be seen in the lounge area. Sparkling leaded-glass doors usher diners into a high-ceilinged room with fans revolving slowly overhead.

201 N. Cortez St. (a block from Courthouse Plaza). ☏ **520/445-4044.** Reservations recommended for parties of 5 or more. Main courses $7–$13 lunch, $13–$27 dinner. AE, DISC, MC, V. Sun–Thurs 11am–9pm; Fri–Sat 11am–10pm. Stays open later in summer.

The Palace *Finds* SOUTHWESTERN/STEAKHOUSE/SEAFOOD The Palace is the oldest saloon in Arizona (in business for more than 120 years), and in 1996 was beautifully renovated and returned to the way it might have looked around the turn of the last century. If you bump into someone carrying a shotgun, don't panic! It's probably just the owner, who likes to dress the part of a Wild West saloonkeeper. While the front of the Palace is centered around the old bar, most of the cavernous space is dedicated to an always bustling dining room. The menu includes choices such as an appetizer of grilled tiger prawns wrapped in basil and prosciutto; citrus salmon; corn chowder; and generous portions of steak, pork chops, and seafood. While other self-styled cowboy steakhouses around the state are just tourist traps, this place is the genuine article.

120 S. Montezuma St. ☏ **520/541-1996.** www.historicpalace.com. Reservations suggested on weekends. Main courses $6–$8 at lunch, $11–$22 at dinner. AE, DISC, MC, V. Sun–Thurs 11am–3pm and 4:30–9:30pm; Fri–Sat 11am–3pm and 4:30–10:30pm.

The Rose Restaurant ✵✵ CONTINENTAL Chef Linda Rose worked for nearly a decade at the Hassayampa Hotel's Peacock Room, and now she brings her creative flair to her own restaurant. The manicotti and double-cut lamb chops are house specialties well worth trying. The dining rooms here are small, and tables close together, but that doesn't dissuade both locals and visitors from enjoying the excellent food and reasonably priced wines.

234 S. Cortez St. ☏ **520/777-8308.** Reservations recommended. Main courses $16–$28. AE, DC, DISC, MC, V. Wed–Sun 5–9pm.

INEXPENSIVE

Gurley St. Grill ITALIAN/AMERICAN   The Gurley St. Grill is located a block off Courthouse Plaza and run by the same people who operate Murphy's. Brick walls, ceiling fans, and beveled glass reflect the building's historic heritage. Families come for the pastas, pizzas, steaks, and rotisserie chicken. At lunch the Sonoran corn chowder is a good bet; at dinner the Cajun chicken with house-made fettuccine is not only delicious but also plentiful.

230 W. Gurley St. (𝐶) **520/445-3388.** Reservations accepted for parties of 5 or more at dinner. Main courses $7–$15. AE, DISC, MC, V. Daily 11am–10pm; late-night menu daily 10pm–midnight.

Kendall's Famous Burgers & Ice Cream BURGERS   Ask anyone in town where to get the best burger in Prescott, and you'll be sent to Kendall's on Courthouse Plaza. This bright and noisy luncheonette serves juicy burgers with a choice of more than a dozen condiments.

113 S. Cortez St. (𝐶) **520/778-3658.** Burgers $4–$6. DISC, MC, V. Mon–Sat 11am–8pm; Sun 11am–6pm.

Machu Picchu Peruvian Restaurant ★ (𝑉𝑎𝑙𝑢𝑒) PERUVIAN   This little cottage restaurant offers beguilingly low prices, along with food that's both flavorful and filling. To start, the ceviche, with its piquant lime and chile flavorings, is pleasantly offset by the sweetness of an accompanying yam. For more intriguing flavors, try the fried rockfish, squid, shrimp, mussels, and potatoes covered with a spicy shredded onion salsa (served weekends). For dessert, don't miss the *budin* (bread pie with raisins), which is flamed table side with a blowtorch. The restaurant is small and quite popular, so expect a wait.

111 Grove St. (𝐶) **520/717-8242.** Reservations not accepted. Main courses $7–$13. AE, MC, V. Mon–Sat 11am–2pm and 4–9pm.

Prescott Brewing Company AMERICAN/PUB FARE   Popular primarily with a younger crowd, this brewpub keeps a good selection of its own beers and ales on tap, but is just as popular for its cheap and filling meals. Fajitas are a specialty, along with such pub standards as fish and chips, bangers and mash, and not-so-standard spent-grain beer-dough pizzas and vegetarian dishes. The Caesar salad with chipotle dressing packs a wallop.

130 W. Gurley St. (𝐶) **520/771-2795.** www.prescottbrewingcompany.com. Main courses $6–$13. AE, DISC, MC, V. Sun–Thurs 11am–10pm; Fri–Sat 11am–11pm (pub stays open 2 hr. after kitchen closes).

PRESCOTT AFTER DARK

Back in the days when Prescott was the territorial capital and a booming mining town, it supported dozens of rowdy saloons, most of which were concentrated along Montezuma Street on the west side of Courthouse Plaza. This section of town was known as **Whiskey Row,** and legend has it there was a tunnel from the courthouse to one of the saloons so lawmakers wouldn't have to be seen ducking into the saloons during regular business hours. On July 14, 1900, a fire consumed most of Whiskey Row. However, concerned cowboys and miners managed to drag the tremendously heavy bar of the Palace saloon across the street before it was damaged.

Today Whiskey Row is no longer the sort of place where respectable women shouldn't be seen, although it does still have a few noisy saloons with genuine Wild West flavor. Most of them feature live country music on weekends and are the dark, dank sorts of places that cowboys tend to gravitate to. If, however, you'd rather see what this street's saloons looked like back in the old days, drop by the **Palace,** 120 S. Montezuma St. ((𝐶) **520/541-1996**), which still has a classic bar up front (though it's now primarily a restaurant). Just push through the swinging doors and say howdy to the fellow with the six-guns or shotgun; he's the owner. A couple of times a month, the Palace presents dinner theater performances; call to find out if anything is happening while you're in town. Just around the corner is the **Prescott Brewing Company,** 130 W. Gurley St. (© **520/771-2795**), which is today's answer to the saloons of yore, brewing and serving its own tasty microbrews. Good pub fare is also served.

If you're feeling lucky, head up to **Bucky's Casino,** 1500 Hwy. 69 (© **800/ SLOTS-44** or 520/776-5695), located at the Prescott Resort. In addition to 300 slot machines, the casino has a poker room and keno. Across the street from the entrance to the Prescott Resort is the **Yavapai Casino,** which is under the same management and offers slot machines and bingo.

The **Prescott Fine Arts Association,** 208 N. Marina St. (© **520/445-3286;** www.pfaa.net), sponsors plays, music performances, children's theater, and art exhibits. The association's main building, a former church built in 1899, is on the National Register of Historic Places.

EN ROUTE TO OR FROM PHOENIX

If you crave a taste of the country life, stop by **Young's Farm** (© **520/632-7272;** www.youngsfarminc.com), a country store at the intersection of Ariz. 69 and 169 between I-17 and Prescott. Located in the middle of the desert, this farm stand sells a wide variety of produce as well as gourmet and unusual foods. You might find any of a number of various seasonal festivals going on here, such as a Pumpkin Festival during the month of October.

3 Jerome

35 miles NE of Prescott; 28 miles W of Sedona; 130 miles N of Phoenix

Few towns anywhere in Arizona make more of an impression on visitors than Jerome, a historic mining town that clings to the slopes of Cleopatra Hill high on Mingus Mountain. The town is divided into two sections that are separated by an elevation change of 1,500 vertical feet, with the upper part of town 2,000 feet above the Verde Valley. On a clear day, the view from Jerome is stupendous—it's possible to see for more than 50 miles, with the red rocks of Sedona, the Mogollon Rim, and the San Francisco Peaks visible in the distance. Add to the unforgettable views the abundance of interesting shops and galleries and the winding narrow streets, and you have a town that should not be missed.

Jerome had its start as a copper-mining town, but it was never easy to mine the copper ore here. For many years, the mountain's ore was mined using an 88-mile-long network of underground railroads. However, in 1918, a fire broke out in the mine tunnels, and mining companies were forced to abandon the tunnels in favor of open-pit mining. One unforeseen hazard of this type of mining was the effect dynamiting would have on a town built on a 30° slope. Buildings in Jerome began sliding downhill, and eventually the town jail broke loose and slid 225 feet downhill (now that's a jailbreak).

Between 1883 and 1953, Jerome experienced an economic roller-coaster ride as the price of copper rose and fell. In the early 1950s, when it was no longer profitable to mine the copper ore of Cleopatra Hill, the last mining company shut down its operations, and almost everyone left town. By the early 1960s, Jerome looked as though it were on its way to becoming just another ghost town, but then artists who had discovered the phenomenal views and dirt-cheap rents began moving in, and slowly the would-be ghost town developed a reputation as an artists' community. Soon tourists began visiting to see and buy the artwork that was being created in Jerome, and old storefronts turned into galleries.

Jerome is now far from a ghost town, and on summer weekends the streets are packed with visitors browsing the galleries and crafts shops. The same remote and rugged setting that once made it difficult and expensive to mine copper has now become one of the town's main attractions. Because Jerome is built on a slope, streets through town switch back from one level of houses to the next, and narrow alleys and stairways connect the different levels of town. Old brick and wood-frame buildings are built into the side of the mountain. The entire town has been designated a National Historic Landmark. Today, residences, studios, shops, and galleries stand side by side looking (externally, anyway) much as they did when Jerome was an active mining town.

ESSENTIALS

GETTING THERE   Jerome is on Ariz. 89A roughly halfway between Sedona and Prescott. Coming from Phoenix, take Ariz. 260 from Camp Verde.

VISITOR INFORMATION   Contact the **Jerome Chamber of Commerce** (© 520/634-2900; www.jeromechamber.com) for information.

EXPLORING THE TOWN

Wandering the streets, soaking up the atmosphere, and shopping are the main pastimes in Jerome. However, before you launch yourself on a shopping tour, you can learn about the town's past at the **Jerome State Historic Park,** off U.S. 89A on Douglas Road in the lower section of town (© 520/634-5381). Located in a mansion built in 1916 as a home for mine owner "Rawhide Jimmy" Douglas and as a hotel for visiting mining executives, the Jerome State Historic Park contains exhibits on mining as well as a few of the mansion's original furnishings. Set on a hill above Douglas's Little Daisy Mine, the mansion overlooks Jerome and, dizzyingly far below, the Verde Valley. Constructed of adobe bricks made on the site, the mansion contained a wine cellar, billiards room, marble shower, steam heat, and central vacuum system. The library has been restored as a period room; other rooms have exhibits on copper mining and local history. Admission is $2.50 for adults, $1 for children 7 to 13. It's open daily from 8am to 5pm, except Christmas.

To learn more about Jerome's history, stop in at the **Jerome Historical Society's Mine Museum,** 200 Main St. (© 520/634-5477), which has some small and old-fashioned displays on mining. It's open daily from 9am to 4:30pm; admission is $1. For that classic mining-town tourist-trap experience, follow the signs up the hill from downtown Jerome to the **Gold King Mine and Ghost Town** (© 520/634-0053), where you can see lots of old, rusting mining equipment and maybe even catch a demonstration.

To get a wider perspective on both the mining history and Native American history of this area, try a four-wheel-drive tour with **Arizona Time Expeditions** (© 520/634-3497; www.arizonahealingtours.com), operated by Clay Miller (who also works as a guide on the nearby Verde Canyon Railroad and is a fount of information on this region). Clay also offers hiking explorations.

Most visitors come to Jerome for the shops, which offer an eclectic blend of urban art, chic jewelry, one-of-a-kind handmade fashions, unusual imports and gifts, and the inevitable tacky souvenirs and ice cream (alas, no place stays undiscovered for long anymore; at least there's no McDonald's). To see what local artists are creating, stop in at the **Jerome Artists Cooperative** (© 520/ 639-4276), on the west side of the street where Hull Avenue and Main Street fork as you come up the hill into town. The **Raku Gallery,** 250 Hull Ave. (© **520/639-0239**), has gallery space on two floors and walls of glass across the back, with views of the red rocks of Sedona in the distance. The **Jerome Gallery,** 240 Hull Ave. (© **520/634-7033**), has good-quality ceramics, jewelry, and home furnishings. **Sky Fire,** 140 Main St. (© **520/634-8081**), features an interesting collection of Southwestern and ethnic gifts and furnishings. On this same block, you'll also find **Nellie Bly,** 136 Main St. (© **520/634-0255**), with a room full of colorful, handmade kaleidoscopes (ask to see the ones in the back room), and **Nellie Bly II,** 130 Main St. (© **520/634-7825**), which specializes in jewelry made from semiprecious stones. **Guilt Complex** (also the House of Joy), on Hull Avenue (© **520/634-7101**), stocks an eclectic assortment of greeting cards, hearts, handmade bears, and old tobacco art.

WHERE TO STAY

Connor Hotel of Jerome   Housed in a recently renovated historic hotel, this is now the most up-to-date lodging in Jerome. Some rooms are quite spacious, with large windows to let in lots of light. Views of the valley, however, are limited. The only real drawback is that most of the rooms are directly above the hotel's popular bar, which can be quite noisy on weekends. Ask for a room at the end of the building away from the bar.

164 Main St. (P.O. Box 1177), Jerome, AZ 86331. © **800/523-3554** or 520/634-5006. www.connorhotel. 10 units. $75–$105 double. AE, MC, V. **Amenities:** Bar. *In room:* TV, coffeemaker, fridge.

Ghost City Inn   With its long verandas on both floors, this restored old house is hard to miss as you drive into town from Clarkdale. It manages to capture the spirit of Jerome, with a mix of Victorian and Southwestern decor. Most bedrooms have great views across the Verde Valley (and these are definitely worth requesting). Two units feature antique brass beds, while a third has a high bed that you have to use a footstool to climb into. The accommodations are on the small side, so if space is a priority, opt for the suite.

541 N. Main St. (P.O. Box 382), Jerome, AZ 86331. © **888/63-GHOST** or 520/63-GHOST. www. ghostcityinn.com. 6 units (2 with private bathroom). $85–$100 double; $125 suite. Rates include full breakfast. AE, DISC, MC, V. **Amenities:** Jacuzzi. *In room:* TV, no phone.

The Inn at Jerome   This inn is located above a restaurant on Main Street. It has similar styling to the Ghost City Inn, but only two of its rooms have views across the valley. One unit has a rustic log bed so high that you have to climb up into it; the other rooms' options, including a wrought-iron bed, a spool bed, and a sleigh bed, are equally attractive. All units come with terry robes, ceiling fans, and evaporative coolers (almost as good as air-conditioning).

309 Main St. (P.O. Box 901), Jerome, AZ 86331. © **800/634-5094** or 520/634-5094. 8 units (2 with private bathroom). $55–$85 double. AE, DISC, MC, V. **Amenities:** Restaurant. *In room:* TV, no phone.

The Surgeon's House ⊛   Built in 1917 as the home of Jerome's resident surgeon, this Mediterranean-style building has a jaw-dropping view of the Verde Valley and is surrounded by beautiful gardens. All units are suites, but the old chauffeur's quarters, located in a separate cottage across the gardens, is the one to request. This unconventionally designed room has a wall of glass opposite the bed (so you can take in the view from under the covers), an old tub in one corner, and a wall of glass blocks around the toilet. The rooms in the main house are much more traditional, filled with antiques that conjure up Jerome's heyday.

101 Hill St. (P.O. Box 998), Jerome, AZ 86331. **©** **800/639-1452** or 520/639-1452. www.surgeonshouse.com. 4 units. $100–$150 suite. Rates include full breakfast. MC, V. Pets accepted ($25 per night). **Amenities:** Massage. *In room:* A/C, dataport, fridge, hair dryer.

WHERE TO DINE

Apizza Heaven PIZZA/SOUTHERN ITALIAN   These folks specialize in East Coast–style pizza. We like to get it to go (this place isn't very big) and then grab a seat with a view at the nearby public park. You can also dig into such things as a hearty eggplant parmigiana or a sausage and pepper sandwich.

Near the corner of Main St. and Hull Ave. **©** **520/649-1843.** Pizzas, pastas, sandwiches $6.50–$20. No credit cards. Thurs–Mon 11am–7 or 8pm, sometimes later on Fri–Sat.

Flatiron Café BREAKFAST/LIGHT MEALS   The tiny Flatiron Café is a simple breakfast-and-lunch spot in, you guessed it, Jerome's version of a flatiron building. The limited menu includes the likes of lox and bagels, a breakfast quesadilla, black-bean hummus, smoked-salmon quesadillas, fresh juices, and espresso drinks. It looks as though you could hardly squeeze in here, but there's more seating across the street. Definitely not your usual ghost-town lunch counter.

416 Main St. (at the corner of Hull Ave.) **©** **520/634-2733.** Breakfast, salads, sandwiches $4.25–$8. No credit cards. Thurs–Tues 8:30am–3pm.

4 The Verde Valley

Camp Verde: 30 miles S of Sedona; 95 miles N of Phoenix; 20 miles E of Jerome

With its headwaters in the Juniper Mountains of Prescott National Forest, the Verde River flows down through a rugged canyon before meandering slowly across the plains of the Verde Valley. Named by early Spanish explorers who were impressed at the sight of such a verdant valley in an otherwise brown desert landscape, it has long been a magnet for both wildlife and people. Today the valley is one of Arizona's richest agricultural and ranching regions and is quickly gaining popularity with retirees.

Long before the first European explorers entered the Verde Valley, the Sinagua people were living by the river and irrigating their fields with its waters. Sinagua ruins can still be seen at Tuzigoot and Montezuma national monuments, and there are even primitive cave dwellings along the banks of the river. By the time the first pioneers began settling in this region, the Sinaguas had long since disappeared, but Apaches had claimed the valley as part of their territory. Inevitably there were clashes with the Apaches, and the U.S. Army established Fort Verde to protect the settlers. Hundreds of years of Verde Valley history and prehistory can be viewed at sites such as Fort Verde State Park and the national monuments. This valley is also the site of the most scenic railroad excursion in the state.

ESSENTIALS

GETTING THERE   Camp Verde is just off I-17 at the junction with Ariz. 260. The latter highway leads northwest through the Verde Valley for 12 miles to Cottonwood.

VISITOR INFORMATION   Contact the **Cottonwood/Verde Valley Chamber of Commerce,** 1010 S. Main St., Cottonwood (**©** **520/634-7593;** http://chamber.verdevalley.com).

A RAILWAY EXCURSION

Verde Canyon Railroad   When the town of Jerome was busily mining copper, a railway was built to link the booming town with the territorial capital at nearby Prescott. Because of the rugged mountains between Jerome and Prescott, the railroad was forced to take a longer but less difficult route north along the Verde River before turning back south toward Prescott. Today you can ride these same tracks aboard the Verde Canyon Railroad. The route through the Verde River Canyon traverses both the remains of a copper smelter and unspoiled desert that's inaccessible by car and is part of the Prescott National Forest. The views of the rocky canyon walls and green waters of the Verde River are quite dramatic, and if you look closely along the way, you'll see ancient Sinagua cliff dwellings. In late winter and early spring, nesting bald eagles can also be spotted. Of the two excursion train rides in Arizona, this is by far the more scenic (although the Grand Canyon Railway certainly has a more impressive destination). Live music and a very informative narration make the ride entertaining as well.

300 N. Broadway, Clarkdale. ℭ **800/293-7245** or 520/639-0010. www.verdecanyonrr.com. Tickets $35.95 adults, $32.95 seniors, $20.95 children 2–12; first-class tickets $54.95. Call for schedule and reservations.

NATIONAL MONUMENTS & STATE PARKS

Fort Verde State Historic Park   Just south of Montezuma Castle and Montezuma's Well, in the town of Camp Verde, you'll find Fort Verde State Historic Park. Established in 1871, Fort Verde was the third military post in the Verde Valley and was occupied until 1891, by which time tensions with the Indian population had subsided and made the fort unnecessary. The military had first come to the Verde Valley in 1865 at the request of settlers who wanted protection from the local Tonto Apache and Yavapai. The tribes, traditionally hunters and gatherers, had been forced to raid the settlers' fields for food after their normal economy was disrupted by the sudden influx of whites and Mexicans into the area. Between 1873 and 1875, most of the Indians in the area were rounded up and forced to live on various reservations. An uprising in 1882 led to the last clash between local tribes and Fort Verde's soldiers.

Today the state park, which covers 10 acres, preserves three officers' quarters, an administration building, and some ruins. The buildings that have been fully restored house exhibits on the history of the fort and what life was like here in the 19th century. With their white lattices and picket fences, gables, and shake-shingle roofs, the buildings of Fort Verde suggest that life at this remote post was not so bad, at least for officers. Costumed military reenactments are held here on the second Saturday in October.

125 Holloman St. ℭ **520/567-3275.** Admission $2 adults, $1 children 7–13. Daily 8am–5pm.

Montezuma Castle National Monument ⭐   Despite the name, the ruins within this monument are neither castle nor Aztec dwelling—as the reference to Aztec ruler Moctezuma (traditionally Montezuma) implies. Rather, the Sinagua cliff dwelling, among the best preserved in Arizona, consists of two impressive stone pueblos that were, for some as-yet-unknown reason, abandoned by the Sinagua people, who disappeared without a trace in the early 14th century.

The more intriguing of the two ruins is set in a shallow cave 100 feet up a cliff overlooking Beaver Creek. Construction on this five-story, 20-room village began sometime in the early 12th century. Because Montezuma Castle has been protected from the elements by the overhanging roof of the cave in which it was built, the original adobe mud that was used to plaster over the stone walls of the dwelling is still intact. Another structure, containing 45 rooms on a total of six levels, stands at the base of the cliff. This latter dwelling, which has been subjected to rains and floods over the years, is not nearly as well preserved as the cliff dwelling. In the visitor center, you'll see artifacts that have been unearthed from the two ruins.

Located 11 miles north of Montezuma Castle (although still part of the national monument), **Montezuma Well** is a water-filled sinkhole that has for centuries served as an oasis in the desert. Occupied first by the Hohokam and later by the Sinagua, this sunken pond was formed when a cavern in the porous limestone bedrock collapsed. Underground springs quickly filled the sinkhole, which today contains a pond measuring 368 feet across and 65 feet deep. Over the centuries, the presence of year-round water attracted both the Hohokam and the Sinagua peoples, who built irrigation canals to use the water for growing crops. Some of these channels can still be seen. An excavated Hohokam pit house, built around 1100, and Sinagua houses and pueblos are clustered around the sinkhole.

Exit 289 off I-17. ✆ **520/567-3322.** www.nps./gov/moca. Admission $3 adults, free for children 16 and under; no charge to see Montezuma Well. Late May to early Sept daily 8am–7pm; early Sept to late May daily 8am–5pm.

Tuzigoot National Monument   Perched atop a hill overlooking the Verde River, this small, stone-walled pueblo was built by the Sinagua people, contemporaries of northern Arizona's Anasazi, and was inhabited between 1125 and 1400. The Sinagua, whose name is Spanish for "without water," were traditionally dry-land farmers relying entirely on rainfall to water their crops. When the Hohokam, who had been living in the Verde Valley since A.D. 600, moved on to more fertile land around 1100, the Sinagua moved into this valley. Their buildings progressed from individual homes called pit houses to communal pueblos.

An interpretive trail leads through the Tuzigoot ruins, explaining different aspects of Sinaguan life, and inside the visitor center is a small museum displaying many of the artifacts unearthed here. Desert plants, many of which were used by the Sinagua, are identified along the trail.

Just outside Clarkdale off U.S. 89A. ✆ **520/634-5564.** www.nps.gov/tuzi. Admission $2 adults, free for children 16 and under. Late May to early Sept daily 8am–7pm; early Sept to late May daily 8am–5pm.

Dead Horse Ranch State Park   On the outskirts of Cottonwood, not far from Tuzigoot National Monument, you'll find this state park. Set on the banks of the Verde River, it offers picnicking, fishing, swimming, hiking, and camping. Trails in the park lead through the riparian forests along the banks of the river and visit marshes that offer good bird-watching; they also lead into the adjacent national forest, so you can get in many miles of scenic hiking. The ranch was named in the 1940s, when the children of a family looking to buy it told their parents they wanted to buy the ranch with the dead horse by the side of the road.

675 Dead Horse Ranch Rd., Cottonwood. ✆ **520/634-5283.** Admission $4 per car. Daily 8am–8pm. From Main St. on the east side of Cottonwood, drive north on N. 10th St.

OTHER VERDE VALLEY ATTRACTIONS & ACTIVITIES
IN & AROUND CAMP VERDE

If you have an interest in 19th-century reenactments or antique cowboy and military gear, stop in at **Kicking Mule Outfitters,** 545 S. Main St., Camp Verde (✆ **520/567-2501**), which specializes in reproduction Western leather holsters, gun belts, saddles, and the like. It also sells Western antiques and rents equipment to movie companies. Another place worth a look is **White Hills Indian Arts,** 567 S. Main St. (© **520/567-3490**), housed in an 1883 stagecoach stop and specializing in Native American arts and crafts.

Horseback Adventures (© **520/567-5502**) offers rides ranging from 1 hour ($29) to all day ($120). One- and 2-hour rides along Beaver Creek and around Montezuma Castle are probably the most enjoyable if you haven't spent much time in the saddle.

For a completely different sort of entertainment, drop by the **Cliff Castle Casino,** 555 Middle Verde Rd. (© **800/381-SLOT**), at exit 289 off I-17.

If you want to do some wine tasting, visit the **San Dominique Winery** (© **480/945-8583**), 11 miles south of Camp Verde. To get here, take exit 278 off I-17 (the Cherry Road exit), go east, and then before the road turns to gravel, turn right on the dirt road that leads to the winery. You might have to look hard to see the winery's small sign. There are always plenty of wines available for tasting. The winery also sells lots of garlic-flavored foods, as well as different types of pickles. Sandwiches and light meals are available.

IN & AROUND COTTONWOOD & CLARKDALE

Cottonwood, 6 miles from Jerome, isn't nearly as atmospheric as the old copper town, but there are a few blocks of historic buildings slowly filling up with interesting shops that seem to be spillovers from the old hippie days in Jerome. A pleasant place to stroll is old-town Cottonwood's **Main Street,** one side of which has a covered sidewalk, along with several shops, galleries, and cafes. Also in town, though not right downtown, you'll find the **Clemenceau Heritage Museum,** 1 N. Willard St. (© **520/634-2868**), housed in an old school building. The most interesting display is a model railroad layout of the region's old system of mining railroads. It's open Wednesday from 9am to noon, Friday through Sunday from 11am to 3pm. Admission is free.

WHERE TO STAY

The Lodge at Cliff Castle   Although most people staying at this motel just off I-17 at exit 289 are here to do a little gambling in the adjacent Cliff Castle Casino, it also makes a good base for exploring the Verde Valley, the Sedona area, and even north to the Grand Canyon. Rooms are standard motel issue. There are a total of eight eating and drinking establishments, including one designed to look like a cave, plus a bowling alley.

333 Middle Verde Rd., Camp Verde, AZ 86322. © 800/524-6343 or 520/567-6611. Fax 520/567-9455. www.cliffcastle.com. 82 units. $59–$79 double. AE, DC, DISC, MC, V. **Amenities:** 5 restaurants (American, steakhouse), 3 lounges; outdoor pool (summer only); Jacuzzi; game room; baby-sitting; casino. *In room:* A/C, TV, coffeemaker, hair dryer.

WHERE TO DINE

Blazin' M Ranch Chuckwagon Suppers _Kids_ AMERICAN   Located adjacent to Dead Horse State Park, the Blazin' M Ranch is classic Arizona-style family entertainment—steaks and beans accompanied by cowboy music and comedy. This place is geared primarily toward the young 'uns, with pony rides, farm animals, and a little cow town for the kids to explore. If you're young at heart, you might enjoy the Blazin' M, but it's definitely more fun if you bring the whole family.

Off 10th St., Cottonwood. © 800/WEST-643 or 520/634-0334. www.blazinm.com. Reservations recommended. Dinner $19.95 adults, $9.95 children 10 and under. AE, DISC, MC, V. Wed–Sat gates open at 5pm, dinner at 6:30pm, show at 7:30pm. Closed Jan and Aug.

Gas Works Mexican Restaurant MEXICAN   If you happen to be hungry and can't hold out for Jerome (or couldn't handle the crowds up at the top of the hill), check out this colorful and eclectic hole in the wall in old Cottonwood. Basic homey cooking includes burritos, enchiladas, and, for the vegetarians among us, vegetable tamales and salads. Be sure to try the green corn tamales.

1033 N. Main St., Cottonwood. © **520/634-7426.** Meals $3–$7. No credit cards. Sun–Fri noon–4pm.

Main Street Cafe ⊛ SOUTHWESTERN   You'll find this casual and very reasonably priced restaurant between the modern strip malls and old-town Cottonwood. The menu is a mix of both the familiar (fajitas and seafood linguine) and more creative dishes. It is in the latter realm that the restaurant usually shines. The green corn tamale in chipotle cream sauce makes a savory starter, or try the Southwest corn chowder. Steak fans shouldn't miss the Southwest blackened sirloin with fresh salsa. In case the extensive wine list throws you for a loop, the chef offers his own wine recommendations for each dish.

315 S. Main St., Cottonwood. © **520/639-4443.** www.main-street-cafe.net. Reservations recommended. Main courses $10–$24. DISC, MC, V. Tues–Sat 11am–3pm and 5–9 or 10pm.

Murphy's Grill ⊛ AMERICAN   With a cheerful and lively atmosphere reminiscent of other Murphy's properties in Prescott, the main focus here is on decently prepared salads, sandwiches, pastas, pizzas, and rotisserie chicken. Service is speedy, and there's a full bar.

747 S. Main St. © **520/634-7272.** Main courses $6–$17. AE, DISC, MC, V. Daily 11am–10pm.

Old Town Café *Finds* CAFE   The almond croissants at this European-style cafe in downtown Cottonwood are the best we've ever had, period. If that isn't recommendation enough for you, there are also good salads and sandwiches, such as a grilled panini of smoked turkey, spinach, and tomatoes.

1025 "A" N. Main St. © **520/634-5980.** Sandwiches $5–$6. No credit cards. Tues–Fri 7am–4pm; Sat 8am–3pm.

Pinon Bistro ⊛⊛ NEW AMERICAN   Tucked into a small, nondescript office plaza next door to a budget motel, this restaurant is the most upscale and sophisticated place in Cottonwood. Pinon's style and menu, which changes every week, both draw heavily on the bistros of southern France for inspiration. Not only can you savor such dishes as a chevre-and-leek tart or butternut squash–filled ravioli with sage cream and toasted pine nuts, but there's also often opera on the stereo and lots of good wine to accompany your meal.

1075 Hwy. 260, Cottonwood. © **520/649-0234.** Reservations recommended. Main courses $15–$21. No credit cards. Thurs–Sun 5–8 or 9pm.

5 Sedona & Oak Creek Canyon ⊛⊛

106 miles S of the Grand Canyon; 116 miles N of Phoenix; 56 miles NE of Prescott

Although in recent years housing developments and strip malls have sprawled across the hills at the mouth of Oak Creek Canyon, the town of Sedona can still claim the most beautiful setting in the Southwest. Red-rock buttes, eroded canyon walls, and mesas rise into blue skies. Off in the distance, the Mogollon Rim looms, its forests of juniper and ponderosa pine dark against the rocks. Imagine a cross between Monument Valley and a wealthy Southern California suburb, and you have a pretty good idea of Sedona today.

However, with national forest surrounding the city (and even extending fingers of forest into what would otherwise be the city limits), Sedona has some of the best outdoor access of any city in the Southwest. All over, alongside highways and down side streets in suburban neighborhoods, there are trailheads. Head down any one of these trails, and you leave the city behind and enter the world of the red rocks. Just don't be surprised if you come around a bend in the trail and find yourself in the middle of a wedding ceremony or a group of 30 people doing tai chi.

Located at the mouth of Oak Creek Canyon, Sedona was first settled by pioneers in 1877 and named for the first postmaster's wife. Word of Sedona's beauty did not begin to spread until Hollywood filmmakers began using the region's red rock as backdrop to their Western films. Next came artists, lured by the landscapes and desert light (it was here in Sedona that the Cowboy Artists of America organization was formed). Although still much touted as an artists' community, Sedona's art scene these days is geared more toward tourists than toward collectors of fine works.

More recently, the spectacular views and mild climate were discovered by retirees. Sedona's hills are now alive with the sound of construction as ostentatious retirement mansions and celebrity trophy homes sprout from the dust like desert toads after an August rainstorm. When, quite a few years back, a New Age channeler discovered the "Sedona vortexes," yet another group discovered that Sedona was where their cosmic energy fields converged. Most recently, mountain bikers have begun to ride the red rock, and word is spreading that the biking here is almost as good as up north in Moab, Utah.

The waters of Oak Creek were what first attracted settlers and native peoples to this area, and today this stream still lures visitors to Sedona—especially in summer, when the cool shade and even cooler creek waters are a glorious respite from the heat of the desert. Two of Arizona's finest swimming holes are located on Oak Creek, only a few miles from Sedona, and one of these, Slide Rock, has been made into a state park.

With its drop-dead scenery, dozens of motels and resorts, and plethora of good restaurants, Sedona makes an excellent base for exploring central Arizona. Several ancient Indian ruins (including an impressive cliff dwelling), the "ghost town" of Jerome, and the scenic Verde Canyon Railroad are all within easy driving distance, and even the Grand Canyon is but a long day trip away.

ESSENTIALS

GETTING THERE Sedona is on Ariz. 179 at the mouth of scenic Oak Creek Canyon. From Phoenix, take I-17 to Ariz. 179 north. From Flagstaff, head south on I-17 until you see the turnoff for Ariz. 89A and Sedona. Ariz. 89A also connects Sedona with Prescott.

Sedona Phoenix Shuttle (© **800/448-7988** in Arizona, or 520/282-2066) operates several trips daily between the Phoenix Sky Harbor Airport and Sedona. The fare is $35 one way, $60 round-trip.

VISITOR INFORMATION The **Sedona–Oak Creek Chamber of Commerce** (© **800/288-7336** or 520/282-7722; www.sedonachamber.com) operates a visitor center at the corner of Ariz. 89A and Forest Road near uptown Sedona.

GETTING AROUND Whether traveling by car or on foot, you'll need to cultivate patience when trying to cross major roads in Sedona. Traffic here, especially on weekends, is some of the worst in the state. Also be prepared for slow traffic on roads that have good views; drivers are often distracted by the red rocks. You may hear or see references to the **"Y,"** which refers to the intersection

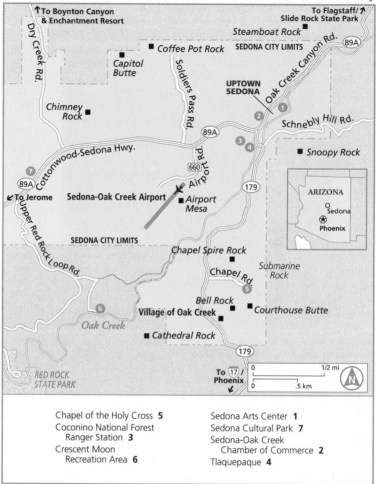

Chapel of the Holy Cross **5**
Coconino National Forest
   Ranger Station **3**
Crescent Moon
   Recreation Area **6**

Sedona Arts Center **1**
Sedona Cultural Park **7**
Sedona-Oak Creek
   Chamber of Commerce **2**
Tlaquepaque **4**

of Ariz. 179 and Ariz. 89A between the Tlaquepaque shopping plaza and uptown Sedona.

Rental cars are available through **Enterprise** (© **800/RENT-A-CAR** or 520/282-2052), **Practical Rent-a-Car** (© **800/464-8697** or 520/282-6702), and **Sedona Car Rentals** (© **800/879-JEEP or** 520/282-2227). For about $150 a day, you can rent a Jeep from **Sedona Jeep Rentals** (© **800/879-JEEP** or 520/282-2227).

For taxi service, call **Bob's Taxi** (© **520/282-1234**).

SPECIAL EVENTS The **Sedona International Film Festival** (© **800/ 780-ARTS** or 520/203-4TIX; www.sedonaculturalpark.org), held in early March, has been booking quite a few interesting films.

One of the year's biggest events is the world-class **Sedona Chamber Music Festival,** held in mid-May; call © **520/204-2415** or go to www. chambermusicsedona.org for details.

The **Jazz on the Rocks Benefit Festival** is held on the fourth weekend in September in an outdoor amphitheater with a superb view of the red rocks. Tickets range from $40 to $200. For information, call ℂ **520/282-1985** or see www.sedonajazz.com.

In early October (usually a week after the jazz festival), an annual benefit for the Native American Scholarship Project called the **Verde Valley Music Festival** is staged by Jackson Browne. This concert always includes musical friends of Browne's, such as Bruce Cockburn, Crosby, Stills & Nash, and Marc Cohn. The concert is held at the Verde Valley School's Warren Amphitheater; for information, contact the school at ℂ **520/284-2272,** ext. 130.

In early December, Sedona celebrates the **Festival of Lights** at Tlaquepaque (ℂ **800/288-7336** or 520/282-4838) by lighting thousands of luminárias (paper bags partially filled with sand and containing a single candle). From Thanksgiving eve until early January, more than a million lights illuminate Los Abrigados Resort (ℂ **520/282-1777**) in a **Red-Rock Fantasy.**

EXPLORING RED-ROCK COUNTRY

Rugged cliffs, needlelike pinnacles, and isolated buttes rise up from the green forest floor at the mouth of Oak Creek Canyon in Sedona. Layers of different-colored stone deposited during various prehistoric ages form bands through the cliffs above. Because this rosy sandstone predominates around Sedona, the region has come to be known as the red-rock country. Each evening at sunset, the rocks put on a light show that is reason enough for visiting Sedona.

Days can be spent exploring the red-rock country in any of half a dozen different modes of transport. There are Jeep tours, hot-air-balloon flights, horseback rides, mountain-bike trails, hiking trails, and scenic drives suitable for standard cars. (See the following sections, "Organized Tours" and "Sports & Outdoor Pursuits.")

Although in the past it has been possible for passenger cars to drive **Schnebly Hill Road** for superb views of Sedona, the road is no longer regularly maintained. However, it is worth checking at the visitor center (see "Visitor Information," above) to see if it is once again passable in a regular car. If so, head south out of Sedona on Ariz. 179, turn left after you cross the bridge over Oak Creek, and head up the dirt road. The road climbs up into the hills above town, every turn yielding a new and breathtaking view, and eventually reaching the top of the Mogollon Rim. At the rim is the Schnebly Hill overlook, offering the very best view in the area.

Just south of Sedona, on Ariz. 179, you'll see the aptly named **Bell Rock** on the east side of the road. There's a parking area at the foot of Bell Rock and trails leading up to the top. From Bell Rock, you can see **Cathedral Rock** to the west. This rock is the most photographed formation in Sedona. Adjacent to Bell Rock is **Courthouse Rock,** and not far from Bell Rock and visible from Chapel Road are **Eagle Head Rock** (from the front door of the Chapel of the Holy Cross—see "Attractions & Activities Around Town," below—look three-quarters of the way up the mountain to see the eagle's head), the **Twin Nuns** (two pinnacles standing side by side), and **Mother and Child Rock** to the left of the Twin Nuns.

If you head west out of Sedona on U.S. 89A and turn left onto Airport Road, you'll drive up onto **Airport Mesa,** which consists of three small hills commanding an unobstructed panorama of Sedona and the red rocks. About halfway up the mesa is a small parking area from which trails radiate. The views from here are among the best in the region, and the trails are very easy.

C **Vortex Power**

In recent years, Sedona has been one of the world's centers for the New Age movement; large numbers of people come to experience the "power vortexes" of the surrounding red-rock country. You'll see local bulletin boards and publications advertising such diverse New Age services as past-life regressions, crystal healing, angelic healing, tarot readings, reiki, axiatonal therapy, electromagnetic field balancing, soul recovery, channeling, aromatherapy, myofacial release, and aura photos and videos.

According to believers, a vortex is a site where the earth's unseen lines of power intersect to form a particularly powerful energy field. Page Bryant, an adherent of New Age beliefs, determined through channeling that there were four vortexes around Sedona. Scientists may scoff, but Sedona's vortexes have become so well known that the visitor center has several handouts to explain them and a map to guide you to them. (Many of the most spectacular geological features of the Sedona landscape also happen to be vortexes.)

The four main vortexes include Bell Rock, Cathedral Rock, Airport Mesa, and Boynton Canyon. **Bell Rock** and **Airport Mesa** are both said to contain masculine or electric energy that boosts emotional, spiritual, and physical energy. **Cathedral Rock** is said to contain feminine or magnetic energy, good for facilitating relaxation. The **Boynton Canyon** vortex is considered an electromagnetic energy site, which means it has a balance of both masculine and feminine energy.

If you're not familiar with vortexes and want to learn more about the ones in Sedona, consider a vortex tour. These are offered by several companies, including **Earth Wisdom Tours** (*C* **800/482-4714** or 520/282-4714), **Spirit Steps** (*C* **800/728-4562** or 520/282-4562), and **Vortex Tours** (*C* **520/282-2733**). All three offer tours that combine aspects of Native American and New Age beliefs. Tours last about 3 hours and cost about $55 to $60 per person.

You can also stock up on books, crystals, and other spiritual supplies at stores such as **Crystal Magic**, 2978 W. Hwy. 89A (*C* **520/282-1622**), or **Center for the New Age**, 341 Hwy. 179 (*C* **520/282-2085**).

One of the most beautiful areas around Sedona is **Boynton Canyon**, located 8 miles from the "Y." To get here, drive west out of Sedona on U.S. 89A, turn right on Dry Creek Road, take a left at the T intersection, and at the next T take a right. On the way to Boynton Canyon, look north from U.S. 89A, and you'll see **Coffee Pot Rock,** which is also known as Rooster Rock, rising 1,800 feet above Sedona. Three pinnacles, known as the **Three Golden Chiefs** by the Yavapai tribe, stand beside Coffee Pot Rock. As you drive up Dry Creek Road, on your right you'll see **Capitol Butte,** which resembles the U.S. Capitol building. Just outside the gates of Enchantment Resort is a parking area for the **Boynton Canyon Trail.** From the parking area, the trail leads 3 miles up into the canyon. The ancient Sinagua people once lived in Boynton Canyon, and the ruins of their homes can still be seen.

The High Cost of Red-Rock Views

A quick perusal of any Sedona real-estate magazine will convince you that property values around these parts are as high as the Mogollon Rim. However, red-rock realty is also expensive for those who want only a glimpse of the rocks. With the land around Sedona split up into several types of National Forest Service day-use sites, state parks, and national monuments, visitors find themselves pulling out their wallets just about every time they turn around to look at another rock. Here's the lowdown on what it's going to cost you to do the red rocks right.

Depending on how long you're spending in the area and how much you want to see, you'll want to get a **Red Rock Pass,** which will allow you to visit Palatki Ruins and the V-Bar-V petroglyph site and park at any national forest trailhead parking areas. The cost is $5 for a 1-day pass, $15 for a 7-day pass, and $20 for a 12-month pass. Passes are good for everyone in your vehicle. If you plan to be in the area for more than a week and also want to visit Grasshopper Point (a swimming hole), Banjo Bill (a picnic area), Call of the Canyon (the West Fork Oak Creek trailhead), and Crescent Moon recreation sites (Sedona's top photo-op site), you'll want to buy a **Red Rock Grand Pass** for $40. Individually, these sites each charge a $5 admission, so if you aren't planning on going to all of them or you don't expect to be around for more than a week, the Red Rock Grand Pass is not a good deal.

There are also two state parks in the area—Slide Rock and Red Rock—both of which charge $5 per car. However, for $15 you can also get a pass good for admission to five state parks. Admission to Montezuma Castle or Tuzigoot national monuments will cost you $2 or $3 per adult. However, if there are two or more of you traveling together and you are planning on visiting the Grand Canyon and three or four other national parks or monuments, you might want to consider getting a National Parks Pass ($50) or a Golden Eagle Pass ($65). These passes are good for a year and will get you into any national park or national monument in the country. If you're 62 or older, definitely get a Golden Age Pass; it's only $10 and is good for the rest of your life. A Golden Age Pass will also get you a Red Rock Pass for half price.

In this same area, you can visit the well-preserved Sinagua cliff dwellings at **Palatki Ruins,** set in a beautiful canyon. To reach the ruins, follow the directions to Boynton Canyon, but instead of turning right at the second T intersection, turn left onto unpaved Boynton Pass Road (Forest Road 152), which is one of the most scenic roads in the area and is well worth driving even if you don't go to Palatki. Follow this road to another T intersection and go right onto FR 125, then veer right onto FR 795, which dead-ends at the ruins. You can also get here by taking Ariz. 89A west from Sedona to FR 525, a gravel road leading north to FR 795. To visit Palatki, you'll need a Red Rock Pass (see "The High Cost of Red-Rock Views," below); ruins are usually open daily from 9:30am to 4:30pm. Don't try coming out here if the roads are at all muddy.

South of Ariz. 89A and a bit west of the turnoff for Boynton Canyon is Upper Red Rock Loop Road, which leads to **Crescent Moon Recreation Area** (formerly known as Red Rock Crossing), a National Forest Service recreation area that has become a must-see for almost everyone who visits Sedona. Its popularity stems from a beautiful photograph of Oak Creek with **Cathedral Rock** in the background—an image that has been reproduced countless times in Sedona promotional literature and on postcards. Hiking trails lead up to Cathedral Rock. Admission is $5, unless you have previously purchased a Red Rock Grand Pass (see "The High Cost of Red-Rock Views," below, for details).

If you continue on Upper Red Rock Loop Road, it becomes gravel for a while before turning into Lower Red Rock Loop Road and reaching **Red Rock State Park** (② 520/282-6907), which flanks Oak Creek. The views here take in many of the rocks listed above, and you have the additional bonus of being right on the creek (but no swimming or wading is allowed). The park entry fee is $5 per vehicle.

South of Sedona, near the junction of I-17 and Ariz. 179, you can visit an ancient petroglyph site at the **V Bar V Ranch.** To reach this site, head east several miles on the marked dirt road that leads to the Beaver Creek Campground. The entrance to the petroglyph site is just past the campground. From the parking area, it's about a half-mile walk to the petroglyphs. The site is open Friday through Monday from 9:30am to 4pm. To visit this site, you'll need to purchase a Red Rock Pass for $5.

OAK CREEK CANYON

The **Mogollon Rim** (pronounced *Mug-ee-un* by the locals) is a 2,000-foot escarpment cutting diagonally across central Arizona and on into New Mexico. At the top of the Mogollon Rim are the ponderosa pine forests of the high mountains, while at the bottom the lowland deserts begin. Of the many canyons cutting down from the rim, Oak Creek Canyon is the most beautiful (and one of the few that has a paved road down through it).

Ariz. 89A runs through the canyon from Flagstaff to Sedona, winding its way down from the rim and paralleling Oak Creek. Along the way are overlooks, parks, picnic areas, campgrounds, cabin resorts, and small inns.

If you have a choice of how first to view Oak Creek Canyon, approach it from the north. Your first stop after traveling south from Flagstaff will be the **Oak Creek Canyon Vista,** which provides a view far down the valley to Sedona and beyond. The overlook is at the edge of the Mogollon Rim, and the road suddenly drops in tight switchbacks just south of here. You may notice that one rim of the canyon is lower than the other. This is because Oak Creek Canyon is on a geologic fault line; one side of the canyon is moving in a different direction from the other.

Although the top of the Mogollon Rim is a ponderosa pine forest and the bottom a desert, Oak Creek Canyon supports a forest of sycamores and other deciduous trees. There is no better time to drive scenic Ariz. 89A than between late September and mid-October, when the canyon is ablaze with red and yellow leaves.

In the desert, swimming holes are powerful magnets during the hot summer months, and consequently **Slide Rock State Park** (② 520/282-3034), located 7 miles north of Sedona on the site of an old homestead, is the most popular spot in all of Oak Creek Canyon. What pulls in the crowds of families and teenagers is the park's natural water slide and great little swimming hole. On hot days the park is jammed with people splashing in the water and sliding over the algae-covered sandstone bottom of Oak Creek. Sunbathing and fishing are other popular pastimes. If you aren't intending to swim, you could probably give this place a miss, but if you've got the kids along, don't leave the area without spending an afternoon here. The park is open daily; admission is $5 per vehicle. There's another popular swimming area at **Grasshopper Point,** several miles closer to Sedona. Admission is $5 per vehicle, unless you have previously purchased a Red Rock Grand Pass.

Within Oak Creek Canyon, several hikes of different lengths are possible. By far the most spectacular and popular is the 6-mile round-trip hike up the **West Fork of Oak Creek.** This is a classic canyon-country hike with steep canyon walls rising up from the creek. At some points, the canyon is no more than 20 feet wide with walls rising up more than 200 feet. You can extend the hike many more miles up the canyon for an overnight backpacking trip. The trailhead for the West Fork hike is at the Call of the Canyon Recreation Area, which charges a $5 day-use fee unless you have already purchased a Red Rock Grand Pass.

Stop by the Sedona–Oak Creek Chamber of Commerce to pick up a free map listing hikes in the area. The **Coconino National Forest's Sedona Ranger Station** (© 520/282-4119), on Brewer Road just west of the intersection of Ariz. 89A and Ariz. 179, is also a good source of hiking information. Also check out www.redrockcountry.org.

If you get thirsty while driving through the canyon, hold out for **Garlands General Store,** in Indian Gardens, about 4 miles north of Sedona. Here you can get delicious organic apple juice made from apples grown in the canyon. For one last view down the canyon, stop at **Midgely Bridge** (just watch for the parked cars and small parking area at the north end of the bridge).

ATTRACTIONS & ACTIVITIES AROUND TOWN

Sedona's most notable architectural landmark is the **Chapel of the Holy Cross** (© 520/282-4069), a small church built right into the red rock on the south side of town. If you're driving up from Phoenix, you can't miss the chapel. It sits high above the road just off Ariz. 179. With its contemporary styling, the chapel is one of the most architecturally important modern churches in the country. Marguerite Brunswig Staude, a devout Catholic painter, sculptor, and designer, had the inspiration for the chapel in 1932, but it wasn't until 1957 that her dream was finally realized. The chapel's design is dominated by a simple cross forming the wall that faces the street. The cross and the starkly beautiful chapel seem to grow directly from the rock, allowing the natural beauty of the red rock to speak for itself. It's open Monday through Saturday from 9am to 5pm, Sunday from 10am to 5pm.

The **Sedona Arts Center,** Ariz. 89A at Art Barn Road (© **520/282-3865** or 520/282-3809), near the north end of town, serves both as a gallery for work by local and regional artists and as a theater for plays and music performances.

To learn a bit about the local history, stop by the **Sedona Heritage Museum,** 735 Jordan Rd. (© **520/282-7038**), in Jordan Historical Park. The museum, which is housed in a historic home, is furnished with antiques and contains exhibits on the many movies that have been filmed in the area over the years. The farm was once an apple orchard, and there's still apple-processing equipment in the barn. It's open daily from 11am to 4pm, with a suggested donation of $3.

Out on the west side of town, the **Sedona Cultural Park,** on Ariz. on 89A
(✆ **800/780-2787** or 520/282-0747; www.sedonaculturalpark.org), is home to
an amphitheater; buildings for classes, workshops, and exhibitions; and nature
trails and picnic areas.

While Sedona isn't yet a resort destination on par with Phoenix or Tucson, it
does have a few **spas** and treatment centers that might add just the right bit of
pampering to your vacation. **Therapy on the Rocks,** 676 N. Hwy. 89A
(✆ **520/282-3002**), with its creek-side setting, is a long-time local favorite that
offers myofacial release and great views of the red rocks. At Los Abrigados resort,
you'll find the more traditional **Sedona Health Spa,** 160 Portal Lane
(✆ **520/282-1777**), with a wide selection of body and beauty treatments,
including seaweed facials and mineral wraps.

ORGANIZED TOURS

For an overview of Sedona, take a tour on the **Sedona Trolley** (✆ **520/
282-5400**), which leaves several times daily on two separate tours. One tour visits Tlaquepaque, the Chapel of the Holy Cross, and several art galleries, while
the other goes out through west Sedona to Boynton Canyon and Enchantment
Resort. Tours are $8 for adults and $3 for children 12 and under. Call for the
trolley stop nearest you.

The red-rock country surrounding Sedona is the city's greatest natural attraction, and there's no better way to explore it than by four-wheel-drive vehicle. If
you're not inclined to rent your own Jeep, there are plenty of tour options. For
more than 35 years, **Pink Jeep Tours,** 204 N. Hwy. 89A (✆ **800/873-3662** or
520/282-5000; www.pinkjeep.com), has been heading deep into the Coconino
National Forest. It offers tours ranging in length from 1½ to 2½ hours. For a
trip over the red rocks and for better value, you're best off springing for the
2-hour "Broken Arrow" tour ($60). **Sedona Adventures,** 276 N. Hwy. 89A
(✆ **800/888-9494** or 520/282-3500; www.sedonaadventures.com), is affiliated
with Pink Jeep Tours, but offers a couple of different excursions. Ask for the
Premier Tour, which visits one of the area's unusual sinkholes.

Sedona Red Rock Jeep Tours, 270 N. Hwy. 89A (✆ **800/848-7728** or
520/282-6826; www.redrockjeep.com), offers similar tours for $32 to $58, as
well as helicopter-Jeep tours, horseback rides, and even a seasonal canoe tour to
cave dwellings on the Verde River. If you want some photographic tips while you
tour red-rock country, try **Sedona Photo Tours,** 252 N. Hwy. 89A (✆ **800/
973-3662** or 520/282-4320; www.adayinthewest.com), which operates the
Kodak-yellow Jeeps you see around town.

Several companies can give an aerial view of the area. **Arizona Helicopter
Adventures** (✆ **800/282-5141** or 520/282-0904) and **Skydance Helicopters**
(✆ **800/882-1651** or 520/282-1651) both offer short flights to different parts
of this colorful region. Prices start around $40 for a 10-minute flight. **AeroVista**
(✆ **520/282-7768;** www.aerovista.com) and **Sky Safari Air Tours** (✆ **888/
TOO-RIDE** or 520/204-5939; www.sedonaairtours.com) offer a variety of
flights in small planes. Prices start at around $45 to $55 for 25 minutes. Flights
as far afield as the Grand Canyon and Canyon de Chelly can be arranged.

Our favorite is **Red Rock Biplane Tours** (✆ **888/TOO-RIDE** or
520/204-5939), which operates modern Waco open-cockpit biplanes. With the
wind in your hair, you'll feel as though you've entered the world of *The English
Patient.* A 20-minute tour is about $65 per person.

If something a bit slower is more your speed, try a peaceful ride on a hot-air balloon. **Northern Light Balloon Expeditions** (© 800/230-6222 or 520/282-2274) and **Red Rock Balloon Adventures** (© 800/258-3754 or 520/284-0040; www.redrockballoons.com) fly over the sculpted red buttes of Sedona and charge $145 to $155 per person. **Sky High Balloon Adventures** (© 800/551-7597 or 520/204-1395; www.skyhighballoons.com) floats 14 miles outside of Sedona over the Verde River and charges $135 per person.

OUTDOOR PURSUITS

Hiking is by far the most popular outdoor activity in the Sedona area, and with dozens of trails leading off into the red rocks, it's easy to understand why. The easiest and most convenient place to get some red dust on your boots is along the **Bell Rock Pathway,** which begins alongside Ariz. 179 just north of the Village of Oak Creek. This trail winds around the base of Bell Rock and accesses many other trails that lead up on to the slopes of Bell Rock. It's about 5 miles to go all the way around Bell Rock. The ¾-mile **Cathedral Rock Trail** is another great route on the south side of Sedona. This trail follows cairns (piles of rocks) up the slick-rock slopes on the north side of Cathedral Rock. To reach this trail, turn off Ariz. 179 at the sign for the Back o' Beyond housing development and watch for the trailhead at the end of the paved road. Perhaps the most popular trails in the area are those that lead into Boynton Canyon (site of Enchantment Resort). Here you'll glimpse ancient Native American ruins built into the red-rock cliffs. Although the scenery is indeed stupendous, the great numbers of other hikers on the trail detract considerably from the experience. The 1½-mile **Vultee Arch Trail,** which leads to an impressive sandstone arch, is another great hike. The trailhead is 2 miles up Dry Creek Road. For the hands-down best views in Sedona, hike all or part of the **Airport Mesa Trail,** a 3½-mile loop that circles Airport Mesa. With virtually no elevation gain, this is an easy hike. You'll find the trailhead about halfway to the top of Airport Mesa on Airport Road. For more information on hiking in Oak Creek Canyon (site of the famous West Fork Trail), see "Oak Creek Canyon," above. For more information on all these hikes, contact the **Coconino National Forest's Sedona Ranger Station** (© 520/282-4119), on Brewer Road just west of the intersection of Ariz. 89A and Ariz. 179.

Sedona is rapidly becoming one of the Southwest's meccas for **mountain biking.** The red rock here is every bit as challenging and scenic as the famed slick-rock country of Moab, Utah, and much less crowded. Using Sedona as a base, mountain bikers can ride year-round by heading up to Flagstaff in summer and down to the desert lowlands in winter. One of our favorite places to ride is around the base of Bell Rock. Starting at the trailhead parking area just north of the Village of Oak Creek, you'll find not only the easy Bell Rock Path but also numerous more challenging trails. Another great ride starts above uptown Sedona, where you can ride the Jim Thompson Trail to Midgely Bridge or the network of trails that head toward Soldier Pass. The riding here is moderate and the views are superb. To reach these trails, take Jordan Road to a left onto Park Ridge Road, and follow this road to where it ends at a dirt trailhead parking area. You can rent bikes from **Sedona Sports,** Creekside Plaza below the "Y" (© 520/282-1317), or **Mountain Bike Heaven,** 1695 W. Hwy. 89A (© 520/282-1312). Rates are around $25 to $35 per day. **Sedona Bike & Bean,** 6020 Hwy. 179 (© 520/284-0210; www.bike-bean.com), across the street from the popular Bell Rock Pathway and its adjacent mountain-bike trails, rents bikes (and serves coffee). Bikes go for $35 for a full day. Any of these stores can sell you the *Epic Sedona* map or Cosmic Ray's *Fat Tire Tales and Trails* guidebook to the best rides in Arizona.

Trail Horse Adventures at Kachina Stables, Lower Red Rock Loop Road (© **800/SADDLE-UP** or 520/282-7252; www.trailhorseadventures.com), offers guided horseback trail rides. Prices range from $30 for a 1-hour ride to $135 for an all-day ride (minimum two people; includes lunch). There are also breakfast, lunch, sunset, and multiday pack trips. Lower Red Rock Loop Road is west of Sedona on Ariz. 89A. **Sedona Red Rock Jeep Tours** (© **800/848-7728** or 520/282-6826; www.redrockjeep.com) offers horseback rides ($42 for 1 hour, $55 for 2 hours) that include transportation by Jeep to the ranch where the rides are held.

Oak Creek is well known in Arizona as an excellent trout stream, and **fly-fishing** is quite popular here. The creek is stocked with trout during the summer. If you're looking for a fly-fishing guide, call Jim McInnis of **Gon' Fishen** (© **520/282-0788**). If you want to take the family fishing, try the **Rainbow Trout Farm,** 3500 N. Ariz. 89A (© **520/282-3379**), 4 miles north of Sedona.

Surprisingly, Sedona has not yet been ringed with **golf** courses. However, what few courses there are offer superb views to distract you from your game. The **Oak Creek Country Club,** 690 Bell Rock Blvd. (© **520/284-1660**), south of town off Ariz. 179, has stunning views from the course. Greens fees are $50 to $80. The **Sedona Golf Resort** ✸✸, 35 Ridge Trail Dr. (© **520/284-9355**), south of town on Ariz. 179, offers similarly excellent views of the red rocks; greens fees are $82 to $99.

SHOPPING

Ever since the Cowboy Artists of America organization was founded in Sedona back in 1965 (at what is now the Cowboy Club restaurant), this town has had a reputation as an artists' community. Today, with dozens of galleries around town, it's obvious that art is one of the driving forces behind the local economy. Most of Sedona's galleries specialize in traditional Western, contemporary Southwestern, and Native American art, and in some galleries, you'll see works by members of the Cowboy Artists of America. You'll find the greatest concentration of galleries and shops in the uptown area of Sedona (along Ariz. 89A just north of the "Y") and in the Tlaquepaque Arts and Crafts Village.

With more than 40 stores and restaurants, **Tlaquepaque Arts & Crafts Village,** on Ariz. 179 at the bridge over Oak Creek on the south side of Sedona (© **520/282-4838;** www.tlaquepaque.net), is designed to resemble a Mexican village and is named after a famous arts-and-crafts neighborhood in the suburbs of Guadalajara. The maze of narrow alleys, connecting courtyards, fountains, and even a chapel and a bell tower, are worth a visit even if you aren't in a buying mood. We wish all shopping centers were such fascinating places. Most of the shops sell high-end art.

Unfortunately, many of Sedona's shops now specialize in cheap Southwestern gifts that have little to do with art, and weeding through the tackiness to find the real galleries can be difficult. One place to start is at **Hozho,** with a couple of Sedona's better galleries, on Ariz. 179 just before you cross over the Oak Creek bridge in Sedona.

Compass Rose Gallery   Oddly out of place, but certainly welcome on the souvenir-oriented Sedona shopping scene, this store sells old maps (up to $3,000), old prints, and Edward S. Curtis sepia-toned photos. Hillside Sedona, 671 Ariz. 179. © **520/282-7904.** www.oldmaps.com.

Cowboy Corral   If you want to adopt the Wyatt Earp or Annie Oakley look, this shop can outfit you. Definitely not your standard urban cowboy shop, Cowboy Corral goes for the vintage look. Classic firearms are available to accessorize your ensemble. 219 N. Hwy. 89A. 📞 800/457-2279 or 520/282-2040.

Garland's Indian Jewelry   A great location in the shade of scenic Oak Creek Canyon and a phenomenal collection of concho belts, squash blossom necklaces, and bracelets make this a worthwhile stop. At Indian Gardens, 4 miles north on Ariz. 89A. 📞 520/282-6632.

Garland's Navajo Rugs   With a large collection of both contemporary and antique Navajo rugs (claimed to be the biggest in the world), Garland's is the premier Navajo rug shop in Sedona. It also carries a line of Native American baskets and pottery, Hopi kachina dolls, and Navajo sand paintings. 411 Hwy. 179. 📞 520/282-4070. www.garlandsrugs.com.

Hillside Sedona   This shopping center is dedicated to art galleries, retail shops, and a couple of restaurants. Here you'll find the Clay Pigeon, with some nice ceramics and glass, and the Scherer Gallery (see below). 671 Hwy. 179. 📞 520/282-4500. www.hillsidesedona.com.

Hoel's Indian Shop   Located 10 miles north of Sedona in a private residence in Oak Creek Canyon (just past Hoel's Cabins), this Native American arts-and-crafts gallery is one of the finest in the region and sells pieces of the highest quality. Most customers are serious collectors. It's a good idea to call before coming out to make sure the store will be open. 9440 N. Hwy. 89A. 📞 520/282-3925. www.hoels.com.

Prime Outlets   Yes, even Sedona (or, more correctly, the community of the Village of Oak Creek) has an outlet mall. If you aren't in the market for art, but do need some cut-rate fashions, this is the place. Hwy. 179, Village of Oak Creek. 📞 888/545-7227 or 520/284-2150. www.primeoutlets.com.

Scherer Gallery   What makes this gallery unique is its collection of kaleidoscopes, which may be the largest in the country. More than 100 kaleidoscope artists from around the world create these colorful concoctions. You'll also find art glass, tasteful contemporary paintings, and Jack Acrey's large-format photographs of red-rock landscapes. Hillside Sedona, 671 Hwy. 179. 📞 800/957- or 2673 520/203-9000.

Sedona Arts Center Gallery Shop   Located at the north end of uptown Sedona, this shop is the best place in town to see the work of area artists—everything from jewelry and fiber arts to photography and ceramics. Since it's a nonprofit shop, you won't pay any tax here. Ariz. 89A and Art Barn Rd. 📞 520/282-3865.

Son Silver West   For those who love everything Southwestern, this shop is a treasure trove of all kinds of interesting stuff, including Native American and Hispanic arts and crafts, antique *santo* (saint) carvings, rifles, imported pots, chile garlands (*ristras*), and garden art. 1476 Hwy. 179 (on the south side of town). 📞 520/282-3580.

WHERE TO STAY

Sedona is one of the most popular destinations in the Southwest, with dozens of inexpensive and moderately priced motels in town. However, keep in mind that accommodations are often relatively expensive for what you get. Blame it on the incomparable views. Below are some of our favorites of the many hotels, resorts, and B&Bs in the Sedona area.

EXPENSIVE

Briar Patch Inn ★★ Value   If you're searching for tranquility or a romantic retreat amid the cool shade of Oak Creek Canyon, this is the place. Located 3 miles north of Sedona on the banks of Oak Creek (there are even swimming holes here), this inn's cottages are surrounded by beautiful grounds where bird-song and the babbling creek set the mood. The cottages date from the 1930s, but have been attractively renovated and updated (some with flagstone floors). A Western style predominates. Some units have fireplaces and kitchenettes. Breakfast is often served on a terrace above the creek, and there's a stone gazebo for creek-side massages. All in all, the Briar Patch offers a delightful combination of solitude and sophistication.

3190 N. Hwy. 89A, Sedona, AZ 86336. ✆ 888/809-3030 or 520/282-2342. Fax 520/282-2399. www. briarpatchinn.com. 18 units. $159–$295 double. Rates include full breakfast. AE, MC, V. **Amenities:** Massage. *In room:* A/C, fridge, coffeemaker.

Canyon Villa ★★   Located in the Village of Oak Creek, 6 miles south of Sedona, this bed-and-breakfast offers luxurious accommodations and spectacular views of the red rocks. All rooms but one have views, as do the pool area, living room, and dining room, so if you want to just hole up at the inn, you won't be missing the best of the area—it's right out your window. Guest rooms are varied in style—Victorian, Santa Fe, country, rustic, Americana, wicker—but no matter what the decor, the furnishings are impeccable, accompanied by such amenities as terry robes, whirlpool tubs, and double sinks. All rooms have balconies or patios, and several have fireplaces. Breakfast is a lavish affair meant to be lingered over, and in the afternoon there's an elaborate spread of snacks.

125 Canyon Circle Dr., Sedona, AZ 86351. ✆ 800/453-1166 or 520/284-1226. Fax 520/284-2114. www.canyonvilla.com. 11 units. $160–$250 double. Rates include full breakfast. AE, MC, V. **Amenities:** Small outdoor pool; concierge; massage; dry cleaning. *In room:* A/C, TV, hair dryer, iron.

Enchantment Resort ★★★   Located at the mouth of Boynton Canyon, this resort more than lives up to its name. The setting is breathtaking, the pueblo-style architecture blends in with the canyon landscape, and the new Mii Amo spa is one of the finest in the state. The individual casitas can be booked as two-bedroom suites, one-bedroom suites, or single rooms; it's worth reserving a suite just so you can enjoy the casita living rooms, which feature high beamed ceilings, beehive fireplaces, Native American crafts, and patios with dramatic views of the canyon (ask for one of the newer units). Both the Yavapai Dining Room (see "Where to Dine," below) and a less formal bar and grill offer tables outdoors; lunch on the terrace should not be missed.

Mii Amo spa is actually a separate entity within the resort and has its own restaurant, guest rooms, and rates. However, Enchantment Resort guests have access to the spa facilities and can avail themselves of treatments. No other spa in the state has a more Southwestern feel than this relatively small but well-designed facility.

525 Boynton Canyon Rd., Sedona, AZ 86336. ✆ 800/826-4180 or 520/282-2900. Fax 520/282-9249. www.enchantmentresort.com. 220 units. Enchantment Resort: $195–$350 double; $295–$450 casita parlor; $390–$650 1-bedroom suite; $655–$1,050 2-bedroom suite. Mii Amo spa: 3-day package from $1,590 per person (double occupancy). AE, DC, DISC, MC, V. **Amenities:** 2 restaurants (new American, spa cuisine); lounge; 5 pools; 6-hole pitch-and-putt golf course; putting green; 7 tennis courts; croquet court; exercise room; full-service spa; 2 Jacuzzis; bike rentals; children's programs; concierge; business center; salon; room service; massage; baby-sitting; laundry service; dry cleaning. *In room:* A/C, TV, dataport, minibar, coffeemaker, hair dryer, iron, safe.

The Graham Bed & Breakfast Inn & Adobe Village ★★   Located in the Village of Oak Creek, 6 miles south of Sedona, this inn lies almost at the foot of Bell Rock and features a variety of individually decorated rooms and suites. The casitas, the Sundance room, and the Sedona suite are the most impressive rooms in the Sedona area. The Purple Lizard opts for a colorful Taos-style interior and an amazing rustic canopy bed. The Wilderness is like a log cabin, with a fireplace that can be seen from both the living room and the double whirlpool tub. The Lonesome Dove is a sort of upscale cowboy cabin with a fireplace, potbelly stove, and round hot tub in a "barrel." Can you say *romantic?* While the views here aren't as good as at the nearby Canyon Villa, the accommodations are unforgettable.

150 Canyon Circle Dr., Sedona, AZ 86351. ℂ **800/228-1425** or 520/284-1425. Fax 520/284-0767. www.sedonasfinest.com. 11 units. $149–$249 double; $309–$349 suite; $389–$439 casita. Rates include full breakfast. AE, DISC, MC, V. **Amenities:** Small outdoor pool; Jacuzzi; bikes; concierge; tour desk; massage. *In room:* A/C, TV, coffeemaker, hair dryer, iron, safe.

The Inn on Oak Creek ★★   Located right on Oak Creek and just around the corner from the Tlaquepaque shopping plaza, this luxurious modern inn offers the best of both worlds. A shady creek-side setting lends it the air of a forest retreat, yet much of Sedona's shopping and many of its best restaurants are within walking distance. There is even a private little park on the bank of the creek. Guest rooms vary considerably in size, but all have interesting theme decors. Some of our favorites are the Garden Gate (with a picket-fence headboard), Hollywood Out West (with old movie posters), the Rose Arbor (with creek views from both the tub and the bed), and the Angler's Retreat (with bentwood furniture, fly-fishing decor, and a fabulous view). Because the inn is built out over the creek, you can look straight down into the water from your balcony. All rooms have gas fireplaces and whirlpool tubs.

556 Hwy. 179, Sedona, AZ 86336. ℂ **800/499-7896** or 520/282-7896. Fax 520/282-0696. www.sedona-inn.com. 11 units. $170–$260 double. Rates include full breakfast. AE, DISC, MC, V. **Amenities:** Concierge; self-service laundry. *In room:* A/C, TV/VCR, dataport, hair dryer.

Junipine Resort ★ *(Kids)*   If you're with the kids and are looking for a place in the cool depths of Oak Creek Canyon (rather than amid the red-rock views in Sedona proper), this condominium resort is a good bet. All the condos have loads of space (some with lofts), skylights, decks, stone fireplaces, decorative quilts on the walls, full kitchens, and contemporary styling. Some have hot tubs. Best of all, the creek is right outside the door of most units. The dining room serves a surprisingly sophisticated Southwestern and regional American menu at reasonable prices, so there's no need to drive all the way into Sedona for a good meal.

8351 N. Hwy. 89A, Sedona, AZ 86336. ℂ **800/742-PINE** or 520/282-3375. Fax 520/282-7402. www. junipine.com. 32 units. $170–$210 1-bedroom unit; $240–$275 2-bedroom unit (lower rates Nov–Feb). AE, DISC, MC, V. **Amenities:** Restaurant; concierge; room service; coin-op laundry; laundry service. *In room:* TV, kitchen, fridge, coffeemaker.

L'Auberge de Sedona ★★   Located in the heart of uptown Sedona, this resort claims an enviable location on a hillside above Oak Creek and amid the shade trees along the banks of the creek. Although L'Auberge is extremely luxurious and provides excellent service, the country French styling seems out of place in such a quintessentially Southwestern setting. Likewise, room decor is for the most part quite fussy. However, if you had to forgo your vacation in France this year, you might enjoy a stay here. For spectacular views and sunsets, opt for a room in the resort's Orchards wing, which faces the red rocks but lacks the secluded setting of the main lodge or cottages. While the creek-side cottages set beneath shady sycamores look utterly rustic from the outside, the log cabins actually hide rooms done in flowery country decor. With two restaurants (one serving formal six-course French dinners, the other a much more casual place) but only a pool and whirlpool for activities, this lodge is more romantic getaway than recreational resort.

301 L'Auberge Lane (P.O. Box B), Sedona, AZ 86339. © **800/272-6777** or 520/282-1661. Fax 520/282-2885. www.lauberge.com. 100 units. Late Nov to Feb (excluding holidays) $170–$235 double, $210–$265 suite, $260–$370 cottage; Mar to late Nov and holidays $185–$250 double, $240–$295 suite, $330–$430 cottage. AE, DC, DISC, MC, V. **Amenities:** 2 restaurants (French, regional American); small outdoor pool; access to nearby health club; Jacuzzi; concierge; room service; in-room massage; baby-sitting; laundry service; dry cleaning. *In room:* A/C, TV, minibar, coffeemaker, hair dryer.

MODERATE

Best Western Inn of Sedona ★   Located about midway between uptown and west Sedona, this hotel has great views of the red rocks from its wide terraces and the outdoor pool area. Unfortunately, although the rooms are comfortable enough, not all of them have views. However, the modern Southwestern decor and the setting, surrounded by native landscaping and out of the tourist mainstream, make this an appealing choice.

1200 W. Hwy. 89A, Sedona, AZ 86336. © **800/292-6344** or 520/282-3072. Fax 520/282-7218. www.innofsedona.com. 110 units. $110–$155 double. Rates include continental breakfast. AE, DC, DISC, MC, V. Pets accepted ($10 nonrefundable deposit). **Amenities:** Small outdoor pool; exercise room; Jacuzzi; concierge; laundry service; dry cleaning. *In room:* A/C, TV, fridge, coffeemaker, hair dryer, iron.

Garland's Oak Creek Lodge ★ *(Finds)*   Located 8 miles north of Sedona in the heart of Oak Creek Canyon, this lodge may be the hardest place in the area to get a reservation. People have been coming here for so many years and like it so much that they reserve a year in advance (last-minute cancellations do occur, so don't despair). What makes the lodge so special? Maybe it's that you have to drive *through* Oak Creek to get to your log cabin (don't worry—the water's shallow, and the creek bottom is paved). Maybe it's the beautiful gardens overlooking the creek. Or maybe it's the slow, relaxing atmosphere of an old-time summer getaway. The well-maintained cabins are rustic but comfortable; the larger ones have their own fireplaces. Meals include organic fruits and vegetables grown on the property.

P.O. Box 152, Sedona, AZ 86339. © **520/282-3343.** www.garlandslodge.com. 16 units. $178–$208 double (plus 15% gratuity). Rates include breakfast and dinner. 2-night minimum. MC, V. Closed mid-Nov to Mar 31 and Sun throughout the year. **Amenities:** Dining room, lounge; tennis court; massage; baby-sitting. *In room:* No phone.

Hilton Sedona Resort ★★   This is Sedona's newest resort and is still adding to its many amenities. It boasts not only one of the most breathtaking golf courses in the state, but also the best pool area north of Phoenix. While golf is the driving force behind most stays here, all those looking for an active vacation will keep busy here. Guest rooms are suites of varying sizes, with fireplaces and balconies or patios. The resort's main restaurant plays up its views of the golf course and red rocks, while the other dining option is a poolside bar and grill. About the only drawback to this place is that it's quite a ways outside Sedona itself (actually south of the Village of Oak Creek), so it's a bit of a drive to Sedona's restaurants and Oak Creek Canyon.

90 Ridge Trail Dr., Sedona, AZ 86351. © **800/HILTONS** or 520/284-4040. Fax 520/284-6940. www. hiltonsedona.com. 219 units. Mar–June $159–$209 double; July–Sept $119–$139 double; Oct to mid-Nov

$119–$159 double; mid-Nov to Feb $119–$159 double. AE, DC, DISC, MC, V. **Amenities:** 2 restaurants (Southwestern, American), lounge; 3 pools; 18-hole golf course; 4 tennis courts; racquetball courts; exercise room; access to nearby health club and spa; 2 Jacuzzis; children's programs; concierge; business center; salon; room service; massage; baby-sitting; complimentary laundry room; laundry service; dry cleaning. *In room:* A/C, TV, dataport, minibar, coffeemaker, hair dryer, iron, safe.

The Lodge at Sedona ⭐ Located in the west Sedona part of town, this B&B is surrounded by desert landscaping that includes pine trees, rock gardens, waterfalls, sculptures, and a stone labyrinth. The bedrooms are individually decorated; our favorites are the Lariat Room and the Master Suite (which is absolutely huge and has a stone fireplace). Upstairs units tend to be small and have showers only (no tubs), so if you can afford to spend a little more, opt for a downstairs room, and ask for one with a whirlpool tub. Owners Barb and Mark Dinunzio make all their guests feel very much at home.

125 Kallof Place, Sedona, AZ 86336. ☎ 800/619-4467 or 520/204-1942. Fax 520/204-2128. www.lodgeatsedona.com. 14 units. $130–$260 double. Rates include full breakfast. AE, DISC, MC, V. **Amenities:** Access to nearby health club; concierge; massage. *In room:* A/C, hair dryer, no phone.

Radisson Poco Diablo Resort ⭐ Although not nearly as lavish as golf resorts down in Phoenix, this older golf and tennis resort, located on the southern outskirts of Sedona, benefited from a complete renovation a couple of years ago. Oak Creek runs through the 22-acre grounds, and the fairways of the nine-hole golf course provide a striking contrast to the red rocks and blue skies. The views here are not as good as at other comparable properties in the area, but the staff is courteous and helpful. With its Mission-style furnishings, contemporary Southwestern art, and Native American baskets and pottery, the lobby has the feel of a small inn, while the rest of the grounds all say resort. Ask for one of the guest rooms with a view of the golf course or the red rocks. These units have whirlpool tubs and fireplaces and are done in a modern rustic Southwest style. However, the upper-end rooms seem a bit overpriced.

1752 S. Hwy. 179, Sedona, AZ 86336. ☎ 800/528-4275 or 520/282-7333. Fax 520/282-3729. www.pocodiablo.com. 137 units. Early Mar to early July and early Sept to mid-Nov $159–$239 double, $279–$299 suite; early July to early Sept and mid-Nov to early Mar $129–$199 double, $229–$249 suite. AE, DISC, MC, V. **Amenities:** Restaurant (Southwestern), lounge; 2 pools; 9-hole golf course; 4 tennis courts; 2 racquetball courts; exercise room; 3 Jacuzzis; game room; concierge; room service; massage; laundry service; dry cleaning. *In room:* A/C, TV, fridge, coffeemaker, hair dryer.

Rose Tree Inn *Finds* This little inn, only a block from Sedona's uptown shopping district, is tucked amid pretty gardens (yes, there are lots of roses) on a quiet street. The property consists of an eclectic cluster of older buildings that have all been renovated. Four guest rooms have kitchenettes, which makes them good choices for families or for longer stays. All units are furnished differently— one Victorian, one Southwestern, another with a gas fireplace. Complimentary coffee and tea are available.

376 Cedar St., Sedona, AZ 86336. ☎ 888/282-2065 or 520/282-2065. Fax 520/282-0083. www.rosetreeinn.com. 5 units. $85–$135 double. AE, MC, V. **Amenities:** Access to nearby health club; Jacuzzi; bike rentals; concierge; self-service laundry; laundry service. *In room:* A/C, TV/VCR, coffeemaker.

Saddle Rock Ranch ⭐ The stunning views alone would make this one of Sedona's better lodging choices, but on top of that, you get classic Western ranch styling (the house was built in 1926) in a home that once belonged to Barry Goldwater. Walls of stone and adobe, a flagstone floor in the living room, huge exposed beams, and plenty of windows to take in the scenery are enough to enchant guests even before they reach their rooms. And the rooms don't disappoint, either. In one you'll find Victorian elegance, in another an English canopy bed and stone fireplace. Dressing areas and private gardens add to the charm. The third room is a separate little cottage with a lodgepole-pine bed, flagstone floors, and beamed ceiling. The pool and whirlpool are surrounded by a flagstone terrace and enjoy one of the best red-rock views in town.

255 Rock Ridge Dr., Sedona, AZ 86336. ⊘ 866/282-7640 or 520/282-7640. Fax 520/282-6829. www. saddlerockranch.com. 3 units. $159–$179 double. Rates include full breakfast. MC, V. **Amenities:** Small outdoor pool; access to nearby health club; Jacuzzi; concierge; laundry service. *In room:* A/C, TV/VCR, hair dryer.

INEXPENSIVE

Cedars Resort on Oak Creek   Located right at the "Y" (where it is often difficult to get out of the parking lot) and within walking distance of uptown Sedona, this economical motel has a fabulous view across Oak Creek to the towering red rocks. In addition to the pool and Jacuzzi, there's a long stairway (77 steps) leading down to Oak Creek. Guest rooms are large and have been recently refurbished. For the best views, ask for a king-size room.

20 W. Hwy. 89A (P.O. Box 292), Sedona, AZ 86339. ⊘ **520/282-7010.** Fax 520/282-5372. 38 units. $77–$119 double. AE, DC, DISC, MC, V. **Amenities:** Small outdoor pool; access to nearby health club; Jacuzzi; coin-op laundry. *In room:* A/C, TV, fridge, coffeemaker, hair dryer, iron.

Los Abrigados Lodge *(Value)*   Located behind the tourist shops and Jeep tour offices in uptown Sedona, this modest motel can claim some of the best views in town. Most of the rooms, although quite basic, are large, and some have balconies. Just be sure you ask for a room with a view; they're only $10 more than the cheapest units. Behind the motel, you'll find a small pool and hot tub with the same great red-rock views.

270 N. Hwy. 89A, Sedona, AZ 86336. ⊘ **800/542-8484** or 520/282-7125. Fax 520/ 282-1825. www. ilxresorts.com. 40 units. $69–$119 double; $105–$150 suite. AE, DISC, MC, V. **Amenities:** Small outdoor pool; Jacuzzi. *In room:* A/C, TV, fridge, coffeemaker.

Matterhorn Lodge   Located in the heart of the uptown shopping district, this choice is convenient to restaurants and shopping, and all guest rooms have excellent views of the red-rock canyon walls. Although the Matterhorn overlooks busy U.S. 89A, if you lie in bed and keep your eyes on the rocks, you'll never notice the traffic below. This place may not have a lot of character, but it is a good value for Sedona.

230 Apple Ave., Sedona, AZ 86336. ⊘ **520/282-7176.** Fax 520/282-0727. www.sedona.net/hotel/ matterhorn. 23 units. Mid-Feb to Nov $79–$119 double; Dec to early Feb $59–$89 double. AE, MC, V. Small pets accepted. **Amenities:** Small outdoor pool; Jacuzzi. *In room:* A/C, TV, dataport, fridge, coffeemaker.

Oak Creek Terrace Resort   Wedged between the highway and Oak Creek about 5 miles north of Sedona, this is a sort of budget romantic getaway. For as little as $79, you can get a room with a fireplace, and for $89, you get an in-room whirlpool. Rooms range from cramped to spacious, and most have a modern woodsy feel (with a bit of Southwest styling thrown in). To get closer to the creek and farther from the highway, ask for a unit in back. You can stretch out in the shade in one of the hammocks beside the creek, and save money on your dining budget by taking advantage of the picnic area with barbecue grills. There are even on-site Jeep rentals.

4548 N. Hwy. 89A, Sedona, AZ 86336. ⊘ **800/224-2229** or 520/282-3562. Fax 520/282-6061. www.oakcreekterrace.com. 20 units. $72–$210 double. AE, DISC, MC, V. Small dogs accepted ($25 nonrefundable fee). **Amenities:** Jeep-rental desk. *In room:* A/C, TV.

Sedona Motel *Value* Although the Sedona Motel looks like any other older motel from the outside, once you check in, you'll find a few surprises. First and foremost is the view across the parking lot to the red rocks. You can pay twice as much in Sedona and not have views this good. Despite being right on the highway, the double-paned windows help keep the rooms quiet.

P.O. Box 1450 (almost at the intersection of Ariz. 179 and Ariz. 89A), Sedona, AZ 86339. (C) **520/282-7187.** 16 units. $49–$89 double. DISC, MC, V. *In room:* A/C, TV, fridge, coffeemaker, hair dryer, iron, safe.

Sky Ranch Lodge This motel is located atop Airport Mesa and has the most stupendous view in town. From here you can see the entire red-rock country, with Sedona filling the valley below. Although the rooms are fairly standard motel issue, some have such features as gas fireplaces, barn-wood walls, and balconies.

Airport Rd. (P.O. Box 2579), Sedona, AZ 86339. (C) **888/708-6400** or 520/282-6400. Fax 520/282-7682. www.skyranchlodge.com. 94 units. $75–$200 double. AE, MC, V. Pets accepted ($10). **Amenities:** Small outdoor pool; access to nearby health club; Jacuzzi; coin-op laundry. *In room:* A/C, TV, dataport.

CAMPGROUNDS

Within the reaches of Oak Creek Canyon along U.S. 89A, there are five National Forest Service campgrounds. Of these, **Bootlegger,** 9 miles north of town, is the largest, but **Manzanita,** 6 miles north of town, is the most pleasant (and the only one open in winter). Other Oak Creek Canyon campgrounds include **Pine Flat,** 13 miles north of town, and **Cave Springs,** 12 miles north of town. The **Beaver Creek Campground,** 3 miles east of I-17 on FR 618, which is an extension of Ariz. 179 (take exit 298 off I-17), is a pleasant spot near the V-Bar-V petroglyph site. For more information on area campgrounds, stop by the **Coconino National Forest's Sedona Ranger Station** ((C) **520/ 282-4119**), on Brewer Road just west of the intersection of U.S. 89A and Ariz. 179. Reservations can be made for Pine Flat and Cave Springs campgrounds by contacting the **National Recreation Reservation Service** ((C) **800/280-2267;** www.reserveusa.com).

WHERE TO DINE

Restaurants in Sedona tend to be expensive, so your best bets for economical meals are sandwich shops or ethnic restaurants. For filling sandwiches, try **Sedona Memories,** 321 Jordan Rd. ((C) **520/282-0032**), 1 block off Ariz. 89A in the uptown shopping area. As you wait for your order, peruse the collection of old Western movie posters and photos. For breakfast, locals swear by the **Coffee Pot Restaurant,** 2050 W. Hwy. 89A ((C) **520/282-6626**). Having a picnic? Get your supplies from the take-out counter at **New Frontiers Natural Foods,** 1420 W. Hwy. 89A ((C) **520/282-6311**). For baked goods such as croissants and bread made with organic flour, visit the **Desert Flour Bakery & Bistro,** in Oak Creek Village at 6446 Hwy. 179 ((C) **520/284-4633**).

EXPENSIVE

Cowboy Club SOUTHWESTERN With its big booths, huge steer horns over the bar, and cowboy gear adorning the walls, this place looks like a glorified cowboy steakhouse, but when you see the menu, you'll know it's more than your average meat-and-potatoes joint. This is big flavor country, and the menu isn't the sort any real cowboy would likely have anything to do with. Start out with fried cactus strips with black-bean caramel gravy or barbecued snake. For an entree, grilled salmon with chipotle hollandaise or the buffalo sirloin with

> ### 🄲 Super Sedona Sunset Spots
>
> If you thought the rocks were beautiful at noon, wait till you see the way they glow in the setting sun. Some of the best spots for taking in Sedona's sunsets are the following:
>
> - Airport Mesa (arrive early to get a parking space at the trailhead, which is near the top of the mesa).
> - Bell Rock Pathway, at the foot of Bell Rock between Sedona and the Village of Oak Creek.
> - Crescent Moon Recreation Area on Red Rock Loop Road (west of Sedona off Ariz. 89A).
> - Dry Creek and Boynton Pass roads, which are both near Enchantment Resort (avoid the latter if it's muddy).
> - Enchantment Resort's restaurant, lounge, or adjacent terraces, all of which are very civilized and very popular.

dried cherries are almost too good to pass by. At lunch, burgers and sandwiches are mainstays, but you can also get such dishes as ginger black-bean pasta with shrimp. Service is relaxed and friendly. It was in this building that the Cowboy Artists of America organization was formed back in 1965.

The Cowboy Club also operates the adjacent Silver Saddle Room, a more upscale spin on the same concept. It offers huge suede-covered booths, Western paintings, and a similar menu with prices equivalent to those of the Cowboy Club at dinner.

241 N. Hwy. 89A. 🄲 **520/282-4200.** www.cowboyclub.com. Reservations recommended. Main courses $7–$13 lunch, $15–$35 dinner. AE, DISC, MC, V. Daily 11am–10pm.

René at Tlaquepaque ⭑ CONTINENTAL/AMERICAN   Slightly less expensive than the dining room at L'Auberge de Sedona resort, this elegant restaurant (with lace curtains and paintings by Southwestern artists) offers the same sort of formal dining experience and traditional French fare. Located in Tlaquepaque, the city's upscale south-of-the-border–themed shopping center, René's is a great place for a special lunch or dinner. You might start off with escargots or the spinach salad, followed by the house specialty rack of lamb. More adventurous diners may want to try the excellent tenderloin of venison with whiskey–juniper berry sauce, or the roasted duck with sun-dried cherry sauce. Finish with a flambéed dessert and selections from the after-dinner drink cart. At lunch, try the coriander-crusted pork tenderloin.

Tlaquepaque, Suite 118 (on Ariz. 179). 🄲 **520/282-9225.** www.rene-sedona.com. Reservations recommended. Main courses $10–$16 lunch, $19–$33 dinner. MC, V. Sun–Thurs 11:30am–2:30pm and 5:30–8:30pm; Fri 11:30am–2:30pm and 5:30–9pm; Sat 11:30am–3pm and 5:30–9pm. Closes earlier weekdays in summer.

Yavapai Dining Room ⭑⭑ SOUTHWESTERN   Because the view of the red rocks of Boynton Canyon are so much a part of the experience of dining here, we recommend coming out to this classy resort for lunch or, preferably, a sunset dinner. Much of the dinner menu changes regularly, but usually includes a few popular signature dishes such as the surprisingly complex black-bean soup, which gets a special touch with applewood-smoked bacon and cumin-scented tortilla strips. Among the entrees, tasty standouts include rack of lamb with a pistachio crust.

In the Enchantment Resort, 525 Boynton Canyon Rd. ℂ 520/204-6000. Reservations highly recommended at both lunch and dinner, and required for Sun brunch. Main courses $10–$18 lunch, $22–$38 dinner; Sun brunch $28.50. AE, DISC, MC, V. Daily 7am–2:15pm and 5:30–8:45pm; Sun brunch 10:30am–2:15pm.

MODERATE

Dahl & DiLuca ★★ ROMAN ITALIAN   In an atmosphere that's both romantic and humorous, brightly colored cherubs dance across the ceiling amid opulent decor. Maybe they're joyous because they've just eaten some *pane romano*, which, as far as we're concerned, is the best garlic bread west of New York's Little Italy. Pasta predominates here, and portions are big. We like the linguine with calamari and mushrooms. The kitchen also serves up a panoply of deftly prepared veal, seafood, chicken, and vegetarian dishes. Sautéed prawns in a wine sauce with lemon, garlic, and parsley are a real standout. Genial and efficient service, reasonably priced wines, and occasional live piano music make this place even more enjoyable. An amaretto crème brûlée or a deceptively light chocolate espresso mousse torte—that's the sort of difficult decision you'll have to make when it comes time for dessert.

2321 W. Hwy. 89A (in west Sedona diagonally across from the Safeway Plaza). ℂ 520/282-5219. Reservations recommended. Main courses $10–$24. AE, DC, DISC, MC, V. Daily 5–10pm.

Fournos Restaurant ★ *Finds* MEDITERRANEAN   In contrast to the glitz and modern Southwest decor of so many of Sedona's restaurants, Fournos is a refreshingly casual place run by the husband-and-wife team of Shirley and Demetrios Fournos. There's even a white board out front for prospective guests to write in their reservations. Pots and ladles hang from the kitchen ceiling in this tiny place, where chef Demetrios cooks up a storm, preparing such dishes as Greek salads with homemade kalamata olives and shrimp flambéed in ouzo and baked with feta cheese. The menu includes specialties such as lamb Cephalonian with herbs and potatoes, and poached fish Mykonos with a sauce of yogurt, onions, mayonnaise, and butter. Other specialties are rack of lamb and lamb Wellington, for a slightly higher price than the usual dinners. A flourless semolina-honey sponge cake comes with ice cream and fruit for a delicious dessert.

3000 W. Hwy. 89A. ℂ 520/282-3331. Reservations highly recommended. Main courses $15–$17. No credit cards. Thurs–Sat seatings at 6 and 8pm.

The Heartline Cafe ★★ SOUTHWESTERN/INTERNATIONAL   The heart line, from Zuni mythology, is a symbol of health and longevity; it is also a symbol for the food here—healthful and very creative. Service is great, and crusty rolls appear on the table immediately (usually accompanied by an unusual spread made from butternut squash). Attention to detail and creative flavor combinations are the order of the day. Large salads, such as watercress with grapes and pistachios or spinach with Gorgonzola cheese and pecans, make tasty starters. Memorable entrees include halibut with ginger-lemongrass butter and smoked mozzarella ravioli. Lunch fare leans toward imaginative sandwiches and salads. Those searching out variety in vegetarian choices will find it here. A beautiful courtyard and a traditionally elegant interior are good places to savor a meal accompanied by a selection from the reasonably priced wine list.

1610 W. Hwy. 89A. ℂ 520/282-0785. www.heartlinecafe.com. Reservations recommended. Main courses $7–$15 lunch, $14–$27 dinner. AE, DC, DISC, MC, V. Fri–Mon 11am–3pm; daily 5–9:15pm.

Pietro's Italian Restaurant ✦ TUSCAN ITALIAN   Pietro's pushes the envelope of Italian creativity. You'll find appetizers such as calamari with smoked tomato-and-basil aioli and grilled eggplant rolled with goat cheese in a red-pepper sauce. Pastas include fettuccine with duck confit, shiitake mushrooms, and figs in a port-wine sauce. Main courses are not quite as daring, but such dishes as boneless game hen with fresh rosemary, lemon, and garlic are certainly tasty. A wide range of wines, including many rare Italian reds and American boutique wines, are available by the glass. Sunday through Wednesday until 6:30pm, less expensive dinners are served.

2445 W. 89A (in west Sedona diagonally across from the Safeway Plaza). ⓒ 520/282-2525. Reservations recommended. Main courses $16–$24; pastas $15–$18. AE, DC, DISC, MC, V. Sun–Thurs 5:30–9pm; Fri–Sat 5:30–9:30pm. Parking is in back of the restaurant—look sharp for the driveway, which is to the east of the building.

Robert's Creekside Café and Grill ✦ SOUTHWESTERN   This place bustles, and tables are small and close together, so we try to grab a seat on the patio if possible. Lunch features salads and sandwiches, such as a hearty eggplant sandwich with goat cheese and roasted red pepper. We especially like the nibble-perfect house-smoked salmon paté. Dinner sees the likes of well-prepared seafoods and New York steak with a cognac and shiitake mushroom glaze. There are several choices here that will appease the vegetarians among us. Don't forget to top it all off with Robert's justifiably famous peach cobbler. If you show up on a weekend night, you just might catch some live music.

Creekside Plaza, 251 Ariz. 179. ⓒ 520/282-3671. Reservations recommended. Main courses $8–$9 lunch, $15–$21 dinner. AE, DISC, MC, V. Daily 11am–4pm and 5–9pm.

Takashi Japanese Restaurant JAPANESE   A peaceful respite from the hustle of uptown Sedona though just steps away, Takashi soothes with soft-spoken service and a simple decor. Although it's a long way from the red rocks to the sea, we like to order the soft-shell crab appetizer and a selection of sushi (yellowtail, eel, and salmon in particular). Traditional plates include the expected teriyaki, tempura, and sukiyaki, but all are well prepared. Refreshing genmai tea is a nice accompaniment to the meal.

465 Jordan Rd., uptown Sedona. ⓒ 520/282-2334. www.takashisedona.com. Reservations recommended. Main courses $11–$21; sushi $3–$8. AE, MC, V. Tues–Fri 11:30am–1:30pm and 5–9pm; Sat–Sun 5–9pm.

INEXPENSIVE

The Hideaway Restaurant ITALIAN/DELI   Hidden away at the back of a shopping plaza near the "Y," this casual family restaurant is as popular with locals as it is with visitors. Basic pizzas, subs, sandwiches, salads, and pastas are the choices here, and though none are particularly remarkable, the views from the deck certainly are. From the shady porch, you can see the creek below and the red rocks rising up across the canyon. An early sunset dinner is your best bet.

Country Sq., Ariz. 179. ⓒ 520/282-4204. Reservations accepted for parties of 10 or more. Main courses $4.50–$8.50 lunch, $8.50–$11 dinner. AE, DC, DISC, MC, V. Spring and summer daily 11am–10pm; fall and winter daily 11am–9pm.

India Palace NORTHERN INDIAN   Good Indian food in a no-frills atmosphere is what you have here. We like the nicely marinated chicken tandoori and breads such as garlic nan and parantha stuffed with spicy vegetables. There are lots of veggie options here, even at the all-you-can-eat buffet lunch, which goes for $5.95 per person.

1910 W. Hwy. 89A ((next to Basha's). ⓒ 520/204-2300. Complete dinners $12–$14; entrees $7–$13. AE, DC, DISC, MC, V. Daily 11am–2:30pm and 5–10pm.

Javelina Cantina MEXICAN Although Javelina Cantina is part of a chain of Arizona restaurants, the formula works, and few diners leave disappointed. Sure, the restaurant is touristy, but what it has going for it is good Mexican food, a lively atmosphere, decent views, and a convenient location in the Hillside shops (so you can do a bit of browsing before or after your meal). Shrimp *albondigas* soup (available Friday and Saturday) comes in a rich and hearty broth, and the grilled fish tacos are tasty. There are also the usual combo dishes and fajitas, with plenty of different margaritas and tequilas to accompany your meal. Expect a wait.

671 Hwy. 179 (in the Hillside Sedona shopping plaza). (© 520/203-9514. Reservations recommended at dinner. Main courses $9–$19. AE, DC, MC, V. Daily 11:30am–9:30pm.

SEDONA PERFORMING ARTS & NIGHTLIFE

The **Sedona Cultural Park** ((© **800/780-2787** or 520/282-0747; www.sedona-culturalpark.org) is Sedona's premier outdoor performing-arts space and takes full advantage of the magnificent scenery. The main attraction is the amphitheater, which hosts a wide variety of performances each summer. Also here at the cultural park, you'll find a visitor center that sells the Red Rock Pass you'll need if you plan to park at any national forest trailheads in the Sedona area. **Shakespeare Sedona** (http://shakespearesedona.com) stages plays both here and at another venue in Sedona. Tickets are $16 to $22. You can also catch frequent music performances and theater productions at the **Sedona Arts Center,** U.S. 89A at Art Barn Road ((© **520/282-3809;** www.sedonaartscenter.com).

If all the entertainment you need is a pleasant place for a sunset cocktail, head out to the **Enchantment Resort** ((© **520/282-2900**), where the lounge and patio boast some of the best sunsets in the state. (See "Where to Stay," above, for directions.) If it's microbrewed beer you're after, drop by the **Oak Creek Brewing Co.,** 2050 Yavapai Dr. ((© **520/204-1300**), north of Ariz. 89A off Coffee Pot Drive.

The Grand Canyon & Northern Arizona

The Grand Canyon—the name is at once apt and inadequate. How can words sum up the grandeur of 2 billion years of the earth's history sliced open by the power of a single river? Once an impassable and forbidding barrier to explorers and settlers, the Grand Canyon is today a magnet that each year attracts millions of visitors from all over the world. The pastel layers of rock weaving through the rugged ramparts of the canyon, the interplay of shadows and light, the wind in the pines and the croaking of ravens on the rim are the sights and sounds that never fail to transfix the hordes of visitors who annually gaze awestruck into the canyon's seemingly infinite depths.

Yet other parts of northern Arizona contain worthwhile, and less crowded, attractions. Only 60 miles south of the great yawning chasm stand the San Francisco Peaks, the tallest of which, Humphreys Peak, rises to 12,643 feet. These peaks, sacred to the Hopi and Navajo, are ancient volcanoes that today are popular with skiers, hikers, and mountain bikers. The eruption in this region of smaller volcanoes in the not-too-distant past helped turn the land northeast of Flagstaff into fertile farmland that supported the Sinagua people, who have long since disappeared, leaving only the ruins of their ancient villages.

Amid northern Arizona's miles of windswept plains and ponderosa pine forests stands the city of Flagstaff, which at 7,000 feet in elevation is one of the highest cities in the United States. Flagstaff is home to Northern Arizona University, whose students ensure that it's a lively town. Born of the railroads and named for a flagpole, Flagstaff is best known as the jumping-off point for trips to the Grand Canyon. However, the city has preserved its Western heritage in its restored downtown historic district, and is well worth a visit on its own.

While it's the Grand Canyon that brings most people to northern Arizona, the region actually has much more to offer, and since most visitors spend only a day or so in Grand Canyon National Park, you may want to take a look at what else there is to do in this part of the state. If, on the other hand, you only want to visit the canyon, there are many different ways to accomplish this goal. You can do so in a group or alone, on foot or by raft, from a mule or a helicopter. Regardless of what you decide, you'll find that the Grand Canyon more than lives up to its name.

1 Flagstaff ★★

150 miles N of Phoenix; 32 miles E of Williams; 80 miles S of Grand Canyon Village

At 7,000 feet above sea level, Flagstaff, a classic Western mountain town, is one of the highest cities in the country and is best known as the jumping-off point for trips to the South Rim of the Grand Canyon. With its wide variety of accommodations and restaurants, the great outdoors at the edge of town, three national monuments nearby, one of the state's finest museums, and a university that supports a lively cultural community, Flagstaff makes an ideal base for exploring much of northern Arizona.

The San Francisco Peaks, just north of the city, are the site of the Arizona Snowbowl ski area, one of the state's main winter playgrounds. In summer, miles of trails through these same mountains attract hikers and mountain bikers, and it's even possible to ride the chairlift at Arizona Snowbowl for a panoramic vista that stretches 70 miles north to the Grand Canyon. Of the area's national monuments, two preserve ancient Indian ruins and one preserves an otherworldly landscape of volcanic cinder cones.

It was as a railroad town that Flagstaff made its fortunes, and after several years of renovations, the historic downtown offers a glimpse of the days when the city's fortunes rode the rails. The railroad still runs right through the middle of Flagstaff, much to the dismay of many visitors, who find that most of the city's inexpensive motels (and even some of the more expensive places) are too close to the busy tracks to allow them to get a good night's sleep.

ESSENTIALS

GETTING THERE   Flagstaff is on I-40, one of the main east-west interstates in the United States. I-17 starts here and heads south to Phoenix. U.S. 89A connects Flagstaff to Sedona by way of Oak Creek Canyon. U.S. 180 connects Flagstaff with the South Rim of the Grand Canyon, and U.S. 89 connects to Page.

Flagstaff's Pulliam Airport, 3 miles south of town off I-17, is served by **America West/Mesa Airlines** (© 800/235-9292) from Phoenix. **Amtrak** (© 800/872-7245) offers service to Flagstaff from Chicago and Los Angeles. The train station is at 1 E. Rte. 66.

VISITOR INFORMATION   The **Flagstaff Visitor Center** is at 1 E. Rte. 66 (© 800/842-7293 or 520/774-9541; www.flagstaffarizona.org).

ORIENTATION   Downtown Flagstaff is just north of I-40. Milton Road, which at its southern end becomes I-17 to Phoenix, leads past Northern Arizona University on its way into downtown, where it becomes Route 66. Route 66 runs parallel to the railroad tracks. Downtown's main street is San Francisco Street; Humphreys Street leads north out of town toward the San Francisco Peaks and the South Rim of the Grand Canyon.

GETTING AROUND   Car rentals are available from **Avis** (© 800/331-1212 or 520/774-8421), **Budget** (© 800/527-0700 or 520/779-5235), **Enterprise** (© 800/736-8222 or 520/526-1377), **Hertz** (© 800/654-3131 or 520/774-4452), and **National** (© 800/227-7368 or 520/774-3321).

If you need a taxi, call **A Friendly Cab** (© 520/774-4444). **Pine Country Transit** (© 520/779-6624) provides public bus transit around the city; the fare is 75¢.

OUTDOOR PURSUITS

Flagstaff is northern Arizona's center for outdoor activities. Chief among them is skiing at **Arizona Snowbowl** (© 520/779-1951 for information, or 520/779-4577 for snow report; www.arizonasnowbowl.com), on the slopes of Mount Agassiz, from which you can see all the way to the North Rim of the

The Grand Canyon & Northern Arizona

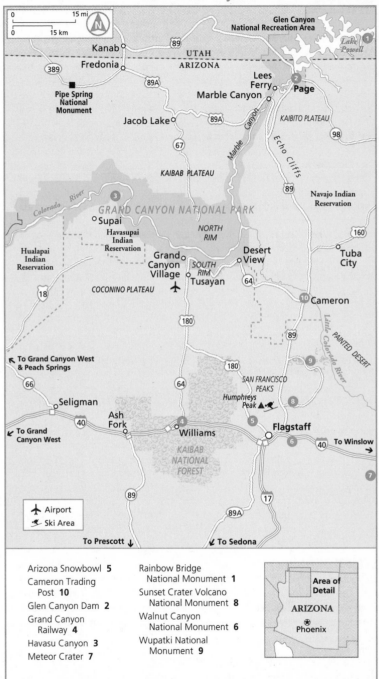

Grand Canyon. There are four chairlifts, 32 runs, 2,300 vertical feet of slopes, ski rentals, and a children's ski program. With an excellent mix of beginner, intermediate, and advanced slopes, Snowbowl attracts many different types of skiers. As the ski area that's most accessible from Phoenix, it sees a lot of weekend traffic from the snow-starved denizens of the desert. Snow conditions are, however, very unreliable. All-day lift tickets are $37 for adults, $20 for children 8 to 12, $17 for seniors, and free for children under 8 and seniors over 69. In summer, you can ride a chairlift almost to the summit of Mount Agassiz and enjoy the expansive views across seemingly all of northern Arizona. The round-trip lift-ticket price is $9 for adults, $6.50 for seniors, and $5 for children 8 to 12. To get here, take U.S. 180 north from Flagstaff for 7 miles and turn right onto Snow Bowl Road.

Snowbowl also operates the **Flagstaff Nordic Center,** 16 miles north of Flagstaff (© **520/779-1951,** ext. 195), which has 40 kilometers of groomed track and 15 kilometers of snowshoe trails. Equipment rentals and ski lessons are available. Trail passes are $10 ($5 for a snowshoe pass).

When there's no snow on the ground, there are plenty of **hiking trails** throughout the San Francisco Peaks, and many national forest trails are open to mountain bikes. Late September, when the aspens have turned a brilliant golden yellow, is one of the best times of year for a hike in Flagstaff's mountains. If you've got the stamina, do the **Humphreys Peak Trail,** which climbs 3,000 feet in 4½ miles. Needless to say, the views from the 12,633-foot summit are stupendous. To reach the trailhead, take U.S. 180 north out of Flagstaff for 7 miles, turn right on Snow Bowl Road, and continue to the parking area by the ski lodge. For information on other hikes in the Coconino National Forest, contact the **Peaks Ranger District,** Coconino National Forest, 5075 N. Hwy. 89, Flagstaff (© **520/526-0866**).

If you feel like saddlin' up and hittin' the trail, contact **Hitchin' Post Stables,** 4848 Lake Mary Rd. (© **520/774-1719**). This horseback-riding stable offers guided trail rides, sunset steak rides, and cowboy breakfast rides. The most popular ride goes into Walnut Canyon, site of ancient cliff dwellings. Prices range from $45 for a 2-hour ride to $95 for a full-day Walnut Canyon ride. **Flying Heart Ranch** (© **520/526-2788**), 4½ miles north of I-40 on U.S. 89, leads rides up into the foothills of the San Francisco Peaks and out through the juniper and piñon forests of the lower elevations. Rides are $25 for 1 hour and $35 for 1½ hours.

If you want to rent a mountain bike and head out on the trails around town, stop by **Mountain Sports,** 1800 S. Milton Rd. (© **800/286-5156** or 520/779-5156), which charges $25 per day for a front-suspension bike.

SEEING THE SIGHTS

Downtown Flagstaff along Route 66, San Francisco Street, Aspen Avenue, and Birch Avenue is the city's **historic district.** These old brick buildings are now filled with shops selling Native American handcrafts, arts and crafts by local artisans, Route 66 souvenirs, and various other Arizona souvenirs such as rocks, minerals, and crystals. This historic area is worth a walk-through even if you aren't shopping.

In summer, **Nava-Hopi Tours** (© **877/467-3329** or 520/774-5003; www.navahopitours.com) operates a tour that takes in most of the city's museums and other attractions. It costs $19.50 for adults and $9.50 for children 5 to 15.

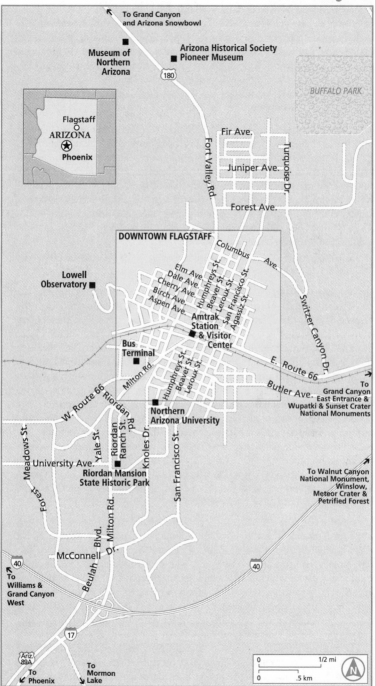

To Grand Canyon
and Arizona Snowbowl

Museum of
Northern
Arizona

Arizona Historical Society
Pioneer Museum

180

BUFFALO PARK

Flagstaff
ARIZONA
Phoenix

Fir Ave.

Juniper Ave.

Turquoise Dr.

Fort Valley Rd.

Forest Ave.

DOWNTOWN FLAGSTAFF

Columbus Ave.

Lowell
Observatory

Elm Ave.
Dale Ave.
Cherry Ave.
Birch Ave.
Aspen Ave.

Humphreys St.
Beaver St.
Leroux St.
San Francisco St.
Agassiz St.

Switzer Canyon Dr.

Amtrak
Station
& Visitor
Center

Bus
Terminal

Milton Rd.

E. Route 66

W. Route 66

Riordan Rd.

Humphreys St.
Beaver St.
Leroux St.

Butler Ave.

To
Grand Canyon
East Entrance &
Wupatki & Sunset Crater
National Monuments

Northern
Arizona University

Meadows St.

Yale St.

Riordan Ranch St.

Knoles Dr.

San Francisco St.

To Walnut Canyon
National Monument,
Winslow,
Meteor Crater &
Petrified Forest

University Ave.

Riordan Mansion
State Historic Park

Forest

Beulah Blvd.

Dr. Milton Rd.

40

McConnell

40

40
To
Williams &
Grand Canyon
West

17

Ariz.
89A
To
Phoenix

To
Mormon
Lake

0   1/2 mi
0   .5 km

N

MUSEUMS, PARKS & CULTURAL ACTIVITIES

The Arboretum at Flagstaff   Covering 200 acres, this arboretum, the highest-elevation research garden in the United States, focuses on plants of the high desert, coniferous forests, and alpine tundra, all of which are environments found in the vicinity of Flagstaff. On the grounds are a butterfly garden, an herb garden, a shade garden, and a passive solar greenhouse.

4001 Woody Mountain Rd. © 520/774-1442. www.thearb.org. Admission $4 adults, $3 seniors, $1 children 6–17. Daily 9am–5pm. Guided tours at 11am and 1pm. Closed mid-Dec to Mar.

Arizona Historical Society Pioneer Museum   The main museum building here is a large stone structure built in 1908 as a hospital for the indigent (Poor Farm). Today, the old hospital houses a historical collection from northern Arizona's pioneer days. Among the exhibits are pieces of camera equipment used by Emery Kolb at his studio on the South Rim of the Grand Canyon; many of Kolb's photos are on display as well. Several small exhibit rooms cover various aspects of life in northern Arizona during the pioneer days and later. You'll see a doctor's office filled with frightening instruments, barbed wire and brands, dolls, saddles, and trapping and timber displays.

2340 N. Fort Valley Rd. © 520/774-6272. Admission by donation. Mon–Sat 9am–5pm. Closed New Year's Day, Easter, Thanksgiving, and Christmas.

Lowell Observatory ⌀   Located atop aptly named Mars Hill is one of the oldest astronomical observatories in the Southwest. Founded in 1894 by Percival Lowell, the observatory has played important roles in contemporary astronomy. Among the work carried out here was Lowell's study of the planet Mars and his calculations that led him to predict the existence of Pluto. It wasn't until 13 years after Lowell's death that Pluto was finally discovered, almost exactly where he had predicted it would be. Today the observatory is still an important research facility, but most astronomical observations are now carried out at Anderson Mesa, 10 miles farther away from the lights of Flagstaff.

The facility consists of several observatories, a large visitor center with numerous fun and educational exhibits, and outdoor displays. Keep in mind that the telescope domes are not heated, so if you come up to observe the stars, be sure to dress appropriately.

1400 W. Mars Hill Rd. © 520/774-3358. www.lowell.edu. Admission $4 adults, $3.50 seniors, $2 children 5–17. Mar–Dec daily 9am–5pm (tours at 10am, 1pm, and 3pm); Jan–Feb Wed–Sun noon–5pm (tours at 1pm and 3pm). Call for hours and days of evening telescope viewings.

Museum of Northern Arizona ⌀⌀   This small but surprisingly thorough museum is the ideal first stop on an exploration of northern Arizona. You'll learn, through state-of-the-art exhibits, about the archaeology, ethnology, geology, biology, and fine arts of the region. The cornerstone of the museum is an exhibit that explores life on the Colorado Plateau from 15,000 B.C. to the present. Among the other displays are a life-size kiva ceremonial room and a small but interesting collection of kachinas. The large gift shop is full of contemporary Native American arts and crafts, and throughout the summer there are special exhibits and sales focusing on Hopi, Navajo, and Zuni arts and crafts.

The museum building itself is made of native stone and incorporates a courtyard featuring vegetation from the six life zones of northern Arizona. Outside is a short, self-guided nature trail that leads through a narrow canyon strewn with boulders.

3101 N. Fort Valley Rd. (3 miles north of downtown Flagstaff on U.S. 180). © 520/774-5213. www.musnaz.org. Admission $5 adults, $4 seniors, $3 students, $2 children 7–17. Daily 9am–5pm. Closed Thanksgiving, Christmas, and New Year's Day.

Riordan Mansion State Historic Park (★)   Built in 1904 for local timber barons Michael and Timothy Riordan, this 13,000-square-foot mansion is actually two houses connected by a large central hall. Each brother and his family occupied half of the house (they had the rooflines constructed differently so that visitors could tell the two sides apart). The home is built in the Craftsman style, and although it looks like a log cabin, it's actually only faced with log slabs. Guided tours provide a glimpse into the lives of two of Flagstaff's most influential pioneers.

409 E. Riordan Rd. (off Milton Rd./U.S. 89A, just north of the junction of I-40 and I-17). (✆) 520/779-4395. www.pr.state.az.us. Admission $5 adults, $2.50 children 7–13. May–Sept daily 8:30am–5pm; Oct–Apr daily 11:30am–5pm. Guided tours on the hour. Closed Christmas.

NEARBY ATTRACTIONS

If you find yourself traveling U.S. 89 between the entrances to Sunset Crater and Wupatki national monuments, keep an eye out for **Sacred Mountain Trading Post** ((✆) 520/679-2255). Though small, is has the look and feel of a trading post of 50 years ago. The shelves are full of Navajo pottery.

Sunset Crater Volcano National Monument (★)   Dotting the landscape northeast of Flagstaff are more than 400 volcanic craters, of which Sunset Crater Volcano is the youngest. Taking its name from the sunset colors of the cinders near its summit, Sunset Crater Volcano stands 1,000 feet tall and began forming in A.D. 1064. Over a period of 100 years, the volcano erupted repeatedly (creating the red-and-yellow cinder cone we see today), and eventually covered an area of 800 square miles with ash, lava, and cinders. A 1-mile interpretive trail passes through a desolate landscape of lava flows, cinders, and ash as it skirts the base of this volcano. In the visitor center (at the west entrance to the national monument), you can learn more about the formation of Sunset Crater and about volcanoes in general. Near the visitor center is a small campground that's open spring through fall.

18 miles north of Flagstaff off U.S. 89. (✆) 520/526-0502. www.nps.gov/sucr. Admission $3 adults, free for children under 17 (admission also valid for Wupatki National Monument). Daily sunrise to sunset; visitor center daily 8am–5pm (until 6pm in summer). Closed Christmas.

Walnut Canyon National Monument (★)   The remains of 300 small 13th-century Sinagua cliff dwellings can be seen in the undercut layers of limestone in this 400-foot-deep wooded canyon east of Flagstaff. The cliff dwellings constructed here, though not nearly as impressive as those at nearby Montezuma Castle or Wupatki national monuments, are worth a visit for the chance to poke around inside the well-preserved rooms, which were well protected from the elements (and from enemies). The Sinagua were the same people who built and then abandoned the stone pueblos found in Wupatki National Monument to the north. It's theorized that when the land to the north lost its fertility, the Sinagua began migrating southward, settling for 150 years in Walnut Canyon.

A self-guided trail leads from the visitor center on the canyon rim down 185 feet to a section of the canyon wall where 25 cliff dwellings can be viewed up close (some can even be entered). Bring binoculars so you can scan the canyon walls for other cliff dwellings. There's also a picnic area near the visitor center.

7 miles east of Flagstaff on Walnut Canyon Rd. (take exit 204 off I-40). (✆) 520/526-3367. www.nps. gov/waca. Admission $3 adults, free for children under 17. June–Aug daily 8am–6pm; Mar–May and Sept–Nov daily 8am–5pm; Dec–Feb daily 9am–5pm; trail closes 1 hr. earlier.

Wupatki National Monument ⚐⚐   The landscape northeast of Flagstaff is desolate and windswept, a sparsely populated region carpeted with volcanic ash deposited in the 11th century. It comes as quite a surprise, then, to learn that this area contains hundreds of Native American habitation sites. The most impressive ruins are those left by the Sinagua (the name means "without water" in Spanish), who inhabited this area from around A.D. 1100 until shortly after 1200. The Sinagua people built small villages of stone similar to the pueblos on the nearby Hopi reservation, and today the ruins of these ancient villages can be seen in this national monument.

The largest of the pueblos is Wupatki Ruin, in the southeastern part of the monument. Here the Sinagua built a sprawling three-story pueblo containing nearly 100 rooms. They also constructed what is believed to be a ball court, which, although quite different in design from the courts of the Aztec and Maya, leaves no doubt that a similar game was played. Another circular stone structure just below the main ruins may have been an amphitheater or dance plaza.

The most unusual feature of Wupatki, however, is a natural phenomenon: a blowhole, which may have been the reason this pueblo was constructed here. A network of small underground tunnels and chambers acts as a giant barometer, blowing air through the blowhole when the underground air is under greater pressure than the outside air. On hot days, cool air rushes out of the blowhole with amazing force.

Several other ruins within the national monument are easily accessible by car. They include Nalakihu, Citadel, and Lomaki, which are the closest to U.S. 89, and Wukoki, near Wupatki. Wukoki Ruin, built atop a huge sandstone boulder, is particularly picturesque. The visitor center is adjacent to the Wupatki ruins and contains interesting exhibits on the Sinagua and Anasazi people who once inhabited the region.

36 miles north of Flagstaff off U.S. 89. ✆ 520/679-2365. www.nps.gov/wupa. Admission $3 adults, free for children under 17. Daily sunrise to sunset; visitor center daily 8am–5pm (until 6pm in summer). Closed Christmas.

ORGANIZED TOURS
Gray Line/Nava-Hopi Tours (✆ 877/467-3329 or 520/774-5003; www. navahopitours.com) operates several tours of northern Arizona, including excursions to the South Rim of the Grand Canyon ($42 for adults, $21 for children 5–15); Lake Powell and Page, with a float trip on the Colorado River ($109 for adults, $59 for children); Sedona and the Verde Valley ($40 for adults, $20 for children); the Navajo Indian Reservation ($74 for adults, $37 for children); and the Petrified Forest, Painted Desert, and Meteor Crater ($58 for adults, $29 for children).

JOINING AN ARCHAEOLOGICAL DIG
On the north side of Flagstaff on U.S. 89 is a small archaeological site called Elden Pueblo, which is open to the public free of charge. These Sinagua ruins are not much to look at, but if you're interested, you can help out with the excavation of the site. Each summer, the **Elden Pueblo Archaeological Project,** P.O. Box 3496, Flagstaff, AZ 86003 (✆ 520/527-3475), hosts several public days as well as field schools for members of the Arizona Archaeological Society (AAS). Field schools cost $100 per week plus the $30 AAS membership dues.

WHERE TO STAY
EXPENSIVE

The Inn at 410 ★★   Located only 2 blocks from downtown Flagstaff, this restored 1907 bungalow is one of the best B&Bs in Arizona, providing convenience, pleasant surroundings, comfortable rooms, and delicious breakfasts. Guests lounge about on the large front porch (complete with swing), in a comfortably furnished living room and dining room, and out on the pleasant garden patio. Bedrooms feature distinctive themes, and eight have their own fireplaces. A separate adjacent building contains some of the units, one of which is wheelchair accessible. The Dakota Suite and the Southwest Room are our favorites, as they conjure up the inn's Western heritage. Breakfasts are multicourse affairs, and if you're lucky, you might get innkeeper Sally Krueger's award-winning curried corn-bread pudding with pumpkin sauce.

410 N. Leroux St., Flagstaff, AZ 86001. ℂ 800/774-2008 or 520/774-0088. Fax 520/774-6354. www.inn410.com. 9 units. $135–$190 double. Rates include full breakfast. MC, V. *In room:* A/C, fridge, coffeemaker, hair dryer, no phone.

MODERATE

Arizona Mountain Inn *(Kids)*   Just a few minutes south of downtown Flagstaff, this family-oriented inn is a quiet mountain retreat set beneath shady pine trees. Although there are three bed-and-breakfast rooms in the main building, the rest of the accommodations are cabins that sleep 2 to 16 people. Many of the rustic cabins are A-frames or chalets, and each is a little different. The property consists of 13 acres, beyond which are miles of national forest.

4200 Lake Mary Rd., Flagstaff, AZ 86001. ℂ 520/774-8959. Fax 520/774-8837. www.arizonamountaininn. com. 20 units. $90–$110 double; $80–$390 cabin. AE, DISC, MC, V. Pets accepted ($5 per night; $50 refundable cleaning fee). **Amenities:** Access to nearby health club; volleyball court; playground; horseshoe pits; coin-op laundry. *In room:* Fridge, coffeemaker, no phone.

Jeanette's Bed & Breakfast ★★   If you've ever wanted to step back in time and live in the early decades of the 20th century, then you might want to spend some time at this unusual B&B a few miles from downtown. Innkeeper Jeanette West and her husband built this new "old house" a few years ago, and their attention to detail is astounding. There are vintage tubs and sinks, vintage heat grates, vintage light switches, and, of course, plenty of antique furniture. What you might not expect is that wardrobes, dressers, and trunks are filled with vintage clothing. The house was designed as a 1912 Victorian that has been updated to a less cluttered 1920s look. One bedroom has a fireplace, while another has a porch with a view of nearby Mount Elden. Mornings start with coffee in the parlor and then an elaborate Victorian breakfast.

3380 E. Lockett Rd., Flagstaff, AZ 86004. ℂ 800/752-1912 or 520/527-1912. Fax 520/527-1713. www.jeanettesbb.com. 4 units. $99–$145 double. Rates include full breakfast. MC, V. *In room:* A/C, dataport, hair dryer, no phone.

Little America Hotel ★ *(Value)*   At first it might seem like Little America is little more than a giant truck stop on the east side of Flagstaff, but on closer inspection you'll find that behind the truck stop stands an excellent economy motel beneath shady pines. The decor is dated but fun, with a sort of suburban French-provincial styling predominating. Rooms vary in size, but all have small private balconies. There's a casual dining room plus a more formal restaurant that serves steaks and Continental dishes.

2515 E. Butler Ave., Flagstaff, AZ 86004. ℂ 800/352-4386 or 520/779-7900. Fax 520/779-7983. www.flagstaff.littleamerica.com. 248 units. $79–$119 double; $89–$129 suite. AE, DC, DISC, MC, V. Take exit

198 off I-40. **Amenities:** 2 restaurants (American, Continental/steakhouse), lounge; outdoor pool; exercise room; access to nearby health club; Jacuzzi; volleyball court; croquet court; horseshoe pits; concierge; car-rental desk; courtesy car; business center; room service; massage; coin-op laundry; laundry service; dry cleaning. *In room:* A/C, TV, dataport, fridge, coffeemaker, hair dryer, iron.

Radisson Woodlands Hotel Flagstaff ★★   With its elegant marble-floored lobby, the Woodlands Hotel is easily the most upscale hotel in Flagstaff. A white baby grand piano, crystal chandelier, traditional European furnishings, and contemporary sculpture all add to the unexpected luxury in the public spaces, as do intricately carved pieces of furniture and architectural details from different Asian countries. Guest rooms are comfortable, but not overly luxurious.

1175 W. Rte. 66, Flagstaff, AZ 86001. © **800/333-3333** or 520/773-8888. Fax 520/773-0597. www.radisson.com/flagstaff. 183 units. $79–$129 double; $119–$149 suite. AE, DC, DISC, MC, V. **Amenities:** 2 restaurants (Japanese, American/Southwestern), lounge; outdoor pool; exercise room; 2 Jacuzzis; sauna; steam room; room service; laundry service; coin-op laundry; dry cleaning. *In room:* A/C, TV, dataport, coffeemaker, hair dryer.

The Sled Dog Inn ★★ *(Finds)*   For outdoor-sports enthusiasts, this is *the* place to stay in the Flagstaff area. Located on the edge of a meadow south of the city, the Sled Dog is a contemporary building that abounds in wood, much of which was salvaged from buildings being torn down. The inn has more than a dozen Siberian huskies, and when there's enough snow in the winter, dog-sled rides are offered. Rock-climbing, cross-country skiing, and mountain-biking excursions are also on the program here. At the end of an active day, the hot tub out back is always welcome. Guest rooms are modern lodge rustic, comfortable and uncluttered. Don't be surprised if you wake up to see elk grazing right outside your window.

10155 Mountainaire Rd., Flagstaff, AZ 86001. © **800/754-0664** or 520/525-6212. Fax 520/525-1855. www.sleddoginn.com. 10 units. $95–$135 double; $160–$185 suite. Rates include full breakfast. AE, MC, V. No children under 7 accepted. **Amenities:** Exercise room; Jacuzzi; sauna; bike rentals. *In room:* A/C, no phone.

INEXPENSIVE

In addition to the options listed below, you'll find numerous budget chain motels in Flagstaff. They include **Motel 6,** 2440 E. Lucky Lane (© **520/774-8756**), and **Motel 6,** 2745 S. Woodlands Village (© **520/779-3757**), both charging $46 to $56 for a double. Flagstaff has dozens of old Route 66 motels that aren't for the fussy, but usually charge under $30.

Hotel Monte Vista   If you don't mind roughing it a bit for a chance to sleep in a hotel once frequented by the likes of Clark Gable, John Wayne, Jane Russell, Spencer Tracy, Carole Lombard, and Gary Cooper, try the Monte Vista. Originally opened in 1927, this hotel was renovated in the mid-1980s and today appeals mostly to a younger crowd, especially college students and young European travelers who appreciate the economical rates (and the hotel bar). In the small, dark lobby (a bit the worse for wear) are painted ceiling beams and Victorian furniture. The rooms vary in size, and many are furnished with oak furniture and ceiling fans. Although the hotel has plenty of old-fashioned flair, don't expect top-notch accommodations. Check out a room first to see if this is your kind of place.

100 N. San Francisco St., Flagstaff, AZ 86001. © **800/545-3068** or 520/779-6971. Fax 520/779-2904. www.hotelmontevista.com. 50 units (6 with shared bathrooms). $50 double with shared bathroom; $65–$90 double with private bathroom; $100–$120 suite (lower rates in winter). AE, DISC, MC, V. **Amenities:** Restaurant (American), lounge; room service; coin-op laundry. *In room:* TV.

Hotel Weatherford *(Value)* For many years, this historic lodging was known primarily as a youth hostel frequented by backpacking Europeans. As part of an ongoing 20-year restoration, it has now risen above hostel level. Although only a few of the rooms have yet been renovated, budget-conscious fans of historic hotels will want to check them out. The distinctive stone-walled 1897 building has a wraparound veranda on its second floor, where you'll find the beautifully restored Zane Grey Ballroom (now an elegant bar). Downstairs are a diner and the ever-popular Charly's Pub & Grill, which has been booking live rock, blues, and jazz acts for more than 2 decades. This place isn't fancy, but it has loads of character.

23 N. Leroux St., Flagstaff, AZ 86001. © **520/779-1919.** Fax 520/773-8951. www.weatherfordhotel.com. 8 units (5 with private bathroom); 2 dorms. $45–$50 double with shared bathroom, $49–$55 double with private bathroom. AE, DC, DISC, MC, V. **Amenities:** Restaurant (American/Southwestern), 2 lounges. *In room:* No phone.

WHERE TO DINE
MODERATE

Chez Marc Bistro ★ FRENCH Housed in an elegant little cottage in downtown Flagstaff, this French restaurant could pass for a country inn if not for the busy road out front. Once inside, you can easily forget where you are. For many years now, this has been northern Arizona's bastion of all things Gallic. You want frogs' legs in garlic butter or escargot in a phyllo tulip? You got 'em. Other influences creep onto the menu as well: You might find buffalo steak in a Beaujolais sauce or guinea hens in sun-dried cranberry demi-glace. Regardless of what you order, rest assured you won't find a more rarefied atmosphere in Flagstaff. The wine list is excellent.

503 Humphreys St. © **520/774-1343.** www.chezmarc.com. Reservations recommended. Main courses $19.50–$29. AE, MC, V. Daily 5–9pm.

Cottage Place Restaurant ★★ CONTINENTAL/NEW AMERICAN Located on the south side of the railroad tracks in a neighborhood mostly frequented by college students, Cottage Place is just what its name implies—an unpretentious little cottage. But despite the casual appearance, dining is a formal affair. The menu, which tends toward the rich side, is primarily Continental, with Southwestern and Middle Eastern influences as well. The house specialties are chateaubriand and rack of lamb (both served for two), and there are always several choices for vegetarians. The appetizer sampler, with stuffed mushrooms, charbroiled shrimp, and *tiropitas* (cheese-stuffed phyllo pastries), is a winner. There's a long wine list, priced on the high side.

126 W. Cottage Ave. © **520/774-8431.** www.cottageplace.com. Reservations recommended. 3-course meals $16.50–$27. AE, MC, V. Tues–Sun 5–9:30pm.

Down Under New Zealand Restaurant NEW ZEALAND Restaurants specializing in the cuisine of New Zealand are, to say the least, not very common in the United States, so to find one in Flagstaff seems even more unusual. If you're curious to find out what Kiwi cooking is all about, try the Hoki fish cakes (made with coconut cream), the lamb, or the venison. Okay, so the menu preparations here display more than a hint of Southwestern influence. All the better as far as we're concerned. For dessert, don't miss the Pavlova.

6 E. Aspen Ave. © **520/774-6677.** www.downundernz.com. Reservations recommended on weekends. Main courses $8.50–$24. AE, DISC, MC, V. Daily 11am–3pm and 5–10pm (earlier closings in winter).

Pasto 🌟 ITALIAN   Operated by the same folks who run Café Espress, Pasto is a health-conscious Italian restaurant in downtown Flagstaff that's very popular with the hip and young at heart. Billing itself as "Fun Italian Dining," Pasto has a flamboyant decor and casual atmosphere. The menu includes a good assortment of pastas, of course, as well as dishes such as chicken Marsala and rolled eggplant stuffed with roasted red peppers and ricotta.

19 E. Aspen St. ℂ 520/779-1937. Reservations recommended. Main courses $9–$16. AE, MC, V. Sun–Thurs 5–9pm; Fri–Sat 5–9:30pm (until 10pm in summer).

INEXPENSIVE

Beaver Street Brewery *Value* BURGERS/PIZZA   This big microbrewery and cafe, in a former supermarket on the south side of the railroad tracks in downtown Flagstaff, serves up several good brews, but it also does great pizzas and salads. The Beaver Street pizza, made with roasted-garlic pesto, sun-dried tomatoes, fresh basil, and soft goat cheese, is particularly tasty. There are robust salads, such as a Mongolian beef salad with sesame-ginger dressing, and even fondue. This place stays packed with college students, but a good pint of ale helps any wait pass quickly, especially if you can grab a seat by the woodstove.

11 S. Beaver St. ℂ 520/779-0079. www.beaverstreetbrewery.com. Main courses $7.50–$10. AE, DISC, MC, V. Sun 11:30am–10pm; Mon–Thurs 11:30am–11pm; Fri–Sat 11:30am–midnight.

Café Espress INTERNATIONAL/VEGETARIAN   Grab a newspaper from the basket by the door, sit down at one of the tables by the front window, and ensconce yourself in college life all over again. If you happen to be a student (or one at heart), this place will become your favorite dining spot in Flagstaff. You can start the day with granola (or something much more substantial), grab a tempeh or turkey burger for lunch, and then have spinach enchiladas or quiche of the day for dinner. There are good sandwiches, a salad bar, and espresso as well.

16 N. San Francisco St. ℂ 520/774-0541. Sandwiches/plates $4.50–$13. AE, MC, V. Daily 7am–9pm.

Macy's European Coffee House & Bakery COFFEEHOUSE/BAKERY   Good espresso and baked goodies draw people in here the first time, but there are also decent vegetarian pasta dishes, soups, salads, and other college-town standbys. This is Flagstaff's counterculture hangout, attracting both students and professors. For the true Macy's experience, order one of the huge lattes and a scone or other pastry.

14 S. Beaver St. ℂ 520/774-2243. www.macyscoffee.com. Meals $3.50–$7. No credit cards. Sun–Wed 6am–8pm; Thurs–Sat 6am–midnight.

FLAGSTAFF AFTER DARK

For events taking place during your visit, check *Flagstaff Live*, a free weekly arts-and-entertainment newspaper available at shops and restaurants downtown. The university has many musical and theatrical groups that perform throughout most of the year, and several clubs around town book a variety of live music acts.

The **Flagstaff Symphony Orchestra** (ℂ 888/520-7214 or 520/523-5661; www.flagstaffsymphony.org) provides the city with a full season of classical music. Most performances are held at Ardrey Auditorium on Knoles Drive on the campus of Northern Arizona University. Ticket prices range from $13 to $36.

The city's community theater group, **Theatrikos** (ℂ 520/774-1662), performs at the Flagstaff Playhouse, 11 W. Cherry St. Tickets are $8 to $14.

Flagstaff has a couple of good brewpubs. Our favorite is the **Beaver Street Brewery,** 11 S. Beaver St. (℘ **520/779-0079**), described under "Where to Dine," above, but not far away, you'll also find the **Mogollon Brewing Co.,** 15 N. Agassiz St. (℘ **520/773-8950**). For a livelier scene, check out the **Museum Club,** 3404 E. Rte. 66 (℘ **520/526-9434**), a Flagstaff institution and one of America's classic roadhouses. Built in the early 1900s and often called the Zoo Club, this cavernous log saloon is filled with deer antlers, stuffed animals, and trophy heads. There's live music on weekends and everything from karaoke to country other nights. Other places worth checking out include **Kiwi Blue,** 6 E. Aspen St. (℘ **520/774-6677**), which is the bar at the Down Under New Zealand Restaurant (see "Where to Dine," above), or **Campus Coffee Bean,** 1800 S. Milton Rd. (℘ **520/556-0660**), a coffeehouse with live music nightly.

2 Williams

58 miles S of the Grand Canyon; 32 miles W of Flagstaff; 220 miles E of Las Vegas

Although it's almost 60 miles south of the Grand Canyon, Williams is still the closest real town. Consequently, it has dozens of motels catering to those unable to get a room at or just outside the park. Williams, founded in 1880 as a railroading and logging town, also has a bit of Western history to boast about, which make it not only a good place to get a room but also an interesting place to spend a little time exploring. Old brick commercial buildings dating from the late 19th century line the main street, while modest Victorian homes sit on the tree-shaded streets that spread south from the railroad tracks. In recent years, mid-20th-century history has taken center stage: Williams was the last town on historic Route 66 to be bypassed by I-40, and the town plays up its Route 66 heritage.

Most important for many visitors, however, is that Williams is where you'll find the Grand Canyon Railway depot. The excursion train that departs from here not only provides a fun ride on the rails but also serves as an alternative to dealing with traffic congestion in Grand Canyon National Park. Of course, there are also the obligatory on-your-way-to-the-Grand-Canyon tourist traps nearby.

Named for famed mountain man Bill Williams, the town sits at the edge of a ponderosa pine forest atop the Mogollon Rim, and surrounding Williams is the Kaibab National Forest. Within the forest and not far out of town are good fishing lakes, hiking and mountain-biking trails, and a small downhill ski area.

ESSENTIALS
GETTING THERE   Williams is on I-40 just west of the junction with Ariz. 64, which leads north to the South Rim of the Grand Canyon.

Amtrak (℘ **800/872-7245**) now has service to Williams on its *Southwest Chief* line. There's no station, though—the train stops on the outskirts of town. Be sure you have previously arranged to have your hotel pick you up.

The **Grand Canyon Railway** ✸✸★, Grand Canyon Railway Depot, Grand Canyon Boulevard (℘ **800/843-8724** or 520/773-1976; www.thetrain.com), operates vintage steam and diesel locomotives and 1920s coaches between Williams and Grand Canyon Village. Round-trip fares range from $54.95 to $139.95 for adults and $24.95 to $109.95 for children 16 and under (fares do not include tax or national park entrance fee). Although this is primarily a day-excursion train, it's possible to ride up one day and return on a different day—just let the reservations clerk know. If you stay overnight, you'll want to be sure you have a reservation at one of the hotels right in Grand Canyon Village; otherwise, you'll end up having to take a shuttle bus or taxi out of the park to your hotel, which can be inconvenient and add a bit to your daily costs.

VISITOR INFORMATION For more information on the Williams area, including information on hiking, mountain biking, and fishing, contact the **Williams–U.S. Forest Service Visitor Center,** 200 W. Railroad Ave., Williams (© **800/863-0546** or 520/635-4061; www.williamschamber.com). The visitor center, which includes some interesting historic displays, is open daily from 8am to 5pm. The shop here carries books on the Grand Canyon and trail maps for the adjacent national forest.

WHAT TO SEE & DO: ROUTE 66 & BEYOND

These days, most people coming to Williams are here to board the Grand Canyon Railway (see "Getting There," above, for details).

Route 66 fans will want to drive Williams's main street, which, not surprisingly, is named Route 66. Along this stretch of the old highway, you can check out the town's vintage buildings, many of which now house shops selling Route 66 souvenirs. There are also a few antiques stores selling collectibles from the heyday of Route 66.

Both east and west of town, there are other parts of the "Mother Road" that you can drive. However, with the exception of the section of road that begins at exit 139, these stretches of road are not very remarkable and are recommended only for die-hard fans of Route 66. East of town, take exit 167 off I-40 and follow the graveled Old Trails Highway (the predecessor to Route 66). A paved section of Route 66 begins at exit 171 on the north side of the interstate and extends for 7 miles to the site of the Parks General Store. From Parks, you can continue to Brannigan Park on a graveled section of Route 66.

West of Williams, take exit 157 and go south. If you turn east at the T intersection, you'll be on a gravel section of the old highway; if you turn west, you'll be on a paved section. Another stretch can be accessed at exit 106. If you continue another 12 miles west and take exit 139, you'll be on the longest uninterrupted stretch of Route 66 left in the country. It extends from here through the town of Seligman, which has several interesting buildings, and all the way to Kingman.

WHERE TO STAY
MODERATE

Best Western Inn of Williams Although this modern motel is not within walking distance of historic downtown Williams, the contemporary styling and location in the pines at the west end of town make it a good bet for comfortable, quiet accommodations.

2600 W. Rte. 66 (P.O. Box 275), Williams, AZ 86046. © **800/635-4445** or 520/635-4400. Fax 520/635-4488. www.bestwestern.com. 79 units. Late May to Dec $69–$139 double; Jan to late May $59–$119. Rates include full breakfast. AE, DC, DISC, MC, V. **Amenities:** Lounge; year-round outdoor pool; Jacuzzi. *In room:* A/C, TV, coffeemaker, hair dryer, iron.

Fray Marcos Hotel ★★ Named for Fray (Father) Marcos de Niza, who some say was the first European to set foot in what is today Arizona, this hotel is affiliated with the Grand Canyon Railway and is named for the Williams hotel once run by the famous Fred Harvey Company. The hotel combines modern comforts with the style of a classic Western railroad hotel, and the high-ceilinged lobby features a large flagstone fireplace and original paintings of the Grand

Canyon. The very comfortable guest rooms feature Southwestern styling. Ask for a unit in the new wing (which is where you'll find the fitness room, pool, and hot tub). The hotel's elegant lounge, which features a 100-year-old English bar, serves simple meals, and there's an adjacent cafeteria-style restaurant. The original Fray Marcos now serves as the railway station (ticket office, gift shop, railroad museum, and display trains).

235 N. Grand Canyon Blvd., Williams, AZ 86046. © **800/843-8724** or 520/635-4010. Fax 520/773-1610. www.thetrain.com. 196 units. Mid-Mar to mid-Oct (and holidays) $119 double; late Oct to early Mar $79 double. Railroad packages available. AE, DISC, MC, V. **Amenities:** Restaurant, lounge; indoor pool; exercise room; Jacuzzi; tour desk. *In room:* A/C, TV.

Quality Inn Mountain Ranch ★

Located 6 miles east of town, this motel is surrounded by 26 acres of forest and meadow that give it a secluded feeling. That seclusion and the hotel's many recreational amenities make this a good out-of-town choice in the Williams area. However, the rooms, although large and mostly with views of forest and mountains, are strictly motel issue. Keep an eye out for elk.

6701 E. Mountain Ranch Rd. (exit 171 off I-40), Williams, AZ 86046. © **800/228-5151** or 520/635-2693. www.mountainranchresort.com. 73 units. Apr to mid-May and Oct $69–$89 double; mid-May to Sept $89–$129 double. Rates include deluxe continental breakfast. AE, DC, DISC, MC, V. Closed Nov–Feb. Supervised pets accepted. **Amenities:** Restaurant; outdoor pool; 2 tennis courts; volleyball and basketball courts; Jacuzzi; sauna; horseback riding. *In room:* A/C, TV, dataport, coffeemaker, hair dryer.

The Sheridan House Inn ★ *Kids*

Located on a pine-shaded hillside a few blocks from downtown Williams, this place isn't fancy, but it's plenty comfortable. Innkeepers Steve and Evelyn Gardner make people feel right at home in a B&B with the amenities of a resort (hot tub on the flagstone patio, pool table and bar in the basement, fitness room, and plenty of movies to watch on in-room VCRs). Guest rooms are comfortably furnished; our favorite is the Cedar Room. The complimentary buffet dinner each evening is a welcome alternative to the basic burgers-and-steaks menus that predominate in Williams, and breakfast always includes an impressive array of fruits. This inn is child-friendly, so it makes a good base of operations for families.

460 E. Sheridan Ave., Williams, AZ 86046. © **888/635-9345** or 520/635-9441. www.grandcanyonbbinn. com. 8 units. $110–$225 double. Rates include full breakfast and buffet dinner. AE, DISC, MC, V. Closed mid-Jan to mid-Feb. **Amenities:** Exercise room, Jacuzzi; game room. *In room:* A/C, TV, fridge, coffeemaker, hair dryer, no phone.

Terry Ranch Bed & Breakfast

This modern log inn on the edge of town looks as though it should be surrounded by a big cattle spread, but instead it's close to the train depot and the restaurants in downtown Williams. The guest rooms, furnished in Western-country style, have king beds and antiques and are named for brides who lived at the Terry Ranch in Utah back in the 1800s. Two rooms have claw-foot tubs, two have whirlpool tubs, and two have fireplaces.

701 Quarterhorse St., Williams, AZ 86046. © **800/210-5908** or 520/635-4171. Fax 520/635-2488. www.grand-canyon-lodging.net. 4 units. $110–$155 double. Rates include full breakfast. AE, DISC, MC, V. *In room:* TV, no phone.

INEXPENSIVE

In addition to the following choices, there are numerous budget chain motels in Williams, including two Motel 6s, two Super 8s, and an Econo Lodge.

The New Canyon Motel ★ *Finds*

You'll find this recently restored old motel on the eastern outskirts of Williams, tucked against the trees. While the setting and new rooms in duplex stone cabins are nice enough, the real attractions are the railroad cars parked in the front yard. You can stay in a caboose or a Pullman car, which makes this a fun place to overnight if you're planning on taking the excursion train to the Grand Canyon. We prefer the caboose rooms, which have a more authentic feel.

1900 E. Rodeo Rd., Williams, AZ 86046. (C) **800/482-3955** or 520/635-9371. Fax 520/635-4138. 18 units. $50–$80 double; $80–$120 caboose or pullman double. AE, DISC, MC, V. **Amenities:** Small indoor pool. *In room:* A/C, TV, no phone.

Norris Motel *(Value)*   Run by a British family, the Norris Motel may not look like anything special from the street, but the friendliness of the welcome will immediately tell you that this is not your ordinary motel. Most of the guest rooms have been remodeled and have a homey feel, and many have refrigerators. Keep an eye out for the prairie dogs in the back field.

1001 W. Rte. 66, P.O. Box 388, Williams, AZ 86046. (C) **800/341-8000** or 520/635-2202. Fax 520/635-9202. www.thegrandcanyon.com/bestvalue. 33 units. Mid-May to mid-Sept $55–$107 double; Apr to early May and late Sept to Oct $44–$87 double; Nov–Mar $26–$59 double. AE, DISC, MC, V. **Amenities:** Small outdoor pool; Jacuzzi. *In room:* A/C, TV, fridge.

The Red Garter Bed & Bakery *(★ (Finds)*   The Wild West lives again at this restored 1897 bordello, but these days the only tarts that come with the rooms are in the bakery downstairs. Located across the street from the Grand Canyon Railway terminal at the top of a steep flight of stairs, this B&B sports high ceilings, new carpets, attractive wood trim, and reproduction period furnishings. A couple of rooms even have graffiti written by bordello visitors in the early 20th century.

137 W. Railroad Ave., Williams, AZ 86046. (C) **800/328-1484** or 520/635-1484. www.redgarter.com. 4 units. $85–$120 double. Lower rates off-season. Rates include continental breakfast. AE, DISC, MC, V. **Amenities:** Bakery. *In room:* TV, no phone.

CAMPGROUNDS

There are several campgrounds near Williams in the Kaibab National Forest. They include **Cataract Lake** (2 miles northwest of Williams on Cataract Lake Road), **Dogtown Lake** (8 miles south of Williams off Fourth Street/County Road 73), **Kaibab Lake** (4 miles northeast of Williams off Ariz. 64), and **Whitehorse Lake** (15 miles south of Williams off Fourth Street/County Road 73). All campgrounds are first-come, first-served.

WHERE TO DINE

Cruiser's Café 66 AMERICAN   If you're looking for a taste of old-fashioned Route 66 atmosphere, this is the place. Dig into some smoked baby-back pork ribs or a platter of fajitas at Cruiser's, which is partly housed in a 1930s gas station and is full of all manner of Route 66 memorabilia. You'll usually see a couple of classic cars parked out front, and just inside the front door is a stuffed bison with a saddle on its back. The menu runs the gamut from steaks and spicy wings to pizza and calzones.

233 W. Rte. 66. (C) 520/635-2445. www.thegrandcanyon.com/cruisers. Main courses $6–$17. AE, DISC, MC, V. Daily noon–10pm (Oct to mid-May 4–10pm).

Rod's Steak House STEAKHOUSE/SEAFOOD   For a good dinner in Williams, just look for the red neon steer at the east end of town. This is the sign that beckons hungry canyon explorers to come on in and have a great steak. The menu, printed on a paper cutout of a steer, may be short, but the food is reliable. Prime rib au jus, the house specialty, comes in three different weights to fit your hunger. If you're not in a mood for a steak, opt for barbecued ribs, trout, chicken, or shrimp.

301 E. Rte. 66. ✆ **520/635-2671.** www.rods-steakhouse.com. Reservations recommended. Main courses $8–$26. MC, V. Daily 11:30am–9:30pm.

3 The Grand Canyon South Rim ★★★

60 miles N of Williams; 80 miles NE of Flagstaff; 230 miles N of Phoenix; 340 miles N of Tucson

Whether you merely stand on the rim gazing in awe, spend several days hiking deep in the canyon, or ride the roller-coaster rapids of the Colorado River, the Grand Canyon is a landscape not to be missed. A mile deep, 277 miles long, and up to 18 miles wide, the Grand Canyon is so large as to be overwhelming in its grandeur, truly one of the great wonders of the world. The cartographers who mapped this land were obviously deeply affected by the spiritual beauty of the canyon, and named the landscape features accordingly. Their reverence is reflected in such names as Solomon Temple, Angels Gate, the Tabernacle, Apollo Temple, Venus Temple, Thor Temple, Zoroaster Temple, Horus Temple, Buddha Temple, Vishnu Temple, Krishna Temple, Shiva Temple, and Confucius Temple.

Something of this reverence infects nearly every first-time visitor. Nothing in the slowly changing topography of the approach to the Grand Canyon prepares you for what awaits. You hardly notice the elevation gain or the gradual change from windswept scrubland to pine forest. Suddenly, it's there. No preliminaries, no warnings. Stark, quiet, a maze of colors and cathedrals sculpted by nature.

Banded layers of sandstone, limestone, shale, and schist give the canyon its colors, and the interplay of shadows and light from dawn to dusk creates an ever-changing palette of hues and textures. Written in these bands of stone are more than 2 billion years of history. Formed by the cutting action of the Colorado River as it flows through the Kaibab Plateau, the Grand Canyon is an open book exposing the secrets of the geologic history of this region. Geologists believe it has taken between 3 million and 6 million years for the Colorado River to carve the Grand Canyon, but the canyon's history extends much further back in time.

Millions of years ago, vast seas covered this region. Sediments carried by sea water were deposited and over millions of years were turned into limestone and sandstone. When the ancient seabed was thrust upward to form the Kaibab Plateau, the Colorado River began its work of cutting through the plateau. Today, 21 sedimentary layers, the oldest of which is more than a billion years old, can be seen in the canyon. Beneath all these layers, at the very bottom, is a stratum of rock so old that it has metamorphosed, under great pressure and heat, from soft shale to a much harder stone. Called Vishnu schist, this layer is the oldest rock in the Grand Canyon and dates from 2 billion years ago.

In the more recent past, the Grand Canyon has been home to several Native American cultures, including the Anasazi, who are best known for their cliff dwellings in the Four Corners region. About 150 years after the Anasazi and Coconino peoples abandoned the canyon in the 13th century, another tribe, the Cerbat, moved into the area. The Hualapai and Havasupai tribes, descendants of the Cerbat people, still live in and near the Grand Canyon on the south side of the Colorado River. On the North Rim lived the Southern Paiute, and in the west, the Navajo.

In 1540, Spanish explorer Garcia Lopez de Cárdenas became the first European to set eyes on the Grand Canyon. It would be another 329 years before the first expedition would travel through the entire canyon. John Wesley Powell, a one-armed Civil War veteran, was deemed crazy when he set off to navigate the Colorado River in wooden boats. His small band of men spent 98 days traveling 1,000 miles down the Green and Colorado rivers. So difficult was the journey that when some of the expedition's boats were wrecked by powerful rapids, part of the group abandoned the journey and set out on foot, never to be seen again.

How wrong the early explorers were about this supposedly Godforsaken landscape. Instead of being abandoned as a worthless wasteland, the Grand Canyon has become one of the most important natural wonders on the planet, a magnet for people from all over the world. By raft, by mule, on foot, and in helicopters and small planes—some five million people each year come to the canyon to gaze into this great chasm.

However, there have been those in the recent past who regarded the canyon as mere wasted space, suitable only for filling with water. Upstream of the Grand Canyon stands Glen Canyon Dam, which forms Lake Powell, while downstream lies Lake Mead, created by Hoover Dam. The same thing could have happened to the Grand Canyon, but luckily the forces for preservation prevailed. Today the Grand Canyon is the last major undammed stretch of the Colorado River.

The Colorado River, named by early Spanish explorers for the pinkish color of its muddy waters, once carried immense loads of silt. Due to the Glen Canyon Dam, the water in the Grand Canyon is much clearer (and colder) than it once was and no longer flows murky and pink from heavy loads of eroding sandstone. The water that now rumbles through the Grand Canyon flows cold and clear from the bottom of the Glen Canyon Dam after it has had a chance to deposit its silt on the bottom of Lake Powell.

While the waters of the Colorado are now clearer than before, the same cannot be said for the air in the canyon. Yes, you'll find smog here, smog that has been blamed on both Las Vegas and Los Angeles to the west and a coal-fired power plant to the east, near Page. Scrubbers installed on the power plant's smokestacks should help the park's air quality, but there isn't much to be done about smog drifting up from Las Vegas.

However, the most visible and frustrating negative impact on the park in recent years has been the traffic congestion at the South Rim during the busy months from spring to fall. With five million visitors each year, traffic during the summer months has become almost as bad at the South Rim as it is during rush hour in any major city, and finding a parking space can be the biggest challenge of a visit to Grand Canyon National Park. This may all change in the next few years if the park goes through with the proposed construction of a new light-rail system connecting the community of Tusayan with the South Rim. The light rail would in turn connect with the alternative-fuel buses that operate along the South Rim. As part of the overall new vision for the park, there are also plans to build a multiuse greenway trail along the South Rim. Unfortunately, as of this writing, the light-rail plan has been put on hold due to falling visitor numbers (and thus, park revenues) and escalating costs.

The first phase of this plan was implemented in late 2000, when the new Canyon View Information Plaza opened. However, this information plaza was designed specifically as part of the light-rail system, which has not yet been built. Consequently, there is no parking near the information plaza, and getting here from the far end of Grand Canyon Village can take 45 minutes or more, which makes the plaza very inconvenient for visitors. Until the light-rail system or some other people-moving system is in place, you can expect continued parking problems, traffic congestion, and the added inconvenience of trying to get to the information plaza. But don't let these inconveniences dissuade you from visiting. Despite the crowds, the Grand Canyon still more than lives up to its name and is one of the most amazing sights on earth.

GETTING THERE

BY CAR   In the past few years, parking problems, traffic jams, and traffic congestion have become the norm at Grand Canyon Village during the popular summer months (and are becoming common in spring and fall as well). If at all possible, travel into the park by some means other than car. (Alternatives include taking the Grand Canyon Railway from Williams, flying into the Grand Canyon Airport and then taking the Tusayan–Grand Canyon Shuttle or a taxi, or taking the Nava-Hopi Tours bus service from Flagstaff.) There are plenty of scenic overlooks, hiking trails, restaurants, and lodges in the village area, and depending on the time of year, free shuttle buses operate along both the West Rim Drive and the East Rim Drive.

If you do drive, be sure you have plenty of gasoline in your car before setting out for the canyon; there are few service stations in this remote part of the state. The South Rim of the Grand Canyon is 60 miles north of Williams and I-40 on Ariz. 64 and U.S. 180. Flagstaff, the nearest city of any size, is 78 miles away. From Flagstaff, it's possible to take U.S. 180 directly to the South Rim or U.S. 89 to Ariz. 64 and the east entrance to the park.

Grand Canyon National Park is currently developing a combination light-rail and alternative-fuel bus system for transporting visitors to and around the South Rim and Grand Canyon Village. Plans are to have a light-rail system connect Tusayan, outside the park's south entrance, with the new Canyon View Information Plaza, which is the South Rim's main orientation area for visitors. From this transit center, alternative-fuel buses shuttle visitors to various points along the South Rim. If and when the light-rail system is built, day visitors will park outside the park; by leaving their vehicles outside the park and taking light rail to the South Rim, much of the traffic congestion should be alleviated. This new transportation plan may be implemented over the next few years if funding is forthcoming.

BY PLANE   The Grand Canyon Airport is 6 miles south of Grand Canyon Village in Tusayan. Airlines flying from Las Vegas include **Scenic Airlines** (© 800/446-4584), which charges $227 round-trip, and **Air Vegas** (© 800/255-7474), which charges $278 round-trip. Alternatively, you can fly into Flagstaff and then arrange another mode of transportation the rest of the way to the national park (see "Flagstaff," earlier in this chapter, for details).

BY TRAIN   The **Grand Canyon Railway** operates excursion trains between Williams and the South Rim of the Grand Canyon. See "Williams," earlier in this chapter, for details.

For long-distance connections, **Amtrak** (© 800/872-7245) provides service to Flagstaff and Williams. From Flagstaff, it's then possible to take a bus directly to Grand Canyon Village. From Williams, you can take the Grand Canyon

Railway excursion to Grand Canyon Village. Note that the Williams stop is undeveloped and is on the outskirts of town. If you plan to take the train to Williams, arrange in advance to get picked up by your hotel.

BY BUS Bus service between Phoenix, Flagstaff, and Grand Canyon Village is provided by **Nava-Hopi Tours** (© **800/892-8687** or 520/774-5003; www.navahopitours.com). Round-trip fares are $76 between Phoenix and Grand Canyon Village, $28 between Flagstaff and Grand Canyon Village.

VISITOR INFORMATION
You can get advance information on the Grand Canyon by contacting **Grand Canyon National Park,** P.O. Box 129, Grand Canyon, AZ 86023 (© **520/ 638-7888;** www.nps.gov/grca).

When you arrive at the park, stop by the **Canyon View Visitor Center,** at Canyon View Information Plaza, 6 miles north of the south entrance. Here you'll find informative indoor and outdoor exhibits about the canyon, an information desk where you can pick up various brochures and maps, and a large shop selling maps as well as books and videos about the canyon. The center is open daily (hours vary with the seasons). Unfortunately, the information plaza, which is well designed for handling large crowds, has no adjacent parking, so you'll have to park where you can and then walk or take a free shuttle bus. The nearest places to park are at Mather Point, Market Plaza, park headquarters, and Yavapai Observation Station. If you're parked anywhere in Grand Canyon Village, you'll want to catch the Village Route bus. If you happen to be parked at Yaki Point, you can take the Kaibab Trail Route bus. *The Guide,* a small newspaper crammed full of useful information about the park, is available at both South Rim park entrances.

For information on services outside the park in Tusayan, contact the **Grand Canyon Chamber of Commerce,** P.O. Box 3007, Grand Canyon, AZ 86023 (© **520/638-2901;** www.grandcanyonchamber.com).

ORIENTATION
Grand Canyon Village is built on the South Rim of the canyon and divided roughly into two sections. At the east end of the village are the Canyon View Information Plaza, Yavapai Lodge, Trailer Village, and Mather Campground. At the west end are El Tovar Hotel and Bright Angel, Kachina, Thunderbird, and Maswik lodges, as well as several restaurants, the train depot, and the trailhead for the Bright Angel Trail.

GETTING AROUND
As mentioned earlier, the Grand Canyon Village area can be extremely congested, especially in summer. If possible, you may want to use one of the transportation options below to avoid the park's traffic jams and parking problems. To give you an idea, in summer you can expect at least a 20- to 30-minute wait at the South Rim entrance gate just to get into the park. You can cut the waiting time here by acquiring a national park pass (Golden Eagle, Golden Age, or Golden Access) before arriving. With pass in hand, you can use the express lane for seasonal pass holders.

BY BUS The **Cassi Grand Canyon–Tusayan Shuttle** (© **520/638-0821;** www.cassitours.com) operates between the Grand Canyon Airport in Tusayan, at the park's south entrance, and Grand Canyon Village, with stops in Tusayan at the Canyon Squire Inn, the IMAX Theater, and Babbitt's Store, and in Grand Canyon Village at Maswik Transportation Center. The fare is $6 each way, with service between 9:30am and 6:30pm in summer (reduced hours in other months). By taking this shuttle into the park, you get a reduced park admission of $4 per adult (free for children under 17). So, not only can you avoid parking problems by taking this shuttle, but you can also save money—a win-win situation!

March through November, free shuttle buses operate on three routes within the park. The **Village Route** bus circles through Grand Canyon Village throughout the day with frequent stops at the Canyon View Information Plaza, Market Plaza (site of general store, bank, laundry, and showers), hotels, campgrounds, restaurants, and other facilities. The **Hermit's Rest Route** bus takes visitors to eight canyon overlooks west of Bright Angel Lodge. The **Kaibab Trail Route,** which stops at the Canyon View Information Plaza, the South Kaibab Trailhead, Yaki Point, Mather Point, and Yavapai Observation Station, provides the only access to Yaki Point, the trailhead for the South Kaibab Trail to the bottom of the canyon. Hikers needing transportation to or from Yaki Point when the bus is not running can use a taxi (© **520/638-2822**).

Trans Canyon (© **520/638-2820**) offers shuttle-bus service between the South Rim and the North Rim. The vans leave the South Rim at 1:30pm and arrive at the North Rim at 6:30pm. The return trip leaves the North Rim at 7am, arriving back at the South Rim at noon. The fare is $65 one way; reservations are required.

BY CAR   There are **service stations** outside the south entrance to the park in Tusayan, at Desert View near the east entrance (this station is seasonal), and east of the park at Cameron. Because of the long distances within the park and to towns outside the park, be sure you have plenty of gas before setting out on a drive. Gas at the canyon is very expensive.

BY TAXI   There is taxi service available to and from the airport, trailheads, and other destinations (© **520/638-2822**). The fare from the airport to Grand Canyon Village is $10 for up to two adults ($5 for each additional person).

FAST FACTS: **The Grand Canyon**

Accessibility Check *The Guide* for park programs, services, and facilities that are partially or fully accessible. You can also get *The Grand Canyon National Park Accessibility Guide* at park entrances, Canyon View Center, Yavapai Observation Station, Kolb Studio, Tusayan Museum, and Desert View Information Center. Temporary accessibility permits are available at the park entrances, Canyon View Center, and Yavapai Observation Station. The national park has wheelchairs available at no charge for temporary use inside the park. You can usually find one of these wheelchairs at the Canyon View Center. Wheelchair-accessible tours are offered by prior arrangement through any lodge transportation desk or by calling Grand Canyon National Park Lodges (© **520/638-2631**). Accessible shuttle buses are also available with a 48-hour advance reservation (© **520/638-0591**).

Admission Admission to Grand Canyon National Park is $20 per car (or $10 per person if you happen to be coming in on foot or by bicycle). Your admission ticket, which is good for 7 days, is nothing more than a small paper receipt similar to what you might get at a store. Don't lose it, or you'll have to pay again.

Banks & ATM Networks There's an ATM at the Bank One (© **520/ 638-2437**) at Market Plaza, which is near Yavapai Lodge. The bank is open Monday through Thursday from 10am to 3pm and Friday from 10am to 5pm.

Bus Tours If you'd rather leave the driving to someone else and enjoy more of the scenery, you can opt for a bus or van tour of one or more sections of the park. Grand Canyon National Park Lodges (© **520/638-2631**) offers several different tours within the park. Tours can be booked by calling or by stopping at one of the transportation desks, which are at Bright Angel, Maswik, and Yavapai lodges (see "Where to Stay," later in this chapter). Prices range from $11.50 for a 1½-hour sunset tour to $32 for a combination tour to both Hermit's Rest and Desert View.

Climate The climate at the Grand Canyon is quite different from that of Phoenix, and between the rim and the canyon floor there's a considerable difference. Because the South Rim is at 7,000 feet, it gets very cold in winter. You can expect snow anytime between November and May, and winter temperatures can be below 0°F at night, with daytime highs in the 20s or 30s. Summer temperatures at the rim range from highs in the 80s to lows in the 50s. The North Rim of the canyon, which is slightly higher than the South Rim and stays a bit cooler throughout the year, is open to visitors only from May to October because the access road is not kept cleared of snow.

On the canyon floor, temperatures are considerably higher. In summer, the mercury can reach 120°F with lows in the 70s, while in winter, temperatures are quite pleasant with highs in the 50s and lows in the 30s. July, August, and September are the wettest months because of frequent afternoon thunderstorms. April, May, and June are the driest months, but it still might rain or even snow. Down on the canyon floor, there is much less rain year-round.

Festivals The **Grand Canyon Music Festival** (© **800/997-8285** or 520/638-9215; www.grandcanyonmusicfest.org) is held each year in mid-September.

Hospitals/Clinics The **Grand Canyon Clinic** (© **520/638-2551**) is on Clinic Drive, off Center Road (the road that runs past the National Park Service ranger office). The clinic is open Monday through Friday from 9am to 6pm and Saturday from 9am to 1pm. It provides 24-hour emergency service.

Laundry A coin-operated laundry is located near Mather Campground in the Camper Services building.

Lost & Found Report lost items or turn in found items at the Canyon View Center. Call © **520/638-7798**. For items lost or found at a hotel, restaurant, or lounge, call © **520/638-2631**.

Parking If you want to avoid parking headaches, try using the lot in front of the Canyon Village Marketplace (the general store), which is up a side road near Yavapai Lodge and the Canyon View Information Plaza. From this large parking area, a paved hiking trail leads to the historic section of the village in less than 1½ miles, and most of the route is along the rim. Another option is to park at the Maswik Transportation Center parking lot, which is served by the Village Route shuttle bus.

Police In an emergency, dial © **911.** Ticketing speeders is one of the main occupations of the park's police force, so obey the posted speed limits.

Post Office The post office is at Market Plaza near Yavapai Lodge.

Radio KSGC, 92.1 FM, provides news, music, the latest weather forecasts, and travel-related information for the Grand Canyon area.

Road Conditions Information on road conditions in the Grand Canyon area is available by calling © **888/411-7623** or 520/638-7888.

Safety The most important safety tip to remember is to be careful near the edge of the canyon. Footing can be unstable and may give way. Be sure to keep your distance from wild animals, no matter how friendly they may appear. Avoid hiking alone if at all possible and keep in mind that the canyon rim is more than a mile above sea level (it's harder to breathe up here). Don't leave valuables in your car or tent.

GRAND CANYON VILLAGE & VICINITY: YOUR FIRST LOOK AT THE CANYON

Grand Canyon Village is the first stop for the vast majority of the more than five million people who visit the Grand Canyon every year. Consequently, it is the most crowded area in the park, but it also has the most overlooks and visitor services. Its many historic buildings, while nowhere near as impressive as the canyon itself, add to its popularity of the village, which, if it weren't so crowded all the time, would have a pleasant mountain village atmosphere.

For most visitors, that all-important initial glimpse of the canyon comes at **Mather Point,** the first canyon overlook you reach if you enter the park through the south entrance. From this overlook, there's a paved path to the Canyon View Information Plaza. Continuing west toward the village proper, you next come to **Yavapai Point,** a favorite spot for sunrise and sunset photos and the site of the **Yavapai Observation Station.** This historic building houses a small museum and has excellent views. Yavapai point is at the east end of a paved pathway that extends for more than 3 miles to the west side of Grand Canyon Village. At press time, a trail connecting Mather Point and Yavapai Point was under construction.

Continuing west from Yavapai Point, you'll come to a parking lot at park headquarters and a side road that leads to parking at the Market Plaza, which is one of the closest parking lots to the Canyon View Information Plaza.

West of these parking areas is Grand Canyon Village proper, where a paved pathway leads along the rim providing lots of good (though crowded) spots for taking pictures. The village is also the site of such historic buildings as **El Tovar Hotel** and **Bright Angel Lodge,** both worth brief visits. Adjacent to El Tovar are two historic souvenir and curio shops. **Hopi House Gift Store and Art Gallery,** the first shop in the park, was built in 1905 to resemble a Hopi pueblo and to serve as a place for Hopi artisans to work and sell their crafts. Today, it's full of Hopi and Navajo arts and crafts, including expensive kachinas, rugs, jewelry, and pottery. The second floor of the Hopi House is an art gallery. The nearby **Verkamps Curios** originally opened in a tent in 1898, but John Verkamp soon went out of business. However, the store reopened in 1905 and ever since has been the main place to look for souvenirs and crafts. Just inside the door is a 535-pound meteorite. Both shops are open daily; hours vary seasonally.

Impressions

We are imprisoned three quarters of a mile in the depths of the earth
and the great unknown river shrinks into insignificance as it dashes its
angry waves against the walls and cliffs that rise to the world above.
                                                    —Maj. John Wesley Powell,
                                        on his successful trip through the Grand Canyon

---

To the west of Bright Angel Lodge, two buildings cling precariously to the rim of the canyon. These are the **Lookout** and **Kolb studios,** both of which are listed on the National Register of Historic Places. **Kolb Studio** is named for Ellsworth and Emory Kolb, two brothers who set up a photographic studio on the rim of the Grand Canyon in 1904. The construction of this studio generated one of the Grand Canyon's first controversies—over whether buildings should be allowed on the canyon rim. Because the Kolbs had friends in high places, their sprawling studio and movie theater remained. Emory Kolb lived here until his death in 1976, by which time the studio had been listed as a historic building. Today it serves as a bookstore, while the auditorium houses special exhibits. **Lookout Studio,** built in 1914 from a design by Mary Elizabeth Jane Colter, was the Fred Harvey Company's answer to the Kolb brothers' studio. Photographs and books about the canyon were sold at the studio, which incorporates architectural styles of the Hopi and the Anasazi. The use of native limestone and an uneven roofline allow the studio to blend in with the canyon walls and give it the look of an old ruin. It now houses a souvenir store and two lookout points. Both the Kolb and Lookout studios are open daily; hours vary seasonally.

HERMIT ROAD

Hermit Road leads 8 miles west from Grand Canyon Village to Hermit's Rest; mile for mile, it has the greatest concentration of breathtaking viewpoints in the park. Because it is closed to private vehicles March through November, it is also one of the most pleasant places to do a little canyon viewing or easy hiking during the busiest times of year. No traffic jams, no parking problems, and plenty of free shuttle buses to hop on and off of along the route. Westbound shuttle buses stop at eight overlooks (Trailview, Maricopa Point, Powell Point, Hopi Point, Mohave Point, The Abyss, Pima Point, and Hermit's Rest); eastbound buses stop only at Mohave Point and Hopi Point. From December to February, you can drive your own vehicle along this road, but keep in mind that winters usually include a lot of snow and the road can sometimes be closed due to hazardous driving conditions.

Since you probably won't want to stop at every viewpoint along this route, here are some tips to help you get the most out of an excursion along Hermit Road. First of all, keep in mind that the earlier you catch a shuttle bus, the more likely you are to avoid the crowds (buses start an hour before sunrise so photographers can get good sunrise shots). Second, remember that the closer you are to Grand Canyon Village, the larger the crowds will be. So, head out early and get a couple of miles between you and the village before getting off the shuttle bus.

The first two stops are **Trailview Overlook** and **Maricopa Point,** both on the paved section of the Rim Trail and within 1½ miles of the village, so consequently usually pretty crowded. If you just want to do a short, easy walk on

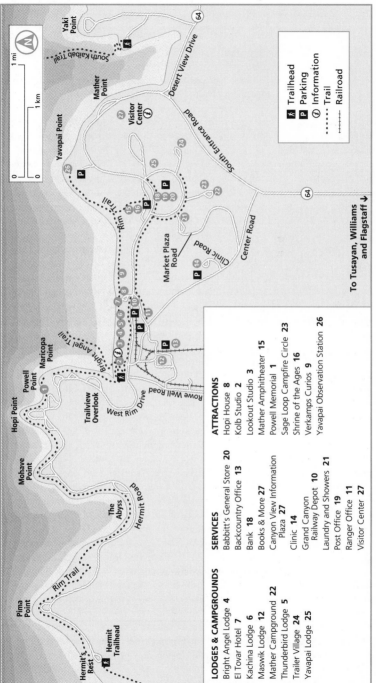

Trailhead
Parking
Information
Trail
Railroad

LODGES & CAMPGROUNDS
Bright Angel Lodge **4**
El Tovar Hotel **7**
Kachina Lodge **6**
Maswik Lodge **12**
Mather Campground **22**
Thunderbird Lodge **5**
Trailer Village **24**
Yavapai Lodge **25**

SERVICES
Babbitt's General Store **20**
Backcountry Office **13**
Bank **18**
Books & More **27**
Canyon View Information Plaza **27**
Clinic **14**
Grand Canyon Railway Depot **10**
Laundry and Showers **21**
Post Office **19**
Ranger Office **11**
Visitor Center **27**

ATTRACTIONS
Hopi House **8**
Kolb Studio **2**
Lookout Studio **3**
Mather Amphitheater **15**
Powell Memorial **1**
Sage Loop Campfire Circle **23**
Shrine of the Ages **16**
Verkamps Curios **9**
Yavapai Observation Station **26**

To Tusayan, Williams and Flagstaff →

pavement, get out at Maricopa Point and walk back to the village. From either overlook, you have a view of the Bright Angel Trail winding down into the canyon from Grand Canyon Village. The trail, which leads to the bottom of the canyon, crosses the Tonto Plateau about 3,000 feet below the rim. This plateau is the site of Indian Garden, where there's a campground in a grove of cotton-wood trees. Because the views from these two overlooks are not significantly dif-ferent from those in the village, we'd suggest skipping these stops if you've already spent time gazing into the canyon from the village.

Powell Point, the third stop, is the site of a memorial to John Wesley Powell, who, in 1869 with a party of nine men, became the first person to navigate the Colorado River through the Grand Canyon. Visible at Powell Point are the remains of the Orphan Mine, which began operation in 1893. The mine went out of business because transporting the copper to a city where it could be sold was too expensive. Uranium was discovered here in 1954, but in 1966 the mine was shut down, and the land became part of Grand Canyon National Park. Again, we recommend continuing on to the more spectacular vistas that lie ahead.

The next stop is **Hopi Point,** which is one of the three best stops along this route. From here you can see a long section of the Colorado River far below you. Because of the great distance, the river seems to be a tiny, quiet stream, but in reality the section you see is more than 100 yards wide and races through Gran-ite Rapids. Because Hopi Point juts out into the canyon, it is one of the best spots in the park for taking sunrise and sunset photos; shuttle buses operate from 1 hour before sunrise to 1 hour after sunset.

The view is even more spectacular at the next stop, **Mohave Point.** Here you can see the river in two directions. Three rapids are visible from this overlook, and on a quiet day, you can sometimes even hear Hermit Rapids. As with almost all rapids in the canyon, these are formed at the mouth of a side canyon where boulders loosened by storms and carried by flooded streams are deposited in the Colorado River. Don't miss this stop; it's got the best view on Hermit Road!

Next you come to **The Abyss,** the appropriately named 3,000-foot drop created by the Great Mojave Wall. This vertiginous view is one of the most awe-inspiring in the park. The walls of the Abyss are red sandstone that's more resistant to erosion than the softer shale in the layer below. Other layers of erosion-resistant sandstone have formed the freestanding pillars that are visible from here. The largest of these pillars is called the Monument. If you're looking for a good hike along this road, get out here and walk westward to either Pima Point (2.9 miles distant) or Hermit's Rest (4 miles away).

The **Pima Point** overlook, because it is set back from the road, is another good place to get off the bus. From here, the Rim Trail leads through the forest near the canyon rim, providing good views undisturbed by traffic on Hermit Road. From this overlook, it's also possible to see the remains of Hermit Camp on the Tonto Plateau. Built by the Santa Fe Railroad, Hermit Camp was a pop-ular tourist destination between 1911 and 1930 and provided cabins and tents. Only foundations remain.

The final stop on Hermit Road is at **Hermit's Rest,** which was named for Louis Boucher, a prospector who came to the canyon in the 1890s and was known as the Hermit. The log-and-stone Hermit's Rest building, designed by Mary Elizabeth Jane Colter and built in 1914, is on the National Register of Historic Places and is one of the most fascinating structures in the park. With

Tips Shooting the Canyon: Tips for Photographers

By the time most people leave the Grand Canyon, they've shot several rolls of film. This is not at all surprising considering the beauty of this rugged landscape. But it's not always easy to capture the canyon's spirit. Here are some tips to help you bring back the best possible photos from your trip:

- A polarizing filter is a great investment if you have the kind of camera that accepts lens filters. A polarizing filter reduces haze, lessens the contrast between shadowy areas and light areas, and deepens the color of the sky.

- The best times to photograph the canyon are at sunrise and sunset, when filtered and sharply angled sunlight paints the canyon walls in beautiful shades of lavender and pink. At these times, the shadows are at their most dramatic. To capture these ephemeral moments, it's best to use a tripod and a long exposure. The worst time to photograph the canyon is at noon when there are almost no shadows, and thus little texture or contrast. The National Park Service includes a table with sunrise and sunset times in *The Guide*, the park's official visitor newspaper.

- Something else to keep in mind is that the Grand Canyon is immense. A wide-angle lens may leave the canyon looking on paper like a distant plane of dirt. Try zooming in on narrower sections of the canyon to emphasize a single dramatic landscape element. If you're shooting with a wide-angle lens, try to include something in the foreground (people or a tree branch) to give the photo perspective and scale.

- When shooting portraits against a sunrise or sunset, use a flash to illuminate your subjects; otherwise, your camera meter may expose for the bright light in the background and leave your subjects in shadow.

its snack bar, it makes a great place to linger while you soak up a bit of park history. The steep Hermit Trail, which leads down into the canyon, begins just past Hermit's Rest.

DESERT VIEW DRIVE

Desert View Drive extends for 25 miles from Grand Canyon Village to Desert View, which is just inside the east entrance to the park. Along this route, you'll find not only good viewpoints but also several picnic areas. Much of this drive is through forests, and canyon views are limited, which should make it your second choice for views, especially if you are short on time. Also keep in mind that shuttle buses operate only as far as Yaki Point, so any time of year, you're going to need a car to do this drive.

The first stop is **Yaki Point,** near the trailhead for the South Kaibab Trail. The spectacular view from here encompasses a wide section of the central canyon. The large, flat-topped butte to the northeast is Wotan's Throne, one of the canyon's easily recognizable features. March through November, Yaki Point is closed to private vehicles and can be reached only via the Kaibab Trail Route shuttle bus, which begins its route at the Canyon View Information Plaza. The South Kaibab Trail is the preferred hiking route down to Phantom Ranch and is a more scenic route down into the canyon than the Bright Angel Trail, so if you're planning a day hike into the canyon, this should be your number-one choice.

The next stop, **Grandview Point,** affords a view of Horseshoe Mesa, another interesting feature of the canyon landscape. The mesa was the site of the Last Chance Copper Mine in the early 1890s. Later that same decade, the Grandview Hotel was built and served canyon visitors until its close in 1908. The steep, unmaintained Grandview Trail leads down to Horseshoe Mesa from here.

Next along the drive is **Moran Point,** from which you can see a bright red layer of shale in the canyon walls. This point is named for 19th-century landscape painter Thomas Moran, whose artwork shared the beauty of the West with people of the eastern cities.

The free **Tusayan Museum** (open daily in summer, as staffing permits in other months) is the next stop. This small museum is dedicated to the Hopi tribe and ancient Anasazi people who inhabited the region 800 years ago; inside are artfully displayed exhibits on various aspects of Anasazi life. Outside is a short, self-guided trail through the ruins of an Anasazi village. Free guided tours are available.

At **Lipan Point,** you get one of the park's best views of the Colorado River; you can even see a couple of major rapids. From here you can also see the Grand Canyon *supergroup:* several strata of rock tilted at an angle to the other layers of rock in the canyon. Their angle indicates there was a period of geological mountain building before the depositing of layers of sandstone, limestone, and shale. The red, white, and black rocks of the supergroup are composed of sedimentary rock and layers of lava. From nearby **Navajo Point,** the Colorado River and Escalante Butte are both visible, and there's a good view of Desert Tower.

Desert View, with its trading post, general store, snack bar, service station, information center, bookstore, and watchtower, is the end of this scenic drive. The road does continue east from here, but it soon leaves the park (outside the park, there are still some good views to be had of the Little Colorado River). The scenery is breathtaking from anywhere at Desert View, but the very best perspective is from atop the Desert View Watchtower (open daily; admission 25¢). Although the watchtower looks as though it had been built centuries ago, it actually dates from 1932. Architect Mary Elizabeth Jane Colter, who is responsible for much of the park's historic architecture, designed it to resemble the prehistoric towers that dot the Southwestern landscape. Built as an observation tower and rest stop for tourists, the watchtower incorporates Native American designs and art. The curio shop on the ground floor is a replica of a kiva (sacred ceremonial chamber) and has lots of interesting souvenirs, regional crafts, and books. The tower's second floor features work by Hopi artist Fred Kabotie. Covering the walls are pictographs incorporating traditional designs. On the walls and ceiling of the upper two floors are more traditional images by artist Fred Geary, this time reproductions of petroglyphs from throughout the Southwest. From the roof, the highest point on the South Rim (7,522 ft. above sea level), it's possible to see the Colorado River, the Painted Desert to the northeast, the San Francisco Peaks to the south, and Marble Canyon to the north.

Coin-operated binoculars provide close-up views of some of the noteworthy landmarks of this end of the canyon. Several black-mirror "reflectoscopes" provide interesting darkened views of some of the most spectacular sections of the canyon. The gift shop offers a pamphlet describing the watchtower in detail.

HIKING THE CANYON

No visit to the canyon is complete without journeying below the rim on one of the park's hiking trails. While the views don't necessarily get any better than they are from the top, they do change considerably. Gazing up at all those thousands of feet of vertical rock walls provides a very different perspective than that from atop the rim. Should you venture far below the rim, you also stand a chance of seeing fossils, old mines, petroglyphs, wildflowers, and wildlife. However, with more than five million people visiting the Grand Canyon annually, you can forget about finding any solitude on the park's main hiking trails.

That said, there is no better way to see the canyon than on foot (our apologies to the mules). You can get away from *most* of the crowds simply by heading down the Bright Angel or South Kaibab trail for 2 or 3 miles. Keep in mind, though, that these are the two busiest trails below the canyon rim and can see hundreds of hikers per day. If you want to see fewer other hikers and are in good shape, consider heading down the Grand View Trail or the Hermit Trail instead. If you're just looking for an easy hike that doesn't involve hiking back up out of the canyon, the Rim Trail is for you.

The Grand Canyon offers some of the most rugged and strenuous hiking anywhere in the United States, and for this reason anyone attempting even a short walk should be well prepared. Each year, people are injured or killed because they set out to hike the canyon without preparing properly. Most of these injuries and fatalities are suffered by day hikers who set out without sturdy footgear and without food or adequate amounts of water. Even a short 30-minute hike in summer can dehydrate you (carry and drink at least 2 qt. of water), and a long hike in the heat can necessitate drinking more than a gallon of water. Don't attempt to hike from the rim to the Colorado River and back in 1 day. Many people who have tried this have died. Also remember that mules have the right of way.

DAY HIKES

Hikers tend to gravitate to loop trails, but here on the South Rim, you'll find no such trails. So day hikers must reconcile themselves to out-and-back hikes. Still, the vastly different scenery in every direction makes out-and-back hikes here as interesting as any loop trail could be. The only problem is that most of the out-and-back trails are the reverse of what you'll find most places. Instead of starting out by slogging up a steep mountain, you let gravity assist you in hiking down into the canyon. With little negative reinforcement and few natural turnaround destinations, it is easy to hike so far that the return trip back up the trail becomes an arduous death march. Know your limits and turn around before you become tired, and your hike down into the canyon will likely be the highlight of your visit. On the canyon rim, the only hiking trail is the Rim Trail, while the Bright Angel, South Kaibab, Grandview, and Hermit trails all head down into the canyon.

For an easy, flat hike, your only option is the **Rim Trail,** which stretches from Yavapai Point east of Grand Canyon Village to Hermit's Rest, 8 miles west of the village. Just over 3 miles of this trail are paved, and because this paved portion passes through Grand Canyon Village, it is always the most crowded stretch of trail in the park. To the west of the village, after the pavement ends, the Rim Trail leads another 6.7 miles out to Hermit's Rest. For most of this distance, the trail follows the Hermit Road, which means you'll have to deal with traffic noise (mostly from shuttle buses). To get the most enjoyment out of a hike along this stretch, we like to head out as early in the morning as possible (to avoid the crowds) and get off at the Abyss shuttle stop. From here it's a 4-mile hike to Hermit's Rest; for more than half of this distance, the trail isn't as close to the road as it is at the Grand Canyon Village end of the route. Plus, Hermit's Rest makes a great place to rest, and from there you can catch a shuttle bus back to the village. Alternatively, you could start hiking from Grand Canyon Village (it's just over 8 miles from the west end of the village to Hermit's Rest) or any of the seven shuttle-bus stops en route, or take the shuttle all the way to Hermit's Rest and then hike back.

The **Bright Angel Trail,** which starts just west of Bright Angel Lodge in Grand Canyon Village, is the most popular trail into the canyon because it starts right where the greatest number of park visitors tend to congregate (near the ice-cream parlor and the hotels). It is also the route used by mule riders headed down into the canyon. Bear in mind that this trail follows a narrow side canyon for several miles down into the Grand Canyon and thus has somewhat limited views. For these reasons, this trail is worth avoiding if you're on foot. On the other hand, it's the only maintained trail into the canyon that has potable water, and there are four destinations along the trail that make good turnaround points. Both 1½ Mile Resthouse (1,131 ft. below the rim) and 3 Mile Resthouse (2,112 ft. below the rim) have water (except in winter, when the water is turned off). Keep in mind that these rest houses take their names from their distance from the rim; if you hike to 3 Mile Resthouse, you still have a 3-mile hike back up. Destinations for longer day hikes include Indian Garden (9.2 miles round-trip) and Plateau Point (12.2 miles round-trip), which are both just over 3,000 feet below the rim. There is year-round water at Indian Garden.

The **South Kaibab Trail** begins near Yaki Point east of Grand Canyon Village and is the preferred route down to Phantom Ranch. This trail also offers the best views of any of the day hikes into the canyon, so should you have time for only one day hike into the canyon, make it this trail (not the more popular Bright Angel Trail, which, in its upper stretch, is in a side canyon with limited views). From the trailhead, it's 3 miles round-trip to Cedar Ridge or 6 miles round-trip to Skeleton Point. The hike is very strenuous, and there's no water available along the trail.

If you're looking to escape the crowds and are an experienced mountain or desert hiker with good, sturdy boots, consider the unmaintained **Hermit Trail,** which begins at Hermit's Rest, 8 miles west of Grand Canyon Village at the end of Hermit Road. It's a 5-mile round-trip to Santa Maria Spring. An additional 2 miles (for a total of 7 miles) will bring you to Dripping Springs, which is on the Dripping Springs Trail. This hike loses almost all of its elevation (1,600–1,700 ft.) in the first 1½ miles. Beyond Santa Maria Spring, the Hermit Trail descends to the Colorado River, but it is a 17-mile hike, one way, from the trailhead. Water from either of the two springs along this route must be treated with a water filter, iodine, or purification tablets, or by boiling for at least 10 minutes, so you're better off just carrying sufficient water for your hike. Hermit Road is closed to private vehicles March through November, so chances are you'll need to take the free shuttle out to the trailhead. If you take the first shuttle of the day, you'll probably have the trail almost all to yourself.

The **Grandview Trail,** which begins at Grandview Point 12 miles east of Grand Canyon Village, is another steep and unmaintained trail that's a good choice for physically fit hikers with good boots. The strenuous 6-mile round-trip hike leads down to Horseshoe Mesa, 2,600 feet below the rim-top trailhead. There's no water available, so carry at least 2 quarts. Allow at least 7 hours for this rugged hike. Just to give you an idea of how steep this trail is, you'll lose more than 2,000 feet of elevation in the first three-quarters of a mile down to Coconino Saddle!

BACKPACKING

Backpacking the Grand Canyon is an unforgettable experience. Although most people are content to simply hike down to Phantom Ranch and back, there are many miles of trails deep in the canyon. Keep in mind, however, that to backpack the canyon, you'll need to do a lot of planning. A **Backcountry Use Permit** is required of all hikers planning to overnight in the canyon, unless you'll be staying at Phantom Ranch in one of the cabins or a dormitory.

Because a limited number of hikers are allowed into the canyon on any given day, it's important to make reservations as soon as it is possible to do so. Reservations are taken in person, by mail, by fax (but not by phone), and online. Contact the **Backcountry Office,** Grand Canyon National Park, P.O. Box 129, Grand Canyon, AZ 86023 (© **520/638-7875** from 1–5pm for information; fax 520/638-2125; www.nps.gov/grca). Holiday periods are the most popular. The office begins accepting reservations on the first of every month for the following 5 months. If you want to hike over the Labor Day weekend, be sure you make your reservation on May 1! If you show up without a reservation, go to the Backcountry Information Center (open daily from 8am–noon and 1–5pm), adjacent to the Maswik Lodge, and put your name on the waiting list. When applying for a permit, you must specify your exact itinerary, and once in the canyon, you must stick to this itinerary. Backpacking fees include a nonrefundable $10 backcountry permit fee and a $5 per person per night backcountry camping fee. Visa and MasterCard are accepted for permit fees. Keep in mind that you'll still have to pay park admission when you arrive at the Grand Canyon.

There are **campgrounds** at Indian Garden, Bright Angel Campground (near Phantom Ranch), and Cottonwood, but hikers are limited to 2 nights per trip at each of these campgrounds (except Nov 15–Feb 28, when 4 nights are allowed at each campground). Other nights can be spent camping at undesignated sites in certain regions of the park.

The *Backcountry Trip Planner* contains information to help you plan your itinerary. It's available through the Backcountry Office. Maps are available through the **Grand Canyon Association,** P.O. Box 399, Grand Canyon, AZ 86023 (© **800/858-2808;** fax 520/638-2484; www.grandcanyon.org), and at bookstores and gift shops within the national park, including Canyon View Information Plaza, Kolb Studio, Desert View Information Center, Yavapai Observation Station, Tusayan Museum, and, on the North Rim, in Grand Canyon Lodge.

The best times of year to backpack are spring and autumn. In summer, temperatures at the bottom of the canyon are frequently above 100°F, while in winter, ice and snow at higher elevations make footing on trails precarious (crampons are recommended). Plan to carry at least 2 quarts, and preferably 1 gallon, of water whenever backpacking in the canyon.

If you'd like to have a guide lead you on a backpacking trip through some of the more remote and little visited parts of the park, contact **Grand Canyon Trail Guides** (© 888/283-3194 or 520/638-3194; http://grandcanyontrailguides. com), which offers guided hikes in the backcountry for around $205 to $275 per person per day, including most of your supplies and gear (lower rates apply if you supply some of your own gear and food). Guided day hikes are also available. A wide range of guided backpacking trips are offered by the Grand Canyon Field Institute (see below for details).

OTHER WAYS TO SEE THE CANYON
MULE RIDES

Mule rides into the canyon are some of the most popular activities in the Grand Canyon and have been since the turn of the last century, when the Bright Angel Trail was a toll road. However, after having a look at the steep drop-offs and narrow path of the Bright Angel Trail, you might decide this isn't exactly the place to trust your life to a mule. Never fear: Wranglers will be quick to reassure you they haven't lost a rider yet. Trips of various lengths and to different destinations are offered. The 1-day trip descends to Plateau Point, where there's a view of the Colorado River 1,300 feet below. This grueling trip requires riders to spend 6 hours in the saddle. Those who want to spend a night down in the canyon can choose an overnight trip to Phantom Ranch, where cabins and dormitories are available at the only lodge actually in the canyon. From mid-November to March, there's a 3-day/2-night trip to Phantom Ranch, but other times of year, you'll ride down one day and back up the next. Mule trips range in price from $118 for a 1-day ride to Plateau Point to $332 for an overnight ride to Phantom Ranch to $584 for a 2-night ride to Phantom Ranch. Couples get discounts on overnight rides.

A few rider qualifications to keep in mind before calling to make a reservation: You must weigh less than 200 pounds fully dressed, stand at least 4 feet 7 inches tall, and speak fluent English. Pregnant women are not allowed on mule trips.

Because these trail rides are very popular (especially in summer), they often book up 6 to 11 months in advance (reservations are taken up to 23 months in advance). Try to make a reservation as soon as you know when you'll be visiting. For more information or to make a reservation, contact **Grand Canyon National Park Lodges/AMFAC Parks & Resorts** (© 303/297-2757; fax 303/297-3175; www.amfac.com). If at the last minute (5 days or fewer from the day you want to ride) you decide you want to go on a mule trip, contact Grand Canyon National Park Lodges at its Arizona phone number (© 520/638-2631) for the remote possibility that there may be space available. If you arrive at the canyon without a reservation and decide that you'd like to go on a mule ride, stop by the Bright Angel Transportation Desk to get your name on the next day's waiting list.

HORSEBACK RIDES
Trail rides on the rim (but not into the canyon) are available from Moqui Lodge's **Apache Stables** (© 520/638-2891; www.apachestables.com), at the south entrance to the park. There are rides of various lengths, with prices ranging from $30 for a 1-hour ride to $95 for a 4-hour ride. Evening wagon rides ($12) are also offered. The stables are usually open April through mid-October (depending on the weather).

RIDING THE RAILS

In the early part of the 20th century, most visitors to the Grand Canyon arrived by train, and it's still possible to travel to the canyon along the steel rails. The **Grand Canyon Railway** (© 800/843-8724 or 520/773-1976; www.thetrain. com), which runs from Williams to Grand Canyon Village, uses turn-of-the-last-century steam engines (Memorial Day through Sept) and 1950s-vintage diesel engines (during other months) to pull 1920s passenger cars as well as a dome coach car. Trains depart from the Williams Depot, housed in the renovated Fray Marcos Hotel. Built in 1908, the hotel now houses a railroad museum, gift shop, and cafe. (Grand Canyon Railway also operates a new Fray Marcos Hotel, which really is a hotel.) At Grand Canyon Village, the trains use the 1910 log railway terminal in front of El Tovar Hotel.

Passengers have the choice of five classes of service: coach, club, first class, deluxe observation class (upstairs in the dome car), and luxury parlor car. Actors posing as cowboys provide entertainment, including music performances, aboard the train. The round-trip takes 8 hours (including 3¼ hr. at the canyon). Fares range from $55 to $140 for adults and from $25 to $110 for children 16 and under (not including tax or the park admission fee).

Not only is this a fun trip that provides great scenery and a trip back in time, but taking the train also allows you to avoid the traffic congestion and parking problems in Grand Canyon Village. When booking your train trip, you can also book a bus tour in the park, which will help you see more than you would on foot. The railway offers different room/train packages as well.

A BIRD'S-EYE VIEW

Despite controversies over noise and safety (there have been a few crashes over the years), airplane and helicopter flights over the Grand Canyon remain one of the most popular ways to see this natural wonder. Personally, we would rather enjoy the canyon on foot or from a saddle. However, the volume of flights over the canyon each day would indicate that quite a few people don't share our opinion. If you want to join the crowds buzzing the canyon, you'll find several companies operating out of the Grand Canyon Airport in Tusayan. Air tours last anywhere from 30 minutes to about 2 hours.

Companies offering tours by small plane include **Air Grand Canyon** (© 800/ 247-4726 or 520/638-2686; www.airgrandcanyon.com), **Airstar Airlines** (© 800/962-3869 or 520/638-2139; www.airstar.com), and **Grand Canyon Airlines** (© 800/528-2413 or 520/638-2407; www.grandcanyonairlines.com). Rates for 50-minute flights range from $71 to $89 for adults and $45 to $51 for children.

Helicopter tours are available from **Airstar Helicopters** (© 800/962-3869 or 520/638-2622; www.airstar.com), **Kenai Helicopters** (© 800/541-4537 or 520/638-2764; www.flykenai.com), and **Papillon Grand Canyon Helicopters** (© 800/528-2418 or 520/638-2419; www.papillon.com). Rates range from $94 to $99 for a 30-minute flight to between $154 and $161 for a 45- to 55-minute flight.

INTERPRETIVE PROGRAMS

Numerous interpretive programs are scheduled throughout the year at various South Rim locations. There are ranger-led walks that explore different aspects of the canyon, geology talks, lectures on the cultural and natural resources of the canyon, nature hikes, trips to fossil beds, and stargazing gatherings. At Tusayan

Ruin, there are guided tours. Evening programs are held at Mather Amphi-theater or the Shrine of the Ages. Consult your copy of *The Guide* for information on times and meeting points.

THE GRAND CANYON FIELD INSTITUTE

If you're the active type or would just like to turn your visit to the Grand Canyon into more of an educational experience, you may want to consider doing a trip with the **Grand Canyon Field Institute**, P.O. Box 399, Grand Canyon, AZ 86023 (© **520/638-2485**; www.grandcanyon.org/fieldinstitute). Cosponsored by Grand Canyon National Park and the Grand Canyon Association, the field institute schedules an amazing variety of guided, educational trips, such as challenging backpacking trips through the canyon (some for women only) and programs lasting anywhere from 2 to 10 days. Subjects covered include wilderness studies, geology, natural history, human history, photography, and art.

JEEP TOURS

If you'd like to see some parts of Grand Canyon National Park that most visitors never see, try a Jeep tour with **Grand Canyon Jeep Tours & Safaris** (© **800/320-JEEP** or 520/638-JEEP; www.grandcanyonjeeptours.com), which offers three different tours that visit the park as well as the adjacent Kaibab National Forest. One tour stops at a lookout tower where you get an elevated view of the canyon, while another visits an Indian ruin and site of petroglyphs and cave paintings. Prices range from $35 to $83 for adults and $25 to $65 for children 12 and under.

RAFTING THE COLORADO RIVER

Rafting down the Colorado River as it roars and tumbles through the mile-deep gorge of the Grand Canyon is the adventure of a lifetime. Ever since John Wesley Powell ignored everyone who knew better and proved that it was possible to travel by boat down the tumultuous Colorado, running the big river has become a passion and an obsession with adventurers. Today, anyone from grade-schoolers to grandmothers can join the elite group who have made the run. Be prepared for some of the most furious white water in the world.

There are 16 companies offering trips through various sections of the canyon. You can spend as little as half a day on the Colorado (downstream from Glen Canyon Dam; see "Lake Powell & Page" in chapter 7, "The Four Corners Region: Land of the Hopi & Navajo") to as many as 19 days. You can go down the river in a huge motorized rubber raft (the quickest way to see the entire canyon), a paddled- or oar-powered raft (more thrills and more energy expended on your part if you have to help paddle), or a wooden dory (the biggest thrill of all). In a motorized raft, you can travel the entire canyon from Lees Ferry to Lake Mead in only 8 days. Should you opt for an oar- or paddle-powered raft or dory, expect to spend 5 or 6 days getting from Lees Ferry to Phantom Ranch or 7 to 9 days getting from Phantom Ranch to Diamond Creek, just above Lake Mead. Aside from the half-day trips near Glen Canyon Dam, any Grand Canyon rafting trip will involve lots of monster rapids. Variables to consider include hiking in or out of Phantom Ranch for a combination rafting-and-hiking adventure.

Most trips start from Lees Ferry near Page and Lake Powell. It's also possible to start (or finish) a trip at Phantom Ranch, hiking in or out from either the North or South Rim. The main rafting season is April through October, but some companies operate year-round. Rafting trips tend to book up well in advance, and most companies begin taking reservations between March and May for the following year's trips. Expect to pay anywhere from $200 to $280 per day for your white-water adventure, depending on the length of the trip and the type of boat used.

The following companies are currently authorized to operate trips through the Grand Canyon:

- **Aramark-Wilderness River Adventures,** P.O. Box 717, Page, AZ 86040 (© 800/992-8022 or 520/645-3296; www.riveradventures.com); 7- and 8-day motorized-raft trips and 12- and 14-day oar trips.
- **Arizona Raft Adventures,** 4050 E. Huntington Dr., Flagstaff, AZ 86004 (© 800/786-7238 or 520/526-8200; www.azraft.com); 6- to 15-day motor, oar, and paddle trips.
- **Arizona River Runners,** P.O. Box 47788, Phoenix, AZ 85068-7788 (© 800/477-7238 or 602/867-4866; www.raftarizona.com); 6- and 7-night motorized-raft trips and 13-day oar trips.
- **Canyoneers,** P.O. Box 2997, Flagstaff, AZ 86003 (© 800/525-0924 or 520/526-0924; www.canyoneers.com); 6-night motorized-raft trips and 13-night oar-powered trips, plus several short trips.
- **Canyon Explorations/Canyon Expeditions,** P.O. Box 310, Flagstaff, AZ 86002 (© 800/654-0723 or 520/774-4559; www.canyonx.com); 13- to 18-day oar or paddle trips, some including inflatable kayaks.
- **Colorado River & Trail Expeditions,** P.O. Box 57575, Salt Lake City, UT 84157-0575 (© 800/253-7328 or 801/261-1789; www.crateinc.com); 4- to 11-day motor and oar trips, some with an accompanying paddle raft.
- **Diamond River Adventures,** P.O. Box 1300, Page, AZ 86040 (© 800/343-3121 or 520/645-8866; www.diamondriver.com); 4- to 8-day motorized-raft trips and 5- to 13-day oar trips.
- **Grand Canyon Dories,** P.O. Box 216, Altaville, CA 95221 (© 800/877-3679 or 209/736-0805; www.oars.com/gcdories); 8- to 19-day dory trips.
- **Grand Canyon Expeditions Company,** P.O. Box O, Kanab, UT 84741 (© 800/544-2691 or 435/644-2691; www.gcex.com); 8-day motorized trips and 14-day dory trips.
- **Hatch River Expeditions,** P.O. Box 1200, Vernal, UT 84078 (© 800/433-8966 or 435/789-3813); 4- and 6-day motorized trips.
- **High Desert Adventures,** P.O. Box 40, St. George, UT 84771-0040 (© 800/673-1733 or 435/673-1733; www.funboat.com); 6- to 14-day motor and oar trips.
- **Moki Mac River Expeditions,** P.O. Box 21242, Salt Lake City, UT 84121 (© 800/284-7280 or 801/268-6667; www.mokimac.com); 6-, 9-, and 13-day oar trips and 8-day motorized trips.
- **OARS,** P.O. Box 67, Angels Camp, CA 95222 (© 800/346-6277 or 209/736-2924; www.oars.com); 8- to 19-day oar and dory trips.
- **Outdoors Unlimited,** 6900 Townsend Winona Rd., Flagstaff, AZ 86004 (© 800/637-7238 or 520/526-2852; www.outdoorsunlimited.com); 5- to 15-day oar and paddle trips.
- **Tour West,** P.O. Box 333, Orem, UT 84059 (© 800/453-9107 or 801/225-0755; www.twriver.com); 3- and 6-night motorized-raft trips and 12-night oar-powered trip.

- **Western River Expeditions,** 7258 Racquet Club Dr., Salt Lake City, UT 84121 (© 800/453-7450 or 801/942-6669; www.westernriver.com); 2-, 3-, and 6-night motorized trips and a single 11-night oar-powered trip.

For information on 1-day rafting trips at the west end of the Grand Canyon, see "South Rim Alternatives: Havasu Canyon & Grand Canyon West," later in this chapter. For information on half- and full-day trips near Page, see "Lake Powell & Page" in chapter 7, "The Four Corners Region: Land of the Hopi & Navajo".

ACTIVITIES OUTSIDE THE CANYON

If you aren't completely beat at the end of the day, you might want to take in an evening of **Navajo storytelling and dancing** at the Grand Hotel (© **520/ 638-3333**) in Tusayan; call for schedule.

For a virtual Grand Canyon experience, take in a show at the **Grand Canyon IMAX Theater,** Ariz. 64/U.S. 180 (© **520/638-2203;** www. grandcanyonimaxtheater.com), in Tusayan outside the south entrance to the park. A short IMAX film covering the history and geology of the canyon is shown throughout the day on the theater's seven-story screen. Admission is $9.50 for adults and $6.50 for children 3 to 11. March through October, there are shows daily between 8:30am and 8:30pm; November through February, daily between 10:30am and 6:30pm.

Outside the east entrance to the park, the **Cameron Trading Post** (© **800/ 338-7385** or 520/679-2231), at the crossroads of Cameron where Ariz. 64 branches off U.S. 89, is the best trading post in the state. The original stone trading post, a historic building, now houses a gallery of old and antique Indian artifacts, clothing, and jewelry. This gallery offers museum-quality pieces, and even if you don't have $10,000 to drop on a rug or basket, you can still look around. The main trading post is a more modern building and is the largest trading post in northern Arizona. Don't miss the beautiful old terraced gardens in back of the original trading post.

WHERE TO STAY

Keep in mind that the Grand Canyon is one of the most popular national parks in the country, and hotel rooms both within and just outside the park are in high demand. Make reservations as far in advance as possible. Don't expect to find a room if you head up here in summer without a reservation. You'll likely wind up driving back to Williams or Flagstaff to find a vacancy. There, is, however, one long-shot option. See "Inside the Park," below, for details. Who knows? You might get lucky.

INSIDE THE PARK

All hotels inside the park are operated by **Amfac Parks & Resorts.** Reservations are taken up to 23 months in advance, beginning on the first of the month. If you want to stay in one of the historic rim cabins at Bright Angel Lodge, reserve at least a year in advance. However, rooms with shared bathrooms at Bright Angel Lodge are often the last in the park to book up, and although they're small and very basic, they're your best bet if you're trying to get a last-minute reservation. The Yavapai Lodge, because it is set back from the rim, is also a good bet for last-minute reservations.

To book reservations at any of the in-park hotels listed below (as well as Moqui Lodge, just outside the park), contact **Grand Canyon National Park**

Lodges/Amfac Parks & Resorts, 14001 E. Iliff Ave., Suite 600, Aurora, CO 80014 (© **303/297-2757;** fax 303/297-3175; www.amfac.com or www. grandcanyonlodges.com). It is sometimes possible, due to cancellations and no-shows, to get a same-day reservation; it's a long shot, but it happens. Same-day reservations can be made by calling © **520/638-2631.** Amfac accepts American Express, Discover, MasterCard, and Visa.

Moderate

El Tovar Hotel ★★   El Tovar Hotel, which first opened its doors in 1905, is the park's premier lodge. Built of local rock and Oregon pine by Hopi crafts-men, it's a rustic yet luxurious mountain lodge that perches on the edge of the canyon (but with views from only a few rooms). The lobby, entered from a veranda set with rustic furniture, has a small fireplace, cathedral ceiling, and log walls on which moose, deer, and antelope heads are displayed. The guest rooms feature modern Mission-style furnishings that are somewhat in keeping with the period when the hotel was built. The standard units are rather small, as are the bathrooms. For more legroom, book a deluxe unit. Suites, with private terraces and stunning views, are extremely spacious and done mostly in new Southwest-ern style.

The El Tovar Dining Room (see "Where to Dine," below) is the best restau-rant in the village. Just off the lobby is a cocktail lounge with a view (and a TV directly above the picture window in case the Grand Canyon isn't interesting enough for you).

78 units. $116–$174 double; $199–$284 suite. **Amenities:** Restaurant (Continental/Southwestern), lounge; concierge; tour desk; room service. *In room:* TV.

Maswik Lodge   Set back a quarter mile or so from the rim, the Maswik Lodge offers spacious rooms and rustic cabins. If you crave modern appoint-ments, opt for one of the Maswik North rooms. If you don't mind roughing it a bit, the old cabins have lots of character and are comfortable enough. These have bathtubs but not showers.

278 units, including 28 cabins (available summer only). $73–$136 double (winter discounts sometimes avail-able); $63 cabin. **Amenities:** Cafeteria, lounge; tour desk. *In room:* TV.

Thunderbird & Kachina Lodges   Despite the use of native sandstone in their construction, these 1960s-vintage motel-style lodgings are probably far from your idea of what a national park lodge should look like, and the dated "modern" styling clashes with the traditional design of the adjacent historic lodges. However, if you want "modern" amenities and a fairly large room, these should be your in-park choice in this price range. The rooms in both lodges have large windows, although you'll have to request a canyon-side room on the sec-ond floor if you want a view of something more than a parking lot (the canyon-view rooms cost only $10 more than those without views). Thunderbird Lodge registration is handled by Bright Angel Lodge, and Kachina Lodge registration is handled by El Tovar Hotel.

104 units. $114–$124 double. *In room:* TV.

Yavapai Lodge   Located in several buildings at the east end of Grand Canyon Village (a 1-mile hike from the main section of the village but convenient to the new Canyon View Information Plaza), the Yavapai is the largest lodge in the park, and thus is where you'll likely wind up if you wait too long to make a reser-vation. There are no canyon views here, which is why this place is less expensive than the Thunderbird and Kachina lodges. The rooms in the Yavapai East section of the hotel are set under shady pines and are more attractive than the rooms in the Yavapai West section (well worth the price difference).

358 units. $88–$102 double (winter discounts sometimes available). **Amenities:** Cafeteria; tour desk. *In room:* TV.

Inexpensive

Bright Angel Lodge & Cabins ☆   Bright Angel Lodge, which began operation in 1896 as a collection of tents and cabins on the edge of the canyon, is the most affordable lodge in the park, and, with its flagstone-floor lobby and huge fireplace, it has a genuine, if crowded, mountain-lodge atmosphere. It offers the greatest variety of accommodations in the park and has undergone the most recent renovations. In addition to rooms with shared bathrooms, there are cabins, including rim cabins that are the lodge's best and most popular accommodations (book a year in advance for summer). Outside the winter months, other rooms should be booked at least 6 months in advance. Most of the rooms and cabins feature rustic furnishings. The Buckey Suite, the oldest structure on the canyon rim, is arguably the best room in the park, with a canyon view, fireplace, and king-size bed. The rim cabins with fireplaces aren't worth the extra cost, since the fireplaces don't work very well. The tour desk, fireplace, museum, and restrooms account for the constant crowds in the lobby.

89 units (20 with shared bathroom). $46 double with sink only; $50 double with sink and toilet; $63 double with bathroom; $73–$234 cabin. **Amenities:** 2 restaurants (American, steakhouse/Southwestern), lounge, ice-cream parlor; tour desk. *In room:* No phone.

Phantom Ranch ☆   Built in 1922, Phantom Ranch is the only lodge at the bottom of the Grand Canyon and has a classic ranch atmosphere. The accommodations are in rustic stone-walled cabins or 10-bed gender-segregated dormitories. Evaporative coolers keep both the cabins and the dorms cool in summer. Make reservations as early as possible (up to a year in advance) and don't forget to reconfirm. It's also sometimes possible to get a room on the day of departure if there are any last-minute cancellations. To attempt this, you must put your name on the waiting list at the Bright Angel Lodge transportation desk the day before you want to stay at Phantom Ranch.

Family-style meals must be reserved in advance. The menu consists of beef-and-vegetable stew ($18), a vegetarian dinner ($18), or steak ($29). Breakfasts ($15) are hearty, and sack lunches ($8) are available. Between meals, the dining hall becomes a canteen selling snacks, drinks, gifts, and necessities. After dinner, it becomes a beer hall. There's a public phone here, and mule-back baggage transfer between Grand Canyon Village and Phantom Ranch can be arranged ($52 each way).

Reconfirmations ✆ **520/638-3283** or 520/638-2631. 11 cabins, 40 dorm beds. $69 double in cabin; $23 dormitory bed. Mule-trip overnights (with all meals and mule ride included) $332 for 1 person, $595 for 2 people. 2-night trips available mid-Nov through Mar. **Amenities:** Restaurant, lounge. *In room:* No phone.

IN TUSAYAN (OUTSIDE THE SOUTH ENTRANCE)

If you can't get a reservation for a room in the park, this is the next closest place to stay. Unfortunately, this area can be very noisy because of the many helicopters and airplanes taking off from the airport. Also, hotels outside the park are very popular with tour groups, which during the busy summer months keep many hotels full. All of the hotels listed here are lined up along U.S. 180/ Ariz. 64.

There is one other motel in town, the **Seven Mile Lodge** (✆ **520/638-2291**), which is usually the least expensive place in town ($68 double). However, this motel does not take reservations and is usually full by 2pm in summer (it starts renting rooms at 9am).

Best Western Grand Canyon Squire Inn ⭐⭐ *Kids*   If you prefer playing tennis to riding a mule, this may be the place for you. Of all the hotels in Tusayan, this one has the most resortlike feel due to its restaurants, lounges, and extensive recreational amenities (there's even a bowling alley and pool room). With so much to offer, it almost seems as if the hotel were trying to distract guests from the canyon itself. Even if you don't bowl or play tennis, you'll likely appreciate the large rooms with comfortable easy chairs and big windows. In the lobby, which is more Las Vegas glitz than mountain rustic, are cases filled with old cowboy paraphernalia. Down in the basement is an impressive Western sculpture and waterfall wall.

Ariz. 64 (P.O. Box 130), Grand Canyon, AZ 86023-0130. ✆ **800/622-6966** or 520/638-2681. Fax 520/638-0162. www.grandcanyonsquire.com. 250 units. Apr to mid-Oct and Christmas holidays $105–$175 double; mid-Oct to Mar $60–$125 double. AE, DC, DISC, MC, V. **Amenities:** 3 restaurants (Continental, American), 2 lounges; seasonal outdoor pool; 2 tennis courts; exercise room; Jacuzzi; sauna; game room; tour desk; salon; coin-op laundry. *In room:* A/C, TV, dataport, coffeemaker, hair dryer, iron.

Grand Hotel ⭐⭐   This is the newest hotel in Tusayan, and its mountain-lodge-style lobby is certainly quite grand. There's a flagstone fireplace, log-beam ceiling, and fake ponderosa pine tree trunks holding up the roof. Just off the lobby (past the large gift shop), are a dining room (with evening entertainment ranging from Native American dancers to country-music bands) and a small bar that even has a few saddles for barstools. Guest rooms are spacious, with a few Western touches, and some have small balconies. Try to get a room on the back side of the hotel; these face the forest rather than the parking lot.

Ariz. 64 (P. O. Box 3319), Grand Canyon, AZ 86023. ✆ **888/63-GRAND** or 520/638-3333. Fax 520/638-3131. www.gcanyon.com. 120 units. $69–$138 double. AE, DISC, MC, V. **Amenities:** Restaurant (American), lounge; indoor pool; exercise room; Jacuzzi. *In room:* A/C, TV, dataport, coffeemaker, hair dryer.

Holiday Inn Express—Grand Canyon   This is one of the newest lodgings in the area and has modern, well-designed, if a bit sterile and characterless, guest rooms. With no pool or restaurant, this place is really just somewhere to crash at the end of the day. The Holiday Inn Express also manages an adjacent 32-suite property that has theme suites. Although these are fairly pricey, they're among the nicest rooms inside or outside the park.

Ariz. 64 (P.O. Box 3245), Grand Canyon, AZ 86023. ✆ **888/473-2269** or 520/638-3000. Fax 520/638-0123. www.gcanyon.com/HI. 197 units. $69–$129 double; $80–$149 suite. Rates include continental breakfast. AE, DC, DISC, MC, V. *In room:* A/C, TV, hair dryer.

Moqui Lodge   Although the Moqui Lodge is managed by the same company that operates all the lodges within the park, this motel is located just outside the park's south entrance on the outskirts of the community of Tusayan. The location makes it a last-choice sort of place. The building's A-frame construction gives it the look of a ski lodge, but everything else says "captive audience." The best of accommodations here are standard motel-style rooms with large windows (that for the most part look out onto the parking lot), while the worst rooms are cramped, poorly furnished, and overpriced.

Amfac Parks & Resorts, 14001 E. Iliff Ave., Suite 600, Aurora, CO 80014. ✆ **303/297-2757**. Fax 303/297-3175. www.amfac.com. 136 units. $94–$118 double. AE, DISC, MC, V. Closed Nov–Mar. **Amenities:** Restaurant (Mexican/American), lounge; horseback riding; tour desk. *In room:* TV.

Quality Inn & Suites Grand Canyon This relatively luxurious hotel at the park's south entrance is built around two enclosed skylit courtyards, one of which houses a restaurant and the other a bar and large whirlpool. The rooms are large and comfortable and have balconies or patios. Most also have minibars. For extra space, there are suites with separate small living rooms, microwaves, and refrigerators. The hotel is next to the IMAX Theater and is very popular with tour groups.

P.O. Box 520, Grand Canyon, AZ 86023. © **800/228-5151** or 520/638-2673. Fax 520/638-9537. www. grandcanyonqualityinn.com. 232 units. Apr to mid-Oct $118 double, $168 suite; late Oct–Mar $78 double, $128 suite. AE, DC, DISC, MC, V. **Amenities:** Restaurant, lounge; outdoor pool; 2 Jacuzzis; courtesy airport shuttle. *In room:* A/C, TV, dataport, coffeemaker, hair dryer.

Rodeway Inn Red Feather Lodge *Kids* With more than 200 rooms, this motel is often slow to fill up, so it's a good choice for last-minute bookings. Try to get one of the newer rooms, which are a bit more comfortable than the older ones. The pool here makes this place a good bet for families.

Ariz. 64 (P.O. Box 1460), Grand Canyon, AZ 86023. © **800/228-2000** or 520/638-2414. Fax 520/638-9216. www.redfeatherlodge.com. 231 units. $59–$119 double. AE, DC, DISC, MC, V. Pets accepted ($50 deposit, $45 refundable). **Amenities:** Restaurant (American); seasonal outdoor pool; exercise room; Jacuzzi; game room. *In room:* A/C, TV, dataport, coffeemaker, hair dryer.

OTHER AREA ACCOMMODATIONS

Cameron Trading Post Motel ★★ *Finds* Located 54 miles north of Flagstaff on U.S. 89 at the junction with the road to the east entrance of the national park, this motel offers some of the most attractive rooms in the vicinity of the Grand Canyon and is part of one of the best trading posts in the state. The motel, adjacent to the historic Cameron Trading Post, is built around the old trading post's terraced gardens, which are a shady oasis. The rooms feature Southwestern-style furniture and attractive decor. Most have balconies, and some have views of the canyon of the Little Colorado River.

P.O. Box 339, Cameron, AZ 86020. © **800/338-7385** or 520/679-2231. Fax 520/679-2350. www. camerontradingpost.com. 62 units. Feb–Mar $49–$69 double; Mar–May $69–$99 double; June to mid-Oct $89–$119 double; mid-Oct to Jan $59–$79 double. Suites $99–$159 year-round. AE, DC, DISC, MC, V. Well-behaved pets accepted. **Amenities:** Restaurant. *In room:* A/C, TV, coffeemaker.

CAMPGROUNDS
Inside the Park

On the South Rim, there are two campgrounds and an RV park. **Mather Campground,** in Grand Canyon Village, has 313 campsites. Reservations can be made up to 5 months in advance and are required for stays between April 1 and November 30 (reservations not accepted for other months). Contact the National Park Reservation Service (© **800/365-2267** or 301/722-1257; http://reservations.nps.gov). Between late spring and early fall, don't even think of coming up here without a reservation; you'll just be setting yourself up for disappointment. If you don't have a reservation, your next best bet is to arrive in the morning, when campsites are being vacated. Campsite fees range from $10 to $15 depending on the season.

Desert View Campground, with 50 sites, is 25 miles east of Grand Canyon Village and open from mid-May to mid-October only. No reservations are accepted for this campground. Campsites are $10 per night.

The **Trailer Village RV park,** with 80 RV sites, is in Grand Canyon Village and charges $20 per night for full hookup. Reservations can be made up to

23 months in advance; contact Amfac Parks & Resorts, 14001 E. Iliff Ave., Suite 600, Aurora, CO 80014 (© **303/297-2757;** fax 303/297-3175).

Outside the Park

Getting a campsite inside the park is no easy feat, and if you get shut out, your next best choices lie within a few miles of the south entrance. In Tusayan, you'll find **Grand Canyon Camper Village,** P.O. Box 490, Grand Canyon, AZ 86023-0490 (© **520/638-2887**), open year-round. This is primarily an RV park, but it also has sites for tents. The only drawback is that you're right in town, which is probably not what you were dreaming of when you planned your trip to the Grand Canyon. Rates range from $18 to $26.

Two miles south of Tusayan is the U.S. Forest Service's **Ten-X Campground.** It's open May through September, charging $10 for campsites. This is usually your best bet for finding a site late in the day.

You can also camp just about anywhere within the **Kaibab National Forest,** which borders Grand Canyon National Park, as long as you are more than a quarter mile away from Ariz. 64/U.S. 180. Several dirt roads lead into the forest from the highway, and although you won't find designated campsites or toilets along these roads, you will find spots where others have obviously camped before. This so-called dispersed camping is usually used by campers who have been unable to find sites in campgrounds. Anyone equipped for backpacking could just hike in a bit from any forest road rather than camping right beside the road. One of the most popular roads for this sort of camping is on the west side of the highway between Tusayan and the park's south entrance. For more information, contact the **Tusayan Ranger District,** Kaibab National Forest, P.O. Box 3088, Grand Canyon, AZ 86023 (© **520/638-2443;** www.fs.fed.us/r3/kai).

WHERE TO DINE
INSIDE THE PARK

If you're looking for a quick, inexpensive meal, there are plenty of options. In Grand Canyon Village, choices include **cafeterias** at the Yavapai and Maswik lodges and a **delicatessen** at Canyon Village Marketplace on Market Plaza. The **Bright Angel Fountain,** at the back of the Bright Angel Lodge, serves hot dogs, sandwiches, and ice cream and is always crowded on hot days. The most atmospheric food outlet in the park is **Hermit's Rest Snack Bar,** at the west end of Hermit Road. The stone building that houses this snack bar was designed by Mary Jane Colter, who also designed several other buildings on the South Rim. At Desert View (near the east entrance to the park), is the **Desert View Trading Snack Bar.** All of these places are open daily for all three meals, and all serve meals for $8 and under.

The Arizona Room SOUTHWESTERN   Meals other than steaks here can be very uneven, so stick to the slabs of beef and hope for the best. Despite the lackluster food, this place is always packed (can you say "captive audience"?)— primarily because the steaks are relatively cheap and there's a decent view out the window. There's almost always a wait for a table, so try to show up early. Keep in mind that once the sun goes down, the view out the window is absolutely black (which means you could be dining anywhere). Arrive early and enjoy the sunset.

In the Bright Angel Lodge. © **520/638-2631.** Reservations not accepted. Dinners $14–$22. AE, DC, DISC, MC, V. Daily 4:30–10pm.

Bright Angel Coffee Shop AMERICAN   As the least expensive of the three restaurants right on the rim of the canyon, this casual Southwestern-themed coffeehouse in the historic Bright Angel Lodge stays packed throughout the day. Meals are simple and none too memorable, but if you can get one of the few tables near the windows, at least you get something of a view. The menu includes everything from Southwestern favorites such as chili, tacos, and fajitas to spaghetti and meatballs (foods calculated to comfort tired and hungry hikers). Wines are available, and service is generally friendly and efficient.

In the Bright Angel Lodge. (C) **520/638-2631.** Reservations not accepted. Main courses $6–$18. AE, DC, DISC, MC, V. Daily 6:30–10:45am and 11:15am–10pm.

El Tovar Dining Room ★★ CONTINENTAL/SOUTHWESTERN   If you're staying at El Tovar, you'll want to have dinner in the hotel's rustic-yet-elegant dining room. But before making reservations at the most expensive restaurant in the park, be aware that meals can be uneven, and few tables have views of the canyon. With this knowledge in hand, decide for yourself whether you want to splurge on a meal that will definitely be the best food available inside the park, but that might not be as good as you would hope after seeing the prices. The menu leans heavily to the spicy flavors of the Southwest (pan-seared salmon with chile-lime rice, blue-corn tamales, grilled prickly pear shrimp). Plenty of milder, more familiar dishes are offered as well. Service is generally quite good.

In the El Tovar Hotel. (C) **520/638-2631,** ext. 6432. Reservations required for dinner. Main courses $16.50–$23. AE, DC, DISC, MC, V. Daily 6:30–11am, 11:30am–2pm, and 5–10pm.

TUSAYAN (OUTSIDE THE SOUTH ENTRANCE)

In addition to the restaurants listed below, you'll also find a steakhouse, a pizza place, and a Chinese restaurant, as well as familiar chains such as McDonald's, Taco Bell, Pizza Hut, and Wendy's.

Canyon Star ★ AMERICAN/MEXICAN   While the food here may not be all that memorable, at least you'll have some live entertainment while you chow down on barbecued ribs, steaks, and Mexican standards. Evening shows include performances of Native American songs and dances, as well as traditional cowboy songs or country music. This place is big, so there usually isn't too long a wait for a table, and even if there is, you can head for the saloon and saddle up a bar stool (some of the stools have saddles instead of seats) while you wait.

The Grand Hotel, Ariz. 64. (C) **520/638-3333.** Main courses $11–$21. AE, DISC, MC, V. Daily 8am–2pm and 5–9pm.

Coronado Room ★ CONTINENTAL/SOUTHWESTERN   If you should suddenly be struck with an overpowering desire to have escargot for dinner, don't despair—head for the Best Western Grand Canyon Squire Inn. Now, we're well aware that Best Western and escargot go together about as well as the Grand Canyon and escargot, but this place really does serve classic Continental fare way out here in the Arizona high country. French onion soup or oysters on the half shell? You got it. Realistically, you'll probably want to stick to the steaks; after all, this is beef country. No need to leave the kids in the room, as there's an extensive children's menu.

Best Western Grand Canyon Squire Inn, Ariz. 64. (C) **520/638-2681.** Reservations recommended. Main courses $16–$20. AE, DC, DISC, MC, V. Daily 5–9pm.

4 South Rim Alternatives: Havasu Canyon ⭐⭐ & Grand Canyon West

Havasu Canyon: 200 miles W of Grand Canyon Village; 70 miles N of Ariz. 66; 155 miles NW of Flagstaff; 115 miles NE of Kingman

Grand Canyon West: 240 miles W of Grand Canyon Village; 70 miles N of Kingman; 115 miles E of Las Vegas

With five million people each year visiting the South Rim of the Grand Canyon, and traffic congestion and parking problems becoming the most memorable aspects of most people's visits, you might want to consider an alternative to the South Rim. For most people, this means driving around to the North Rim; however, it's open only from mid-May to late October and itself is not immune to parking problems and traffic congestion.

There are a couple of other lesser-known alternatives. A visit to Havasu Canyon, on the Havasupai Indian Reservation, entails a 20-mile round-trip hike or horseback ride similar to that from Grand Canyon Village to Phantom Ranch, although with a decidedly different setting at the bottom of the canyon. Visiting Grand Canyon West, on the Hualapai Indian Reservation, is much less strenuous, and is favored by people short on time or who want to fly down into the canyon (something that isn't permitted within Grand Canyon National Park). Note that the drive to and from Grand Canyon West involves spending some 28 miles on gravel, so expect lots of dust and some stretches of rough road. Also remember that Grand Canyon West is particularly popular with tour buses from Las Vegas, and the constant helicopter traffic here precludes any sort of tranquil canyon experience.

ESSENTIALS

GETTING THERE   Havasu Canyon   It isn't possible to drive all the way to Supai village or Havasu Canyon. The nearest road ends 8 miles from Supai at Hualapai Hilltop. This is the trailhead for the trail into the canyon and is at the end of Indian Route 18, which runs north from Ariz. 66. The turnoff is 7 miles east of Peach Springs and 31 miles west of Seligman. Many Arizona maps show an unpaved road between U.S. 180 south of Tusayan and Hualapai Hilltop, but this road is not maintained on a regular basis and is passable only to four-wheel-drive vehicles *when* no fallen logs block the way.

The easiest and fastest (and by far the most expensive) way to reach Havasu Canyon is by helicopter from Grand Canyon Airport. Flights are operated by **Papillon Grand Canyon Helicopters** (© **800/528-2418** or 520/638-2419; www.papillon.com). The round-trip air-and-ground day excursion is $461; the overnight excursion is $503.

Grand Canyon West   If you're headed to Grand Canyon West, you've got several options, two of which entail driving nearly 50 miles of gravel roads that aren't even passable if it has rained any time recently. The best route is to head northwest out of Kingman on U.S. 93, and in 27 miles turn right onto the Pearce Ferry Road (signed for Dolan Springs and Meadview). After 28 miles on this road, turn right onto gravel Diamond Bar Road, which is signed for Grand Canyon West. Another 14 miles down this road brings you to the Hualapai Indian Reservation. A little farther along, you'll come to the Grand Canyon West Terminal (there's actually an airstrip here), where visitor permits and bus tour tickets are sold. You can also drive to Grand Canyon West from Peach Springs via Buck and Doe Road, which adds almost 50 more miles of gravel to your trip.

VISITOR INFORMATION   For information on Havasu Canyon, contact the **Havasupai Tourist Enterprises,** P.O. Box 160, Supai, AZ 86435 (© **520/ 448-2121**), which handles all campground reservations. For information on Grand Canyon West, contact **Hualapai Reservations,** P.O. Box 538, Peach Springs, AZ 86434-0538 (© **888/255-9550** or 520/769-2230; fax 520/ 769-2372; www.hualapaitours.com).

HAVASU CANYON ⊛

Imagine hiking for hours through a dusty brown landscape of rocks and cacti. The sun overhead is blistering and bright. The air is hot and dry. Rock walls rise up higher and higher as you continue your descent through a mazelike canyon. Eventually the narrow canyon opens up into a wide plain shaded by cottonwood trees, a sure sign of water, and within a few minutes you hear the sound of a babbling stream. The water, when you finally reach it, is cool and crystal clear, a pleasant surprise. Following the stream, you pass through a dusty (usually cluttered and unkempt, some say dirty and depressing) Indian village of small homes. Not surprisingly in a village 8 miles beyond the last road, every yard seems to be a corral for horses. Passing through the village, you continue along the stream. As the trail descends again, you spot the first waterfall.

The previously crystal-clear water is now a brilliant turquoise blue at the foot of the waterfall. The sandstone walls look redder than before. No, you aren't having a heat-induced hallucination—the water really is turquoise, and it fills terraces of travertine that form deep pools of cool water at the base of three large waterfalls. Together these three waterfalls form what many claim is the most beautiful spot in the entire state.

This is Havasu Canyon, the canyon of the Havasupai tribe, whose name means "people of the blue-green waters." For centuries, the Havasupai have called this idyllic desert oasis home.

The waterfalls are the main attraction here, and most people are content to go for a dip in the cool waters, sun themselves on the sand, and gaze for hours at the turquoise waters. When you tire of these pursuits, you can hike up the small side canyon to the east of Havasu Falls. Another trail leads along the west rim of Havasu Canyon and can be reached by carefully climbing up a steep rocky area near the village cemetery. There's also a trail that leads all the way down to the Colorado River, but this is an overnight hike.

In Supai village is a small museum dedicated to the culture of the Havasupai people. Its exhibits and old photos will give you an idea of how little the lives of these people have changed over the years.

The Havasupai entry fee is $20 per person to visit Havasu Canyon, and everyone entering the canyon is required to register at the tourist office in the village of Supai. Because it's a long walk to the campground, be sure you have a confirmed reservation before setting out from Hualapai Hilltop. It's good to make reservations as far in advance as possible, especially for holiday weekends. Havasupai Tourist Enterprises operates on a cash-only basis, so remember to bring enough money for your entire stay.

If you plan to hike down into the canyon, start early to avoid the heat of the day. The hike is beautiful, but it's 10 miles to the campground. The steepest part of the trail is the first mile or so from Hualapai Hilltop. After this section, it's relatively flat.

Through **Havasupai Tourist Enterprises** (© **520/448-2121**) you can hire a horse to carry you or your gear down into the canyon from Hualapai Hilltop. Horses cost $78.75 each way. Many people who hike in decide that it's worth the money to ride out, or at least have their backpacks carried out. Be sure to confirm your horse reservation a day before driving to Hualapai Hilltop. Sometimes no horses are available, and it's a long drive back to the nearest town.

GRAND CANYON WEST

Located on the Hualapai Indian Reservation on the south side of the Colorado River, **Grand Canyon West** (② 888/255-9550) overlooks the rarely visited west end of Grand Canyon National Park. Although the view is not as spectacular as at either the South Rim or the North Rim, Grand Canyon West is noteworthy for one thing. This is the only place where you can legally fly down into the canyon. The reason this is possible is because the helicopters operate on land that is part of the Hualapai Indian Reservation. At this point, the south side of the Colorado lies within the reservation while the north side of the river is within Grand Canyon National Park. The tours are operated by **Papillon Helicopters** (② 520/699-3993), which charges $79 per person for a quick trip to the bottom of the canyon.

There are also **guided bus tours** along the rim of the canyon. These include a barbecue lunch and time to do a bit of exploring at a canyon overlook. Tours stop at Eagle Point, where rock formations resemble various animals and people, and at Guano Point, where bat guano was once mined commercially. The tours, which operate daily throughout the year, cost $35 for adults and $22 for children 2 to 12. No reservations are accepted, so it's a good idea to arrive around 9am when Grand Canyon West opens (if you're coming from Kingman, allow at least 1½ hr. to get here).

If you'd just like to take in the view from this end of the canyon, head to **Quartermaster Point,** after first purchasing your sightseeing permit ($10) at the Grand Canyon West terminal. At Quartermaster Point, you'll find a trail that leads down a few hundred yards to a viewpoint overlooking the Colorado River.

Because this is about the closest spot to Las Vegas that actually provides a glimpse of the Colorado River and Grand Canyon National Park, the bus tours and helicopter rides are very popular with tour groups from Las Vegas. Busloads of visitors come and go throughout the day, and the air is always filled with the noise of helicopters ferrying people down into the canyon.

While we can only recommend a trip out to Grand Canyon West as a side trip from Las Vegas or for travelers who absolutely must fly down into the canyon, the drive out here is almost as scenic as the destination itself. Along Diamond Bar Road, you'll be driving below the Grand Wash Cliffs, and for much of the way, the route traverses a dense forest of Joshua trees.

OTHER AREA ACTIVITIES

If you long to raft the Grand Canyon but have only a couple of free days in your schedule to realize your dream, then you have only a couple of options. Here at the west end of the canyon, it's possible to do a 1-day rafting trip that begins on the Hualapai Indian Reservation. These trips are operated by **Hualapai River Runners,** P.O. Box 538, Peach Springs, AZ 86434 (② 888/255-9550; www. river-runners.com), a tribal rafting company, and operate between March and October. Expect a mix of white water and flat water (all of it very cold). Although perhaps not as exciting as longer trips in the main section of the canyon, you'll still plow through some pretty big waves. Be ready to get wet. These trips stop at a couple of side canyons where you can get out and do some exploring. One-day trips cost $250 per person.

Also in this area, you can visit **Grand Canyon Caverns** (© 520/422-3223), just outside Peach Springs. The caverns, which are accessed via a 210-foot elevator ride, are open from Memorial Day to October 15, daily from 8am to 6pm (hours vary other months). Admission is $9.50 for adults, $6.75 for children 4 to 12.

WHERE TO STAY & DINE
IN & NEAR PEACH SPRINGS

Grand Canyon Caverns Inn   If you're planning to hike or ride into Havasu Canyon, you'll need to be at Hualapai Hilltop as early in the morning as possible, and because it's a 3- to 4-hour drive to the trailhead from Flagstaff, you might want to consider staying here at one of only two lodgings for miles around. As the name implies, this motel is built on the site of the Grand Canyon Caverns, which are open to the public. On the premises is a general store with camping supplies and food. For much of the year, this motel is used by Elderhostel and stays full.

P.O. Box 180, Peach Springs, AZ 86434. © 520/422-3223. 48 units. Summer $50 double; winter $35 double. AE, DISC, MC, V. Pets accepted ($50 deposit). **Amenities:** Restaurant, lounge; outdoor pool; coin-op laundry. *In room:* A/C, TV.

Hualapai Lodge ★ *Finds*   Located in the Hualapai community of Peach Springs, this lodge is by far the most luxurious accommodation anywhere in this region. Guest rooms are spacious and modern, with a few bits of regional decor for character. The dining room is just about the only place in town to get a meal. Most people staying here are in the area to visit Grand Canyon West, to go rafting with Hualapai River Runners, or to hike in to Havasu Canyon.

900 Rte. 66, P.O. Box 538, Peach Springs, AZ 86434. © 888/255-9550 or 520/769-2230. Fax 520/769-2372. www.hualapaitours.com. 60 units. May–Sept $75–$85 double; Oct–Apr $60–$70 double. AE, DISC, MC, V. **Amenities:** Restaurant (American); concierge; tour desk; coin-op laundry. *In room:* A/C, TV, dataport.

IN HAVASU CANYON

Havasu Campground   The campground is 2 miles below Supai village, between Havasu Falls and Mooney Falls, and the campsites are mostly in the shade of cottonwood trees on either side of Havasu Creek. Picnic tables are provided, but no firewood is available. Cutting any trees or shrubs is prohibited, so be sure to bring a camp stove. Spring water is available, and although it's considered safe to drink, we advise treating it first.

Havasupai Tourist Enterprise, P.O. Box 160, Supai, AZ 86435. © 520/448-2121. 100 sites. $10 per person per night. MC, V.

Havasupai Lodge   Located in Supai village, this lodge is, aside from the campground, the only accommodation in the canyon. The two-story building features standard motel-style rooms that are lacking only TVs and telephones, neither of which are much in demand at this isolated retreat. The only drawback of this comfortable-though-basic lodge is that it's 2 miles from Havasu Falls and 3 miles from Mooney Falls. The Havasupai Café, across from the general store, serves breakfast, lunch, and dinner. It's a very casual place, and the prices are high for what you get because all ingredients must be packed in by horse.

P.O. Box 159, Supai, AZ 86435. © 520/448-2201. 24 units. $80 double. MC, V. **Amenities:** Restaurant. *In room:* A/C, no phone.

5 The Grand Canyon North Rim ★★★

42 miles S of Jacob Lake; 216 miles N of Grand Canyon Village (South Rim); 354 miles N of Phoenix; 125 miles W of Page/Lake Powell

Although the North Rim of the Grand Canyon is only 10 miles from the South Rim as the crow flies, it's more than 200 miles by road. It is this much greater distance from population centers such as Phoenix and Las Vegas that has helped keep this rim of the canyon much less crowded than the South Rim. Additionally, due to heavy snowfalls, the North Rim is open only from mid-May to late October or early November. There are far fewer activities on the North Rim than there are on the South Rim (no helicopter or plane rides, no IMAX theater, no McDonald's). For these reasons, most of the millions of people who annually visit the Grand Canyon never make it to this side—and that is exactly why quite a few people think the North Rim is a far superior place to visit. If Grand Canyon Village turns out to be more human zoo than the wilderness experience you expected, the North Rim will probably be much more to your liking, although crowds, traffic congestion, and parking problems are not unheard of here, either.

The North Rim is on the Kaibab Plateau, which is more than 8,000 feet high on average and takes its name from the Paiute word for "mountain lying down." The higher elevation of the North Rim means that instead of the junipers and ponderosa pines of the South Rim, you'll see dense forests of ponderosa pines, Douglas firs, and aspens interspersed with large meadows. Consequently, the North Rim has a much more alpine feel than the South Rim. The 8,000-foot elevation (1,000 ft. higher than the South Rim) means that the North Rim gets considerably more snow in winter than the South Rim. The highway south from Jacob Lake is not plowed in winter, when the Grand Canyon Lodge closes down.

ESSENTIALS

GETTING THERE   The North Rim is at the end of Ariz. 67 (the North Rim Parkway), reached from U.S. 89A. **Trans Canyon** (© 520/638-2820) operates a shuttle between the North Rim and South Rim of the Grand Canyon during the months the North Rim is open. The trip takes 5 hours; the fare is $65 one way (reservations are required).

FEES   The park admission fee is $20 per car and is good for 1 week. Remember not to lose the little paper receipt that serves as your admission pass.

VISITOR INFORMATION   For information before leaving home, contact **Grand Canyon National Park,** P.O. Box 129, Grand Canyon, AZ 86023 (© 520/638-7888; www.nps.gov/grca).

At the entrance gate, you'll be given a copy of *The Guide,* a small newspaper with information on park activities. There's also an **information desk** in the lobby of the Grand Canyon Lodge.

Important note: Visitor facilities at the North Rim are open only from mid-May to mid-October. From mid-October to November (or until snow closes the road to the North Rim), the park is open for day use only. The campground may be open after mid-October, weather permitting.

EXPLORING THE PARK

While it's hard to beat the view from a rustic rocking chair on the terrace of the Grand Canyon Lodge, the best spots for viewing the canyon are Bright Angel Point, Point Imperial, and Cape Royal. **Bright Angel Point** is at the end of a half-mile trail near the Grand Canyon Lodge, and from here you can see and hear Roaring Springs, which is 3,600 feet below the rim and is the North Rim's only water source. You can also see Grand Canyon Village on the South Rim.

At 8,803 feet, **Point Imperial** is the highest point on the North Rim. A short section of the Colorado River can be seen far below, and off to the east the Painted Desert is visible. The Nankoweap Trail leads north from here along the rim of the canyon, and if you're looking to get away from the crowds, try hiking a few miles out along this trail.

Cape Royal is the most spectacular setting on the North Rim, and along the 23-mile road to this viewpoint you'll find several other scenic overlooks. Across the road from the **Walhalla Overlook** are the ruins of an Anasazi structure, and just before reaching Cape Royal, you'll come to the **Angel's Window Overlook,** which gives you a breathtaking view of the natural bridge that forms Angel's Window. Once at Cape Royal, you can follow a trail across this natural bridge to a towering promontory overlooking the canyon.

Once you've had your fill of simply taking in the views, you may want to get out and stretch your legs on a trail or two. Quite a few day hikes of varying lengths and difficulty are possible. The shortest is the half-mile paved trail to Bright Angel Point, along which you'll have plenty of company but also plenty of breathtaking views. If you have time for only one hike while you're here, make it down the **North Kaibab Trail.** This trail is 14 miles long and leads down to Phantom Ranch and the Colorado River. To hike the entire trail, you'll have to have a camping permit and be in very good physical condition (it's almost 6,000 ft. to the canyon floor). For a day hike, most people make Roaring Springs their goal. This hike is 9.4 miles round-trip, involves a descent and ascent of 3,000 feet, and takes 6 to 8 hours. You can shorten this hike considerably by turning around at the Supai Tunnel, which is fewer than 1,500 feet below the rim at the 2-mile point. For a relatively easy hike away from the crowds, try the Widforss Point Trail

If you want to see the canyon from a saddle, contact **Grand Canyon Trail Rides** (℡ 435/679-8665; www.canyonrides.com), which offers mule rides varying in length from 1 hour to a full day. Prices range from $20 for an hour up to $95 for a day.

EN ROUTE TO OR FROM THE NORTH RIM

Between Page and the North Rim of the Grand Canyon, U.S. 89A crosses the Colorado River at **Lees Ferry** in Marble Canyon. The **Navajo Bridge** over the river was replaced a few years ago, and the old bridge is now open to pedestrians, along with the Navajo Bridge Interpretive Center. Lees Ferry is the starting point for raft trips through the Grand Canyon, and for many years was the only place to cross the Colorado River for hundreds of miles in either direction. This stretch of the river is legendary among anglers for its trophy trout fishing, and when the North Rim closes and the rafting season comes to an end, about the only folks you'll find up here are anglers and hunters. Lees Ferry has a 51-site campground (℡ 520/355-2234) that does not take reservations.

Lees Ferry Anglers (℡ 800/962-9755 or 520/355-2261; www.leesferry. com), 3 miles west of the bridge at Lees Ferry, is fishing headquarters for the region. Not only does it sell all manner of fly-fishing tackle and offer advice about good spots to try your luck, but it also operates a guide service and rents waders and boats. A guide will cost $280 per day for one person or $350 for two people.

Continuing west, the highway passes under the **Vermilion Cliffs,** so named for their deep red coloring. At the base of these cliffs are huge boulders balanced

Return of the Condors

California condors are among the most endangered bird species in North America, but the Grand Canyon is playing a part in helping these huge scavengers return from the brink of extinction. Since 1996, the Vermillion Cliffs have become home to a small population of California condors that has been released here in hopes of reestablishing a wild condor population. Condors have also been released at the eastern end of the canyon in the Hurricane Cliffs area, now part of the newly designated Grand Canyon–Parashant National Monument. So far, 35 birds have been released in the area, and most of the birds in the canyon have survived. Occasionally, Grand Canyon visitors spot these huge birds. Should you be so lucky as to see a condor, do not approach the bird or offer it food.

on narrow columns of eroded soil. The balanced rocks give the area an otherworldly appearance. Along this unpopulated stretch of road are a couple of very basic lodges.

Seventeen miles west of Marble Canyon, you'll see a sign for **House Rock Ranch.** This wildlife area, managed by the Arizona Game and Fish Department, is best known for its herd of bison (American buffalo). From the turnoff, it's a 22-mile drive on a gravel road to reach the ranch.

One last detour to consider before or after visiting the national park is an area known as the East Rim. This area lies just outside the park in Kaibab National Forest and can be reached by turning east on gravel Forest Service Road 610 across from the Kaibab Lodge, a few miles north of the park entrance. For the best view, continue to the end of FR 610 and the Saddle Mountain Viewpoint. Another good view can be had from the Marble viewpoint at the end of FR 219, a dead-end spur road off FR 610. For more information, contact the **North Kaibab Ranger District** (© 520/643-7395).

NORTH OF THE PARK

To learn more about the pioneer history of this remote and sparsely populated region of the state (known as the Arizona Strip), continue west from Jacob Lake 45 miles on Ariz. 389 to **Pipe Spring National Monument** (© 520/643-7105; www.nps.gov/pisp), which preserves an early Mormon fort. In summer, living-history demonstrations are held. The monument is open daily (except Thanksgiving, Christmas, and New Year's Day) from 7:30am to 5:30pm June through September, and from 8am to 5pm the rest of the year. Admission is $3 per adult.

Southwest of Pipe Spring, in an area accessible only via long gravel roads, lies the **Grand Canyon–Parashant National Monument.** Dedicated by President Clinton in early 2000, this monument preserves a vast and rugged landscape north of the east end of Grand Canyon National Park. The monument has no facilities and no paved roads. For more information, contact the Arizona Strip Field Office of the **Bureau of Land Management,** 345 E. Riverside Dr., St. George, UT 84790-9000 (© 435/688-3200; www.az.blm.gov).

WHERE TO STAY
INSIDE THE PARK

Grand Canyon Lodge ★★   Perched right on the canyon rim, this classic mountain lodge is listed on the National Register of Historic Places and is as impressive a lodge as you will find in any national park. The stone-and-log main lodge building has a soaring ceiling and a viewing room set up with chairs facing a wall of glass, and on either side of this room are flagstone terraces set with rustic chairs that face out toward the canyon. The guest rooms vary from standard motel units to rustic mountain cabins to comfortable modern cabins. Although the modern cabins have been recently renovated, our favorites are still the little cabins, which, although cramped and paneled with dark wood, capture the feeling of a mountain retreat better than any of the other rooms. A few units have views of the canyon, but most are tucked back away from the rim. The dining hall has two walls of glass to take in the awesome canyon views.

Amfac Parks & Resorts, 14001 E. Iliff Ave., Suite 600, Aurora, CO 80014. ✆ **303/297-2757,** or 520/638-2611 (for same-day reservations). Fax 303/297-3175. www.grandcanyonnorthrim.com. 201 units. $80–$99 double. AE, DC, DISC, MC, V. Closed Oct 15–May 15. **Amenities:** Restaurant, lounge, snack bar; tour desk; coin-op laundry.

OUTSIDE THE PARK

In addition to this hotel, and the other lodges mentioned below, you'll find numerous budget motels in Fredonia, Arizona (30 miles west of Jacob Lake), and Kanab, Utah (37 miles west of Jacob Lake).

Kaibab Lodge   Located 5 miles north of the entrance to the Grand Canyon's North Rim, the Kaibab Lodge was built in the 1920s and is situated on the edge of a large meadow where deer can often be seen grazing. Nights here are cool even in summer, and a favorite pastime of guests is to sit by the fireplace in the lobby. The rooms are mostly in small rustic cabins set back in the pines from the main lodge building. The dining room serves all meals, and the kitchen prepares box lunches.

P.O. Box 2997, Flagstaff, AZ 86003. ✆ **800/525-0924** or 520/526-0924 (520/638-2389 May 15–Oct 31). Fax 520/638-9864. www.canyoneers.com. 29 units. Mid-May to late Oct $80–$130 double. DISC, MC, V. Closed Nov to mid-May. Pets accepted. **Amenities:** Restaurant, lounge. *In room:* No phone.

EN ROUTE TO THE PARK

If you don't have a reservation at either of the North Rim area lodges listed above, you may want to stop at one of the places recommended below and continue on to the North Rim the next morning. Lodges near the canyon fill up early in the day if they aren't already fully booked with reservations made months in advance.

Cliff Dwellers Lodge   To give you some idea of how remote an area this is, the Cliff Dwellers Lodge is marked on official Arizona state maps; there just isn't much else out here, so a single lodge can be as important as a town. The newer, more expensive rooms are standard motel units with combination bathtub/ showers, while the older rooms, in a stone-walled building, have more character but showers only. The lodge is close to some spectacular balanced rocks, and it's about 11 miles east to Lees Ferry. The views here are great.

U.S. 89A (H.C. 67-30), Marble Canyon, AZ 86036. ✆ **800/433-2543** for reservations, or 520/355-2228. Fax 520/355-2229. www.cliffdwellerslodge.com. 21 units. $57–$78 double. DISC, MC, V. **Amenities:** Restaurant (American). *In room:* A/C, no phone.

Lees Ferry Lodge   Located at the foot of the Vermillion Cliffs, 3½ miles west of the Colorado River, the Lees Ferry Lodge, built in 1929 of native stone and rough-hewn timber beams, is a small place with rustic accommodations. The rafters and anglers who stay here don't seem to care much about the condition of the rooms, and besides, the patio seating area in front of all the rooms has fabulous views of the Vermilion Cliffs. Unfortunately, the highway is only a few yards away, so traffic noises can disturb the tranquility. Boat rentals and fly-fishing guides can be arranged through the lodge.

U.S. 89A (H.C. 67-Box 1), Marble Canyon, AZ 86036. © **520/355-2231**. www.leesferrylodge.com. 11 units. $50–$75 double. MC, V. Pets accepted. **Amenities:** Restaurant. *In room:* A/C, no phone.

Marble Canyon Lodge   Just 4 miles from Lees Ferry, the Marble Canyon Lodge was built in the 1920s and is popular with rafters preparing to head down the Grand Canyon. The room styles vary considerably in size and age, with some rustic units in old stone buildings and other newer motel-style rooms as well. You're right at the base of the Vermilion Cliffs here, and the views are great. In addition to the cozy restaurant, there's a trading post.

P.O. Box 6001, Marble Canyon, AZ 86036. © **800/726-1789** or 520/355-2225. Fax 520/355-2227. 60 units. $60–$125 double. AE, DISC, MC, V. Pets accepted. **Amenities:** Restaurant. *In room:* A/C, TV, no phone.

CAMPGROUNDS

Located just north of Grand Canyon Lodge, the **North Rim Campground,** with 75 sites and no hookups for RVs, is the only campground at the North Rim. It opens in mid-May and sometimes stays open past the mid-October closing of other North Rim visitor facilities. Reservations can be made up to 5 months in advance by calling the **National Park Reservation Service** (© **800/365-2267;** www.reservations.nps.gov). The fee is $15 to $20 per site per night.

There are two nearby campgrounds outside the park in the Kaibab National Forest. They are **DeMotte Park Campground,** which is the closest to the park entrance and has only 23 sites, and **Jacob Lake Campground,** which is 30 miles north of the park entrance and has 53 sites. Both charge $10 per night and do not take reservations. You can camp anywhere in the Kaibab National Forest as long as you're more than a quarter mile from a paved road or water source. So if you can't find a site in a campground, simply pull off the highway in the national forest and park your RV or pitch your tent.

The **Kaibab Camper Village** (© **520/643-7804** in summer, or 520/526-0924 in winter), is a privately owned campground in the crossroads of Jacob Lake, 30 miles north of the park entrance. The campground has around 100 sites; rates are $12 per night for tent sites and $22 per night for RV sites with full hookups. Make reservations well in advance.

7

The Four Corners Region: Land of the Hopi & Navajo

There is only one place in the United States where you can stand in four states at the same time, and that spot is in northeast Arizona where Colorado, Utah, New Mexico, and Arizona all come together. Known as Four Corners, this spot is the site of a Navajo Tribal Park. However, Four Corners also refers to this entire region. Most of it is Navajo and Hopi reservation land, and it's also some of the most spectacular countryside in the state, with majestic mesas, rainbow-hued deserts, towering buttes, multi-colored cliffs, deep canyons, a huge cliff-rimmed reservoir, and even a meteorite crater. Among the most spectacular of the landscape features are the 1,000-foot buttes of Monument Valley, which for years have symbolized the Wild West of John Wayne movies and car commercials.

The Four Corners region is also home to Arizona's most scenic reservoir—Lake Powell—which is sort of a flooded version of the Grand Canyon. With its miles of blue water mirroring red-rock canyon walls hundreds of feet high, Lake Powell is one of northern Arizona's curious contrasts—a vast artificial reservoir in the middle of barren desert canyons. Although 40 years ago there was a bitter fight over damming Glen Canyon to form Lake Powell, today the lake is among the most popular attractions in the Southwest.

While this region certainly offers plenty of scenery, it also provides one of the nation's most fascinating cultural experiences. This is Indian country, the homeland of both the Navajo and the Hopi, tribes that have lived on these lands for hundreds of years and have adapted different means of surviving in this arid region. The Navajo, with their traditional log homes scattered across the countryside, have become herders of sheep, goats, and cattle. The Hopi, on the other hand, have congregated in villages atop mesas and built houses of stone. They farm the floors of narrow valleys at the feet of their mesas in much the same way the indigenous peoples of the Southwest have done for centuries.

These two tribes are only the most recent Native Americans to inhabit what many consider to be a desolate, barren wilderness. The ancient Anasazi (ancestral Puebloans) left their mark throughout the canyons of the Four Corners region. Their cliff dwellings date back 700 years or more, the most spectacular in Arizona being the ruins in Canyon de Chelly and Navajo national monuments. No one is sure why the Anasazi moved up into the cliff walls, but there is speculation that unfavorable growing conditions brought on by drought may have forced them to use every possible inch of arable land. Likewise, no one is certain why the Anasazi abandoned their cliff dwellings in the 13th century, and with no written record, their disappearance may forever remain a mystery.

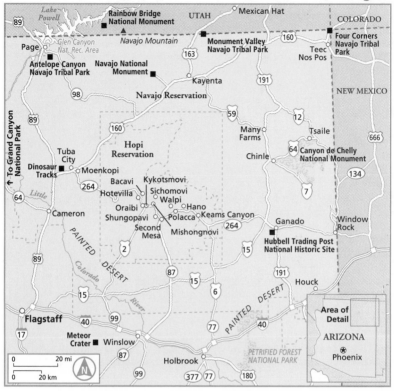

The Hopi, who claim the Anasazi as their ancestors, have for centuries had their villages on the tops of mesas in northeastern Arizona. They claim that Oraibi, on Third Mesa, is the oldest continuously inhabited community in the United States. Whether or not this is true, several of the Hopi villages are quite old, and for this reason have become tourist attractions. Most of the villages are built on three mesas, known simply as First, Second, and Third Mesa, which are numbered from east to west. These villages have always maintained a great deal of autonomy, which over the years has sometimes led to fighting. The appearance of missionaries and the policies of the Bureau of Indian Affairs have also created conflicts among and within villages. Today the Hopi Reservation is completely surrounded by the much larger Navajo Reservation.

Roughly the size of West Virginia, the Navajo Reservation covers an area of 25,000 square miles in northeastern Arizona, as well as parts of New Mexico, Colorado, and Utah. It's the largest Native American reservation in the United States and is home to nearly 200,000 Navajo. Although the reservation today has modern towns with supermarkets, malls, and hotels, many Navajo still follow a pastoral lifestyle as herders of goats and sheep. As you travel the roads of the reservation, you'll frequently encounter these flocks as well as herds of cattle and horses. These animals have free range of the reservation and often graze beside the highways.

Unlike the pueblo tribes such as the Hopi and Zuni, the Navajo are relative newcomers to the Southwest. Their Athabascan language is most closely related to the languages spoken by Native Americans in the Pacific Northwest, Canada, and Alaska. It's believed that the Navajo migrated southward from northern Canada beginning around A.D. 1000, arriving in the Southwest sometime after 1400. At this time, they were still hunters and gatherers, but contact with the pueblo tribes, which had long before adopted an agricultural lifestyle, began to change the Navajo into farmers. When the Spanish arrived in the Southwest in the early 17th century, the Navajo acquired horses, sheep, and goats through raids and adopted a pastoral way of life, grazing their herds in the high plains and canyon bottoms.

The continued raids, made even more successful with the acquisition of horses, put the Navajo in conflict with the Spanish settlers who were beginning to encroach on Navajo land. In 1805, the Spanish sent a military expedition into the Navajo's chief stronghold, Canyon de Chelly, and killed 115 people, who, by some accounts, may have been all women, children, and old men. This massacre, however, did not stop the conflicts between the Navajo and Spanish settlers.

In 1846, when this region became part of the United States, American settlers encountered the same problems that the Spanish had. Military outposts were established to protect the new settlers, and numerous unsuccessful attempts were made to establish peace. In 1863, after continued attacks, a military expedition led by Col. Kit Carson burned crops and homes late in the summer, effectively obliterating the Navajo's winter supplies. Thus defeated, the Navajo were rounded up and herded 400 miles to an inhospitable region of New Mexico near Fort Sumner. This march became known as the Long Walk. Living conditions at Fort Sumner were deplorable, and the land was unsuitable for farming. In 1868, the Navajo were allowed to return to their homeland.

Upon returning home, and after continued clashes with white settlers, the Navajo eventually settled into a lifestyle of herding. In recent years, however, the Navajo have had to turn to different livelihoods. Although weaving and silver work have become lucrative businesses, the amount of money they garner for the tribe as a whole is not significant. Many Navajo now take jobs as migrant workers, and gas and oil leases on the reservation provide additional income.

Although the reservation covers an immense area, much of it is of no value other than as scenery. Fortunately, the Navajo are recognizing the income potential of their spectacular land. Monument Valley is operated as a tribal park, as is the Four Corners park. Numerous Navajo-owned tour companies also operate on the reservation.

As you travel the reservation, you may notice small hexagonal buildings with rounded roofs. These are hogans, the traditional homes of the Navajo, and are usually made of wood and earth. The doorway of the hogan always faces east to greet the new day. At the Canyon de Chelly and Navajo National Monument visitor centers, you can look inside hogans that are part of the parks' exhibits. If you take a tour at Canyon de Chelly or Monument Valley, you may have an opportunity to visit a hogan that is still someone's home. Most Navajo now live in modest houses or mobile homes, but a family will usually also have a hogan for religious ceremonies.

All over the reservation, you'll see roadside stalls selling jewelry and crafts. While you can sometimes find quality merchandise and bargain prices at these stalls, you'll usually get better quality at trading posts, museum and park gift shops, and established shops where you receive some guarantee of quality.

The Navajo and Hopi reservations cover a vast area and are laced with a network of good paved roads, as well as many unpaved roads that are not always passable to cars that don't have four-wheel drive. Keep your gas tank filled, since distances are great, and keep an eye out for livestock on the road, especially at night.

Before taking a photograph of a Navajo, always ask permission. If it's granted, a tip of $1 or more is expected. Photography is not allowed at all in Hopi villages. Unlike the rest of Arizona, the Navajo Reservation observes daylight saving time. However, the Hopi Reservation does not. Another important thing to keep in mind: *Alcohol is not allowed on either reservation.*

1 Winslow

55 miles E of Flagstaff; 70 miles S of Second Mesa; 33 miles W of Holbrook

It's hard to imagine a town that could build its entire tourist fortunes on a mention in a pop song, but that is exactly what Winslow has done for a couple of decades, ever since the Eagles sang about "standin' on a corner in Winslow, Arizona," in their hit song "Take It Easy." They've even built an official Standin' on the Corner Park (complete with a mural of a girl in a flatbed Ford) on the corner of Second Street and Kinsley Avenue.

Popular songs aside, Winslow can claim a couple of more significant attractions. Right in town is one of the Southwest's historic railroad hotels, La Posada, which is undergoing ongoing renovations that have returned it to its original glory. Twenty miles west of town is mile-wide Meteor Crater. And east of town is Homolovi Ruins State Park, which has ancient ruins as well as extensive petroglyphs.

ESSENTIALS

GETTING THERE Winslow is on I-40 at the junction with Ariz. 87, which leads north to the Hopi mesas and south to Payson. **Amtrak** (© **800/ 872-7245**) trains stop in Winslow on East Second Street (at La Posada).

VISITOR INFORMATION Contact the **Winslow Chamber of Commerce,** 300 W. North Rd. (© **520/289-2434,** ext. 300; www.winslowarizona.org).

THE ORIGINAL DEEP IMPACT

Meteor Crater ⭑⭑ Northern Arizona has more than its fair share of natural attractions, and while most of the region's big holes in the ground were created by the slow process of erosion, there is one hole that has far more dramatic origins. At 570 feet deep and 3 miles in circumference, Meteor Crater, the best-preserved meteorite impact crater on earth, is billed as "this planet's most penetrating natural attraction." The meteorite, which estimates put at roughly 100 feet in diameter, was traveling at 45,000 miles per hour when it slammed into the earth 49,000 years ago. Within seconds, more than 300 million tons of rock had been displaced, leaving a gaping crater and a devastated landscape. Today you can stand on the rim of the crater (there are observation decks and a short trail) and marvel at the power, equivalent to 15 million tons of TNT, that created this otherworldly setting. In fact, so closely does this crater resemble craters on the surface of the moon that in the 1960s, NASA came here to train Apollo astronauts.

A small museum on the rim features exhibits on astrogeology and space exploration, as well as a film on meteorites. On display are a 1,400-pound meteorite and an Apollo space capsule.

20 miles west of Winslow at exit 233 off I-40. © 800/289-5898 or 520/289-2362. www.meteorcrater.com. Admission $10 adults, $9 seniors, $5 children 6–17. May 15–Sept 15 daily 6am–6pm; Sept 16–May 14 daily 8am–5pm.

OTHER AREA ATTRACTIONS

In downtown Winslow, near that famous corner, you'll find the little **Old Trails Museum,** 212 N. Kinsley Ave., at Second Street (© **520/289-5861**), which has exhibits on Route 66 and the Harvey Girls (who once worked in the nearby La Posada hotel). From April to October, it's open Tuesday through Saturday from 1 to 5pm, and from November to March, it's open Tuesday, Thursday, and Saturday from 1 to 5pm. Admission is free.

Even if you aren't planning on staying the night at the restored **La Posada,** 303 E. Second St. (© **520/289-4366**), be sure to stop by just to see this historic railway hotel. Self-guided tours are available for a $2 donation, and guided tours are arranged through Winslow's Harvey Girls association ($5 suggested donation).

On the windswept plains north of Winslow (1.3 miles north of I-40 at exit 257), you'll find **Homolovi Ruins State Park** (© **520/289-4106**), which preserves more than 300 ancient Anasazi archaeological sites, several of which have been partially excavated. Although these ruins are not nearly as impressive as those at Wupatki or Walnut Canyon, a visit here will give you a better understanding of the interrelationship of the many ancient pueblos of this region. Also in the park are numerous petroglyphs; ask directions at the visitor center. Admission is $4 per vehicle. The ruins are open daily from 7am to sunset, but the visitor center is open only from 8am to 5pm. There's also a campground, charging $10 to $15 per site.

Continuing north from the state park, you'll find the little known and little visited **Little Painted Desert** ⚘, a 660-acre county park. To reach the park and its viewpoint overlooking the painted hills of this stark yet colorful landscape, continue north on Ariz. 87 from Homolovi State Park for another 12 miles. Although the trail down into the desert itself is closed, unofficially, the parks department doesn't mind if you hike down. For information, contact Navajo County Parks (© **520/524-4251**).

If you're in the market for some Route 66 memorabilia, drop by **Roadworks Gifts & Souvenirs,** 206 Kinsley Ave. # 6 (© **520/289-5423**), directly across the street from Standin' on the Corner Park. If you're more interested in Native American crafts, check out the **Arizona Indian Arts Cooperative,** 523 W. Second St. (© **520/289-3986**), which is housed in the historic Lorenzo Hubbell Co. trading post.

WHERE TO STAY

In addition to the following historic hotel, you'll find lots of budget chain motels in Winslow.

La Posada ⭐⭐ *Finds*   Designed by Mary Elizabeth Jane Colter, who designed many of the buildings on the South Rim of the Grand Canyon, this railroad hotel opened in 1930. Colter gave La Posada the feel of an old Spanish hacienda, and even created a fictitious history surrounding the building. The hotel is currently being restored (20 more rooms are scheduled to open in 2001) and is reason enough to overnight in Winslow. In the lobby are several pieces of original furniture as well as reproductions of pieces once found in the hotel. The nicest rooms at press time are the large units named for famous guests—Clark Gable, Howard Hughes, Gary Cooper, Charles Lindbergh, the Marx brothers. The management's artistic flair comes across in these rooms, one of which (the Frank & Joanne Randall Room) has wide plank floors, murals, a fireplace, a rustic bed and armoire, Art Deco chairs, and a kilim rug. The bathroom is a classic of black-and-white tile and original fixtures. In 2000, the hotel opened a restaurant (the best in the Four Corners region) and a lounge.

303 E. Second St. (Route 66), Winslow, AZ 86047. © **520/289-4366.** Fax 520/289-3873. www.laposada.org. 23 units. $79–$99 double. AE, DC, DISC, MC, V. Pets accepted ($5 fee). **Amenities:** Restaurant (see "Where to Dine," below), lounge. *In room:* A/C, TV, no phone.

WHERE TO DINE

The Turquoise Room ★★ *Value* NEW AMERICAN/SOUTHWESTERN When Fred Harvey began his railroad hospitality career, his objective was to provide decent meals to the traveling public. (See "Fred Harvey & His Girls," on p. 258.) Here, in La Posada's reincarnated dining room, you'll get not just decent meals, but superb meals the likes of which you won't find anywhere else in northern Arizona. The menu includes dishes from original Fred Harvey menus as well as contemporary Southwestern cuisine such as incredibly tender elk medallions with cherry sauce. In summer, herbs and vegetables often come from the hotel's own gardens, and wild game is a specialty. At breakfast, don't miss the baked egg dishes, which were a mainstay of Fred Harvey menus. On top of all this, you can watch the trains rolling by just outside the window.

In La Posada, 303 E. Second St. © **520/289-2888.** www.laposada.org. Main courses $7–$10 lunch, $12–$20 dinner. MC, V. Tues–Sun 7–9:30am, 11:30am–2pm, and 5:30–9pm.

2 The Hopi Reservation

250 miles NE of Phoenix; 67 miles N of Winslow; 100 miles SW of Canyon de Chelly; 140 miles SE of Page/Lake Powell

This remote region of Arizona, with its flat-topped mesas and barren landscape, is the center of the universe for the Hopi people. The Hopi Reservation is completely surrounded by the Navajo Reservation, and has at its center the grouping of mesas upon which the Hopi have lived for nearly 1,000 years. Here the Hopi follow their ancient customs, and many aspects of pueblo culture remain intact. However, much of the culture is hidden from the view of non-Hopi, and although the Hopi perform elaborate religious and social dances throughout the year, many of these dances are not open to outsiders.

The mesas are home to two of the oldest continuously inhabited villages in North America—Walpi and Old Oraibi. Although these two communities show their age and serve as a direct tie to the pueblos of the ancient Anasazi culture, most of the villages on the reservation are scattered collections of modern homes. These villages are not destinations unto themselves, but along Ariz. 264 are numerous craft shops and studios selling kachinas, Hopi basketry and pottery, and silver jewelry. The chance to buy crafts and jewelry directly from the Hopi is the main reason for a visit to this area, although you can also go on a guided tour of Walpi village.

Important note: When visiting the Hopi pueblos, remember that you are a guest and your privileges can be revoked at any time. Respect all posted signs at village entrances, and remember that *photographing, sketching, and recording are prohibited in the villages and at ceremonies.* Also, kivas (ceremonial rooms) and ruins are off-limits.

ESSENTIALS

GETTING THERE   This is one of the state's most remote regions. Distances are great, but highways are generally in good condition. Ariz. 87 leads from Winslow to Second Mesa, and Ariz. 264 runs from Tuba City in the west to the New Mexico state line in the east.

The **Navajo Transit System** (© **520/729-4002**) operates bus service Monday through Friday throughout the Navajo and Hopi reservations, with service between the following towns: Farmington, Gallup, and Crown Point (all in New Mexico), and Window Rock, Kayenta, Chinle, and Tuba City. The route between Window Rock and Tuba City stops at several of the Hopi villages, including Second Mesa.

VISITOR INFORMATION   For advance information, contact the **Hopi Tribal Council,** P.O. Box 123, Kykotsmovi, AZ 86039 (© **520/734-3000;** www.hopi.nsn.us), or the **Hopi Cultural Preservation Office** (© **520/ 734-2244;** www.nau.edu/~hcpo-p).

Because each of the Hopi villages is relatively independent, you might want to contact the **Community Development Office** of a particular village for specific information: **Bacavi** (© 520/734-9360), **Sichomovi** (© 520/737-2670), **Hotevilla** (© 520/734-2420), **Kykotsmovi** (© 520/734-2472), **Mishongnovi** (© 520/737-2520), **Upper Moenkopi** (© 520/283-8054), **Lower Moenkopi** (© 520/283-5212), **Shipaulovi** (© 520/737-2570), **Shungopavi** (© 520/ 734-7135), and **Walpi** (© 520/737-5435). These offices are open Monday through Friday from 8am to 5pm.

THE VILLAGES

With the exception of Moenkopi, which is located near the Navajo town of Tuba City, the Hopi villages are scattered along roughly 20 miles of U.S. 264. With its organized tours, Walpi is the best of the villages to visit. Although Old Oraibi is older, there are no tours of the village and visitors are not likely to feel very welcome here. We mention all the Hopi villages to provide a bit of history and perspective on this area. However, for the most part, these villages (with the exception of Walpi and Old Oraibi) are not at all picturesque. Most do have quite a few crafts galleries and stores selling silver jewelry.

FIRST MESA   At the top of First Mesa is the village of **Walpi,** which was located lower on the slopes of the mesa until the Pueblo Revolt of 1680 brought on fear of reprisal from the Spanish. The villagers moved Walpi to the very top of the mesa so they could better defend themselves in the event of a Spanish attack. Walpi looks much like the Anasazi villages of the Arizona canyons. Small stone houses seem to grow directly from the rock of the mesa top, and ladders jut from the roofs of kivas. The view from here stretches for hundreds of miles around.

Immediately adjacent to Walpi are the two villages of **Sichomovi,** which was founded in 1750 as a colony of Walpi, and **Hano,** which was founded by Tewa peoples who were most likely seeking refuge from the Spanish after the Pueblo Revolt. Neither of these villages has the ancient character of Walpi. At the foot of First Mesa is **Polacca,** a settlement founded in the late 1800s by Walpi villagers who wanted to be closer to the trading post and school.

SECOND MESA   Second Mesa is today the center of tourism in Hopiland, as the Hopi country is called, and this is where you'll find the Hopi Cultural Center. Villages on Second Mesa include **Shungopavi,** which was moved to its present site after Old Shungopavi was abandoned in 1680 following the Pueblo

Revolt against the Spanish. Old Shungopavi is said to be the first Hopi village. It's notable for its silver jewelry and its coiled plaques.

Mishongnovi, which means "place of the black man," is named for the leader of a clan that came here from the San Francisco Peaks around A.D. 1200. The original Mishongnovi village, located at the base of the mesa, was abandoned in the early 1700s and the village was reestablished at the current site atop the mesa. The Snake Dance is held here during odd-numbered years and in nearby Gray Spring in even years. However, it is doubtful that these dances will be open to non-Hopis, though you could try calling Mishongnovi's Community Development Office (see "Visitor Information," above) to check.

Shipaulovi, which is located on the eastern edge of the mesa, was founded after the Pueblo Revolt of 1680.

THIRD MESA   Oraibi, which the Hopi claim is the oldest continuously occupied town in the United States, is located on Third Mesa. The village dates from 1150 and, according to legend, was founded by people from Old Shungopavi. A Spanish mission was established in Oraibi in 1629, and the ruins are still visible north of the village. Today Oraibi is a mix of old stone houses and modern ones, usually of cinder block. With permission, you can wander around in Oraibi, where you'll likely be approached by village women offering to sell you various local crafts.

For centuries, Oraibi was the largest of the Hopi villages, but in 1906, a schism occurred over Bureau of Indian Affairs policies and many of the villagers left to form **Hotevilla.** This is considered the most conservative of the Hopi villages and has had frequent confrontations with the federal government. **Kykotsmovi,** also known as Lower Oraibi or New Oraibi, was founded in 1890 by villagers from Oraibi who wanted to be closer to the school and trading post. This village is the seat of the Hopi Tribal Government. **Bacavi** was founded in 1907 by villagers who had helped found Hotevilla but who later decided that they wanted to return to Oraibi. The people of Oraibi would not let them return, and rather than go back to Hotevilla, they founded a new village.

MOENKOPI   One last Hopi village, **Moenkopi,** is located 40 miles to the west. Founded in 1870 by people from Oraibi, Moenkopi sits in the center of a wide green valley where plentiful water makes farming more reliable. Moenkopi is only a few miles from Tuba City off U.S. 160 and is divided into the villages of Upper Moenkopi and Lower Moenkopi.

EXPLORING THE WORLD OF THE HOPI

Start your visit to the Hopi pueblos at the **Hopi Cultural Center,** on Ariz. 264 in Second Mesa (© **520/734-6650**). This combination museum, motel, and restaurant is the tourism headquarters for the area. Be sure to take notice of signs indicating when villages are open to visitors. The museum is open Monday through Friday from 8am to 5pm; in summer, it's also open on Saturday and Sunday from 9am to 3pm. Admission is $3 for adults and $1 for children.

Although it's possible to get permission to visit most Hopi villages, the easiest to see is **Walpi** ⍟, on First Mesa. Guided tours of this tiny village are offered daily, between 9am and 5pm in summer and between 9:30am and 4pm other months. Admission is $8 for adults, $5 for children 5 to 17. To sign up for a tour, drive to the top of First Mesa (in Polacca, take the road that says First Mesa village) and continue through the village to **Punsi Hall Visitor Center** (© **520/ 737-2262**), where you'll see signs for the tours. The tours, which last 45 minutes to 1 hour, are led by Hopis who will tell you the history of the village and explain a bit about the local culture. On the third weekend in September, a harvest festival features 2 days of dancing. As of this writing, the festival is open to the public.

CULTURAL TOURS

Perhaps the best way to see the Hopi mesas is on a guided small-group tour. With a guide, you will likely learn much more about this rather insular culture than you ever could on your own. Tour companies frequently use local guides and stop at the homes of working artisans. This all adds up to a more in-depth and educational visit to one of the oldest cultures on the continent. Gary Tso is one local guide who gives tours through his **Left-Handed Hunter Tour Co.** (© **520/734-2567;** lhhunter58@hotmail.com). Gary will take you to Walpi, old Oraibi, a petroglyph site, and the studios of a kachina carver, a potter, and a silver- and goldsmith. All-day tours (including lunch, transportation, and entry fees) range from $195 for one person to $345 for four.

Other companies offering Hopi tours include **Crossing Worlds Journeys & Retreats** (© **800/350-2693** or 520/203-0024; www.crossingworlds.com) and **Discovery Passages** (© **520/717-0519**). One-day tours to the mesas run about $165 per person.

DANCES & CEREMONIES

The Hopi have developed the most complex religious ceremonies of any of the Southwest tribes. Masked kachina dances, for which they are most famous, are held from January to July. Most kachina dances are closed to the non-Hopi public. Social dances (usually open to the public) are held August through February, and Snake Dances (closed to the non-Hopi public) are held August through December.

Kachinas, whether in the form of dolls or as masked dancers, are representative of the spirits of everything from plants and animals to ancestors and sacred places. More than 300 kachinas appear on a regular basis in Hopi ceremonies, and another 200 appear occasionally. The kachina spirits are said to live in the San Francisco Peaks to the south and at Spring of the Shadows in the east. According to legend, the kachinas lived with the Hopi long ago, but the Hopi people made the kachinas angry, causing them to leave. Before leaving, though, the kachinas taught the Hopi how to perform their ceremonies.

Today the kachina ceremonies, performed by men wearing elaborate costumes and masks, serve several purposes. Most important, they bring clouds and rain to water the all-important corn crop, but they also ensure health, happiness, long life, and harmony in the universe. As part of the kachina ceremonies, dancers often bring carved wooden kachina dolls to village children to introduce them to the various spirits.

The kachina season lasts from the winter solstice until shortly after the summer solstice. The actual dates for dances are determined by the position of the sun and usually are announced only shortly before the ceremonies are to be held. Preparations for the dances take place inside kivas (circular ceremonial rooms) that are entered from the roof by means of a ladder; the dances themselves are usually held in a village square or street.

With ludicrous and sometimes lewd mimicry, clowns known as *koyemsi, koshares,* and *tsukus* entertain spectators between the dances, bringing a lighthearted counterpoint to the very serious nature of the kachina dances. Be aware that non-Hopis at kachina dances often become the focus of attention for these clowns.

Despite the importance of the kachina dances, it is the **Snake Dance** that has captured the attention of many non-Hopis. The Snake Dance is held every other year in Mishongnovi and Gray Spring and involves the handling of both poisonous and nonpoisonous snakes. The ceremony takes place over 16 days, with the first 4 days dedicated to collecting all the snakes from the four cardinal directions. Later, footraces are held from the bottom of the mesa to the top. On the last day of the ceremony, the actual Snake Dance is performed. Men of the Snake Society form pairs of dancers—one to carry the snake in his mouth and the other to distract the snake with an eagle feather. When all the snakes have been danced around the plaza, they are rushed down to their homes at the bottom of the mesa to carry the Hopi prayers for rain to the spirits of the underworld.

Due to the disrespectful attitude of some visitors in the past, many ceremonies and dances are now closed to non-Hopis. However, several Hopi villages do allow visitors to attend some of their dances. The best way to find out about attending dances is to contact the **Community Development Office** of the individual villages (see phone numbers under "Visitor Information," above).

SHOPPING

Most visitors come to the reservation to shop for Hopi crafts. There are literally dozens of small shops selling crafts and jewelry of different quality, and some homes have signs indicating that they sell crafts. Shops often sell the work of only a few individuals, so you should stop at several to get an idea of the variety of work available. Also, if you tour Walpi or wander around in Oraibi, you will likely be approached by villagers selling various crafts, including kachinas. The quality is not usually as high as in shops, but neither are the prices.

One of the best places to get a quick education in Hopi art and crafts is **Tsakurshovi** (© 520/734-2478), a tiny shop 1½ miles east of the Hopi Cultural Center on Second Mesa. This shop has an amazing selection of crafts, old-style kachina dolls, native herbs, and coil and wicker plaque baskets. The owners are very friendly and are happy to share their expertise with visitors. Open daily from 9am to 6pm.

If you're in the market for Hopi silver jewelry, stop in at **Hopi Arts and Crafts-Silvercraft** (© 520/734-2463), 100 yards from the Hopi Cultural Center on Second Mesa. This arts-and-crafts cooperative shows work by artisans from all the villages of the Hopi mesas. The selection is most extensive in the summer. Open Monday through Friday from 8am to 5pm. The **Honani Crafts Gallery** (© 520/737-2238), at the intersection of Highway 264 and the road up to Second Mesa, sells both silver and the less common gold jewelry. Open daily from 9am to 5:30pm.

If you're interested in kachina dolls, be sure to visit Oraibi's **Monongya Gallery** (© 520/734-2344), a big turquoise-and-cream building west of the Hopi Cultural Center on Ariz. 264. It usually has one of the largest selections of kachina dolls in the area, and holds a Christmas Eve sale at 50% off. Open Monday through Saturday from 9am to 5pm and Sunday from 10am to 4pm.

Also in Oraibi is **Old Oraibi Crafts** (no phone), which sells artwork and crafts based on kachina images. At Keams Canyon, almost 30 miles east of the cultural center, is **McGee's Indian Art** (© 520/738-2295; www.hopiart.com), another great place to shop for high-quality kachina dolls. This shop is adjacent to a grocery store and has been a trading post for more than 100 years.

(C) A Native American Crafts Primer

The Four Corners region is taken up almost entirely by the Navajo and Hopi reservations, so Native American crafts are ubiquitous. You'll see jewelry for sale by the side of desolate, windswept roads, Navajo rugs in tiny trading posts, and Hopi kachinas being sold out of village homes. If you decide you want to take home a work by a local crafts-person, the information below will help you make an informed pur-chase. It is also possible now to shop for Native American crafts online at **www.hopimarket.com**.

Hopi Kachinas   These elaborately decorated wooden dolls are repre-sentations of spirits of plants, animals, ancestors, and sacred places. Traditionally, they were given to children to initiate them into the pan-theon of kachina spirits, who play important roles in ensuring rain and harmony in the universe. However, kachinas are popular with collec-tors of Native American crafts, and Hopi carvers have changed their style to cater to the new market. Older kachinas were carved from a single piece of cottonwood, sometimes with arms simply painted on. This older style is much simpler and stiffer than the currently popular style that emphasizes action poses and realistic proportions. A great deal of carving and painting goes into each kachina, and prices today are in the hundreds of dollars for even the simplest. Currently very popular with tourists and collectors are the *tsuku*, or clown kachinas, which are usually painted with bold horizontal black and white stripes and are often depicted in humorous situations or carrying slices of watermelon.

Navajo Silver Work   While the Hopi create overlay silver work from sheets of silver and the Zuni use silver work simply as a base for their skilled lapidary or stone-cutting work, the Navajo silversmiths highlight the silver itself. Just as rug weaving did not begin until the latter part of the 19th century, silversmithing did not catch on with the Navajo until the 1880s, when Lorenzo Hubbell decided to hire Mexican silver-smiths as teachers. When tourists began visiting the area after 1890, the demand for Navajo jewelry increased. The earliest pieces of Navajo jew-elry were replicas of Spanish ornaments, but as the Navajo silversmiths became more proficient, they began to develop their own designs. Sand-casting, stamp work, repoussé, and file-and-chisel work give Navajo jewelry its unique look. The squash-blossom necklace, with its horseshoe-shaped pendant, is perhaps the most distinctive Navajo jew-elry design. Wide bracelets and concha belts are also popular.

Hopi Overlay Silver Work   Most Hopi silver work is done in the overlay style, which was introduced to Hopi artisans after World War II, when the GI Bill provided funds for Hopi soldiers to study silversmithing at a school founded by Hopi artist Fred Kabotie. The overlay process basically uses two sheets of silver, one with a design cut from it. Heat fuses the two sheets, forming a raised image. Designs used in overlay jewelry are often borrowed from other Hopi crafts such as basketry and pottery, as well as from ancient Anasazi pottery designs. Belt buckles, earrings, bolo ties, and bracelets are all popular.

Hopi Baskets   Although the Tohono O'odham of central and southern Arizona are the state's best-known basket makers, the Hopi also produce beautiful work. On Third Mesa, wicker plaques and baskets are made from rabbit brush and sumac and colored with bright aniline dyes, and on Second Mesa, coiled plaques and baskets are created from dyed yucca fibers. Throughout the reservation, yucca-fiber sifters are made by plaiting over a willow ring.

Hopi Pottery   With the exception of undecorated utilitarian pottery that's made in Hotevilla on Third Mesa, most Hopi pottery is produced on First Mesa. Contemporary Hopi pottery comes in a variety of styles, including a yellow-orange ware decorated with black-and-white designs. This style is said to have been introduced by the potter Nampeyo, a Tewa from the village of Hano who stimulated the revival of Hopi pottery in 1890. White pottery with red-and-black designs is also popular. Hopi pottery designs tend toward geometric patterns.

Navajo Rugs   After they acquired sheep and goats from the Spanish, the Navajo learned weaving from the pueblo tribes, and by the early 1800s, their weavings were widely recognized as being the finest in the Southwest. The Navajo women primarily wove blankets, but by the end of the 19th century, the craft began to die out when it became more economical to purchase a ready-made blanket. When Lorenzo Hubbell set up his trading post, he immediately recognized a potential market in the East for the woven blankets—if they could be made heavy enough to be used as rugs. Having great respect for Hubbell, the Navajo adapted his ideas and soon began doing a brisk business. Although today the cost of Navajo rugs, which take hundreds of hours to make, has become almost prohibitively expensive, there are still enough women practicing the craft to keep it alive and provide plenty of rugs for shops and trading posts all over Arizona.

The best rugs are those made with homespun yarn and natural vegetal dyes. However, commercially manufactured yarns and dyes are increasingly used to keep costs down. There are more than 15 regional styles of rugs and quite a bit of overlapping and borrowing. Bigger and bolder patterns are likely to cost quite a bit less than very complex and highly detailed patterns.

WHERE TO STAY & DINE

If you've brought your food along, there are picnic tables with an amazing view just east of Oraibi on top of the mesa.

Hopi Cultural Center Restaurant & Inn Although it isn't much, this is the only lodging for miles around—so be sure you have a reservation before heading up for an overnight visit. The rooms have all been remodeled in the past couple of years. The restaurant has a good salad bar and serves American and traditional Hopi meals, including *piki* bread (a paper-thin bread made from blue corn) and Hopi stew with hominy, lamb, and green chile. Prices are very reasonable, considering the remoteness of the location. There's also a museum and a very basic campground.

P.O. Box 67, Second Mesa, AZ 86043. ℂ **520/734-2401.** Fax 520/734-6651. www.hopionline.com. 33 units. Mar 15–Oct 15 $95 double; Oct 16–Mar 14 $65–$70 double. AE, DC, DISC, MC, V. **Amenities:** Restaurant (American/Hopi); shopping arcade. *In room:* A/C, TV, coffeemaker.

EN ROUTE TO OR FROM THE HOPI MESAS

On the west side of the reservation, in Tuba City, is the **Tuba City Trading Post** (ℂ **520/283-5441**), at Main Street and Moenave Avenue. This octagonal trading post was built in 1906 of local stone and is designed to resemble a Navajo hogan (there's also a real hogan on the grounds). The trading post sells Native American crafts, with an emphasis on books, music, and jewelry. Open Monday through Saturday from 8am to 5pm.

On the western outskirts of Tuba City, on U.S. 160, you'll find **Van's Trading Co.** (ℂ **520/283-5343**), in the corner of a large grocery store. Van's has a dead-pawn auction on the 15th of each month at 3pm (any pawned item not reclaimed by the owner by a specified date is considered "dead pawn"). The auction provides opportunities to buy older pieces of Navajo silver-and-turquoise jewelry.

In mid-October, Tuba City is the site of the **Western Navajo Fair,** which provides another opportunity for buying Native American crafts.

West of Tuba City and just off U.S. 160, you can see **dinosaur footprints** 𝕣 preserved in the stone surface of the desert. There are usually a few people waiting at the site to guide visitors to the best footprints (these guides will expect a tip). The scenery out your car window is some of the strangest in the region—red-rock sandstone formations that resemble petrified sand dunes.

The **Cameron Trading Post** 𝕣 (ℂ **520/679-2231**), 16 miles south of the junction of U.S. 160 and U.S. 89, is well worth a visit. The main trading post is filled with souvenirs, but has large selections of rugs and jewelry as well. In the adjacent stone-walled gallery are museum-quality Native American artifacts (with prices to match). The trading post also includes a motel (see "Where to Stay" under "The Grand Canyon South Rim" in chapter 6, "The Grand Canyon & Northern Arizona").

WHERE TO STAY

Quality Inn Tuba City Located in the bustling Navajo community of Tuba City (where you'll find gas stations, fast-food restaurants, and grocery stores), this modern motel is adjacent to the historic Tuba City Trading Post. It offers comfortable rooms of average size. If you're unable to get a room either in Kayenta or at the Hopi Cultural Center on Second Mesa, this is the next closest acceptable lodging. There's also an RV park here.

Main St. and Moenave Ave. (P.O. Box 247), Tuba City, AZ 86045. ℂ **800/228-5151** or 520/283-4545. Fax 520/283-4144. www.qualityinn.com. 80 units. Apr–Oct $95–$140 double; Nov–Mar $75–$105 double. AE, DC, DISC, MC, V. **Amenities:** Restaurant (American/Mexican/Navajo). *In room:* A/C, TV, coffeemaker.

3 The Petrified Forest & Painted Desert ⭐

25 miles E of Holbrook; 90 miles E of Flagstaff; 118 miles S of Canyon de Chelly; 180 miles N of Phoenix

Petrified wood has intrigued people for generations, and although it can be found in almost every state, the "forests" of downed logs in northeastern Arizona are by far the most extensive. But don't head out this way expecting to see standing trees of stone, leaves and branches intact. Though there are enough petrified logs scattered across this landscape to fill a forest, they are, in fact, logs and not standing trees. Many a visitor has shown up expecting to find some sort of national forest of stone trees. The reality is much less impressive than the petrified forest of the imagination.

However, this area is still unique. When, in the 1850s, this vast treasure trove of petrified wood was discovered scattered like kindling across the landscape, enterprising people began exporting it wholesale to the East. By 1900, so much had been removed that in 1906 several areas were set aside as the Petrified Forest National Monument, which, in 1962, became a national park. Today, a 27-mile scenic drive winds through the petrified forest (and a small corner of the Painted Desert), providing a fascinating high desert experience.

It may be hard to believe when you drive across this arid landscape, but at one time this area was a vast humid swamp. That was 225 million years ago, when dinosaurs and huge amphibians ruled the earth and giant now-extinct trees grew on the high ground around the swamp. Fallen trees were washed downstream, gathered in piles in still backwaters, and were eventually covered over with silt, mud, and volcanic ash. As water seeped through this soil, it dissolved the silica in the volcanic ash and redeposited this silica inside the cells of the logs. Eventually the silica recrystalized into stone to form petrified wood. Minerals such as iron, manganese, and carbon contribute the distinctive colors.

This region was later inundated with water, and thick deposits of sediment buried the logs ever deeper. Eventually the land was transformed yet again as a geologic upheaval thrust the lake bottom up above sea level. This upthrust of the land cracked the logs into the segments we see today. Wind and water gradually eroded the landscape to create the Painted Desert and northern Arizona's many other spectacular features, and the petrified logs were once again exposed on the surface of the land.

In gift shops throughout this region, you'll see petrified wood in all sizes and colors, natural and polished. This petrified wood comes from private land. No piece of petrified wood, no matter how small, may be removed from Petrified Forest National Park.

ESSENTIALS

GETTING THERE   The north entrance to Petrified Forest National Park is 25 miles east of Holbrook on I-40. The south entrance is 20 miles east of Holbrook on U.S. 180. There is **Amtrak** (℃ 800/872-7245) passenger rail service to Winslow, 33 miles west of Holbrook.

VISITOR INFORMATION   For further information on the Petrified Forest or the Painted Desert, contact **Petrified Forest National Park** (℃ 520/ 524-6228; www.nps.gov/pefo). The park is open daily from 8am to 5pm, with longer hours in summer. Admission is $10 per car.

For information on Holbrook and the surrounding region, contact the **Holbrook Chamber of Commerce,** 100 E. Arizona St. (℃ 800/524-2459 or 520/524-6558; www.ci.holbrook.az.us/Chamber.shtml).

EXPLORING A UNIQUE LANDSCAPE

Although Petrified Forest National Park has both a north and a south entrance, it's probably better to start at the southern entrance and work your way north along the park's 27-mile scenic road, which has more than 20 overlooks. This way, you'll see the most impressive displays of petrified logs early in your visit and save the Painted Desert overlooks for last.

Just inside the south entrance to the park is the **Rainbow Forest Museum,** the best place to learn about petrified wood and orient yourself within the park. Exhibits chronicle the area's geologic and human history. There's also a display of letters written by people who took pieces of petrified wood and who later felt guilty and returned the stones. The museum sells maps and books and also issues free backpacking permits. It's open daily from 8am to 5pm. Adjacent to the museum is a snack bar.

The **Giant Logs self-guided trail** starts behind the museum. The trail winds across a hillside strewn with huge logs and certainly lives up to its name. Almost directly across the parking lot from the museum is the entrance to the **Long Logs** and **Agate House** areas. On the half-mile Long Logs trail, you can see more big trees, while at Agate House, a 1.6-mile round-trip hike will lead you to the ruins of a pueblo built from colorful agatized petrified wood.

Heading north, you pass by the unusual formations known as **The Flattops.** These structures were caused by the erosion of softer soil deposits from beneath a harder and more erosion-resistant layer of sandstone. The Flattops is one of the park's wilderness areas. The **Crystal Forest** is the next stop to the north, named for the beautiful amethyst and quartz crystals once found in the cracks of petrified logs. Concern over the removal of these crystals was what led to the protection of the petrified forest. A 0.75-mile loop trail winds past the logs that once held the crystals.

At the **Jasper Forest Overlook,** you can see logs that include petrified roots, and a little bit farther north, at the **Agate Bridge** stop, you can see a petrified log that forms a natural agate bridge. Continuing north, you come to **Blue Mesa,** where pieces of petrified wood form capstones over easily eroded clay soils. As wind and water wear away at the clay beneath a piece of stone, the balance of the stone becomes more and more precarious until it eventually comes toppling down. A 1-mile loop trail here leads into the badlands.

Erosion has played a major role in the formation of the Painted Desert, and to the north of Blue Mesa you'll see some of the most interesting erosional features of the area. It's quite evident why these hills of sandstone and clay are known as **The Teepees.** The layers of different color are due to manganese, iron, and other minerals in the soil.

By this point, you've probably seen as much petrified wood as you'd ever care to see, so be sure to stop at **Newspaper Rock,** where instead of staring at more ancient logs, you can see a dense concentration of petroglyphs left by generations of Native Americans. At nearby **Puerco Pueblo,** the park's largest archaeological site, you can view the remains of homes built by the people who created the park's petroglyphs. This pueblo was probably built sometime around 1400. Don't miss the petroglyphs on its back side.

North of Puerco Pueblo, the road crosses I-40. From here to the Painted Desert Visitor Center, there are eight overlooks onto the southernmost edge of the **Painted Desert.** Named for the vivid colors of the soil and stone that cover the land here, the Painted Desert is a dreamscape of pastel colors washed across a barren expanse of eroded hills. The colors are created by minerals dissolved in sandstone and clay soils that were deposited during different geologic periods. There's a picnic area at Chinde Point overlook, and at Kachina Point is the **Painted Desert Inn,** a restored historic building that's open daily from 8am to 4pm. From here, there's access to the park's other wilderness area. The inn, which was built by the Civilian Conservation Corps, is noteworthy for both its architecture and the Fred Kabotie murals on the interior walls. Ranger-guided tours start here, and you'll usually see Native American craftspeople giving demonstrations. Between Kachina Point and Tawa Point, you can do an easy 1-mile round-trip hike along the rim of the Painted Desert. An even more interesting route leads down into the Painted Desert from behind the Painted Desert Inn at Kachina Point.

Just inside the northern entrance to the park is the **Painted Desert Visitor Center,** where you can watch a short film that explains the process by which wood becomes fossilized. Adjacent to the visitor center are a cafeteria and a gas station.

OTHER REASONS TO LINGER IN HOLBROOK

Although the Petrified Forest National Park is the main reason for visiting this area, you might want to stop by downtown Holbrook's **Historic Courthouse Museum,** 100 E. Arizona St. (© **520/524-6558**), which also houses the Holbrook Chamber of Commerce visitor center. This old and dusty museum has exhibits on local history, but is most interesting for its old jail cells. It's open daily from 8am to 5pm. June through July, the Holbrook Chamber sponsors Native American dances weekday evenings on the lawn in front.

Although it is against the law to collect petrified wood inside Petrified Forest National Park, there are several **rock shops** in Holbrook where you can buy pieces of petrified wood in all shapes and sizes. You'll find them lined up along the main street through town and out on U.S. 180, the highway leading to the south entrance of Petrified Forest National Park.

Three miles west of town is the **International Petrified Forest Visitor Center and Museum of the Americas,** 1001 Forest Dr. (© **520/524-9178**), at exit 292 off I-40. Although this place may seem at first like just another tourist trap, it actually contains the largest collection of pre-Columbian artifacts in the Southwest, with an emphasis on Mayan and Aztec artifacts, along with plenty of Anasazi and Hohokam pieces. There's also a "rock yard" full of petrified wood, dinosaur fossils, geodes, and other interesting rocks, and a 3-mile drive takes you past Triassic dig sites and more petrified wood. The museum is open from 7am to 7pm in summer (with shorter hours the rest of the year); admission is $5. There's also a warehouse-size rock shop.

Route 66 fans will find plenty to keep them entertained. Hopi Drive, the town's main street, is old Route 66, home to the Wigwam Motel (see "Where to Stay," below). At **Julien's Roadrunner,** 109 W. Hopi Dr. (© **520/524-2388**), you can investigate all manner of memorabilia, from Route 66 signs to enameled replicas of old advertising signs for Mobil Gas and the Santa Fe Railroad. West of Holbrook at exit 269 off I-40, the **Jack Rabbit Trading Post** (© **520/288-3230**) is another fun Route 66–era tourist trap, with all kinds of fun, kitschy stuff straight out of the 1960s.

In town on the north side of I-40 is **McGee's Gallery,** 2114 N. Navajo Blvd. (© **520/524-1977**), a Native American crafts gallery with a wide selection of typical crafts at reasonable prices.

If you're interested in **petroglyphs,** you may want to schedule a visit to the **Rock Art Ranch** ⚔ (© 520/288-3260), southwest of Holbrook on part of the old Hashknife Ranch, which was the largest ranch in the country during the late 19th century. Within the bounds of this ranch, pecked into the rock walls of Chevelon Canyon, are hundreds of Anasazi petroglyphs. The setting, a narrow canyon that is almost invisible until you are right beside it, is enchanting, making this the finest place in the state to view petroglyphs. Tours are available on Saturdays from May to October.

WHERE TO STAY

Holbrook, the nearest town to Petrified Forest National Park, offers lots of budget chain motels charging very reasonable rates.

Wigwam Motel *(Finds* If you're willing to sleep on a saggy mattress for the sake of reliving a bit of Route 66 history, don't miss this collection of concrete wigwams (tepees, actually). This unique motel was built in the 1940s, when unusual architecture was springing up all along famous Route 66. The motel has been owned by the same family since it was built and still has the original rustic furniture. Old cars are kept in the parking lot for an added dose of Route 66 character.

811 W. Hopi Dr. (P.O. Box 788), Holbrook, AZ 86025. © **800/414-3021** or 520/524-3048. 15 units. $36–$42 double. MC, V. Pets accepted. *In room:* A/C, TV.

WHERE TO DINE

Butterfield Stage Co. STEAK/SEAFOOD   It's natural to assume that finding a decent meal in an out-of-the-way town might be nearly impossible, so the Butterfield Stage Co. comes as a pleasant surprise. Meals here are pretty good, with a soup-and-salad bar that is usually fresh. Tables have historical panels with amusing information to read while waiting for your pepper steak or filet mignon. The restaurant is named for the famous overland stagecoach line that carried the mail from St. Louis to San Francisco in the mid–19th century.

609 W. Hopi Dr. © **520/524-3447.** Main courses $8–$18. AE, MC, V. Daily 4–10pm.

4 The Window Rock & Ganado Areas

190 miles E of Flagstaff; 68 miles SE of Canyon de Chelly National Monument; 74 miles NE of Petrified Forest National Park; 91 miles E of Second Mesa

Window Rock, the capital of the Navajo nation, is less than a mile from the New Mexico state line and is named for a huge natural opening in a sandstone cliff just outside town. Today that landmark is preserved as the **Window Rock Tribal Park,** located 2 miles north of Ariz. 264. As the Navajo nation's capital, Window Rock is the site of government offices, a museum and cultural center, and a zoo. About a half hour's drive west is the community of Ganado, the location of two historic sites—St. Michael's Mission and the Hubbell Trading Post. Window Rock's Navajo Nation Inn makes a good base for exploring this corner of the reservation.

ESSENTIALS

GETTING THERE   To reach Window Rock from Flagstaff, take I-40 east to Lupton and go north on Indian Route 12. There's **Amtrak** (**800/872-7245**) passenger rail service to Winslow, south of the reservation.

The **Navajo Transit System** (© **520/729-4002**) operates bus service throughout the Navajo nation, with service between the cities of Farmington,

---

Tips A Reminder about the Time

The Navajo nation observes daylight saving time, contrary to the rest of Arizona, so if you are coming from elsewhere in Arizona, the time here will be 1 hour later in months when daylight saving is in effect.

Gallup, and Crown Point (all in New Mexico), and Window Rock, Kayenta, Chinle, and Tuba City.

VISITOR INFORMATION   For advance information, contact **Navajo Tourism,** P.O. Box 663, Window Rock, AZ 86515 (© **520/871-7371**).

SPECIAL EVENTS   Unlike the village ceremonies of the pueblo-dwelling Hopi, Navajo religious ceremonies tend to be held in the privacy of family hogans. However, there are numerous fairs, powwows, and rodeos throughout the year that the public is welcome to attend. The biggest of these is the **Navajo Nation Fair** (© **520/871-6478** or 520/871-6703), held in Window Rock in early September. At this fair are traditional dances, a rodeo, a powwow, a parade, a Miss Navajo Pageant (contestants are judged on, among other things, their sheep-butchering skills), and arts-and-crafts exhibits and sales.

AREA ATTRACTIONS

Hubbell Trading Post National Historic Site ⚔   Located just outside the town of Ganado, 26 miles west of Window Rock, the Hubbell Trading Post was established in 1876 by Lorenzo Hubbell and is the oldest continuously operating trading post on the Navajo Reservation. Hubbell did more to popularize the arts and crafts of the Navajo people than any other person and was in large part responsible for the revival of Navajo weaving in the late 19th century. Although Hubbell Trading Post is still in use, today it is more of a living museum. You can explore the grounds on your own or take a guided tour, and you can often watch Navajo weavers in the slow process of creating a rug.

The rug room is filled with a variety of traditional and contemporary Navajo pieces. And although it's possible to buy a small 12-by-18-inch rug for around $100, most cost in the thousands of dollars. In another room are baskets, kachinas, and several cases of jewelry by Navajo, Hopi, and Zuni artisans.

Glance around the general store, and you'll see basic foodstuffs (not much variety here) and bolts of cloth used by Navajo women for sewing their traditional skirts and blouses. Much more than just a place to trade crafts for imported goods, trading posts were for many years the main gathering spot for meeting people from other parts of the reservation and served as a sort of gossip fence and newsroom.

Ariz. 264, Ganado. © **520/755-3475.** www.nps.gov/hutr. Free admission. May–Sept daily 8am–6pm; Oct–Apr daily 8am–5pm. Closed Thanksgiving, Christmas, and New Year's Day.

The Navajo Nation Museum   Sponsored by the Navajo Nation Historic Preservation Society, this museum and cultural center is housed in a large modern building patterned after a traditional hogan. Inside, you'll find temporary exhibits of contemporary crafts and art, as well as exhibits on contemporary Navajo culture, a library, and a gift shop. There are plans to eventually add an exhibit of historic Navajo artifacts and old photos.

Ariz. 264 at Post Office Loop Rd. (across from the Navajo Nation Inn), Window Rock. © **520/871-7941.** Free admission. Sept–May Mon–Fri 8am–5pm; June–Aug Mon–Fri 8am–5pm, Sat 9am–5pm.

Navajo Nation Zoo & Botanical Park *(Kids)*   Located in back of the Navajo Nation Inn, this zoo and botanical garden features animals and plants that are significant in Navajo history and culture. Bears, cougars, and wolves are among the animals you'll see. The setting, which includes several sandstone "haystack" rocks, is very dramatic, and some of the animal enclosures are quite large and incorporate natural rock outcroppings. Also exhibited are examples of different styles of hogans. Well worth a stop.

Ariz. 264, Window Rock. **©** **520/871-6573.** Free admission. Daily 8am–5pm. Closed Christmas and New Year's Day.

St. Michael's Historical Museum   Located in the town of St. Michael's, 4 miles west of Window Rock, this historical museum chronicles the lives and influence of Franciscan friars who started a mission in this area in the 1670s. The museum is in a small building adjacent to the impressive stone mission church.

St. Michael's, just south of Ariz. 264. **©** **520/871-4171.** Free admission. Memorial Day to Labor Day daily 9am–5pm. Closed the rest of the year.

A TOUR FROM THE NAVAJO PERSPECTIVE

The best way to understand the Navajo culture is through the eyes of a Navajo. Stanley M. Perry (**©** **520/871-2484;** best after 7pm), a Navajo born and raised on the reservation, is a storyteller and guide who will accompany you in your vehicle to tour the Window Rock, Canyon de Chelly, and Monument Valley areas. The rate is $100 per day for up to four people; for larger groups, rates depend on the number in the party.

SHOPPING

The Hubbell Trading Post, although it is a National Historic Site, is still an active trading post and has an outstanding selection of rugs, as well as lots of jewelry (see "Area Attractions," above). In Window Rock, be sure to visit the **Navajo Arts and Crafts Enterprise** (**©** **520/871-4090**), which is next to the Navajo Nation Inn and has been operating since 1941. Here you'll find silver-and-turquoise jewelry, Navajo rugs, baskets, pottery, and Native American clothing.

WHERE TO STAY

Navajoland Days Inn   This is the newest hotel on the reservation, located 2 miles west of Window Rock near the historic St. Michael's Mission. The location is centrally located for exploring west to the Hopi mesas, north to Canyon de Chelly, and south to Petrified Forest National Park. Because this hotel is so new, it makes a better choice than the nearby Navajo Nation Inn.

392 W. Hwy. 264 (P.O. Box 905), St. Michael's, AZ 86511. **©** **800/DAYSINN** or 520/871-5690. Fax 520/871-5699. www.daysinn.com. 73 units. $75–$90 double; $85–$125 suite. Rates include continental breakfast. AE, DC, DISC, MC, V. **Amenities:** Sandwich shop; indoor pool; exercise room; Jacuzzi; sauna; coin-op laundry. *In room:* A/C, TV, dataport, coffeemaker.

Navajo Nation Inn   Located on the edge of Window Rock, the administrative center of the Navajo Reservation, the Navajo Nation Inn is an older motel. The restaurant and coffee shop serve American and traditional Navajo dishes daily.

48 W. Hwy. 264 (P.O. Box 2340), Window Rock, AZ 86515. **©** **800/662-6189** or 520/871-4108. Fax 520/871-5466. 56 units. $62–$72 double. AE, DC, MC, V. Pets accepted ($50 deposit). **Amenities:** Restaurant (American/Navajo), coffee shop. *In room:* A/C, TV, dataport.

WHERE TO DINE

In Window Rock, your best bet is the **Navajo Nation Inn** (see "Where to Stay," above). In Ganado, you can get good, inexpensive, cafeteria-style food at **Cafe Sage** (© 520/755-3411), on the grounds of Ganado's health clinic, which is across Ariz. 264 and a half mile east of the trading post.

5 Canyon de Chelly ★★★

222 miles NE of Flagstaff; 68 miles NW of Window Rock; 110 miles SE of Navajo National Monument; 110 miles SE of Monument Valley Navajo Tribal Park

It's hard to imagine narrow canyons less than 1,000 feet deep being more spectacular than the Grand Canyon, but in some ways **Canyon de Chelly National Monument** is just that. Gaze down from the rim at an ancient Anasazi cliff dwelling as the whinnying of horses and clanging of goat bells drift up from far below, and you'll be struck by the continuity of human existence. For nearly 5,000 years, people have called these canyons home, and today there are not only the summer homes of Navajo farmers and sheepherders but also more than 100 prehistoric dwelling sites.

Canyon de Chelly National Monument consists of two major canyons— Canyon de Chelly (which is pronounced canyon *shay* and is derived from the Navajo word *tséyi,* meaning "rock canyon") and *Canyon del Muerto* (Spanish for "Canyon of the Dead")—and several smaller canyons. The canyons extend for more than 100 miles through the rugged slick-rock landscape of northeastern Arizona, draining the seasonal runoff from the snowmelt of the Chuska Mountains.

In summer, Canyon de Chelly's smooth sandstone walls of rich reds and yellows contrast sharply with the deep greens of corn, pasture, and cottonwood on the canyon floor. Vast stone amphitheaters form the caves in which the ancient Anasazi built their homes, and as you watch shadows and light paint an ever-changing canyon panorama, it's easy to see why the Navajo consider this sacred ground. With mysteriously abandoned cliff dwellings and breathtaking natural beauty, Canyon de Chelly is certainly as worthy of a visit as the Grand Canyon.

ESSENTIALS

GETTING THERE   From Flagstaff, the easiest route to Canyon de Chelly is I-40 to U.S. 191 to Ganado. At Ganado, drive west on Ariz. 264 and pick up U.S. 191 north to Chinle. If you're coming down from Monument Valley or Navajo National Monument, Indian Route 59, which connects U.S. 160 and U.S. 191, is an excellent road with plenty of beautiful scenery.

Chinle, 3 miles from the entrance to Canyon de Chelly National Monument, is served by the **Navajo Transit System** (© 520/729-4002).

FEES   Monument admission is free.

VISITOR CENTER & INFORMATION   Before leaving home, you can contact **Canyon de Chelly National Monument** (© 520/674-5500; www.nps.gov/cach). The visitor center is open daily, May through September from 8am to 6pm (on daylight saving time) and October through April from 8am to 5pm. The monument itself is open daily from sunrise to sunset.

SPECIAL EVENTS   The **Central Navajo Fair** is held in Chinle each year in August.

SEEING THE CANYON

Your first stop should be the **visitor center,** in front of which is an example of a traditional crib-style hogan, a hexagonal structure of logs and earth that Navajos use as both a home and a ceremonial center. Inside, a small museum acquaints visitors with the history of Canyon de Chelly, and there's often a silversmith demonstrating Navajo jewelry-making techniques. Interpretive programs are offered at the monument from Memorial Day to Labor Day. Check at the visitor center for daily activities, such as campfire programs and natural-history programs, that might be scheduled.

From the visitor center, most people tour the canyon by car. Very different views of the canyon are provided by the 15-mile North Rim and 16-mile South Rim drives. The North Rim Drive overlooks Canyon del Muerto, while the South Rim Drive overlooks Canyon de Chelly. With stops, either rim drive can easily take 2 to 3 hours. If you have time for only one, make it the South Rim Drive, which provides both a dramatic view of Spider Rock and the chance to hike down into the canyon on the only trail you can explore without hiring a guide. If on the other hand you're more interested in the history and prehistory of this area, opt for the North Rim Drive, which overlooks several historically significant sites within the canyon.

THE NORTH RIM DRIVE

The first stop on the North Rim is the **Ledge Ruin Overlook.** On the opposite wall, about 100 feet up from the canyon floor, you can see the Ledge Ruin. This site was occupied by the Anasazi between A.D. 1050 and 1275. Nearby, at the Dekaa Kiva Viewpoint, you can see a lone kiva (circular ceremonial building). This structure was reached by means of toeholds cut into the soft sandstone cliff wall.

The second stop is at the **Antelope House Overlook.** The Antelope House ruin takes its name from the paintings of antelopes on a nearby cliff wall. It's believed that they were done in the 1830s. Beneath the ruins of Antelope House, archaeologists have found the remains of an earlier pit house dating from A.D. 693. Although most of the Anasazi cliff dwellings were abandoned sometime after a drought began in 1276, Antelope House had already been abandoned by 1260, possibly because of damage caused by flooding. Across the wash from Antelope House, an ancient tomb, known as the Tomb of the Weaver, was discovered by archaeologists in the 1920s. The tomb contained the well-preserved body of an old man wrapped in a blanket of golden eagle feathers and accompanied by cornmeal, shelled and husked corn, pine nuts, beans, salt, and thick skeins of cotton. Also visible from this overlook is Navajo Fortress, a red-sandstone butte that the Navajo once used as a refuge from attackers. A steep trail leads to the top of Navajo Fortress, and by using log ladders that could be pulled up into the refuge, the Navajo were able to escape their attackers.

The third stop is at **Mummy Cave Overlook,** named for two mummies found in burial urns below the ruins. Archaeological evidence indicates that this giant amphitheater consisting of two caves was occupied for 1,000 years, from A.D. 300 to 1300. In the two caves and on the shelf between are 80 rooms, including three kivas. The central structure between the two caves includes an interesting three-story building characteristic of the architecture in Mesa Verde in New Mexico. Archaeologists speculate that a group of Anasazi migrated here from New Mexico. Much of the original plasterwork is still intact and indicates that the buildings were colorfully decorated.

The fourth and last stop on the North Rim is at the **Massacre Cave Overlook,** which got its name after an 1805 Spanish military expedition killed more than 115 Navajo at this site. The Navajo at the time had been raiding Spanish settlements that were encroaching on Navajo territory. Accounts of the battle at Massacre Cave differ. One version claims there were only women, children, and old men taking shelter in the cave, but the official Spanish records claim 90 warriors and 25 women and children were killed. Also visible from this overlook is Yucca Cave, which was occupied about 1,000 years ago.

THE SOUTH RIM DRIVE

The South Rim Drive climbs slowly but steadily, and at each stop you're a little bit higher above the canyon floor. Near the mouth of the canyon is the **Tunnel Overlook** and, nearby, the **Tséyi Overlook.** *Tséyi* means "rock canyon" in Navajo, and that's just what you'll see when you gaze down from this viewpoint. A short narrow canyon feeds into Chinle Wash, which is formed by the streams cutting through the canyons of the national monument.

The next stop is at the **Junction Overlook,** so named because it overlooks the junction of Canyon del Muerto and Canyon de Chelly. Visible here is the Junction Ruin, with its 10 rooms and kiva. The Anasazi occupied this ruin during the great pueblo period, which lasted from around 1100 until the Anasazi disappeared shortly before 1300. Also visible is First Ruin, which is perched precariously on a long narrow ledge. In this ruin are 22 rooms and two kivas.

The third stop is at **White House Overlook,** from which you can see the 80-room White House Ruins, among the largest ruins in the canyon. These buildings were inhabited between 1040 and 1275. From this overlook, you have your only opportunity for descending into Canyon de Chelly without a guide or ranger. The **White House Ruins Trail** ☆ descends 600 feet to the canyon floor, crosses Chinle Wash, and approaches the White House Ruins. The buildings of this ruin were constructed both on the canyon floor and 50 feet up the cliff wall in a small cave. Although you cannot enter the ruins, you can get close enough to get a good look. Do not wander off this trail, and please respect the privacy of those Navajo living here. It's a 2½-mile round-trip hike and takes about 2 hours. Be sure to carry water.

Notice the black streaks on the sandstone walls above the White House Ruins. These streaks, known as desert varnish, are formed by seeping water, which reacts with iron in the sandstone (iron is what gives the walls their reddish hue). To create the canyon's many petroglyphs, Anasazi artists would chip away at the desert varnish. Later the Navajo used paints to create pictographs of animals and historic events, such as the Spanish military expedition that killed 115 Navajo at Massacre Cave. Many of these petroglyphs and pictographs can be seen if you take one of the guided tours into the canyon.

The fifth stop is at **Sliding House Overlook.** These ruins are built on a narrow shelf and appear to be sliding down into the canyon. Inhabited from about 900 until 1200, Sliding House contained between 30 and 50 rooms. This overlook is already more than 700 feet above the canyon floor, with sheer walls giving the narrow canyon a very foreboding appearance. The **Face Rock Overlook** provides yet another dizzying glimpse of the ever-deepening canyon. Here you gaze 1,000 feet down to the bottom of the canyon.

The last stop on the South Rim is one of the most spectacular: **Spider Rock Overlook.** This viewpoint overlooks the junction of Canyon de Chelly and Monument Canyon, where the monolithic pinnacle called Spider Rock rises 800 feet from the canyon floor, its two freestanding towers forming a natural

Fred Harvey & His Girls

Unless you grew up in the Southwest and can remember back to pre–World War II days, you may have never heard of Fred Harvey and the Harvey Girls. However, if you spend much time in northern Arizona, you're likely to run into quite a few references to the Harvey Girls and their boss.

Fred Harvey was the Southwest's most famous mogul of railroad hospitality and an early promoter of tourism in the Grand Canyon State. Harvey, who was working for a railroad in the years shortly after the Civil War, had developed a distaste for the food served at railroad stations. He decided he could do a better job, and in 1876 opened his first Harvey House railway-station restaurant for the Santa Fe Railroad. At the time of his death in 1901, Harvey operated 47 restaurants, 30 diners, and 15 hotels across the West.

The women who worked as waitresses in the Harvey House restaurants came to be known as Harvey Girls. Known for their distinctive black dresses, white aprons, and black bow ties, Harvey Girls had to adhere to very strict behavior codes and were the prim and proper women of the late-19th- and early-20th-century American West. In fact, in the late 19th century, they were considered the only real "ladies" in the West, aside from schoolteachers. So celebrated were they in their day that in the 1940s, Judy Garland starred in a Technicolor MGM musical called *The Harvey Girls*. Garland played a Harvey Girl who battles the evil town dance-hall queen (played by Angela Lansbury) for the soul of the local saloonkeeper.

monument. Across the canyon from Spider Rock stands the similarly striking **Speaking Rock,** which is connected to the far canyon wall.

ALTERNATIVE WAYS OF SEEING THE CANYON

Access to the floor of Canyon de Chelly is restricted; unless you're on the White House Ruins trail (see "The South Rim Drive," above), you must be accompanied by either a park ranger or an authorized guide in order to enter the canyon. **Navajo guides** charge $15 per hour with a 3-hour minimum and will lead you into the canyon on foot or in your own four-wheel-drive vehicle. **De Chelly Tours** (© 520/674-3772; www.dechellytours.com) charges $20 per hour to go out in your four-wheel-drive vehicle (3-hour minimum); if it supplies the vehicle, the cost goes up to a total of $125 for three people for 3 hours. Similar tours are offered by **De Chelly Unimog & Private Jeep Tours** (© 520/674-1044 or 520/674-5433), which will take you into the canyon in a Unimog truck or a Jeep. Unimog tours are $40 for adults and $25 for children 12 and under. Tours depart from the Holiday Inn parking lot. Reservations are recommended. The monument visitor center also maintains a list of guides.

Another way to see Canyon de Chelly and Canyon del Muerto is on what locals call **shake-and-bake tours** , via six-wheel-drive truck. In summer, these excursions really live up to the name. (In winter, the truck is enclosed to keep out the elements.) The trucks operate out of **Thunderbird Lodge** (© **800/ 679-2473** or 520/674-5841) and are equipped with seats in the bed. Tours make frequent stops for photographs and to visit ruins, Navajo farms, and rock art. Half-day trips cost $39 per person ($30 for children 11 and under), while full-day tours cost $63.50 for all ages. Full-day tours, offered in summer only, leave at 9am and return at 5pm.

If you'd rather use a more traditional means of transportation, you can go on a guided horseback ride. Stables offering horseback tours into the canyon include **Justin's Horse Rental** (© **520/674-5678**), which charges $10 per hour per person for a horse and $15 per hour per group for a guide (2-hr. minimum). To visit a more remote part of the canyon (including the Spider Rock area), arrange a ride through **Tsotsonii Ranch** (© **520/755-6209**), 1¼ miles past the end of the pavement on the South Rim Drive. Rides are $10 per hour per person for the horse and $10 per hour per group for the guide.

SHOPPING

The **Thunderbird Lodge Gift Shop** (© **520/674-5841**) in Chinle is well worth a stop while you're in the area. It has a huge collection of rugs, as well as good selections of pottery and plenty of souvenirs. In the canyon wherever visitors gather (at ruins and petroglyph sites), you're likely to encounter craftspeople selling jewelry and other types of handiwork. These craftspeople, most of whom live in the canyon, accept cash, personal checks, and traveler's checks and sometimes credit cards.

WHERE TO STAY & DINE

Best Western Canyon de Chelly Inn   This motel, located right in the center of Chinle, is both the farthest from the national monument and the least attractive of the three motels in town. Consequently, although the rooms are decent enough, you should make this your last choice. The restaurant is large and reminiscent of a suburban chain establishment.

100 Main St. (P.O. Box 295), Chinle, AZ 86503. © **800/327-0354** or 520/674-5874. Fax 520/674-3715. www.bestwestern.com. 99 units. May–Oct $109 double; Nov–Apr $69–$89 double. AE, DC, DISC, MC, V. **Amenities:** Restaurant (American/Navajo); indoor pool. *In room:* A/C, TV, dataport, coffeemaker, hair dryer.

Coyote Pass Hospitality   Looking for something a little out of the ordinary? How about spending the night in a traditional Navajo hogan? Coyote Pass Hospitality runs a very rustic sort of bed-and-breakfast operation. Guests stay in a dirt-floored hogan and enjoy a traditional Navajo breakfast. With advance reservations, lunch ($15) and dinner ($20) can be arranged as well. When you call to book your stay, you can also arrange for customized, off-the-beaten-path Navajo cultural and historic tours with the hosts.

P.O. Box 91-B, Tsaile, AZ 86556 © **520/724-3383** or 520/787-2295. www.navajocentral.org/cppage.htm. $100 double. Rates include Navajo breakfast. Credit cards not accepted.

Holiday Inn—Canyon de Chelly   Located between the town of Chinle and the national monument entrance, this modern hotel is on the site of the old Garcia Trading Post, which has been incorporated into the restaurant and giftshop building (although the building no longer has any historic character). All guest rooms have patios or balconies and big windows and bathrooms, and most face the cottonwood-shaded pool courtyard. The hotel restaurant serves the best food in town.

Indian Rte. 7 (P.O. Box 1889), Chinle, AZ 86503. ✆ **800/HOLIDAY** or 520/674-5000. Fax 520/674-8264. www.holiday-inn.com/chinle-garcia. 108 units. July–Sept $109 double; Oct–June $69–$99 double. AE, DC, DISC, MC, V. **Amenities:** Restaurant (American/Navajo); outdoor pool; exercise room; concierge; room service; laundry service. *In room:* A/C, TV, dataport, fridge, coffeemaker, hair dryer.

Thunderbird Lodge ✪   Built on the site of an early trading post right at the mouth of Canyon de Chelly, the Thunderbird Lodge is the most appealing of the hotels in Chinle and is the closest to the national monument. The lodge's buildings back on to a low hill, and to one side is a large campground in a grove of cottonwoods. The red adobe construction of the lodge itself is reminiscent of ancient pueblos, and the presence on the property of an old stone-walled trading post gives this place more character than any of the other choices in the area. Guest rooms have both ceiling fans and air-conditioning. The old trading post now serves as the lodge cafeteria. There is also a gift shop and rug room.

P.O. Box 548, Chinle, AZ 86503. ✆ **800/679-BIRD** or 520/674-5841. Fax 520/674-5844. www. tbirdlodge.com. 72 units. $101–$106 double; $138 suite. Lower rates mid-Nov to Mar. AE, DC, DISC, MC, V. **Amenities:** Restaurant (American/Navajo); tour desk. *In room:* A/C, TV, hair dryer.

CAMPGROUNDS

Adjacent to the Thunderbird Lodge is the free **Cottonwood Campground,** which has 96 sites but does not take reservations. The campground has water and restrooms in summer, but in winter you must bring your own water and only portable toilets are available. On South Rim Drive 10 miles east of the Canyon de Chelly visitor center is another option, the private **Spider Rock Campground** (✆ 520/674-8261), which charges $10 per night. The next nearest campgrounds are at **Tsaile Lake** and **Wheatfields Lake,** both south of the town of Tsaile on Indian Route 12. Tsaile is at the east end of the North Rim Drive.

<h2>6 Navajo National Monument ✪</h2>

140 miles NE of Flagstaff; 90 miles E of Page; 60 miles SW of Monument Valley; 110 miles NW of Canyon de Chelly

Navajo National Monument, although set in a less spectacular landscape than National Monument (see the following section), is no less interesting: It is here where you will find some of the largest cliff dwellings in Arizona. Located 30 miles west of Kayenta and 60 miles northeast of Tuba City, Navajo National Monument encompasses three of the best-preserved Anasazi cliff dwellings in the region—Betatakin, Keet Seel, and Inscription House. It's possible to visit both Betatakin and Keet Seel, but fragile Inscription House is closed to the public. The name Navajo National Monument is a bit misleading. Although the Navajo people do inhabit the area now, it was the ancient Anasazi who built the cliff dwellings. The Navajo arrived centuries after the Anasazi had abandoned the area.

The inhabitants of Tsegi Canyon were ancestral Hopi and Pueblo peoples known as the Kayenta Anasazi. For reasons unknown, the Anasazi began abandoning their well-constructed homes around the middle of the 13th century. Tree rings suggest that a drought in the latter part of the 13th century prevented the Anasazi from growing sufficient crops. However, in Tsegi Canyon there's another theory for the abandonment. The canyon floors were usually flooded each year by spring and summer snowmelt, which made farming quite productive, but in the mid-1200s, weather patterns changed and streams running through the canyons began cutting deep into the soil, forming deep, narrow canyons called arroyos, which lowered the water table and made farming much more difficult.

ESSENTIALS

GETTING THERE   Navajo National Monument can be reached by taking U.S. 89 north to U.S. 160 to Ariz. 564 north.

FEES   Monument admission is free.

VISITOR CENTER & INFORMATION   Contact **Navajo National Monument** (© **520/672-2366** or 520/672-2700; www.nps.gov/nava). The visitor center is open daily from 8am to 5pm; closed Thanksgiving, Christmas, and New Year's Day. The monument is open daily from sunrise to sunset.

EXPLORING NAVAJO NATIONAL MONUMENT

Unlike a visit to nearby Monument Valley, a visit to Navajo National Monument requires physical effort. The shortest distance you'll have to walk here is 1 mile, which is the round-trip from the visitor center to the Betatakin overlook. However, if you want to actually climb around inside these ruins, you're looking at strenuous daylong or overnight hikes.

Your first stop should be the **visitor center,** which has informative displays on the ancestral Pueblo and Navajo cultures, including numerous artifacts from Tsegi Canyon. You can watch a couple of short films or a slide show.

Betatakin ✯   Betatakin means "ledge house" in Navajo, and it's the only one of the monument's three ruins that can be seen easily. Built in a huge amphitheater-like alcove in the canyon wall, Betatakin was occupied only from 1250 to 1300, and at its height of occupation may have housed 125 people. A 1-mile round-trip paved trail from the visitor center leads to overlooks of Betatakin. The strenuous 5-mile round-trip hike to Betatakin itself is led by a ranger, takes about 5 hours, and involves descending more than 700 feet to the floor of Tsegi Canyon and later returning to the rim. These guided hikes are usually offered twice a day (at 9am and noon) between Memorial Day and Labor Day. All participants should carry 1 to 2 quarts of water. This very popular hike is limited to 25 people per tour; many people line up at the visitor center an hour or more before it opens.

Keet Seel ✯   Keet Seel, which means "broken pieces of pottery" in Navajo, has a much longer history than Betatakin, with occupation beginning as early as A.D. 950 and continuing until 1300. At one point, Keet Seel may have housed 150 people. The 17-mile round-trip hike or horseback ride is quite strenuous, and hikers may stay overnight at a primitive campground near the ruins. You must carry enough water for your trip (2 gal.), since none is available along the trail. Only 20 people a day are given permits to visit Keet Seel, and the trail is open only from Memorial Day to Labor Day. You can apply for a permit up to 2 months in advance of your visit.

WHERE TO STAY

There is no lodge at the national monument, but there is a free campground with 30 campsites. It's open from mid-May to October. In summer, the campground is usually full by dark, but there is an overflow camping area.

The nearest reliable motels are 30 miles away in Kayenta. See "Monument Valley," below, for details.

7 Monument Valley (★(★(★

200 miles NE of Flagstaff; 60 miles NE of Navajo National Monument; 110 miles NW of Canyon de Chelly; 150 miles E of Page

In its role as sculptor, nature has, in the north-central part of the Navajo Reservation, created a garden of monoliths and spires unequaled anywhere on earth. Whether you've ever been here or not, you almost certainly have seen **Monument Valley** before. This otherworldly landscape has been an object of fascination for years, and since Hollywood director John Ford first came here in the 1930s, it has served as backdrop for countless movies, TV shows, and commercials.

Located 30 miles north of Kayenta and straddling the Arizona-Utah state line (you actually go into Utah to get to the park entrance), Monument Valley is a vast flat plain punctuated by natural sandstone cathedrals. These huge monoliths rise up from the sagebrush with sheer walls that capture the light of the rising and setting sun and transform it into fiery hues. Evocative names reflect the shapes the sandstone has taken under the erosive forces of nature: The Mittens, Three Sisters, Camel Butte, Elephant Butte, the Thumb, and Totem Pole are some of the most awe-inspiring natural monuments.

The Navajo have been living in the valley for generations, herding their sheep through the sagebrush scrublands, and some families continue to reside here today. However, human habitation in Monument Valley dates back much further. Within the park are more than 100 ancient Anasazi archaeological sites, ruins, and petroglyphs dating from before A.D. 1300.

ESSENTIALS

GETTING THERE   Monument Valley Navajo Tribal Park is 200 miles northeast of Flagstaff. Take U.S. 89 north to U.S. 160 to Kayenta, and then drive north on U.S. 163.

The **Navajo Transit System** (© **520/729-4002**) operates bus service Monday through Friday throughout the Navajo nation, with service between the cities of Farmington, Gallup, and Crown Point (all in New Mexico), and Window Rock, Kayenta, Chinle, and Tuba City.

FEES   Admission is $3 for adults, $1 for seniors, and free for children 7 and under. *Note:* Because this is tribal park and not a federal park, neither the National Park Service's National Park Pass nor its Golden Eagle Pass are valid here.

VISITOR CENTER & INFORMATION   For more information, contact **Monument Valley Navajo Tribal Park,** P.O. Box 360289, Monument Valley, UT 84536 (© **435/727-3353** or 435/727-3287). The park is open May through September, daily from 7am to 7pm; October through April, daily from 8am to 5pm (from 8am–noon on Thanksgiving).

EXPLORING THE TRIBAL PARK

This is big country, and, like the Grand Canyon, is primarily a point-and-shoot experience for most visitors. Because this is reservation land and people still live in Monument Valley, backcountry or off-road travel is prohibited unless you're with a licensed guide. So basically the only ways to see the park are from the overlook at the visitor center, by driving the park's scenic (but very rough) 17-mile dirt loop road, or by taking a four-wheel-drive, horseback, or guided-hiking tour. At the park's valley overlook parking area, you'll find a small museum, gift shop, restaurant, snack bar, campground, and tour desk for companies operating Jeep and hiking tours through the park.

For four-wheel-drive adventures, try **Roland's Navajoland Tours** (© 520/ 697-3524). Prices range from $15 for a 1½-hour tour to $80 for an all-day tour. **Sacred Monument Tours** (© 435/727-3218) charges $20 for a 1-hour Jeep tour and then $10 per person per hour after that; hiking and horseback tours are also available. **Totem Pole Tours** (© 800/345-8687 or 435/727-3313) offers similar options.

If you want to see the park on foot, you can arrange a guided hike through **Sacred Monument Tours** (© 435/727-3218), which charges $15 per person for a 1-hour hike and $10 for each additional hour. Keep in mind that it will take you a while to get away from the traffic around the visitor center, and summers can be very hot.

If nothing but the cowboy thing will do for you in this quintessential Wild West landscape, contact **Ed Black's Monument Valley Trail Rides** (© 435/ 683-2327), located near the visitor center. It charges $30 for a 1½-hour ride and $100 for an all-day ride.

Another option is **Goulding's Tours** (© 435/727-3231), which has its office on the edge of the valley at Goulding's Lodge (see below), just a few miles from the park entrance. Goulding's offers 2½-hour tours ($25.50 for adults, $15.50 for children under 8), half-day tours ($30.50 for adults, $18.50 for children), and full-day tours ($60.50 for adults, $45.50 for children). In summer, full-moon tours ($30.50 for adults, $18.50 for children) are another option.

ACTIVITIES OUTSIDE THE PARK

Before leaving the area, you might want to visit **Goulding's Museum and Trading Post,** at Goulding's Lodge (see "Where to Stay & Dine," below). This old trading post was the home of the Gouldings for many years and is set up as they had it back in the 1920s and 1930s. There are also displays about the many movies that have been shot here. The trading post is usually open April through November, daily from 7:30am to 9pm (limited hours other months); admission is by donation. Also in the area is the **Oljato Trading Post & Museum** (© 435/727-3210), 11 miles west of Monument Valley on the scenic stretch of road that leads past Goulding's. Although this trading post, which dates from 1921, is in Utah, it was originally located in Arizona. The old building, which is open daily from 7am to 7pm, still has a classic trading-post feel—and few tourists venture out this way. Horseback rides are available for $25 for 1 hour, up to $100 for a full-day ride. We like riding from Oljato because you get to escape the crowds within the tribal park.

If you're interested in learning about Navajo culture, stop at Kayenta's **Navajo Cultural Center,** U.S. 160 (© 520/697-3170), located between the Burger King and the Hampton Inn. The center is basically just a display of hogans and other traditional structures, but the explanatory signs are very informative. In summer, you might encounter Navajo artisans giving demonstrations. Inside the adjacent Burger King, there's an interesting exhibit on the Navajo code talkers of World War II. The code talkers were Navajo soldiers who used their own language to transmit military messages, primarily in the South Pacific.

WHERE TO STAY & DINE

In addition to the lodgings listed here, you'll find several budget motels north of Monument Valley in the towns of Mexican Hat and Bluff, both of which are in Utah.

Best Western Wetherill Inn   Located in Kayenta a mile north of the junction of U.S. 160 and U.S. 163 and 20 miles south of Monument Valley, the Wetherill Inn offers neither the convenience of Goulding's Lodge nor the amenities of the nearby Holiday Inn. However, the rooms here are comfortable enough. A cafe next door serves Navajo and American food.

1000 Main St. (P.O. Box 175), Kayenta, AZ 86033. ✆ **800/WESTERN** or 520/697-3231. Fax 520/697-3233. 54 units. May 1–Oct 15 and Nov 16–Dec 31 $89–$98 double; Oct 16–Nov 15 and Apr $63–$70 double; Jan–Mar $50–$55 double. AE, DISC, MC, V. **Amenities:** Indoor pool; tour desk. *In room:* A/C, TV, coffeemaker.

Goulding's Lodge ✯   This is the only lodge actually located in Monument Valley, and it offers superb views from the private balconies of the large guest rooms, which feature Southwestern decor. The restaurant serves Navajo and American dishes, and its views are enough to make any meal an event. Unfortunately, although the setting is memorable, the service can be somewhat lacking. Also on the grounds are a museum, a video library of films shot in Monument Valley, and a gas station.

P.O. Box 360001, Monument Valley, UT 84536-0001. ✆ **435/727-3231.** Fax 435/727-3344. www. gouldings.com. 62 units. Mar 15–Oct 15 $108–$148 double; Oct 16–Mar 14 $62–$72 double. AE, DC, DISC, MC, V. Pets accepted ($50 deposit). **Amenities:** Restaurant (American/Navajo); indoor pool; exercise room; tour desk; coin-op laundry. *In room:* A/C, TV/VCR, dataport, fridge, coffeemaker, hair dryer.

Hampton Inn—Navajo Nation   Located in the center of Kayenta, this is the newest lodging in the area and as such should be your second choice after Goulding's. The hotel is built in a modern Santa Fe style and has spacious, comfortable rooms. It's adjacent to the small Navajo Cultural Center and a Burger King that has an interesting display on the Navajo code talkers of World War II.

U.S. 160 (P.O. Box 1217), Kayenta, AZ 86033. ✆ **800/HAMPTON** or 520/697-3170. Fax 520/697-3189. www.hampton-inn.com. 73 units. May–Sept $91–$96 double; Oct and mid-Mar to Apr $71–$79 double; Nov to mid-Mar $59–$66 double. Rates include continental breakfast. AE, DC, DISC, MC, V. Pets accepted. **Amenities:** Restaurant (American/Navajo); small outdoor pool. *In room:* A/C, TV, dataport, coffeemaker, iron.

Holiday Inn—Kayenta   Located in the center of Kayenta, 23 miles south of Monument Valley and 29 miles east of Navajo National Monument, this Holiday Inn is very popular with tour groups and is almost always crowded. Although the grounds are dusty and a bit run-down, the rooms are spacious and clean. We like the poolside units best. Part of the on-site restaurant is designed to look like an Anasazi ruin, and the menu offers both American and Navajo meals.

At the junction of U.S. 160 and U.S. 163 (P.O. Box 307), Kayenta, AZ 86033. ✆ **800/HOLIDAY** or 520/697-3221. Fax 520/697-3349. www.basshotels.com. 160 units. Apr–Oct $99–$129 double; Nov–Mar $79–$89 double. AE, DC, DISC, MC, V. **Amenities:** Restaurant (American/Navajo); small outdoor pool; exercise room; tour desk; room service; coin-op laundry. *In room:* A/C, TV, coffeemaker, hair dryer, iron.

CAMPGROUNDS

If you're headed to Monument Valley Navajo Tribal Park, you can camp in the park at the **Mitten View Campground** (✆ **435/727-3287**), which has 99 sites and charges $10 per night April through September ($5 per night Oct–Mar, when there are no facilities and you must be self-contained), or just outside the park at **Goulding's Campground** (✆ **435/727-3231**), which charges $15 to $24 per night, is open mid-March through October, and even has an indoor swimming pool.

DRIVING ON TO COLORADO OR NEW MEXICO: THE FOUR CORNERS MEET

Other attractions you might want to visit while you're in this part of the state include the **Four Corners Monument Navajo Tribal Park** (© 520/871-6647), north of Teec Nos Pos in the very northeast corner of the state. This is the only place in the United States where the corners of four states come together, and though the scenery is not exactly the most dramatic in the region, plenty of people go out of their way to come here and stand in four states—Arizona, Colorado, Utah, and New Mexico—at the same time (and, of course, get someone to snap a photo). The point is marked by a cement pad surrounded by flags. The park also offers a picnic ground, crafts vendors, and a snack bar serving, among other things, Navajo fry bread. It's open daily from 7am to 8pm between May and late August and from 8am to 5pm between late August and April. The park is closed Thanksgiving, Christmas, and New Year's. Admission is $2 for adults, free for children 6 and under.

Also in the area, in the community of Teec Nos Pos, is the **Teec Nos Pos Trading Post** (© 520/656-3224) and **Teec Nos Pos Arts and Crafts** (© 520/656-3228), both of which have good selections of rugs and other crafts. At the former shop, you'll also find a cafe with a small courtyard patio.

8 Lake Powell ★★ & Page

272 miles N of Phoenix; 130 miles E of Grand Canyon North Rim; 130 miles NE of Grand Canyon South Rim

Imagine the Grand Canyon filled with water instead of air, and you have a pretty good picture of **Lake Powell.** Had the early Spanish explorers of Arizona suddenly come upon this lake after traipsing for months across desolate desert, they would have either taken it for a mirage or fallen to their knees and rejoiced. Surrounded by hundreds of miles of parched desert land, this reservoir, created by the damming of the Colorado River at Glen Canyon, seems unreal when first glimpsed. Yet real it is, and, like a magnet, it draws everyone in the region toward its promise of relief from the heat.

Construction of the Glen Canyon Dam came about despite the angry outcry of many who felt that this canyon was even more beautiful than the Grand Canyon and should be preserved in its natural state. Preservationists lost the battle, and construction of the dam began in 1960 and was completed in 1963. It took another 17 years for Lake Powell to fill to capacity. Today the lake is a watery powerboat playground, and houseboats and skiers cruise where birds and waterfalls once filled the canyon with their songs. These days most people seem to agree that Lake Powell is as amazing a sight as the Grand Canyon, and it draws almost as many visitors each year as its downriver neighbor.

While Lake Powell is something of a man-made wonder of the world, one of the natural wonders of the world—**Rainbow Bridge**—can be found on the shores of the lake. Called *nonnozhoshi,* or "the rainbow turned to stone," by the Navajo, this is the largest natural bridge on earth and stretches 275 feet across a side canyon of Lake Powell.

The town of **Page,** a work camp constructed to house the workers who built the dam, has now become much more than a construction camp. With its many motels and restaurants, it's the main base for visitors who come to explore Lake Powell.

ESSENTIALS

GETTING THERE   Page is connected to Flagstaff by U.S. 89. Ariz. 98 leads southeast onto the Navajo Indian Reservation and connects with U.S. 160 to Kayenta and Four Corners. Currently there is no regularly scheduled air service to Page, but there are rumors that a small commuter airline was considering establishing service. Check with the chamber of commerce for updates.

FEES   Admission to Glen Canyon National Recreation Area is $10 per car (good for 1 week). There is also a $10-per-week boat fee if you bring your own boat.

VISITOR INFORMATION   For further information on the Lake Powell area, contact **Glen Canyon National Recreation Area** (© **520/608-6404;** www. nps.gov/glca); **Page/Lake Powell Chamber of Commerce,** 644 N. Navajo Dr., Page (© **888/261-7243** or 520/645-2741; www.pagelakepowellchamber. org); or the **John Wesley Powell Museum and Visitor Information Center,** 6 N. Lake Powell Blvd., Page (© **520/645-9496;** www.powellmuseum.org). You can also go to **www.powellguide.com**.

GETTING AROUND   Rental cars are available at the Page Airport from **Avis** (© **800/331-1212** or 520/645-2024).

GLEN CANYON NATIONAL RECREATION AREA

Until the flooding of Glen Canyon formed Lake Powell, this area was one of the most remote regions in the contiguous 48 states. However, with the construction of Glen Canyon Dam at a spot where the Colorado River was less than ⅓ mile wide, this remote and rugged landscape became one of the country's most popular national recreation areas. Today, the lake and much of the surrounding land is designated the Glen Canyon National Recreation Area and attracts nearly four million visitors each year. The otherworldly setting (imagine the Grand Canyon, only flooded) amid the slick-rock canyons of northern Arizona and southern Utah is a tapestry of colors, the blues and greens of the lake contrasting with the reds and oranges of the surrounding sandstone cliffs. This interplay of colors and vast desert landscapes easily makes Lake Powell the most beautiful of Arizona's many reservoirs.

Built to provide water for the desert communities of the Southwest and West, **Glen Canyon Dam** stands 710 feet above the bedrock and contains almost 5 million cubic yards of concrete. The dam also provides hydroelectric power, and deep within its massive wall of concrete are huge power turbines. Most visitors to the area are, however, more interested in water-skiing and powerboating than they are in drinking water and power production. Without the dam, however, there would be no lake, so any visit to this area ought to start with a tour of the dam and a stop at the **Carl Hayden Visitor Center** (© **520/608-6404**), which is located beside the dam on U.S. 89 just north of Page. Here you can learn about the construction of the dam and then descend into the dam itself for a free guided 1-hour tour (call ahead if you want to do the tour). Hours are daily from 7am to 7pm between Memorial Day weekend and Labor Day weekend, and from 8am to 5pm other months.

More than 500 feet deep in some places, and bounded by nearly 2,000 miles of shoreline, Lake Powell is a maze of convoluted canyons where rock walls often rise hundreds of feet straight out of the water. In places, the long, winding canyons are so narrow there isn't even room to turn a motorboat around. The only way to truly appreciate this lake is from a boat, whether a houseboat, a runabout, or a sea kayak. Water-skiing, riding personal watercraft, and fishing are by far the most popular on-water activities, and consequently, you'll be hard-pressed to find a quiet corner of the lake if you happen to be a solitude-seeking sea kayaker. However, with 2,000 miles of shoreline, you're bound to find someplace where you can get away from it all. Your best bet for solitude is to head up-lake from Wahweap Marina. This will get you away from the crowds and into some of the narrower reaches of the lake.

In addition to the Carl Hayden Visitor Center mentioned above, there is the **Bullfrog Visitor Center,** in Bullfrog, Utah (© 435/684-7400). It's open May through late October, daily from 8am to 5pm (closed November through February; open intermittently in March).

BOAT & AIR TOURS

There are few roads penetrating the Glen Canyon National Recreation Area, so the best way to appreciate this rugged region is by boat. If you don't have your own boat, you can at least see a small part of the lake on a boat tour. A variety of tours depart from **Wahweap Marina** (© 800/528-6154 or 520/645-1070; www.visitlakepowell.com). The paddle-wheeler *Canyon King* does a 1-hour tour ($11 for adults, $8 for children) that unfortunately doesn't really show you much more of the lake than you can see from shore. The *Canyon King* also offers sunset ($28) and dinner cruises ($60). A better choice for those with limited time or finances would be the **Navajo Tapestry Cruise** ($43 for adults, $31 for children) or the **Antelope Canyon Cruise** ($27 for adults, $21 for children). To see the most of the lake, opt for the full-day tour to Rainbow Bridge (see below for details).

The Glen Canyon National Recreation Area covers an immense area, much of it only partially accessible by boat. If you'd like to see more of the area than is visible from car or boat, consider taking an air tour with **Lake Powell Airlines** (© 800/245-8668), which offers several tours of northern Arizona and southern Utah, including flights over Rainbow Bridge, the Escalante River, the Grand Canyon, Canyonlands, Bryce Canyon, Monument Valley, and the Navajo nation. Sample rates are $83 for a 30-minute flight over Rainbow Bridge and $160 for a 90-minute flight over Monument Valley.

RAINBOW BRIDGE NATIONAL MONUMENT

Roughly 40 miles up Lake Powell from Wahweap Marina and Glen Canyon Dam, in a narrow side canyon of the lake, rises **Rainbow Bridge** ★★★, the world's largest natural bridge and one of the most spectacular sights in the Southwest. Preserved in Rainbow Bridge National Monument, this natural arch of sandstone stands 290 feet high and spans 275 feet. Carved by wind and water over the ages, Rainbow Bridge is an awesome reminder of the powers of erosion that have sculpted this entire region into the spectacle it is today.

Rainbow Bridge is accessible only by boat or on foot (a hike of minimum 13 miles); going by boat is by far the more popular method. **Lake Powell Resorts and Marinas** (© 800/528-6154 or 520/645-2433; www.visitlakepowell.com) offers half-day ($80 for adults, $55 for children) and full-day ($106 for adults, $69 for children) tours that not only get you to Rainbow Bridge in comfort, but also cruise through some of the most spectacular scenery on earth. The full-day tours include a box lunch and explore two other major canyons after visiting Rainbow Bridge.

Rainbow Bridge National Monument is administered by Glen Canyon National Recreation Area, and additional information is available from sources for the recreation area, mentioned above. For information on hiking to Rainbow Bridge, contact the **Navajo Parks and Recreation Department,** P.O. Box 9000, Window Rock, AZ 86515 (© 520/871-6647 or 520/871-7307).

ANTELOPE CANYON

Antelope Canyon Navajo Tribal Park ★★   If you've spent any time in Arizona, chances are you've seen photos of a narrow sandstone canyon only a few feet wide. The walls of the canyon seem to glow with an inner light, and beams of sunlight slice down through the darkness of the deep slot canyon. Sound familiar? If you have seen such a photo, chances are you were looking at **Antelope Canyon** (also sometimes known as Corkscrew Canyon). Located 2½ miles outside Page off Ariz. 98 (at milepost 299), this photogenic canyon comprises the Antelope Canyon Navajo Tribal Park, which is on the Navajo Indian Reservation and is divided into upper and lower canyons.

There are currently two options for visiting Antelope Canyon. The most convenient and reliable way is to take a 1½-hour tour with **Lake Powell Jeep Tours** (© 866/645-5501 or 520/645-5501; www.jeeptour.com), **Roger Ekis' Antelope Canyon Tours** (© 520/645-9102 or 520/645-8579; www.antelopecanyon.com), or **Grand Circle Adventures** (© 800/835-8859 or 520/645-5594), all of which charge $20 (plus Navajo permit fee) per adult for a basic tour (photographic tours are $35).

Alternatively, at both Upper Antelope Canyon and Lower Antelope Canyon, you'll find Navajo guides collecting park admission fees and fees for guide services. These guides charge $12.50. At Upper Antelope Canyon, the guide will drive you from the highway to the canyon and then pick you up again after your hike. At Lower Antelope Canyon, the guide will likely just show you the entrance to the slot canyon. You'll get more out of your experience on one of the guided tours mentioned above, but you'll save a little money by visiting the canyon on your own.

Just remember that if there is even the slightest chance of rain anywhere in the region, you should not venture into this canyon, which is subject to flash floods. In the past, people who have ignored bad weather have been killed by flash floods.

2½ miles outside Page off Ariz. 98 (at milepost 299). © **520/698-3347.** Admission $5 adults, free for children 7 and under. Apr–Oct daily 8am–5pm. Closed Nov–Mar.

WATERSPORTS

While simply exploring the lake's maze of canyons on a narrated tour is satisfying enough for many visitors, the most popular activities are still houseboating, water-skiing, riding personal watercraft, and fishing. Five marinas (only Wahweap is in Arizona) help boaters explore the lake. At the **Wahweap Marina** (© 800/528-6154 or 520/645-2433; www.visitlakepowell.com), you can rent various types of boats, along with personal watercraft and water skis. Rates in summer range from about $75 to $310 per day depending on the type of boat. Weekly rates are also available. Small boats and personal watercraft can also be rented from **Lake Powell Water World,** 920 Hemlock St. (© **520/645-8845;** www.lakepowellwaterworld.com), and **Doo Powell,** 130 Sixth Ave. (© **800/ 350-1230** or 520/645-1230; www.doopowell.com). For information on renting houseboats, see "Houseboats" under "Where to Stay," below.

If roaring engines aren't your speed, you might want to consider exploring Lake Powell by sea kayak. While afternoon winds can sometimes make paddling difficult, mornings are often quiet. With a narrow sea kayak, you can even explore canyons too small for powerboats. Rentals are available at **Twin Finn Dive Center,** 811 Vista Ave. (© **520/645-3114;** www.twinfinn.com). Sea kayaks rent for $45 to $55 per day, and sit-on-top kayaks for $35 to $48.50.

While most of Glen Canyon National Recreation Area consists of the impounded waters of Lake Powell, within the recreation area there is also a short stretch of the Colorado River that still flows swift and free. If you'd like to see this stretch of river, try a float trip from Glen Canyon Dam to Lees Ferry, operated by **Wilderness River Adventures,** 50 S. Lake Powell Blvd. (© **800/ 528-6154** or 520/645-3279; www.visitlakepowell.com), between March and mid-September. Half-day trips cost $57 for adults and $49 for children 12 and under. Full-day trips are $77 for adults, $71 for children. Try to reserve at least 2 weeks in advance.

If you have a boat (either your own or a rental), avail yourself of some excellent year-round **fishing.** Smallmouth, largemouth, and striped bass, as well as walleye, catfish, crappie, and carp are all plentiful. Because the lake lies within both Arizona and Utah, you'll need to know which state's waters you're fishing in whenever you cast your line out, and you'll need the appropriate license. (Also, be sure to pick up a copy of the Arizona and Utah state fishing regulations, or ask about applicable regulations at any of the marinas.) You can arrange licenses to fish the entire lake at **Wahweap Lodge and Marina** (© **520/ 645-2433**), which also sells bait and tackle and can provide you with advice on fishing this massive reservoir. Other marinas on the lake also sell licenses, bait, and tackle. The best season is March through November, but walleye are most often caught during the cooler months. If you'd rather try your hand at catching enormous rainbow trout, try downstream of the Glen Canyon Dam, where cold waters provide ideal conditions for trophy trout. Unfortunately, there isn't much access to this stretch of river. You'll need a trout stamp to fish for the rainbows.

If you're just looking for a good place for a swim near Wahweap Lodge, take the Coves Loop just west of the marina. Of the three coves, the third one is the best, with a sandy beach. The Chains area, another good place to jump off the rocks and otherwise lounge by the lake, is outside Page down a rough dirt road just before you reach Glen Canyon Dam. The view underwater at Lake Powell is as scenic as the view above it; to explore the underwater regions of the canyon, contact **Twin Finn Diving Center,** 811 Vista Ave. (© **520/645-3114;** www. twinfinn.com), which charges $45 a day for scuba gear and also rents snorkeling equipment.

OTHER OUTDOOR PURSUITS

While most activity within the national recreation area revolves around water, the short hike to the **Horseshoe Bend** ✦ viewpoint is not to be missed (be sure to bring your camera). Horseshoe Bend is a huge loop of the Colorado River, and the viewpoint is hundreds of feet above the water on the edge of a sheer cliff. Far below, you can often see people camped at a riverside site that is accessible only by boat. It's about a half mile to the viewpoint from the trailhead, which is 5 miles south of the Carl Hayden Visitor Center on U.S. 89 just south of milepost 545.

At Lees Ferry, 39 miles from Page at the southern tip of the national recreation area, you'll find three short trails (Cathedral Wash, River Trail, and Spencer Trail). The 20-mile **Cathedral Wash Trail** is the most interesting of the three day hikes and follows a dry wash through a narrow canyon with unusual rock formations. The trailhead is at the second turnout after turning off U.S. 89A. Be aware that this wash is subject to flash floods. The **Spencer Trail,** which begins along the River Trail, leads up to the top of a 1,500-foot cliff. Lees Ferry is also the southern trailhead for the famed **Paria Canyon** ✦, a favorite of canyoneering backpackers. This trail is 37 miles long and follows the meandering route of a narrow slot canyon for much of its length. Most hikers start from the northern trailhead, which is in Utah on U.S. 89. For more information on hiking this remote and narrow canyon, contact **Arizona Strip Interpretive Association,** 345 E. Riverside Dr., St. George, UT 84790 (✆ **435/688-3246;** http://paria.az.blm.gov).

The 27-hole **Lake Powell National Golf Course,** 400 Clubhouse Dr. (✆ **520/645-2023**), is one of the most spectacular golf courses in the state. The fairways wrap around the base of the red-sandstone bluff atop which sits the town of Page. In places, walls of eroded sandstone come right down to the greens, and alongside one fairway, water is pumped up the rock to create a waterfall. The views stretch on forever. Greens fees range from $35 to $62.50 in the warmer months.

OTHER AREA ATTRACTIONS

In addition to the museum listed here, you can learn about Navajo culture at **Navajo Village,** a sort of living-history center located on the south side of Page off Haul Road. Programs here, which run May through October, include demonstrations by weavers, silversmiths, basket-makers, and potters. Prices range from $24.95 ($18.95 for children 6–13) for a 1-hour tour to $49.95 ($34.95 for children) for a 4-hour evening tour that includes dinner and traditional dances. Between 9am and 3pm, it is sometimes possible to visit and see Navajo artisans at work ($10 for adults, $7 for children). Although this is definitely a tourist attraction, you will come away with a better sense of Navajo culture. For information or to make reservations, contact the John W. Powell Memorial Museum, listed below.

John Wesley Powell Memorial Museum & Visitor Information Center

In 1869, John Wesley Powell, a one-armed Civil War veteran, and a small band of men spent more than 3 months fighting the rapids of the Green and Colorado rivers to become the first people to travel the length of the Grand Canyon. It is for this intrepid—some said crazy—adventurer that Lake Powell is named and to whom this small museum is dedicated. Besides documenting the Powell expedition with photographs, etchings, and artifacts, the museum displays Indian artifacts from Anasazi pottery to contemporary Navajo and Hopi crafts. The exhibit of fluorescent minerals is particularly interesting, and there are several informative videos shown in the small auditorium. The museum also acts as an information center for Page, Lake Powell, and the surrounding region.

6 N. Lake Powell Blvd. ✆ 520/645-9496. www.powellmuseum.org. Admission $1 adults, 50¢ children grades K–8. May–Sept Mon–Fri 8am–6pm; Nov to mid-Dec and mid-Feb to Apr Mon–Fri 9am–5pm. Closed mid-Dec to mid-Feb.

WHERE TO STAY
HOUSEBOATS

Lake Powell Resorts and Marinas ★★ *Kids*   Although there are plenty of hotels and motels in and near Page, the most popular accommodations here are not waterfront hotel rooms but houseboats, which function as floating vacation homes. With a houseboat, which is as easy to operate as a car, you can explore Lake Powell's beautiful red-rock country, far from any roads. No special license or prior experience is necessary, and plenty of hands-on instruction is offered before you leave the marina. Because Lake Powell houseboating is extremely popular with visitors from all over the world, it's important to make reservations as far in advance as possible, especially if you plan to visit in summer.

Houseboats range in size from 36 to 59 feet, sleep anywhere from 6 to 12 people, and come complete with hot shower, refrigerator/freezer, heating system (more expensive houseboats also have heat pumps or evaporative coolers), stove, oven, and gas grill. Kitchens come equipped with everything you need to prepare meals. The only things you really need to bring are bedding and towels. We recommend going for the largest boat you can afford (you'll appreciate the space), and if you're coming in the heat of summer, splurge on a boat with some sort of cooling system.

P.O. Box 1597, Page, AZ 86040. ☎ **800/528-6154.** Fax 602/331-5258. www.visitlakepowell.com. May to mid-Oct $1,862–$6,021 per week; mid-Oct to Apr approximately 50% less. 3-, 4-, 5-, and 6-night rates also available. AE, DISC, MC, V.

HOTELS & MOTELS

Best Western Arizonainn   Perched right at the edge of the mesa on which Page is built, this modern motel has a fine view across miles of desert. Half the guest rooms have views. The hotel's pool has a 100-mile view.

716 Rimview Dr. (P.O. Box 250), Page, AZ 86040. ☎ **800/826-2718** or 520/645-2466. Fax 520/645-2053. 103 units. Apr–Oct $80–$140 double; Nov–Mar $52–$77 double. Rates include continental breakfast. AE, DC, DISC, MC, V. Pets accepted ($10 fee). **Amenities:** Small outdoor pool; exercise room; Jacuzzi; coin-op laundry. *In room:* A/C, TV, iron.

Best Western at Lake Powell   This Best Western is on the edge of town overlooking Lake Powell, right next door to the Arizonainn. The rooms are comfortable and modern, and the pool has a great view.

208 N. Lake Powell Blvd. (P.O. Box 4899), Page, AZ 86040. ☎ **888/794-2888,** 800/528-1234, or 520/645-5988. Fax 520/645-2578. 132 units. May–Sept $79–$109; Oct and Apr $59–$79; Nov–Mar $49–$69. Rates include continental breakfast. AE, DC, DISC, MC, V. **Amenities:** Small outdoor pool; exercise room; Jacuzzi; courtesy airport shuttle. *In room:* A/C, TV.

Courtyard by Marriott   Located at the foot of the mesa on which Page is built and adjacent to the Lake Powell National Golf Course, this is the top in-town choice—and it's the closest you'll come to a golf resort in this corner of the state. The rooms are larger than those at most lodgings; you'll pay a premium for views of the golf course or lake. Moderately priced meals are served in a casual restaurant that has a terrace overlooking the distant lake. The 18-hole golf course has great views of the surrounding landscape.

600 Clubhouse Dr. (P.O. Box 4150), Page, AZ 86040. ☎ **800/851-3855,** 800/321-2211, or 520/645-5000. Fax 520/645-5004. www.courtyard.com. 153 units. July to early Sept $109–$139 double; late Sept to June $79–$109 double. AE, DC, DISC, MC, V. **Amenities:** Restaurant (American), lounge; outdoor pool; 18-hole golf course; exercise room; Jacuzzi; concierge; room service; massage; laundry service; dry cleaning. *In room:* A/C, TV, dataport, coffeemaker, hair dryer, iron.

Lake Powell Motel   Situated on a barren hill set back from the lake, the Lake Powell Motel offers an alternative away from the traffic and lights of downtown Page and the bustle of activity at the Wahweap Marina. The accommodations are standard motel rooms with two queen-size beds.

U.S. 89 near Wahweap Marina (mailing address: P.O. Box 1597, Page, AZ 86040). ☎ **800/528-6154** or 520/645-2477. Fax 602/331-5258. www.visitlakepowell.com. 24 units. $89 double. AE, DC, DISC, MC, V. Closed Nov–May. Pets accepted. Drive 3 miles west of the Wahweap Marina or 4 miles north of the Glen Canyon Dam on U.S. 89. *In room:* A/C, TV, coffeemaker.

Wahweap Lodge   The Wahweap Marina is a sprawling complex 5 miles north of Page on the shores of Lake Powell. As the biggest and busiest hotel in the area, Wahweap features many of the amenities and activities of a resort. The guest rooms are arranged in several long two-story wings, and every room has either a balcony or a patio. Only half the rooms have lake views, though, and of these, those in the west wing have the better views (the east wing overlooks the

Navajo coal-fired power plant). The Rainbow Room (see "Where to Dine," below) offers fine dining with a sweeping panorama of the lake and desert. This place stays packed with tour groups from around the world, and getting a reservation can be difficult.

100 Lakeshore Dr. (mailing address: P.O. Box 1597, Page, AZ 86040). © 800/528-6154 or 520/645-2433. Fax 602/331-5258. www.visitlakepowell.com. 350 units. Apr–Oct $159–$169 double, $180 suite; Nov–Mar $111–$118 double, $125 suite. AE, DC, DISC, MC, V. Pets accepted. **Amenities:** 2 restaurants (American/Southwestern, pizza), snack bar, lounge; 2 outdoor pools; Jacuzzi; watersports; boat rentals; tour desk; room service; coin-op laundry. *In room:* A/C, TV, fridge, coffeemaker, hair dryer.

CAMPGROUNDS & RV PARKS

There are campgrounds at **Wahweap** (© **520/645-1059**) and **Lees Ferry** (© **520/608-6404**) in Arizona, and at Bullfrog, Hite, and Halls Crossing in Utah. Some scrubby trees provide a bit of shade at the Wahweap campground, but the winds and sun make this a rather bleak spot in summer. Nevertheless, because of the lake's popularity, these campgrounds stay packed for much of the year. Reservations are not accepted.

WHERE TO DINE

Butterfield Stage Co. STEAKHOUSE/AMERICAN   Located adjacent to the Best Western Arizonainn, this steakhouse is the only in-town restaurant with a view, and although that view is somewhat marred by the number of power lines that stretch out from the dam, it's still the best in town. Sunrises and sunsets are gorgeous. Steaks and seafood are the menu mainstays.

704 Rimview Dr. © **520/645-2467**. Main courses $9–$19. AE, MC, V. Daily 4–9pm (until 10pm in summer).

The Dam Bar & Grille AMERICAN   Page's first and only theme restaurant is a warehouse-size space designed to conjure up images of the Glen Canyon Dam. Big industrial doors are the first hint this is more than your usual small-town dining establishment. Inside, cement walls, hard hats, and a big transformer that sends out bolts of neon "electricity" put you in a dam good mood. Sandwiches, pastas, and steaks dominate the menu, with a smattering of seafood. There's a large lounge area that's a popular locals' hangout, and next door is the affiliated Gunsmoke Saloon.

644 N. Navajo Dr. © **520/645-2161**. www.damplaza.com. Reservations recommended in summer. Main courses $12–$24. AE, DISC, MC, V. Tues–Sat 4–10pm (longer hours in summer).

Rainbow Room AMERICAN/SOUTHWESTERN   With sweeping vistas of Lake Powell out the walls of glass, the Rainbow Room at the Wahweap Lodge is Page's premier restaurant. As such, be prepared for a wait; this place regularly feeds busloads of tourists. The menu features American dishes, such as blackened chicken breast and Caesar salad, but there are also specials such as grilled rainbow trout with crab stuffing and lemon-caper sauce. If you're heading out on the water for the day, the kitchen will fix you a box lunch.

In the Wahweap Lodge, Lakeshore Dr. © **520/645-1162**. Reservations recommended. Main courses $5–$10 lunch, $9–$22 dinner. AE, DC, DISC, MC, V. Daily 6am–2pm and 5–9pm (until 10pm in summer).

Zapata's MEXICAN   Zapata's, a little place in the shopping plaza diagonally across the intersection from the Powell Museum, serves some of the best Mexican food (and margaritas) in town. You can count on finding spicy chile verde burritos and somewhat milder, although flavorful, chicken enchiladas. The crowd here is usually more local than tourist.

614 N. Navajo Dr. © **520/645-9006**. Main courses $7.50–$13.50. AE, DC, DISC, MC, V. Daily 11am–9pm.

8

Eastern Arizona's High Country

Cactus and desert landscapes are what come to mind when most people think of Arizona. But that's only part of the picture. Arizona actually has more mountainous country than Switzerland and more forest than Minnesota, and most of these mountains and forests are here in the highlands of eastern Arizona.

In this sparsely populated region, towns with such apt names as Alpine, Lakeside, and Pinetop have become summer retreats for the people who live in the state's low-lying, sun-baked deserts. Folks from Phoenix and its surrounding cities discovered long ago how close the cool mountain forests were. In only a few hours, you can drive up from the cacti and creosote bushes to the meadows and pine forests of the White Mountains.

Dividing the arid lowlands from the cool pine forests of the highlands is the Mogollon Rim (pronounced *Mug-ee-un* by the locals), a 2,000-foot-high escarpment that stretches for 200 miles from central Arizona into New Mexico. Along this impressive wall, the climatic and vegetative change is dramatic. Imagine sunshine at the base and snow squalls at the top, and you have an idea of the Mogollon Rim's variety. This area was made famous by Western author Zane Grey, who lived in a cabin near Payson and set many of his novels in this scenic yet oft-overlooked part of Arizona. Fans of Zane Grey's novels can follow in the author's footsteps and visit a small museum dedicated to Grey.

Trout fishing, hiking, horseback riding, and hunting are the main warm-weather pastimes of eastern Arizona, and when winter weather reports from up north have Phoenicians dreaming about snow (it's true, they really do), many head up this way to the White Mountains for a bit of skiing. Sunrise Park Resort, operated by the White Mountain Apache Tribe, is the state's biggest and busiest downhill ski area, and there are also plenty of cross-country ski trails in the area.

Much of eastern Arizona is Apache Reservation land. Recreational activities abound on this land, but remember that the Apache tribe requires visitors to have reservation fishing permits and outdoor recreation permits. Fishing is particularly popular on the reservation, which isn't surprising considering there are 400 miles of trout streams and 25 lakes stocked with rainbow and brown trout.

1 Payson & the Mogollon Rim Country

94 miles NE of Phoenix; 90 miles SW of Winslow; 90 miles SE of Flagstaff; 100 miles W of Pinetop-Lakeside

Payson, 94 miles from Phoenix and 5,000 feet above sea level, is one of the closest places for Phoenicians to find relief from the summer heat. Payson may not be quite high enough to be considered the mountains, but it certainly isn't the desert (summer temperatures are 20° cooler than in the Valley of the Sun). The 2,000-foot-high, 200-mile-long Mogollon Rim is only 22 miles north of town, and the surrounding Tonto National Forest provides opportunities for hiking, swimming, fishing, and hunting. The nearly perfect climate of Payson has also made the town a popular retirement spot. Summer highs are usually in the 80s or 90s, while winter highs are usually in the 50s and 60s.

ESSENTIALS

GETTING THERE Ariz. 87, the Beeline Highway, connects Payson to Phoenix and Winslow. Ariz. 260 runs east from Payson, climbing the Mogollon Rim and continuing into the White Mountains.

VISITOR INFORMATION Contact the **Rim Country Regional Chamber of Commerce,** 100 W. Main St., Payson (© **800/672-9766** or 520/474-4515; www.rimcountrychamber.com).

SPECIAL EVENTS The **World's Oldest Continuous Rodeo** takes place on the third weekend in August, while another **PRCA Rodeo** is held in May.

OUTDOOR PURSUITS

The area's most popular attraction is **Tonto Natural Bridge State Park** (© **520/ 476-4202**), which is 15 miles north of Payson on Ariz. 87 and preserves the largest natural travertine bridge in the world. In 1877, gold prospector David Gowan, while being chased by Apaches, became the first white man to see this natural bridge, which stand 183 feet high and 150 feet across at its widest point. Although this all sounds very impressive, this natural bridge looks nothing like the sandstone arches in southern Utah. Tonto Natural Bridge creates something of a tunnel rather than a free-standing arch. This state park also preserves a historic lodge built by Gowan's nephew and the nephew's sons. The lodge has been restored to the way it looked in 1927, but is not open for overnight accommodations. Admission to the park is $5 per car. It's open daily from 9am to 5pm in winter, 8am to 6pm in spring and fall, and 8am to 7pm Memorial Day through Labor Day.

If you'd like to go horseback riding between Memorial Day and late September, contact **O.K. Corral Stables** (© **520/476-4303**) in Pine, which is 14 miles north of Payson on Ariz. 87, or **Kohl's Stables,** on Highway 260 17 miles north of Payson (© **520/478-0030**). Rates range from $20 for a 1-hour ride to $80 for a half-day ride.

The **Highline Trail** is a 51-mile hike along the lower slope of the Mogollon Rim. You can find out more about this and other area trails, as well as which trails are open to mountain bikes, at the **Payson Ranger Station,** 1009 E. Hwy. 260 (© **520/474-7900**), at the east end of town.

You can also hike this area in the company of llamas that will carry your gear for you. **Fossil Creek Llamas** (© **520/476-5178;** www.fossilcreekllamas.com) offers both day trips and overnight hikes starting at $65 per person. A tepee "bed-and-breakfast," wellness courses, and retreats are also offered.

OTHER AREA ATTRACTIONS

About 5 miles north of town, off Ariz. 87 on Houston Mesa Road, you can visit the ruins of **Shoofly Village,** in the Tonto National Forest. This village was first occupied nearly 1,000 years ago by peoples related to the Hohokam and Salado. It once contained 87 rooms, though today only rock foundations remain. An interpretive trail helps bring the site to life.

To learn more about the history of the area, stop by the **Rim Country Museum,** 700 Green Valley Pkwy. (© **520/474-3483**), which has displays on the region as well as a special Zane Grey exhibit. The museum, located in Green

Valley Park, is open Wednesday through Sunday from noon to 4pm; admission is $3 for adults, $2.50 for seniors, and $2 for children 12 to 17.

You'll find more Zane Grey memorabilia at the **Zane Grey Museum of Payson,** 503 W. Main St. (© **520/474-6243**). The museum includes a shop, and Zane Grey book searches are a specialty. It's open Monday through Saturday from 10am to 3pm. Admission is $3.50 for adults and $1 for students.

If you're feeling lucky, spend some time and money at the **Mazatzal Casino** (© **800/777-PLAY**), half a mile south on Ariz. 87. The casino is run by the Tonto Apaches.

SCENIC DRIVES

Scenic drives through this region are among the favorite pastimes of visitors. One of the most popular drives is along the top of the Mogollon Rim on 45-mile-long **Forest Road 300.** On the road, which clings to the edge of the rim, are numerous views of the forest far below and plenty of places to stop, including lakes, picnic areas, trailheads, and campgrounds. This is a good gravel road in summer and can be negotiated in a standard passenger car. In winter, however, the road is not maintained. To access the rim road, head east on Ariz. 260 or north on Ariz. 87 for 30 miles and watch for signs.

About 15 miles north of Payson on Ariz. 87 is the village of **Pine,** and another 3 miles beyond this, the village of **Strawberry.** Here, in a quiet setting in the forest, you'll find a few antiques and crafts shops and, in Pine, a small museum that chronicles the history of this area. In Strawberry, on the road that leads west from the center of the village, is the old Strawberry schoolhouse, a restored log building dating from 1885.

Another interesting drive starts west of the old Strawberry schoolhouse. If you continue west on this road, you'll be on the gravel Fossil Creek Road, which leads 10 miles down a deep and spectacular canyon. It's a bit hair-raising, but if you like views, it's well worth the white knuckles and dust. At the bottom, **Fossil Creek** offers some of the most idyllic little swimming holes you could ever hope to find. If you make it down here on a weekday, you just might have a swimming hole all to yourself.

WHERE TO STAY

Kohl's Ranch Lodge *(Kids*   This casual family-oriented resort makes an excellent base for exploring the Mogollon Rim region. Located 17 miles east of Payson on Ariz. 260, Kohl's Ranch is surrounded by pine forest on the banks of Tonto Creek and is the most comfortable mountain retreat in the area. Although the exterior of the main lodge looks like an aging mountain motel, inside you'll find that renovations in recent years have thoroughly upgraded the property. All guest rooms feature a contemporary rustic look, and all cabins and some of the smaller lodge rooms have fireplaces. The creek-side cabins are the best accommodations, but they may seem somewhat overpriced. The dining room is done up like an old log cabin; there's a cowboy bar and pool hall across the parking lot.

E. Hwy. 260, Payson, AZ 85541. ✆ 800/521-3131 or 520/478-4211. Fax 520/478-0353. www.ilxresorts.com. 49 units. May 1–Sept 30 $95–$115 double, $230– $295 cabin; Oct 1–Apr 30 $75–$95 double, $200–$270 cabin. AE, DISC, MC, V. **Amenities:** Restaurant (American), 2 lounges; outdoor pool; putting green; tennis court; volleyball and basketball courts; boccie ball; horseshoes; exercise room; Jacuzzi; sauna; bike rentals; playground; horseback riding. In room: A/C, TV, kitchenette, fridge, coffeemaker.

Majestic Mountain Inn   Although it's located in town, this motel was built in an attractive, modern mountain-lodge style that makes it the most appealing place to stay right in Payson. There's a large stone chimney and fireplace in the lobby, and several of the deluxe rooms have fireplaces of their own. These deluxe units also have tile floors and double whirlpool tubs facing the fireplace. The standard rooms aren't as spacious or luxurious, but are still quite comfortable. A restaurant is scheduled to open later in 2001.

602 E. Ariz. 260, Payson, AZ 85541. ✆ 800/408-2442 or 520/474-0185. Fax 520/472-6097. www. majesticmountaininn.com. 50 units. $67–$140 double. AE, DC, DISC, MC, V. Pets accepted ($6 per night). **Amenities:** Outdoor pool; access to nearby health club. In room: A/C, TV, dataport, fridge, coffeemaker, hair dryer.

CAMPGROUNDS

East of Payson on Ariz. 260 are several national forest campgrounds. These include (from west to east) Lower Tonto Creek and Upper Tonto Creek campgrounds (neither of which take reservations) and Christopher Creek Campground. You can make reservations for the latter through the **National Recreation Reservation Service** (✆ 800/280-2267; www.reserveusa.com). Information is available from the **Payson Ranger Station** (✆ 520/474-7900), on Ariz. 260 at the east end of town.

WHERE TO DINE

Mogollon Grill AMERICAN   The old Payson and the new Payson come together at this restaurant, set amid shady trees just off busy Ariz. 87 at the south end of town. While it serves familiar American fare such as steaks (the filet mignon is great), the ambience is a mix of Phoenix chic and country cottage.

Service is good, and the large lounge area is a pleasant place to hang out after a day exploring the forest.

202 W. Main St. ✆ 520/474-5501. Reservations recommended on weekends. Main courses $6–$8 lunch, $6–$19 dinner. AE, MC, V. Mon–Fri 11:30am–3pm and 4–9pm; Sat–Sun 1:30am–3:30pm and 5–9pm (closed Sun Nov–Mar).

2 Pinetop-Lakeside

185 miles NE of Phoenix; 140 miles SE of Flagstaff; 50 miles S of Holbrook; 90 miles NE of Payson

With dozens of motels and cabin resorts strung along Ariz. 260 as it passes through town, Pinetop-Lakeside, actually two towns that grew together over the years, is the busiest community in the White Mountains. At first glance, it's easy to dismiss it as too commercial, what with all the strip malls and budget motels, but this area has spent many years entertaining families during the summer months, and it still has plenty of diversions to keep visitors busy. You just have to look a little harder than you might in other White Mountains communities.

With Apache-Sitgreaves National Forest on one side of town and the unspoiled lands of the White Mountain Apache Indian Reservation on the other, Pinetop-Lakeside is well situated for anyone who enjoys getting outdoors. Nearby are several lakes with good fishing; nearly 200 miles of hiking, mountain-biking, and cross-country ski trails; horseback riding; and downhill skiing. Although summer is the busy season, Pinetop-Lakeside becomes a ski resort in winter. The Sunrise ski area is only 30 miles away, and on weekends the town is packed with skiers.

Pinetop-Lakeside is definitely the family destination of the White Mountains, so if you're looking for a romantic weekend or solitude, continue farther into the White Mountains to Greer or Alpine.

ESSENTIALS

GETTING THERE   Pinetop and Lakeside are both located on Ariz. 260.

VISITOR INFORMATION   For information on this area, contact the **Pinetop-Lakeside Chamber of Commerce,** 102C W. White Mountain Blvd., Lakeside (✆ **800/573-4031** or 520/367-4290; www.pinetoplakesidechamber. com). For information on the White Mountain Apache Reservation, contact the **White Mountain Apache Tribe Office of Tourism,** P.O. Box 710, Fort Apache, AZ 85926 (✆ **520/338-1230;** www.wmat.nsn.us).

OUTDOOR PURSUITS

Old forts and casinos aside, it's the outdoors (and the cool weather) that really draws people here. Fishing, hiking, mountain biking, and horseback riding are among the most popular activities. If you want to saddle up, call **Porter Mountain Stable,** 4048 Porter Mountain Rd. (✆ **520/368-5306**), which charges $20 for a 1-hour ride.

In the forests surrounding Pinetop-Lakeside is the 180-mile **White Mountain Trail system.** Many of these trails are easily accessible (in fact, some are right in town) and are open to both hikers and mountain bikers. The trails at Pinetop's **Woodland Lake Park** are among our favorites. The park is just off Ariz. 260 near the east end of Pinetop and has 6 miles of trails, including a paved trail around the lake. For a panoramic vista of the Mogollon Rim, you can hike the short **Mogollon Rim Nature Walk** off Ariz. 260 on the west side of Lakeside. For another short but pleasant stroll, check out the **Big Springs Environmental Study Area,** on Woodland Road in Lakeside. This quiet little preserve encompasses a small meadow through which flows a spring-fed stream. There is often good bird-watching here. You can spot more birds at Woodland Lake Park, mentioned above, and at **Jacques Marsh,** 2 miles north of Lakeside on Porter Mountain Road. For more information on area trails, contact the **Lakeside Ranger Station** (© 520/368-5111), on Ariz. 260 in Lakeside, or the **Pinetop-Lakeside Chamber of Commerce** (see "Visitor Information," above).

If you're up here to catch the big one, you've got plenty of options. Area lakes hold native Apache trout, as well as stocked rainbows, browns, and brookies. This is also the southernmost spot in the United States where you can fish for Arctic graylings. Right in the Pinetop-Lakeside area, try **Rainbow Lake,** which is a block south of Ariz. 260 in Lakeside and has boat rentals available; **Woodland Lake,** in Woodland Lake Park, toward the east end of Pinetop and just south of Ariz. 260; or **Show Low Lake,** east of Lakeside and north of Ariz. 260. On the nearby White Mountain Apache Indian Reservation, there's good fishing in **Hawley Lake** and **Horseshoe Lake,** both of which are east of Pinetop-Lakeside and south of Ariz. 260. If you plan to fish at either of these latter two lakes, be sure to get your reservation fishing license ($6 per day). They're available at the **Hon-Dah Convenience Store,** at the junction of Ariz. 260 and Ariz. 73 (© 520/369-4311), **Hon-Dah Ski & Outdoor Sport,** also at the junction of Ariz. 260 and Ariz. 73 (© 877/CAN-HUNT or 520/369-7669), and **Hawley Lake Store,** south of Ariz. 260 between Hon-Dah and Sunrise (© 520/335-7511).

Several area golf courses are open to the public, including **Pinetop Lakes Golf Club,** Buck Springs Road, Pinetop-Lakeside (© 520/369-4531), considered one of the best executive courses in the state (play this one if you have time for only one round while you're in the area); **Silver Creek Golf Club,** White Mountain Lake Road, Show Low (© 520/537-2744); and the **Show Low Country Club,** Ariz. 260 and Old Linden Road, Show Low (© 520/537-4564).

About 50 miles south of Show Low, U.S. 60 crosses a bridge over the narrow, scenic canyon of the Salt River. This stretch of the river is a favorite of white-water rafters, and several companies offer rafting trips of varying lengths. Try **Far Flung Adventures** (© 800/231-7238 or 520/425-7272; www.farflung.com), **Sun Country Rafting** (© 800/272-3353 or 602/493-9011), or **Mild to Wild Rafting** (© 800/567-6745). Prices start at $80 to $100 for a day trip.

OTHER AREA ATTRACTIONS

If you're curious to learn more about the Apaches, drive south from Pinetop-Lakeside to **Fort Apache Historic Park** (© 520/338-4625), in the town of Fort Apache, which, along with the White Mountain Apache Reservation, was established in 1870 by the U.S. government. The park, approximately 22 miles south of Pinetop on Ariz. 73, includes more than 20 historic buildings, but don't expect to see a Hollywood-style fort (this "fort" has more the look of a military base). You'll also find a reconstructed Apache village and the Apache Museum/Cultural Center, which has a few small but informative displays. The cultural center is open Monday through Friday from 8am to 5pm. Admission is $3 for adults, $2 for seniors and children 7 to 14. You'll get much more out of your visit if you take a 1½-hour guided tour, which costs $8 for adults and $7 for seniors.

Also in this area is **Kinishba Ruins,** up a gravel road 2 miles west of Fort Apache on Ariz. 73 and then 3 miles down a rough gravel road. This 200-room

---

Tips **A Pleasant Valley Detour**

For a bit of back roads adventure, head south from the Mogollon Rim to the remote community of Young, which sits in the middle of the aptly named Pleasant Valley. Be prepared for gravel roads: The town can be reached only via well-graded gravel roads (24 miles of gravel if you come from the north, 32 miles from the south).

Why visit Young? Most people come just to see the land that spawned the worst range war and family feud in the West. Known as the Pleasant Valley War or Graham-Tewksbury Feud, it likely erupted over conflicts about sheep grazing in the valley and took dozens of lives. Zane Grey memorialized the 1880s feud in his novel *To the Last Man.*

You'll find Young on Ariz. 288, which heads south from Ariz. 260 about midway between Payson and Heber and connects to Ariz. 88 north of Globe (near Theodore Roosevelt Lake).

---

pueblo ruin is more than 1,000 years old and was visited by Coronado when he passed through in search of the Seven Cities of Cíbola. Get directions to the ruins at the Cultural Center. The best way to visit is as an add-on to the guided tours offered at Fort Apache Historic Park.

For more information on visiting the White Mountain Apache Reservation, contact the **White Mountain Apache Tribe Office of Tourism** (© 520/ 338-1230), also located in Fort Apache Historic Park.

If you're looking for something to do after dark, head out to the **Hon-Dah Casino** (© 800/WAY-UP-HI or 520/369-0299), owned and operated by the White Mountain Apache Tribe. It's open daily around the clock and is at the junction of Ariz. 73 and Ariz. 260, about 4 miles east of Pinetop.

WHERE TO STAY

Hon-Dah Resort This hotel, adjacent to the Hon-Dah Casino a few miles east of Pinetop-Lakeside, is the largest and most luxurious lodging in the White Mountains. As with most casino hotels, it was designed to impress. The portico is big enough to hold a basketball court, and inside the front door is an artificial rock wall upon which are mounted stuffed animals, including a cougar, bobcat, bear, ducks, and even a bugling elk. Guest rooms are for the most part very large.

777 Hwy. 260 (P.O. Box 3250), Hon-Dah, AZ 85935. © 800/WAY-UP-HI or 520/369-0299. Fax 520/369-0382. www.hon-dah.com. 128 units. $79–$109 double; $150–$180 suite. AE, DC, DISC, MC, V. Located at the junction of Ariz. 260 and Ariz. 73. **Amenities:** 2 restaurants; 2 lounges; casino; outdoor heated pool; Jacuzzi; sauna. *In room:* A/C, TV, dataport, fridge, iron.

Lake of the Woods *Kids* Set on its own private lake right on Ariz. 260, Lake of the Woods is a rustic mountain resort that caters primarily to families. Cabins and houses range from tiny to huge, with rustic and modern side by side. The smallest sleep two or three, while the largest can take up to 18; several have kitchens and fireplaces. Some are on the edge of the lake, while others are tucked away under the pines; be sure to request a location away from the busy highway and ask for a newer cabin, as they vary considerably in quality. Kids in particular love this place: They can fish in the lake, row a boat, or play in the snow.

Ariz. 260 (P.O. Box 777), Lakeside, AZ 85929. © 520/368-5353. www.l-o-w.com. 31 units. $51–$168 cabin for 2; $93–$303 house for 2. 3- to 5-night minimum in summer and on some holidays. DISC, MC, V. **Amenities:** Exercise room; Jacuzzi; sauna; boat rentals; horseshoes; playground; game room; coin-op laundry. *In room:* TV, kitchen, fridge, coffeemaker, no phone.

Sierra Springs Ranch ⭐   Located off a gravel road east of Pinetop, the Sierra Springs Ranch is the most upscale property around and as idyllic a mountain retreat as you'll find in Arizona. Set in a wide clearing in the forest, each of the eight cabins is a little bit different, but all are spacious and comfortable (the largest cabin sleeps 13). Our favorite is the honeymoon cottage, which is built of logs and has a stone fireplace. All units have full kitchens, which makes up for the lack of a restaurant on the premises. The ranch also has its own trout pond (fishing gear is available) and meadows.

HC 62, Box 32100, Pinetop, AZ 85935. © **800/492-4059** or 520/369-3900. Fax 520/369-0741. www. sierraspringsranch.com. 8 units. $175 cabin for 2. 2-night minimum (longer on holidays and in summer). AE, MC, V. **Amenities:** Tennis court; horseshoes; exercise room; sauna; bikes; game room; laundry service. *In room:* Kitchen, fridge, coffeemaker.

CAMPGROUNDS

There are four campgrounds in the immediate Pinetop-Lakeside area, including Show Low Lake, Fool Hollow, Lewis Canyon, and Lakeside. Of these, **Show Low Lake County Park** (© **520/537-4126**) and **Fool Hollow Lake Recreation Area** (© **520/537-3680**) are the nicest. There are also numerous campgrounds nearby on the White River Apache Indian Reservation. For information about these campgrounds, contact the **White Mountain Wildlife and Outdoor Recreation Division** (© **520/338-4385;** www.wmatoutdoors.com) or the **White Mountain Apache Tribe Office of Tourism** (© **520/338-1230;** www.wmat.nsn.us).

WHERE TO DINE

Charlie Clark's Steak House STEAKHOUSE/SEAFOOD   Charlie Clark's, the oldest steakhouse in the White Mountains, has been serving up thick, juicy steaks since 1938 (before that, during Prohibition, the building was used as a sort of backwoods speakeasy). Mesquite-broiled steaks and chicken, as well as seafood and prime rib, fill the menu. To find the place, just look for the building with a fake horse on the roof.

Ariz. 260 at Penrod Ave., Pinetop. © **520/367-4900**. Main courses $10–$22. Early bird dinners Sun–Thurs 5–6:30pm. AE, DC, DISC, MC, V. Daily 5–10pm.

The Christmas Tree Restaurant AMERICAN/CONTINENTAL   Located in a quiet setting off the main drag, this country restaurant serves good old-fashioned American food as well as a few standard Continental offerings. Chicken and dumplings are the specialty of the house, but you can also get a New York steak accompanied by your choice of seafood. Meals are filling, accompanied by everything from delicious pickled beets to Boston clam chowder. As the name implies, a Christmas theme prevails year-round, and there's also a country gift store.

455 Woodland Rd., Lakeside. © **520/367-3107**. Reservations recommended on Sat. Main courses $11–$30. DISC, MC, V. Wed–Sun 5–9pm.

3 Greer & Sunrise Park ⭐

51 miles SE of Show Low; 98 miles SE of Holbrook; 222 miles NE of Phoenix

The tiny community of Greer, set in the lush meadows on either side of the Little Colorado River and surrounded by forests, holds the distinction of being the most picturesque mountain community in Arizona. The elevation of 8,525 feet ensures plenty of snow in winter and pleasantly cool temperatures in summer, and together these two factors have turned Greer into something of an upscale mountain getaway that's popular among lowlanders with an eye for aesthetics. Modern log homes are springing up all over the valley, but Greer is still free of the sort of strip-mall developments that have forever changed the character of Payson and Pinetop-Lakeside.

The Little Colorado River, which flows through the middle of Greer on its way to the Grand Canyon, is little more than a babbling brook up here. Still, it's known for trout fishing, one of the main draws in these parts. Several lakes and ponds also provide good fishing. In winter, cross-country skiing, ice-skating, ice fishing, and sleigh rides are popular. Greer also happens to be the closest community to the Sunrise ski area, which is what gives the village its ski-resort atmosphere.

ESSENTIALS

GETTING THERE   From Phoenix, take U.S. 87 north to Payson and then go east on Ariz. 260, or take U.S. 60 east from Phoenix through Globe and Show Low to Ariz. 260 east. Greer is just a few miles south of Ariz. 260 on Ariz. 373.

VISITOR INFORMATION   Contact the **Round Valley Chamber of Commerce,** 318 E. Main St., Springerville (© **520/333-2123;** www.az-tourist.com).

OUTDOOR PURSUITS

Winter is one of the busiest seasons in Greer, since it's so close to the **Sunrise Park Resort** ski area (© **520/735-7669;** www.sunriseskipark.com). Located just off Ariz. 260 on Ariz. 273, this ski area, the largest and most popular in Arizona, is operated by the White Mountain Apache Tribe. It usually opens in November, but thaws and long stretches without snow can make winters a bit unreliable (snow-making machines enhance the sometimes sparse natural snowfall). Although there are some good advanced runs, beginner and intermediate skiers will be in heaven. We've rarely seen so many green runs starting from the uppermost lifts of a ski area, all of which translates into a very family-oriented place. At the top of 11,000-foot Apache Peak is a day lodge providing meals and a view that goes on forever. A ski school offers lessons for everyone from beginners to advanced skiers. Lift tickets cost $34 for adults and $19 for children. Ski rentals are available here and at numerous shops in Pinetop-Lakeside.

More than 13½ kilometers of groomed cross-country ski trails wind their way through forests of ponderosa pines and across high snow-covered meadows. These trails begin at the **Sunrise Sports Center,** located in the service station at the turnoff for the downhill area. There are also good opportunities for cross-country skiing in Greer, which has 35 miles of developed trails. At 8,500 feet, the alpine scenery is quiet and serene. You can also go for a sleigh ride near Sunrise, offered by **Lee Valley Stables** (© **520/735-7454**) at a cost of $16 ($8 for children) for 45 minutes.

Come summer, the cross-country ski trails become **mountain-biking trails,** and when combined with the nearby **Pole Knoll trail system,** provide mountain bikers with 35 miles of trails of varying degrees of difficulty. Sunrise Park Resort also opens up its slopes to mountain bikers. Bikes can be rented for $15 to $25 for 1 to 2 hours; a lift ticket for the day will run you another $15.

This area offers some of the finest mountain **hiking** in Arizona, and most recommended of all the area trails is the hike up 11,590-foot **Mount Baldy,** the second-highest peak in Arizona. This peak lies on the edge of the White Mountain Apache Indian Reservation and is sacred to the Apaches. Consequently, the summit is off limits to non-Apaches. There are two trailheads for the hike up Mount Baldy. The most popular and scenic route begins 6 miles south of Sunrise Ski Resort (off the gravel extension of Ariz. 273) and follows the West

---

Finds **A Worthwhile Museum**

The **Butterfly Lodge Museum** (© 520/735-7514; www.wmonline.com/ butterflylodge.htm) is a restored historic cabin built in 1914. Owned by James Willard Schultz (a writer) and his son Hart Merriam Schultz (a painter), the museum is a memorial to these two unusual and creative individuals who once called Greer home. It's just off Ariz. 373 between Ariz. 260 and Greer. Memorial Day through Labor Day, it's open Friday through Sunday plus holidays from 10am to 5pm. Admission is $2 for adults and $1 for youths 12 to 17.

Fork of the Little Colorado River. This trail climbs roughly 2,000 feet and is moderately strenuous, and the high elevation often leaves lowland hikers gasping for breath. Hikers can also catch a lift to the top of the hill at Sunrise Ski Resort, which keeps its lifts running in summer for hikers and anyone else interested in the view from on high. A single-ride lift ticket is $8 for adults and $4 for children.

To explore the Greer area from the back of a horse, contact **Lee Valley Stables** (© 520/735-7454), which is located between Greer and Ariz. 260 and offers rides of varying lengths ($20 for 1 hr., $32 for 2 hr.). This company also does wagon rides and cookout rides.

The three Greer Lakes on the outskirts of town—Bunch, River, and Tunnel reservoirs—are popular **fishing** spots. All three hold brown and rainbow trout. On River Reservoir, try the shallows at the south end. On Tunnel Reservoir, you can often do well from shore, especially if fly-fishing, though there is a boat launch. However, it's Big Lake, south of Greer, that has the biggest fishing reputation around these parts. Fishing is also good on Sunrise Lake, but be sure to get a White Mountain Apache Indian Reservation fishing license (available at the Sunrise service station). If you'd like a guide to take you out for a day of fishing the Arizona high country, contact **Troutback Flyfishing Guide Service** (© 800/903-4092 or 520/532-3474; www.troutback.com), which charges $175 per day for one angler and $250 for two.

Sunrise Lake, near the Sunrise ski area, is a popular spot in the summer. Boat rentals are available at the **Sunrise Lake Marina** (© 520/735-7669, ext. 2155). A fishing boat with an outboard motor rents for $45 per day.

WHERE TO STAY
IN GREER

Cattle Kate's Bed & Breakfast ⭐ Consisting of several modern log buildings with a classic mountain feel, Cattle Kate's seems to have patterned itself after the nearby Greer Lodge, but it's much more comfortable than its more rustic (and more famous) neighbor. The rooms, although Spartanly furnished in classic western style, have high ceilings and look out on small trout ponds and the meadows along the Little Colorado River. In the large breakfast room, an elk head is mounted over the fireplace, while an antler chandelier hangs from the ceiling. The only drawback is that you're right on the main road through Greer, though this road is rarely very busy.

80 N. Main St. (P.O. Box 21), Greer, AZ 85927. © 520/735-7744. Fax 520/735-7386. www.wmonline. com/cattlekates. 9 units. $95 double; $135 suite. Rates include continental breakfast. MC, V. **Amenities:** Restaurant (American), lounge; trout ponds, fly-fishing lessons. *In room:* No phone.

Greer Lodge   Only 20 minutes from the Sunrise ski area and boasting its own trout ponds and section of the Little Colorado River, this old lodge is a good choice for both skiers and anglers. Rooms in the main building have nice views of the mountains or river, but tend to get quite a lot of noise from the lobby (which doubles as a TV room). If you're seeking quiet, request a cabin, although these have not been well maintained in recent years. The lodge's multilevel restaurant has walls of glass that look out over a river, meadows, and trout pond, and in the winter, there's a cozy fireplace. In addition to the restaurant, where entrees range from $17 to $26, there's a barbecue area.

44 Main St. (P.O. Box 244), Greer, AZ 85927. © **888/475-6343** or 520/735-7216. Fax 520/735-7720. www.greerlodge.com. 11 units. $120 double; $95 cabin for 2; $210–$280 house. AE, DC, DISC, MC, V. **Amenities:** Restaurant, lounge; fishing ponds, fly-fishing classes; volleyball court; horseshoe pits. *In-room:* No phone.

Red Setter Inn & Cottage ★★   If you're headed up to the mountains for a romantic weekend getaway, this three-story log lodge, the most luxurious in Greer, should be your first choice. The inn is built on the bank of the Little Colorado River, which is only steps away from the decks of some guest rooms. Several units have fireplaces and whirlpool tubs, while others have vaulted ceilings and skylights. Cases full of antique toys and a game room with old arcade games make this inn fun as well as romantic. There's also a housekeeping "cottage" with four bedrooms, three bathrooms, and three fireplaces; two new cabins were under construction at press time. If you stay for 2 nights or more, you get a complimentary picnic lunch to take with you on an outing.

8 Main St. (P.O. Box 133), Greer, AZ 85927. © **888/99-GREER** or 520/735-7441. Fax 520/735-7425. www.redsetterinn.com. 14 units. $135–$195 double; $225 cottage (8-person maximum). Rates include full breakfast. AE, MC, V. **Amenities:** Game room; river fishing. *In room:* Hair dryer, no phone.

Snowy Mountain Inn *Kids*   Set back from the main road down a gravel driveway and shaded by tall pines, the Snowy Mountain Inn has a remote yet very comfortable feel about it. The modern cabins, although a bit cramped inside, are great for family vacations; they come equipped with gas fireplaces, porches, and sleeping lofts, and some have private hot tubs as well. Surrounding the log cabins and main lodge are 100 acres of private forest, so guests have plenty of room to roam. The 1½-acre trout pond is one of the largest in the area.

38721 Rte. 373, Greer, AZ 85927. © **520/735-7576.** Fax 520/735-7705. www.snowymountaininn.com. 12 units. $150–$165 cabin; $205–$385 house. Room rates include continental breakfast. 3- to 5-night minimum during busy times. AE, DISC, MC, V. Pets accepted. **Amenities:** Restaurant, lounge; exercise room; children's playroom; fishing ponds; coin-op laundry. *In room:* TV, kitchen, fridge, coffeemaker, no phone in cabins.

White Mountain Lodge Bed & Breakfast and Cabins   Situated on the road into Greer with a view across an open, marshy stretch of the valley, this recently remodeled lodge was built in 1892 and is the oldest building in Greer (but you'd never know it to look at it). Knotty pine throughout gives the lodge a classic cabin feel, but the many large windows prevent the rooms from feeling too dark. Guest rooms are done up in a Southwestern or country theme; our favorite has a king-size bed and a view up the valley. The cabins, which are perfect for families or two couples to share, are even more comfortable—one has a stone fireplace and a porch swing.

140 Main St. (P.O. Box 143), Greer, AZ 85927. © **888/493-7568** or 520/735-7568. Fax 520/735-7498. www.wmlodge.com. 12 units. $85–$95 double; $85–$195 cabin for 2. Lodge room rates include full breakfast. 2-night minimum on weekends, 3- to 4-night minimum on holidays. AE, DC, DISC, MC, V. **Amenities:** Jacuzzi; coin-op laundry. *In room:* Hair dryer, no phone in rooms.

IN MCNARY

Sunrise Park Lodge   Located 20 miles outside Greer in McNary, this is the closest lodge to the Sunrise ski area and thus a favorite of downhill skiers. About half the rooms overlook Sunrise Lake, and these are worth requesting. The two on-site restaurants are about your only dinner options in the vicinity; there's also a cozy lounge for après-ski drinks.

Hwy. 273, near intersection of Hwy. 260 (P.O. Box 217), McNary, AZ 85930. © **800/772-7669** or 520/735-7669. Fax 520/735-7315. www.sunriseskipark.com. 100 units. Winter $59–$112 double, $155–$295 suite; summer $59–$72 double, $155–$195 suite. AE, DC, DISC, MC, V. **Amenities:** 2 restaurants (American), lounge; small indoor pool; exercise room; 2 Jacuzzis; sauna; volleyball court; bike rentals; courtesy ski-area shuttle. *In room:* A/C, TV.

CAMPGROUNDS

In the immediate vicinity of Greer, there are three campgrounds in Apache-Sitgreaves National Forest. Reservations can be made for the Rolfe C. Hoyer Campground, 1 mile north of Greer on Ariz. 373, and the Winn Campground, 12 miles southwest of Greer on Ariz. 273 (the road past Sunrise Park Resort), by contacting the **National Recreation Reservation Service** (© **800/280-2267;** www.reserveusa.com). Benny Creek, 2 miles north of Greer, does not take reservations. Because of its proximity to Greer and the Greer lakes, Rolfe C. Hoyer is the top choice in the area. There are also several campgrounds nearby on the White Mountain Apache Indian Reservation (no reservations accepted).

WHERE TO DINE

Your best bets in Greer are the dining rooms at the Greer Lodge and Cattle Kate's, both of which serve reasonably priced meals. Both feature a bit of Southwestern fare plus familiar American standards. Hours vary considerably with the seasons and the snowfall. See "Where to Stay," above, for details.

4 Springerville & Eagar

56 miles E of Show Low; 82 miles SE of Holbrook; 227 miles NE of Phoenix

Together the adjacent towns of Springerville and Eagar constitute the northeastern gateway to the White Mountains. Although the towns themselves are at the foot of the mountains, the vistas from around Springerville and Eagar take in all the area's peaks. The two towns like to play up their Wild West backgrounds—in fact, John Wayne liked the area so much that he had a ranch along the Little Colorado River just west of Eagar. Today, large ranches still run their cattle on the windswept plains north of the towns.

It was volcanic activity between 300,000 and 700,000 years ago that gave the land north of Springerville and Eagar its distinctive character. This area, known as the Springerville Volcanic Field, is the third largest volcanic field of its kind in the continental United States (the San Francisco Field near Flagstaff and the Medicine Lake Field in California are both larger). The Springerville Volcanic Field covers an area bigger than the state of Rhode Island and contains 405 extinct volcanic vents. It's the many cinder cones dotting the landscape that give this region such a distinctive appearance. For a brochure outlining a tour of the volcanic field, contact the Round Valley Chamber of Commerce (see "Visitor Information," below).

One other thing you might be curious about is that big dome—it's the Round Valley Ensphere, one of the only domed high-school football stadiums in the country.

ESSENTIALS

GETTING THERE   Springerville and Eagar are in the northeast corner of the White Mountains at the junction of U.S. 60, U.S. 180/191, and Ariz. 260. From Phoenix, there are two routes: Ariz. 87 north to Payson and then Ariz. 260 east, or U.S. 60 east to Globe and then north to Show Low and on to Springerville (or you can take Ariz. 260 from Show Low to Springerville). From Holbrook, take U.S. 180 southeast to St. Johns and U.S. 180/191 south to Springerville. From southern Arizona, U.S. 191 is slow but very scenic.

VISITOR INFORMATION   For information on the Springerville and Eagar areas, contact the **Round Valley Chamber of Commerce** (© **520/333-2123;** www.az-tourist.com).

ANASAZI RUINS

Casa Malpais Archaeological Park *Finds*   Casa Malpais, another Mogollon ruin, is unique in that the pueblo, which dates from A.D. 1250 and was occupied until about 600 years ago, was built to take advantage of existing caves. Many of these caves form a system of catacombs under the pueblo. The only way to visit the ruins is on guided tours that leave from the Casa Malpais museum, which is located in downtown Springerville. At the museum, you'll find exhibits on both the Mogollon people and on dinosaurs that once roamed this region.

318 Main St., Springerville. © 520/333-5375. www.casamalpais.com. Guided tours $5 adults, $4 students and seniors, $3 children under 12. Daily 8am–4pm.

Lyman Lake State Park   Within this state park are the early Anasazi ruins of Rattlesnake Point Pueblo, as well as petroglyphs that date from 10,000 B.C. Some of the petroglyphs are accessible only by boat, and during the summer months you can see them on guided tours.

18 miles north of Springerville. © 520/337-4441. www.pr.state.az.us. Admission $4 per car; tours $2 per person. Park daily daylight hours; tours May–Sept Sat–Sun 10am.

White Mountain Archaeological Center/Raven Site Ruin ⭐   If you've ever dreamed of being an archaeologist, you've got a chance to realize your fantasy here in eastern Arizona. This field school and research center is located on a 5-acre pueblo site where Mogollon and Anasazi artifacts have been found. Hands-on archaeological programs allow visitors to assist in excavating the site while learning the basics of archaeology. Tours of the ruins are also offered.

H.C. 30, Box 30, St. Johns, AZ 85936. © 888/333-5859 or 520/333-5857. www.ravensite.com. Programs $59 adults, $39 children 9–17 (children under 9 not accepted); tours $4 adults, $3 seniors and children 12–17, free for children under 12. May 1–Oct 15 Mon–Sat 10am–4pm. Located 12 miles north of Springerville off U.S. 180/191.

MUSEUMS

A couple of small museums are worth a look if you have the time. The **Reneé Cushman Art Collection** is housed in the L.D.S. (Mormon) Church in Springerville. It consists of one woman's personal collection of European art and antiques. Among the works are an etching attributed to Rembrandt and three pen-and-ink drawings by Tiepolo. The antique furniture dates back to the Renaissance. The museum is open by appointment only; arrange a visit through Reed's Lodge (© **520/333-4323**).

Local history and old automated musical instruments are the focus of the **Little House Museum** (© **520/333-2286**), 7 miles west of Eagar on South Fork Road, off Ariz. 260. Tales of colorful Wild West characters as told by the guide are as much a part of the museum as the displays themselves. To visit,

---

Finds Cowboy Golf

If you've spent much time in Arizona souvenir shops, you've probably seen humorous drawings of cowboys playing golf on the range. Well, each year in June, the **X Diamond Ranch** (② 520/333-2286; www.xdiamondranch. com) west of Springerville actually does hold a cowboy golf tournament. What sets cowboy golf apart from regular golf? Well, first of all, the caddies are horses. Then there's the golfers' attire—cowboy boots, blue jeans, and cowboy hats. And, of course, there are the coffee-can holes and the tall-grass fairways, which are really just cow pastures, filled with all the hazards one would expect in a cow pasture. (A chip shot on this golf course can be a very messy affair!)

---

you'll have to take a guided 90-minute tour. These are offered Thursday through Sunday at 11am and 1pm; the cost is $5 for adults and $2 for children 12 and under.

OUTDOOR PURSUITS

If you're interested in fishing, contact **Troutback Flyfishing Guide Service** (② 800/903-4092 or 520/532-3474; www.troutback.com), which charges $175 per day for one angler and $250 for two. Alternatively, you can head out to the **X Diamond Ranch** (② 520/333-2286), off Ariz. 260 between Eagar and Greer (take County Road 4124). The ranch maintains a section of the Little Colorado River as a fishing habitat. Half-day fishing rates are $25, while a full day will cost $35.

Lyman Lake State Park (② 520/337-4441), 18 miles north of Springerville, is popular for lake fishing. And if it's high summer and you feel like swimming, this is the place to take a dip or even plan a day of water-skiing or sailing.

WHERE TO STAY

Paisley Corner Bed & Breakfast ✦ *Finds*   This lovingly restored 1910-vintage Colonial Revival house in Eagar is one of the most authentic B&Bs we've visited and as such is one of our favorites in the state. (For authentic, read Victorian antiques and dark color schemes.) In contrast to all that authenticity is a room done up to resemble an old soda fountain, complete with vintage jukeboxes and telephone booth. The inn's kitchen features a 1910 gas stove and looks as though it came straight out of a 1920s Sears and Roebuck catalog. Guest rooms on the second floor have antique beds, and two have bathrooms with claw-foot tubs and old pull-chain toilets.

287 N. Main St. (P.O. Box 458), Eagar, AZ 85938. ② 520/333-4665. 4 units. $75–$95 double. Rates include full breakfast. MC, V. **Amenities:** Jacuzzi. *In room:* A/C, hair dryer, no phone.

X Diamond Ranch   Long known for its Little House Museum and trout fishing on the Little Colorado River, this ranch also rents a variety of cabins, ranging from an updated old log cabin to a couple of new ones. Activities include fishing, horseback riding, and touring the ranch's two archaeological sites (for $10 per hr., you can also help excavate these ruins). Perhaps most surprising of all, there's a small day spa on the property. There's no restaurant on the premises, but cabins have full kitchens.

P.O. Box 791, Springerville, AZ 85938. ② 520/333-2286. Fax 520/333-5009. www.xdiamondranch.com. 5 units. $95–$225 double. AE, DISC, MC, V. Off Ariz. 260 between Eagar and Greer (take County Road 4124). **Amenities:** Spa; horseback riding. *In room:* Kitchen, fridge, coffeemaker, no phone.

CAMPGROUNDS

Lyman Lake State Park (✆ 520/337-4441), 18 miles north of Springerville on U.S. 180/191, has a campground. It's very popular with water-skiers, so don't expect much peace and quiet.

WHERE TO DINE

Vintage Hideaway Restaurant *(Finds)* AMERICAN Set in an old house beneath big shade trees, this casual Victorian-inspired restaurant may be most popular with the women of the Springerville-Eagar area, but it still makes a good place for lunch if you're passing through. There's a good selection of sandwiches on homemade bread, as well as soups and salads. Dinners focus on steaks and simple seafood dishes.

389 N. Eagar St. (behind the Community First Bank). ✆ **520/333-4398.** Main courses $7–$17. No credit cards. Mon–Thurs 7am–3pm; Fri 7am–3pm and 5–8:30pm; Sat 5–8:30pm.

5 The Coronado Trail ⊛

Alpine: 28 miles S of Springerville and Eagar; 95 miles N of Clifton and Morenci; 75 miles E of Pinetop-Lakeside

Winding southward from the Springerville-Eagar area to Clifton and Morenci, the Coronado Trail (U.S. 191) is one of the most remote and little-traveled paved roads in the state. Because this road is so narrow and winding, it's slow going—meant for people who aren't in a hurry to get anywhere anytime soon. If you are *not* prone to carsickness, you may want to take a leisurely drive down this scenic stretch of asphalt.

The Coronado Trail is named for the Spanish explorer Francisco Vásquez de Coronado, who came to Arizona in search of gold in the early 1540s. Although he never found it, his party did make it as far north as the Hopi pueblos and would have traveled through this region on their march northward from Mexico. Centuries later, the discovery of huge copper reserves would make the fortunes of the towns of Clifton and Morenci, which lie at the southern end of the Coronado Trail.

It's **Alpine,** at the northern end of the Coronado Trail, that is the main base for today's explorers, who tend to be outdoor types in search of uncrowded trails and trout streams where the fish are still biting. Not far from the New Mexico state line, Alpine offers a few basic lodges and restaurants, plus easy access to the region's many trails.

This area is known as the Alps of Arizona, and Alpine's picturesque setting in the middle of a wide grassy valley at 8,030 feet certainly lives up to this image. Alpine is surrounded by **Apache-Sitgreaves National Forest,** which has miles of trails and several campgrounds. In spring, wildflowers abound and the trout fishing is excellent. In summer, there's hiking on forest trails. In autumn, the aspens in the Golden Bowl on the mountainside above Alpine turn a brilliant yellow, and in winter, visitors come for the cross-country skiing and ice fishing.

ESSENTIALS

GETTING THERE Alpine is 28 miles south of Springerville-Eagar at the junction of U.S. 191, which continues south to Clifton and Morenci, and U.S. 180, which leads east into New Mexico.

VISITOR INFORMATION For more information on the region, contact the **Alpine Area Chamber of Commerce** (✆ 520/339-4330; www.alpine-az.com).

For outdoor information, contact the Apache-Sitgreaves National Forest's **Alpine Ranger District,** P.O. Box 469, Alpine, AZ 85920 (© **520/339-4384**).

OUTDOOR PURSUITS

Fall, when the aspens turn the mountainside gold, is probably the most popular time of year in this area—there are only a few places in Arizona where fall color is worth a drive, and this is one of them.

Not far outside Alpine, there's cross-country skiing at the **Williams Valley Winter Recreation Area,** which doubles as a mountain-biking trail system in summer.

Visitors can play a round of golf at the **Alpine Country Club** (© **520/ 339-4944**), 3 miles east of town off U.S. 180. At 8,500 feet in elevation, this is one of the highest golf courses in the country. Greens fees are $15 for 18 holes.

If you're looking for fish to catch, try **Luna Lake,** east of Alpine off U.S. 180. Here at the lake, you'll also find some easy to moderate mountain-bike trails that usually offer good wildlife-viewing opportunities.

The best hike in the area is the trail up **Escudilla Mountain,** just outside Alpine, where you'll see some of the best displays of aspens in the autumn.

Summer or winter, **Hannagan Meadows,** 23 miles south of Alpine, is the place to be. Here you'll find excellent hiking, mountain biking, and cross-country ski trails. Hannagan Meadows also provides access to the **Blue Range Primitive Area,** which is popular with hikers. The Eagle Trail, which starts 5 miles south of Hannagan Meadows off Eagle Creek Road, is a good place to spot wildlife. It is in the remote wilderness areas near here that a Mexican gray wolf recovery project has been underway for several years. The reintroduction has so far met with mixed success, as wolves have been killed by cars, people, disease, and even mountain lions. Some of the wolves have had to be recaptured because they had strayed out of the area set aside for them or because they had had encounters with humans.

WHERE TO STAY & DINE

Between Springerville-Eagar and Clifton-Morenci, there are nearly a dozen National Forest Service campgrounds. If fishing and boating interest you, head to **Luna Lake Campground,** just east of Alpine on U.S. 180. Reserve for Luna Lake Campground by contacting the **National Recreation Reservation Service** (© **800/280-2267;** www.reserveusa.com). For a more tranquil forest setting, try **Hannagan Meadows Campground** (no reservations accepted), which makes a good base for exploring the Coronado Trail. For information on these camp-grounds, contact the **Alpine Ranger District** (© **520/339-4384**).

If you're looking for someplace to eat, you'll find a couple of basic restaurants in Alpine.

Tal-Wi-Wi Lodge Located 3 miles north of Alpine on U.S. 191, the Tal-Wi-Wi Lodge is nothing fancy—just a rustic lodge popular with anglers and hunters—but it's the best choice in the Alpine area. The deluxe rooms come with a hot tub or woodstove (one unit has both), heat sources that are well appreciated on cold winter nights (Alpine is often the coldest town in Arizona). The furnishings are rustic yet comfortable, and the wood-paneled walls and large front porches give the lodge a classic country flavor. The dining room serves country breakfasts and dinners.

U.S. 191 (P.O. Box 169), Alpine, AZ 85920. © **520/339-4319.** Fax 520/339-1962. www.talwiwilodge.com. 20 units. $65–$95 double. 2-night minimum on holidays. MC, V. Dogs accepted ($10). **Amenities:** Restaurant (American). *In room:* Coffeemaker, no phone.

Tucson

Encircled by mountain ranges and bookended by the two units of Saguaro National Park, Tucson is Arizona's second largest city, and for the vacationer it has everything that Phoenix has to offer, plus a bit more. There are world-class golf resorts, excellent restaurants, art museums, and galleries, an active cultural life, and, of course, plenty of great weather. Tucson also has a long history that melds Native American, Hispanic, and Anglo roots. And with a national park, a national forest, and other natural areas just beyond the city limits, Tucson is a city that celebrates its Sonoran Desert setting.

At Saguaro National Park, you can marvel at the massive saguaro cacti that have come to symbolize the desert Southwest, while at the Arizona–Sonora Desert Museum (actually a zoo), you can acquaint yourself with the myriad flora and fauna of this region. Take a hike or a horseback ride up one of the trails that leads into the wilderness from the edge of the city, and you might even meet up with a few desert denizens on their own turf. Look beyond the saguaros and prickly pears, and you'll find a desert oasis, complete with waterfalls and swimming holes, and, a short drive from the city, a pine forest that's home to the southernmost ski area in the United States.

Founded by the Spanish in 1775, Tucson was built on the site of a much older Native American village. The city's name comes from the Pima

Indian word *chukeson,* which means "spring at the base of black mountain," a reference to the peak now known simply as "A Mountain." From 1867 to 1877, Tucson was the territorial capital of Arizona, but eventually the capital was moved to Phoenix. Consequently, Tucson did not develop as quickly as Phoenix and still holds fast to its Hispanic and Western heritage.

Tucson has a history of valuing quality of life over development. Back in the days of urban renewal, Tucson's citizens turned back the bulldozers and managed to preserve at least some of the city's old Mexican character. Likewise, today, in the face of the sort of sprawl that has given Phoenix the feel of a landlocked Los Angeles, advocates for controlled growth are fighting hard to preserve both Tucson's desert environment and the city's unique character.

The struggle to retain an identity distinct from other Southwestern cities is ongoing, and despite long, drawn-out attempts to breathe life into the city's core, known as the Tucson Downtown Arts District, the past few years have seen the loss of downtown's vibrancy as shops, galleries, and restaurants have moved out to the suburbs. However, downtown Tucson still has its art museum, convention center, and historic neighborhoods, and there is still a belief that this part of the city will one day find its stride.

Despite this minor shortcoming, Tucson remains Arizona's most beautiful and most livable city. With the

Tucson at a Glance

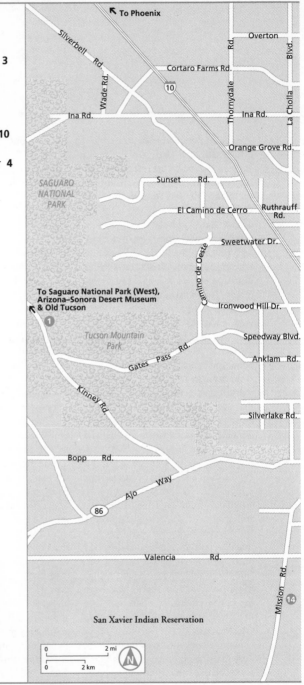

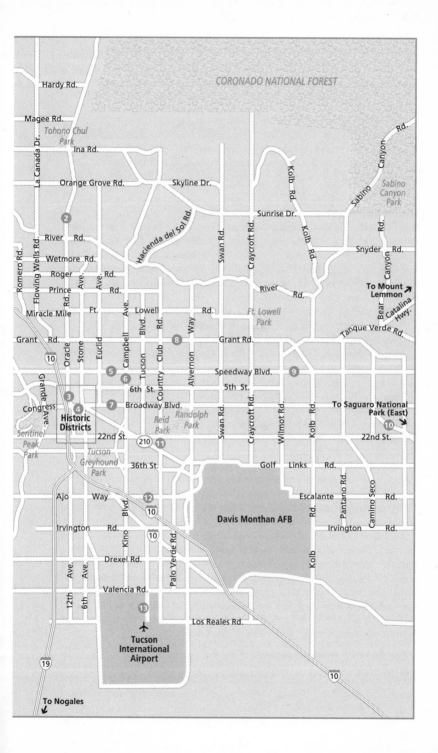

Hardy Rd.

Magee Rd.

Tohono Chul Park

Ina Rd.

La Canada Dr.

Orange Grove Rd.

Skyline Dr.

CORONADO NATIONAL FOREST

Sabino Canyon Rd.

Kolb Rd.

Sunrise Dr.

Sabino Canyon Park

Romero Rd.

Flowing Wells Rd.

River Rd.

Wetmore Rd.

Roger Rd.

Prince Rd.

Miracle Mile

Grant Rd.

Oracle Rd.

Stone Ave.

Euclid Ave.

Ft. Rd.

Campbell Ave.

Lowell Blvd.

Tucson Blvd.

Country Club Rd.

Alvernon Way

Rd.

Kolb Rd.

Snyder Rd.

River Rd.

Ft. Lowell Park

Bear Canyon Rd.

Catalina Hwy.

To Mount Lemmon ↗

Tanque Verde Rd.

Grant Rd.

Speedway Blvd.

5th St.

6th St.

Broadway Blvd.

Congress

Grande Ave.

Historic Districts

Sentinel Peak Park

22nd St.

Tucson Greyhound Park

36th St.

Ajo Way

Irvington Rd.

12th Ave.

6th Ave.

Kino Blvd.

Drexel Rd.

Valencia Rd.

Reid Park

Randolph Park

Swan Rd.

Craycroft Rd.

Wilmot Rd.

Kolb Rd.

Golf Links Rd.

To Saguaro National Park (East) ↘

22nd St.

Escalante

Pantano Rd.

Camino Seco Rd.

Irvington Rd.

Kolb Rd.

Davis Monthan AFB

Palo Verde Rd.

Tucson International Airport

Los Reales Rd.

To Nogales ↙

Santa Catalina Mountains for a backdrop, Tucson boasts one of the most dramatic settings in the Southwest, and whether you're taking in the mountain vistas from the tee box of the 12th hole, the saddle of a palomino, or a table for two, we're sure you'll agree that Tucson makes a superb winter vacation destination.

1 Orientation

Not nearly as large and spread out as Phoenix and the Valley of the Sun, Tucson is small enough to be convenient, yet large enough to be sophisticated. Compared to Phoenix, the mountains ringing the city of Tucson are bigger and closer to town, and the desert is equally close.

ARRIVING

BY PLANE Located 6 miles south of downtown, **Tucson International Airport** (© 520/573-8000) is served by many airlines, including **Aero México** (© 800/237-6639; www.aeromexico.com), **Alaska** (© 800/426-0333; www.alaskaair.com), **American** (© 800/433-7300; www.im.aa.com), **America West** (© 800/235-9292; www.americawest.com), **Continental** (© 800/525-0280; www.continental.com), **Delta** (© 800/221-1212; www.delta.com), **Northwest/KLM** (© 800/225-2525; www.nwa.com), **Shuttle by United** (© 800/748-8853; www.united.com), **Southwest** (© 800/435-9792; www.iflyswa.com), and **United** (© 800/241-6522; www.united.com).

At the airport, you'll find car-rental desks, regularly scheduled shuttle vans to downtown, and taxis. **Visitor information centers** in both baggage-claim areas can give you brochures and reserve a hotel room if you haven't done so already.

Many resorts and hotels in Tucson provide free or competitively priced airport shuttle service. **Arizona Stagecoach** (© **520/889-1000**) operates daily 24-hour van service to downtown Tucson and the foothills resorts. You'll find the vans outside the center of the baggage-claim area. Fares for two people range from about $16.50 to downtown to $32.50 to the foothills resorts. It takes between 45 minutes and 1 hour to reach the foothills resorts. To return to the airport, it's best to call at least a day before your scheduled departure.

You'll find taxis waiting in the same area, or you can call **Yellow Cab** (© **520/624-6611**) or **Allstate Cab** (© **520/798-1111**). A taxi to downtown costs around $16, to the resorts about $24 to $38.

Sun Tran (© **520/792-9222;** www.suntran.com), the local public transit, operates bus service to and from the airport, although you'll have to make a transfer to reach downtown. The bus at the airport is no. 25 (ask for a transfer when you board); at the Roy Laos Transit Center, transfer to no. 16 for downtown. The fare is $1. Route 25 from the airport operates Monday through Friday from about 6:30am to 7:30pm, Saturday from about 7:30am to 7:30pm, and Sunday from about 8:30am to 7:30pm. Departures are every hour. It takes between 45 minutes and 1 hour to reach downtown.

BY CAR **I-10,** the main east-west interstate across the southern United States, passes through Tucson as it swings north to Phoenix. **I-19** connects Tucson with the Mexican border at Nogales. **Ariz. 86** heads southwest into the Papago Indian Reservation, and **Ariz. 79** leads north toward Florence and eventually connects with **U.S. 60** into Phoenix.

If you're headed downtown, take the Congress Street exit off I-10. If you're going to one of the foothills resorts north of downtown, you'll probably want to take the Ina Road exit.

BY TRAIN   Tucson is served by **Amtrak** (© **800/872-7245;** www.amtrak.com) passenger rail service. The *Sunset Limited,* which runs between Orlando and Los Angeles, stops in Tucson. The **train station** is at 400 E. Toole Ave. (© **520/623-4442**), in the heart of downtown and within walking distance of the Tucson Convention Center, El Presidio Historic District, and a few hotels. You'll see taxis waiting to meet the train.

BY BUS   Greyhound (© **800/231-2222** or 520/792-3475) connects Tucson to the rest of the United States through its extensive system. The bus station is at 2 S. Fourth Ave., across the street from the Hotel Congress in the Downtown Arts District.

VISITOR INFORMATION

The **Metropolitan Tucson Convention and Visitors Bureau (MTCVB),** 110 S. Church St. (on the corner of Broadway), Suite 9100 (© **800/638-8350,** 888/2-TUCSON, or 520/624-1817; www.visitTucson.org), is an excellent source of information on Tucson and environs. You can contact the bureau before leaving home or stop in at the visitor center, which is stocked with brochures and has helpful staff members to answer your questions. The visitor center is open Monday through Friday from 8am to 5pm, Saturday and Sunday from 9am to 4pm

CITY LAYOUT

MAIN ARTERIES & STREETS   Tucson is laid out on a grid that's fairly regular in the downtown areas, but becomes less orderly the farther you go from the city center. In the foothills, where Tucson's most recent growth has occurred, the grid system breaks down completely because of the hilly terrain. Major thoroughfares are spaced at 1-mile intervals, with smaller streets filling in the squares created by the major roads.

The main **east-west roads** are (from south to north) 22nd Street, Broadway Boulevard, Speedway Boulevard, Grant Road (with Tanque Verde Road as an extension), and Ina Road/Skyline Drive. The main **north-south roads** are (from west to east) Miracle Mile/Oracle Road, Stone/Sixth Avenue, Campbell Avenue, Country Club Road, and Alvernon Road. **I-10** cuts diagonally across the Tucson metropolitan area from northwest to southeast.

In **downtown Tucson,** Congress Street and Broadway Boulevard are the main east-west streets; Stone Avenue, Sixth Avenue, and Fourth Avenue are the main north-south streets.

FINDING AN ADDRESS   Because Tucson is laid out on a grid, finding an address is relatively easy. The zero (or starting) point for all Tucson addresses is the corner of Stone Avenue, which runs north and south, and Congress Street, which runs east and west. From this point, streets are designated either north, south, east, or west. Addresses usually, but not always, increase by 100 with each block, so that an address of 4321 E. Broadway Blvd. should be 43 blocks east of Stone Avenue. In the downtown area, many of the streets and avenues are numbered, with numbered streets running east and west and numbered avenues running north and south.

STREET MAPS   The best way to find your way around Tucson is to pick up a map at the visitor information center at the airport or at the MTCVB (see "Visitor Information," above) for $2. The MTCVB offers a free map in the *Tucson Official Visitors Guide.* The maps handed out by car-rental agencies are not very detailed, but will do for some purposes. Local gas stations also sell detailed maps.

NEIGHBORHOODS IN BRIEF

El Presidio Historic District
Named for the Spanish military garrison that once stood on this site, the neighborhood is bounded by Alameda Street on the south, Main Avenue on the west, Franklin Street on the north, and Church Avenue on the east. El Presidio was the city's most affluent neighborhood in the 1880s, and many large homes from that period have been restored and now house restaurants, arts-and-crafts galleries, and a bed-and-breakfast inn. The Tucson Museum of Art anchors the neighborhood.

Barrio Histórico District   Another 19th-century neighborhood, the Barrio Histórico is bounded on the north by Cushing Street, on the west by the railroad tracks, on the south by 18th Street, and on the east by Stone Avenue. The Barrio Histórico is characterized by Sonoran-style adobe row houses that directly abut the street with no yards, a style typical in Mexican towns. Although a few restaurants and galleries dot the neighborhood, most restored buildings serve as offices. This is still a borderline neighborhood where restoration is a slow, ongoing process, so try to avoid it late at night.

Armory Park Historic District
Bounded by 12th Street on the north, Stone Avenue on the west, 19th Street on the south, and Second Avenue and Third Avenue on the east, the Armory Park neighborhood was Tucson's first historic district. Today this area is undergoing a renaissance.

Downtown Arts District   This neighborhood encompasses a bit of the Armory District, a bit of El Presidio District, and the stretch of Congress Street and Broadway Boulevard west of Toole Avenue. Although the area is home to several galleries, nightclubs, and hip cafes, it continues to struggle to survive as an arts district. It is mostly frequented by the young and the homeless. Many young travelers make the Hotel Congress their base while in Tucson.

Fourth Avenue   Running from University Boulevard in the north to Ninth Street in the south, Fourth Avenue is the favored shopping district of cash-strapped college students. Shops specialize primarily in ethnic and used/vintage clothing as well as handcrafted items from around the world. Twice a year, in spring and late fall, the street is closed to traffic for a colorful street fair. Plenty of restaurants, bars, and clubs make this the city's favorite college nightlife district as well.

The Foothills   Encompassing a huge area of northern Tucson, the foothills contain the city's most affluent neighborhoods. Elegant shopping plazas, modern malls, world-class resorts, golf courses, and expensive residential neighborhoods are surrounded by hilly desert at the foot of the Santa Catalina Mountains.

2 Getting Around

BY CAR

Unless you plan to stay by the pool or on the golf course, you'll probably want to rent a car. See "Getting Around" in chapter 2, "Planning Your Trip to Arizona," for details on car rentals in Arizona. Luckily, rates are fairly economical. At press time, Budget was charging $183 per week or $32 per day for a compact car with unlimited mileage in Tucson.

The following agencies have offices at Tucson International Airport; several have offices in other parts of the city as well, so be sure to ask if there's a more convenient location for pickup or drop-off of your car. Because taxes, use fees, and surcharges add up to about 20% on car rentals at the airport, you might want to consider renting at some other location, where you can avoid paying some of these taxes. Among the Tucson car-rental agencies are **Alamo** (© 800/327-9633; www.alamo.com), **Avis** (© 800/331-1212; www.avis.com), **Budget** (© 800/527-0700; www.budget.com), **Dollar** (© 800/800-4000; www. dollar.com), **Enterprise** (© 800/736-8222; www.enterprise.com), **Hertz** (© 800/654-3131; www.hertz.com), **National** (© 800/227-7368; www. nationalcar.com), and **Thrifty** (© 800/367-2277; www.thrifty.com).

Downtown Tucson is still a relatively easy place to find a parking space, and parking fees are low. There are two huge parking lots at the south side of the Tucson Convention Center, a couple of small lots on either side of the Tucson Museum of Art (one at Main Avenue and Paseo Redondo, south of El Presidio Historic District, and one at the corner of Council Street and Court Avenue), and parking garages beneath the main library and El Presidio Park. You'll find plenty of metered parking on the smaller downtown streets. Almost all Tucson hotels and resorts provide free parking.

Lanes on several major avenues in Tucson change direction at rush hour to facilitate traffic flow, so pay attention to signs. These tell you the time and direction of traffic in the lanes.

BY PUBLIC TRANSPORTATION

BY BUS   Covering much of the Tucson metropolitan area, **Sun Tran** (© 520/792-9222; www.suntran.com) public buses are $1 for adults or students, 40¢ for seniors, and free for children 5 and under.

The **Downtown-Ronstadt Transit Center,** at Congress Street and Sixth Avenue, is served by about 30 regular and express bus routes to all parts of Tucson. The bus system does not extend to such tourist attractions as the Arizona–Sonora Desert Museum, Old Tucson, Saguaro National Park, or the foothills resorts, and thus is of limited use to visitors. However, Sun Tran does provide a shuttle for sports games and special events. Call the above phone number for information.

BY TROLLEY   Although they don't go very far, the restored electric streetcars of **Old Pueblo Trolley** (© 520/792-1802) are a fun way to get from the Fourth Avenue shopping district to the University of Arizona. The trolleys operate on Friday from 6 to 10pm, Saturday from noon to midnight, and Sunday from noon to 6pm. The fare is $1 for adults and 50¢ for children 6 to 12. On Sunday, the fare is 25¢ for everyone.

T.I.C.E.T., or Tucson Inner City Express Transit (© 520/747-3778), operates three free downtown-area shuttles. For visitors, the only route that is of much use is the Blue Route, which has stops near the visitor center, the Tucson Convention Center, the Tucson Children's Museum, Old Town Artisans, and the Tucson Museum of Art. Buses operate Monday through Saturday.

BY TAXI

If you need a taxi, you'll have to phone for one. **Yellow Cab** (© 520/624-6611) and **Allstate Cab** (© 520/798-1111) provide service throughout the city. Fares start at about $1.50, and after that it's about $1.50 per mile. Although distances in Tucson are not as great as those in Phoenix, it's still a good 10 or more miles from the foothills resorts to downtown Tucson, so expect to pay at least $10 for any taxi ride. Most resorts offer or can arrange taxi service to major tourist attractions.

Shoppers should keep in mind that several Tucson malls offer free shuttle service from hotels and resorts. Be sure to ask at your hotel before paying for a ride to a mall.

ON FOOT

Downtown Tucson is compact and easily explored on foot. Many old streets in the downtown historic neighborhoods are narrow and much easier to appreciate if you leave your car in a parking lot. On the other hand, several major attractions, including the Arizona–Sonora Desert Museum, Old Tucson Studios, Saguaro National Park, and Sabino Canyon, require quite a bit of walking, often on uneven footing, so be sure to bring a good pair of walking shoes.

FAST FACTS: Tucson

Baby-Sitters Most hotels can arrange a baby-sitter for you, and many resorts feature special programs for children on weekends and throughout the summer. If your hotel can't help, call **A-1 Messner Sitter Service** (② 520/881-1578), which will send a sitter to your hotel.

Car Rentals See "Getting Around," earlier in this chapter.

Climate See "When to Go," in chapter 2.

Dentist Call the Arizona Dental Association (② **800/866-2732**) or Dental Referral Service (② **800/577-7317**) for a referral.

Doctor For a doctor referral, ask at your hotel or call University Health Connection (② **520/694-8888**).

Emergencies For fire, police, or medical emergency, phone ② **911.**

Eyeglass Repair **Alvernon Optical** has several stores around town where you can have your glasses repaired or replaced. Locations include 440 N. Alvernon Way (② **520/327-6211**), 7043 N. Oracle Rd. (② **520/297-2501**), and 7123 E. Tanque Verde Rd. (② **520/296-4157**).

Hospitals The **Tucson Medical Center** is at 5301 E. Grant Rd. (② **520/327-5461**), and the **University Medical Center** is at 1501 N. Campbell Ave. (② **520/694-0111**).

Information See "Visitor Information" under "Orientation," earlier in this chapter.

Internet Access The hot spot in downtown Tucson is the **Library of Congress,** at the Hotel Congress, 311 E. Congress St. (② **520/622-2708**). The rate for Internet access is $6 per hour. Access is free at the main public **library,** in downtown Tucson at 101 N. Stone Ave. (② **520/791-4393**).

Lost Property If you lose something at the airport, call ② **520/573-8156;** if you lose something on a Sun Tran bus, call ② **520/792-9222.** If you lose something and you have no idea where, try the **Tucson Police Department Found-Recovered Property Office** (② 520/791-4458).

Newspapers & Magazines The *Arizona Daily Star* is Tucson's morning daily, while the *Tucson Citizen* is the afternoon daily. The *Tucson Weekly* is the city's news-and-arts journal, published on Thursdays.

Pharmacies Walgreens has stores all over Tucson. Call ✆ 800/WALGREENS for the Walgreens pharmacy that's nearest you or that's open 24 hours a day.

Police In case of an emergency, phone ✆ 911.

Post Office There's a post office in downtown Tucson at 141 S. 6th Ave. (✆ 800/275-8777), open Monday through Friday from 8:30am to 5pm and Saturday from 9am to noon.

Radio KXCI (91.3 FM) has an alternative mix of programming and is a favorite with local Tucsonans, while KUAT (90.5 FM) has all-classical programming and is a good station for news. KUAZ (89.1 FM) is the National Public Radio station.

Safety Tucson is surprisingly safe for a city of its size. However, the Downtown Arts District isn't all that lively after dark, and you should be particularly alert if you're down here for a performance of some sort. An exception is during Downtown Saturday Night festivities.

Just to the south of downtown lies a poorer section of the city that's best avoided after dark unless you are certain of where you're going. Otherwise, take the same precautions you would in any other city.

When driving, be aware that many streets in the Tucson area are subject to flooding when it rains. Heed warnings about possible flooded areas and don't try to cross a low area that has become flooded. Find an alternate route instead.

Taxes In addition to the 5% state sales tax, Tucson levies a 2% city sales tax. State car-rental tax is 5% (plus there are other taxes and surcharges on car rentals; at the airport, these add up to around 20%). The hotel tax is 9.5% to 10.5% in Tucson. Outside the city limits, you'll likely pay 7.5% to 8.5%

Taxis See "Getting Around," earlier in this chapter.

Transit Information For information on Sun Tran public buses, call ✆ 520/792-9222.

Weather Phone ✆ 520/881-3333 for the local weather forecast.

3 Where to Stay

Although Phoenix still holds the title of Resort Capital of Arizona, Tucson is not far behind, and this city's resorts boast much more spectacular settings than most comparable properties in Phoenix and Scottsdale. As far as nonresort accommodations go, Tucson has a wider variety than Phoenix—partly because several historic neighborhoods have become home to bed-and-breakfast inns. The presence of several guest ranches within a 20-minute drive of Tucson adds to the city's diversity of accommodations. Business and budget travelers are well served with all-suite and conference hotels, as well as plenty of budget chain motels.

At the more expensive hotels and resorts, summer rates, usually in effect from May to September or October, are often less than half what they are in winter. Surprisingly, temperatures usually aren't unbearable in May or September, which makes these good times to visit if you're looking to save money. When making late spring reservations, always be sure to ask when rates are scheduled to go up

Tucson Accommodations

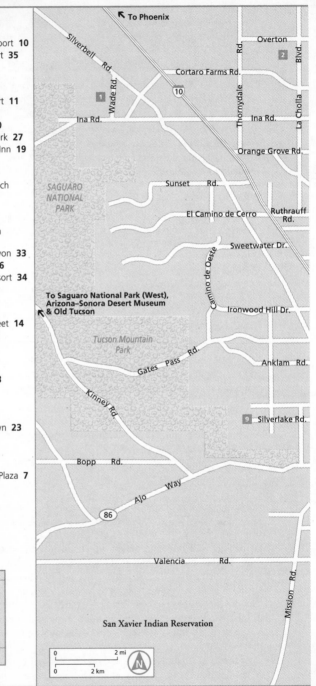

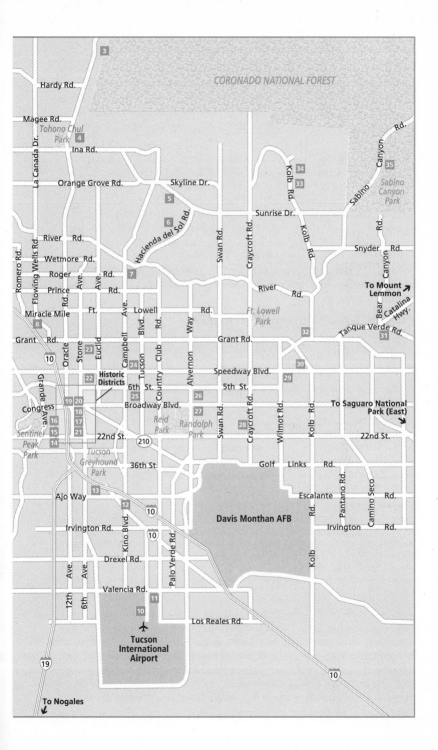

or down. If you aren't coming to Tucson specifically for the winter gem and mineral shows, then you'll save quite a bit if you avoid the last week in January and the first 2 weeks in February, when hotels around town generally charge exorbitant rates.

Most hotels offer special packages, weekend rates, various discounts (such as for AARP members), and free accommodations for children, so it helps to ask about these when you reserve. Nearly all hotels have smoke-free and wheelchair-accessible rooms.

BED & BREAKFASTS   If you're looking to stay in a B&B, several agencies can help. The **Arizona Association of Bed and Breakfast Inns,** P.O. Box 22086, Phoenix, AZ 86002-2086 (℗ **800/284-2589;** www.arizona-bed-breakfast.com), has several members in Tucson. **Advance Reservations Inn Arizona/Mi Casa-Su Casa Bed & Breakfast Reservation Service,** P.O. Box 950, Tempe, AZ 85280-0950 (℗ **800/456-0682** or 480/990-0682; www.azres.com), will book you into one of its many homestays in the Tucson area (or elsewhere in the state), as will **Arizona Trails Bed & Breakfast Reservation Service,** P.O. Box 18998, Fountain Hills, AZ 85269-8998 (℗ **888/799-4284** or 480/837-4284; fax 480/816-4224; www.arizonatrails.com), which also books tour and hotel reservations.

DOWNTOWN & THE UNIVERSITY AREA
EXPENSIVE

Arizona Inn ✦✦✦   With its pink-stucco buildings and immaculately tended gardens, the historic Arizona Inn, opened in 1930, is an oasis offering Old Arizona charm and modern levels of comfort. Most guest rooms have original furniture as well as reproductions of period furnishings. Some units have fireplaces, and most suites have private patios or enclosed sun porches, as well as sitting rooms. Although bathrooms are generally fairly small and have their original fixtures, this only adds to the charm. Strolling the grounds, relaxing in the antiques-filled library, or cozying into your room, it's easy to conjure up those slower-paced days when guests would spend the entire winter here. The inn's main dining room is a casually elegant hall with plenty of outdoor seating as well (see "Where to Dine," later in this chapter). Although the pool is small, it's surrounded by fragrant flowering trees and vines.

2200 E. Elm St., Tucson, AZ 85719. ℗ 800/933-1093 or 520/325-1541. Fax 520/320-2182. www.arizona inn.com. 89 units. Late Jan to mid-Apr $225–$245 double, from $299 suite; mid-Apr to May $189 double, from $235 suite; June to mid-Sept $134 double, from $184 suite; mid-Sept to mid-Dec $140 double, from $193 suite; mid-Dec to mid-Jan $163 double, from $224 suite. AE, DC, MC, V. **Amenities:** 2 restaurants (new American, Southwestern), 2 lounges; small outdoor pool; 2 Har-Tru tennis courts; croquet court; well-equipped exercise room; saunas; concierge; room service; massage; baby-sitting. *In room:* A/C, TV, dataport, hair dryer, iron.

Doubletree Hotel at Reid Park ✦   Located across the street from Randolph Park municipal golf course, the Doubletree is midway between the airport and downtown Tucson and could be thought of as an in-town budget golf resort. Although the hotel does a lot of convention business and sometimes feels crowded, the gardens, with their citrus trees and roses, are almost always tranquil. The rooms are divided between a nine-story building that offers views of the valley (even-numbered rooms face the pool, odd-numbered rooms face the mountains) and a two-story building with patio rooms overlooking the garden and pool area. All are comfortably appointed with contemporary furnishings.

445 S. Alvernon Way, Tucson, AZ 85711. ☎ **800/222-TREE** or 520/881-4200. Fax 520/323-5225. www.double treehotels.com. 295 units. Nov–early Apr $79–$159 double, from $215 suite; mid-Apr to mid-May and late Sept to mid-Dec $99–$159 double, from $175 suite; late May to mid-Sept $59–$79 double, from $175 suite; late Dec–early Jan $69–$99 double, from $175 suite. AE, DC, DISC, MC, V. Pets accepted ($50 deposit). **Amenities:** 2 restaurants (Southwestern, Mexican), 2 lounges; outdoor pool; adjacent municipal 18-hole golf course; 3 tennis courts; exercise room; access to nearby health club; Jacuzzi; business center; room service; laundry service; dry cleaning. *In room:* A/C, TV, dataport, minibar, coffeemaker, hair dryer.

The Lodge on the Desert ⚘⚘   Dating from 1936, the Lodge on the Desert is a restored romantic getaway in central Tucson. Set amid neatly manicured lawns and flower gardens shaded by palm, orange, and eucalyptus trees, the lodge offers a lush and relaxing retreat comparable in many ways to the Arizona Inn (though certainly not as deluxe). On the grounds are numerous hacienda-style adobe buildings tucked amid the cactus and orange trees. Inside the rooms, you'll find a mix of contemporary and Southwestern furnishings; many units have beamed ceilings or fireplaces, and some are carpeted while others have tile floors. Although the pool (the original) is very small, it has a good view of the Catalinas.

306 N. Alvernon Way, Tucson, AZ 85711. ☎ **800/456-5634** or 520/325-3366. Fax 520/327-5834. www. lodgeonthedesert.com. 35 units. Mid-Jan to May $169–$289 double; June–Sept $79–$159 double; Oct to mid-Jan $119–$209 double. AE, DC, DISC, MC, V. Pets accepted ($10 per day, $50 deposit). **Amenities:** Restaurant (Southwestern), lounge; small outdoor pool; concierge; room service; baby-sitting; dry cleaning. *In room:* A/C, TV, coffeemaker, hair dryer, iron.

MODERATE

Adobe Rose Inn ⚘   Located in a quiet residential neighborhood a few blocks from the University of Arizona campus, this B&B, with its strikingly angular adobe buildings, has the feel of a little village. Our favorite room is right off the entrance hall and has a brick floor, beehive fireplace, and colorful stained-glass windows. For extra privacy, you can opt for the room in the cottage out back. Almost the first thing you see as you step through the front door is the blue of the swimming pool through a large picture window. Furnishings throughout the inn are of peeled lodgepole pine logs for a sort of contemporary Southwestern rustic look.

940 N. Olsen Ave., Tucson, AZ 85719. ☎ **800/328-4122** or 520/318-4644. Fax 520/325-0055. www. aroseinn.com. 5 units. Mid-Dec to May $95–$125 double; June–Aug $65–$85 double; Sept to mid-Dec $75–$95 double. Rates include full breakfast. AE, MC, V. **Amenities:** Small outdoor pool; access to nearby health club; Jacuzzi. *In room:* A/C, TV, coffeemaker, hair dryer.

Catalina Park Inn ⚘⚘   Located close to downtown and overlooking a shady park, this inn has the look of a Mediterranean villa. Built in 1927, the home has been lovingly restored by owners Mark Hall and Paul Richard, and many interesting and playful touches enliven the classic interior (a crystal chandelier in a bathroom, a formal dining room, and a rustic breakfast room). The huge basement room is one of our favorites. Not only does it conjure up the inside of an adobe, but there's also a whirlpool tub in a former cedar closet and a separate toilet room with a display of colorful Fiesta Ware. Two upstairs rooms have balconies, while two units in a separate cottage across the garden offer more contemporary styling than the rooms in the main house.

309 E. First St., Tucson, AZ 85705. ☎ **800/792-4885** or 520/792-4541. www.catalinaparkinn.com. 6 units. $114–$144 double (lower rates in summer and fall). Rates include full breakfast. AE, DISC, MC, V. *In room:* A/C, TV, hair dryer, iron.

El Presidio Bed & Breakfast Inn ★★ Built in 1886 and lovingly restored by innkeeper Patti Toci and her husband, Jerry, El Presidio is a mix of Victorian and adobe architectural styles. Only steps from the Tucson Museum of Art, Old Town Artisans, and El Charro Cafe, this is the quintessential Tucson territorial home. There are two high-ceilinged suites in the main house, while the other two units, both with kitchenettes, are arranged around a shady courtyard at the center of which is a Mexican fountain. All are decorated with antiques and original art (much of it by Jerry). In addition to the filling breakfast in the sunroom, complimentary drinks, fruit, and treats are served in the afternoon and evening.

297 N. Main Ave., Tucson, AZ 85701. © 800/349-6151 or 520/623-6151. Fax 520/623-3860. 4 units. $95–$125 double. Rates include full breakfast. 2-night minimum. No credit cards. **Amenities:** Access to nearby health club; guest laundry. *In room:* A/C, TV, hair dryer.

Elysian Grove Market *Finds* Located in the Barrio Histórico just a block away from El Tiradito shrine, this former general store (the building still has the old store name painted on the front wall) is now an unusual little inn filled with rustic Mexican antiques and Hispanic folk art. The two suites contain high-ceilinged living rooms that incorporate all manner of salvaged architectural details, colorful textiles, and original grocery-store fixtures (including an old walk-in meat locker that has been turned into a kitchen). Each suite has a bedroom on the ground level and a second bedroom (rather dark but cool) down a flight of steps. Although this funky barrio B&B isn't for everyone, the old Mexican atmosphere and abundance of art will appeal to travelers searching for a place with the feel of Old Tucson.

400 W. Simpson St., Tucson, AZ 85701. © 520/628-1522. www.bbonline.com/az/elysiangrove. 2 units. $85 double. Rates include continental or Mexican breakfast. No credit cards. *In room:* No phone.

The Royal Elizabeth ★★ Located only a block away from the Temple of Music and Art in downtown Tucson, the Royal Elizabeth is situated in an 1878 Victorian adobe home. The odd combination of architectural styles makes for a uniquely Southwestern-style inn. In classic 19th-century Tucson fashion, the old home looks thoroughly unpretentious from the outside. Inside, however, you'll find beautiful woodwork and gorgeous Victorian-era antique furnishings. Guest rooms open off a large, high-ceilinged central hall.

204 S. Scott Ave., Tucson, AZ 85701. © 877/670-9022 or 520/670-9022. Fax 520/629-9710. www.royal elizabeth.com. 6 units. Sept–May $120–$170 double; June–Aug $85–$115 double. Rates include full breakfast. AE, DISC, MC, V. **Amenities:** Small outdoor pool; access to nearby health club; Jacuzzi. *In room:* A/C, TV/VCR, dataport, fridge, safe.

INEXPENSIVE

In addition to the choices listed below, you'll find dozens of budget chain motels along I-10 as it passes through downtown. Among the better ones are **Days Inn Tucson,** 222 S. Freeway, exit 258 (© **520/791-7511**), charging $55 to $135 double; **Motel 6—Tucson/Congress Street,** 960 S. Freeway, exit 258 (© **520/628-1339**), and **Motel 6—Tucson/22nd Street,** 1222 S. Freeway, exit 259 (© **520/624-2516**), both charging $40 to $54; and **Super 8—Tucson/Downtown,** 1248 N. Stone St., exit 257 (© **520/622-6446**), with rates of $39 to $99.

Clarion Hotel & Suites Santa Rita ★ *Value* This hotel, only a block from the convention center and close to El Presidio Historic District, isn't exactly luxurious, and you'd never know that it's nearly 100 years old. However, it was completely remodeled a few years ago and makes a decent, economical

---

Kids **Family-Friendly Hotels**

Loews Ventana Canyon Resort *(see p. 305)* With a playground, kids' club, croquet court, table tennis, basketball hoop, and its own waterfall, this resort has plenty to keep the kids busy. There's a hiking trail that starts from the edge of the property, and Sabino Canyon Recreation Area is nearby.

Smuggler's Inn *(see p. 304)* Built around a large central courtyard with a very tropical feel, this hotel is a good choice for families on a budget. In addition to a pool and whirlpool, there are lawns for the kids to play on and a meandering pond that's home to fish and ducks.

Westin La Paloma *(see p. 306)* Kids get their own lounge and game room here. In the summer and during holiday periods, there are special children's programs so parents can have a little free time. To top it all off, there's a great water slide in the pool area.

Guest Ranches *(see p. 311)* The Tucson area has several guest ranches, most of which are family oriented. Kids can play cowboy to their hearts' content, riding the range and singing songs by campfire.

---

downtown address. Some of the guest rooms have balconies. Although the place stays busy with conventioneers, it can also be a good choice for vacationers. Best of all: This hotel is home to Café Poca Cosa, Tucson's most innovative Mexican restaurant (see "Where to Dine," later in this chapter).

88 E. Broadway Blvd., Tucson, AZ 85701. ✆ 800/CLARION or 520/622-4000. Fax 520/620-0376. 153 units. Oct–May $89–$249 double; June–Sept $69–$189 double. Rates include full breakfast. AE, DC, DISC, MC, V. Pets accepted ($50 deposit, $25 nonrefundable). **Amenities:** Small outdoor pool; access to nearby health club; Jacuzzi; sauna; business center; coin-op laundry; dry cleaning. *In room:* A/C, TV, dataport, fridge, coffeemaker, hair dryer, iron.

Ghost Ranch Lodge ★ *(Finds* Although Miracle Mile was once Tucson's main drag, today it's looking a bit shabby. One exception is the Ghost Ranch Lodge, which opened in 1941 and was for many years one of the desert resorts that catered to northern visitors who stayed for the winter. If you're looking for affordable Old Tucson, this is it. Situated on 8 acres, the lodge has a justly famous cactus garden, orange grove, and extensive lawns that together create an oasis atmosphere. The guest rooms were refurbished recently but retain a bit of western flavor, with beamed ceilings, painted brick walls, and patios covered by red-tile roofs. The lodge's dining room has a poolside patio and a view of the Santa Catalina Mountains.

801 W. Miracle Mile, Tucson, AZ 85705. ✆ 800/456-7565 or 520/791-7565. Fax 520/791-3898. www.ghost ranchlodge.com. 83 units. Mid-Jan to early Apr $86–$135 double; early Apr–early June $50–$80 double; early June–early Oct $44–$75 double; early Oct to mid-Jan $46–$90 double. Rates include continental breakfast. AE, DISC, MC, V. Pets accepted. **Amenities:** Restaurant (American); small outdoor pool; Jacuzzi; coin-op laundry. *In room:* A/C, TV.

Hotel Congress *(Finds* Located in the heart of downtown Tucson conveniently near the Greyhound and Amtrak stations, the Hotel Congress, built in 1919 to serve railroad passengers, once played host to John Dillinger. Today, it operates as a budget hotel and youth hostel catering primarily to backpacking European travelers. Although the place is far from luxurious, the lobby has been restored to its original Southwestern elegance (straight out of a film-noir set). With antique telephones and old radios that really work, guest rooms remain true to their historical character, so don't expect anything fancy (like TVs). Some bathrooms have tubs only, while others have showers only. There's a classic little diner/cafe off the lobby (think Edward Hopper meets Gen X), as well as a tiny though very genuine Western bar. At night, the Club Congress is a popular (and loud) dance club (guests can pick up free earplugs at the front desk). There's even a cybercafe called the Library of Congress.

311 E. Congress St., Tucson, AZ 85701. (*C*) **800/722-8848** or 520/622-8848. Fax 520/792-6366. www. hotcong.com. 40 units. $30–$80 double; $16 per person in shared hostel rooms. AE, DISC, MC, V. Pets accepted ($25 nonrefundable deposit plus $10 per night). **Amenities:** Restaurant, saloon, nightclub.

EAST TUCSON
MODERATE

Doubletree Guest Suites ★★ *Value* With surprisingly reasonable rates throughout the year, this all-suite hotel is a good choice for both those who need plenty of space and those who want to be in the east-side business corridor. The five-story brick building is arranged around two long garden courtyards, one of which has a large pool and whirlpool. In fact, the pool and gardens are the best reason for vacationers to stay here. The two-room suites feature contemporary furnishings and such amenities as refrigerators, microwaves, and irons.

6555 E. Speedway Blvd., Tucson, AZ 85710. (*C*) **800/222-TREE** or 520/721-7100. Fax 520/721-1991. www.doubletreetucson.com. 304 suites. $69–$170 double. AE, DC, DISC, MC, V. Pets accepted ($50 nonrefundable fee). **Amenities:** Restaurant (American); large outdoor pool; exercise room; access to nearby health club; Jacuzzi; concierge; business center; room service; coin-op laundry; dry cleaning. *In room:* A/C, TV, dataport, fridge, coffeemaker, hair dryer.

Hawthorn Suites Ltd. ★ Although it looks rather stark from the outside and is located adjacent to an older shopping center, the Hawthorn Suites is surprisingly pleasant inside. Built around four tranquil and lushly planted garden courtyards, the motel has large rooms (for the most part), some with kitchenettes. There's no restaurant on the premises, but Tanque Verde Road is Tucson's restaurant row, making this a good choice for a foodie on a budget.

7007 E. Tanque Verde Rd., Tucson, AZ 85715. (*C*) **800/527-1133** or 520/298-2300. Fax 520/298-6756. www.hawthorn.com. 90 units. Jan–Mar $79–$149 double; Apr–May $59–$89; June–Sept $55–$69 double; Oct–Dec $79–$89 double. Rates include full breakfast and evening cocktails. AE, DC, DISC, MC, V. Pets accepted ($25 nonrefundable fee). **Amenities:** Small outdoor pool; access to nearby health club; Jacuzzi; coin-op laundry; dry cleaning. *In room:* A/C, TV, dataport, coffeemaker, hair dryer, iron.

Smuggler's Inn ★ *Value* *Kids* Built around an attractive garden and pond, the Smuggler's Inn is a very comfortable and economically priced hotel. There's nothing about this place to remind you that you're in the middle of the desert—in fact, the neatly trimmed lawns and tall palm trees give the garden a tropical look—but the grounds are much nicer than those at most comparably priced hotels in the area. Amid these tropical surroundings are a pool, whirlpool, and putting green. If you bring the family, the kids will have plenty of space in which to run around. The spacious guest rooms, which are generally in good shape, have modern furnishings and balconies or patios.

6350 E. Speedway Blvd. (at Wilmot), Tucson, AZ 85710. (*C*) **800/525-8852** or 520/296-3292. Fax 520/722-3713. www.smugglersinn.com. 150 units. Jan–Mar $99–$119 double, $125–$135 suite; Apr–Dec $59–$99 double, $99–$125 suite. Rates include continental breakfast. AE, DISC, DC, MC, V. **Amenities:** Restaurant, lounge; outdoor pool; access to nearby health club; Jacuzzi; putting green; coin-op laundry; dry cleaning. *In room:* A/C, TV, dataport, coffeemaker, hair dryer, iron.

SunStone Guest Ranch ★ *(Finds)*   Although not exactly a guest ranch, this inn offers a beautiful ranchlike setting in a pocket of grassland surrounded by desert and suburbs. Although you'll feel as if you're on a remote spread, the gourmet dining of Tucson's restaurant row is only a 10-minute drive away. Accommodations are in a pair of 1920s baked-adobe buildings fronted by long verandas. Rooms are large and decorated in modern Southwest style, with the occasional Mission-style antique. Surrounding the buildings are lush green lawns and huge old mesquite trees that keep the grounds delightfully shady.

2545 N. Woodland Rd., Tucson, AZ 85749. © 520/749-1928. Fax 520/749-2456. www.sunstoneguest ranch.com. 12 units. Sept–May $145 double; June–Aug $95 double. Rates include continental breakfast. MC, V. **Amenities:** Outdoor pool; tennis court; basketball court; volleyball court; horseshoes; Jacuzzi. *In room:* A/C, hair dryer.

THE FOOTHILLS
VERY EXPENSIVE

The Lodge at Ventana Canyon ★★★   Golf is the name of the game at this small boutique resort, set within a gated country-club community at the base of the Santa Catalina Mountains. The lodge, though small, manages to offer plenty of big-resort amenities and places an emphasis on personal service. Thanks to the two spectacular Tom Fazio–designed golf courses, this place appeals almost exclusively to avid golfers. The Mountain Course's third hole plays across a deep ravine and is one of the most photographed holes in the West. The accommodations are in spacious suites, most of which have walls of windows facing the Catalinas, modern Mission-style furnishings, small kitchens, and large bathrooms with oversized tubs (some of the old-fashioned footed variety). Some suites have balconies, cathedral ceilings, and spiral stairs that lead to sleeping lofts.

6200 N. Clubhouse Lane, Tucson, AZ 85750. © 800/WYNDHAM or 520/577-1400. Fax 520/577-4065. www.wyndham.com. 49 units. Jan–early Apr $279–$519 1-bedroom suite, $449–$719 2-bedroom suite; early Apr to late May $189–$419 1-bedroom suite, $359–$619 2-bedroom suite; late May to early Sept $139–$175 1-bedroom suite, $239–$275 2-bedroom suite; early Sept to Dec $179–$399 1-bedroom suite, $349–$599 2-bedroom suite (plus $16 nightly service charge, year-round). AE, DC, DISC, MC, V. **Amenities:** Restaurant (new American), 2 lounges, snack bar; outdoor pool; 2 acclaimed 18-hole golf courses; 12 tennis courts; exercise room; Jacuzzi; saunas; concierge; pro shop; salon; room service; massage and spa treatments; babysitting; laundry service; dry cleaning. *In room:* A/C, TV/VCR, dataport, kitchen, minibar, coffeemaker, hair dryer, iron, safe.

Loews Ventana Canyon Resort ★★★ *(Kids)*   For breathtaking scenery, fascinating architecture, and superb resort facilities (including two Tom Fazio golf courses and a full-service spa), no other Tucson accommodation can compare. The Santa Catalina Mountains rise up behind the property, and despite its many amenities, the resort is firmly planted in the desert. Flagstone floors in the lobby and tables with boulders for bases give the public rooms a rugged but luxurious appeal. Guest rooms have beds angled out from corners and drapes hung from the headboards. Balconies overlook city lights or mountains, and some rooms have fireplaces. Bathrooms include tiny TVs and bathtubs built for two. The Ventana Room is one of Tucson's finest restaurants, while the Flying V has good food and good views (see "Where to Dine," later in this chapter, for both). The lobby lounge serves afternoon tea before becoming an evening piano bar. In addition to numerous other amenities, there are jogging and nature trails and a playground on the grounds.

7000 N. Resort Dr., Tucson, AZ 85750. © 800/23-LOEWS or 520/299-2020. Fax 520/299-6832. www.loews hotels.com. 398 units. Early Jan to late May $185–$365 double, from $750 suite; late May to early Sept $95–$150 double, from $295 suite; early Sept to early Jan $175–$325 double, from $700 suite. AE, DC, DISC,

MC, V. **Amenities:** 4 restaurants (new American, Southwestern, American), 2 lounges; 2 outdoor pools with mountain views; 2 acclaimed 18-hole golf courses; 8 tennis courts; basketball court; croquet court; exercise room; full-service spa; 2 Jacuzzis; bike rentals; children's programs; concierge; tour desk; courtesy shuttle; business center; salon; 24-hour room service; massage; baby-sitting; laundry service; dry cleaning. *In room:* A/C, TV, dataport, minibar, coffeemaker, hair dryer, iron, safe.

Omni Tucson National Golf Resort & Spa ★★★   As the name implies, golf is the driving force behind most stays at this boutique resort, which is the site of the annual Tucson Open PGA golf tournament; if you don't have your own clubs, you might feel a bit out of place. Then again, you could just avail yourself of the full-service health spa, which underwent a $3-million renovation in 2000 and is one of the best in Arizona. Most of the spacious guest rooms cling to the edges of the golf course and have their own patios or balconies; hand-carved doors and Mexican tile counters in the bathrooms contribute a Spanish colonial feel, while the furniture has a classically modern Mediterranean style. Aside from the least expensive rooms, the accommodations here are the best and most luxurious in Tucson.

2727 W. Club Dr. (off Magee Rd.), Tucson, AZ 85742-8919. (2) **800/528-4856** or 520/297-2271. Fax 520/297-7544. www.omnihotels.com. 167 units. Jan to early Apr $275–$295 double, $295–$395 suite; early Apr to late May $175–$220 double, $220–$260 suite; late May to early Sept $110–$135 double, $175–$195 suite; early Sept to Dec $190–$210 double, $210–$310 suite (plus $7 nightly service charge). AE, DC, DISC, MC, V. **Amenities:** 2 restaurants (American, Southwestern), 2 lounges; 2 large pools; championship 27-hole golf course; 4 tennis courts; basketball court; volleyball court; health club; full-service spa; 2 Jacuzzis; concierge; pro shop; salon; 24-hour room service; massage; laundry service; dry cleaning. *In room:* A/C, TV, dataport, minibar, coffeemaker, hair dryer, iron, safe.

Sheraton El Conquistador Resort & Country Club ★★★   With the Santa Catalina Mountains rising up behind the property, this resort in Tucson's northern foothills boasts a spectacular setting. However, keep in mind that if you stay here, you'll be at least 30 minutes from downtown. Most guest rooms are built around a central courtyard with a large pool and manicured lawns. This area is often taken over by conventioneers, so those seeking peace and quiet may want to opt for a room in the separate casitas area, which has its own pool. For the full Tucson experience, ask for a mountain-view room. All accommodations feature Southwestern-influenced contemporary furniture, spacious marble bathrooms, and balconies or patios. While golf on the resort's three nine-hole courses is the favorite pastime here, nongolfers have plenty of options, too. In the Mexican restaurant, strolling mariachis entertain, while in the steakhouse, cowboy vittles and cancan dancers are the order of the day.

10000 N. Oracle Rd., Tucson, AZ 85737. (2) **800/325-7832** or 520/544-5000. Fax 520/544-1222. www. sheratonelconquistador.com. 428 units. Jan to late May $259–$490 double, from $339 suite; late May to early Sept $119–$290 double, from $179 suite; late Sept to Dec $219–$420 double, from $299 suite (plus $8 service fee, year-round). AE, DC, DISC, MC, V. Pets accepted. **Amenities:** 4 restaurants (Southwestern, steakhouse, Mexican, American), 2 lounges; snack bar; four pools; 45-hole golf course; 31 tennis courts; 7 racquetball courts; basketball court; volleyball court; 2 exercise rooms; spa; 6 Jacuzzis; sauna; bike rentals; horseback riding; children's programs; concierge; tour desk; car-rental desk; courtesy shopping shuttle; business center; shopping arcade; salon; room service; massage; baby-sitting; laundry service; dry cleaning. *In room:* A/C, TV, dataport, minibar, coffeemaker, hair dryer, iron, safe.

Westin La Paloma ★★★ *Kids*   If grand scale is what you're looking for in a resort, this is the place. Everything about the Westin is big—big portico, big lobby, big lounge, big pool area—and from the resort's sunset-pink Mission-revival buildings, set in the middle of Tucson's prestigious foothills, there are also very big views. While adults appreciate the resort's tennis courts, exercise facilities, and abundant poolside lounge chairs, kids love the 177-foot water slide.

Guest rooms are situated in 27 low-rise buildings surrounded by desert land-scaping. Couples should opt for the king rooms (ask for a mountain- or golf-course view if you don't mind spending a bit more). French-inspired Southwestern cuisine is the specialty at Janos, one of Tucson's finest restaurants (see "Where to Dine," later in this chapter).

3800 E. Sunrise Dr., Tucson, AZ 85718. (*)' **800/WESTIN-1** or 520/742-6000. Fax 520/577-5878. www.westin.com. 487 units. Jan to late May $299–$349 double, from $429 suite; late May to early Sept $139–$159 double, from $239 suite; early Sept to Dec $239–$279 double, from $359 suite (plus $10 service fee, year-round). AE, DC, DISC, MC, V. **Amenities:** 3 restaurants (Southwester, American), 2 lounges, 3 snack bars (including a swim-up bar); 3 pools (1 for adults only); 27-hole golf course; 10 tennis courts; racquetball court; volleyball court; croquet court; health club; full-service Elizabeth Arden Red Door spa; three Jacuzzis; bike rentals; children's programs; game room; concierge; car-rental desk; business center; shopping arcade; pro shops; salon; 24-hour room service; massage; baby-sitting; laundry service; dry cleaning. In room: A/C, TV, dataport, minibar, coffeemaker, hair dryer, iron, safe.

EXPENSIVE

Hacienda del Sol Guest Ranch Resort ★★ (Finds)   With its colorful South-west styling, historic character, mature desert gardens, and ridge-top setting, Hacienda del Sol is one of the most distinctive hotels in Tucson. The small resort, once a guest ranch, exudes the sort of Old Tucson atmosphere available at only a couple of other lodgings in the city. The lodge's basic rooms are evoca-tive of Spanish posadas and old Mexican inns and have rustic and colorful Mex-ican character, with a decidedly artistic flair. These units are in the resort's oldest buildings, set around flower-filled courtyards. If you prefer more modern, spa-cious accommodations, ask for a suite; if you want loads of space and the chance to stay where Katherine Hepburn and Spencer Tracy may have once stayed, ask for a casita. With large terraces for alfresco dining, the Grill is one of Tucson's best restaurants (see "Where to Dine," later in this chapter).

5601 N. Hacienda del Sol Rd., Tucson, AZ 85718. (*)' **800/728-6514** or 520/299-1501. www.haciendadelsol. com. 33 units. Nov to mid-May $140 double, $210 hacienda, $305 suite, $345–$425 casita; mid-May to mid-Sept $75 double, $95 hacienda, $145 suite, $180–$225 casita; mid-Sept to Nov $120 double, $150 hacienda, $215 suite, $265–$335 casita. Rates include continental breakfast. AE, MC, V. **Amenities:** Small outdoor pool with view of the Catalinas; tennis court; Jacuzzi; horseback riding; massages. In room: A/C, TV.

Westward Look Resort ★★ (Value)   Built in 1912 as a dude ranch, the West-ward Look is the oldest resort in Tucson and one of the most reasonably priced resorts in the city. Set in the Catalina foothills, the property is surrounded by desert, and although it doesn't have its own golf course, it does have an excellent health spa and plenty of tennis courts. There are also jogging and nature trails. If you aren't a golfer but do enjoy resort amenities, this is one of your best Tucson choices. Upstairs from the lobby, you'll find an interesting little natural-history exhibit, which is part of this resort's emphasis on nature and the out-doors. The large guest rooms, all of which were recently renovated, have a Southwestern flavor and private patios or balconies with great views of the city. The Gold Room restaurant serves reliably excellent Continental and South-western cuisine (see "Where to Dine," later in this chapter).

245 E. Ina Rd., Tucson, AZ 85704. (*)' **800/722-2500** or 520/297-1151. Fax 520/297-9023. www.westwardlook. com. 244 units. Jan to Apr $169–$349 double; May $129–$189 double; June–Sept $99–$189 double; Oct–Dec $149–$209 double. AE, DC, DISC, MC, V. Pets accepted. **Amenities:** Restaurant (Continental/Southwestern), lounge; 3 pools; 8 tennis courts; basketball court; volleyball court; health club; full-service spa; 3 Jacuzzis; bike rentals; horseback riding; concierge; tour desk; business center; tennis pro shop; salon; room service; mas-sage; baby-sitting; laundry service; dry cleaning. In room: A/C, TV, dataport, minibar, coffeemaker, hair dryer, iron, safe.

MODERATE

Windmill Inn at St. Philip's Plaza ⭐ *Value*   Located in St. Philip's Plaza, which has several great restaurants and an array of upscale shops, this all-suite hotel offers a good location and spacious accommodations. Every unit contains a work desk, double vanity, wet bar, refrigerator, microwave, three phones (one in the bathroom), two TVs—basically everything to make the business traveler or vacationer comfortable for a long stay. Extras include free local calls, a lending library, and complimentary use of bicycles (the Rillito River bike path starts in back of the hotel).

4250 N. Campbell Ave., Tucson, AZ 85718. ℂ 800/547-4747 or 520/577-0007. Fax 520/577-0045. www.windmillinns.com. 122 units. Mid-Jan to mid-Apr $135–$145 double; late Apr to early June and mid-Sept to mid-Jan $99–$120 double; early June to mid-Sept $67–$85 double. Rates include continental breakfast. AE, DC, DISC, MC, V. **Amenities:** Outdoor pool; access to nearby health club; Jacuzzi; bikes; coin-op laundry; laundry service; dry cleaning. *In room:* A/C, TV, fridge, microwave.

WEST OF DOWNTOWN
EXPENSIVE

La Tierra Linda Guest Ranch Resort ⭐⭐ *Finds*   Set on 30 acres in northwest Tucson and adjacent to Saguaro National Park, this guest ranch balances convenience to the city with a desert setting. Originally opened as a dude ranch back in the 1930s, La Tierra Linda is now a surprisingly resortlike little property. Guest rooms vary in size and layout, and the suites, which give you plenty of extra space, are generally worth the added expense. Throughout the property is lots of interesting stonework incorporated into the buildings; a viewing deck provides an excellent view of Sombrero Peak in the Tucson Mountains. The ranch's restaurant serves good Southwestern dishes, so there's little need to make the long drive into town. An "Old West" town is the setting for cookouts and hayrides, as well as a collection of antique wagons. There's also a petting zoo for the kids.

7501 N. Wade Rd., Tucson, AZ 85743. ℂ 888/872-6241 or 520/744-7700. Fax 520/579-9742. www.latierralinda.com. 14 units. Early Dec to mid-May $155–$165 double, $215–$335 suite; mid-May to early Sept $90–$100 double, $125–$200 suite; early Sept to early Dec $115–$125 double, $160–$250 suite. Rates include full breakfast (American plan also available). AE, DC, DISC, MC, V. **Amenities:** Restaurant (Southwestern), lounge; small outdoor pool; access to nearby health club; tennis court; Jacuzzi in a stone gazebo; horseback riding; bike rentals; volleyball court; horseshoe pits. *In room:* A/C, TV, fridge, coffeemaker, hair dryer.

Starr Pass Golf Suites ⭐⭐   Located 3 miles west of I-10, Starr Pass is both the closest golf resort to downtown and the most economically priced golf resort in the city. It's a condominium resort, however, which means you won't find the sort of service you get at Tucson's other resorts (but neither will you pay as much). Accommodations are in privately owned Santa Fe–style casitas that can be rented as two-bedroom units or broken down into a master suite and a standard hotel-style room. The master suites are more comfortable, with fireplaces, full kitchens, and a Southwestern style throughout. The smaller hotel-style rooms are a bit cramped and much less lavishly appointed. The desert-style 18-hole golf course is one of the best courses in the city. There are also hiking/biking trails on the property.

3645 W. Starr Pass Blvd., Tucson, AZ 85745. ℂ 800/503-2898 or 520/670-0500. Fax 520/670-0427. www.starrpasstucson.com. 80 units. Mid-Jan to mid-May $179 double, $309 suite, $429 casita; mid-May to Sept $89 double, $139 suite, $199 casita; Oct to mid-Jan (except Dec 24–Jan 1) $119 double, $179 suite, $249 casita; Dec 24–Jan 1 $169 double, $299 suite, $419 casita. AE, DC, DISC, MC, V. **Amenities:** Restaurant (Continental/Southwestern), lounge; outdoor pool; 18-hole golf course; 2 tennis courts; exercise room; Jacuzzi; pro shop. *In room:* A/C, TV, kitchen, coffeemaker, hair dryer.

MODERATE

Casa Tierra ⋆ If you've come to Tucson to be in the desert and you really want to be a *part* of the desert, then this secluded B&B is well worth considering. Built to look as if it has been here since Spanish colonial days, the modern adobe home is surrounded by 5 acres of cactus and palo verde trees on the west side of Saguaro National Park. There are great views, across a landscape full of saguaros, to the mountains to the north, and sunsets are enough to take your breath away. The guest rooms open onto a landscaped central courtyard, which is surrounded by a covered seating area. The outdoor whirlpool spa makes a perfect stargazing spot.

11155 W. Calle Pima, Tucson, AZ 85743. ℂ 886/254-0006 or 520/578-3058. Fax 520/578-8445. www.casatierratucson.com. 4 units. Aug 15–June 15 $125–$185 double, $175–$300 suite. Rates include full breakfast. 2-night minimum. AE, MC, V. Closed June 16–Aug 14. **Amenities:** Well-equipped exercise room; Jacuzzi; concierge. *In room:* A/C, TV, hair dryer.

NEAR THE AIRPORT
MODERATE

Best Western Inn at the Airport If you're the type who likes to get as much sleep as possible before rising to catch a plane, this motel right outside the airport entrance will do it for you—there's no place closer.

7060 S. Tucson Blvd., Tucson, AZ 85706. ℂ 800/772-3847 or 520/746-0271. Fax 520/889-7391. 149 units. Jan–Mar $69–$129 double; Apr–May and Sept–Oct $59–$89 double; June–Aug and Nov–Dec $49–$79 double. Rates include continental breakfast. AE, DC, DISC, MC, V. **Amenities:** Restaurant (American), lounge; small outdoor pool; Jacuzzi; tennis court; exercise room. *In room:* A/C, TV, dataport.

Clarion Hotel Tucson Airport Located just outside the airport exit, this hotel provides convenience and some great amenities, including a complimentary nightly cocktail reception. The rooms are generally quite large; the king rooms are particularly comfortable. The poolside units, in addition to being convenient for swimming and lounging, have small fridges.

6801 S. Tucson Blvd., Tucson, AZ 85706. ℂ 800/526-0550 or 520/746-3932. Fax 520/889-9934. www. clarionhotel.com. 191 units. Jan–Mar $89–$129 double; Apr–Aug $59–$79 double; Sept–Oct $69–$89 double; Nov–Dec $59–$79 double. Rates include full breakfast. AE, DC, DISC, MC, V. **Amenities:** Restaurant (eclectic), lounge; outdoor pool; Jacuzzi; courtesy airport shuttle; exercise room; room service; coin-op laundry; laundry service; dry cleaning. *In room:* A/C, TV, coffeemaker.

INEXPENSIVE

There are numerous budget motels near the Tucson Airport. These include **Motel 6**, 755 E. Benson Hwy., exit 262 off I-10 (ℂ **520/622-4614**), and **Motel 6**, 1031 E. Benson Hwy., exit 262 off I-10 (ℂ **520/628-1264**), both charging $46 to $52 double; and **Super 8—Tucson/East**, 1990 S. Craycroft Rd., exit 265 off I-10 (ℂ **520/790-6021**), with double rates of $43 to $86.

OUTLYING AREAS
NORTH OF TUCSON

Across the Creek at Aravaipa Farms ⋆⋆ *Finds* Located 60 miles north of Tucson on one of the only year-round streams in southern Arizona, this B&B is a romantic getaway near one of the state's most spectacular desert wilderness areas. Because the inn is 3 miles up a gravel road and then across a stream (high-clearance vehicles recommended), it's a long way to a restaurant. Consequently, innkeeper Carol Steele, who formerly operated restaurants in the Scottsdale area, provides all meals. Guests entertain themselves hiking in the nearby Aravaipa Canyon Wilderness, bird-watching, and cooling off in Aravaipa Creek. The casitas are eclectically designed and decorated with a mix of folk art and rustic Mexican furniture. There are tile floors, stone-walled showers, and shady verandas. For either a romantic weekend or a vigorous vacation exploring the desert, this inn makes an ideal base.

89395 Aravaipa Rd., Winkelman, AZ 85292. ✆ **520/357-6901**. www.aravaipafarms.com. 5 units. $225 double. Rates include all meals. 2-night minimum on weekends and holidays. No credit cards. **Amenities:** Dining room. *In room:* No phone.

C.O.D. Ranch ★ *Finds* Located 45 minutes north of Tucson, this place is primarily used by groups and family reunions, but with its two restored 1880s adobe houses and remote setting overlooking the San Pedro Valley, the lovingly restored ranch is also an ideal spot for a tranquil getaway between the desert and the mountains. The decor is a mix of rustic Mexican furnishings and contemporary art by regional artists. Several of the casitas have full kitchens, and two have fireplaces. A section of the Arizona Trail is within a few miles of the property, and you can arrange horseback rides to a ranch where Buffalo Bill Cody once lived. Wagon rides are also available.

P.O. Box 241, Oracle, AZ 85623. ✆ **800/868-5617** or 520/615-3211. Fax 520/896-2271. www.codranch.com. 12 units (2 with shared bathroom). $95–$225 double. Meals $40–$50 per person per day extra. MC, V. **Amenities:** Dining room; small outdoor pool; Jacuzzi; horseback riding; massage.

SOUTH OF TUCSON

Santa Rita Lodge This lodge in the shady depths of Madera Canyon is used almost exclusively by bird-watchers, and getting a room in late spring, when the birds are out in force, can be difficult. The rooms and cabins are large and fairly comfortable; natural-history programs and guided bird walks are offered between March and August. Note that the nearest restaurants are 13 miles away, so you should bring food for your stay.

H.C. 70, Box 5444, Sahuarita, AZ 85629. ✆ **520/625-8746**. Fax 520/648-1186. www.santaritalodge.com. 12 units. $73–$78 double in lodge; $83–$93 double in cabins. AE, MC, V. *In room:* A/C, TV, kitchen.

SPAS

Canyon Ranch Health Resort ★★★ Canyon Ranch, one of America's premier health spas, offers the sort of complete spa experience that's available at only a handful of places around the country. On staff are doctors, nurses, psychotherapists and counselors, fitness instructors, massage therapists, and tennis, golf, and racquetball pros. Services offered include health and fitness assessments; health, nutrition, exercise, and stress-management consultations, seminars, presentations, and evaluations; fitness classes and activities; massage therapy; herbal and aroma wraps; facials, manicures, pedicures, haircuts, and styling; private sports lessons; makeup consultations; cooking demonstrations; and art classes. Guests stay in a variety of spacious and very comfortable accommodations. Three gourmet, low-calorie meals are served daily with options for total daily caloric intake (don't worry, you won't go hungry).

8600 E. Rockcliff Rd., Tucson, AZ 85750. ✆ **800/742-9000** or 520/749-9000. Fax 520/749-7755. www.canyonranch.com. 185 units. Oct to mid-June 4-night package from $3,730 double; mid-June to Sept 4-night package from $2,010 double. Rates include all meals and a variety of spa services and programs. AE, DC, DISC, MC, V. No children under 14 accepted (with exception of infants in the care of personal nannies). **Amenities:** Dining room; aquatic center and 4 pools; 7 tennis courts; basketball court; racquetball and squash courts; 7 exercise rooms; 62,000-square-foot spa complex; Jacuzzis; saunas; steam rooms; bike rentals; concierge; tour desk; courtesy airport shuttle; salon; room service; massage; coin-op laundry; laundry service; dry cleaning. *In room:* A/C, TV/VCR, dataport, hair dryer, safe.

Miraval ✸✸✸ Focusing on what it calls "life balancing," Miraval, one of the country's most exclusive health spas, emphasizes stress management, self-discovery, and relaxation rather than facials and mud baths. To this end, activities at the all-inclusive resort include meditation, tai chi, Pilates, and yoga; more active types can go hiking, mountain biking, and rock climbing (on an outdoor climbing wall). Of course, such desert classics as horseback riding, tennis, volleyball, and swimming are also available. However, staying busy isn't really the objective here; learning a new way of life is the ultimate goal. Miraval offers lifestyle-management workshops, fitness/nutrition consultations, cooking demonstrations, exercise classes, an "equine experience" program, massage, and skin care and facials. Of the three swimming pools, one is a three-tiered leisure pool surrounded by waterfalls and desert landscaping. Guest rooms, many of which have views of the Santa Catalina Mountains, are done in a Southwestern style. For the most part, the very large bathrooms have showers but no tubs.

5000 E. Via Estancia Miraval, Catalina, AZ 85739. © **800/232-3969** or 520/825-4000. Fax 520/825-5163. www.miravalresort.com. 106 units. Mid-Jan to late May $990–$1,140 double, $1,540–$1,840 suite; late May–Sept $650–$930 double, $1,1,180–$1,480 suite; Oct to mid-Jan $940–$1,190 double, $1,590–$1,890 suite (plus 17.5% service charge, year-round). Rates include all meals and a variety of spa services and programs. AE, DISC, MC, V. **Amenities:** 2 restaurants, 2 snack lounges; 4 pools; 2 tennis courts; volleyball court; croquet court; superbly equipped exercise room; spa; 3 Jacuzzis; saunas; steam rooms; horseback riding; concierge; courtesy airport shuttle; salon; room service; massage; guest laundry; laundry service; dry cleaning. *In room:* A/C, TV/VCR, dataport, fridge, coffeemaker, hair dryer, iron, safe.

GUEST RANCHES

Lazy K Bar Ranch ✸ Homesteaded in 1933 and converted to a dude ranch in 1936, the Lazy K Bar Ranch covers 160 acres adjacent to Saguaro National Park. There are plenty of nearby hiking and riding trails, and if you have a hankering for city life, downtown Tucson is only 20 minutes away. Ranch activities include horseback rides, hayrides, cattle drives, and cookouts, as well as nature talks, guided hikes, rappelling, and stargazing. The guest rooms vary in size and comfort level (some have whirlpool tubs); try for one of the newest units, which are absolutely gorgeous. Family-style meals consist of hearty American ranch food, with cookouts some nights.

8401 N. Scenic Dr., Tucson, AZ 85743. © **800/321-7018** or 520/744-3050. Fax 520/744-7628. www. lazykbar.com. 23 units. Oct to mid-Dec $245–$309 double; mid-Dec to Apr $284–$362 double; May–Sept $206–$252 double (plus 16% service charge, year-round). Rates include all meals and horseback riding. 3-night minimum. AE, DISC, MC, V. **Amenities:** Dining room, lounge; small outdoor pool; 2 tennis courts; volleyball court; basketball court; horseshoe pits; Jacuzzi; horseback riding and lessons; bikes; courtesy airport shuttle. *In room:* A/C, no phone.

Tanque Verde Ranch ✸✸ Want to spend long days in the saddle but don't want to give up resort luxuries? Then Tanque Verde Ranch, which was founded in the 1880s and still has some of its original buildings, is for you. This is far and away the most luxurious guest ranch in Tucson. It borders Saguaro National Park and the Coronado National Forest, ensuring plenty of room for horseback riding. The bird-watching here is excellent (more than 220 species have been seen), and there are nature trails and guided hikes, wildlife-viewing ramadas (shaded patios), a nature center, and evening lectures and performances. The guest rooms are spacious and comfortable, with fireplaces and patios in many units. The new casitas are absolutely huge and among the most luxurious accommodations in the state. The dining room, which overlooks the Rincon Mountains, sets impressive buffets. There are also breakfast horseback rides, poolside luncheons, and cookout rides. An old foreman's cabin houses a cantina.

14301 E. Speedway Blvd., Tucson, AZ 85748. © 800/234-DUDE or 520/296-6275. Fax 520/721-9426. www.tanqueverderanch.com. 75 units. Mid-Dec to Apr $320–$500 double; May–Sept $260–$375 double; Oct to mid-Dec $280–$395 double. Rates include all meals. AE, DISC, MC, V. **Amenities:** Dining room, lounge; indoor and outdoor pools; 5 tennis courts; exercise room; Jacuzzi; saunas; horseback riding and lessons; horseshoe pits; basketball and volleyball courts; children's programs; car-rental desk; courtesy airport shuttle with 4-night stay; tennis pro shop; baby-sitting; self-service laundry; dry cleaning. *In room:* A/C, dataport, fridge.

White Stallion Ranch ✺ *Kids*　Set on 3,000 acres of desert just over the hill from Tucson, the White Stallion Ranch is perfect for those who crave wide-open spaces. Operated since 1965 by the True family, this spread has a more authentic feel than any other guest ranch in the area. Three or four horseback rides are offered Monday through Saturday, and a petting zoo keeps kids entertained. There are also nature trails, guided nature walks and hikes, and hayrides. The guest rooms vary considerably in size and comfort, from tiny, spartan single units to deluxe two-bedroom suites. The family-style meals, mostly familiar American fare, are served in the main dining room, which is housed in a 90-year-old building. There's also an honor bar.

9251 W. Twin Peaks Rd., Tucson, AZ 85743. © 888/977-2624 or 520/297-0252. Fax 520/744-2786. www.wsranch.com. 41 units Oct to mid-Dec $232–$268 double, $286–$328 suite; mid-Dec to May $252–$310 double, $328–$368 suite (plus 15% service charge). Rates include all meals. 4- to 6-night minimum stay in winter. No credit cards. Closed June–Sept. **Amenities:** Dining room, lounge; small outdoor pool; access to nearby health club; 2 tennis courts; basketball court; volleyball court; Jacuzzi; horseback riding and lessons; bikes; game room; concierge; tour desk; courtesy airport shuttle; business center; coin-op laundry. *In room:* A/C, fridge, hair dryer, no phone.

4 Where to Dine

Variety, they say, is the spice of life, and Tucson certainly dishes up plenty of variety (and spice) when it comes to eating out. Tucson is a city that lives for spice, and in the realm of spicy foods, Mexican reigns supreme. There's historic Mexican at El Charro Café and El Minuto, nouveau Mexican at Café Poca Cosa and J Bar, Mexico City Mexican at La Parilla Suiza, and family-style Mexican at Casa Molina. So if you like Mexican food, you'll find plenty of places in Tucson to get all fired up.

On the other hand, if Mexican leaves you cold, don't despair—there are dozens of other restaurants serving everything from the finest French cuisine to innovative American, Italian, and Southwestern food. Southwestern cuisine is almost as abundant in Tucson as Mexican, and you should be sure to dine at a Southwestern restaurant early in your visit. This cuisine can be brilliantly creative, and after trying it you may want *all* your meals to be Southwestern.

Foodies fond of the latest culinary trends will find plenty of spots to satisfy their cravings. Concentrations of creative restaurants can be found along East Tanque Verde Road, which has long been known as Tucson's restaurant row, and at foothills resorts and shopping plazas. On the other hand, if you're on a tight dining budget, you might want to look for early bird dinners, which are particularly popular with retirees.

DOWNTOWN & THE UNIVERSITY AREA
EXPENSIVE
Arizona Inn ✺✺ NEW AMERICAN　The dining room at the Arizona Inn, one of the state's first resorts, has established itself as a consistently excellent restaurant. The rose-pink stucco pueblo-style buildings are surrounded by neatly

manicured gardens that have matured gracefully, and it's romantic to dine in the courtyard or on the bar patio overlooking the colorful gardens. The menu is not extensive, but every dish, such as roasted duck breast with a honey-Riesling sauce, is perfectly prepared. Flavors are predominantly Southwestern, with hints of Mediterranean and Asian. Presentation is artistic but not overly so, and fresh ingredients are emphasized more than sauces. The homemade ice creams, such as ginger-cappuccino, are fabulous. On weekends, you might catch some live music.

2200 E. Elm St. ⓒ **520/325-1541**. Reservations recommended. Main courses $7–$16 lunch, $21–$34 dinner. AE, DC, MC, V. Mon–Sat 7–10am, 11:30am–2pm, and 6–10pm; Sun 7–10am, 11am–2pm (brunch), and 6–10pm.

MODERATE

Barrio ✪ SOUTHWESTERN   Located at the edge of the Barrio Histórico, this neighborhood restaurant is packed throughout the day with both downtown professionals and the art crowd. The food, on the whole, is pleasantly spicy and served with zippy Southwestern accents. If you're not too hungry, one of the little plates will do—try the tasty Anaheim chile stuffed with black beans, garlic, and goat cheese on a red-pepper cream sauce. The jalapeño burger is thick, juicy, and just spicy enough, while the pork tenderloin with a mango-ginger chutney offers an interesting mélange of flavors.

135 S. Sixth Ave. ⓒ **520/629-0191**. Reservations recommended for dinner. Main courses $8–$22. AE, DC, MC, V. Tues–Thurs 11am–10pm; Fri 11am–midnight; Sat 5pm–midnight; Sun 5–9pm.

Café Poca Cosa ✪✪ (Value NUEVO MEXICAN   Created by owner/chef Suzana Davila, the food here is not just *any* Mexican food; it's imaginative and different, and the flamboyant atmosphere of red and purple walls and Mexican and Southwestern artwork is equally unusual. The cuisine—which has been compared to the dishes dreamed up in *Like Water for Chocolate*—consists of creations such as grilled beef with a jalapeño chile and tomatillo sauce, and chicken with a dark mole sauce made with Kahlúa, chocolate, almonds, and chiles. The staff is courteous and friendly and will recite the menu for you in both Spanish and English. This lively restaurant is an excellent value, especially at lunch (which is served until 4pm).

Another (smaller and simpler) **Café Poca Cosa,** 20 S. Scott St., is open Monday through Friday from 7:30am to 2:30pm.

Clarion Hotel & Suites Santa Rita, 88 E. Broadway Blvd. ⓒ **520/622-6400**. Reservations highly recommended. Main courses $8–$9.50 lunch, $14–$20 dinner. MC, V. Mon–Thurs 11am–9pm; Fri–Sat 11am–10pm.

The Dish Bistro & Wine Bar ✪✪ NEW AMERICAN   Located in the rear of the Rumrunner Wine and Cheese Co., this tiny, minimalist restaurant is brimming with urban chic. On a busy night, the space could be construed as either cozy or crowded, so if you like it more on the quiet side, come early or late. The chef has a well-deserved reputation for daring, and turns out such dishes as roast duck with a port-and-chile glaze and grilled salmon with a champagne-lavender beurre blanc. Naturally, since this place is associated with a wine shop, the wine list is great; the servers, who are well informed about the menus, will be happy to help you choose a bottle.

3200 E. Speedway Blvd. (at the Rumrunner). ⓒ **520/326-1714**. Reservations highly recommended. Main courses $14.50–$25. AE, DC, MC, V. Tues–Thurs 5–9pm; Fri–Sat 5–10pm.

Tucson Dining

Anthony's in the Catalinas **9**
Arizona Inn **22**
Barrio **4**
Bistro Zin **14**
Café Poca Cosa **3**
Café Terra Cotta **10**
Casa Molina **32,18,33**
Cielos **28**
Dakota Café **36**
Daniel's Restaurant & Trattoria **15**
The Dish Bistro & Wine Bar **25**
El Charro Café **1, 30**
El Corral Restaurant **13**
El Cubanito Restaurant **23**
Elle **27**
El Minuto Cafe **24**
Firecracker **34**
Flying V Bar & Grill **40**
Fuego **37**
The Gold Room **8**
The Grill **12**
Hidden Valley Inn **39**
Janos **11**
J Bar **11**
Kingfisher **21**
La Cocina/Two Micks Cantina **2**
La Parilla Suiza **19, 29**
Le Bistro **20**
Le Rendez-Vous **26**
Little Anthony's Diner **31**
McMahon's Prime Steakhouse **38**
Native Café **16**
Ocotillo Café **5**
Ovens **15**
Pastiche Modern Eatery **17**
Pinnacle Peak Steakhouse **32**
The Tack Room **35**
Tohono Chul Tea Room **6**
Ventana Room **41**
Vivace Restaurant **15**
Wildflower **7**

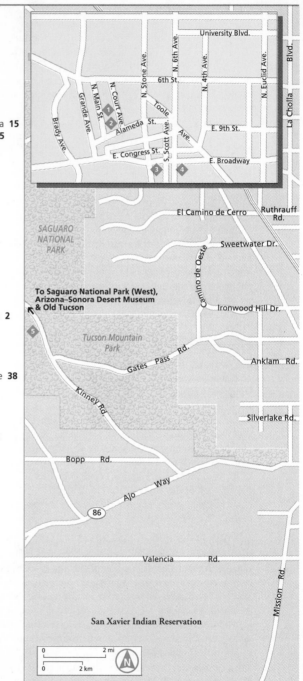

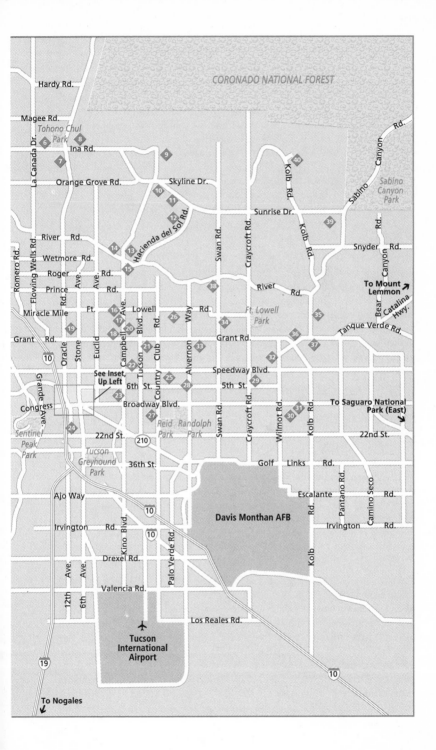

CORONADO NATIONAL FOREST

Hardy Rd.

Magee Rd.
Tohono Chul Park
Ina Rd.

La Canada Dr.

Orange Grove Rd.

Skyline Dr.

River Rd.

Wetmore Rd.

Roger Rd.

Prince Rd.

Miracle Mile

Grant Rd.

Congress

Sentinel Peak Park

Romero Rd.

Flowing Wells Rd.

Hacienda del Sol Rd.

Swan Rd.

Craycroft Rd.

Kolb Rd.

Sabino Canyon Rd.

Sabino Canyon Park

Snyder Rd.

Sunrise Dr.

River Rd.

To Mount Lemmon

Bear Canyon

Catalina Hwy.

Ft. Lowell Park

Lowell Blvd.

Way Rd.

Grant Rd.

Tanque Verde Rd.

Speedway Blvd.

5th St.

To Saguaro National Park (East)

6th St.

Broadway Blvd.

Reid Park

Randolph Park

22nd St.

Wilmot Rd.

Kolb Rd.

22nd St.

Tucson Greyhound Park

36th St.

Golf Links Rd.

Pantano Rd.

Camino Seco Rd.

Ajo Way

Davis Monthan AFB

Escalante

Irvington Rd.

Irvington Rd.

Drexel Rd.

Kino Blvd.

Palo Verde Rd.

Kolb Rd.

Valencia Rd.

12th Ave.

6th Ave.

Los Reales Rd.

Tucson International Airport

To Nogales

See Inset, Up Left

Grande Ave.

Oracle

Stone

Euclid

Campbell Ave.

Tucson Blvd.

Country Club

Alvernon

Ft. Lowell Rd.

El Charro Café ☆ SONORAN MEXICAN   El Charro, housed in an old stone building in El Presidio Historic District, lays claim to being Tucson's oldest family-operated Mexican restaurant and is legendary around these parts for its unusual *carne seca*, a traditional air-dried beef that is a bit like shredded beef jerky. To see how they make carne seca, just glance up at the restaurant's roof as you approach. The large metal cage up there is filled with beef drying in the desert sun. You'll rarely find carne seca on a Mexican menu outside of Tucson, so indulge in it while you're here—and although other area restaurants serve it, El Charro's is the best. *A warning:* The cafe can be packed at lunch, so arrive early or late.

The adjacent **¡Toma!,** a colorful bar/cantina, is under the same ownership. Other El Charro branches can be found at 6310 E. Broadway (✆ **520/ 745-1922**) and in the Tucson International Airport (✆ **520/573-8222**).

311 N. Court Ave. ✆ **520/622-1922.** Reservations recommended for dinner. Main courses $4.50–$13.50. AE, DC, DISC, MC, V. Sun–Thurs 11am–9pm; Fri–Sat 11am–10pm.

Elle ☆☆ MEDITERRANEAN   Located in the historic Broadway Village shopping plaza, Elle bills itself as a wine-country restaurant. Okay, so Tucson isn't Napa, but the menu does include more than 40 wines by the glass. French posters lend the high-ceilinged room a feel of the 1880s, and the dining experience is comfortable without being noisy. We like to start a meal here with a bowl of steamed mussels and a spinach salad with apples, blue cheese, and walnuts. Grilled pork chops with white cheddar potato gratin were recommended by two people before we even got to the restaurant, and we're happy to report their opinions were right on.

In Broadway Village, 3048 E. Broadway. ✆ **520/327-0500.** Reservations recommended. Main courses $11–$24. AE, MC, V. Mon–Fri 11:30am–10pm; Sat 4:30–10pm.

Kingfisher ☆ SEAFOOD   If you're serious about seafood, the Kingfisher is definitely your best bet in Tucson. The freshest seafood, artfully blended with bright flavors and imaginative ingredients, is deftly prepared as appetizers, sandwiches, and main dishes. You may have difficulty deciding whether to begin with Umpqua Bay oysters, seared ahi tuna salad, or the delicately smoked red trout—so why not tackle them all? Meat eaters as well as vegetarians will find items on the menu. The atmosphere is upscale and lively, and the bar and late-night menu are a hit with night owls.

2564 E. Grant Rd. ✆ **520/323-7739.** www.kingfisherbarandgrill.com. Reservations recommended on weekends. Main courses $7–$12.50 lunch, $12–$22 dinner. AE, DC, DISC, MC, V. Mon–Fri 11am–midnight; Sat–Sun 5pm–midnight.

La Cocina/Two Micks Cantina SOUTHWESTERN/AMERICAN   Housed in the same historic 1850s adobe building as the Old Town Artisans shopping plaza, La Cocina is one of the few good restaurants left in downtown Tucson, and its convenience to both shopping and the Tucson Museum of Art recommends it as a lunch spot. The tree-shaded patio area in the courtyard is surrounded by colorful gardens, making it a pleasant place for a light lunch (salads, sandwiches, and Mexican specialties). The more formal dining room is decorated with regional artwork. On the far side of the courtyard is the restaurant's rustic cantina.

201 N. Court St. ✆ **520/622-0351.** Reservations recommended. Main courses $6–$8. AE, DC, DISC, MC, V. Mon–Sat 11am–3pm; Sun noon–3pm.

North-of-the-Border Margaritaville

Jimmy Buffet may have had a problem keeping his flip-flops on after a few margaritas, but he certainly knew a good thing when he tasted it. Nothing takes the heat out of a hot desert day like an icy, limey margarita. While the rest of the country is busy sipping single malts and designer martinis, Tucson has quietly become a north-of-the-border Margaritaville.

Today, with dozens of premium tequilas making their way north from Mexico, tequila is no longer something to be slammed back as quickly as possible with enough salt and lime to hide its flavor. A margarita makes far better use of salt and lime, which, when combined with a dash of Triple Sec or Cointreau, produce the perfect drink for the desert. When the tequila in a margarita is a premium *reposado* (rested or aged), 100% blue agave tequila, and the lime juice is fresh-squeezed instead of from a bottle or a margarita mix, you have the makings of the perfect margarita. Of course, the question of on the rocks or frozen is a matter of personal taste; we prefer our margaritas on the rocks. It allows the flavors to better express themselves. And yes, with salt. However, we do make an exception for prickly pear margaritas. These hot-pink concoctions, made with the fruit of the prickly pear cactus, are best when served blended.

The following are some restaurants and bars that we think make the best margaritas in Tucson and where you, too, can ponder the question, "Is this the perfect margarita?"

Barrio, 135 S. Sixth Ave. (© 520/629-0191). Downtown bars and margaritas just seem to go together. At the Barrio, you can sip your sour-and-salty with Tucson's art crowd.

Café Poca Cosa, 88 E. Broadway Blvd. (© 520/622-6400). Great food, great atmosphere, and you'll never wonder if the bartender forgot the tequila in your margarita.

Casa Molina, 6225 E. Speedway Blvd. (© 520/886-5468). Although not the best in town, the margaritas at this economical Mexican restaurant are cheap and good. They go well with the fiery salsa and chips here. No pretension.

Flying V Bar & Grill, in Loews Ventana Canyon Resort, 7000 N. Resort Dr. (© 520/299-2020). While the prickly pear margaritas here aren't necessarily better than others around town, the view from the deck is superb. You can not only see all of Tucson spread out below, but also watch the golfers double bogey the 18th hole of the Canyon Course.

¡Toma!, 311 N. Court Ave. (© 520/622-1922). Another downtown favorite next door to El Charro Café, Tucson's famous *carne seca* restaurant. These margaritas are just plain good.

Le Bistro 🍴 FRENCH/EUROPEAN   Etched mirrors, lace, and live palm trees full of twinkling lights set the scene for casual bistro cuisine on a rather nondescript stretch of road. European specialties include the likes of duck pâté, roast quail, blackened sea scallops, and bouillabaisse. Salads are quite good, there are dozens of choices for wine, and prices are reasonable. On the extravagant side is the showcase of desserts, with names such as Tuxedo (a double-chocolate mousse) and Opera (a creation with hazelnut and mocha crème). The bar is a good place for a glass of wine and one of these rich, decadent desserts.

2574 N. Campbell Ave. ⊘ **520/327-3086.** Reservations recommended for dinner. Main courses $7.50–$10 lunch, $12–$22 dinner. AE, DISC, MC, V. Mon 11am–2:30pm; Tues–Fri 11am–2:30pm and 5–10pm; Sat–Sun 5–10pm.

Pastiche Modern Eatery ★★ NEW AMERICAN   Located in a shopping plaza that has lots of Tucson character, this high-energy bistro is currently one of *the* places to dine in Tucson. The colorful artwork and vibrant contemporary food fairly shout out *trendy,* but the restaurant manages to appeal to a broad spectrum of the population. The main attraction is the wide variety of creative dishes. From ginger crab cakes to a Southwestern club sandwich to spicy jerked chicken, there's enough here to keep everyone at the table happy. Light eaters (and drinkers) can get half orders of entrees, desserts, and even glasses of wine. The crowded bar is a popular watering hole that turns out some tasty margaritas and a bloody Mary from hell (made with chipotle-infused vodka).

3025 N. Campbell Ave. ⊘ **520/325-3333.** www.pasticheme.com. Reservations recommended. Main courses $7–$22. AE, DC, DISC, MC, V. Mon–Fri 11:30–midnight; Sat–Sun 4:30pm–midnight.

INEXPENSIVE

El Cubanito Restaurant *(Finds* CUBAN   With shocking purple walls and Latino soap operas playing on TV, this place has a very authentic feel. El Cubanito is popular with students not only because of its proximity to the University of Arizona, but also for the reasonably priced Cuban specialties, including a Cuban sandwich (a meat- and cheese-filled baguette pressed and warmed on the grill). Also worth trying are the fried plantains and yucca, and fruity shakes made with mango, banana, or guanabana.

1150 E. Sixth St. ⊘ **520/623-8020.** Main courses $4–$9. No credit cards. Mon–Sat 11am–8pm.

El Minuto Cafe MEXICAN   El Minuto, located downtown at the edge of the Barrio next to the El Tiradito shrine, is a meeting ground for both Anglos and Latinos who come here for the lively atmosphere and Mexican home cooking. In business since 1939, this establishment is a neighborhood landmark and a prototype that other Mexican restaurants often try to emulate. Cheese crisps (Mexican pizza) are a specialty, and enchiladas, especially *carne seca,* are tasty. This is a fun place for people-watching—you'll find all types, from kids to guys in suits.

354 S. Main Ave. ⊘ **520/882-4145.** Main courses $6–$12. AE, MC, V. Daily 11am–10pm.

Native Café ★ NATURAL FOODS   With a mellow, arty atmosphere and a comfortable patio, the Native Café is a good place for a leisurely light meal or snack. Opulent salads brimming with the freshest of veggies and delicious sandwiches made with handcrafted bread are the norm here. There are plenty of choices for everyone from vegans to meat eaters—and it's all healthful and impeccably fresh. You can choose among juices, smoothies, or coffees to accompany a sweet treat of scones or cardamom-cinnamon coffeecake.

3073 N. Campbell Ave. ⊘ **520/881-8881.** Salads and sandwiches $5.50–$9. DISC, MC, V. Daily 8am–4:30pm.

EAST TUCSON
EXPENSIVE

Cielos ⭐ CONTINENTAL   Arriving at Cielos is like taking a step back to a more tranquil time. Against a backdrop of rosy terra-cotta walls, the colorful gardens, candlelight, and fragrant woods burning in the open fireplaces create a romantic ambience. Ask for a table on the terrace, where you'll have garden and fireplace views. Cielos tends to be popular with an older clientele and families out on special occasions, so perhaps for that reason the menu is fairly conservative. Look for familiar favorites such as rack of lamb or filet mignon with blue cheese.

At Lodge on the Desert, 306 N. Alvernon Way. ℂ **520/325-3366.** www.lodgeonthedesert.com. Reservations recommended. Main courses $13–$25; Sun brunch $19.95. AE, DC, DISC, MC, V. Mon 7–10am and 11am–2pm; Tues–Fri 7–10am, 11am–2pm, and 5–9:30pm; Sat 7–10am and 5–9:30pm; Sun 7–10am.

Le Rendez-Vous ⭐ FRENCH   While this rather casual French restaurant serves all the dishes you would expect (escargots, pâté, vichyssoise, veal sweetbreads), it has become legendary among Tucson's foodies for its phenomenal duck à l'orange, and you would be remiss if someone at your table didn't order this dish. If you want to leave more room for a selection from the pastry tray, you can order from the limited spa menu. You might expect such rich, savory fare to be served amid rarefied elegance, but Le Rendez-Vous is housed in an unpretentious little stucco cottage, where the atmosphere is strictly bistro.

3844 E. Ft. Lowell Rd. (at Alvernon Way). ℂ **520/323-7373.** Reservations recommended. Main courses $8.50–$13.50 at lunch, $17–$30 at dinner. AE, DC, DISC, MC, V. Tues–Fri 11:30am–2pm; Tues–Sun 6–9:30pm.

MODERATE

Dakota Café ⭐⭐ INTERNATIONAL   Located in a mock cow town favored by families with small children, this restaurant, with its contemporary cowboy decor, lures a more sophisticated and adult crowd. Start your meal out on the patio with fruity apricot iced tea (very refreshing on a hot day) and a blue crab quesadilla. The grilled ahi tuna sandwich with pickled ginger is tasty. For dinner, we like the pistachio-jalapeño–crusted salmon. The food here is hearty yet inventive enough to try on a regular basis, and vegetarians will find many choices.

6541 E. Tanque Verde Rd. (in Traildust Town). ℂ **520/298-7188.** Reservations recommended. Main courses $7–$9 lunch, $10–$22 dinner. AE, DC, DISC, MC, V. Year-round Mon–Thurs 11am–9pm; Fri–Sat 11am–10pm. Oct–May also Sun 11am–4pm.

Fuego ⭐ NEW AMERICAN/SOUTHWESTERN   In Spanish, *Fuego* means "fire," and this place takes its name seriously. Not only are there spicy dishes, but there are actual flambéed dishes on the menu. The atmosphere is slightly formal but unpretentious, with tables set close together. Waiters bustle about serving such flavorful dishes as the signature Field of Greens salad, with blue cheese, chile-roasted walnuts, and dried cranberries, or prickly pear pork tenderloin that is so tender you can cut it with a fork. There are also daily seafood, game, and ostrich specials. Artful presentation can be amusing, if a little difficult to approach with a fork. Lively yet intimate, Fuego appeals to couples, families, and retirees alike, and casual to dressy attire fits in just fine.

6958 E. Tanque Verde Rd. (in Santa Fe Square). ℂ **520/886-1745.** Reservations recommended. Main courses $14–$24. AE, DC, MC, V. Sun–Thurs 5:30–9:30pm; Fri–Sat 5–10pm.

INEXPENSIVE

Casa Molina MEXICAN   For years, this has been Tucson's favorite family-run Mexican restaurant. Casa Molina sports a festive atmosphere and is usually abuzz with families, groups, and couples. The margaritas are inexpensive yet tasty, and the *carne seca* (sun-dried beef) shouldn't be missed. Lighter eaters will enjoy a layered topopo salad made with tortillas, refried beans, chicken, lettuce, celery, avocado, tomato, and jalapeños. The food is good, and the service efficient. The patio is pleasant in almost any weather.

There are other locations at 3001 N. Campbell Ave. (© **520/795-7593**), and 4240 E. Grant Rd. (© **520/326-6663**).

6225 E. Speedway Blvd. (near the northwest corner with Wilmot Rd.). © **520/886-5468**. Reservations recommended. Dinners $13–$18; a la carte $6–$13. AE, DC, DISC, MC, V. Daily 11am–10pm.

La Parilla Suiza MEXICO CITY MEXICAN   Most Mexican food served in the United States is limited to Sonoran style, originating just south of the border. In actuality, the cuisine of Mexico is nearly as varied as that of China, and the meals served at La Parilla Suiza are based on the style popular in Mexico City, where most of the chain's restaurants are located. Many menu items are sandwiched between two tortillas, much like a quesadilla, but the charcoal broiling of meats and cheeses lends the sandwiches special status. For an appetizer, we like the grilled green scallions with lime.

There's another La Parilla Suiza at 2770 N. Oracle Rd. (© **520/624-4300**).

5602 E. Speedway Blvd. © **520/747-4838**. Main courses $6–$20. AE, DC, DISC, MC, V. Sun–Thurs 11am–10pm; Fri–Sat 11am–11pm.

Little Anthony's Diner *(Kids* AMERICAN   This is a place for kids, although lots of big kids (including us) enjoy the 1950s music and decor. A video-game room will keep the children entertained while you finish your meal. The menu includes such offerings as a Jailhouse Rock burger and Chubby Checker triple-decker club sandwich. Daily specials and bottomless soft drinks make feeding the family fairly inexpensive. The Gaslight Theatre next door stages old-fashioned melodramas; together, these two places make for a fun night out with the family.

7010 E. Broadway Blvd. (in back of the Gaslight Plaza). © **520/296-0456**. Pizza and burgers $4–$7. MC, V. Mon 11am–9pm; Tues–Thurs 11am–10pm; Fri 11am–11pm; Sat 8am–11pm; Sun 8am–10pm.

THE FOOTHILLS
EXPENSIVE

Anthony's in the Catalinas *(★★* NEW AMERICAN/CONTINENTAL   Anthony's, housed in a modern Italianate-style building overlooking the city, exudes Southwestern elegance from the moment you drive up and let the valet park your car. The waiters are smartly attired in tuxedos, and guests (the cigar-and-single-malt foothills set) are nearly as well dressed. In such a rarefied atmosphere, you'd expect only the finest meal and service, and that's exactly what you get. Terrine de foie gras is a fitting beginning, followed by the likes of Chateaubriand with Béarnaise and a red-wine sauce. Wine is not just an accompaniment but a reason for dining out at Anthony's; at more than 100 pages, the wine list may be the most extensive in the city. Don't miss out on the next best part of a meal here (after the wine): the day's soufflé (order early).

6440 N. Campbell Ave. © **520/299-1771**. Reservations highly recommended. Main courses $12–$16 lunch, $24–$34 dinner. AE, DC, MC, V. Mon–Fri 11:30am–2:30pm and 5:30–10pm; Sat–Sun 5:30–10pm.

Daniel's Restaurant & Trattoria *(★★* NORTHERN ITALIAN/MEDITER-RANEAN   Although the elegant atmosphere here translates into as good a place for a romantic evening out as Anthony's (described above), Daniel's appeals to an equally affluent but younger and more casual crowd. For an appetizer, we recommend the intriguing antipasto misto, consisting of dried figs, prosciutto, marinated mushrooms, roasted red peppers, and fresh mozzarella. The signature dish is rack of lamb, but it's difficult to pass up a luscious seafood risotto in a lemon cream sauce. Attempt to save room for the warm chocolate truffle cake with vanilla-bean gelato. An outstanding wine list emphasizes Italian wines and includes about 30 selections by the glass. Lots of single malts, too, and insanely decadent after-dinner coffee drinks.

In St. Philip's Plaza, 4340 N. Campbell Ave. ℂ **520/742-3200.** Reservations recommended. Lunch $7.50–$10; dinner pastas $21–$26, main courses $24–$35. AE, DC, DISC, MC, V. Mon–Sat 11:30am–2:30pm and 5–10pm (bar menu from 2:30pm); Sun 10am–2pm (brunch) and 5–10pm.

The Gold Room ★★ REGIONAL AMERICAN/CONTINENTAL Located in the Westward Look Resort, the Gold Room is a tastefully casual restaurant featuring Southwestern ranch decor and a terrace for alfresco dining. Despite the casual atmosphere, the place settings are elegant and the service is very professional. Satisfying all tastes, the menu is equally divided between classic dishes (filet mignon and roast rack of lamb) and regional specialties, all of which are beautifully presented. We favor the regional cuisine—tender mesquite-grilled buffalo with purple Peruvian potatoes or veal piccata with a charred tomato, chipotle peppers, and lime beurre blanc—which emphasizes flavor over fire. The length of the wine list is staggering, and there's a welcome range of prices. Desserts are delectably rich and amusingly presented—the chocolate bombé is an event in itself. Although you can eat here on the cheap if you come at lunch, the restaurant is most remarkable at night, when the cityscape of Tucson twinkles below.

In the Westward Look Resort, 245 E. Ina Rd. ℂ **520/297-1151.** Reservations recommended. Main courses $10.75–$15 lunch, $19–$38 dinner; Sun brunch $23.50. AE, DC, DISC, MC, V. Daily 7am–10am, 11am–2pm, and 5:30–10pm.

The Grill ★★ REGIONAL AMERICAN Located in a 1920s hacienda-style building at a former foothills dude ranch, the Grill has been one of Tucson's hottest restaurants for several years now, and is known not only for its well-prepared meats and vegetables (grilled over pecan wood), but also for its classic Southwestern styling and great views of the city. For openers, consider the roasted tomato soup, which comes with garlic and goat cheese crostini, or something from the Spanish-style tapas menu such as *camarrones de las planchas* (flat-iron grilled shrimp). The dry-aged Angus New York strip steak is the most popular entree, but anyone seeking greater creativity would do well to opt for the pecan-grilled duckling with blood orange and pomegranate glaze. This is a great place to come just for tapas and a selection from the nearly 500 bottles on the wine list. Sunday brunch here is a treat. The patio overlooks the Catalinas and the fairways of the Westin La Paloma's golf course.

At the Hacienda del Sol Guest Ranch Resort, 5601 N. Hacienda del Sol Rd. ℂ **520/529-3500.** Reservations recommended. Main courses $23–$34; tapas $4–$16; Sun brunch $24.95. AE, DC, DISC, MC, V. Daily 5:30–9:30pm; Sun 10am–2pm.

Janos ★★★ SOUTHWESTERN/REGIONAL AMERICAN Janos Wilder is Tucson's most celebrated chef and has been satisfying Tucsonans' tastes for creative cuisine for many years now. Janos started out downtown in a historic adobe, but now exercises his culinary imagination in a luxuriously appointed dining room just outside the front door of the Westin La Paloma. The menu changes both daily and seasonally, with such complex offerings as lobster with papaya in champagne sauce, a pistachio-crusted rack of lamb with couscous and fig baklava, and at least one nightly vegetarian entree with sophisticated embellishments. In summer, there's sometimes a low-priced sampler menu that is one of Tucson's best values. There's an award-winning wine list. This is about as formal a restaurant as you'll find in this otherwise very casual city. If you can't afford the high prices here, try Janos's adjacent J Bar, which dishes up equally memorable flavor combinations at much more moderate prices (see below).

At the Westin La Paloma, 3770 E. Sunrise Dr. © **520/615-6100.** Reservations highly recommended. Main courses $24–$45; 5-course tasting menu $75 ($110 with wines). AE, DC, MC, V. Mon–Sat 5:30–9pm.

McMahon's Prime Steakhouse ★★ STEAKHOUSE/SEAFOOD If a perfectly done steak is your idea of a memorable meal out, then you'll enjoy McMahon's. With a decidedly modern opulence that's a far cry from steakhouses of yore, McMahon's boasts an atmosphere that's calculated to impress. A large glass-walled wine room dominates the main dining room, which is ringed with plush booths. You can drop a bundle on dinner here, but no more than you'd spend at such high-end restaurants as Janos, the Tack Room, or the Ventana Room. The main difference is that your choices at McMahon's are simpler: steak, seafood, or steak and seafood. You'd be wasting a night out, though, if you didn't order a steak; the aged prime-beef steaks are the best we've ever had. There's a separate piano lounge and cigar bar.

2959 N. Swan Rd. © **520/327-7463.** Reservations recommended. Main courses $20–$37. AE, DC, DISC, MC, V. Mon–Thurs 11am–10pm; Fri 11am–11pm; Sat 5–11pm; Sun 5–10pm.

The Tack Room ★★★ SOUTHWESTERN/NEW AMERICAN Housed in an older Southwestern-style hacienda with a casually elegant atmosphere, the Tack Room is most prestigious with Tucson's old-money set and is formal enough that jackets are requested for men. This is a place to feel pampered: From the time that little marinated salads appear on the table to the moment the last bit of chocolate is savored, service (by a bevy of tuxedoed waiters) is attentive and discreet. Although the filet mignon with Béarnaise sauce is the most popular dish on the menu, plump Guaymas shrimp shows up regularly in various incarnations and is always delicious. Coffee, which comes with a condiment tray that includes whipped cream and crumbled Belgian chocolate, could double as dessert, but don't let it. Of course, you'll pay for all this, but you'll leave truly satisfied with your dining experience.

7300 E. Vactor Ranch Trail. © **520/722-2800.** Reservations recommended. Jackets recommended for men. Main courses $26–$40. AE, DC, DISC, MC, V. Tues–Sun 5:30–9pm.

Ventana Room ★★★ NEW AMERICAN *Ventana* means "window" in Spanish, and the views through the windows of this restaurant are every bit as memorable as the food that comes from the kitchen. Whether you're seated overlooking the resort's waterfall or the lights of Tucson far below, you'll likely have trouble concentrating on your food, but do try; you wouldn't want to miss any of the subtle nuances of such dishes as the velvety fillet of Dover sole or the translucent and moist house-smoked salmon. With such creations as an indecently rich crème brûlée with raspberry sauce, neither should you allow the dessert cart to pass you by. In the restaurant's rarefied atmosphere, you'll be pampered by a bevy of wait staff providing professional and unobtrusive service.

In Loews Ventana Canyon Resort, 7000 N. Resort Dr. © **520/299-2020.** www.ventanaroom.com. Reservations highly recommended. Jackets recommended for men. Main courses $30–$40; chef's 5-course tasting menu $75 without wine, $110 with wine; 4-course spa menu $55. AE, DC, DISC, MC, V. Daily 6–9pm (closed Tues June–Aug).

MODERATE

Bistro Zin ★★ REGIONAL AMERICAN   Sophisticated and urbane, Bistro Zin, Tucson's premier wine bar/restaurant, effects an urban feel with its black-and-white photos of jazz greats on wine-colored walls. It's all very classy and cool, the perfect place to sample wines from around the world, and more than 20 different wine flights are available on any given day. There's also plenty of good food to accompany the many wines. Try the salmon with mashed potatoes and a very winey zinfandel sauce. Don't miss the restrooms—they're straight out of *Architectural Digest.*

In Joesler Village, 1865 E. River Rd., Suite 101. ⓒ **520/299-7799.** Reservations recommended. Main courses $8–$11 lunch, $11–$21 dinner. AE, DC, DISC, MC, V. Mon–Sat 11am–2:30pm and 5–11:30pm; Sun 5–11:30pm.

Café Terra Cotta ★★ SOUTHWESTERN   Café Terra Cotta is Arizona's original Southwestern restaurant, and has only gotten better since its recent move to a large and very modern building in the foothills. The combination of creative Southwestern cooking, a casual atmosphere, and local artwork appeals to trendy Tucsonans. A large brick oven is used to make pizzas, while salads, sandwiches, small plates, and main dishes flesh out the long menu. With so many choices, it's often difficult to decide, but for starters the must-have signature dish is garlic custard, served with a warm salsa vinaigrette. Other standouts include the poblano chile rellenos stuffed with pork and sweet potato on red pepper chipotle sauce. The wine list includes the largest collection of zinfandels in the country.

3500 Sunrise Dr. ⓒ **520/577-8100.** www.cafeterracotta.com. Reservations recommended. Main courses $8–$23. AE, DC, DISC, MC, V. Daily 11am–9:30pm.

Firecracker ★★ PAN-ASIAN   With a menu that knows no boundaries and a wild decor that includes flames issuing from torches atop the building and faux tree trunks in the bar, Firecracker is one of Tucson's hot spots. Hip decor aside, it's the large portions and reasonable prices that keep people coming back. The spicy-chicken lettuce-cup appetizers (sort of roll-your-own burritos) are a fun finger-food starter. Seafood is definitely the strong suit here, and the wok-charred chunks of salmon covered with cilantro pesto is just about the best thing on the menu. Expect a wait even if you have a reservation; the wine bar is a fine place to do so.

2990 N. Swan Rd. (at Ft. Lowell). ⓒ **520/318-1118.** Reservations recommended. Main courses $10–$17. AE, DISC, MC, V. Sun–Thurs 11am–10pm; Fri–Sat 11am–10:30pm. Sunset dinners ($7–$10) 4–6pm daily.

Flying V Bar & Grill ★★ SOUTHWESTERN   If it's bold Southwestern fare you're after, you won't do better than the Flying V. Take a seat out on the large deck and watch the koi in the pond below or the golfers struggling not to double bogey on the 18th hole of the Canyon Course. Mixing creative Southwestern and gourmet Mexican, this is one of only a couple of menus in Tucson that competes with the flair of downtown's Café Poca Cosa or J Bar (at the Westin La Paloma). There aren't too many places where you'll find ostrich fajitas, venison nachos, and duck tacos. The guacamole prepared table side is a lot of fun, as are the hot-pink prickly pear margaritas.

In Loews Ventana Canyon Resort, 7000 N. Resort Dr. ⓒ **520/299-2020.** Reservations recommended for dinner. Main courses $10–$18 lunch, $18–$29 dinner. AE, DC, DISC, MC, V. Tues–Sat 11am–2:30pm and 5–10pm; Sun 11am–2:30pm (brunch) and 5–10pm; tapas Tues–Sun 2–5pm.

J Bar ★★★ SOUTHWESTERN   The mouthwatering culinary creations of celebrity chef Janos Wilder at half price? Sounds impossible, but that's pretty much what you'll find here at J Bar, Janos's casual bar and grill adjacent to his famed foothills restaurant. Ask for a seat out on the heated patio, and with the lights of Tucson twinkling in the distance, dig into the best nachos you'll ever taste—here made with chorizo sausage and chili con queso. No matter what you order, you'll likely find that the ingredients and flavor combinations are most memorable. Who can forget spicy jerked pork with cranberry-habañero chile pepper chutney or Yucatan-style plantain-crusted chicken with green coconut milk curry? There are plenty of drink options, and the margaritas are tasty (and strong). You won't want to miss sampling one of the *postres* (desserts). The *cajeta* (Mexican caramel) sundae with Kahlúa ice cream is a delicious spin on an old favorite.

At the Westin La Paloma, 3770 E. Sunrise Dr. ℂ 520/615-6100. Reservations highly recommended. Main courses $13.50–$16.50. AE, DC, MC, V. Mon–Sat 5:30–10pm.

Ovens ★ *Value* INTERNATIONAL   We like this restaurant because it's low-key, unpretentious, and relatively quiet. The wood-fired oven turns out pizzas topped with imaginative ingredients, from spicy peanut-ginger sauce to barbecued chicken. Or if you'd rather, there are salads, handmade pastas, and grilled meats and fish. Sit out on the patio on the St. Philip's mall or inside the lounge, where you can sample one of the many wines by the glass or choose from a long list of wine-tasting flights (2-oz. pours of several different, though related, wines). The margaritas are pretty tasty, too. Whimsical art on the walls lends a playful atmosphere.

In St. Philip's Plaza, corner of Campbell Ave. at River Rd. ℂ 520/577-9001. www.ovensbistro.com. Reservations recommended. Main courses $8–$20. AE, MC, V. Sun–Thurs 11am–9:30pm; Fri–Sat 11am–10pm.

Vivace Restaurant ★★ NORTHERN ITALIAN   With a beautiful new Tuscan-like setting in the former Café Terra Cotta space, this restaurant serves reasonably priced, creative dishes. The atmosphere here isn't as formal as that at Daniel's (see above), and the food is more down-to-earth. For starters, we like to indulge in the luscious antipasto platter for two, containing garlic-flavored spinach, roasted red peppers, marinated artichoke hearts, creamy eggplant, and goat cheese. Pasta dishes, such as penne with sausage and roasted-pepper sauce or fettuccine with seafood, come nicely presented and in generous portions. The wine list has plenty of selections, many fairly reasonably priced.

In St. Philip's Plaza, 4310 N. Campbell Rd. ℂ 520/795-7221. Reservations recommended. Main courses $8.50–$11.50 lunch, $12.50–$21 dinner. AE, DC, DISC, MC, V. Mon–Thurs 11:30am–9pm; Fri–Sat 11:30am–10pm.

Wildflower ★★ NEW AMERICAN   Stylish comfort foods in gargantuan proportions are the order of the day at this chic and casually elegant north Tucson bistro. A huge wall of glass creates minimalist drama, and large flower photographs on the walls enhance the bright and airy decor. The marinated Chinese chicken salad tossed with napa cabbage and wontons and the heaping plate of fried calamari with mizuna greens are both well worth trying. Entrees run the gamut from rack of lamb with a Dijon crust to a simple roasted chicken. Pasta and salmon both show up in various guises. With so many tempting, reasonably priced dishes to sample, Wildflower is a foodie's delight.

7037 N. Oracle Rd. (in the Casa Adobes Shopping Plaza, between Oracle and Ina rds.). ℂ 520/219-4230. Reservations recommended. Main courses $8–$9 lunch, $11.50–$22 dinner. AE, MC, V. Mon–Thurs 11:30am–2:30pm and 5–9pm; Fri–Sat 11:30am–2:30pm and 5–10pm; Sun 5–9pm.

(Kids) **Family-Friendly Restaurants**

Hidden Valley Inn *(see p. 326)*   This cavernous restaurant has a false-front cow-town façade in bright colors, and inside are stables and a dance hall that serve as the dining rooms. Kids will love the miniature action dioramas of funny Western scenes.

Little Anthony's Diner *(see p. 320)*   As you might guess from the name, this place has a 1950s theme that's fun for both kids and adults. The staff is good with children, and there's a video-game room inside and an old-fashioned melodrama theater next door.

Pinnacle Peak Steakhouse *(see p. 326)*   Dinner here is a Wild West event, and there's an entire western town outside complete with carousel, train rides, and gold panning. Kids love it.

INEXPENSIVE

Tohono Chul Tea Room REGIONAL AMERICAN   Located in a brick territorial-style building in 37-acre Tohono Chul Park, this is one of the most tranquil restaurants in the city, and the garden setting provides a wonderful opportunity to experience the desert. Before or after lunching on grilled raspberry-chipotle chicken or tortilla soup, you can wander through the park's desert landscaping and admire the many species of cacti. The tearoom's patios, surrounded by natural vegetation and plenty of potted flowers, are frequented by many species of birds. The adjacent gift shop is packed with Mexican folk art, nature-theme toys, household items, T-shirts, and books. For a description of the park, see "Parks, Gardens & Zoos" under "Seeing the Sights," below.

7366 N. Paseo del Norte (1 block west of the corner of Ina Rd. and Oracle Rd. in Tohono Chul Park). ⓒ 520/797-1222. www.tohonochulpark.org. Reservations accepted for parties of 6 or more. Main courses $5–$9. AE, MC, V. Daily 8am–5pm.

WEST TUCSON

Ocotillo Café ✦ REGIONAL AMERICAN   With a terrace set in a beautiful desert garden and backed by colorful walls, the Ocotillo Café could be a destination in itself. Add to that the experience of visiting the Arizona–Sonora Desert Museum (see "The Top Attractions," below), and you have a superb day's outing. You can watch a hummingbird drink from a penstemon flower while you dine on a delicious Caesar salad made with spicy grilled chicken, dried cranberries, roasted peppers, and toasted pine nuts. Chile-rubbed pork chops are another winner. In summer, the cafe is open Saturday nights only, which is a good time to view the museum's desert inhabitants in their more active nocturnal state.

At the Arizona–Sonora Desert Museum, 2021 N. Kinney Rd. ⓒ 520/883-5705. Reservations required Sat nights. Main courses $15–$17.50. AE, MC, V. Dec 26–Apr Mon–Sat 11am–3pm, Sun 10:30am–3pm (brunch); June–Sept Sat 5:30–9pm. Closed other months.

COWBOY STEAKHOUSES

El Corral Restaurant (Value) STEAKHOUSE   Owned by the same folks who brought you Tucson's Pinnacle Peak Steakhouse, El Corral is another inexpensive steakhouse. What you'll find here is good steak, cheap, which makes the place popular with retirees and families. The restaurant doesn't accept reservations, so expect long lines or come before or after regular dinner hours. Inside, the hacienda building has a genuine old-timey feeling, with flagstone floors and wood paneling that make it dark and cozy. In keeping with the name, there's a traditional corral fence of mesquite branches around the restaurant parking lot. Prime rib is the house specialty, but there are steaks, chicken, pork ribs, and burgers for the kids.

2201 E. River Rd. ℂ **520/299-6092.** Reservations not accepted. Complete dinner $8–$14. AE, DC, DISC, MC, V. Mon–Thurs 5–10pm; Fri–Sun 4:30–10pm.

Hidden Valley Inn ⭐ (*Kids*) STEAKHOUSE   Kids will love this brightly colored, false-fronted cow town, whose most entertaining features are the walls of glass cases containing miniature action dioramas of humorous Western scenes. A very authentic dance hall and stable serve as dining rooms, and there's also the Red Garter Saloon where adults can imbibe. This steakhouse is the kind of place where people come to celebrate a family birthday and inevitably leave with large doggie bags. Cowpuncher-size steaks and barbecued ribs are the main attraction, although there are some seafood and chicken choices as well.

4825 N. Sabino Canyon Rd. ℂ **520/299-4941.** www.hiddenvalleyinntuc.com. Reservations not accepted. Main courses $6–$20. AE, DC, DISC, MC, V. Daily 11am–10pm.

Pinnacle Peak Steakhouse ⭐ (*Kids*) STEAKHOUSE   Located in Trail Dust Town, a Wild West–themed shopping and dining center, the Pinnacle Peak Steakhouse specializes in family dining in a fun cowboy atmosphere. Stroll the wooden sidewalks past the opera house and saloon to the grand old dining rooms of the restaurant. Once through the doors, you'll be surprised at the authenticity of the place, which really does resemble a dining room in Old Tombstone or Dodge City. Be prepared for crowds—this place is very popular with tour buses. Oh, and by the way, wear a neck tie into this place, and it will be cut off!

6541 E. Tanque Verde Rd. ℂ **520/296-0911.** Reservations not accepted. Main courses $5.50–$14. AE, DC, MC, V. Daily 5–10pm.

LATE-NIGHT NOSHING
If the movie didn't let out until 10pm and the popcorn wasn't enough to fill you up, where do you go to satisfy your hunger? Try **Barrio,** 135 S. Sixth Ave. (ℂ **520/629-0191**); **Kingfisher,** 2564 E. Grant Rd. (ℂ **520/323-7739**); **Pastiche,** 3025 N. Campbell Ave. (ℂ **520/325-3333**); **Presidio Grill,** 3352 E. Speedway Blvd. (ℂ **520/327-4667**); or **Firecracker,** 2990 N. Swan Rd. (ℂ **520/318-1118**), all of which stay open on Friday and Saturday until about 11pm or midnight.

QUICK BITES, CAFES & COFFEEHOUSES
A student hangout near the University of Arizona, **Café Paraíso,** 820 E. University Blvd. (ℂ **520/624-1707**), has a shady, cool patio and delectable salads and sandwiches. **Cuppuccinos,** 3400 E. Speedway Blvd. (ℂ **520/323-7205**), bills itself as a Seattle-style coffeehouse, with another location at 5575 E. River Rd. (ℂ **520/615-0051**). The **Epic Café,** 745 N. Fourth Ave. (ℂ **520/624-6844**), is a popular neighborhood place with colorful artwork, delicious scones, and other light fare. For eight-layer cakes and light food in an edgy atmosphere, we buzz on over to **The Cup,** at Club Congress, 311 E. Congress St. (ℂ **520/798-1618**). With comfy couches and a place to plug in your laptop, the **Coffee X Change,** 2415 N. Campbell Ave. (ℂ **520/327-6784**), makes a

good stop between downtown and the foothills. The **Bristol Espresso Bus,** a 1937 British double-decker bus and probably the oldest double-decker bus in the United States, is parked at 5775 E. Broadway (no phone), waiting to serve you espresso. The bus will probably be closed in summer.

When we need a quick lunch, we dart over to **Baggins Gourmet Sandwiches** for a delicious sandwich. Baggins has several locations, three of which are at Kolb Road and Speedway Boulevard (© **520/290-9383**), Campbell Avenue and Fort Lowell Road (© **520/327-1611**), and downtown at Church Avenue and Pennington Street (© **520/792-1344**). The best pizza in town can be had at **Magpies Gourmet Pizza,** downtown at Fourth Avenue and Fifth Street (© **520/628-1661**), Speedway Boulevard and Swan Road (© **520/795-5977**), Broadway Boulevard and Houghton Road (© **520/751-9949**), and Ina and Oracle roads (© **520/297-2712**). **Wild Oats Market** is a good place to get picnic supplies: organic fruit, delicious baked goods, cheese, meats, and wine, the kind of things you'd expect from a specialty market. Locations are at 3360 E. Speedway Blvd. (© **520/795-9844**), at Oracle and Ina roads (© **520/ 297-5394**), and in the foothills at Sunrise Drive and Swan Road (© **520/ 299-8858**).

5 Seeing the Sights

THE TOP ATTRACTIONS

While there are plenty of interesting things to see and do all over the Tucson area, anyone interested in the desert Southwest or the cinematic Wild West should go west—to Tucson's western outskirts, that is. Here you'll find not only the west unit of Saguaro National Park (with the biggest and best stands of saguaro cactus) but also the Arizona–Sonora Desert Museum (one of Arizona's most popular attractions) and Old Tucson Studios (film site over the years for hundreds of Westerns). Together, these three attractions make a great day's outing.

THE TUCSON AREA'S (MOSTLY) NATURAL WONDERS

Arizona–Sonora Desert Museum ★★ *(Kids)* Don't be fooled by the name. This is a zoo, and it's one of the best in the country. The Sonora Desert, which encompasses much of central and southern Arizona as well as parts of northern Mexico, contains within its boundaries not only arid lands but also forested mountains, springs, rivers, and streams. To reflect this diversity, exhibits here encompass the full spectrum of Sonora Desert life—from plants to insects to fish to reptiles to mammals—and all are on display in very natural settings. Coyotes and javelinas (peccaries) seem very much at home in their compounds, which are surrounded by almost invisible wire mesh fences that make it seem as though there is nothing between you and the animals. These display areas are along the new Desert Loop Trail, which currently has numerous new exhibits under construction. In only slightly less natural surroundings, you'll find black bears and mountain lions, beavers and otters, frogs and fish, tarantulas and scorpions, prairie dogs and desert bighorn sheep. Our favorite exhibit is the walk-in hummingbird aviary. The tiny birds buzz past your ears and stop only inches in front of your face. A separate aviary contains many other bird species, and a garden is devoted specifically to displays on pollinators (insects, birds, and mammals that pollinate desert flowers).

You'll find this zoological park 14 miles west of downtown near Tucson Mountain Park, Saguaro National Park West, and Old Tucson Studios. The museum has two dining options (the cafeteria-style Ironwood Terraces and the

Tucson Attractions

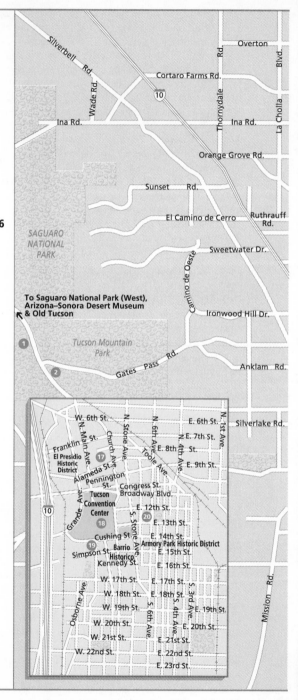

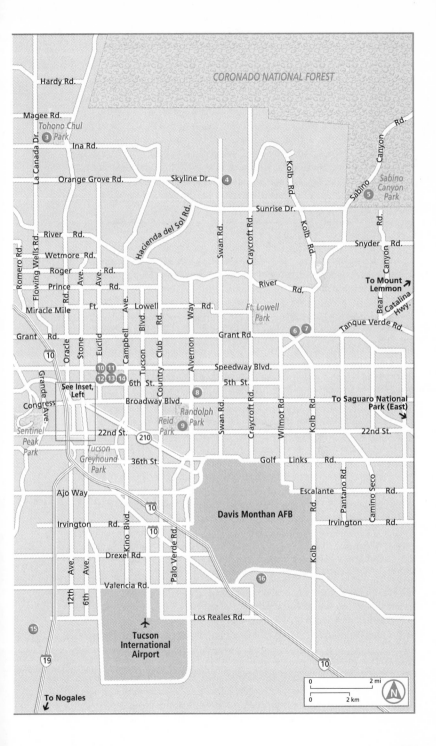

CORONADO NATIONAL FOREST

Hardy Rd.

Magee Rd.
Tohono Chul
Park ③
Ina Rd.

La Canada Dr.

Orange Grove Rd.
Skyline Dr. ④

Kolb Rd.

Sabino Canyon Rd.

Sabino ⑤
Sabino
Canyon
Park

Sunrise Dr.

River Rd.
Wetmore Rd.
Roger Rd.
Prince Rd.
Miracle Mile

Romero Rd.
Flowing Wells Rd.
Oracle Rd.
Stone Ave.
Ft. Ave.
Campbell Ave.
Tucson Blvd.
Country Club Rd.
Alvernon Way

Hacienda del Sol Rd.

Swan Rd.

Craycroft Rd.

Kolb Rd.

Snyder Rd.

To Mount Lemmon ↗

Bear Canyon Rd.

Catalina Hwy.

Lowell Rd.

Ft. Lowell Park

Grant Rd. ⑥ ⑦

Tanque Verde Rd.

Grant Rd. ⑩
Interstate 10

Euclid

Speedway Blvd.
6th St.
5th St.

⑩ ⑪
⑫ ⑬ ⑭

See Inset, Left

Congress
Grande Ave.

Sentinel Peak Park

Broadway Blvd. ⑧

Randolph Park

22nd St.
210

Reid Park ⑨

To Saguaro National Park (East) →

Wilmot Rd.
Kolb Rd.

22nd St.

Tucson Greyhound Park

36th St.

Golf Links Rd.

Escalante Rd.

Pantano Rd.
Camino Seco Rd.

Ajo Way
10

Irvington Rd.

Kino Blvd.
10

Palo Verde Rd.

Davis Monthan AFB

Irvington Rd.

Kolb Rd.

Drexel Rd.

12th Ave.
6th Ave.

Valencia Rd.

⑯

⑮

19

✈
Tucson
International
Airport

Los Reales Rd.

10

To Nogales ↓

0   2 mi
0   2 km

N ↑

Moments **Driving the Catalina Highway**

Within a span of only 25 miles, the Catalina/Mount Lemmon Highway climbs roughly 1 mile in elevation from the lowland desert landscape of cactus and ocotillo bushes to forests of ponderosa pines. Passing through several different life zones, this route is the equivalent of driving from Mexico to Canada. When you look at it this way, the $5 use fee is small compared to what a flight to Canada would cost. Along the way are numerous overlooks, some of which are nauseatingly vertiginous. Other spots are particularly popular with rock climbers. There are numerous hiking trails, picnic areas, and campgrounds along the route. For more information, contact the **Coronado National Forest Santa Catalina Ranger District,** 5700 N. Sabino Canyon Rd. (© **520/749-8700**).

---

sit-down restaurant Ocotillo Cafe), which both serve good food. The grounds here are extensive, so wear good walking shoes; a sun hat of some sort is advisable. Don't be surprised if you end up staying here hours longer than you had intended; there's an awful lot to see and do.

2021 N. Kinney Rd. © 520/883-2702 or 520/883-1380. www.desertmuseum.org. Admission $9.95 adults Nov–Apr, $8.95 May–Oct; $1.75 children 6–12. Oct–Feb daily 8:30am–5pm; Mar–Sept daily 7:30am–5pm. From downtown Tucson, go west on Speedway Blvd., which becomes Gates Pass Rd., and follow the signs.

Colossal Cave Mountain Park *Kids*   It seems nearly every cave in the Southwest has its legends of bandits and buried loot, and Colossal Cave is no exception. A tour through this dry cavern, which isn't exactly colossal but is certainly impressive, combines a bit of Western lore with a bit of geology for an experience that both kids and adults will enjoy. Not surprisingly for this desert location, this is a dry cave, which means that the stalactites, stalagmites, and other formations are no longer actively growing. The 50-minute tour covers about half a mile, and the temperature is a comfortable 70° to 72°F. This private park also encompasses the adjacent La Posta Quemada Ranch, a historic working cattle ranch that has been in operation since the 1870s. On the ranch, you can go horseback riding, visit a small museum, have a picnic, sluice for gemstones (sort of like panning for gold), go for a hike, or attend one of the annual events (including a chili cook-off in February and a Halloween howl-in).

16 miles east of Tucson in Vail. © 520/647-7275. www.colossalcave.com. Admission $7.50 adults, $4 children 6–12, in addition to $3 per car for park entry. Mar 16–Sept 15 Mon–Sat 8am–6pm, Sun and holidays 8am–7pm; Sept 16–Mar 15 Mon–Sat 9am–5pm, Sun and holidays 9am–6pm. Take Old Spanish Trail southeast from east Tucson or take I-10 and get off at the Vail exit.

Sabino Canyon *★★*   Located in the Santa Catalina Mountains of Coronado National Forest on the northeastern edge of the city, Sabino Canyon is a desert oasis that has attracted people and animals for thousands of years. Today it's by far the most spectacular and accessible corner of the desert in the Tucson area, containing not only impressive desert scenery, but also hiking trails and a stream. The chance to splash and swim in the canyon's waterfalls and pools (water conditions permitting) attracts many visitors, but it is equally enjoyable simply to gaze at the beauty of crystal-clear water flowing through a rocky canyon guarded by saguaro cacti. There are numerous picnic tables in the canyon, and many miles of hiking trails wind their way into the Catalinas from here, making it one of the best places in the city for a day hike (the farther you hike, the fewer people you'll see).

A road once allowed cars to drive up into the canyon, but cars are now prohibited; instead, a narrated tram shuttles visitors up and down the lower canyon throughout the day. Moonlight tram rides take place three times each month (usually the nights before the full moon) between April and November (but not July or August). The Bear Canyon tram is used by hikers heading to the picturesque Seven Falls, which are at the end of a 2.6-mile trail and are our favorite destination within this recreation area. Bring at least 1 quart of water per person if you plan to do any hiking here.

Another good way to experience the park is by bicycling up the paved road during the limited hours when bikes are allowed (Thurs–Fri, Sun–Tues before 9am and after 5pm). This is a strenuous uphill ride for most of the way, but the scenery is beautiful; if you get an early enough start in the morning, you'll even avoid most of the crowds.

5900 N. Sabino Canyon Rd. ⓒ **520/749-2861**, or 520/749-2327 for moonlight reservations. Parking $5. Sabino Canyon tram ride $6 adults, $2.50 children 3–12; Bear Canyon tram ride $3 adults, $1 children 3–12. Park daily dawn–dusk. Sabino Canyon tram rides daily 9am–4:30pm; Bear Canyon tram rides daily 9am–4pm (both trams more limited in summer). Take Grant Rd. east to Tanque Verde Rd., continuing east; at Sabino Canyon Rd., turn north and watch for the sign.

Saguaro National Park ⭐⭐   Saguaro cactus are the quintessential symbol of the American desert and occur naturally only here in the Sonoran Desert. Sensitive to fire and frost and exceedingly slow to mature, these massive, treelike cacti grow in great profusion around Tucson but have long been threatened by both development and plant collectors. In 1933, to protect these desert giants, the federal government set aside two large tracts of land as a saguaro preserve. This preserve eventually became Saguaro National Park. The two units of the park, one on the east side of the city (Rincon Mountain District) and one on the west (Tucson Mountain District), preserve not only dense stands of saguaros, but also the many other wild inhabitants of this part of the Sonoran Desert. Both units have loop roads, nature trails, hiking trails, and picnic grounds.

The west unit of the park, because of its proximity to both the Arizona–Sonora Desert Museum and Old Tucson Studios, is the more popular area to visit. This also happens to be where you'll see the most impressive stands of saguaros. Coyotes, foxes, squirrels, and javelinas all eat the sweet fruit of the saguaro, and near the west unit's Red Hills Information Center is a water hole that attracts these and other wild animals, which you're most likely to see at dawn and dusk or during the night. Be sure to drive the scenic Bajada Loop Drive, where you'll find good views and several hiking trails (the Hugh Morris Trail involves a long steep climb, but great views are the reward). To reach the west unit of the park, take Speedway Boulevard west from downtown Tucson (it becomes Gates Pass Boulevard).

The east section of the park contains an older area of saguaro "forest" at the foot of the Rincon Mountains. This section is popular with hikers because most of it has no roads. It does contain a visitor center, a loop scenic drive, a picnic

---

⟮*Moments* **Sunset on Signal Hill**

A hike to Signal Hill, located off the Bajada Loop Drive in Saguaro National Park West and only a quarter-mile walk from the parking area, will reward you with not only a grand sunset vista away from the crowds at Gates Pass, but also the sight of dozens of petroglyphs.

area, and a trail open to mountain bikes (and the paved loop drive is a great road-bike ride). To reach the east unit of the park, take Speedway Boulevard east, then head south on Freeman Road to Old Spanish Trail.

East district visitor center: 3693 S. Old Spanish Trail. Ⓒ 520/733-5153. West district visitor center: 2700 N. Kinney Rd. Ⓒ 520/733-5158. www.nps.gov/sagu. Entry fee $6 per car, $3 per hiker (charged in the east section only). Park daily 7am–sunset, visitor centers daily 8:30am–5pm; open to hikers 24 hours a day.

HISTORIC ATTRACTIONS BOTH REAL & REEL

Mission San Xavier del Bac ⋒ Called the White Dove of the Desert, Mission San Xavier de Bac, a blindingly white adobe building rising from a sere, brown landscape, is considered the finest example of mission architecture in the Southwest. The beautiful church, which was built between 1783 and 1797, incorporates Moorish, Byzantine, and Mexican Renaissance architectural styles. The church, however, was never actually completed, which becomes apparent when the two bell towers are compared. One is topped with a dome, while the other has none. The mission underwent an extensive restoration in recent years, and much of the elaborate interior has taken on a new luster. Restored murals cover the walls, and behind the altar are colorful and elaborate decorations. To the left of the main altar, in a glass sarcophagus, is a statue of St. Francis Xavier, the mission's patron saint, who is believed to answer the prayers of the faithful. A visit to San Xavier's little museum provides a bit of historical perspective and a chance to explore more of the mission.

To the east of the church, atop a small hill, you'll find not only an interesting view of the church but also a replica of the famous grotto in Lourdes, France. This is an active Roman Catholic church serving the San Xavier Indian Reservation. Masses are held daily at 8:30am, Saturday at 5:30pm, and Sunday at 8am, 11am, and 12:30pm.

1950 W. San Xavier Rd. Ⓒ 520/294-2624. Free admission; donations accepted. Daily 8am–5pm. Take I-19 south to exit 92 and turn right.

Old Tucson Studios ⋒⋒ *(Kids* Despite the name, this is not the historic location of the old city of Tucson—it's a Western town originally built as the set for the 1939 movie *Arizona*. In the years since, Old Tucson has been used during the filming of John Wayne's *Rio Lobo, Rio Bravo,* and *El Dorado;* Clint Eastwood's *The Outlaw Josey Wales;* Kirk Douglas's *Gunfight at the O.K. Corral;* Paul Newman's *The Life and Times of Judge Roy Bean;* and, more recently, *Tombstone* and *Geronimo.*

Today, Old Tucson is far more than just a movie set. In addition to serving as a site for frequent film, TV, and advertising productions (call ahead to find out if any filming is scheduled), it has become a Wild West theme park with diverse family-oriented activities and entertainment. Throughout the day, there are staged shootouts in the streets, stunt demonstrations, a cancan musical revue, and other performances. Train rides, stagecoach rides, kiddie rides, restaurants, and gift shops round out the experience. Educational shows explain the history of the West, and several multimedia and video presentations complement the live performances.

201 S. Kinney Rd. Ⓒ 520/883-0100. www.oldtucson.com. Admission $14.95 adults, $9.45 children 4–11 (Pima County residents $12.95 adults and $8.95 children). Daily 10am–6pm. Closed Thanksgiving and Christmas. Take Speedway Blvd. west, continuing in the same direction when it becomes Gates Pass Blvd., and turn left on S. Kinney Rd.

MORE TO SEE & DO
ART MUSEUMS

Center for Creative Photography   Have you ever wished you could see an original Ansel Adams print up close, or perhaps an Edward Weston or a Richard Avedon? You can at the Center for Creative Photography. Originally conceived by Ansel Adams, the center now holds more than 500,000 negatives, 200,000 study prints, and 60,000 master prints by the greatest photographers, making it one of the best and largest collections in the world. Although the center mounts excellent exhibits year-round, it's also a research facility that preserves the complete photographic archives of various photographers, including Adams. Prints may be examined in a special room. It's highly recommended that you make an appointment and decide beforehand whose works you'd like to see. You're usually limited to two photographers per visit.

University of Arizona campus, east of the corner of Park Ave. and Speedway Blvd. © 520/621-7968. www.creativephotography.org. Suggested donation $2. Mon–Fri 9am–5pm; Sat–Sun noon–5pm. Bus: 1, 4, 5, 6, 9X, 102, or 103.

De Grazia Gallery in the Sun   Southwestern artist Ettore "Ted" De Grazia is a Tucson favorite son, and his gallery, set in an adobe home in the foothills, is a Tucson landmark. De Grazia is said to be the most reproduced artist in the world because many of his impressionistic images of big-eyed children were used as greeting cards during the 1950s and 1960s. Connected to the gallery is a small adobe chapel that De Grazia built in honor of the missionary explorer Father Eusebio Kino. No original works are for sale, but there are many reproductions and other objects with De Grazia images.

6300 N. Swan Rd. © 800/545-2185 or 520/299-9191. www.degrazia.org. Free admission. Daily 10am–4pm.

Tucson Museum of Art & Historic Block ⋆   The Tucson Museum of Art is situated in a modern building surrounded by historic adobes and a spacious plaza frequently used to display sculptures. The museum boasts an excellent collection of pre-Columbian art, representing 3,000 years of life in Mexico and Central and South America. A large collection of Western art depicts cowboys, horses, and the wide-open spaces of the American West. In addition, the museum hosts temporary exhibitions and frequently presents shows with a Western theme. The museum has preserved five historic homes on this same block, all open to the public. See "History Museums & Landmark Buildings," below, for details.

140 N. Main Ave. © 520/624-2333. www.tucsonarts.com. Admission $5 adults, $4 seniors, $3 students, free for children 12 and under; free on Sun. Mon–Sat 10am–4pm; Sun noon–4pm. Closed Mon Memorial Day to Labor Day and all national holidays. All downtown-bound buses.

The University of Arizona Museum of Art ⋆⋆   With European and American works from the Renaissance to the 20th century, this collection is even more extensive and diverse than that of the Tucson Museum of Art. Tintoretto, Rembrandt, Picasso, O'Keeffe, Warhol, and Rothko are all represented. Another attraction, the *Retable of Ciudad Rodrigo*, consists of 26 paintings from 15th-century Spain that were originally placed above a cathedral altar. The museum also has an extensive collection of 20th-century sculpture that includes more than 60 clay and plaster models and sketches by Jacques Lipchitz.

University of Arizona campus, Park Ave. and Speedway Blvd. © 520/621-7567. http://artmuseum. arizona.edu. Free admission. Mon–Fri 9am–5pm; Sun noon–4pm. Closed major holidays. Bus: 1, 4, 5, 6, 9X, 102, or 103.

HISTORY MUSEUMS & LANDMARK BUILDINGS

In addition to the attractions listed below, downtown Tucson has a couple of historic neighborhoods that are described in "Walking Tour—Downtown Historic Districts," below. Among the more interesting buildings are those maintained by the Tucson Museum of Art, located on the block surrounding the museum. These restored homes date from between 1850 and 1907 and are all built on the former site of the Tucson presidio. A map and descriptive brochures are available at the museum's front desk, and free (with admission to the museum) guided tours of the historic block are available.

Arizona Historical Society Tucson Museum   As the state's oldest historical museum, this repository of all things Arizonan is a treasure trove for the history buff. If you've never explored a real mine, you can do the next best thing by looking at the museum's full-scale reproduction of an underground mine tunnel. You'll see an assayer's office, miner's tent, stamp mill, and blacksmith's shop in the mining exhibit. A transportation exhibit, displaying stagecoaches and horseless carriages that revolutionized life in the Southwest, along with temporary exhibits, which cover a wide range of topics, give a pretty good idea of what it was like back then. The museum has a research library and a decent gift shop.

949 E. Second St. ℂ **520/628-5774.** Admission by donation. Mon–Sat 10am–4pm; Sun noon–4pm. Closed major holidays. Bus: 1, 4, 5, 6, 9X, 102, or 103.

Arizona State Museum   This museum, which is the oldest anthropological museum in the Southwest, houses one of the state's most interesting exhibits on prehistoric and contemporary Native American cultures of the Southwest. The exhibit, called *Paths of Life: American Indians of the Southwest,* has extensive displays on 10 different tribes from around the Southwest and northern Mexico. The exhibit not only displays a wide range of artifacts but also explores the lifestyles and cultural traditions of Indians living in the region today. The museum also showcases a collection of some 20,000 whole-vessel ceramic pieces. This pottery spans 2,000 years of life in the desert Southwest.

University of Arizona campus, University Blvd. and Park Ave. ℂ **520/621-6302.** www.statemuseum. arizona.edu. Free admission; donations accepted. Mon–Sat 10am–5pm; Sun noon–5pm. Closed major holidays. Bus: 1, 4, 5, 6, 9X, 102, or 103.

Sosa-Carillo-Frémont House Museum   Located on the shady grounds of the modern Tucson Convention Center, the Sosa-Carillo-Frémont House is a classic example of Sonoran-style adobe architecture. Originally built in 1858 as a small adobe house, the structure was enlarged after 1866. In 1878, it was rented to territorial governor John Charles Frémont, who had led a distinguished military career as an explorer of the West. The building has been restored in the style of this period, with the living room and bedrooms opening off a large central hall known as a *zaguán.* All rooms are decorated with period antiques. The flat roof is made of pine beams called *vigas,* covered with saguaro cactus ribs, and topped by a layer of hard-packed mud. From November to March, this museum offers Saturday tours of historic Tucson ($10 for adults, free for children under 12).

151 S. Granada Ave. (in the Tucson Convention Center complex). ℂ **520/622-0956.** Free admission. Wed–Sat 10am–4pm. Closed major holidays. All downtown-bound buses.

SCIENCE & TECHNOLOGY MUSEUMS

Biosphere 2   For 2 years, beginning in September 1991, four men and four women were locked inside this airtight, 3-acre greenhouse in the desert 35 miles north of Tucson near the town of Oracle. During their tenure in Biosphere 2

Moments **Stumbling on the Boneyard**

Driving along Kolb and Valencia roads between I-10 and east Tucson, you'll pass right by the Davis Monthan Air Force Base boneyard, which is more correctly known as the AMARC (Arizona Maintenance and Regeneration Center) facility and is a storage facility for hundreds of mothballed aircraft.

(earth is considered Biosphere 1), they conducted experiments on how the earth, basically a giant greenhouse, manages to support all the planet's life forms. Although there are no longer people living in Biosphere 2, similar experiments continue (but this giant science project is now more of a tourist attraction than a research facility).

Tours, including one that takes you into the interior of Biosphere 2, are offered daily. Before heading out on the basic tour (which doesn't go inside the greenhouse), you can learn about the project at an orientation center. On the basic tour, you'll get to see the Ocean Viewing Gallery, the test module, demonstration labs, and video presentations. An interactive display provides entertainment for children. The latest addition here is a 24-inch telescope that allows nighttime visitors to do a bit of stargazing (call for schedule). Whether you consider it science or a tourist attraction, there's plenty to see and do. Also on the grounds are a hotel, restaurant, and gift shop.

Ariz. 77, mile marker 96.5. ℂ **800/828-2462** or 520/825-1289. www.bio2.edu. Admission $12.95 adults, $8.95 children 13–17, $6 children 6–12. "Under the Glass" tour $10. Discounts for students and seniors. Daily 8:30am–5pm. Closed Christmas. Take Oracle Rd. north out of Tucson and continue north on Ariz. 77 until you see the Biosphere sign.

Flandrau Science Center & Planetarium   Located on the campus of the University of Arizona, the Flandrau Planetarium offers stargazers a chance to learn more about the universe. The planetarium theater presents programs on the stars as well as very popular laser shows set to music. The halls contain a mineral collection (the largest in the state) and hands-on science exhibits for people of all ages. On clear nights, you can gaze through the planetarium's 16-inch telescope. (Arizona has become a magnet for astronomers, and there are several observatories near Tucson. See "Starry, Starry Nights," in chapter 10, "Southern Arizona," for information on the Kitt Peak National Observatory.)

University of Arizona campus, Cherry Ave. and University Blvd. ℂ **520/621-STAR**. www.flandrau.org. Admission to exhibits $3 adults, $2 children 13 and under. Telescope viewing free. Planetarium $5 adults, $4.50 seniors and students, $4 children 3–13, children under 3 not admitted. Daytime Mon–Sat 9am–5pm, Sun 1–5pm; evenings Wed–Sat 7–9pm. Telescope viewing Wed–Sat 7–10pm (weather permitting). Closed major holidays. Bus: 9.

Pima Air & Space Museum ✯   Just south of Davis Monthan Air Force Base, the Pima Air & Space Museum houses one of the largest collections of historic aircraft in the world. On display are more than 250 aircraft, including an SR-71 Blackbird, several Russian MiGs, World War II combat gliders, a "Superguppy," a B-17G "Flying Fortress," and numerous experimental aircraft, including a backpack helicopter known as the "Hopicopter." The collection includes replicas of the Wright brothers' 1903 Wright Flyer and the X-15, the world's fastest aircraft. Tours are available.

The museum offers guided tours of Davis Monthan's AMARC (Arizona Maintenance and Regeneration Center) facility, which goes by the name of the

Boneyard. Here, thousands of mothballed planes are lined up in neat rows under the Arizona sun. Tours last just under an hour and cost $6 for adults, $5 for seniors, and $3 for children 12 and under. Tour reservations (© **520/618-4806**) should be made 2 or 3 days in advance.

6000 E. Valencia Rd. © **520/574-0462**. www.pimaair.org. Admission $9.75 adults, $8.50 seniors and military, $6 children 7–12. Daily 9am–5pm. Closed Thanksgiving and Christmas. Take the Valencia Rd. exit from I-10 and drive east 2 miles to the museum.

Titan Missile Museum ✦   Operated by the Pima Air & Space Museum and located south of Tucson in the retirement community of Green Valley, this museum is a deactivated intercontinental ballistic missile (ICBM) silo and is the only such museum in the world. Tours lead you down into the silo itself so you can get a firsthand look at what it would be like to have your finger on the button.

Duval Mine Rd., Green Valley (exit 69 from I-19). © **520/625-7736**. Advance reservations recommended but not necessary. Admission $7.50 adults, $6.50 seniors, $4 children 7–12. May–Oct Wed–Sun 9am–4pm; Nov–Apr daily 9am–4pm. Closed Thanksgiving and Christmas. Take I-19 south to Green Valley; take exit 69 west ¹⁄₂ mile to main entrance.

PARKS, GARDENS & ZOOS

See "The Tucson Area's (Mostly) Natural Wonders," earlier in this chapter, for details on the Arizona– Sonora Desert Museum, the region's premier zoo.

Reid Park Zoo *Kids*   Although small and overshadowed by Tucson's Arizona– Sonora Desert Museum, the Reid Park Zoo is an important breeding center for several endangered species. Among the animals in the zoo's breeding programs are giant anteaters, white rhinoceroses, tigers, ruffed lemurs, and zebras. A South American exhibit features a capybara (the largest rodent in the world), piranhas, and black jaguars. Get here early, when the animals are more active and before the crowds hit. If you've got the kids along, there's a good playground in the adjacent park.

Lake Shore Lane and 22nd St. (between Country Club Rd. and Alvernon Way). © **520/791-4022**. Admission $4 adults, $3 seniors, 75¢ children 5–14. Daily 9am–4pm. Closed Christmas. Bus: 7 or 14.

Tohono Chul Park ✦✦   Although this public park is fairly small, it provides an excellent introduction to the plant and animal life of the desert. You'll see a forest of cholla cactus and a garden of small and complex pincushion cactus. From mid-February to April, the wildflower displays here are gorgeous (if enough rain has fallen in the previous months), and guided tours are offered. The park also includes an ethnobotanical garden; a garden for children that encourages them to touch, listen, and smell; a demonstration garden; natural areas; an exhibit house for art displays; a tearoom that's great for breakfast, lunch, or afternoon tea (see "Where to Dine," earlier in this chapter); and a very good gift shop.

7366 N. Paseo del Norte (off Ina Rd. west of the intersection with Oracle Rd.). © **520/575-8468**. www.tohonochulpark.org. Suggested donation $2. Grounds daily 7am–sunset. Exhibit house Mon–Sat 9:30am–5pm; Sun 11am–5pm. Tearoom daily 8am–5pm.

Tucson Botanical Gardens   Set amid residential neighborhoods in midtown Tucson, these gardens are an oasis of greenery and, though small, are well worth a visit if you're interested in desert plant life, landscaping, or gardening. On the 5¹⁄₂-acre grounds are several small gardens that not only have visual appeal but are also historical and educational. If you live in the desert, you might want to visit just to learn about harvesting rainfall for your desert garden and designing

C Frommer's Favorite Tucson Experiences

Visiting the Arizona–Sonora Desert Museum. One of the world's finest zoos, the museum focuses exclusively on the animals and plants of the Sonoran Desert of southern Arizona and northern Mexico. See page 327.

Taking a Full-Moon Desert Hike. There's no better time to explore the desert than at night (when the desert comes alive) under a full moon. Drive to the east or west section of Saguaro National Park, where the parking lots at the east ends of Speedway and Broadway are open 24 hours a day. It's also possible to park on Old Spanish Trail outside the main entrance to the east unit of the park. There are places on the west side where you can park outside the gates and walk into the park. See page 331.

Making the Drive to Mount Lemmon 👫👫. From the desert, the road twists and turns up into the Santa Catalina Mountains, with cactus and palo verde gradually replaced by pine and juniper. You'll have breath-taking views of Tucson along the way. The 25-mile Catalina/Mount Lemmon Highway begins on the east side of Tucson off Tanque Verde Road. See page 330.

Spending Time in Sabino Canyon. Biking, hiking, swimming, birding—Sabino Canyon has it all. The canyon, carved by a creek that flows for most of the year, is an oasis in the desert. Although popular with both locals and tourists, it still offers delightful opportunities for escaping the city. See page 330.

Bird-Watching in Madera Canyon. Located south of the city in the Santa Rita Mountains, this canyon attracts many species of birds, some of which can be seen in only a handful of other spots in the United States. Even if you're not into birding, there are hiking trails and lots of shade here. See page 344.

a water-conserving landscape. The sensory garden stimulates all five senses, while in another garden traditional Southwestern crops are grown for research purposes. Also here are a children's garden, a bird garden, a greenhouse with "useful" plants from tropical forests, and a gift shop.

2150 N. Alvernon Way. *C* 520/326-9686. www.tucsonbotanical.org. Admission $4 adults, $3 seniors, $1 children 6–11. Labor Day to Memorial Day daily 8:30am–4:30pm; Memorial Day to Labor Day daily 7:30am–4:30pm. Closed Jan 1, July 4, Thanksgiving, and Dec 24–25. Bus: 11.

ESPECIALLY FOR KIDS

In addition to the museum listed below, two of the greatest places to take kids in the Tucson area are the Arizona–Sonora Desert Museum and Old Tucson Studios. Kids will get a kick out of the tram ride at Sabino Canyon, the Reid Park Zoo, Flandrau Science Center and Planetarium, and the Pima Air & Space Museum. All are described in detail earlier in this chapter.

They'll also enjoy **Trail Dust Town,** 6541 E. Tanque Verde Rd. (*C* **520/ 296-4551**), a Wild West–themed shopping and dining center. It has a full-sized

The Shrine That Stopped a Freeway

The southern Arizona landscape is dotted with roadside shrines, symbols of the region's Hispanic and Roman Catholic heritage. Most are simple crosses decorated with plastic flowers and dedicated to people who have been killed in auto accidents. One shrine in particular stands out from all the rest. It is Tucson's El Tiradito (The Castaway), which is dedicated to a sinner, and not too long ago stopped a freeway.

El Tiradito, on South Granada Avenue at West Cushing Street, is the only shrine in the United States dedicated to a sinner buried in unconsecrated soil. Several stories tell of how this shrine came to be, but the most popularly accepted tells of a young shepherd who fell in love with his mother-in-law some time in the 1880s. When the father-in-law found his wife in the arms of this young man, he shot the son-in-law. The young shepherd stumbled from his in-laws' house and fell dead beside the dusty street. Because he had been caught in the act of adultery and died without confessing his sins, his body could not be interred in the church cemetery, so he was buried where he fell.

The people of the neighborhood soon began burning candles on the spot to try to save the soul of the young man, and eventually people began burning candles in hopes that their own wishes would come true. They believed that if the candle burned through the night, their prayers would be answered. The shrine eventually grew into a substantial little structure and in 1927 was dedicated by its owner to the city of Tucson. In 1940, the shrine became an official Tucson monument.

However, such status was not enough to protect the shrine from urban renewal, and when the federal government announced that it would level the shrine when it built a new freeway through the center of Tucson, the city's citizens were outraged. Their activities and protests led the shrine to be named to the National Register of Historic Places. Thus protected, the shrine could not be destroyed, and the freeway was moved a few hundred yards to the west.

To this day, devout Catholics from the surrounding neighborhood still burn candles at the shrine that stopped a freeway.

carousel, a scaled-down train to ride, shootout shows, and a minigolf course next door. Basically, it's a sort of scaled-down Old Tucson. If the kids are into miniature golf, they'll probably love **Magic Carpet Golf,** 6125 E. Speedway Blvd. (© **520/885-3691**), as much as we do. Putt balls under and around a sphinx, a skull, a giant Easter Island head, and a huge snake.

Tucson Children's Museum This museum, in the old Carnegie Library in downtown Tucson, is filled with fun and educational hands-on activities. Exhibits change every year or so, but have included a doctor's office, a fire station, and a bubble factory. Expect to find such perennial kid favorites as a firetruck, a police motorcycle, and dinosaur sculptures. Weekends generally feature special performances and programs.

200 S. Sixth Ave. © **520/792-9985.** Admission $5.50 adults, $4.50 seniors, $3.50 children 2–16; free on 3rd Sun of month. Tues–Sat 10am–5pm; Sun noon–5pm. Closed New Year's Day, Easter, Thanksgiving, and Christmas. All downtown-bound buses.

DOWNTOWN SATURDAY NIGHT

Throughout the year, on the first Saturday of each month, the Downtown Arts District—which includes East Pennington Street, East Congress Street, and East Broadway Boulevard between Fourth Avenue and Stone Avenue—comes alive from about 7 to 10pm. On these nights, there are gallery openings, music performances on the streets and in cafes, and late-evening shopping. For more information, call the **Tucson Arts District Partnership** (𝄢 **520/624-9977**).

WALKING TOUR	DOWNTOWN HISTORIC DISTRICTS

Start	Old Town Artisans.
Finish	Hotel Congress.
Time	5 hours.
Best Times	Weekends, when restaurants aren't packed at lunch.
Worst Times	Summer, when it's just too hot to do any walking.

Tucson has a long and varied cultural history, which is most easily seen on a walking tour of the downtown historic neighborhoods. Start your explorations in the El Presidio Historic District, which is named for the Presidio of San Augustín del Tucson (1775), the Spanish garrison built here to protect the San Xavier del Bac Mission from the Apaches. For many years it was the heart of Tucson, and although no original buildings are still standing, there are numerous structures from the mid–19th century.

After finding a parking space at the large public parking lot at the corner of Court Avenue and Council Street, walk south on Court Avenue to the corner of Washington Street. Here you'll find Tucson's premier crafts market:

❶ Old Town Artisans

In this adobe building at 186 N. Meyer Ave., dating from 1862, are numerous rooms full of handmade Southwestern crafts (see "Shopping," later in this chapter, for details). The central courtyard has shady gardens. You could spend hours browsing through the amazing assortment of crafts here, but keep in mind you've still got a long walk ahead of you.

Across Meyer Avenue from this building's southwest corner is:

❷ La Casa Cordova

This building at 175 N. Meyer Ave. dates from about 1848 and is one of the oldest in Tucson. Although the art museum owns five historic homes on this block, this is the only one that has been restored to look as it might have

in the late 1800s. Each year from November to March, there is a very elaborate *nacimiento*, a Mexican folk-art nativity scene, with images from the Bible and Latin American history all rolled up into one miniature landscape full of angels, greenery, and Christmas lights.

Through a colorful gate just to the south of La Casa Cordova is the entrance to the:

❸ Tucson Museum of Art

This modern building houses collections of pre-Columbian and Western art, as well as exhibits of contemporary works. A visit will not only allow you to see plenty of art, but you should also be able to see inside a couple of historic buildings that now house some of the museum's galleries.

After touring the museum, walk back up North Meyer Avenue; at the end of the block, you will find the:

❹ Romero House

This 1868 house may incorporate part of the original presidio wall. It was altered numerous times over the years, and at one time served as a gas station. The Romero House now contains the Tucson Museum of Art School.

From the Romero House, turn left onto Washington Street and then left again onto Main Avenue. The first building you'll come to on this side of the art museum's historic block is the:

⑤ Corbett House

This restored Mission Revival–style building at 180 N. Main Ave. was built in 1907. The house, which is set back behind a green lawn, is strikingly different from the older, Sonoran-style adobe homes on this block. The Corbett House is open to the public for tours.

Next door to this home stands the:

⑥ Stevens House

Located at 150 N. Main Ave., this is a Sonoran-style row house completed in 1866. This building currently houses the museum's cafe.

Next door is the:

⑦ Fish House

This house at 120 N. Main Ave. was built in 1867 on the site of old Mexican barracks. Named for Edward Nye Fish, a local merchant, it now houses the museum's Western-art collection. Some of the walls of this house are 2 feet thick, and ceilings in some places are made from old packing crates.

From here, head back up Main Avenue; at the far end of the next block, you will reach the:

⑧ Julius Kruttschnidt House

This house at 297 N. Main Ave. dates from 1886 and now houses El Presidio Bed & Breakfast Inn. Victorian trappings, including a long veranda, disguise the adobe origins of this unique and beautifully restored home.

Across Main Avenue from the B&B is the:

⑨ Steinfeld House

This house at 300 N. Main Ave. was built in 1900 in California Mission Revival style and was designed by Henry Trost, Tucson's most noted

architect. It served as the original Owl's Club, a gentlemen's club for some of Tucson's most eligible turn-of-the-last-century bachelors.

Another block north on Main Avenue stands the:

⑩ Owl's Club Mansion

This impressive mansion at 378 N. Main Ave. was built in 1902 and designed by Henry Trost in the Mission Revival style, albeit with a great deal of ornamentation. It replaced the Steinfeld House as home to the bachelors of the Owl's Club.

TAKE A BREAK
If you started your tour late in the morning, you're probably hungry by now. Backtrack down Main Avenue, cross the street, and walk east on Franklin Street to Court Avenue. Turn right onto Court, and you will find **El Charro Cafe,** Tucson's oldest Mexican restaurant. Be sure to order *carne seca,* the house specialty. (See "Where to Dine," earlier in this chapter, for details.)

From here, continue south on Court Avenue and cross Alameda Street to reach:

⑪ El Presidio Park/Plaza de las Armas

This was once the parade ground for the presidio and is now a shady gathering spot for everyone from the homeless to downtown office workers. Here on the plaza, you'll see a life-size bronze statue of a presidio soldier, as well as a statue commemorating the Mormon Battalion's visit to Tucson in 1846.

Just to the east of the park is the very impressive:

⑫ Pima County Courthouse

Built in 1928, the courthouse located at 115 N. Church St. incorporates Moorish, Spanish, and Southwestern architectural features, including a colorful tiled dome. A portion of the original presidio wall is in a glass case on the second floor.

Walking Tour—Downtown Historic Districts

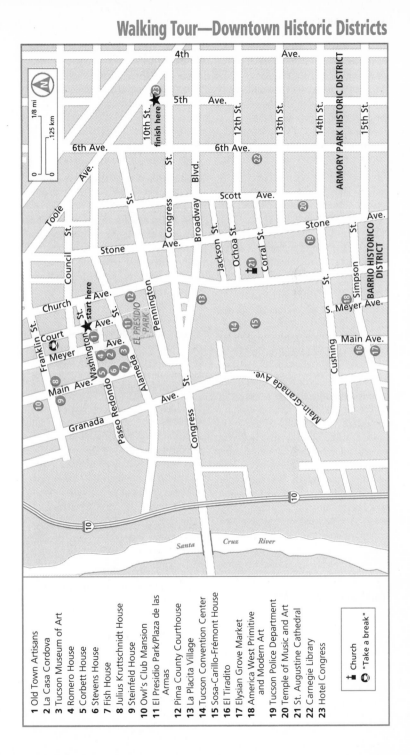

4th Ave.

ARMORY PARK HISTORIC DISTRICT

5th Ave.

10th St.
finish here ★ 23

6th Ave.

6th Ave.

22

Blvd.
Scott Ave.

20

Congress St.
Broadway St.

Stone Ave.

19

Jackson St.
Ochoa St.
Corral St.

✝ 21

BARRIO HISTORICO DISTRICT

Stone Ave.

Toole Ave.

Council St.

Church Ave.
start here

Pennington St.

EL PRESIDIO PARK

12

13

S. Meyer Ave.

18

Simpson

Franklin St.
Court Ave.

★

11

14

15

Main Ave.

16   17

Meyer Ave.

Washington Ave.

1

Alameda St.

2   4   3

Cushing St.

Paseo Redondo

5
6   7

Main Ave.

8

9

10

Granada Ave.

Congress St.

Main-Granada Ave.

Santa   Cruz   River

10

10

1 Old Town Artisans
2 La Casa Cordova
3 Tucson Museum of Art
4 Romero House
5 Corbett House
6 Stevens House
7 Fish House
8 Julius Kruttschnidt House
9 Steinfeld House
10 Owl's Club Mansion
11 El Presidio Park/Plaza de las Armas
12 Pima County Courthouse
13 La Placita Village
14 Tucson Convention Center
15 Sosa-Carillo-Frémont House
16 El Tiradito
17 Elysian Grove Market
18 America West Primitive and Modern Art
19 Tucson Police Department
20 Temple of Music and Art
21 St. Augustine Cathedral
22 Carnegie Library
23 Hotel Congress

✝■ Church
☕ "Take a break"

341

From the courthouse, continue south 2 blocks (across two pedestrian bridges), to:

⑬ La Placita Village

This is a complex of offices and restaurants at 110 S. Church Ave., designed to resemble a Mexican village. It houses Tucson's visitor center and also incorporates the Samaniego House, a Sonoran-style row house that dates from the 1880s.

Near the fountains in the center of the convention center complex is the historic:

⑭ Tucson Convention Center

This sprawling complex includes a sports arena, grand ballroom, concert hall, theater, pavilions, meeting halls, gardens, restaurants, and craft and souvenir vendors.

It is here you will find the colorfully painted:

⑮ Sosa-Carillo-Frémont House

This adobe structure, located at 151 S. Granada Ave., was built in the 1850s and later served as the home of territorial governor John C. Frémont. The restored building is open to the public and is furnished in the style of the period.

Continue south through the grounds of the convention center complex, and you will come to Cushing Street, across which lies the Barrio Histórico District. With its 150 adobe row houses, this is the largest collection of 19th-century Sonoran-style adobe architecture in the United States. The entire neighborhood was almost razed in the name of urban renewal and highway construction. About half of downtown Tucson, including the neighborhoods that once stood on the site of today's convention center, was razed before the voices for preservation and restoration were finally heard. In fact, if it had not been for the activism of the residents of the Barrio Histórico, I-10 would now run right through much of this area.

Start your exploration of the northern (and more restored) blocks of this neighborhood by crossing Cushing Street and then turning down Main Avenue, where you will find, on the west side of the street in the first block:

⑯ El Tiradito

This is the only shrine in the United States dedicated to a sinner buried in unconsecrated soil. People still light candles here in hopes of having their wishes come true (see "The Shrine That Stopped a Freeway," above).

Continuing south to the corner of West Simpson Street, you will see the:

⑰ Elysian Grove Market

This dilapidated-looking old adobe building, at 400 W. Simpson St., is actually one of the most interesting and artistically decorated bed-and-breakfast inns in the city (see "Where to Stay," earlier in this chapter).

Wander a while through the Barrio Histórico District, admiring the Sonoran-style homes that are built right out to the street. Many of these homes sport colorfully painted façades, signs of the ongoing renovation of this neighborhood.

Before leaving the Barrio, you may want to stop in at:

⑱ America West Primitive and Modern Art

Not only will you get a glimpse inside one of these buildings, located at 363 S. Meyer Ave., but the collection of art for sale in this gallery is fascinating.

From the corner of Cushing Street and South Meyer Avenue, walk 2 blocks east to South Stone Avenue, where you'll find the:

⑲ Tucson Police Department

While most people like to give police stations a wide berth, this one, located at 270 S. Stone Ave., is worth a visit. In the lobby, you'll see a display of John Dillinger memorabilia (Dillinger's capture took place not long after an eventful stay at the nearby Hotel Congress).

Continue another block east on Cushing Street and you will come to the:

⑳ Temple of Music and Art

This building, located at 330 S. Scott Ave., was built in 1927 as a movie and stage theater and is the home of the Arizona Theatre Company (see "Tucson After Dark," later in this chapter).

From here, walk north on South Scott Avenue, turn left on McCormick Street/13th Street, and then turn right onto South Stone Avenue, which will bring you to:

㉑ St. Augustine Cathedral
The cathedral was built in 1896 and modeled after the Cathedral of Queretaro, Mexico. Above the door, you'll see a statue of Saint Augustine as well as symbols of the Arizona desert—the horned toad, the saguaro, and the yucca.

From here, walk east on Corral Street, turn left on South Scott Avenue, and then turn right on 12th Street and right again on South Sixth Avenue to reach the front of the old:

㉒ Carnegie Library
The library dates from 1901 and was designed by Henry Trost. The

building now houses the Tucson Children's Museum (see "Especially for Kids," above).

Now head north on South Sixth Avenue for 2 blocks and turn right on Congress Street. In 1 block, you will see on the far side of the street the:

㉓ Hotel Congress
This hotel, located at 311 E. Congress St., was built as a railroad hotel in 1919 and once played host to John Dillinger, infamous public enemy number one. Today, the restored budget lodging is popular with European travelers and students, and has a classically Western-styled lobby. There's a cybercafe and a regular cafe here; the lobby is well worth a stroll-through.

6 Organized Tours

To get an overview of Tucson, you can take a 1½-hour guided tour ($25) with the friendly and informative folks at **Old Pueblo Tours** (© 520/795-7448). The tours head up to the top of A Mountain for a look at the city from above, then visit the three downtown historic districts and the University of Arizona.

Laurel Cooper at **Desert Paths Tours** (© 520/327-7235) has a Ph.D. in anthropology and many years' experience in leading history, art, and culture-oriented field trips. She offers customized tours of the Saguaro National Park and southeastern Arizona, among other places.

Learning Expeditions, a program run by the **Arizona State Museum,** occasionally offers scholar-led archaeological tours, including a trip to view rock art in Tucson. For information, call the marketing department at the Arizona State Museum (© **520/626-8381;** www.statemuseum.arizona.edu).

For a look at a completely different sort of excavation, head south from Tucson 15 miles to the **ASARCO Mineral Discovery Center,** exit 80 off I-19 to Pima Mine Road (© **520/625-7513;** www.mineraldiscovery.com), where you can tour a huge open-pit copper mine and learn about copper mining past and present. The Mineral Discovery Center is open Tuesday through Saturday from 9am to 5pm; admission is free. One-hour mine tours, which leave the Discovery Center every 20 to 30 minutes, are $6 for adults, $5 for seniors, and $4 for children 5 to 12.

Cowboy Up Adventures (© 520/888-3744) can take you south of Tucson to see ghost towns, old mines, and saloons. You'll also visit film sites of famous Westerns (the tour guide is a former actor and stuntman). Tours are $80, which includes lunch.

Want to taste raw cactus, learn about cholla-extraction devices, and hold a live tarantula or snake? Call **Sunshine Jeep Tours** (© **520/742-1943;** www. sunshinejeeptours.com), which charges $48 for adults, $36 for children 11 to 15, and $24 for children 6 to 10. On these tours, you'll head out across a private ranch northwest of Tucson and pass through some of the densest stands of saguaro cacti in the state.

7 Outdoor Pursuits

BALLOONING **Balloon Rides U.S.A.** (© **520/299-7744;** www.balloon ridesusa.com) offers breakfast flights over the desert (for first-timers) or over the foothills of the Santa Catalina Mountains (a more adventurous trip), both of which include a champagne toast. Flights cost $150 to $250 per person; the ballooning season runs October through June. **Fleur de Tucson Balloon Tours** (© **520/529-1025**) offers rides over the Tucson Mountains and Saguaro National Park. Rates are $150 per person, including brunch and a champagne toast.

BICYCLING Tucson is one of the best bicycling cities in the country, and the dirt roads and trails of the surrounding national forest and desert are perfect for mountain biking. Bikes can be rented for $25 to $45 a day at **Full Cycle,** 3302 E. Speedway Blvd. (© **520/327-3232**), or **Basement Bike,** 428 N. Fremont Ave., near the university (© **520/628-1015**). Either store can set you up with a bicycling map of the area.

If you'd rather confine your pedaling to paved surfaces, there are some great options around town. The number-one choice in town for cyclists in halfway decent shape is the road up **Sabino Canyon** (see "Seeing the Sights," earlier in this chapter). Keep in mind, however, that bicycles are allowed on this road only 5 days a week and then only before 9am and after 5pm (the road's closed to bikes all day Wednesday and Saturday). For a much easier ride, try the **Rillito River Park path,** a 4-mile trail that parallels River Road and the usually dry bed of the Rillito River between Campbell Avenue and La Cholla Boulevard. If you've got knobby tires, you can continue west on this trail after the pavement ends. Another option close to downtown is the 4-mile **Santa Cruz River Park path,** which extends from West Grant Road to 29th Street. Once again, this trail parallels a usually dry riverbed.

If mountain biking is more your speed, there are lots of great rides in the Tucson area. For an easy and very scenic dirt-road loop through forests of saguaros, head to Saguaro National Park West and ride the 6-mile **Bajada Loop Drive.** You can turn this into a 12-mile ride (half on paved road) by starting at the Red Hills Visitor Center. (See Saguaro National Park under "Seeing the Sights," earlier in this chapter, for details.) Also on the west side of Tucson are the many miles of challenging trails in **Tucson Mountain Park.** Primarily for experienced riders, these trails are obstacle courses of cactus spines, sand, rocky trails, and steep climbs. In other words, perfect desert mountain-biking conditions. Before riding here, be sure to visit a bike shop and get a map of the area or call Pima County Parks (© **520/740-5830**) for more information. To reach the trailhead, take the Starr Pass Road exit off I10 and drive 3 miles west to a dirt road near the Starr Pass golf resort.

BIRD-WATCHING Southern Arizona has some of the best bird-watching in the country, and although the best spots are south of Tucson, there are a few places around the city that birders will enjoy seeking out. **Roy P. Drachman**

Agua Caliente Park, 4002 N. Soldier Trail, at Roger Road in the northeast corner of the city, is just about the best place in Tucson to see birds. The year-round warm springs here are a magnet for dozens of species, including waterfowl, great blue herons, black phoebes, soras, and vermilion flycatchers. To find the park, follow Tanque Verde Road east 6 miles from the intersection with Sabino Canyon Road and turn left onto Soldier Trail. Watch for signs.

Other good places include **Sabino Canyon Recreation Area** and the path to the waterfall at **Loews Ventana Canyon Resort.**

The very best area for bird-watching is in **Madera Canyon National Forest Recreation Area** (© 520/281-2296), about 40 miles south of the city in the Coronado National Forest. Because of the year-round water to be found here, Madera Canyon attracts a surprising variety of bird life. Avid birders flock to this canyon from around the country in hopes of spotting more than a dozen species of hummingbirds, an equal number of flycatchers, warblers, tanagers, buntings, grosbeaks, and many rare birds not found in any other state. However, before birding became a hot activity, this canyon was popular with families looking for a way to escape the heat down in Tucson, and the shady picnic areas and trails still get a lot of use by those who don't carry binoculars. If you're heading out for the day, arrive early—parking is very limited. To reach Madera Canyon, take exit 39 off I-19; from the exit, it's another 12 miles southeast. The canyon is open daily from dawn to dusk for day use, but there's also a campground ($10 per night). On weekends, a $2 donation is requested for use of the recreation area. For information on the canyon's Santa Rita Lodge, see "Where to Stay," earlier in this chapter.

GOLF   Although there aren't quite as many golf courses in Tucson as in Phoenix, this is still a golfer's town. For last-minute tee-time reservations, contact **Standby Golf** (© 800/655-5345 or 520/882-2665). No fee is charged for this service.

In addition to the public and municipal links, there are numerous resort courses that allow nonguests to play. Perhaps the most famous of these are the two 18-hole courses at **Ventana Canyon Golf and Racquet Club**, 6200 N. Clubhouse Lane (© 520/577-1400). These Tom Fazio–designed courses offer challenging desert target–style play that is nearly legendary. The third hole on the Mountain Course is one of the most photographed holes in the West. Greens fees are $179 in winter, $80 in summer.

As famous as Ventana Canyon courses are, it's the 27-hole **Omni Tucson National Golf Resort and Spa**, 2727 W. Club Dr. (© 520/297-2271 main number; © 520/575-7540, pro shop), a traditional course, that is perhaps more familiar to golfers as the site of the annual Tucson Open. Greens fees are $149 in winter, $59 in summer.

The **El Conquistador Country Club,** 10555 N. La Cañada Dr. (© 520/544-1800), with two 18-hole courses and a 9-hole course, offers stunning (and very distracting) views of the Santa Catalina Mountains. Greens fees are $99 in winter, $39 in summer.

The **La Paloma Resort and Country Club,** 3660 E. Sunrise Dr. (© 520/299-1500), features 27 holes designed by Jack Nicklaus. Fees are $175 in winter, $85 in summer.

At **Starr Pass Golf Club,** 3645 W. Starr Pass Blvd. (© 520/670-0400), players are seduced by the deceptively difficult 15th hole that plays right through the narrow Starr Pass, which was once a stagecoach route. Greens fees are $135 in winter, $65 or less in summer.

There are many public courses around town. The **Raven Golf Club at Sabino Springs,** 9777 E. Sabino Greens Dr. (© **520/749-3636**), incorporates stands of cactus and rocky outcroppings into the course layout. Greens fees are $155 in winter, $55 in summer. At the **Golf Club at Vistoso,** 955 W. Vistoso Highlands Dr. (© **520/797-9900**), you'll find a championship desert course; fees are $140 in winter, $45 in summer. **Heritage Highlands Golf & Country Club,** 4949 W. Heritage Club Blvd. (© **520/579-7000**), is a newer championship desert course at the foot of the Tortolita Mountains, with fees of $125 in winter and $45 in summer.

Tucson Parks and Recreation operates five municipal golf courses, of which the **Randolph North** and **Dell Urich,** 600 S. Alvernon Way (© **520/ 791-4161**), are the premier courses. The former is the site of the LPGA Open. Other municipal courses include **Trini Alvarez/El Rio,** 1400 W. Speedway Blvd. (© **520/791-4229**); **Silverbell,** 3600 N. Silverbell Rd. (© **520/ 791-5235**); and **Fred Enke,** 8251 E. Irvington Rd. (© **520/791-2539**). Nonresident greens fees for 18 holes are about $32 to $37 between November and May (about $20 in summer). Golf carts are available for $18.

HIKING   Tucson is nearly surrounded by mountains, most of which are protected as city and state parks, national forest, or national park, and within these public areas are hundreds of miles of hiking trails.

Saguaro National Park (© **520/733-5153**) flanks Tucson on both the east and west with units accessible off Old Spanish Trail east of Tucson and past the end of Speedway Boulevard west of the city. In these areas, you can observe Sonoran Desert vegetation and wildlife and hike among the huge saguaro cacti for which the park is named. For saguaro-spotting, the west unit is the better choice. See "Seeing the Sights," earlier in this chapter, for details.

Tucson Mountain Park, at the end of Speedway Boulevard, is adjacent to Saguaro National Park and preserves a similar landscape. The parking area at Gates Pass, on Speedway, is a favorite sunset spot.

Sabino Canyon, off Sabino Canyon Road, is Tucson's most popular recreation area. A cold mountain stream here cascades over waterfalls and forms pools that make great swimming holes. The **Seven Falls Trail,** which follows Bear Canyon deep into the mountains, is 5.2 miles round-trip and the most popular hike in the recreation area. You can take a tram to the trailhead or add extra miles by hiking from the main parking lot.

With the city limits pushing right out to the boundary of the Coronado National Forest, there are some excellent hiking options in Tucson's northern foothills. The **Ventana Canyon Trail** begins at a parking area adjacent to the Loews Ventana Canyon Resort (off Sunrise Drive west of Sabino Canyon Road) and leads into the Ventana Canyon Wilderness. Over near the Westward Look Resort is the **Pima Canyon Trail,** which leads into the Ventana Canyon Wilderness and is reached off Ina Road just east of Oracle Road. Both of these trails provide classic desert canyon hikes of whatever length you feel like hiking (a dam at 3 miles on the latter trail makes a good turnaround point).

Catalina State Park, 11570 N. Oracle Rd. (© **520/628-5798**), is set on the rugged northwest face of the Santa Catalina Mountains, between 2,500 and 3,000 feet high. Hiking trails here lead into the Pusch Ridge Wilderness; however, the favorite park day hike is the 5.6-mile round-trip to Romero Pools, where small natural pools of water set amid the rocks are a refreshing destination on a hot day (expect plenty of other people on a weekend). This hike involves about 1,000 feet of elevation gain. Admission to the park is $5. There are horseback-riding stables adjacent to the park, and within the park is an ancient Hohokam ruin. Guided hikes are offered in the cooler months.

One of the reasons Tucson is such a livable city is the presence of the cool (and, in winter, snow-covered) pine forests of 8,250-foot Mount Lemmon. Within the **Mount Lemmon Recreation Area,** at the end of the Catalina Highway, are many miles of hiking trails, and the hearty hiker can even set out from down in the lowland desert and hike up into the alpine forests. For a more leisurely excursion, drive to the top to start your hike. One of our favorite hikes is the 5.1-mile Aspen-Marshall Gulch loop, which begins beyond the community of Summerhaven at the Marshall Gulch picnic area and offers lots of good views at the start of the hike. This hike involves about 1,000 feet of elevation gain. Keep in mind, however, that in winter, when the weather is pleasant in Tucson, people may be skiing up here. There is a $5-per-vehicle charge to use any of the sites within this recreation area. Even if you only plan to pull off at a roadside parking spot and ogle the view of the desert far below, you'll need to stop at the roadside ticket kiosk at the base of the mountain and pay your fee. For more information, contact the **Coronado National Forest Santa Catalina Ranger District,** 5700 N. Sabino Canyon Rd. (© **520/749-8700**).

HORSEBACK RIDING   If you want to play cowboy or just go for a leisurely ride through the desert, there are plenty of stables around Tucson where you can saddle up. In addition to renting horses and providing guided trail rides, some of the stables below offer sunset rides with cookouts. Although reservations are not always required, they're a good idea. You can also opt to stay at a guest ranch and do as much riding as your muscles can stand.

Pusch Ridge Stables, 13700 N. Oracle Rd. (© **520/825-1664**), is adjacent to Catalina State Park and Coronado National Forest. Rates are $20 for 1 hour, $35 for 2 hours. Pusch Ridge has a satellite stable at the Sheraton El Conquistador.

In the same area, you'll find **Walking Wind Stables,** 10811 N. Oracle Rd. (© **520/742-4422**), at Catalina State Park. Rates are $35 for 1½ hours, $42 for 2 hours, and $55 for 3 hours. Reservations are suggested.

Big Sky Rides, 6501 W. Ina Rd. (© **520/744-3789;** www.bigskyride.com), is 2 miles west of I-10 and offers a variety of rides in the Tucson Mountains and Saguaro National Park West. Rates range from $25 for 1 hour to $95 for a full day with lunch. Reservations are requested.

If your idea of fun is doing the *City-Slicker* thing, call the **Cocoraque Ranch,** 6255 N. Diamond Hills Lane (© **520/682-8594**). This working cattle ranch dates from the 1890s and now offers cattle drives. Rates depend on the number of people, and there is a 12-person minimum, but it is sometimes possible to join another group. Trail rides that go out to check on the cattle ($30 for 2 hr.) are available. The ranch is near the Arizona–Sonora Desert Museum and Old Tucson Studios.

SKIING   Located 1 hour (35 miles) from Tucson, **Mount Lemmon Ski Valley** (© **520/576-1321,** or 520/576-1400 for snow report) is the southernmost ski area in the United States and offers 15 runs for experienced downhill skiers as well as beginners. The season here isn't very reliable, and locals recommend not using your own skis or snowboard (too many exposed rocks). The ski area often opens only after a new dump of snow (at which time the Catalina/Mount Lemmon Highway is usually closed), so be sure to call the road-condition information line (© **520/547-7510**) before driving up. The season runs from December to April. Full-day lift tickets are $28 to $32 for adults and $13 for children.

TENNIS The **Randolph Tennis Center,** 50 S. Alvernon Way (© **520/ 791-4896**), convenient to downtown, offers 25 lighted courts. During the day, court time is $2 per person; at night, it's $6 per court. Many of the city's hotels and resorts provide courts for guest use.

WILDFLOWER-VIEWING Bloom time varies from year to year, but April and May are good times to view native wildflowers in the Tucson area. While the crowns of white blossoms worn by saguaro cacti are among the most visible blooms in the area, other cacti are far more colorful. Saguaro National Park and Sabino Canyon are among the best local spots to see saguaros, other cacti, and various other wildflowers in bloom. If you feel like heading further afield, the wildflower displays at Picacho Peak State Park, between Tucson and Casa Grande, are considered the most impressive in the state.

8 Spectator Sports

BASEBALL The **Colorado Rockies** (© 520/327-9467) pitch spring-training camp in March at Hi Corbett Field, 3400 E. Camino Campestre, in Reid Park (at South Country Club Road and East 22nd Street). Tickets are $2 to $11. Both the **Chicago White Sox** and the **Arizona Diamondbacks** have their spring-training camps and exhibition games at Tucson Electric Park, 2500 E. Ajo Way (© **520/434-1111**), on the south side of the city near the airport. Tickets range from $4 to $16.

Tucson Electric Park is also where you can watch the **Tucson Sidewinders** (© **520/434-1021**), the Triple-AAA Affiliate team of the Arizona Diamond-backs. The season runs April through August, and tickets are $4.50 to $8.

FOOTBALL The **University of Arizona Wildcats** (© 520/621-2287; www. arizcats.com), a Pac-10 team, play at UA's Arizona Stadium.

GOLF TOURNAMENTS The **Touchstone Energy Tucson Open** (© 800/ 882-7660), Tucson's main PGA tournament, is held in mid-February at the Omni Tucson National Golf Resort and Spa. Daily tickets are $15. In mid-March, women golfers compete for big prizes at the **Welch's/Circle K LPGA Championship** (© 520/791-5742), which is held at the Randolph Golf Course Complex. Daily tickets are about $10. The **Tucson Classic Celebrity Golf Tournament** (© 520/623-6165) takes place at the Westin La Paloma in early September, with about 20 celebrity golfers participating. Tickets are $5.

GREYHOUND RACING Greyhounds race year-round at **Tucson Greyhound Park,** 36th Street at Fourth Avenue (© 520/884-7576). Admission is $1.25. To reach the track, take exit 261 off I-10.

HORSE RACING **Rillito Park,** on First Avenue between River and Limberlost roads (© 520/293-5011 during racing season, or 520/740-2690 other months), was the birthplace of both the photo finish and organized quarter-horse and Arabian racing. It has now been restored for both quarter-horse and thoroughbred racing. The ponies run on weekends in February and March. Admission is $2 to $3.

9 Day Spas

If you'd prefer a massage over a round on the links, consider spending a few hours at a day spa. While full-service health spas can cost $400 to $500 or more per day, for less than $100, you can avail yourself of a spa treatment or two (massages, facials, seaweed wraps, loofah scrubs, and the like) and maybe even get to spend the day lounging by the pool at some exclusive resort. Spas are great places to while away an afternoon if you couldn't get a tee time at that golf course you wanted to play or if it happens to be raining. While spas in general still cater primarily to women, those mentioned below also have special programs for men.

For variety of services and gorgeous location, you just can't beat the Spa & Tennis Center at **Loews Ventana Canyon Resort,** 7000 N. Resort Dr. (© 520/ 299-2020), which is wedged between the rugged Catalinas and manicured fairways of some of the most fabled golf courses in the state. Soothed by the scent of aromatherapy, you can treat yourself to herbal wraps, mud treatments, different styles of massage, specialized facials, complete salon services, and much more. Treatments run $80 to $115. With any body treatment, you get use of the spa's fitness facilities and pool and can attend any fitness classes being held that day.

For an equally luxurious day at the spa, you can opt to visit the **Omni Tucson National Golf Resort & Spa,** 2727 W. Club Dr. (© 520/575-7559), off Magee Road in the northwestern foothills. Services and prices here are comparable to those at Loews, and once again, with any body treatment or massage, you have full use of the spa's facilities. Try the hot stone massage!

With five locations around the Tucson area, **Gadabout Day Spa** offers the opportunity to slip a relaxing visit to a spa into a busy schedule. Mud baths, facials, and massages as well as hair and nail services are available. You'll find Gadabout at the following locations: St. Philip's Plaza, 1990 E. River Rd. (© 520/577-2000); 6393 E. Grant Rd. (© **520/885-0000**); Rancho Center, 3382 E. Speedway Blvd. (© **520/325-0000**); Sunrise-Kolb, 6960 E. Sunrise Dr. (© **520/615-9700**); and Plaza Escondida, 7888 N. Oracle Rd. (© 520/ **742-0000**). Body treatments and massages range from about $35 to $150.

10 Shopping

Tucsonans have a very strong sense of their place in the Southwest, and this is reflected in the city's shopping scene. Southwestern clothing, food, crafts, furniture, and art abound (and often at reasonable prices), as do shopping centers built in a Southwestern architectural style.

Although Tucson is overshadowed by Scottsdale and Phoenix, the city provides a very respectable diversity of merchants. Its population center has moved steadily northward for some years, so it is in the northern foothills that you'll find most of the large enclosed shopping malls as well as expensive shops selling the best-quality merchandise.

On Fourth Avenue, between Congress Street and Speedway Boulevard, more than 100 shops, galleries, and restaurants make up the **North Fourth Avenue historic shopping district.** The buildings here were constructed in the early 1900s, and there has been an attempt to keep the neighborhood humming and maintain Tucson's downtown vitality. However, these days the area could best be described as the used-clothing capital of the world. Through the underpass at the south end of Fourth Avenue is Congress Street, the heart of the **Downtown Arts District,** where there are a few art galleries. Despite the city's best efforts for several years now, neither of these neighborhoods seems to have caught on very fast with Tucson shoppers, and both areas seem to be primarily hangouts for college students.

El Presidio Historic District around the Tucson Museum of Art is the city's center for crafts shops. This area is home to Old Town Artisans and the Tucson Museum of Art museum shop. The **"Lost Barrio,"** on the corner of Southwest

Park Avenue and 12th Street (a block off Broadway), is a good place to look for Mexican imports and Southwestern-style home furnishings at good prices. Stores include Rústica, Colonial Frontiers, and Magellan Trading.

ANTIQUES & COLLECTIBLES

In addition to the places listed below, you'll find the greatest concentrations of antiques shops along Grant Road between Campbell Avenue and Alvernon Way. You can pick up a map of Tucson antiques stores at the **American Antique Mall** ((✆ **520/326-3070**), 3130 E. Grant Rd., at Country Club Road.

Antique Center   This mall has about 70 dealers and claims to be the largest antiques mall in southern Arizona. For sale are all manner of collectibles and a few antiques, including old radios and telephones and lots of copper and glassware collectibles. 5001 E. Speedway Blvd. ✆ **520/323-0319.**

Eric Firestone Gallery   Collectors of Stickley and other Arts and Crafts furniture will not want to miss this impressive gallery, which is located in one of the historic buildings at Joesler Village shopping plaza. In addition to the furniture, there are period paintings and accessories. In Joesler Village, 4425 N. Campbell Ave. ✆ **520/577-7711.**

Michael D. Higgins   Located next door to the Eric Firestone Gallery, this little shop specializes in pre-Columbian artifacts, but also carries African, Asian, even ancient Greek and Roman pieces. In Joesler Village, 4429 N. Campbell Ave. ✆ **520/577-8330.**

Morning Star Antiques   In a shop that adjoins Morning Star Traders (see "Native American Arts & Crafts," below), Morning Star Antiques carries an excellent selection of antique Spanish mission and Mexican furniture as well as other unusual and rustic pieces. 2000 E. Speedway Blvd. (next door to the Four Points Sheraton Hotel). ✆ **520/881-3060.** www.morningstartraders.com.

Primitive Arts Gallery   This is the best gallery in Tucson for pre-Columbian art, with an eclectic mix of ancient artifacts focusing on ceramics. You'll see a smattering of other artifacts, from Greek urns to contemporary Argentinian maté gourds. 3026 E. Broadway (in Broadway Village). ✆ **520/326-4852.**

ART

Tucson's gallery scene is not as concentrated as that in many other cities. While there are a handful downtown, most Tucson galleries have in the past few years abandoned downtown in favor of the foothills and other more affluent suburbs. The current art hot spot is the corner of Campbell Avenue and Skyline Drive, where you'll find Sanders Galleries and El Cortijo Arts Annex, which has several art galleries and an upscale restaurant.

One of the best ways to take in the downtown Tucson art scene is on the free Thursday docent-led ArtWalk tours that take place between 5:30 and 7pm. These walks are held every Thursday between October and May and are sponsored by the **Tucson Arts District Partnership** ((✆ **520/624-9977**). Call for information on the tour starting point.

Dinnerware Contemporary Art Gallery   *Contemporary* is the key word at this gallery in the downtown arts district. Artists represented tend to have a very wide range of styles and media, so you never know what you'll find. Regardless, you can be sure it will be at the cutting edge of Tucson art. 135 E. Congress St. ✆ **520/792-4503.** dinnerware@theriver.com.

El Presidio Gallery One of Tucson's premier galleries, El Presidio deals primarily in traditional and contemporary paintings of the Southwest, and is located in a large, modern space in the El Cortijo Arts Annex. Contemporary works tend toward the large and bright and are favorites for decorating foothills homes. Also at Santa Fe Square, 7000 E. Tanque Verde Rd. (© **520/733-0388**). 3001 E. Skyline Dr. © 520/299-1414. www.elpresidiogallery.com.

Etherton Gallery For more than 16 years, this gallery has been presenting some of the finest new art to be found in Tucson, including contemporary and historic photographs. A favorite of museums and serious collectors, Etherton Gallery isn't afraid to present work with strong themes. It has additional exhibition space near its main downtown gallery upstairs at the Temple of Music and Art, 330 S. Scott Ave. There's another location in the foothills at Joesler Village, 4419 N. Campbell Ave. (© **520/615-1441**), where the emphasis is on historic photographs. 135 S. Sixth Ave. © 520/624-7370. www.ethgal@azstarnet.com.

Mark Sublette Medicine Man Gallery This gallery has the finest and most tasteful traditional Western art you'll find just about anywhere in Arizona. Artists represented here include Ed Mell and Howard Post, and most of the gallery's artists have received national attention. There's an excellent selection of Native American crafts as well; see "Native American Arts & Crafts," below, for more details. The shop is near a branch of the El Presidio Gallery (see above). In Santa Fe Square, 7000 E. Tanque Verde Rd. © 520/722-7798.

Philabaum Contemporary Art Glass Visitors can stop by Tom Philabaum's glass studio to watch vases, perfume bottles, and bowls being blown, then browse the gallery full of lovely art-glass pieces by Philabaum and more than 100 other artists from around the country. 711 S. Sixth Ave. © 520/884-7404.

BOOKS

Chain bookstores in the Tucson area include **Barnes & Noble,** 5130 E. Broadway Blvd. (© **520/512-1166**), and 7325 N. La Cholla Blvd., in the Foothills Mall (© **520/742-6402**); and **Borders,** 4235 N. Oracle Rd. (© **520/ 292-1331**), and 5870 E. Broadway, at the Park Place Mall (© **520/584-0111**).

Audubon Nature Shop Nature enthusiasts can pick up field guides and books on natural history, along with educational and children's books. 300 E. University Blvd. © 520/629-0510.

Readers Oasis A small bookstore, but packed with handpicked titles of local and general interest. It occasionally has author readings and book signings (local author Barbara Kingsolver spoke here in early 2001). 3400 E. Speedway Blvd., #114. © 520/319-7887.

Settlers West Book & Print Gallery An impressive selection of books about the West, for both adults and children, is the main attraction, but there are lots of interesting prints of Western themes as well. 3061 N. Campbell Ave. © 520/323-8838. www.settlerswest.com.

CRAFTS

Details & Green Shoelaces If you enjoy highly imaginative and colorful crafts with a sense of humor, you'll get a kick out of this place. Unexpected objets d'art turn up in the form of clocks, ceramics, glass, and other media. 2990 N. Swan Rd. (in Plaza Palomino). © 520/323-0222. www.detailsart.com.

Obsidian Gallery Contemporary crafts by artists of national renown fill this gallery. You'll find luminous art glass, unique and daring jewelry, imaginative

ceramics, and much more. 4340 N. Campbell Ave. (at River Rd. in St. Philip's Plaza).
☏ 520/577-3598.

Old Town Artisans   Housed in a restored 1850s adobe building covering an entire city block of El Presidio Historic District are 15 rooms brimming with traditional and contemporary Southwestern designs by more than 400 artisans. 186 N. Meyer Ave. ☏ 800/782-8072 or 520/623-6024. www.oldtownartisans.com.

Pink Adobe Gallery   This contemporary crafts gallery sells unique and whimsical works produced by artists from all over the United States. On a recent visit, we saw hand-tinted photos, glass, ceramics, one-of-a-kind pieces of furniture, and cases full of unique jewelry. The gallery also features fine-crafted Judaica. 6538 E. Tanque Verde Rd. (in La Plaza Shoppes). ☏ 520/298-5995. www.pinkadobe.com.

Tucson Museum of Art Shop   The museum's gift shop offers a colorful and changing selection of Southwestern arts and crafts, mostly by local and regional artists. 140 N. Main Ave. ☏ 520/624-2333.

FASHION
See also the listing for the Beth Friedman Collection under "Jewelry," below. For cowboy and cowgirl attire, see "Western Wear," below.

Buffalo Exchange   A big hit with the college students—both male and female—this resale shop originated in Tucson and has grown into a chain with stores across the West. Browse through racks of resale and new clothing at fairly reasonable prices, and you're sure to find something to fit your needs. This is a good place to pick up a used leather jacket or last season's hot fashion item. There's another Buffalo Exchange at 6170 E. Speedway Blvd. (☏ **520/885-0114**). 2001 E. Speedway Blvd. ☏ **520/795-0508**.

Jasmine   Natural fibers, including washable silks and some hand-loomed fabrics, are the specialty here. There are plenty of styles to browse, from classic to exotic, plus Southwestern accessories and jewelry to go with the clothes. There's a second store at 423 N. Fourth Ave. (☏ **520/629-0706**). 3025 N. Campbell. ☏ **520/323-1771**.

Maya Palace   This shop features ethnic-inspired but very wearable women's clothing in natural fabrics. The friendly staff helps customers of all ages put together a Southwestern chic look, from casual to dressy. A second shop can be found in Plaza Palomino at 2960 N. Swan Rd. (☏ **520/325-6411**). El Mercado de Boutiques, 6332 E. Broadway Blvd. ☏ **520/748-0817**.

Rochelle K Fine Women's Apparel   With everything from the latest in the little black dress to drapey silks and casual linens, Rochelle K attracts a well-heeled clientele. You'll also find beautiful accessories and jewelry here. 5350 E. Broadway Blvd. in the Plaza at Williams Centre (southwest corner of Broadway and Craycroft). ☏ 520/745-4600.

GIFTS & SOUVENIRS
B&B Cactus Farm   This plant nursery is devoted exclusively to cacti and succulents and is worth a visit just to see the amazing variety on display. It's a good place to stop on the way to or from Saguaro National Park East. The store can pack your purchase for traveling or can ship it anywhere in the United States. 11550 E. Speedway Blvd. ☏ 520/721-4687.

Native Seeds/SEARCH   Gardeners, cooks, and just about anyone in search of an unusual gift will likely be fascinated by this tiny shop, which is operated by a nonprofit organization dedicated to preserving the biodiversity offered by native Southwest seeds. The shelves are full of heirloom beans, corn, chiles, and other seeds from a wide variety of native desert plants. For sale are gourds and inexpensive Tarahumara Indian baskets, bottled sauces and salsas made from native plants, and books about native agriculture. 526 N. Fourth Ave. ✆ 520/622-5561. www.nativeseeds.org.

Picánte   There's a plethora of Hispanic-theme icons and accessories here, including *milagros,* Day of the Dead skeletons, Mexican crosses, jewelry, greeting cards, and folk art from around the world. 2932 E. Broadway. ✆ 520/320-5699.

Tohono Chul Gift Shop and Tea Room   This gift shop is packed with Mexican folk art, nature-theme toys, household items, T-shirts, and books; it makes a good stop after a visit to the surrounding Tohono Chul Park, which is landscaped with desert plants. Add a meal at the park's tearoom, and you've got a good afternoon's outing. For a description of the park, see "Parks, Gardens & Zoos," under "Seeing the Sights," earlier in this chapter. 7366 N. Paseo del Norte (1 block west of the corner of Ina Rd. and Oracle Rd. in Tohono Chul Park). ✆ 520/797-1222. www.tohonochulpark.org.

JEWELRY

In addition to the stores mentioned below, see the listing for the Obsidian Gallery under "Crafts," earlier in this section.

Beth Friedman Collection   Located in the Old Town Artisans complex, this shop sells a well-chosen collection of jewelry by Native American craftspeople and international designers. It also carries some extravagant cowgirl get-ups in velvet and lace. The second location in Joesler Village, 1865 E. River Rd., is much larger, with a greater emphasis on contemporary women's fashions (✆ **520/577-6858**). 186 N. Meyer Ave. ✆ **520/622-5013**.

Turquoise Door   The Southwestern contemporary jewelry here is among the most stunning in the city, made with opals, diamonds, lapis lazuli, amethyst, and the ubiquitous turquoise. In St. Philip's Plaza, 4330 N. Campbell Ave. (at River Rd.). ✆ 520/299-7787.

MALLS & SHOPPING CENTERS

Foothills Mall   This large foothills mall went out of business a few years back but has now been revived as a factory-outlet mall and discount shopping center. You'll find a Nike factory store, Off 5th Saks Fifth Avenue outlet, and Barnes & Noble, as well as Keaton's Arizona Grill. 7401 N. La Cholla Blvd. (at Ina Rd.). ✆ 520/219-0650.

Plaza Palomino   Built in the style of a Spanish hacienda with a courtyard and fountains, this shopping center is home to some of Tucson's fun little specialty shops, galleries, and restaurants. 2970 N. Swan Rd. ✆ 520/622-0077.

St. Philip's Plaza   This upscale Southwestern-style shopping center contains two or three excellent restaurants, a luxury beauty salon, and numerous shops and galleries, including Bahti Indian Arts and Turquoise Door jewelry. Makes a great one-stop Tucson outing. 4280 N. Campbell Ave. (at River Rd.). ✆ 520/529-2775.

Tucson Mall   The foothills of northern Tucson have become shopping-center central, and this is the largest of the malls. You'll find more than 200 retailers in this busy, two-story skylit complex. 4500 N. Oracle Rd. ✆ 520/293-7330. www.tucson-mall.com.

MEXICAN & LATIN AMERICAN IMPORTS

In addition to the shops mentioned below, the **"Lost Barrio,"** on the corner of Southwest Park Avenue and 12th Street (a block off Broadway), is a good place to look for Mexican imports and Southwestern-style home furnishings at good prices.

Antigua de Mexico This is a place for arts and crafts from Mexico—big household items, such as oversized ceramics and painted plates, wooden and wrought-iron furniture, and punched-metal frames and framed mirrors. Smaller items include crucifixes and candlesticks. 3235 W. Orange Grove Rd. ✆ 520/742-7114.

La Buhardilla ("The Attic") Okay, so you just cashed out of your place in California, you bought a big house in Arizona, and now you need some sizable furniture to fill up all that space. Buhardilla has it—the hand-carved Spanish baroque furniture is big—as well as 10-foot-high carved wood doors and larger-than-life-size carvings of angels and archangels. 2360 E. Broadway Blvd. ✆ 520/622-5200.

Zocalo Although large pieces, including colonial-style furniture, comprise much of the inventory here, there are also decorator items such as Mexican ceramics, glassware, and Mexican-style paintings. A visit to Zocalo provides an opportunity to wander around Broadway Village, a historic shopping plaza. 3016 E. Broadway Blvd. ✆ 520/320-1236.

NATIVE AMERICAN ARTS & CRAFTS

Bahti Indian Arts Family-owned for more than 40 years, this store sells fine pieces—jewelry, baskets, sculpture, paintings, books, weavings, kachina dolls, Zuni fetishes, and much more. In St. Philip's Plaza, 4300 N. Campbell Ave. ✆ 520/577-0290. www.bahti.com.

Gallery West Located right below Anthony's restaurant, this very small shop specializes in very expensive Native American artifacts (mostly pre-1940s), such as pots, Apache and Pima baskets, 19th-century Plains Indian beadwork, Navajo weavings, and kachinas. Recent additions include both historic and contemporary jewelry. 6420 N. Campbell Ave. (corner of Skyline Dr. and N. Campbell Rd.). ✆ 520/529-7002.

Indian Territory Despite the location in a shopping plaza in the foothills, it's a bit like an old museum in here, with hardwood floors and antique display cases full of Plains and Southwest Indian arts and crafts and regalia. Although much of the store is devoted to new works, you'll also see rare old pieces, such as beaded gauntlets and moccasins. 5639 N. Swan Rd. (on the northwest corner with Sunrise Dr.). ✆ 520/577-7961. www.indianterritoryaz.com.

Kaibab Courtyard Shops In business for about 50 years, this store offers one of the best selections of Native American arts and crafts in Tucson. You can find high-quality jewelry, Mexican pottery and folk arts, home furnishings, glassware, kachinas, and rugs. 2841 N. Campbell Ave. ✆ 520/795-6905.

Mark Sublette Medicine Man Gallery Collectors of old Navajo rugs seem to agree that this rug shop has the best and biggest selection in the city, and perhaps even the entire state. There are Mexican and other Hispanic textiles, Acoma pottery, basketry, and other Indian crafts, as well as artwork by cowboy artists. In Santa Fe Square, 7000 E. Tanque Verde Rd. ✆ 520/722-7798.

Morning Star Traders With hardwood floors and a museum-like atmosphere, this store features museum-quality goods: antique Navajo rugs, kachinas, furniture, and a huge selection of old Native American jewelry. This just may be the best store of its type in the entire state. An adjoining shop, Morning Star Antiques, carries an astounding selection of antique furniture (see "Antiques & Collectibles," above). 2020 E. Speedway Blvd. (next door to the Four Points Sheraton Hotel). ✆ 520/881-2112. www.morningstartraders.com.

Silverbell Trading   Not your usual run-of-the-mill crafts store, this shop specializes in regional Native American artwork, such as baskets and pottery, and carries unique pieces that the owner has obviously sought out. Small items such as stone Navajo corn maidens, Zuni fetishes, and figures carved from sandstone should not be overlooked. In Casas Adobes Plaza, 7007 N. Oracle Rd. ✆ 520/797-6852.

WESTERN WEAR

Arizona Hatters   Arizona Hatters carries important names in cowboy hats, from Stetson to Bailey to Tilles. Employees custom fit and shape the hat to the wearer's head and face. You'll also find bolo ties, Western belts, and other accessories here. 3600 N. First Ave. ✆ 520/292-1320.

Western Warehouse   If you want to put together your Western-wear ensemble under one roof, this is the place. It's the largest Western-wear store in Tucson and can deck you and your kids out in the latest cowboy fashions, including hats and boots. There are other branches at 3719 N. Oracle Rd. (✆ **520/293-1808**), and 6701 E. Broadway Blvd. (✆ **520/885-4385**). 3030 E. Speedway Blvd. ✆ 520/ 327-8005.

WINE

The Rumrunner   Looking for an Arizona wine or a wine you just haven't been able to locate elsewhere? You might find it here at the Rumrunner, along with imported cheeses, pâtés, and fresh caviar to accompany your libation. 3200 E. Speedway Blvd. ✆ 520/326-0121.

11 Tucson After Dark

Tucson after dark is a much easier landscape to negotiate than the vast cultural sprawl of the Phoenix area. Rather than having numerous performing-arts centers all over the suburbs as in the Valley of the Sun, Tucson has a more concentrated nightlife scene. The **Downtown Arts District** is the center of all the action, with the Temple of Music and Art, the Tucson Convention Center Music Hall, and several nightclubs. The **University of Arizona campus,** only a mile away, is another hot spot for entertainment.

The best place to look for entertainment listings is in the free *Tucson Weekly,* which contains thorough listings of concerts, theater and dance performances, and club offerings. The entertainment section of the *Arizona Daily Star,* "Caliente," comes out each Friday and is another good source.

THE CLUB & MUSIC SCENE
MARIACHI

Tucson is the mariachi capital of the United States, and no one should visit without spending at least one evening listening to some of these strolling minstrels.

La Fuente   La Fuente is the largest Mexican restaurant in Tucson and serves up good food, but what really draws the crowds is the live mariachi music. The performance starts at 6pm, and if you just want to listen and not have dinner, you can hang out in the lounge. The mariachis perform nightly. 1749 N. Oracle Rd. ✆ 520/623-8659. No cover.

COUNTRY

Cactus Moon Café   A 20- to 30-something crowd frequents this large and glitzy nightclub primarily for country music. 5470 E. Broadway Blvd. (on the east side of town at the corner of Craycroft Rd.). ✆ 520/748-0049. Cover $2–$4.

The Maverick, King of Clubs   This country-and-western place is tiny, which as far as a lot of people are concerned makes it a great place to go dancing. It generally attracts an older crowd, but there's usually a mix of people. The house band plays Tuesday through Saturday. 4702 E. 22nd. St. (at Swan Rd.). ✆ **520/748-0456.** No cover.

ROCK, BLUES & REGGAE

Berky's Bar   There's live music wailing 7 nights a week in this dark and smoky tavern. Mondays are open-jam nights, so you never know who or what you might hear. 5769 E. Speedway Blvd. ✆ **520/296-1981.** Cover $3 Fri–Sat.

Boondocks Lounge   Long a popular dive bar, this place north of downtown is now one of the city's best spots to hear live blues and reggae. There's even a swing night complete with dance lessons. Just look for the giant Chianti bottle out front. 3306 N. First Ave. ✆ **520/690-0991.** No cover to $10.

Chicago Bar   Transplanted Chicagoans love to watch their home teams on the TVs at this neighborhood bar, but there's also live music nightly. Sure, blues gets played a lot, but so do reggae and rock and about everything in between. 5954 E. Speedway Blvd. ✆ **520/748-8169.** Cover $3 Wed–Sat.

Club Congress   Just off the lobby of the restored Hotel Congress (now a budget hotel and youth hostel), Club Congress is Tucson's main alternative-music venue. There are usually a couple of nights of live music each week, and over the years such bands as Nirvana, Dick Dale, and the Goo Goo Dolls have played here. 311 E. Congress St. ✆ **520/622-8848.** Cover $3–$15.

The Rialto Theatre   This renovated 1919 vaudeville theater, although not a nightclub, is now Tucson's main venue for performances by bands that are too big to play Club Congress (Robert Cray, Los Lobos, Spyrogyra, Little Feat). 318 E. Congress St. ✆ **520/798-3333.** www.rialtotheatre.com. Tickets $5–$25.

JAZZ

To find out what's happening on the jazz scene in Tucson, call the **Tucson Jazz Society** (✆ **520/903-1265;** www.tucsonjazz.org). Its hot line will give you up-to-date information on jazz clubs and jazz performances, which it sponsors throughout the year.

DANCE CLUBS & DISCOS

El Parador   Tropical decor and an overabundance of potted plants set the mood for lively Latin jazz performances and salsa lessons (Friday and Saturday nights), complete with a salsa band. Customers' ages range from the 20s to the 60s, giving new meaning to the term "all ages" club. 2744 E. Broadway. ✆ **520/881-2808.** Cover $6 Fri–Sat.

COMEDY

Laffs Comedy Caffè   This stand-up comedy club features local comedians and professional comedians from around the country Wednesday through Saturday nights; Sunday is open-mike night. A full bar and a limited menu are available. The Village, 2900 E. Broadway Blvd. ✆ **520/881-8928** or 520/323-8669. Cover $5 Wed–Thurs, $5–$9 Fri–Sat.

THE BAR, LOUNGE & PUB SCENE

The Arizona Inn   If you're looking for a quiet, comfortable scene, the jazz or acoustic music in the Audubon Lounge at the Arizona Inn is sure to soothe your soul. The gardens here are beautiful. 2200 E. Elm St. ✆ **520/325-1541.**

Cascade Lounge   This is Tucson's ultimate piano bar. With a view of the Catalinas and a happy hour (daily from 5–7pm), the plush lounge is perfect for romance or relaxation at the start or end of a night on the town. A couple of nights each week, a harpist performs instead of a pianist, and on the weekends, you'll find a trio here. In Loews Ventana Canyon Resort, 7000 N. Resort Dr. ℂ 520/299-2020.

Gentle Ben's Brewing Co.   Located just off the UA campus, Gentle Ben's, a big, modern place with plenty of outdoor seating, is Tucson's favorite microbrewery. The crowd is primarily college students. Food and drink specials are offered daily. 865 E. University Blvd. ℂ 520/624-4177.

Nimbus Brewing   Located in a warehouse district on the south side of Tucson, this brewpub is basically the front room of Nimbus's brewing and bottling facility. The furniture is straight out of Goodwill, but the beer is good, and there's live rock and jazz several nights a week. Hard to find, and definitely a local scene. 3850 E. 44th St. (2 blocks east of Palo Verde Rd.). ℂ 520/745-9175. www.nimbusbeer.com.

Presidio Grill   With its hip, contemporary decor, Presidio Grill attracts a young, upscale crowd. Although best known as one of the city's premier restaurants, the bar is a great place for a cocktail (martinis are the specialty). 3352 E. Speedway Blvd. ℂ 520/327-4667.

Thunder Canyon Brewery   Located in the Foothills Mall and affiliated with the Prescott Brewing Co. in Prescott, this brewpub is your best bet in Tucson for handcrafted ales and is the most convenient brewpub for anyone staying at a foothills resort. 7401 N. La Cholla Blvd. ℂ 520/797-2652.

¡Toma!   This cafe, set in El Presidio Historic District and owned by the family that operates El Charro Café next door, has a humorous, festive atmosphere complete with a Mexican hat fountain/sculpture in the courtyard. Drop by for cheap margaritas during happy hour, Monday through Friday from 3 to 6pm (in the bar only). 311 N. Court Ave. ℂ 520/622-1922.

COCKTAILS WITH A VIEW

Just about all the best views in town are at foothills resorts, but luckily they don't mind sharing with nonguests. In addition to those listed below, the lounge at **Anthony's in the Catalinas** has a great view. See "Where to Dine," earlier in this chapter, for details.

Desert Garden Lounge   If you'd like a close-up view of the Santa Catalina Mountains, drop by the Desert Garden Lounge (at sunset, perhaps). The large lounge, with its multicolored hardwood floors, affects a sort of Casablanca ambience, with live piano music several nights a week. In the Westin La Paloma, 3800 E. Sunrise Dr. ℂ 520/742-6000.

Flying V Bar & Grill   If you can't afford the lap of luxury, you can at least pull up a chair. Set it next to a waterfall just outside the front door of this popular resort watering hole for one of the best views in the city, looking out over the golf course and Tucson far below. In Loews Ventana Canyon Resort, 7000 N. Resort Dr. ℂ 520/299-2020.

Lookout Bar & Grille   The Westward Look is one of Tucson's oldest resorts and took to the hills long before it became the fashionable place to be. The nighttime view of twinkling city lights and stars is unmatched. On weekend nights, there's live music. In the Westward Look Resort, 245 E. Ina Rd. ℂ 520/297-1151.

SPORTS BARS

Famous Sam's With 10-plus branches around the city, Famous Sam's keeps a lot of Tucson's sports fans happy with their cheap prices and large portions. Other convenient locations include 1830 E. Broadway Blvd. (© **520/ 884-0119**); 7930 E. Speedway Blvd. (© **520/290-9666**); and 4801 E. 29th St. (© **520/748-1975**). 3620 N. First Ave. © **520/292-0314.**

GAY & LESBIAN BARS & DANCE CLUBS

To find out about other gay bars around town, keep an eye out for the *Observer,* Tucson's newspaper for the gay, lesbian, and bisexual community. You'll find it at **Antigone Books,** 411 N. Fourth Ave. (© **520/792-3715**), as well as at the bars listed here.

Ain't Nobody's Bizness Located in a small shopping plaza in midtown, this somewhat upscale bar is *the* lesbian gathering spot in Tucson, and has been for several years. There's a dance floor, two pool tables, and a quiet smoke-free room where you can duck out of the noise. 2900 E. Broadway Blvd. © **520/318-4838.**

IBT's Located on funky Fourth Avenue, IBT's has long been the most popular gay men's dance bar in town. The music ranges from 1980s retro to techno, and regular drag shows add to the fun. There's always an interesting crowd. 616 N. Fourth Ave. © **520/882-3053.**

THE PERFORMING ARTS

To a certain extent, Tucson is a clone of Phoenix when it comes to the performing arts. Three of Tucson's major performance companies—the Arizona Opera Company, Ballet Arizona, and the Arizona Theatre Company—spend half their time in Phoenix. This means that whatever gets staged in Phoenix also gets staged in Tucson. This city does, however, have its own symphony, and manages to sustain a diversified theater scene as well.

Usually, the best way to purchase tickets is directly from the company's box office. Tickets to Tucson Convention Center events (but not the symphony or the opera) and other venues around town may be available by calling the TCC box office at © **520/791-4266. TicketMaster** (© **520/321-1000;** www. ticketmaster.com) sells tickets to some Tucson performances.

CLASSICAL MUSIC, OPERA & DANCE

Both the **Tucson Symphony Orchestra** (© **520/882-8585**), which is the oldest continuously performing symphony in the Southwest, and the **Arizona Opera Company** (© **520/293-4336;** www.azopera.com), the state's premier opera company, perform at the Tucson Convention Center (TCC) Music Hall, 260 S. Church Ave. Symphony tickets run $9 to $36, and opera tickets about $21 to $72.

Tucson's dance scene is dominated by **Ballet Arizona** (© **888/322-5538**), which splits its season between Tucson and Phoenix. Productions usually include well-known ballets as well as new works by regional choreographers. Performances are staged at different venues around town, including the Tucson Convention Center. Most tickets are $16 to $38.

THEATER

Tucson doesn't have a lot of theater companies, but what few it does have staged a surprisingly diverse sampling of both classic and contemporary plays.

Arizona Theatre Company, or ATC (© **520/622-2823;** www.aztheatreco. org), which performs at the Temple of Music and Art, 330 S. Scott Ave., splits its time between here and Phoenix and is the state's top professional theater company. Each season sees a mix of comedy, drama, and Broadway-style musical shows; tickets cost about $23 to $36.

For experimental works, there's the **Invisible Theatre,** 1400 N. First Ave. (℃ **520/882-9721**), a tiny theater in a converted laundry building that has been home to Tucson's most experimental theater for about 30 years (it does off-Broadway shows and musicals). Tickets go for about $13 to $20.

The West just wouldn't be the West without good old-fashioned melodramas, and the **Gaslight Theatre,** 7010 E. Broadway Blvd. (℃ **520/886-9428**), is where evil villains, stalwart heroes, and defenseless heroines pound the boards. You can boo and hiss, cheer and sigh as the predictable stories unfold on stage. It's all great fun for kids and adults. Tickets are $15 for adults, $13 for students and seniors, and $6 for children 12 and under. Performances are held Tuesday through Sunday, with two shows nightly on Friday and Saturday plus a Sunday matinee. Tickets sell out a month in advance, so get them as soon as possible.

PERFORMING-ARTS CENTERS & CONCERT HALLS

Tucson's largest performance venue is the **Tucson Convention Center Music Hall,** 260 S. Church Ave. (℃ **520/791-4266**). It's the home of the Tucson Symphony Orchestra and where the Arizona Opera Company usually performs when they're in town. This hall hosts many touring companies, and Ballet Arizona presents its holiday performance of *The Nutcracker* here. The box office is open Monday through Friday from 10am to 6pm.

The centerpiece of the Tucson theater scene is the **Temple of Music and Art,** 330 S. Scott Ave. (℃ **520/622-2823** or 520/884-4875), a restored historic theater dating from 1927. The 605-seat Alice Holsclaw Theatre is the Temple's main stage, but there's also the 90-seat Cabaret Theatre. You'll also find an art gallery and gift shop here. Free tours of the Temple of Art and Music are given on some Saturday mornings; call for details. The box office is open Monday through Friday from 10am to 6pm (and Sat–Sun and later in the evening Tues–Fri during performance weeks).

Centennial Hall, University Boulevard and Park Avenue, on the UA campus (℃ **520/621-3341**), is Tucson's other main performance hall; it stages performances by touring national musical acts, international performance companies, and Broadway shows. A big stage and excellent sound system permit large-scale productions. The box office is open Monday through Friday from 10am to 5pm and Saturday from noon to 5pm (closed Sat in summer).

Also downtown is the **Tucson Center for the Performing Arts,** 408 S. Sixth Ave. (℃ **520/792-8480**), in a building which was constructed as a church in the 1920s. The center provides an alternative stage for a wide variety of small productions and concerts.

The **University of Arizona School of Music and Dance** hosts a series of performances by faculty, including piano and organ concerts, jazz performances, and vocal recitals. For tickets, which run about $10, call the School of Fine Arts box office at ℃ **520/621-1162.**

The **Center for the Arts,** Pima Community College (West Campus), 2202 W. Anklam Rd. (℃ **520/206-6988**), is another good place to check for classical music performances. It offers a wide variety of shows, including performances by Ballet Tucson and the Tucson Symphony Chamber Orchestra. The box office is open Monday through Friday from 10am to 4pm.

OUTDOOR VENUES & SERIES

Weather permitting, Tucsonans head to Reid Park's **DeMeester Outdoor Performance Center,** at Country Club Road and East 22nd Street (✆ **520/ 791-4079**), for performances under the stars. This amphitheater is the site of performances by the Parks and Recreation Community Theatre and other production companies, as well as frequent music performances.

The **Tucson Jazz Society** (✆ **520/903-1265;** www.tucsonjazz.org), which manages to book a few well-known jazz musicians each year, sponsors different outdoor series at various locations around the city, with the summer series at St. Philip's Plaza shopping center being the most popular. Over the course of the year, the society presents around 40 concerts. Tickets are about $11 to $25.

There are various outdoor concert series downtown throughout the year. The most popular of them are the concerts held in conjunction with the Downtown Saturday/Downtown Saturday Night events. Check the *Tucson Weekly* for details.

FILM

The Loft Cinema   If *Star Wars* wasn't your idea of the best movie ever made, this is the place for you. The screen here is one of the largest around, just right for watching a new independent or foreign release. 3233 E. Speedway Blvd. ✆ **520/795-7777.**

The Screening Room   Operated by the Arizona Center for Media Arts, this theater in the downtown arts district specializes in classic art-house films and contemporary independent and foreign films. This is the place to catch *That Obscure Object of Desire, The Night of the Iguana,* or *Woman in the Dunes* one more time. 127 E. Congress St. ✆ **520/622-2262.**

CASINOS

Casino of the Sun   Located 15 miles southwest of Tucson and operated by the Pascua Yaqui tribe, this is southern Arizona's largest casino and offers slot machines, keno, bingo, and a card room. 7406 S. Camino de Oeste. ✆ **800/344-9435** or 520/883-1700.

Desert Diamond Casino   Operated by the Tohono O'odham tribe and located only 3 miles from Mission San Xavier del Bac, this casino offers the same variety of slot and video poker machines found at other casinos in the state. A card room, bingo, and keno round out the options. 7350 S. Nogales Hwy. ✆ **520/294-7777.**

Southern Arizona

Although southern Arizona has its share of prickly pears and saguaros, much of this region has more in common with the Texas plains than it does with the Sonoran Desert. In the southeastern corner of the state, the mile-high grasslands, punctuated by forested mountain ranges, have long supported vast ranches where cattle range across wide-open plains. It was also here that much of America's now-legendary Western history took place. Wyatt Earp and the Clantons shot it out at Tombstone's O.K. Corral, Doc Holliday played his cards, and Cochise and Geronimo staged the last Indian rebellions. Cavalries charged, and prospectors searched for the mother lode. Today ghost towns litter the landscape of southeastern Arizona, but the past is kept alive by people searching for a glimpse of the Wild West.

Long before even the prospectors and outlaws arrived, this region had gained historical importance as the first part of the Southwest explored by the Spanish. This first Spanish expedition, led by Francisco Vásquez de Coronado in 1540, marched up the San Pedro River valley past present-day Sierra Vista, where today a national memorial commemorates Coronado's unfruitful search for the Seven Cities of Cíbola. These cities were rumored to be filled with gold and precious jewels, but all Coronado found were simple Indian pueblos.

Nearly 150 years later, Father Eusebio Francisco Kino founded a string of Jesuit missions across the region the Spanish called the Pimeria Alta, an area that would later become northern Mexico and southern Arizona. Converting the Indians and building mission churches, Father Kino left a long-lasting mark on this region. Two of the missions he founded—San Xavier del Bac (see chapter 9, "Tucson") and San José de Tumacacori (see the section on the Santa Cruz Valley, below)—still stand to this day.

More than 450 years after Coronado marched through this region, the valley of the San Pedro River is undergoing something of a population explosion, especially in the town of Sierra Vista, where retirement communities sprawl across the landscape. Nearby, in the once nearly abandoned copper-mining town of Bisbee, famous for its Bisbee Blue turquoise, a different sort of boom is underway. Urban refugees and artists have been taking up residence and opening galleries and B&Bs, making this one of the most interesting small towns in the state.

The combination of low deserts, high plains, and even higher mountains has given this region a fascinating diversity of landscapes. Giant saguaros cover the slopes of the Sonoran Desert throughout much of southern Arizona, and in the western parts of this region, organ pipe cacti, similar to saguaros, reach the northern limit of their range. In the cool mountains, cacti give way to pines, and passing clouds bring snow and rain. Narrow canyons and broad valleys, fed by the rain and snowmelt, provide habitat for hundreds of species of birds and other wildlife unique to the region. This is the northernmost range for many birds usually found only south of the border. Consequently, southeastern Arizona has become one of the most important bird-watching spots in the United States. Even nonbirders can appreciate the possibility of seeing more than a dozen different species of hummingbirds.

The region's mild climate has also given rise to the state's small wine industry. Throughout southeastern Arizona are quite a few vineyards and wineries, and touring the wine country is a favorite weekend excursion for residents of Tucson and Phoenix.

1 Organ Pipe Cactus National Monument ☆☆

135 miles S of Phoenix; 185 miles SE of Yuma; 140 miles W of Tucson

Located roughly midway between Yuma and Tucson, **Organ Pipe Cactus National Monument,** a preserve for the rare organ pipe cactus, is one of Arizona's least visited and most remote national monuments. The organ pipe cactus resembles the saguaro cactus in many ways, but instead of forming a single main trunk, organ pipes have many trunks, some 20 feet tall, that resemble—you guessed it—organ pipes.

This is a rugged region with few towns or services. To the west lie the inaccessible **Cabeza Prieta Wildlife Refuge** and the **Barry M. Goldwater Air Force Range** (a bombing range), and to the east is the large **Papago Indian Reservation.** The only motels in the area are in the small town of **Ajo.** This former company town was built around a now-abandoned copper mine, and the downtown plaza, with its tall palm trees and arched and covered walkways, has the look and feel of a Mexican town square. Be sure to gas up your car before leaving Ajo.

ESSENTIALS

GETTING THERE　From Tucson, take Ariz. 86 west to Why and turn south on Ariz. 85. From Yuma, take I-8 east to Gila Bend and drive south on Ariz. 85.

FEES　Park admission is $5 per car.

VISITOR CENTER & INFORMATION　For advance information, contact **Organ Pipe Cactus National Monument** (② **520/387-6849;** www.nps.gov/orpi). The visitor center is open daily from 8am to 5pm, although the park itself is open 24 hours a day.

EXPLORING THE MONUMENT

Two well-graded one-way gravel roads loop through the park. The Puerto Blanco Drive is a 53-mile loop, while the Ajo Mountain Drive is only 21 miles. On the Puerto Blanco Drive, you'll pass **Quitobaquito Spring,** which was relied on by Native Americans and pioneers as the only year-round source of water for miles around. This large spring offers great bird-watching opportunities, but cars are subject to break-ins (a highway is only 100 yd. from the parking lot). Quitobaquito Spring can also be reached at the end of a 15-mile two-way section of the Puerto Blanco Drive. Guides available at the park's visitor center explain natural features of the landscape along both drives. There are also a number of hiking trails along the roads.

WHERE TO STAY

There is one campground within the park (although nonvehicle camping is allowed in the backcountry with a permit). Campsites are $10 per night. The

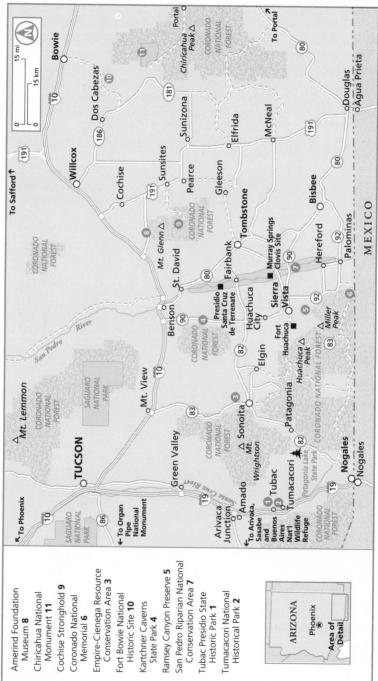

Southern Arizona

Amerind Foundation
Museum **8**
Chiricahua National
Monument **11**
Cochise Stronghold **9**
Coronado National
Memorial **6**
Empire-Cienega Resource
Conservation Area **3**
Fort Bowie National
Historic Site **10**
Kartchner Caverns
State Park **4**
Ramsey Canyon Preserve **5**
San Pedro Riparian National
Conservation Area **7**
Tubac Presidio State
Historic Park **1**
Tumacacori National
Historical Park **2**

ARIZONA

Phoenix ⊛

Area of
Detail

nearest lodgings are in Ajo, where there are several old and very basic motels as well as a B&B. There are also plenty of budget chain motels in the town of Gila Bend, 70 miles north of the monument. They include a **Best Western** (© 800/ **WESTERN**) and a **Super 8** (© 800/800-8000).

Guest House Inn Bed & Breakfast   Built in 1925 as a guesthouse for mining executives, this B&B has attractive gardens in the front yard, a mesquite thicket off to one side, and a modern Southwestern feel to its interior decor. Guest rooms are cool and dark, which is often appreciated in the desert heat here in Ajo. There are also sunrooms on both the north and the south sides of the house.

700 Guest House Rd., Ajo, AZ 85321. © **520/387-6133.** Fax 520/387-3995. 4 units. $79 double. Rates include full breakfast. DC, MC, V. *In room:* A/C, hair dryer.

2 The Santa Cruz Valley ⋆⋆ & Buenos Aires National Wildlife Area ⋆

45 miles S of Tucson; 21 miles N of Nogales; 84 miles W of Sierra Vista

Located in the fertile valley of the Santa Cruz River 45 miles south of Tucson, Tubac and Tumacacori together sum up the early experiences of the Spanish, who were the first Europeans to settle in this region. Established in 1691 by Fr. Eusebio Francisco Kino, Tumacacori was one of the first Spanish missions in what would eventually become Arizona. At that time, Tubac was a Pima village, but by the 1730s, the Spanish had begun settling here in the region they called Pimeria Alta. After a Pima uprising in 1751, Spanish forces were sent into the area to protect the settlers, and in 1752 Tubac became a presidio (fort). Between 1752 and the present, seven different flags have flown over Tubac, including those of Spain, Mexico, the United States, the New Mexico Territory, the Confederacy, the U.S. Territory of Arizona, and the state of Arizona.

Although the European history of this area is more than 300 years old, the area's human habitation actually dates far back into prehistory. Archaeologists have found evidence that there have been people living along the nearby Santa Cruz River for nearly 10,000 years. The Hohokam lived in the area from about A.D. 300 until their mysterious disappearance around 1500, and when the Spanish arrived some 200 years later, they found the Pima people inhabiting this region.

Tubac's other claim to fame is as the site from which Juan Bautista de Anza III, the second commander of the presidio, set out in 1775 to find an overland route to California. De Anza led 240 settlers and more than 1,000 head of cattle on this grueling expedition, and when the group finally reached the coast of California, they founded the settlement of San Francisco. One year later, the garrison was moved from Tubac to Tucson, and, with no protection, Tubac's settlers moved away from the area. Soldiers were once again stationed here beginning in 1776, but lack of funds caused the closure of the presidio when in 1821 Mexican independence brought Tubac under a new flag. It was not until this region became U.S. territory that settlers returned to the area, and by 1860, Tubac was the largest town in Arizona.

Today Tubac is one of Arizona's largest arts communities. The town's old buildings house more than 80 shops selling fine arts, crafts, unusual gifts, and lots of Southwest souvenirs. Although the majority of the shops are thoroughly touristy, there are a few gems worth seeking out. This concentration of shops, artists' studios, and galleries makes Tubac one of southern Arizona's most popular destinations, and a small retirement community is beginning to develop.

After visiting Tubac Presidio State Historic Park and Tumacacori National Monument to learn about the area's history, you'll probably want to spend some time browsing through the shops. Keep in mind, however, that many of the local artists leave town in summer, so it's best to visit on weekends then. The shops are open daily during the busy season of October to May.

ESSENTIALS

GETTING THERE   The Santa Cruz Valley towns of Amado, Tubac, and Tumacacori are all due south of Tucson on I-19.

VISITOR INFORMATION   For information on Tubac and Tumacacori, contact the **Tubac Chamber of Commerce** (© **520/398-2704;** www.tubacaz.com).

SPECIAL EVENTS   The **Tubac Festival of the Arts** is held in February. Artists from all over the country participate. In October, on the weekend nearest to the 23rd, **De Anza Days** commemorates Captain Juan Bautista de Anza's 1775 trek to found San Francisco.

ART & HISTORY IN THE SANTA CRUZ VALLEY

Tubac Center of the Arts ⭐   Tubac is an arts community, and this Spanish colonial building serves as its center for cultural activities. Throughout the season, there are workshops, traveling exhibitions, juried shows, an annual crafts show, and theater and music performances. The quality of the art at these shows is generally better than what's found in the surrounding stores. There is also a gift shop here.

9 Plaza Rd. © **520/398-2371.** Suggested donation $2. Early Sept to mid-May Tues–Sat 10am–4:30pm, Sun 1–4:30pm; mid-Nov to mid-Apr same hours plus Mon 10am–4:30pm. Closed June–Aug and major holidays.

Tubac Presidio State Historic Park   The Tubac Presidio has a long and fitful history. Although the Tumacacori mission was founded in 1691, it was not until 1752 that the Tubac Presidio was established in response to a Pima uprising. In 1775, the presidio's military garrison was moved to Tucson and, with no protection from raiding Apache, most of Tubac's settlers left the area. A military presence was reestablished in 1787, but after Mexican independence in 1821, insufficient funds led to the closing of the presidio. Villagers once again abandoned Tubac because of Apache attacks. After the Gadsden Purchase, Tubac became part of the United States and was again resettled.

Although little but buried foundation walls remains of the old presidio, Tubac Presidio State Historic Park has exhibits that explain its history. There are displays on the Spanish soldiers, Native Americans, religion, and contemporary Hispanic culture in southern Arizona. Also on the grounds is the old Tubac School, which was built in 1885 and is the oldest schoolhouse in the state. Living-history presentations are staged from October to March on Sundays between 1 and 4pm. Among the characters you'll meet are Spanish soldiers, settlers, and friars.

Presidio Dr. © **520/398-2252.** Admission $2 adults, $1 children 7–13. Daily 8am–5pm. Closed Christmas.

Tumacacori National Historical Park ⭐   Founded by Jesuit missionary and explorer Father Eusebio Francisco Kino in 1691 to convert the Pima people, the San José de Tumacacori mission was one of the first Anglo settlements in what is today Arizona. Today the mission ruins are a silent and haunting reminder of the role that Spanish missionaries played in settling the Southwest. Much of the old adobe mission church still stands, and the Spanish architectural influences can readily be seen. A small museum contains exhibits on mission life and the history of the region. On weekends, Native American and Mexican craftspeople give demonstrations of indigenous arts. The **Tumacacori Fiesta,** a celebration of Indian, Hispanic, and Anglo cultures, is held the first weekend of December.

1891 E. Frontage Rd. (C) 520/398-2341. www.nps.gov/tuma. Admission $3 adults, free for children 16 and under. Daily 8am–5pm. Closed Thanksgiving and Christmas. Take I-19 to exit 29; Tumacacori is 3 miles south of Tubac.

SHOPPING

While tourist brochures like to tout Tubac as an artists' community, the town is more of a Southwest souvenir mecca, a land of a million Kokopellis. There are a few genuine art galleries here, but you have to look hard amid the many tourist shops to find the real gems. The interesting **Sonora Trading Company,** in Plaza Antigua on Tubac Street downtown ((C) **520/398-9016**), specializes in carved Zuni fetishes. Some of the better fine art in the area is found at the **Karin Newby Gallery,** Mercado de Baca, 19 Tubac Rd. ((C) **520/398-9662**).

If you want to take the flavor of the area home, stop in at **The Chile Pepper**, on Tubac Road in downtown Tubac ((C) **520/398-2921**), for gourmet foods with a Southwestern accent. Down near Tumacacori National Historical Park, you'll find all things hot (chiles, hot sauces, salsas) arranged on the shelves of one of the more genuine Tubac institutions, the **Santa Cruz Chile and Spice Co.** ((C) **520/398-2591**), a combination store and packing plant. There's an amazing assortment of familiar and obscure spices for sale. In back, you can see various herbs being prepared and packaged. The shop is closed on Sunday.

OUTDOOR PURSUITS

Linking Tubac with Tumacacori is the 8-mile-long **de Anza Trail,** which follows the Santa Cruz River for much of its route and passes through forests and grasslands. This trail is part of the **Juan Bautista de Anza National Historic Trail,** which stretches from Nogales to San Francisco. Bird-watching is the most popular activity; you'll also see an excavation of part of the Spanish colonial settlement of Tubac. The most convenient trailhead is beside Tubac Presidio State Historic Park. **Rex Ranch** ((C) **520/398-2696**) offers horseback rides for $25 per hour between mid-October and mid-May.

If golf is more your speed, you can play a round at the **Tubac Golf Resort** ((C) **520/398-2021**), just north of Tubac off East Frontage Road. Greens fees range from $23 to $66.

BUENOS AIRES NATIONAL WILDLIFE REFUGE ✪

If you're a bird-watcher, you'll definitely want to make the trip over to **Buenos Aires National Wildlife Refuge,** P.O. Box 109, Sasabe, AZ 85633 ((C) **520/ 823-4251;** http://southwest.fws.gov), about 28 miles from Tubac. To get here, head north from Tubac on I-19 to Arivaca Junction, then drive west on a winding two-lane road. The refuge begins just outside the small community of Arivaca.

Your first stop should be at **Arivaca Cienega,** a quarter-mile east of Arivaca. *Cienega* is Spanish for "marsh." A boardwalk leads across this marsh, which is fed by seven springs that provide year-round water and consequently attract an amazing variety of bird life. This is one of the few places in the United States where you can see a gray hawk. Vermilion flycatchers are also common here. Other good birding spots within the refuge include **Arivaca Creek,** 2 miles west of Arivaca, and **Aguirre Lake,** a half mile north of the refuge headquarters and visitor center, which is off Ariz. 286 north of Sasabe.

Moments **The Ruby Road**

If you enjoy scenic drives and don't mind gravel roads, you won't want to pass up the opportunity to drive the Ruby Road through Coronado National Forest to **Peña Blanca Lake** and **Nogales.** This road winds its way through the mountains just north of the Mexican border, passing Arivaca Lake and the privately owned ghost town of **Ruby** (© **520/744-4471** or 520/625-5063; admission $12) before reaching picturesque Peña Blanca Lake, where there are a couple of campgrounds and the pavement resumes.

The **visitor center** is a good place to spot one of the refuge's rarest birds, the masked bobwhite quail. These quail disappeared from Arizona in the late 19th century but have been reintroduced in the refuge. Other birds you might spot outside the visitor center include Bendire's thrasher, Chihuahan ravens, canyon towhees, and green-tailed towhees. The visitor center is open daily from about 7:30am to 4pm. There is also a **refuge information center** in Arivaca, but this center is open only when volunteers are available to staff it.

Other wildlife in the refuge includes pronghorn antelopes, javelinas, coatimundis, white-tailed deer, mule deer, and coyotes. Guided birding and other tours are offered weekends throughout the year. Call for details; reservations are required. There is primitive **camping** at more than 100 designated spots along rough gravel roads. At the refuge information center, a catalog shows pictures of the campsites and provides accessibility information. Look for the brown campsite signs along the road, and bring your own water.

These roads offer good **mountain biking.** If you're looking for a strenuous hike, try the **Mustang Trail,** which has its trailhead 2 miles west of Arivaca. The trail climbs up from Arivaca Creek into the surrounding dry hills and makes for a 5-mile round-trip hike.

WHERE TO STAY
AMADO

Amado Territory Inn Bed & Breakfast ✦   This modern inn just off I-19 in the crossroads of Amado is built in the territorial style and succeeds in capturing the feel of an old Arizona ranch house. Guest rooms are outfitted in a mix of Mexican rustic furnishings and reproduction East Coast antiques, much the way homes would have been furnished in Arizona 100 years ago. While a bit spartan, the rooms have plenty of character; those on the second floor feature balconies with views across the farm fields of the Santa Cruz Valley. The Amado Café is right next door.

3001 E. Frontage Rd. (P.O. Box 81), Amado, AZ 85645. © **888/398-8684** or 520/398-8684. Fax 520/398-8186. www.amado-territory-inn.com. 10 units. Nov–June $105–$135 double; July–Oct $90–$105 double. Rates include full breakfast. MC, V. No children under 12 accepted. **Amenities:** Massage. *In room:* A/C, no phone.

The Rex Ranch ✦ *(Finds*   With its classic Southwestern styling and location adjacent to the de Anza Trail, this place is truly a getaway. Although not all of the guest rooms are as attractively decorated as the public areas, the new rooms and the more recently renovated rooms are quite comfortable. Just getting to this remote property is something of an adventure, since you have to drive *through* the Santa Cruz River to reach it. Primarily a conference center and economical health spa, the family-run ranch offers a wide variety of spa treatments and massages. The attractive little dining room is one of this area's best restaurants.

131 Amado Montosa Rd. (P.O. Box 636), Amado, AZ 85645. ⓒ **888/REX-RANCH** or 520/398-2914. Fax 520/398-8229. www.rexranch.com. 28 units. Oct–May $125–$225 double; June–Sept $105–$205 double. Rates include continental breakfast. AE, DC, DISC, MC, V. **Amenities:** Restaurant (Southwestern); outdoor pool; spa; Jacuzzi; horseback riding; mountain-bike rentals; concierge; massage. *In room:* A/C, no phone.

TUBAC

Tubac Golf Resort ★ ⟨Value⟩   This economical golf resort is built on the Otero Ranch, the oldest Spanish land-grant ranch in the Southwest. Although the ranch dates from 1789, the oldest buildings are the stables, which now house the restaurant and date only from the early 20th century. The red-tile roofs and brick archways, however, help conjure up the Spanish heritage. Guest rooms are in modern buildings set amid expansive lawns that seem a bit out of place here in the desert. Casitas have two patios, beamed ceilings, and beehive fireplaces; newer rooms are worth requesting. The dining room has booths that resemble horse stalls, and the menu focuses on mesquite-broiled steaks and seafood.

1 Otero Rd. (P.O. Box 1297), Tubac, AZ 85646. ⓒ **800/848-7893** or 520/398-2211. Fax 520/398-9261. www.tubacgolfresort.com. 46 units. $80–$150 double; $110–$235 suite. AE, DISC, MC, V. **Amenities:** Restaurant (American), lounge; 18-hole golf course; outdoor pool; tennis court; Jacuzzi; pro shop; coin-op laundry. *In room:* A/C, TV, fridge, coffeemaker, hair dryer.

SASABE

Rancho de la Osa ★★   Steeped in history and sharing a fence line with the Mexican border, this ranch is roughly 200 years old and was one of the last Spanish haciendas built in what later became the United States. Today it's owned by Richard and Veronica Schultz, avid art collectors who have brought to the place an artistic aesthetic unknown at other Arizona guest ranches. The adobe buildings are painted in vibrant shades of pink and turquoise, while the guest rooms are furnished with rustic Mexican antiques. Most have fireplaces and patios. Meals are gourmet Southwestern fare, and there's a rustic little saloon in what may be the oldest building in the state. Although horseback riding is the favorite activity, the ranch attracts birders due to its proximity to Buenos Aires National Wildlife Refuge.

P.O. Box 1, Sasabe, AZ 85633. ⓒ **800/872-6240** or 520/823-4257. Fax 520/823-4238. www.guestranches.com/ranchodelaosa. 18 units. $310–$375 double (plus 15% service charge). 3- to 4-night minimum. Rates include all meals and horseback riding. MC, V. **Amenities:** Dining room (Southwestern), lounge; small outdoor pool; Jacuzzi; bikes; laundry service. *In room:* No phone.

WHERE TO DINE

In addition to the restaurants mentioned below, the **Tubac Golf Resort** (see "Where to Stay," above) has a good restaurant.

AMADO

Amado Café GREEK/AMERICAN   There aren't a lot of dining options out here, making this restaurant, in a handsome territorial-style building just off I-19, an asset to the community. The best part of the experience is sitting out back on the rustic flagstone patio, listening to the gurgling fountain and contemplating the view of the mountains in the distance. The menu includes sandwiches, salads, and more filling fare like leg of lamb and prime rib. The restaurant is owned by a Greek family, so such dishes as the Greek salad, gyro sandwich, and stuffed grape leaves are good bets.

3001 E. Frontage Rd. (exit 48 off I-19), Amado. © **520/398-9211.** Main courses $7–$10 lunch, $11–$17 dinner. AE, DISC, MC, V. Tues–Sun 11:30am–2pm and 5–8pm. Closed Tues in summer and also for 2–3 weeks mid-July to mid-Aug.

Cantina Romantica ★★ SOUTHWESTERN/NEW AMERICAN   Located in a historic adobe hacienda, Cantina Romantica is a culinary oasis in this neck of the woods. The menu has a metropolitan flair, and includes the likes of pecan-crusted pork and filet mignon with mushrooms and black truffle–cabernet sauce. At lunch, a gargantuan grilled chicken salad is a delicious sensory overload. The setting is rustic and colorful, and the inn is reached by driving *through* the Santa Cruz River.

At the Rex Ranch, 6 miles north of Tubac in Amado. © **520/398-2914.** Reservations recommended for dinner. Main courses $7–$10 lunch, $19–$24 dinner. AE, DC, DISC, MC, V. Tues–Sat noon–2pm and 5:30–8pm; Sun 11am–2pm (brunch) and 5:30–8pm. Call ahead during extreme heat in summer; restaurant may be closed.

TUBAC

Melio's Trattoria ITALIAN   With candles flickering in wax-covered Chianti bottles, Italian music playing, and a friendly ambience, this little Tubac trattoria has the feel of a neighborhood restaurant in Little Italy. At lunch you'll find pastas and sandwiches, while dinnertime brings more pastas (spaghetti *alla carbonara,* penne with smoked salmon) and familiar favorites such as veal with lemon sauce.

12 Plaza Rd. © **520/398-8494.** Reservations recommended for dinner. Main courses $7–$9 lunch, $10–$17 dinner. AE, MC, V. Wed 5–8 or 9pm; Thurs–Sun 11:30am–2:30pm and 5–8 or 9pm.

Shelby's Bistro AMERICAN   With only about a dozen tables tucked into the back of the Mercado de Baca shopping plaza, this casual place is usually crammed with tourists at lunchtime, when the pizza and sandwiches really pack 'em in. At dinner, more upscale cuisine—such as Southwest corn-crusted chicken stuffed with spinach, cheese, sun-dried tomatoes, and basil—is offered. Fridays and Saturdays are prime-rib night.

19 Tubac Rd. © **520/398-8075.** Reservations recommended for dinner. Main courses $7–$18. AE, DISC, MC, V. Daily 9am–4pm; Wed–Sat 5–9pm.

3 Nogales

175 miles S of Phoenix; 63 miles S of Tucson; 65 miles W of Sierra Vista

Situated on the Mexican border, the twin towns of Nogales, Arizona, and Nogales, Sonora, Mexico (known jointly as Ambos Nogales), form a bustling border town. All day long, U.S. citizens cross into Mexico to shop for bargains on Mexican handicrafts, pharmaceuticals, and tequila, while Mexican citizens cross into the United States to buy products not available in their country. Nogales is also the busiest produce port in the world. During the harvest season, more than 700 truckloads of produce cross into the United States from Mexico each day.

ESSENTIALS

GETTING THERE   Nogales is the last town on I-19 before the Mexican border. Ariz. 82 leads northeast from town toward Sonoita and Sierra Vista.

VISITOR INFORMATION   Contact the **Nogales–Santa Cruz County Chamber of Commerce,** 123 W. Kino Park Way (© **520/287-3685;** www.nogaleschamber.com).

Starry, Starry Nights

Southern Arizona likes to brag about how many sunny days it has each year, and those clear sunny days give way to clear, starry nights. The absence of lights in the surrounding desert makes the night sky here as brilliant as anywhere on earth. This fact has not gone unnoticed by the world's astronomers—the Tucson vicinity has a greater concentration of astronomical observatories than any other region on earth, and southern Arizona has come to be known as the Astronomy Capital of the World.

Many of these observatories are open to the public. In addition to the ones listed below, the Flandrau Science Center in Tucson offers public viewings, as does Biosphere 2, north of Tucson (see chapter 9, "Tucson"). In Flagstaff, there are public viewing programs at the Lowell Observatory (see chapter 6, "The Grand Canyon & Northern Arizona").

OBSERVATORIES

Fred Lawrence Whipple Observatory   Located atop 8,550-foot Mount Hopkins, this is the largest observatory operated by the Smithsonian Astrophysical Observatory. Tours last about 6 hours. No food is available here, so be sure to bring a picnic lunch.

Near Amado. ☎ 520/670-5707. Tours $7 adults, $2.50 children 6–12, no children under age 6 allowed. Reservations required; call up to 4 weeks in advance. Visitor center Mon–Fri 8:30am–4:30pm. Tours Mar–Nov Mon, Wed, and Fri 9am–3pm. Take I-19 south from Tucson to exit 56, then follow E. Frontage Rd. south 3 miles. Turn left on Elephant Head Rd. and then right on Mount Hopkins Rd. Continue 7 miles to visitor center.

Kitt Peak National Observatory ★   This is the largest and most famous astronomical observatory in the region. Located in the Quinlan Mountains, 56 miles southwest of Tucson, the observatory sits atop 6,882-foot Kitt Peak. There are several major telescopes operating here, including the McMath-Pierce, the world's largest solar telescope. Its system of mirrors channels an image of the sun deep into the mountain before reflecting it back up to the observatory, where scientists study the resulting 30-inch-diameter image. The 158-inch Mayall telescope features a 30,000-pound quartz mirror and is used for studying distant regions of the universe. This is the area's only major observatory to offer public nighttime viewing. Day visitors must be content with a visitor center and museum. A box meal is supplied with evening stargazing programs; day visitors need to pack a lunch. *Tip:* In the winter high

EXPLORING NORTH & SOUTH OF THE BORDER

Most people who visit Nogales, Arizona, are here to cross the border to Nogales, Mexico. The favorable exchange rate makes shopping in Mexico very popular with Americans, although most of the items for sale in Mexico are actually cheaper in Tucson. Many people now cross the border specifically to purchase prescription drugs, and pharmacies line the streets near the border crossing.

To learn more about the history of this area, stop by the **Pimeria Alta Historical Society,** at the corner of Grand Avenue and Crawford Street (☎ 520/287-4621), near the border crossing in downtown Nogales. The society maintains a small museum, library, and archives on this region of northern season, reservations are recommended, but it's sometimes possible to slip in on someone else's cancellation.

Off Ariz. 86. © **520/318-8200,** or 520/318-8726 for stargazing reservations. Suggested donation $2. Nighttime stargazing (reservations required; call 4–8 weeks in advance) $35 adults; $25 students, seniors, and children under 18. Daily 9am–3:45pm. Tours at 10am, 11:30am, and 1:30pm. Closed Thanksgiving, Dec 24–25, and Jan 1. Take Ariz. 86 southwest from Tucson for 40 miles to the turnoff for Kitt Peak.

Mount Graham International Observatory & Discovery Park's Gov Aker Observatory This controversial observatory, one of the nation's newest, stands atop Mount Graham and is partly operated by the Vatican and partly by the University of Arizona. The facilities include the Vatican Advanced Technology Telescope, the Heinrich Hertz Submillimeter Telescope, and the Large Binocular Telescope, which is scheduled to be completed in 2004. When completed, this last telescope will be the most powerful on earth. Tours last 6 hours and include lunch, but do not include actual viewing through the telescopes at the observatory (although the telescopes at Gov Aker Observatory at Discovery Park are open to the public).

Near Safford. © **520/428-6260,** ext. 17. www.discoverypark.com. Tours $15. Reservations required; call at least 2 weeks in advance. Mount Graham International Observatory tours offered mid-May to mid-Nov (weather permitting) Tues–Sat (call or check website for dates). Gov Aker Observatory Tues–Sat 1–10pm.

WHERE TO STAY

Skywatcher's Inn ⚡ Situated on the grounds of the privately owned Vega-Bray Observatory, an amateur observatory with six telescopes and a planetarium, this is one of the most unusual lodgings in the state. The inn provides guests with not only a bed for the night, but also a chance to observe the night sky and the sun through the observatory's telescopes. Although experienced amateur astronomers can rent the facilities for $35 per night, inexperienced guests should opt for one of the astronomer-assisted programs, which range from $59 to $150 per night per group. A kitchen is available to guests.

4 miles outside Benson (call for directions). 5655 N. Via Umbrosa, Tucson, AZ 85750-1357. © and fax **520/615-3886.** www.communiverse.com/skywatcher. 4 units. $75–$160 double. Rates include full breakfast. MC, V. *In room:* A/C, TV.

Mexico and southern Arizona, which was once known as Pimeria Alta. It's open Thursday through Saturday from 10am to 4pm. Admission is by donation.

Just a couple of miles outside Nogales on the road to Patagonia, you'll see signs for the **Arizona Vineyard Winery** (© **520/287-7972**), open daily from 10am to 5pm. You may not think of Arizona as wine country, but the Spanish began growing grapes and making wine as soon as they arrived in the area several centuries ago.

Nogales, Mexico, is a typical border town filled with tiny shops selling crafts and souvenirs and dozens of restaurants serving simple Mexican food. Some of the better deals are on wool rugs, which cost a small fraction of what a Navajo rug costs, but are not nearly as well made. Pottery is another popular buy. Our personal favorites are the ceramic sinks and handblown glasses and pitchers.

All the shops and restaurants in Nogales, Mexico, are within walking distance of the border, so unless you're planning to continue farther into Mexico, it's not a good idea to take your car. There are numerous pay parking lots and garages on the U.S. side of the border where your vehicle will be secure for the day. If you should take your car into Mexico, be sure to get Mexican auto insurance beforehand—your U.S. auto insurance will not be valid. There are plenty of insurance companies set up along the road leading to the border.

Most businesses in Nogales, Mexico, accept U.S. dollars. You may bring back $400 worth of merchandise duty free, including 1 liter of liquor (if you are 21 or older). U.S. citizens need only a driver's license to walk across the border. (For those under driving age, birth certificates are recommended, but not required.)

WHERE TO STAY

Although your best bet is to make this a day trip from Tucson, Tubac, or Patagonia, there are a few budget chain motels in Nogales, including a **Motel 6** (© **800/4-MOTEL 6**) and a **Super 8** (© **800/800-8000**).

Rio Rico Resort & Country Club ★★ *Value* Located a few miles north of Nogales, Rio Rico is a secluded hilltop golf resort that attracts quite a few retirees contemplating relocating to this area. If you want to get away from it all, this is a good bet. The accommodations and amenities are the equal of many of the resorts in Tucson, and the views are almost as good. All guest rooms have excellent views over the golf course and desert (ask for a third-floor room). An abundance of Mexican tile work gives them a little sense of place, too.

1069 Camino Caralampi, Rio Rico, AZ 85648. © **800/288-4746** or 520/281-1901. Fax 520/281-7132. www. rioricoresort.com. 180 units. Jan–Mar $170–$235 double, $255–$700 suite; Apr–May and Sept–Dec $140–$205 double, $235–$500 suite; June–Aug $110–$175 double, $205–$500 suite. AE, DC, DISC, MC, V. **Amenities:** Restaurant (Southwestern/Mediterranean), lounge; Olympic-size outdoor pool; 18-hole golf course; 4 tennis courts; exercise room; access to nearby health club; Jacuzzi; sauna; horseback riding; mountain-bike rentals; business center; pro shop; massage; laundry service. *In room:* A/C, TV, fridge, coffeemaker, hair dryer, iron.

WHERE TO DINE

La Roca Restaurant ★ *Finds* MEXICAN La Roca is as unexpected a restaurant as you're likely to find in a border town. Built into a cliff and cool as a cave, it conjures up images of colonial Mexico. White-jacketed waiters provide a level of professional service found only in the most expensive establishments north of the border. Folk art and paintings in the spacious rooms seem to make the interior glow, and at night the place is lit with candles ensconced on the stone walls. The Guaymas shrimp and chicken mole are our longtime favorites. The shrimp are reliably succulent, and the mole is a brilliantly flavorful balance between chile and chocolate. Don't miss the margaritas.

Calle Elias 91, Nogales, Mexico. © **(52) 631/2-08-91.** Main courses $8–$19. MC, V. Daily 11am–midnight. Walk through the border checkpoint, continue 100 yd., cross the railroad tracks on your left, and look for a narrow side street along the base of the cliff you saw as you crossed into Mexico. The restaurant is about 100 ft. down this street.

4 Patagonia ★★ & Sonoita ★

Patagonia: 171 miles SE of Phoenix; 60 miles SE of Tucson; 50 miles SW of Tombstone; 19 miles NW of Nogales

A mild climate, numerous good restaurants, bed-and-breakfast inns, and a handful of wineries have turned the small communities of Patagonia and

Sonoita into a favorite weekend getaway for Tucsonans. Sonoita Creek, one of the only perennial streams in southern Arizona, is also a major draw, attracting bird-watchers from all over the country. Because this creek flows year-round, it attracts an amazing variety of bird life.

Patagonia and Sonoita are only about 12 miles apart, but they have decidedly different characters. Patagonia is a sleepy little hamlet with tree-shaded streets, quite a few old adobe buildings, and a big park in the middle of town. The Nature Conservancy preserve on the edge of town makes Patagonia popular with bird-watchers. Sonoita, on the other hand, sits out on the windswept high plains and is really just a highway crossroads rather than a real town. The landscape around Sonoita, however, is filled with expensive new homes on small ranches, and not far away are the vineyards of Arizona's wine country.

ESSENTIALS

GETTING THERE   Sonoita is at the junction of Ariz. 83 and Ariz. 82. Patagonia is 12 miles southwest of Sonoita on Ariz. 82.

VISITOR INFORMATION   The **Patagonia Visitor Information Center,** 307 McKeown Ave. (© **888/794-0060** or 520/394-0060; www.patagoniaaz. com), is in the center of Patagonia in the building with Mariposa Bookstore. Open Wednesday through Monday from 10am to 5pm.

BIRD-WATCHING, WINE TASTING & OTHER AREA ACTIVITIES

Patagonia, 18 miles north of Nogales on Ariz. 82, is a historic old mining and ranching town 4,000 feet up in the Patagonia Mountains. Surrounded by higher mountains, the little town has for years been popular with film and television crews. Among the films that have been shot here are *Oklahoma, Red River, A Star Is Born,* and *David and Bathsheba.* TV programs filmed here have included *Little House on the Prairie* and *The Young Riders.* Today, however, bird-watching and tranquility draw people to this remote town.

The **Patagonia–Sonoita Creek Preserve** (© **520/394-2400**) is owned by the Nature Conservancy and protects 1½ miles of Sonoita Creek riparian (riverside) habitat, which is important to migratory birds. More than 250 species of birds have been spotted at the preserve, which makes it a popular spot with birders from all over the world. Among the rare birds that can be seen are 22 species of flycatchers, kingbirds, and phoebes, plus the Montezuma quail. A forest of cottonwood trees, some of which are 100 feet tall, lines the creek and is one of the best remaining examples of such a forest in southern Arizona. At one time, these forests grew along all the rivers here. The sanctuary is just outside Patagonia on a dirt road that parallels Ariz. 82. From April 1 to September 30, hours are Wednesday through Sunday from 6:30am to 4pm; from October 1 to March 31, hours are Wednesday through Sunday from 7:30am to 4pm. A $5 donation is suggested if you're not a Nature Conservancy member. On Wednesdays at 8am and Saturdays at 9am, there are naturalist-guided walks through the preserve; reservations aren't required. If the preserve should be closed when you visit, you are welcome to bird-watch along the road bordering the preserve from dawn to dusk.

Avid birders will also want to visit the **Empire-Cienega Resource Conservation Area** (© **520/722-4289** or 520/455-5522), which has grasslands, wetlands, and oak forests. This is a good place to look for the rarely seen gray hawk. Access is off the east side of Ariz. 83, about 7 miles north of Sonoita.

Patagonia Lake State Park (© **520/287-6965**), about 7 miles south of Patagonia off Ariz. 82, is a popular boating and fishing lake formed by damming

---

Tips **Bird-Watching Update**

To find out what, if any, rare birds have been spotted at the time of your visit, call the **Tucson Audubon Society's Bird Report** (📞 520/798-1005).

Sonoita Creek. The lake is 2½ miles long and stocked in winter with trout. Bass, crappie, bluegill, and catfish can also be found. Park facilities include a picnic ground, campground, and swimming beach. There is also good bird-watching here—elegant trogons, which are among the most beautiful of southern Arizona's rare birds, have been spotted. On Friday and Saturday at 9am, boat tours focus on the birds and history of the area. The park day-use fee is $5.

Sonoita proper is little more than a crossroads with a few shops and restaurants. Surrounding the community are miles of rolling grasslands that are primarily cattle ranches. However, recent years have seen the planting of several vineyards in the area, and the Sonoita area is slowly becoming Arizona's wine country. The **R. W. Webb Winery** (and Dark Mountain Brewery) (📞 520/762-5777), the most accessible of the area's wineries, produces a fairly nice sherry. Its attractive little tasting room is 27 miles north of Sonoita; from Tucson, go east on I-10 to exit 279. In the ghost town of Elgin is the **Village of Elgin Winery** (📞 520/455-9309), open daily from 11am to 5pm; 3 miles south of Elgin is **Sonoita Vineyards,** on Canelo Road (📞 520/455-5893), open daily from 10am to 4pm. **Callaghan Vineyards,** on Elgin Road just west of the village of Elgin (📞 520/455-5322), is open for tastings Friday through Sunday from 11am to 3pm. The above tasting-room hours are subject to change, so you might want to call ahead.

Despite the proliferation of vineyards in the area, this is still ranch country. If you'd like to ride the open range, a couple of area horseback-riding stables can get you back in the saddle. In Patagonia, contact **Arizona Trail Tours** (📞 800/477-0615; www.aztrailtours.com), which offers everything from 2-hour rides ($40) to 6-day pack trips ($1,250). These rides head up into the Patagonia Mountains and the San Rafael Valley. In Sonoita, try **Sonoita Stables** (📞 520/455-9266), which offers rides into the Empire-Cienega Resource Conservation Area on Peruvian Paso horses. Rates range from $25 for 1 hour to $125 for a half day. Expect to see antelope on your ride.

WHERE TO STAY
IN PATAGONIA

Circle Z Ranch 🐎   This is the oldest working cattle ranch in Arizona, and has been a guest ranch since 1925. Over the years it has served as a backdrop for numerous movies and TV shows, including *Gunsmoke* and John Wayne's *Red River.* The 6,000-acre ranch on the banks of Sonoita Creek is bordered by the Nature Conservancy's Patagonia–Sonoita Creek Sanctuary, Patagonia State Park, and the Coronado National Forest. Miles of trails ensure everyone gets in plenty of riding in a variety of terrains, from desert hills to grasslands to the riparian forest along the creek. The adobe cabins provide an authentic ranch feel that's appreciated by guests hoping to find a genuine bit of the Old West.

Ariz. 82 (between Nogales and Patagonia), Patagonia, AZ 85624. 📞 **888/854-2525** or 520/394-2525. Fax 520/394-2058. www.circlez.com. 24 units. $1,700–$2,020 double per week (slightly higher rates for shorter stays). Lower rates for children 17 and under. Rates include all meals and horseback riding. 3-night minimum. No credit cards. Closed mid-May to early Nov. **Amenities:** Dining room; small outdoor pool; tennis court; horseback riding; game room; guest laundry. *In room:* No phone.

Duquesne House B&B ☞ This old adobe building with a shady front porch was built at the turn of the 20th century as a miners' boardinghouse. Each unit has its own entrance, sitting room, and bedroom. Our favorite room has an ornate woodstove and claw-foot tub. At the back of the house, an enclosed porch overlooks the garden and fishpond. The owner of the B&B also runs a local gallery, and artists will feel right at home here.

357 Duquesne Ave., P.O. Box 772, Patagonia, AZ 85624. ℂ 520/394-2732 or 520/394-0054. 4 units. $75 double. Rate includes full breakfast. No credit cards. Pets accepted. *In room:* Fridge, coffeemaker, no phone.

Stage Stop Inn Though nothing fancy, this small hotel in the center of town is large enough that is usually has a few rooms available. Furnishings are motel basic, but there's a small pool in the courtyard if you happen to be here in the heat of summer.

303 W. McKeown St., P.O. Box 777, Patagonia, AZ 85624. ℂ 800/923-2211 or 520/394-2211. Fax 520/394-2212. 43 units. $69 double. AE, DC, DISC, MC, V. Pets accepted ($5). **Amenities:** Small outdoor pool. *In room:* A/C, TV, fridge.

IN SONOITA

Rancho Milagro ☞ Located in the grasslands outside of the village of Elgin, this B&B has just about the biggest skies in the area. There's nothing out here but wide open country and plenty of tranquility. The building, although new, is constructed in a pueblo/territorial style, and each unit has dyed cement floors, a woodstove, and a whirlpool tub. All rooms have separate entrances and are built around a courtyard where breakfast is served.

11 E. Camino del Corral, Elgin, AZ 85611. ℂ 520/455-0381 or 520/455-0380. 3 units. $125 double. Rates include continental breakfast. No credit cards. *In room:* TV/VCR, no phone.

Sonoita Inn Housed in a barnlike building, the Sonoita Inn plays up the area's ranching history. The building was originally constructed by the owner of the famed Triple Crown–winning thoroughbred Secretariat, but in 1999 was converted into an inn. The large lobby, with its wooden floors, huge fireplace, and ranch brands for decoration, is cool and dark. Guest rooms feature Indian rugs and 1950s-inspired bedspreads for a retro cowboy touch. Although it's right on Sonoita's main road, the fascinating decor more than makes up for the less-than-quiet location. A popular steakhouse is adjacent to the inn.

At intersection of Ariz. 82 and Ariz. 83, P.O. Box 99, Sonoita, AZ 85637. ℂ 520/455-5935. Fax 520/455-5069. www.sonoitainn.com. 18 units. $125–$140 double. Rates include deluxe continental breakfast. AE, DC, DISC, MC, V. Pets accepted ($25). *In room:* A/C, TV.

The Vineyard Bed & Breakfast ☞ Set atop a hill just south of Sonoita, the heart of southeast Arizona's wine country, is this pink-adobe ranch house built in 1916. The expansive views of plains and mountains are the inn's biggest selling point. If you're looking for high, wide, and handsome, this is it. The house itself has an unpretentious farm/ranch feel, while the casita, with its own patio and saltillo tile floors, is well worth the extra cost.

92 S. Los Encinos Rd. (P.O. Box 1227), Sonoita, AZ 85637. ℂ 520/455-4749. 4 units. $95 double; $110 casita. Rates include full breakfast. No credit cards. **Amenities:** Jacuzzi. *In room:* Hair dryer, no phone.

WHERE TO DINE
IN PATAGONIA

Cose Buone ☞ ITALIAN It's not often you have a fine-dining experience in a building that also houses a Laundromat, but here it is. Intimate seating and a relaxed atmosphere combine for an experience that seems worlds away from the

---

Tips **Please _Do_ Feed the Tourists**

If you think dining at good restaurants is an integral part of any vacation, don't head down this way on a Monday or Tuesday, when most of the best restaurants in southeastern Arizona are closed. To be absolutely certain of getting good grub during your visit, plan to come between Thursday and Sunday (and make reservations, if possible). You should be on your way somewhere else by Sunday afternoon—some of the good restaurants aren't open Sunday nights, either.

---

urban glitz to the north. The menu changes weekly, but your first course might be a full-flavored antipasto of assorted untraditional vegetables or a Tuscan white-bean soup. For _secondi,_ expect risotto or pasta, moving on to a third course of perhaps shrimp with baby artichokes, shallots, and sun-dried tomatoes. Add an extensive and reasonably priced wine list, and you couldn't ask for more.

436 Naugle Ave. ✆ **520/394-2366.** Reservations highly recommended. 3-course meal $24. MC, V. Fri–Tues 6pm until closing; call ahead to confirm hours. Reduced hours June–July and Sept–Oct; closed Aug.

Marie's European Cuisine ✪ EUROPEAN   Located in the center of Patagonia, this little restaurant sits behind a low wall in a colorful cottage with a few tiled tables and folk art in a "secret garden" setting. The menu offers simple yet very flavorful rustic European food, ranging the continent from the Adriatic to the Baltic. Marie whips up the likes of leek tart, broccoli soufflé, chicken with olives and dried fruit in white-wine sauce, roast lamb so tender it cuts with a fork, and even roast suckling pig.

340 Naugle Ave. ✆ **520/394-2812.** Reservations recommended. Main courses $11–$16. DISC, MC, V. Wed–Sat 5–9pm; Sun 1–7pm.

Velvet Elvis Pizza Company ITALIAN   Marie's and Cose Buone are just the sort of restaurants you might expect to find in wine country, but this casual hangout strikes a very different chord. Faux-finished walls ooze artiness, and paeans to pop culture include shrines to both the Virgin Mary and Elvis. There's even a genuine velvet Elvis painting on display. The menu features pizzas heaped with veggies, cheeses, and meats. Add an organic salad and accompany it with a fresh juice, microbrew, espresso, or organic wine.

292 Naugle Ave. ✆ **520/394-2102.** Pizzas $12–$25. MC, V. Hours vary; call ahead.

IN SONOITA

Grab pastries, hot breakfasts, and sandwiches at the **Grasslands Bakery/Café,** 3119 Ariz. 83 (✆ **520/455-4770**), open Wednesday through Sunday from 8am to 3pm.

Café Sonoita ✪ INTERNATIONAL   A tiny place with just a handful of tables, this cafe is a favorite with locals. In spite of the casual atmosphere, the kitchen turns out some very tasty and creative dishes (with local wines to accompany the meal). For dinner, try roast duckling with dark cherry port sauce, sautéed jumbo shrimp with artichoke hearts and bacon, or a bowl of green chile corn chowder. Lunchtime sandwiches are huge and delicious.

3280 Ariz. 82 (in an old building at the east end of town). ✆ **520/455-5278.** Reservations recommended at dinner for parties of 5 or more. Main courses $6–$15. MC, V. Wed–Thurs 5–8pm; Fri–Sat 11am–2:30pm and 5–8pm; Sun 11am–2:30pm.

Karen's Wine Country Café ⭐ SOUTHWESTERN   With crisp tablecloths and expansive windows, this bright room looks out on panoramic rangeland that seems almost surreal. The view is of the Empire Cienega Ranch, a grassland ringed by mountain ranges—you might see antelope grazing. Inside are well-dressed urbanites sipping wine and grazing on pistachio-wheat bread, pork tenderloin with raspberry-chipotle glaze, and New York steak with blue cheese. Good salads of organic greens are liberally dosed in vinaigrette—a specialty here, along with local jams and jellies, all available for purchase.

3266 Ariz. 82. ℂ 520/455-5282. Reservations recommended. Main courses $8–$9 lunch, $13–$19 dinner; 4-course wine dinner $39.95. MC, V. Mon 11am–3pm, Tues–Thurs 11am–4pm; Fri–Sat 11am–4pm and 5–8pm; Sun 8–10:30am and 11am–4pm.

5 Sierra Vista & the San Pedro Valley ⭐

189 miles SE of Phoenix; 70 miles SE of Tucson; 33 miles SW of Tombstone; 33 miles W of Bisbee

Located at an elevation of 4,620 feet above sea level, Sierra Vista is blessed with the perfect climate—never too hot, never too cold. This fact more than anything else has contributed in recent years to Sierra Vista becoming one of the fastest-growing cities in Arizona. Although the town itself is a modern, sprawling community outside the gates of the U.S. Army's Fort Huachuca, it is wedged between the Huachuca Mountains and the valley of the San Pedro River. Consequently, Sierra Vista, with its many inexpensive motels, makes a good base for exploring the region's natural attractions.

Within a few miles' drive of town are the San Pedro Riparian National Conservation Area, Coronado National Memorial, and the Nature Conservancy's Ramsey Canyon Preserve. No other area of the United States attracts more attention from birders, who come in hopes of spotting some of the 300 species that have been sighted in southeastern Arizona. Also not far north of town is Kartchner Caverns State Park, the region's biggest attraction, located near Benson.

ESSENTIALS
GETTING THERE   Sierra Vista is at the junction of Ariz. 90 and Ariz. 92 about 35 miles south of I-10. **America West** (ℂ 800/235-9292) has regular flights from Phoenix to the Fort Huachuca Airport (also called the Sierra Vista Airport), 2100 Airport Dr.

VISITOR INFORMATION   The **Sierra Vista Convention and Visitors Bureau** is at 21 E. Wilcox Dr. (ℂ 800/288-3861 or 520/458-6940; www.visitsierravista.com). Turn onto Carmichael Avenue from Fry Boulevard; the office is 2 blocks off Fry Boulevard on the left.

SPECIAL EVENTS   In February, cowboy poets, singers, and musicians come together at the **Cochise Cowboy Poetry & Music Gathering** (ℂ 800/288-3861 or 520/459-3868; www.cowboypoets.com).

ATTRACTIONS AROUND BENSON
While Kartchner Caverns is the main draw in the Benson area, there are a few other attractions you might want to check out. North of town is the remarkable **Singing Wind Bookshop** (ℂ 520/586-2425), on a ranch down a dirt road. The store is the brainchild of Winifred Bundy, who, with her late husband, began the business more than 25 years ago with only a couple of shelves of books. Now the inventory is well into the thousands, with an emphasis on the Southwest, natural sciences, and children's literature. To get here, take exit 304

from I-10 in Benson. Drive north 2¼ miles and take a right (east) at the sign that says SINGING WIND ROAD. Drive to the end, opening and closing the green gate.

Kartchner Caverns State Park ★★ These caverns, which opened to the public in 1999, were discovered in 1974 and kept secret for 14 years. The reason for the secrecy was to protect what are among the largest and most beautiful caverns in the country. These are wet caverns, which means that all the cave formations, including stalactites, stalagmites, soda straws, cave popcorn, and "cave bacon," are still growing. To ensure that the cave formations continue to grow as they have for thousands of years, extensive measures, including the construction of air-lock doors, were taken before the caverns were opened to the public. The great effort expended to protect these caverns is in large part the cause of the high admission prices.

Seven acres of the caverns are currently open to the public, and within this area are two huge rooms, each larger than a football field with ceilings more than 100 feet high. In the first room, the Rotunda Room, are thousands of delicate soda straws. In fact, Kartchner Caverns contain the longest soda straw formation in the U.S. (21 ft., 2 in.). The highlight of the cave tour is the Throne Room, at the center of which is a 58-foot-tall column known as Kubla Khan. Within the park are several miles of hiking trails through the hills that hide the caverns, along with a campground charging $20 per night per site.

Because the caverns are a popular attraction and tours are limited, try to make a reservation as far as 3 months in advance, especially if you want to visit on a weekend. It is sometimes possible to get same-day tickets if you happen to be passing by.

Off Ariz. 90, 10 miles south of Benson. (C) **520/586-4100** for information, 520/586-CAVE for tour reservations, or 602/542-4174 for Arizona State Parks. www.pr.state.az.us. Admission $10 per car to enter the park and visit aboveground exhibits; cave tours $14 adults, $6 children 7–13. Park hours daily 7:30am–6pm; cave tours approximately every 20 minutes 8:40am–4:40pm.

ATTRACTIONS AROUND SIERRA VISTA

Arizona Folklore Preserve Set beneath the shady cottonwoods and sycamores of Ramsey Canyon, the Arizona Folklore Preserve is an ongoing project, the brainchild of Dolan Ellis, Arizona's official state balladeer, and his wife, Rose. Ellis was first appointed state balladeer back in 1966 and has been writing songs about Arizona for more than 30 years. He performs most weekends and often welcomes guests to the stage (currently in an old house on the property). In the past, there have been cowboy poets, folk artists, a fiddle maker, saddle makers, and musicians.

44 Ramsey Canyon Rd. (Ariz. 92 south of Sierra Vista). (C) **520/378-6165**. www.arizonafolklore.com. Admission by donation. Showtimes Sat–Sun 2pm. Reservations required.

Fort Huachuca Museum Fort Huachuca, an army base at the mouth of Huachuca Canyon northeast of Sierra Vista, was established in 1877 and, although it has been closed a couple of times, is active today. The buildings of the old post have been declared a National Historic Landmark, and one is now a museum dedicated to the many forts that dotted the Southwest in the latter part of the 19th century. Interesting aspects of the exhibits include the quotes by soldiers that give an idea of what it was like to serve back then. Nearby is the **U.S. Army Military Intelligence Museum,** at Hungerford and Cristi streets ((C) **520/533-1127**). On display are early code machines, surveillance drones, and other pieces of equipment formerly used for intelligence gathering. The museum is open Monday, Wednesday, and Friday from 10am to 2pm; admission is free.

Inside the Fort Huachuca U.S. Army base, Grierson Rd., Sierra Vista. (℃ 520/533-5736. Free admission (suggested donation $2). Mon–Fri 9am–4pm; Sat–Sun 1–4pm.

BIRDING HOT SPOTS & OTHER NATURAL AREAS

Bird-watching has become big business over the past few years, with birders' B&Bs, bird refuges, and even birding festivals. The **Southwest Wings Birding Festival** (℃ **800/288-3861** or 520/459-EVNT) is held in Sierra Vista each year in August.

If you'd like to join a guided bird walk along the San Pedro River or up Carr Canyon in the Huachuca Mountains, an owl-watching night hike, or a hummingbird banding session, contact the **Southeastern Arizona Bird Observatory** (℃ **520/432-1388;** www.sabo.org). Most activities take place between April and September and cost $12 to $18. Workshops and tours are also offered.

Serious birders who want to be sure of adding lots of rare birds to their life lists might want to visit this area on a guided tour. **High Lonesome Ecotours** (℃ **800/743-2668;** www.hilonesome.com) charges about $750 per person for a 4-day birding trip.

In addition to the birding hot spots listed below, there are a few other places that serious birders should not miss. **Garden Canyon,** on Fort Huachuca, has 8 miles of trails, and 350 species of birds have been sighted. There are also Indian pictographs along one of the trails through the canyon. This is a good place to look for elegant trogons and Mexican spotted owls. Get directions at the fort's front gate, and be prepared to show your license, vehicle registration, and proof of vehicle insurance. The canyon is open to the public daily during daylight hours, but is sometimes closed due to military maneuvers, so you must check with the **Range Control Office** (℃ **520/533-7100** or 520/533-7095) before heading out.

South of Ramsey Canyon off Ariz. 92, you'll find **Carr Canyon,** which has a road that climbs up through the canyon to some of the higher elevations in the Huachuca Mountains. Keep your eyes open for buff-breasted flycatchers, red crossbills, and red-faced warblers. The one-lane road is narrow and windy (usually navigable by passenger car), and not for the acrophobic. It climbs 5 miles up into the mountains and goes to Reef Townsite, an old mining camp.

The **Sierra Vista Wastewater Wetlands,** 3 miles east of Ariz. 92 on Ariz. 90, is a good place to see yellow-headed blackbirds, ducks, peregrines, and harriers from fall to spring. The area is open Monday through Friday from 7am to 3pm, Saturday and Sunday from 7am to 1pm.

Coronado National Memorial About 20 miles south of Sierra Vista is a 5,000-acre memorial dedicated to Francisco Vásquez de Coronado, the first European to explore this region. In 1540, Coronado, leading more than 700 people, left Compostela, Mexico, in search of the fabled Seven Cities of Cíbola, said to be rich in gold and jewels. Sometime between 1540 and 1542, Coronado led his band of weary men and women up this valley of the San Pedro River. Forested Montezuma Pass, which is in the center of the memorial, is situated at 6,575 feet and provides far-reaching views of Sonora, Mexico, to the south, the San Pedro River to the east, and several mountain ranges and valleys to the west. A visitor center tells the story of Coronado's fruitless quest for riches and features a wildlife observation area where you might see some of the memorial's 140 or more species of birds. Along the 0.8-mile round-trip Coronado Peak Trail, you'll have good views of the valley and can read quotations from the journals of Coronado's followers.

4101 E. Montezuma Canyon Rd. (✆) 520/366-5515. www.nps.gov/coro. Free admission. Daily 8am–5pm. Closed Thanksgiving and Christmas.

Ramsey Canyon Preserve 🐦   Each year, beginning in late spring, a buzzing fills the air in Ramsey Canyon. This preserve has become internationally known as home to 14 species of hummingbirds—more than anywhere else in the United States. Wear bright red clothing when you visit, and you're certain to attract the little avian dive bombers, which will mistake you for the world's largest flower. Situated in a wooded gorge in the Huachuca Mountains, this Nature Conservancy preserve covers only 380 acres. However, because Ramsey Creek, which flows through the canyon, is a year-round stream, it attracts a wide variety of wildlife, including bears, bobcats, and nearly 200 species of birds. A short nature trail leads through the canyon; a second trail leads higher up the canyon. The preserve offers guided walks as well. April and May are the busiest times here, while August and May are the best times to see hummingbirds.

The preserve also operates the adjacent B&B (see "Where to Stay," below).

27 Ramsey Canyon Rd. (off Ariz. 92, 5 miles south of Sierra Vista). (✆) 520/378-2785. www.tnc.org/arizona. Suggested donation $5 ($3 for Nature Conservancy members). Mar–Oct daily 8am–5pm; Nov–Feb daily 9am–5pm. Closed Thanksgiving, Christmas, and New Year's Day.

San Pedro Riparian National Conservation Area 🐦   Located 8 miles east of Sierra Vista, this conservation area is a rare example of a natural riverside habitat. Over the past 100 years, the Southwestern landscape has been considerably altered by the human hand. Most deleterious of these changes has been the loss of 90% of the region's free-flowing year-round rivers and streams that once provided water and protection to myriad plants, animals, and even humans. Fossil findings from this area indicate that people were living along this river 11,000 years ago. At that time, this area was not a desert, but a swamp, and the San Pedro River is all that remains of the ancient wetland. (Today there isn't much water on the surface, as most of the river water has flowed underground since an earthquake a century ago.) The conservation area is particularly popular with birders, who have a chance of spotting more than 300 species of birds here. Also living in this region are 80 species of mammals, 14 species of fish, and 40 species of amphibians and reptiles.

Also within the riparian area is the **Murray Springs Clovis Site,** where 16 spear points and the remains of a 10,000-year-old mammoth kill were found in the 1960s. Although there isn't much to see other than some trenches, there are numerous interpretive signs along the short trail through the site. It's just north of Ariz. 90 about 5 miles east of Sierra Vista.

For a glimpse of the region's Spanish history, visit the ruins of the **Presidio Santa Cruz de Terrenate,** about 20 miles northeast of Sierra Vista off Ariz. 82 near the ghost town of Fairbanks. This military outpost was established in 1776 by Irish mercenary Hugh O'Conor, who also founded Tucson. Only decaying adobe walls remain of this military outpost, which was never completed due to the constant attacks on the Spanish by Apaches. To reach this site, take Ariz. 82 east from U.S. 90 and drive north 1.8 miles on Kellar Road. It's a 1.2-mile hike to the site.

There are three main parking areas for the conservation area at the bridges over the San Pedro River on Ariz. 92, Ariz. 90, and Ariz. 82. This last parking area is in the ghost town of Fairbank. At the Ariz. 90 parking area, the San Pedro

House, a 1930s ranch, operates as a visitor center and bookstore. It's open daily from 9:30am to 4:30pm.

Ariz. 90. ℂ 520/458-3559. Free admission. Parking areas open sunrise to sunset.

OTHER OUTDOOR PURSUITS

The near-perfect climate of Sierra Vista has made it a great place to golf. You can play a round at the **Pueblo del Sol Country Club,** St. Andrew's Drive (ℂ **520/ 378-6444**), which is off Ariz. 92 on the east side of town and has a great view of the Huachuca Mountains. Greens fees run from $18 to $40.

Horseback riding at Fort Huachuca's Buffalo Corral (ℂ **520/533-5220**) is a good deal, with a cost of $18 for a 2-hour trail ride and special family rates available.

Hikers will find numerous trails in the Huachuca Mountains, which rise up to the west of Sierra Vista. There are trails at Garden Canyon near Fort Huachuca, at Ramsey Canyon Preserve, at Carr Canyon in Coronado National Forest, and at Coronado National Memorial. See "Birding Hot Spots & Other Natural Areas," above, for details. For information on hiking in the Coronado National Forest, contact the **Sierra Vista Ranger District,** 5990 S. Hwy. 92 (ℂ **520/378-0311**), 8 miles south of Sierra Vista in Hereford.

WHERE TO STAY

IN BENSON

If you're looking for lodging close to Kartchner Caverns, try the **Holiday Inn Express,** 630 South Village Loop, Benson (ℂ **888/263-CAVE** or 520/586-8800), which charges $89 for a double.

IN SIERRA VISTA

You'll find numerous budget chain motels in Sierra Vista, including a **Motel 6** (ℂ **800/4-MOTEL-6;**) and a **Super 8** (ℂ **800/800-8000;** 520/459-5380).

Windemere Hotel & Conference Center This three-story conference hotel on the south side of town is one of Sierra Vista's best lodgings, as well as one of the closest to Ramsey Canyon. Although it makes a good choice for avid bird-watchers, it is much more popular with conventions. Guest rooms feature contemporary furnishings.

2047 S. Hwy. 92, Sierra Vista, AZ 85635. ℂ 800/825-4656 or 520/459-5900. Fax 520/458-1347. 149 units. $73 double; $150–$195 suite. Rates include full breakfast and evening cocktail hour. AE, DC, DISC, MC, V. Pets accepted ($50 deposit). **Amenities:** Restaurant (American), lounge; outdoor pool; exercise room; access to nearby health club; Jacuzzi; room service; laundry service; dry cleaning. *In room:* A/C, TV, dataport, fridge, coffeemaker, hair dryer.

IN HEREFORD

Casa de San Pedro Built with bird-watching tour groups in mind, this modern inn is set on the west side of the San Pedro River on 10 acres of land. While the setting doesn't have as much historic character as that of the San Pedro River Inn (see below), the hotel-style guest rooms are large and modern. Built in the territorial style around a courtyard garden, the inn has a large common room where birders gather to swap tales of the day's sightings. This is by far the most upscale inn in the region.

8933 S. Yell Lane, Hereford, AZ 85615. ℂ 800/588-6468 or 520/366-1300. Fax 520/366-0701. www. naturesinn.com. 10 units. $100–$139 double. 2-night minimum in high season. Rates include full breakfast. DISC, MC, V. **Amenities:** Guest laundry. *In room:* A/C.

Ramsey Canyon Inn Bed & Breakfast ✴ Located just outside the gates of the Nature Conservancy's Ramsey Canyon Preserve and operated by the conservancy, this inn is the most convenient choice for avid birders. The property straddles Ramsey Creek, with guest rooms in the main house and apartments in small cabins reached by a footbridge over the creek. A large country breakfast is served in the morning, and in the afternoon you're likely to find a fresh pie made with fruit from the inn's orchard. Guests have 24-hour access to the preserve—a real plus for serious birders. Book early.

29 Ramsey Canyon Rd., Hereford, AZ 85615. © 520/378-3010. Fax 520/803-0819. www.ramseycanyoninn. com. 8 units. $121–$145 double; $145–$158 apt. Room rates include full breakfast. MC, V. **Amenities:** Concierge. *In room:* No phone.

San Pedro River Inn With the character of a small guest ranch, this family-friendly inn is a casual place that will please avid birders who prefer old Arizona character over spotless modern accommodations. Located on the east side of the San Pedro Riparian National Conservation Area, the four eclectically furnished cottages are set beneath huge old cottonwood trees.

8326 S. Hereford Rd., Hereford, AZ 85615. © and fax **520/366-5532.** www.sanpedroriverinn.com. 4 units. $105 double. Rates include continental breakfast. Dogs and horses $5. No credit cards. **Amenities:** Guest laundry. *In room:* TV, kitchen, fridge, coffeemaker.

CAMPGROUNDS

There are two Coronado National Forest campgrounds—16-site Reef Townsite and 8-site Ramsey Vista—up the winding Carr Canyon Road south of Sierra Vista off Ariz. 92. For information, contact the **Coronado National Forest Sierra Vista Ranger District** (© **520/378-0311**). Fort Huachuca has a few campsites charging $3 per night; a rustic cabin is available in Garden Canyon for $25 per night. To reserve a site or a cabin, contact the **Sportsmen Center** (© **520/533-7085**) on base.

WHERE TO DINE

Because Sierra Vista is home to a military base and many of the servicemen have Asian wives, the town supports quite a number of good Asian restaurants, with an emphasis on Chinese, Japanese, and Korean cuisine. Otherwise, it's 30 minutes or so to the restaurants in the towns of Bisbee or Sonoita.

The Outside Inn STEAKHOUSE/SEAFOOD/ITALIAN   Long the special-occasion restaurant in town, the Outside Inn, housed in a cottagelike building south of town and just north of the turnoff for Ramsey Canyon, may not be in the most picturesque of surroundings, but the food is definitely among the best you'll find in the area. In the main dining room or out on the patio, you can enjoy such fare as salmon with spinach fettuccine, blackened swordfish, or mahimahi with a macadamia-nut crust.

4907 S. Ariz. 92. © 520/378-4645. Reservations recommended. Main courses $6–$7 lunch, $11–$18 dinner. MC, V. Mon–Fri 11am–1:30pm and 5–9pm; Sat 5–9pm.

6 Tombstone ⭐

181 miles SE of Phoenix; 70 miles SE of Tucson; 24 miles N of Bisbee

Tombstone, "the town too tough to die," is one of Arizona's most popular attractions, but we'll leave it up to you to decide whether it deserves its reputation (either as a tough town or as a tourist attraction). All it took was a brief blaze of gunfire more than a century ago to seal the fate of this former silver-mining boomtown. It was on these very streets, at a livery stable known as the O.K. Corral, that Wyatt Earp, his brothers Virgil and Morgan, and their friend Doc

Holliday took on the outlaws Ike Clanton and Frank and Tom McLaury on October 26, 1881.

Tombstone was named by Ed Schieffelin, a silver prospector who ventured into this region at a time when the resident Apaches were fighting to preserve their homeland. Schieffelin was warned that all he would find here was his own tombstone, so when he discovered a mountain of silver, he named it Tombstone. Within a few years, Tombstone was larger than San Francisco, and between 1880 and 1887, an estimated $37 million worth of silver was mined here. Such wealth created a sturdy little town, and as the Cochise County seat of the time, Tombstone boasted a number of imposing buildings, including the county courthouse, which is now a state park. In 1887, an underground river flooded the silver mines, and despite attempts to pump the water out, the mines were never reopened. With the demise of the mines, the boom came to an end and the population rapidly dwindled.

Today Tombstone's historic district consists of both original buildings that went up after the town's second fire and newer structures built in keeping with the architectural styles of the time. Most house souvenir shops and restaurants, which should give you some indication that this place is a classic tourist trap, but kids (and adults raised on Louis L'Amour and John Wayne) love it, especially when the famous shootout is reenacted.

ESSENTIALS
GETTING THERE From Tucson, take I-10 east to Benson, from which Ariz. 80 heads south to Tombstone. From Sierra Vista, take Ariz. 90 north to Ariz. 82 heading east.

VISITOR INFORMATION The **Tombstone Chamber of Commerce** (© **888/457-3929** or 520/457-9317; www.tombstone.org) operates a **visitor center** at the corner of Allen Street and Fourth Street.

SPECIAL EVENTS Tombstone's biggest annual celebrations are **Territorial Days,** on the third weekend of March; **Wyatt Earp Days,** in late May; and **Helldorado Days,** on the third weekend in October. The latter celebrates the famous gunfight at the O.K. Corral and includes countless shootouts in the streets, mock hangings, a parade, and contests.

GUNSLINGERS & SALOONS: IN SEARCH OF THE WILD WEST
As portrayed in novels, movies, and TV shows over the years, the shootout has come to epitomize the Wild West, and nowhere is this great American phenomenon more glorified than in Tombstone, where the star attraction is the famous **O.K. Corral.** Located on Allen Street near the corner of Third Street, the site of the 30-second gun battle has taken on mythic proportions over the years. Inside the corral, you'll find not only displays on the shootout, but also exhibits on prostitutes and local photographer C. S. Fly, who ran the boardinghouse where Doc Holliday was staying at the time. For an extra $2 on top of your regular admission, you can take in a shootout reenactment almost on the very site of the original. Next door is **Tombstone's Historama,** a sort of multimedia affair that rehashes the well-known history of Tombstone's "bad old days." Admission is $2.50 at either place.

If you aren't able to catch one of the staged shootouts at the O.K. Corral, don't despair—there are plenty of other shootouts staged in Tombstone. In fact, all over Arizona there are regular reenactments of gunfights, with the sheriff in his white hat always triumphing over the bad guys in black hats. However, nowhere else in the state are there as many modern-day gunslingers entertaining so many people with their blazing six-guns as in Tombstone. Shootouts occur fairly regularly around town between noon and 4pm. Expect to pay $3 or $4 for any of these shows.

When the smoke cleared in 1881, three men lay dead. They were later carted off to the **Boot Hill Graveyard** (© 520/457-9344 or 520/457-3421), on the north edge of town. The cemetery is open to the public and is entered through a gift shop on Ariz. 80. The graves of Clanton and the McLaury brothers, as well as those of others who died in gunfights or by hanging, are well marked. Entertaining epitaphs grace the gravestones; among the most famous is that of Lester Moore—"Here lies Lester Moore, 4 slugs from a 44, No Les, no more." Open 7:30am to 6 or 6:30pm daily; admission is free.

When the residents of Tombstone weren't shooting each other in the streets, they were likely to be found in the saloons and bawdy houses that lined Allen Street. Most famous is the **Bird Cage Theatre,** so named for the cagelike cribs (actually what most people would think of as box seats) that are suspended from the ceiling. These velvet-draped cages were used by prostitutes to ply their trade. For old Tombstone atmosphere, this place is hard to beat. Admission is $4.50; the place is open daily from 8am to 6pm.

If you want to down a cold beer, Tombstone has a couple of very lively saloons that are popular with visitors. The **Crystal Palace,** at Allen and Fifth streets (© **520/457-3611**), was built in 1879 and has been completely restored. This is one of the favorite hangouts for the town's costumed actors and other would-be cowboys and cowgirls. **Big Nose Kate's,** on Allen Street between Fourth and Fifth streets (© **520/457-3107**), is an equally entertaining spot full of Wild West character and characters.

Tombstone has long been a tourist town, and its streets are lined with souvenir shops selling wind chimes, Beanie Babies, and other less-than-wild Western souvenirs. However, there are also several small museums scattered around town. At the **Rose Tree Inn Museum,** at Fourth and Toughnut streets, you can see what may be the world's largest rose bush. Inside, you'll see antique furnishings from Tombstone's heyday in the 1880s. Admission is $2; hours are daily from 9am to 5pm.

The most imposing building in town is the **Tombstone Courthouse State Park,** at Third and Toughnut streets (© **520/457-3311**). Built in 1882, the courthouse is now a state historic park and museum, containing artifacts, photos, and newspaper clippings chronicling Tombstone's lively past. In the courtyard, the gallows that once ended the lives of outlaws and bandits still stands. Open daily from 8am to 5pm, the entrance fee is $2.50 for adults and $1 for children 7 to 13.

At the **Tombstone Epitaph Museum,** on Fifth Street between Allen and Fremont streets, you can inspect the office of the town's old newspaper. Open daily from 9:30am to 5pm; admission is free. To see what life was like for common folk in the old days, pay a visit to the **Pioneer Home Museum,** on Fremont Street (Ariz. 80) between Eighth and Ninth streets. Hours are seasonal; a $2 donation is requested.

At several places along Allen Street, you can hop aboard a reproduction **stagecoach** or **covered wagon,** and for a few dollars get a narrated tour of town. With their rubber tires, these wagons and stagecoaches are much more comfortable than the originals.

WHERE TO STAY

Best Western Lookout Lodge   The biggest and most comfortable motel in Tombstone is a mile north of town overlooking the Dragoon Mountains. Stone walls, porcelain doorknobs, Mexican tiles in the bathrooms, and old-fashioned "gas" lamps give the spacious guest rooms an Old West feel. Ask for a room with a view of the mountains.

Ariz. 80 W. (P.O. Box 787), Tombstone, AZ 85638. ✆ **877/652-6772** or 520/457-2223. Fax 520/457-3870. www.tombstone1880.com/bwlookoutlodge. 40 units. $75–$90 double. Rates include deluxe continental breakfast. AE, DC, DISC, MC, V. Pets accepted ($5 per night plus deposit). **Amenities:** Small outdoor pool. *In room:* A/C, TV, dataport.

Priscilla's Bed & Breakfast   Located 2 blocks from the O.K. Corral, this small Victorian farmhouse has been completely restored and is set behind a white picket fence. Built in 1904, the home reflects a less notorious period of Tombstone's past, a time when lawyers could build houses such as this. Lace curtains hang in the windows, and oak trim and oak furniture throughout the house set a Victorian mood.

101 N. Third St. (P.O. Box 700), Tombstone, AZ 85638. ✆ **520/457-3844**. www.tombstone1880.com/priscilla. 4 units (1 with private bathroom). $59 double with shared bathroom; $69 double with private bathroom. Rates include full breakfast. AE, DC, MC, V. *In room:* No phone.

Tombstone Boarding House   Housed in two whitewashed 1880s adobe buildings with green trim, this inn is in a quiet residential neighborhood only 2 blocks from busy Allen Street. The main house was originally the home of Tombstone's first bank manager, while the guest rooms are in an old boarding-house. Rooms are comfortable and clean, with country decor. Hardwood floors and antiques lend a period feel.

108 N. Fourth St. (P.O. Box 906), Tombstone, AZ 85638-0906. ✆ **888/225-1319** or 520/457-3716. Fax 520/457-3038. 8 units. $65–$80 double. Rates include full breakfast. AE, DISC, MC, V. *In room:* No phone.

WHERE TO DINE

Don Teodoro's Mexican Restaurant MEXICAN   We heard the sweet strains of a guitar wafting through Tombstone, and followed the sound to Don Teodoro's, a little restaurant with a real south-of-the-border atmosphere (and live music 2 nights a week). The experience as a whole was slightly better than the food, which consisted of adequately prepared burritos, chile rellenos, and *carne asada.* What is done well here is the Sonoran-style enchilada.

15 N. Fourth St. ✆ **520/457-3647**. Reservations not accepted; call 30 min. ahead. Main courses $5–$13. AE, MC, V. Sun–Thurs 11am–9pm; Fri–Sat 11am–10pm.

O.K. Café AMERICAN   It's touristy, since it's on the main drag in Tombstone, but we really enjoy the buffalo burgers and homemade soups. Other options include ostrich, emu, veggie, and, of course, beef burgers, as well as bratwurst, BLTs, and chicken. It's also a good place for breakfast.

220 E. Allen St. (corner of Third St.). ✆ **520/457-3980**. Main courses $4–$7. MC, V. Daily 7am–2pm.

7 Bisbee ★★

205 miles SE of Phoenix; 94 miles SE of Tucson; 24 miles NW of Douglas

Arizona has a wealth of ghost towns that boomed on mining profits and then quickly went bust when the mines played out, but none is as impressive as Bisbee, which is built into the steep slopes of Tombstone Canyon on the south side of the Mule Mountains. Between 1880 and 1975, Bisbee's mines produced more than $6 billion worth of metals. When the Phelps Dodge Company shut down its copper mines here, Bisbee nearly went the way of other abandoned mining towns, but because it's the Cochise County seat, it was saved from disappearing into the desert dust.

Bisbee's glory days date from the late 19th and early 20th century, and because the town stopped growing in the early part of the 20th century, it is now one of the best-preserved historic towns anywhere in the Southwest. Old brick buildings line narrow winding streets, and miners' shacks sprawl across the hillsides above downtown. Television and movie producers discovered these well-preserved streets years ago, and Bisbee has doubled as New York, Spain, Greece, Italy, and, of course, the Old West.

The rumor of silver in "them thar hills" is what first attracted prospectors in 1877, and within a few years the diggings attracted the interest of some San Francisco investors, among them Judge DeWitt Bisbee, for whom the town is named. However, it was copper and other less-than-precious metals that would make Bisbee's fortune. With the help of outside financing, large-scale mining operations were begun in 1881 by the Phelps Dodge Company. By 1910, the population had climbed to 25,000, and Bisbee was the largest city between New Orleans and San Francisco. The town boasted that it was the liveliest spot between El Paso and San Francisco—and the presence of nearly 50 saloons and bordellos along Brewery Gulch backed up the boast.

Tucked into a narrow valley surrounded by red hills, Bisbee today has a cosmopolitan air. Many artists call the town home, and urban refugees have been dropping out of the rat race to restore the town's old buildings, opening small inns, restaurants, and galleries. Between the rough edges left over from its mining days and this new cosmopolitan atmosphere, Bisbee is rapidly becoming one of Arizona's most interesting towns.

ESSENTIALS

GETTING THERE   Bisbee is on Ariz. 80, which begins at I-10 in the town of Benson, 45 miles east of Tucson.

VISITOR INFORMATION   Contact the **Bisbee Chamber of Commerce,** 31 Subway St. (© **520/432-5421;** www.bisbeearizona.com).

SPECIAL EVENTS   Bisbee puts on **coaster races** on the Fourth of July; **Brewery Gulch Daze** in September; a **Fiber Arts Festival, Gem and Mineral Show,** and the **1000 Stair Climb** in October; and an **Historic Homes Tour** on Thanksgiving weekend.

EXPLORING THE TOWN

At the Bisbee Chamber of Commerce visitor center, located in the middle of town, pick up walking-tour brochures that will lead you past the most important buildings and sites. Parking is available around the downtown area. On the second floor of the **Copper Queen Library,** across the street from the visitor center, are some great old photographs that give a good idea of what the town looked like in the past century.

Don't miss the **Bisbee Mining and Historical Museum** ✿, 5 Copper Queen Plaza (© **520/432-7071**), housed in the 1897 Copper Queen Consolidated Mining Company office building. This small but comprehensive museum features exhibits on the history of Bisbee. It's open daily from 10am to 4pm; admission is $4 for adults, $3.50 for seniors, and free for children 16 and under.

For another look at early life in Bisbee, visit the **Muheim Heritage House,** up Brewery Gulch at 207 Youngblood Hill (© **520/432-7071**). The house was built between 1902 and 1915 and has an unusual semicircular porch. The interior is decorated with period furniture. It's usually open Thursday through Tuesday from 10am to 4pm; a $2 donation is suggested.

If you climb to the top of **O.K. Street,** there's a path that takes you up to a hill above town for an excellent panorama of the jumble of old buildings. Atop this hill are numerous small colorfully painted shrines built into the rocks and filled with candles, plastic flowers, and pictures of the Virgin Mary. It's a steep climb on a rocky, very uneven path, but the views and the fascinating little shrines make it worth the effort.

You can also see what it was like to work inside Bisbee's copper mines by taking one of the **Queen Mine Tours** ★ (© **520/432-2071**). You can choose either the underground Queen Mine tour or the surface mine and historic tour. Tours are offered daily between 9am and 3:30pm. Underground Queen Mine tours cost $10 for adults, $3.50 for children 7 to 15, and $2 for children 3 to 6; surface mine and historic tours cost $7 per person. The ticket office and mine are just south of the Old Bisbee business district at the Ariz. 80 interchange.

For a personally guided tour of the area, contact **Mary's Walking Tours** (© **520/432-9039**). Mary provides a wealth of information about the area, and she's good with families to boot.

Bisbee has lots of interesting shops and galleries. One of the best and most consistent galleries in town is **Jane Hamilton Fine Art,** 29 Main St. (© **520/ 432-3660**), showing a wide variety of styles. To get a look at some of the quality jewelry created from the minerals mined in the Bisbee area, stop by **Czar Minerals** (© **520/432-2698**), up at the top of Tombstone Canyon Road and Clausen Avenue, or **Bisbee Blue** (© **520/432-5511**), at the Lavender Pit View Point on Ariz. 80. At the former, the specialty is gold- and silversmithing; the latter is an exclusive dealer of the famous Bisbee Blue turquoise, which is a byproduct of copper mining. To protect your face from the burning rays of the sun, visit **Optimo Custom Hat Works,** 47 Main St. (© **520/432-4544**), which sells Panama hats woven by hand in Ecuador and custom-fitted with finesse.

WHERE TO STAY

Bisbee Grand Hotel ★★   The Bisbee Grand Hotel is the sort of place you'd expect Wyatt Earp and his wife to patronize. At street level is a historic saloon with a pressed-tin ceiling and an 1880s bar, while upstairs are beautifully decorated guest rooms. The Oriental Suite features an incredibly ornate Chinese wedding bed, claw-foot tub, and skylight; the Victorian Suite has a red-velvet canopy bed; and the Old Western Suite has a covered wagon for a bed. While all units have private bathrooms, some of them are not in the room itself but across the hall. For 1890s atmosphere, this hotel can't be beat.

61 Main St. (P.O. Box 825), Bisbee, AZ 85603. © **800/421-1909** or 520/432-5900. www.bisbeegrandhotel. com. 15 units. $55–$79 double; $95–$150 suite. Rates include breakfast. AE, DISC, MC, V. *In room:* A/C, no phone.

Copper Queen Hotel   Located in the center of Bisbee, the Copper Queen was built in 1902 by the Copper Queen Mining Company. Today, as the hotel celebrates its centennial, the atmosphere is casual yet quite authentic. The old safe behind the check-in desk has been there for years, as has the oak rolltop desk. Spacious halls lead to guest rooms furnished with antiques. Rooms vary considerably in size (the smallest being quite cramped). Be sure to ask for a renovated unit: While most rooms are up-to-date and attractively furnished, the renovations are an ongoing project. The restaurant serves decent food, and out front is a terrace for alfresco dining. And what would a mining-town hotel be without its saloon?

11 Howell Ave. (P.O. Drawer CQ), Bisbee, AZ 85603. ℰ **520/432-2216.** Fax 520/432-4298. 45 units. $75–$136 double. AE, DC, DISC, MC, V. **Amenities:** Restaurant (American), lounge; small outdoor pool; concierge; room service. *In room:* A/C, TV.

High Desert Inn ⭐ Although small, this is one of Bisbee's two most luxurious hotels and is housed in the former Cochise County Jail (ca. 1901). The guest rooms vary in size, but all feature high ceilings, a cool and sophisticated color scheme, contemporary furnishings (including wrought-iron beds), and small bathrooms with modern fixtures. The inn's dining room is one of the best restaurants in town.

8 Naco Rd. (P.O. Box 145), Bisbee, AZ 85603-9998. ℰ **800/281-0510** or 520/432-1442. Fax 520/432-1410. www.highdesertinn.com. 5 units. $75–$100 double. DISC, MC, V. **Amenities:** Restaurant, lounge; massage. *In room:* A/C, TV.

Le Chêne Hotel ⭐ Located upstairs from the French bistro of the same name (see "Where to Dine," below), this recently opened hotel offers simply furnished rooms, some of which have decent views over the rooftops of town to the nearby hills. Most units are fairly large; big windows and high ceilings make them feel even more spacious. The hotel is right on Brewery Gulch, home to several bars, so you can expect noise on weekend nights.

1 Howard Ave. (P.O. Box DB), Bisbee, AZ 85603. ℰ **520/432-1832.** www.lechenebistro.com. 6 units. $85–$110 double; $120 suite. MC, V. **Amenities:** Restaurant (French), lounge. *In room:* A/C, TV, dataport.

Shady Dell RV Park *Finds* Yes, this really is an RV park, but you'll find neither shade nor dell at this roadside location just south of the Lavender Pit mine. What you will find are eight vintage trailers that have been lovingly restored. Although the trailers don't have their own private bathrooms (there's a bathhouse in the middle of the RV park), they do have all kinds of vintage decor and furnishings—even tapes of period music and radio shows. The latest additions are a vintage Chris Craft boat and a 1947 Flexible Clipper bus that once belonged to the Sacramento Solons baseball team. After numerous write-ups in national publications, the Shady Dell has become so famous that reservations need to be made far in advance. Also here is **Dot's Diner** (ℰ **520/432-2046**), a 1957 vintage diner.

1 Douglas Rd., Bisbee, AZ 85603. ℰ **520/432-3567.** 8 units. $35–$75 per trailer (1–2 people). No credit cards. No pets or children under 10 accepted. **Amenities:** Restaurant. *In room:* No phone.

WHERE TO DINE

Nice baked goods are produced by the **Grateful Bread Bakery,** up at the top of town at 207 Tombstone Canyon (ℰ **520/432-1804**). **Café Cornucopia,** 14 Main St. (ℰ **520/432-4820**), offers fresh juices, smoothies, and homemade sandwiches. For good coffee and a mining-theme decor, check out the **Bisbee Coffee Co.** (ℰ **520/432-7879**), at Copper Queen Plaza at the bottom of Main Street. On nights when most other restaurants are closed, the dining room at the **Copper Queen Hotel** (see "Where to Stay," above) is your best bet for a decent meal. For burgers and homemade Bisbeeberry pie in a vintage diner, drop by **Dot's Diner,** at the Shady Dell RV Park, described above (ℰ **520/432-2046**).

The Bisbee Grille ⭐ REGIONAL AMERICAN Unlike most of the other good restaurants in town, the Bisbee Grille is open almost every day of the week for breakfast, lunch, and dinner. Large photographs of old Bisbee give this place a historic character. Grab a seat by the window for great people-watching. At lunch, the spicy chicken Caesar salad and Southwest Ruben are good bets. Entrees at dinner include pasta dishes, tiger shrimp in garlic, and Bisbee-style fajitas.

Copper Queen Plaza, at the bottom of Main St. © **520/432-6788**. Reservations accepted for parties of 6 or more. Main courses $7–$9 lunch, $13–$19 dinner. AE, DISC, MC, V. Wed–Mon 7am–3pm and 5–9pm.

Café Roka ★★ CONTEMPORARY   Ask almost anyone in southern Arizona where to eat in Bisbee, and this is where they'll send you. Café Roka is a casual and hip find in an out-of-the-way town, offering good value as well as imaginatively prepared food. Menu offerings include grilled salmon with a Gorgonzola crust and artichoke-and-portobello-mushroom lasagna. There's usually a vegetarian dish or two. Flourless chocolate cake with raspberry sauce is an exquisite ending. Local artists display their works, and on some evenings jazz musicians perform.

35 Main St. © **520/432-5153**. Reservations highly recommended. Main courses $13.50–$18.50. AE, MC, V. Mid-Oct to mid-May Wed–Sat 5–9pm; mid-May to mid-Oct call for hours.

High Desert Inn Restaurant ★ INTERNATIONAL   In spite of the fact that it's housed in what was formerly the Cochise County Jail—the back patio used to be the jail cells—this restaurant has a genteel setting that's probably the most formal in town. You'll dine on well-crafted dishes that draw inspiration from around the globe. Such entrees as Southwest chicken with three salsas, mussels in white wine and saffron cream sauce, and three-cheese eggplant torta are representative of the menu here.

8 Naco Rd. © **800/281-0510** or 520/432-1442. www.highdesertinn.com. Reservations recommended 1 week in advance. Main courses $14.50–$18.50. DISC, MC, V. Thurs–Sun 5:30–9pm.

Le Chêne Bistro ★ CONTEMPORARY FRENCH   Ooh-la-la—a French restaurant in Bisbee! Considering the brisk business at the Café Roka and the High Desert Inn, it seemed only a matter of time before the town would get another upscale restaurant. This bistro is housed in a recently restored historic building (with a hotel upstairs). Offerings include pâté maison, escargots, foie gras, coq au vin, trout meunière, cassoulet, basically all the usual suspects. For dessert, don't miss the profiteroles with chocolate and raspberry sauce.

1 Howell Ave. © **520/432-1832**. Reservations recommended. Main courses $12–$22. MC, V. Tues–Sat 5–9pm.

8 Exploring the Rest of Cochise County ★

Willcox: 192 miles SE of Phoenix; 81 miles E of Tucson; 74 miles N of Douglas

Although the towns of Bisbee, Tombstone, and Sierra Vista all lie within Cochise County, much of the county is taken up by the vast Sulphur Springs Valley, which is bounded by multiple mountain ranges. It is across this wide-open landscape that Apache chiefs Cochise and Geronimo once rode. Gazing out across this country today, it is easy to understand why the Apaches fought so hard to keep white settlers out.

The Apaches first moved into this region of southern Arizona sometime in the early 16th century. They pursued a hunting and gathering lifestyle that was supplemented by raiding neighboring tribes for food and other booty. When the Spanish arrived in the area, the Apache acquired horses and became even more efficient raiders. They attacked Spanish, Mexican, and eventually American settlers, and despite repeated attempts to convince them to give up their hostile way of life, the Apache refused to change. Not long after the Gadsden Purchase of 1848 made Arizona U.S. soil, more people than ever began settling in the region. The new settlers immediately became the object of Apache raids, and eventually the U.S. Army was called in to put an end to the attacks; by the mid-1880s, it was embroiled in a war with Cochise, Geronimo, and the Chiricahua Apaches.

Although the Chiricahua and Dragoon mountains, which flank the Sulphur Springs Valley on the east and west, are relatively unknown outside the region, they offer some of the most spectacular scenery in the Southwest. Massive boulders litter the mountainsides, creating fascinating landscapes. The Chiricahua Mountains also have the distinction of being a favorite destination of avid bird-watchers, for it is here that the colorfully plumed elegant trogon reaches the northern limit of its range.

In the southern part of this region lies the town of Douglas, an important gateway to Mexico. Unless you're heading to Mexico, though, there aren't many reasons to visit. But if you do find yourself passing through, be sure to stop in at the historic Gadsden Hotel (see "Where to Stay," below), and if you don't mind driving on gravel roads, the Slaughter Ranch is worth a visit.

ESSENTIALS

GETTING THERE   Willcox is on I-10, with Ariz. 186 heading southeast toward Chiricahua National Monument.

VISITOR INFORMATION   The **Willcox Chamber of Commerce and Agriculture,** 1500 N. Circle I Rd., Willcox (© **800/200-2272** or 520/384-2272; www.willcoxchamber.com), can provide more information.

SPECIAL EVENTS   **Wings Over Willcox,** a festival celebrating the return to the area of more than 12,000 sandhill cranes and other migratory birds, takes place in January.

WILLCOX

Railroad Avenue in downtown Willcox is slowly developing into something of a little historic district. Here you'll find the town's two museums, plus the recently restored **Southern Pacific Willcox Train Depot,** 101 S. Railroad Ave., a redwood depot built in 1880. Inside is a small display of historic Willcox photos. Also worth checking out is the **Willcox Commercial,** 180 N. Railroad Ave. (© **520/384-2448**), a general store that has been around since the days of Geronimo.

Chiricahua Regional Museum & Research Center   If you want to learn more about the history and geology of southeastern Arizona, stop by this small museum, now in its temporary location in an old hardware store. Exhibits done in a folksy and personal style inform visitors about the pioneers, the U.S. Army, and Cochise and the Chiricahua Apaches.

127 E. Maley St. © 800/200-2272 or 520/384-3971. Suggested donation $2 adults, $4 families. Mon–Sat 10am–4pm.

Rex Allen Museum   If you grew up in the days of singing cowboys, then you're probably familiar with Willcox's favorite hometown star. It was Rex Allen who made famous the song "Streets of Laredo," and here at the small museum dedicated to him, you'll find plenty of Rex Allen memorabilia as well as a Cowboy Hall of Fame exhibit. The town celebrates Rex Allen Days every October.

150 N. Railroad Ave. © 520/384-4583. Admission $2 per person, $3 per couple, $5 per family. Daily 10am–4pm.

Finds   A Rest Stop Worth Holding It For

At milepost 320 on I-10 (between Benson and Willcox), you'll find what just might be the most picturesque rest stop in the state. The rest area is set amid the decomposed granite boulders of Texas Canyon and provides one of the only opportunities for getting up close and personal with these beautiful boulders.

SOUTHWEST OF WILLCOX
SCENIC LANDSCAPES

While Chiricahua National Monument claims the most spectacular scenery in this corner of the state, there are a couple of areas southwest of Willcox in the Dragoon Mountains that are almost as impressive. The first of these, **Texas Canyon,** lies right along I-10 between Benson and Willcox and can be enjoyed from the comfort of a speeding car. Huge boulders are scattered across this rolling desert landscape.

South of the community of Dragoon, which is now known for its many pistachio farms (many of which are open to the public), lies a much less accessible area of the Dragoon Mountains known as **Cochise Stronghold** ✰. During the Apache uprisings of the late 19th century, the Apache leader Cochise used this rugged section of the Dragoon Mountains as his hideout and managed to elude capture for years. The granite boulders and pine forests made it impossible for the army to track him and his followers. Cochise eventually died and was buried at an unknown spot somewhere within the area now called Cochise Stronghold. This rugged jumble of giant boulders is reached by a rough gravel road, at the end of which you'll find a campground, picnic area, and hiking trails. For a short, easy walk, follow the 0.4-mile Nature Trail. For a longer and more strenuous hike, head up the Cochise Trail. The Stronghold Divide makes a good destination for a 6-mile round-trip hike. For more information, contact the **Coronado National Forest Douglas Ranger District** (© 520/364-3468).

A MEMORABLE MUSEUM IN AN UNLIKELY LOCALE

Amerind Foundation Museum ✰✰   It may be out of the way and difficult to find, but this museum is well worth seeking out. Established in 1937, the Amerind Foundation is dedicated to the study, preservation, and interpretation of prehistoric and historic Indian cultures. To that end, the foundation has compiled the nation's finest private collection of archaeological artifacts and contemporary items. There are exhibits on the dances and religious ceremonies of the major Southwestern tribes, including the Navajo, Hopi, and Apache, and archaeological artifacts amassed from the numerous Amerind Foundation excavations over the years. Many of the pieces came from right here in Texas Canyon. Fascinating ethnology exhibits include amazingly intricate beadwork from the Plains tribes, a case full of old Zuni fetishes, Pima willow baskets, old kachina dolls, 100 years of Southwestern tribal pottery, and Navajo weavings. The art gallery displays works by 19th- and 20th-century American artists, such as Frederic Remington, whose works focused on the West. The museum store is small but has a surprisingly good selection of books and Native American crafts and jewelry.

Dragoon. © 520/586-3666. Admission $3 adults, $2 seniors and children 12–18, free for children 11 and under. Sept–May daily 10am–4pm; June–Aug Wed–Sun 10am–4pm. Closed major holidays. 64 miles east of Tucson between Benson and Willcox, take the Dragoon Road exit (exit 318) from I-10 and continue 1 mile east.

EAST OF WILLCOX

To explore the Chiricahua Mountains on horseback, contact **Sunglow Guest Ranch** (© **520/824-3334**), which offers rides of anywhere from 1 hour ($18) to all day ($85). Lessons are also available. Reservations are required.

In the town of Bowie, the **Fort Bowie Vineyard,** 156 N. Jefferson St. (© **520/ 847-2593**), has a wine-tasting room and sells locally grown pecans, pistachios, walnuts, and peaches.

Chiricahua National Monument ★★ Sea Captain, China Boy, Duck on a Rock, Punch and Judy—these may not seem like appropriate names for landscape features, but this is no ordinary landscape. These gravity-defying rock formations—called "the land of the standing-up rocks" by the Apache and the "wonderland of rocks" by the pioneers—are the equal of any of Arizona's many amazing rocky landmarks. Rank upon rank of monolithic giants seem to have been turned to stone as they marched across the forested Chiricahua Mountains, and Big Balanced Rock and Pinnacle Balanced Rock threaten to come crashing down at any moment. Formed about 25 million years ago by a massive volcanic eruption, these rhyolite badlands were once the stronghold of renegade Apaches. If you look closely at Cochise Head peak, you can even see the famous chief's profile. If you're in good physical condition, don't miss the chance to hike the 7- to 7½-mile round-trip **Heart of Rocks Trail** ★, which can be accessed from either the Echo Canyon or Massai Point parking areas. This trail leads through the most spectacular scenery in the monument. A shorter loop is also possible. Within the monument are a visitor center, campground, picnic area, many miles of hiking trails, and a scenic drive with views of many of the most unusual rock formations.

Ariz. 186, 36 miles southwest of Willcox. © 520/824-3560. Admission $6 per vehicle. Visitor center daily 8am–5pm. Closed Christmas.

Fort Bowie National Historic Site ★ The Butterfield Stage, which carried mail, passengers, and freight across the Southwest in the mid-1800s, followed a route that climbed up and over Apache Pass, in the heart of the Chiricahua Mountains' Apache territory. Near the mile-high pass, Fort Bowie was established in 1862 to ensure the passage of the slow-moving stage as it traversed this difficult region. The fort was also used to protect the water source for cavalry going east to fight the Confederate army in New Mexico. Later it was from Fort Bowie that federal troops battled Geronimo until the Apache chief finally surrendered in 1886. Today there's little left of Fort Bowie but some crumbling adobe walls, but the hike along the old stage route to the ruins conjures up the ghosts of Geronimo and the Indian Wars.

Off Ariz. 186. © 520/847-2500. Free admission. Visitor center daily 8am–5pm; grounds daily dawn–dusk. Closed Christmas. From Willcox, drive southeast on Ariz. 186; after about 20 miles, watch for signs; it's another 8 miles up a dirt road to the trailhead. Alternatively, drive east from Willcox to Bowie and go 13 miles south on Apache Pass Rd. From the trailhead, it's a 1½-mile hike to the fort.

IN & NEAR DOUGLAS

The town of Douglas abounds in old buildings, and although not many are restored, they hint at the diverse character of this community. Just across the border is Agua Prieta, Sonora, Mexico, where Pancho Villa lost his first battle. Whitewashed adobe buildings, old churches, and sunny plazas provide a contrast to Douglas; curio shops and Mexican restaurants abound. At the **Douglas Chamber of Commerce,** 1125 Pan American Ave. (© **888/315-9999** or 520/ 364-2478; www.discoverdouglas.com), pick up a map to the town's historic buildings as well as a rough map of Agua Prieta. There are also walking tours to Agua Prieta that originate from this office.

Slaughter Ranch Museum ⚑ *Finds*   Down a dusty gravel road lies a little-known Southwestern landmark: the Slaughter Ranch. If you're old enough, you might remember a Walt Disney TV show about Texas John Slaughter. Well, this was his spread (and you can watch videos of the old shows in the ranch's little theater). In 1884, former Texas Ranger John Slaughter bought the San Bernardino Valley and turned it into one of the finest cattle ranches in the West. Slaughter later went on to become the sheriff of Cochise County and helped rid the region of the unsavory characters who had flocked to the many mining towns of this remote part of the state. Today the ranch is a National Historic Landmark and has been restored to its turn-of-the-last-century look. Surrounding the ranch buildings are wide lawns and a large pond that together attract a wide variety of birds, making this one of the best winter birding spots in the state. For the-way-it-was tranquility, this old ranch can't be beat.

About 14 miles east of Douglas. ✆ 520/558-2474. www.vtc.net. Admission $3 adults, free for children under 14. Wed–Sun 10am–3pm. From Douglas, go east on 15th St., which runs into Geronimo Trail; continue east 14 miles.

BIRDING HOT SPOTS

At the **Willcox Chamber of Commerce,** 1500 N. Circle I Rd. (✆ **520/384-2272**), you can pick up several birding maps and checklists for the region.

To the east of Chiricahua National Monument, on the far side of the Chiricahuas, lies **Cave Creek Canyon** ⚑, one of the most important bird-watching spots in America. It's here that the colorful elegant trogon reaches the northern limit of its range. Other rare birds that have been spotted here include sulfur-bellied flycatchers and Lucy's, Virginia's, and black-throated gray warblers. Stop by the visitor center for information on the best birding spots in the area. If you'd like a guide to help you identify the area's many bird species, contact David Jasper, P.O. Box 16430, Portal, AZ 85632 (✆ **520/558-2307**). Cave Creek Canyon is just outside the community of Portal; in summer it can be reached from the national monument by driving over the Chiricahuas on graded gravel roads. In winter, however, you'll have to drive around the mountains, which entails going south to Douglas and then 60 miles north to Portal or north to I-10 and then south 35 miles to Portal.

The **Cochise Lakes** ⚑ (actually the Willcox sewage ponds) are another great bird-watching spot. Birders can see a wide variety of waterfowl and shorebirds, including avocets and ibises. To find the ponds, head south out of Willcox on Ariz. 186, turn right onto Rex Allen Jr. Drive at the sign for the Twin Lakes golf course, and go past the golf course.

Between October and March, as many as 12,000 sandhill cranes gather in the Sulphur Springs Valley south of Willcox, and in January the town holds the **Wings Over Willcox** festival, a celebration of these majestic birds. There are a couple of good places in the area to see sandhill cranes during the winter. Southwest of Willcox on U.S. 191 near the Apache Station electric generating plant and the community of Cochise, you'll find the **Apache Station Wildlife Viewing Area.** About 60 miles south of Willcox, off U.S. 191 near the town of Elfrida, is the **Whitewater Draw Wildlife Area.** To reach the viewing area, go south from Elfrida on Central Highway, turn right on Davis Road, and in another 2½ miles, turn left on Coffman Road and continue 2 miles. The last 2 miles is on a dirt road that should be avoided after rainfall. The Sulphur

Springs Valley is also well known for its large wintering population of raptors, including ferruginous hawks and prairie falcons.

Near Douglas, the **Slaughter Ranch,** which has a large pond, and the adjacent **San Bernardino National Wildlife Refuge** are good birding spots in both summer and winter. See the description of the Slaughter Ranch Museum, above, for directions.

North of Willcox, at the end of a 30-mile gravel road, lies the **Muleshoe Ranch Cooperative Management Area** (© 520/586-7072 or 520/622-3861), a Nature Conservancy preserve that contains seven perennial streams. These streams support endangered aquatic life as well as riparian zones that attract a large number of bird species. To get here, take exit 340 off I-10 and go south; turn right on Bisbee Avenue and then right again onto Airport Road. After 15 miles, watch for a fork in the road and take the right fork. If the road is dry, it is usually passable by passenger car. The headquarters, which includes the visitor center, is open mid-February to mid-May, daily from 8am to 5pm; mid-May through August, Friday through Sunday from 8am to 5pm; and September to mid-February, Thursday through Monday from 8am to 5pm. The backcountry is accessible year-round, 24 hours a day. Overnight accommodations in casitas ($85–$125 double) are available by reservation, but are closed June through August.

WHERE TO STAY
IN & NEAR WILLCOX
Budget chain motels are the only options right in Willcox (you'll find all of the ones listed below off I-10 at exit 340). They include the **Best Western Plaza Inn,** 1100 W. Rex Allen Dr. (© 520/384-3556), charging $69 to $89 double; **Days Inn,** 724 N. Bisbee Ave. (© 520/384-4222), charging $40 to $50; **Motel 6,** 921 N. Bisbee Ave. (© 520/384-2201), with rates of $41; and **Super 8,** 1500 Fort Grant Rd. (© 520/384-0888), charging $52.

Cochise Hotel *Finds* Built in 1882, this historic hotel is about the most authentic in the state. The atmosphere is totally uncontrived, and the rooms are still as simply furnished as travelers on the Southern Pacific Railroad might have found them 100 years ago. In the hotel's parlor, you'll see a working Victrola (guests often end up dancing to old 78 records) and a velvet sofa said to have belonged to Jenny Lind. With 2 days' notice, the hotel can prepare dinners for $8 to $10. Although this place is certainly not for everyone, it is a genuine step back in time. If you're a light sleeper, bring earplugs; the trains still run right past the front door.

P.O. Box 27, Cochise, AZ 85606. © 520/384-3156. 5 units. $50–$65 double. Rates include full breakfast. No credit cards. Take exit 331 off I-10 onto Ariz. 191; drive south 5 miles to Cochise. **Amenities:** Dining room. *In room:* No phone.

IN DOUGLAS
Gadsden Hotel Built in 1907, the Gadsden bills itself as "the last of the grand hotels," and its listing on the National Register of Historic Places backs up that claim. The marble lobby, although dark, is a classic. Vaulted stained-glass skylights run the length of the ceiling, and above the landing of the wide Italian marble stairway is a genuine Tiffany window. Although the carpets in the halls are well worn and rooms aren't always spotless, many units have been renovated and refurnished. The bathrooms are, however, a bit worse for the wear. The lounge is a popular local hangout, with more than 200 cattle brands painted on the walls. The dining room serves Mexican and American fare.

1046 G Ave., Douglas, AZ 85607. © **520/364-4481.** Fax 520/364-4005. www.theriver.com/gadsdenhotel. 156 units. $40–$60 double; $70–$85 suite. AE, DC, DISC, MC, V. **Amenities:** Restaurant (American), lounge; access to nearby health club; room service; coin-op laundry; laundry service; dry cleaning. *In room:* A/C, TV.

IN PORTAL

Portal Peak Lodge, Portal Store & Cafe   This motel-like lodge, located behind the general store/cafe in the hamlet of Portal, has fairly modern guest rooms that face one another across a wooden deck. Meals are available in the adjacent cafe. If you're seeking predictable accommodations in a remote location, you'll find them here.

P.O. Box 364, Portal, AZ 85632. © **520/558-2223.** Fax 520/558-2473. www.portalpeaklodge.com. 16 units. $75 double. AE, DISC, MC, V. **Amenities:** Restaurant (American). *In room:* A/C, TV, coffeemaker.

Southwestern Research Station, The American Museum of Natural History ★ *Finds*   Located far up in Cave Creek Canyon, this is a field research station that takes guests when the accommodations are not filled by scientists doing research. As such, it is the best place in the area for serious bird-watchers, who will find the company of researchers to be a fascinating addition to a visit. Guests stay in simply furnished cabins scattered around the open grounds of the research center. Spring and fall are the easiest times to get reservations and the best times for bird-watching.

P.O. Box 16553, Portal, AZ 85632. © **520/558-2396.** Fax 520/558-2396. http://research.amnh.org/swrs. 15 units. $128 double. Rates include all meals. No credit cards. **Amenities:** Dining room; outdoor pool; volleyball court; guest laundry. *In room:* No phone.

AREA GUEST RANCHES

Grapevine Canyon Ranch ★   Located in the foothills of the Dragoon Mountains adjacent to Cochise Stronghold about 35 miles southwest of Willcox, this guest ranch can be either a quiet hideaway where you can enjoy the natural setting or a place to experience traditional ranch life—horseback riding, rounding up cattle, mending fences. The landscape of mesquite and yucca conjures up images of the high chaparral, and a wide variety of rides are offered, with an emphasis on those for the experienced. If you don't care to go horseback riding, sightseeing excursions can be arranged. The small cabins (with shower-only bathrooms) and larger casitas (with combination shower/tubs) are set under groves of manzanita and oak trees; you can view wildlife and the night sky from the decks. Unfortunately, furnishings and carpets are old, and rooms are short on Western character.

P.O. Box 302, Pearce, AZ 85625. © **800/245-9202** or 520/826-3185. Fax 520/826-3636. www.gcranch.com. 12 units. $270–$370 double. Rates include all meals. 3-night minimum. Various weeklong packages available. AE, DISC, MC, V. No children under 12 accepted. **Amenities:** Dining room; outdoor pool; horseback riding; Jacuzzi; guest laundry. *In room:* A/C, fridge, coffeemaker, hair dryer, no phone.

Sunglow Guest Ranch ★ *Value*   Located in the western foothills of the Chiricahua Mountains roughly 40 miles southeast of Willcox, this remote and tranquil ranch is surrounded by Coronado National Forest. A small lake is just downhill from the ranch buildings, and rising up behind this lake are the peaks of the Chiricahuas. There's great bird-watching both on the ranch and in the nearby hills. Back in the 1880s, Sunglow was a logging boomtown, but all that remains today is an adobe cottage said to have been the home of outlaw Johnny Ringo's girlfriend. The old adobe building now functions as the ranch's dining hall. A reproduction of an old mission church serves as a recreation hall and lounge. Guest rooms are quite large; most have woodstoves. This guest ranch is much less structured than many others in the state, and consequently rates are much lower. Meals are available if arranged in advance ($26 per person per day). Daily maid service is not provided.

H.C. 1, Box 385, Turkey Creek Rd., Pearce, AZ 85625. ✆ **520/824-3334.** Fax 520/824-3176. www. sunglowranch.com. 9 units. $69–$89 double; $149 for 4 in house. AE, DISC, MC, V. **Amenities:** Dining room; horseback riding ($18 per hr.). *In room:* Kitchenette, no phone.

CAMPGROUNDS

Campgrounds in the area include one at **Chiricahua National Monument** (✆ **520/824-3560**) on Ariz. 186, several other small national forest campgrounds on the road to Portal, and a 10-site campground at **Cochise Stronghold,** which is 35 miles southwest of Willcox off U.S. 191. For information on these national forest campgrounds, contact the **Coronado National Forest Douglas Ranger District** (✆ **520/364-3468**). Reservations are not accepted for any of these campgrounds.

WHERE TO DINE
IN WILLCOX

Right across the parking lot from the Willcox Chamber of Commerce Visitor Center/Museum of the Southwest (off I-10 at exit 340), you'll find **Stout's Cider Mill** ★ (✆ **520/384-3696**), which makes delicious concoctions with apples. There's cider, cider floats, "cidersicles," apple cake, and the biggest (and contender for the best) apple pie in the world. Open daily from 8am to 6pm.

Rodney's *Finds* BARBECUE   Willcox doesn't have much in the way of good restaurants, but if you're a fan of barbecue, you'll want to schedule a stop at Rodney's. This little hole in the wall near the Rex Allen Museum is so nondescript that you can easily miss it. Inside, you'll find Rodney Brown, beaming with personality and dishing up lip-smackin' barbecued pork sandwiches and plates of ribs, shrimp, and catfish.

118 N. Railroad Ave. ✆ **520/384-5180.** Main courses $5–$8.50. Credit cards not accepted. Tues–Sun 11am–8pm or later, depending on business.

IN DOUGLAS

The Grand Café MEXICAN   The most interesting part of this cafe is the flamboyant interior and the Marilyn Monroe pictures all over the walls. There are plenty of familiar Mexican choices—enchiladas, tacos, fajitas, and posole, a chile stew with hominy and chicken or pork—with steak and the occasional Italian dish thrown in for good measure. We like the chicken mole, if it's available, with an appetizer of grilled green onions. The guacamole has cottage cheese in it, which seems rather strange, but the green corn tamales are quite good. Don't expect snappy service here.

1119 G Ave. ✆ **520/364-2344.** Main courses $6–$16. MC, V. Mon–Sat 10am–9:30pm.

11

Western Arizona

Separating Arizona from California and Nevada are 340 miles of Colorado River waters, most of which are impounded in huge reservoirs that provide the water and electricity to such sprawling Southwestern boomtowns as Phoenix and Las Vegas. Because of this watery border, the region has come to be known as Arizona's West Coast.

Lake Havasu, Lake Mohave, and Lake Mead are the largest and most popular of these reservoirs, and due to convolutions in the landscape, they offer thousands of miles of shoreline. In some ways Arizona's West Coast is actually superior to California's Pacific coastline. Although there aren't many waves on this stretch of the Colorado River, both the weather and the water are warmer than in California. Consequently, watersports of all types are extremely popular, and the fishing is some of the best in the country.

While the Colorado River has always been the lifeblood of this rugged region, it was not water that first attracted settlers. A hundred years ago, prospectors ventured into this sun-baked landscape hoping to find gold in the desert's mountains. Some actually hit pay dirt. Mining towns sprang up overnight, only to be abandoned a few years later when the gold ran out. Today Oatman is the most famous of these mining boomtowns,

but it has too many people and wild burros to be called a ghost town.

People are still venturing into this region in hopes of striking it rich, but now they head for the casinos in Laughlin, Nevada, just across the Colorado River from Bullhead City, Arizona. Here a miniature version of Las Vegas has grown up on the Nevada shore of the Colorado River.

Laughlin, Nevada, and Bullhead City, Arizona, aren't the only towns in this area with an abundance of waterfront accommodations. As with any warm coastline, Arizona's West Coast is lined with lakefront resorts, hotels, RV parks, and campgrounds. It's for the most part a destination for desert residents, so you won't find any hotels or resorts even remotely as upscale or expensive as those in Phoenix, Tucson, or Sedona. You will, however, see plenty of houseboats for rent. These floating vacation homes are immensely popular with families and groups. With a houseboat, you can get away from the crowds, just dropping anchor and kicking back when you find a remote cove, the best fishing, or the most spectacular views. You can even houseboat to the London Bridge, which is no longer falling down, but rather bridges a backwater of Lake Havasu and is now one of Arizona's biggest tourist attractions.

1 Kingman

90 miles SE of Las Vegas; 180 miles SW of Grand Canyon Village; 150 miles W of Flagstaff; 30 miles E of Laughlin

Although Kingman is the only town of any size between the Grand Canyon and Las Vegas, it is looked upon by most travelers as little more than a place to gas up before heading out across the desert. In fact, Kingman actually has a fairly long history by Arizona standards and contains some interesting downtown historic buildings. The town's other claim to fame is that it is on the longest extant stretch of historic Route 66.

That Kingman today is more way station than destination is not surprising considering its history. In 1857, Lt. Edward Fitzgerald Beale passed through this region leading a special corps of camel-mounted soldiers on a road-surveying expedition. Some 60 years later, the road Beale surveyed would become the National Old Trails Highway, the precursor to Route 66. Gold and silver were discovered in the nearby hills in the 1870s; in the early 1880s, the railroad laid its tracks through what became the town of Kingman. It flourished briefly around the turn of the 20th century as a railroad town; today, it's the buildings constructed during this railroading heyday (including the historic Brunswick Hotel) that give downtown Kingman a bit of character.

In the hills outside of town, such mining towns as Oatman and Chloride sprung up and boomed until the 1920s, when the mines became unprofitable and were abandoned. The lure of gold and silver has never quite died in this area, and in nearby Oatman, the Gold Road Mine is still an operational mine, though giving tours now seems to generate more income than the actual mining of gold.

During the 1930s, Kingman was a stop on the road to the promised land of California, as tens of thousands of unemployed people followed Route 66 from the Midwest to Los Angeles. Route 66 has long since been replaced by I-40, but the longest remaining stretch of the old highway runs east from Kingman to Ash Fork. Over the years, Route 66 has taken on legendary qualities, and today people come from all over the world searching for pieces of this highway's historic past.

Remember Andy Devine? No? Well, Kingman is here to tell you all about its squeaky-voiced native-son actor. Devine starred in hundreds of short films and features in the silent-screen era, but he's perhaps best known as cowboy sidekick Jingles on the 1950s TV Western *Wild Bill Hickok.* In the 1950s and 1960s, he hosted *Andy's Gang,* a popular children's TV show. In the 1960s, he played Captain Hap on *Flipper.* Devine died in 1977, but here in Kingman his memory lives on—in a room in the local museum, on an avenue named after him, and every October when the town celebrates Andy Devine Days.

ESSENTIALS

GETTING THERE   Kingman is on I-40 at the junction with U.S. 93 from Las Vegas. One of the last sections of old Route 66 (Ariz. 66) connects Kingman with Seligman, Arizona.

America West (© 800/235-9292; www.americawest.com) flies between Phoenix and Kingman Airport. Car rentals are available here through **Enterprise** (© 800/325-8007), **Hertz** (© 800/654-3131), and **Thrifty** (© 800/367-2277).

There is **Amtrak** (© 800/872-7245) rail service to Kingman from Chicago and Los Angeles. The station is at 120 W. Andy Devine Ave., downtown.

VISITOR INFORMATION   The **Kingman Area Chamber of Commerce,** 120 W. Andy Devine Ave. (© 520/753-6106; www.arizonaguide.com/visitkingman), operates an information center in this restored 1907 powerhouse, which also houses a Route 66 Museum, a model railroad, and a 1950s-style soda fountain. Open daily from 9am to 6pm.

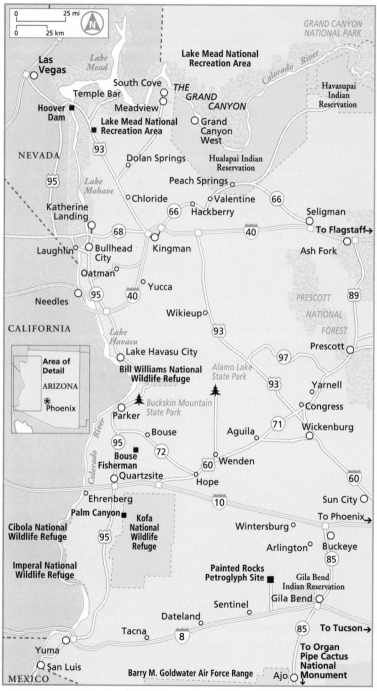

Lake Mead National
Recreation Area

GRAND CANYON
NATIONAL PARK

Las
Vegas

Lake
Mead

South Cove

*THE
GRAND
CANYON*

Colorado River

Havasupai
Indian
Reservation

Temple Bar

Meadview

Hoover
Dam

Lake Mead National
Recreation Area

Grand
Canyon
West

NEVADA

93

Dolan Springs

Hualapai Indian
Reservation

Lake
Mohave

95

Chloride

Peach Springs

Valentine

66

Katherine
Landing

66

Hackberry

Seligman

To Flagstaff→

68

Kingman

40

Laughlin

Bullhead
City

Ash Fork

Oatman

Needles

95

40

Yucca

PRESCOTT

89

CALIFORNIA

Lake
Havasu

Wikieup

NATIONAL

93

FOREST

Lake Havasu City

Prescott

Area of
Detail

ARIZONA

Bill Williams National
Wildlife Refuge

*Alamo Lake
State Park*

97

93

Phoenix

Colorado River

Parker

*Buckskin Mountain
State Park*

Yarnell

Congress

Bouse

Aguila

71

Wickenburg

95

Bouse
Fisherman

72

60

Wenden

Quartzsite

Hope

60

Ehrenberg

10

Sun City

Palm Canyon

Cibola National
Wildlife Refuge

95

Kofa
National
Wildlife
Refuge

To Phoenix→

Wintersburg

Imperial National
Wildlife Refuge

Arlington

Buckeye

85

Painted Rocks
Petroglyph Site

Gila Bend
Indian Reservation

Sentinel

Gila Bend

Dateland

To Tucson→

Tacna

8

85

Yuma

To Organ
Pipe Cactus
National
Monument

San Luis

MEXICO

Barry M. Goldwater Air Force Range

Ajo

EXPLORING THE AREA

There isn't much to do right in Kingman, but while you're in town, you can learn more about local history at the **Mohave Museum of History and Arts,** 400 W. Beale St. ((C) **520/753-3195**). There's also plenty of Andy Devine memorabilia on display. Open Monday through Friday from 9am to 5pm, Saturday and Sunday from 1 to 5pm. Admission is $3 for adults and $2 for seniors. Afterwards, take a drive or a stroll around downtown Kingman to view the town's many historic buildings. (You can pick up a map at the museum.)

If you're interested in historic homes, you can tour the **Bonelli House,** 430 E. Spring St., a two-story stone home built in 1915 and furnished much as it may have been at that time. The house is open Thursday through Monday from 1 to 4pm, but before heading over, check at the Mohave Museum of History and Arts to see if there will be a guide to show you around. Admission is by donation.

The new **Route 66 Museum,** 120 W. Andy Devine Ave. ((C) **520/753-9889**), has exhibits on the history of not just Route 66, but also the roads, railroads, and trails that preceded it. Hours are daily from 9am to 6pm (shorter hours in winter); admission is $3 for adults, free for children 12 and under.

When you're tired of the heat and want to cool off, head southeast of Kingman to **Hualapai Mountain Park,** on Hualapai Mountain Road ((C) **877/ 757-0915** or 520/757-0915; www.hualapaimountainpark.com), which is at an elevation of 7,000 feet and offers picnicking, hiking, camping, and rustic rental cabins built in the 1930s by the Civilian Conservation Corp.

GHOST TOWNS

Located 30 miles southwest of Kingman on what was once Route 66 is the busy little mining camp of **Oatman,** a classic Wild West ghost-town tourist trap full of shops selling tacky souvenirs. Founded in 1906 when gold was discovered here, Oatman quickly grew into a lively town of 12,000 people and was an important stop on Route 66—even Clark Gable and Carole Lombard stayed here (on their honeymoon, no less). In 1942, when the U.S. government closed down many of Arizona's gold-mining operations because gold was not essential to the war effort, Oatman's population plummeted. Today there are fewer than 250 inhabitants, and the once-abandoned old buildings have been preserved as a ghost town. The historic look of Oatman has attracted numerous filmmakers over the years; *How the West Was Won* is just one of the movies that was shot here.

One of the biggest attractions of Oatman is its population of almost-wild burros. These animals, which roam the streets of town begging for handouts, are descendants of burros used by gold miners. Be careful—they bite!

Daily staged shootouts in the streets and dancing to country music on weekend evenings are the other two big draws, but you can also tour an inactive gold mine while you're here. The **Gold Road Mine Tour** ((C) **520/768-1600**) takes you underground and also shows you all the topside workings of a modern gold mine. Tours, which are offered daily between 10am and 4:30pm, last 1 hour and 10 minutes and cost $12 for adults and $6 for children. An extended tour ($24) and an extreme tour ($50) are offered by reservation only. The mine is on historic Route 66 about 2½ miles east of Oatman.

Annual events staged here are among the strangest in the state. There are the bed races in January, a Fourth of July high-noon sidewalk egg fry, a Labor Day burro biscuit toss, and a December Christmas bush festival (bushes along the highway are decorated with tinsel and ornaments). Saloons, restaurants, and a very basic hotel (where you can view the room Clark and Carole rented on their wedding night) provide food and lodging if you decide you'd like to soak up the Oatman atmosphere for a while. For more information, contact the **Oatman Chamber of Commerce** (© 520/768-6222 or 520/763-5885).

Chloride, yet another almost-ghost town, is about 20 miles northwest of Kingman. The town was founded in 1862 when silver was discovered in the nearby Cerbat Mountains, and is named for a type of silver ore that was mined here. By the 1920s, there were 75 mines and 2,000 people in Chloride. When the mines shut down in 1944, the town lost most of its population. Today there are about 300 residents.

Much of the center of the town has been preserved as a historic district that includes the oldest continuously operating post office in Arizona, the old jail, the Silverbelle Playhouse, and the Jim Fritz Museum. Many of the downtown buildings now serve as gift shops.

On the first and third Saturday of each month, Chloride comes alive with staged gunfights in the streets (at high noon, of course) and an afternoon vaudeville show at the Town Hall (no shows during July–Aug). On the last Saturday in June, the town celebrates **Old Miners' Day** with a parade, shootouts, melodramas, music, and dancing.

Chloride's biggest attractions are the **Chloride murals,** painted by artist Roy Purcell in 1966. The murals, sort of colorful hippie images, are painted on the rocks on a hillside about a mile outside town. To find them, drive through town on Tennessee Avenue and continue onward after the road turns to dirt. You can also see old petroglyphs created by the Hualapai tribe on the hillside opposite the murals.

For more information, contact the **Chloride Chamber of Commerce** (© **520/565-2204;** www.chloridearizona.com).

WHERE TO STAY

In addition to the accommodations listed below, most of the budget motel chains have branches in Kingman.

Hotel Brunswick ✦ *(Finds)*   Built in 1909, the Brunswick Hotel is Kingman's only restored historic lodging. Back when the hotel's imposing tufa-stone building was constructed, the railroad was the lifeblood of this town, and inside you'll find rooms furnished with antiques and vintage character from those days. The guest rooms vary considerably in size, and most of those with shared bathrooms have only single beds. Nonetheless, they're quite comfortable, and suites are extremely spacious. Although the railroad tracks are right across the street, triple-paned windows keep things pretty quiet. The restaurant on the premises serves excellent Continental fare.

315 E. Andy Devine Ave., Kingman, AZ 86401. © **888/559-1800** or 520/718-1800. Fax 520/718-1801. www.hotel-brunswick.com. 24 units (15 with private bathroom). $25 single with shared bathroom; $50 double with private bathroom; $75–$115 suite. Rates include deluxe continental breakfast. AE, DC, DISC, MC, V. Pets accepted ($25 deposit plus $10 per night). **Amenities:** Restaurant (Continental), bar; car-rental desk; business center; laundry service; dry cleaning. *In room:* A/C, TV, dataport.

Quality Inn—Kingman   Andy Devine Avenue used to be the famous Route 66, and this motel, 2 miles south of I-40, cashes in on the fame of the historic highway. The public areas are filled with Route 66 memorabilia, while the breakfast room is done up like a 1950s soda shop. Guest rooms are a bit cramped but clean.

1400 E. Andy Devine Ave., Kingman, AZ 86401. © **800/228-5151** or 520/753-4747. 97 units. $47–$65 double. Rates include continental breakfast. AE, DC, DISC, MC, V. **Amenities:** Outdoor pool; exercise room; Jacuzzi; sauna; coin-op laundry. *In room:* A/C, TV, dataport, coffeemaker, hair dryer.

Get Your Kicks on Route 66

It was the Mother Road, the Main Street of America, and for thousands of Midwesterners devastated by the dust bowl days of the 1930s, Route 66 was the road to a better life. However, on the last leg of its journey from Chicago to California, Route 66 meandered across the vast empty landscape of northern Arizona.

Officially dedicated in 1926, Route 66 was the first highway in America to be uniformly signed from one state to the next. Less than half of the highway's 2,200-mile route was paved, and in those days, the stretch between Winslow and Ash Fork was so muddy in winter that drivers had their cars shipped by railroad between the two points. By the 1930s, however, the entire length of Route 66 had been paved, and the westward migration that characterized the Great Depression was underway.

The years following World War II saw Americans take to Route 66 in unprecedented numbers, but this time for a different reason. Steady jobs, a new prosperity, and reliable cars made travel a pleasure, and Americans set out to discover the West—many on the newly affordable family vacation. Motor courts, cafes, and tourist traps sprang up along the highway's length, and these businesses turned to increasingly more eye-catching signs and billboards to lure passing motorists. Neon lights abounded, looming out of the dark Western nights on lonely stretches of highway.

By the 1950s, Route 66 just couldn't handle the amount of traffic it was seeing. With President Eisenhower's initiation of the National Interstate Highway System, Route 66 was eventually replaced by a four-lane divided highway. Many of the towns along the old highway were bypassed, and motorists stopped frequenting such roadside establishments as Pope's General Store and the Oatman Hotel. Many closed, while others were replaced by their more modern equivalents. Some, however, managed to survive, and they appear along the road like strange time capsules from another era, vestiges of Route 66's legendary past.

The **Wigwam Motel** is one of the most distinctive Route 66 landmarks. For many miles out from the town of Holbrook, billboards along I-40 beckon weary motorists to "sleep in a wigwam." The wigwams in question (actually tepees) were built out of concrete around 1940 and still contain many of their original furnishings. Also in Holbrook are several rock shops with giant signs—and life-size concrete dinosaurs—that date from Route 66 days. Nighttime here comes alive with vintage neon.

Continuing west, between Winslow and Flagstaff, you'll find a landmark that made it into the movie *Forrest Gump*. The **Twin Arrows** truck stop, now little more than an abandoned cafe, has as its symbol two giant arrows constructed from telephone poles.

Flagstaff, the largest town along the Arizona stretch of Route 66, became a major layover spot. Motor courts flourished on the road leading into town from the east. Today this road has been officially renamed Route 66 by the city of Flagstaff, and many of the old motor courts remain. Although you probably wouldn't want to stay in many of these old motels, their neon signs were once beacons in the night for tired drivers. Downtown Flagstaff has quite a few shops where you can pick up Route 66 memorabilia.

About 65 miles west of Flagstaff begins the longest remaining stretch of old Route 66. Extending for 160 miles from Ash Fork to Topock, this lonely blacktop passes through some of the most remote country in Arizona (and also goes right through the town of Kingman). In the community of Seligman, at the east end of this stretch of the highway, you'll find the **Snow Cap Drive-In** (℡ 520/422-3291), where owner Juan Delgadillo serves up fast food and quick wit amid outrageous decor. You can't miss it. Next door at **Angel's Barber Shop** (℡ 520/422-3352), owned by Juan's brother Angel, you'll be entertained by one of Route 66's most famous residents and an avid fan of the old highway. Angel still cuts hair, and his one-chair barbershop's walls are covered with photos and business cards of happy customers, many of whom traveled thousands of miles to get their hair cut here. Angel's place also serves as something of a Route 66 information center and souvenir shop, and Angel is president emeritus of the Route 66 Association of Arizona.

After leaving Seligman, the highway passes through such waysides as Peach Springs, Truxton, Valentine, and Hackberry. Before reaching Peach Springs, you'll come to **Grand Canyon Caverns,** once a near-mandatory stop for families traveling Route 66. At Valle Vista, near Kingman, the highway goes into a curve that continues for 7 miles. Some people claim it's the longest continuous curve on a U.S. highway.

After driving through the wilderness west of Seligman, Kingman feels like a veritable metropolis, and its bold neon signs once brought a sigh of relief to the tired and the hungry. Today there are dozens of modern motels in Kingman, but our favorite is the **Quality Inn,** on Andy Devine Avenue. It has lots of Route 66 memorabilia on display, and the breakfast room is done up like a 1950s malt shop. **Mr. D'z Route 66 Diner,** a modern rendition of a 1950s diner (housed in an old gas station/cafe), serves burgers and blue-plate specials and usually has a few classic cars parked out front. Across the street is the restored powerhouse, which dates from 1907 and is home to the **Historic Route 66 Association of Arizona** (℡ 520/753-5001), the **Route 66 Museum** (℡ 520/753-9889), the Kingman Area Chamber of Commerce Visitor Center, a 1950s-style malt shop, and a gallery of photos by a local photographer who once shot for *Arizona Highways* magazine. Each year in late April or early May, Kingman is the site of the **Route 66 Fun Run Weekend,** which consists of a drive along 150 miles of old Route 66 between Topock and Seligman.

The last stretch of Route 66 in Arizona heads southwest out of Kingman through the rugged Sacramento Mountains. It passes through **Oatman,** once almost a ghost town after the local mining industry collapsed and the new interstate pulled money out of town. Today mock gunfights and nosy wild burros entice motorists to stop, and shops playing up Route 66's heritage line the wooden sidewalks.

After dropping down out of the mountains, the road once crossed the Colorado River on a narrow metal bridge. Although the bridge is still there, it now carries a pipeline instead of traffic, and cars must return to the bland I-40 to continue their journey into the promised land of California.

WHERE TO DINE

If you're desperate for an espresso, you'll be glad to know about **Oldtown Coffeehouse,** 616 E. Beale St. (☎ **520/753-2244**), housed in an old cottage in downtown Kingman.

DamBar & Steak House STEAKHOUSE   Operated by the same people who run Murphy's in Prescott, this steakhouse has long been Kingman's favorite place for dinner out. It's hard to miss—just watch for the steer on the roof of a rustic wooden building. Inside, the atmosphere is very casual, with sawdust on the floor and wooden booths. Mesquite-broiled steaks are the name of the game here, but there are plenty of other hearty dishes as well.

1960 E. Andy Devine Ave. ☎ 520/753-3523. Reservations recommended on weekends and in summer. Lunch items $6–$13; main courses $10–$17 at dinner. AE, DISC, MC, V. Daily 11am–10pm (until 11pm in summer).

Hubb's Café CONTINENTAL/FRENCH   Hubb's, a downtown restaurant located in an authentically restored historic 1909 hotel, offers menu items you might not expect to find in a small town like Kingman. The menu ranges the globe from France to Indonesia with escargot, onion soup, tiger prawns in a spicy coconut-milk sauce, and Indonesian chicken curry. There are also plenty of steaks.

At the Hotel Brunswick, 315 E. Andy Devine Ave. ☎ 520/718-1800. www.hotel-brunswick.com. Main courses $10–$40 at dinner. AE, DC, DISC, MC, V. Mon–Sat 5–9pm.

Mr. D'z Route 66 Diner AMERICAN   This 1990s version of a vintage roadside diner is housed in an old gas station now painted an eye-catching turquoise and pink. The retro color scheme continues inside, where you can snuggle into a booth or grab a stool at the counter. This place is a big hit with car buffs and people doing Route 66 (Tuesday night is cruising night, which usually means plenty of vintage cars and hot rods). Punch in a few 1950s tunes on the jukebox, order up a Route 66 bacon cheeseburger and a root-beer float, and you've got an instant trip down memory lane, Route 66 style.

105 E. Andy Devine Ave. ☎ 520/718-0066. Sandwiches $3.25–$5.75; blue-plate specials $7–$9. AE, MC, V. Sun–Thurs 7am–9pm, Fri–Sat 7am–10pm; summer Sun–Thurs 6am–9pm, Fri–Sat 6am–11pm.

Portofino Ristorante Italiano ITALIAN   Long one of Kingman's most enjoyable restaurants, Portofino moved from its downtown location in 2001 and is now on the road to the Hualapai Mountain Park, with views of mountains and desert. The Italian owner and chef do a nice job with Italian standards, including a fresh mozzarella plate with tomato and basil. From there, move on to a selection from the long pasta menu, such as fettuccine with shrimp and mushrooms in a spicy cream sauce, or a choice from the short selection of filling main courses.

2215 Hualapai Mountain Rd. ☎ 520/753-0542. Lunch items $5–$8; main courses $8–$18 at dinner. AE, MC, V. Daily 11am–9pm.

2 Lake Mead National Recreation Area

30 miles SE of Las Vegas; 70 miles NW of Kingman; 256 miles NW of Phoenix

Lake Mead National Recreation Area straddles the border between Arizona and Nevada, and, with its two reservoirs and scenic, free-flowing stretch of the Colorado River, is a watersports playground. Throughout the year, anglers fish for striped bass, rainbow trout, channel catfish, and other sport fish, while during the hot summer months, Lakes Mead and Mohave attract tens of thousands of water-skiers and personal watercraft riders. Due to its proximity to Las Vegas and the fact that there are more facilities on the Nevada side of Lake Mead, the recreation area tends to be more popular with Nevadans than with Arizonans.

The larger reservoir, Lake Mead, was created by the Hoover Dam. Constructed between 1931 and 1935, Hoover Dam was the first major dam on the Colorado River. By supplying huge amounts of electricity and water to Arizona and California, it set the stage for the phenomenal growth the region experienced in the second half of the 20th century.

ESSENTIALS

GETTING THERE   U.S. 93, which runs between Las Vegas and Kingman, crosses over Hoover Dam, and traffic backups at the dam can be horrendous. Don't be surprised if you get stuck for an hour just trying to get across the dam. Several small secondary roads lead to various marinas on the lake. There are also many miles of unpaved roads within the recreation area. If you have a high-clearance or four-wheel-drive vehicle, these roads can take you to some of the least visited shores of the two lakes.

VISITOR INFORMATION   For more information, contact the **Lake Mead National Recreation Area,** 601 Nevada Hwy., Boulder City, NV 89005-2426 (© **702/293-8906**), or stop by the **Alan Bible Visitor Center** (© **702/ 293-8990**), between Hoover Dam and Boulder City.

DAM, LAKE & RIVER TOURS

Standing 726.4 feet tall, from bedrock to the roadway atop it, and tapering from a thickness of 660 feet at its base to only 45 feet at the top, **Hoover Dam** (© **702/294-3524;** www.hooverdam.com) is the tallest concrete dam in the Western Hemisphere. Behind this massive dam lie the waters of **Lake Mead,** which at 110 miles long and with a shoreline of more than 550 miles is the largest artificial lake in the United States. U.S. 93 runs right across the top of the dam, and a visitor center chronicles the dam's construction. It's open daily from 8am to 5:30pm (closed Thanksgiving and Christmas). Two guided tours of the dam are offered. The basic tours last 30 minutes and cost $10 for adults, $8 for seniors, and $3 for children 7 to 16. The Hardhat Tour, a more behind-the-scenes look, lasts about an hour and costs $25.

If you'd like to tour the lake and the dam, call **Lake Mead Cruises** (© **702/ 293-6180**) to book passage on the *Desert Princess* paddle-wheeler. These cruises leave from Lake Mead Cruises Landing off Lakeshore Drive on the Nevada side of Hoover Dam. Day tours, which go to the dam, last 1½ hours and cost $19 for adults and $9 for children 2 to 11. Other options include weekend breakfast cruises ($28.50 for adults, $15 for children), dinner cruises ($39.50 for adults, $21 for children), and weekend dinner-and-dancing cruises ($51).

One of the most interesting ways to see a remote section of Lake Mohave is to take a kayak trip with **Back Bay Canoes & Kayaks,** 1450 Newberry Dr. (at Ariz. 95), Bullhead City (© **888/KAYAKEN** or 520/758-6242), which offers full- and half-day river trips in the Laughlin–Bullhead City area. **Black Canyon Raft Tours** (© **800/696-7238** or 702/293-3776) offers motorized raft trips through Black Canyon, below Hoover Dam. Trips cost $70 for adults, $40 for children 12 and under (which includes lunch, but transportation to and from major hotels costs extra). This is an easy float trip rather than a white-water run.

OUTDOOR PURSUITS

As you would expect, swimming, fishing, water-skiing, sailing, windsurfing, and powerboating are the most popular activities in Lake Mead National Recreation

Area. On Arizona shores, there are swimming beaches at Lake Mohave's Katherine Landing (outside Bullhead City) and Lake Mead's Temple Bar (north of Kingman off U.S. 93). Picnic areas can be found at these two areas and also Willow Beach on Lake Mohave and more than half a dozen spots on the Nevada side of Lake Mead.

Fishing for monster striped bass (up to 50 lb.) is one of the most popular activities on Lake Mead, and while Lake Mohave's striped bass may not reach these awesome proportions, fish in the 25-pound range are not uncommon. Largemouth bass and even rainbow trout are plentiful in the National Recreation Area's waters due to the diversity of habitats. Try for big rainbows in the cold waters that flow out from Hoover Dam through Black Canyon and into Lake Mohave. To fish from shore, you'll need a license from either Arizona or Nevada (depending on which shore you're fishing from). To fish from a boat, you'll need a license from one state and a special use stamp from the other. Most Lake Mead marinas sell both licenses and stamps.

The season for striped bass starts around the beginning of April, when the water begins to warm up. If you don't have your own boat, try fishing from the shore of Lake Mohave near Davis Dam, where the water is deep. Anchovy pieces work well as bait, but be sure to put some shot on your line to get it down to the depths where the fish are feeding. You can get bait, tackle, licenses, and fishing tips at the **Lake Mohave Resort marina** (© **520/754-3245**), at Katherine Landing.

In Arizona, marinas can be found at Katherine Landing on Lake Mohave (just outside Bullhead City), near the north end of Lake Mohave at Willow Beach (best access for trout angling), and at Temple Bar on Lake Mead. There's also a boat ramp at South Cove, north of the community of Meadview at the east end of Lake Mead. This latter boat ramp is the closest to the Grand Canyon end of Lake Mead. On the Nevada side of Lake Mohave, there's a marina at Cottonwood Cove, and on the Nevada side of Lake Mead, you'll find marinas at Boulder Beach, Las Vegas Bay, Callville Bay, and Echo Bay. These marinas offer motels, restaurants, general stores, campgrounds, and boat rentals. At both **Temple Bar** (© **800/752-9669** or 520/767-3211) and **Lake Mohave Resort** (© **800/752-9669** or 520/754-3245), you can rent ski boats, fishing boats, and patio boats for between $75 and $250 per day. Personal watercraft are available for about $50 an hour or $270 a day.

Despite the area's decided watery orientation, there's quite a bit of mountainous desert here that's home to bighorn sheep, roadrunners, and other wildlife. This land was once home to several indigenous tribes that left reminders of their presence in **petroglyphs.** The best place to see these carvings is at Grapevine Canyon, due west of Laughlin, Nevada, in the southwest corner of the National Recreation Area. To reach Grapevine Canyon, take Nev. 163 west from Laughlin to milepost 13 and turn right on the marked dirt road. From the highway, it's about 1½ miles to the turnoff for the parking area. From here, it's less than a quarter-mile to the petroglyph-covered jumble of rocks at the mouth of Grapevine Canyon. Covering the boulders are thousands of cryptic symbols, as well as ancient illustrations of bighorn sheep. To see these petroglyphs, you have to do a lot of scrambling, so wear sturdy shoes (preferably hiking boots).

For information on other **hikes,** contact any of the ranger stations within the National Recreation Area (Katherine Landing and Temple Bar in Arizona; Cottonwood Cove, Boulder Beach, Callville Bay, Echo Bay, and Overton Beach in Nevada).

WHERE TO STAY

All three of the accommodations listed below are operated by Seven Crown Resorts, which also runs two other resorts on the Nevada side of the lake. For more information, contact **Seven Crown Resorts** (✆ **800/752-9669**).

HOUSEBOATS

Seven Crown Resorts ⚓ *(Kids)*   Why pay extra for a lake-view room when you can rent a houseboat that always has a 360° water view? There's no better way to explore Lake Mead than on one of these floating vacation homes. You can cruise for miles, tie up at a deserted cove, and enjoy a wilderness adventure with all the comforts of home. Houseboats come complete with full kitchens, air-conditioning, and room to sleep up to 14 people. Bear in mind that the scenery here on Lake Mead isn't nearly as spectacular as that on Lake Powell, Arizona's other major houseboating lake.

P.O. Box 16247, Irvine, CA 92623-6247. ✆ **800/752-9669.** www.sevencrown.com. $1,150–$2,950 per week. DISC, MC, V. *In room:* A/C, kitchen, no phone.

MOTELS

Lake Mohave Resort *(Kids)*   Just up Lake Mohave from Davis Dam and only a few minutes outside Bullhead City, the Lake Mohave Resort is an older motel, but the huge rooms are ideal for families. Most have some sort of view of the lake, which is across the road. The nautical-theme restaurant and lounge overlook the marina. The resort also has a convenience store and a bait-and-tackle store.

Katherine Landing, Bullhead City, AZ 86430. ✆ **800/752-9669** or 520/754-3245. www.sevencrown.com. 51 units. Mar–Oct $80–$110 double; Nov–Feb $40–$75 double. DISC, MC, V. Pets accepted ($25 deposit plus $5 per day). **Amenities:** Restaurant, lounge; boat and personal watercraft rentals. *In room:* A/C, TV.

Temple Bar Resort   Although basically just a motel, the Temple Bar has a wonderfully remote setting that will have you thinking you're on vacation in Baja California. With a beach right in front, great fishing nearby, and 40 miles of prime skiing waters extending out from the resort, this place makes an excellent getaway. A restaurant and lounge overlook the lake and provide economical meals. The resort offers ski rentals, powerboat rentals, and a convenience store. There are also four very basic fishing cabins here that share shower rooms and toilets.

Temple Bar, AZ 86443. ✆ **800/752-9669** or 520/767-3211. 22 units. Apr–Sept $55–$105 double; Oct–Mar $35–$75 double. DISC, MC, V. Pets accepted ($5 per night). **Amenities:** Restaurant, lounge; boat and personal watercraft rentals. *In room:* A/C, TV.

CAMPGROUNDS

In Arizona, there are campgrounds at Katherine Landing on Lake Mohave and at Temple Bar on Lake Mead. Both of these campgrounds have been heavily planted with trees, so they provide some semblance of shade during the hot, but popular, summer months. In Nevada, you'll find campgrounds at Cottonwood Cove on Lake Mohave and at Boulder Beach, Las Vegas Bay, Callville Bay, and Echo Bay on Lake Mead.

3 Bullhead City & Laughlin, Nevada

30 miles W of Kingman; 216 miles NW of Phoenix; 60 miles N of Lake Havasu City

You may find it difficult at first to understand why anyone would ever want to live in Bullhead City. This is one of the hottest places in North America, with temperatures regularly topping 120°F in summer. To understand Bullhead City, you need only gaze across the Colorado River at the gambling mecca of

Laughlin, Nevada, where the slot machines are always in action and the gaming tables are nearly as hot as the air outside. Laughlin is the southernmost town in Nevada and, before the advent of Indian casinos, was the closest place to Phoenix to do any gambling. The dozen or so large casino hotels across the river in Nevada still make Bullhead City one of the busiest little towns in Arizona.

Laughlin is a perfect miniature Las Vegas. High-rise hotels loom above the desert like so many glass mesas, miles of neon lights turn night into day, and acres of asphalt are always covered with cars and RVs as hordes of hopeful gamblers go searching for Lady Luck. Cheap rooms and meals lure people into spending on the slot machines what they save on food and a bed. It's a formula that works well. Why else would anyone endure the heat of this remote desert?

ESSENTIALS

GETTING THERE   From Phoenix, take U.S. 60, which becomes U.S. 93, northwest to I-40. From Kingman, take Ariz. 68 west to Bullhead City.

The Bullhead City–Laughlin Airport is in Bullhead City. It's served by **America West** (© 800/235-9292) from Phoenix, and by **Air Laughlin** (© 866/359-2386) from Phoenix, Burbank, Ontario (California), and San Jose.

Shuttle-bus services operate between Laughlin and the Las Vegas airport. For information or a reservation, call **Super Shuttle** (© 800/801-8687 or 520/704-9000), which charges $37 one way.

VISITOR INFORMATION   For more information on Bullhead City and Laughlin, Nevada, contact the **Bullhead Area Chamber of Commerce** (© 800/987-7457 or 520/754-4121). In Laughlin, stop by the **Laughlin Visitor Bureau,** 1555 S. Casino Dr. (© 800/452-8445 or 702/298-3321; www.visitlaughlin.com).

GETTING AROUND   Car rentals are available in Bullhead City/Laughlin from **Avis** (© 800/831-2847 or 520/754-4686), **Enterprise** (© 800/325-8007 or 520/754-2700), **Hertz** (© 800/654-3131 or 520/754-4111), and **Thrifty** (© 800/367-2277 or 520/704-0193). **Citizens Area Transit (CAT)** provides public bus service within Laughlin. The fare is $1.50. There is also a shuttle service that operates between the casinos, plus a ferry that operates between the Riverside Resort Hotel & Casino and parking lots on the Arizona side of the Colorado River.

CASINOS & OTHER INDOOR PURSUITS

The casinos of Laughlin, Nevada, just across the Colorado River from Bullhead City, Arizona, are known for having liberal slots—that is, the slot machines pay off frequently. Consequently, Laughlin is a very popular weekend destination for Phoenicians and other Arizonans, who have limited gambling in their own state. In addition to the slot machines, there's keno, blackjack, poker, craps, off-track betting, and sports betting. All the hotels in Laughlin offer live entertainment of some sort, including an occasional headliner, but gambling is still the main event after dark as far as most people are concerned.

If you'd like to learn more about the history of this area, visit the **Colorado River Museum,** 355 Hwy. 95, Bullhead City (© 520/754-3399), a half mile north of the Laughlin Bridge. It's open Tuesday through Sunday from 10am to 4pm (closed July–Aug). Admission is free, but donations are welcome.

BOAT TOURS

If you'd like to get away from the noise of the casinos and see a bit of the Colorado River, daily paddle-wheeler cruises are available through Laughlin

River Tours (© **800/228-9825** or 702/298-1047; www.steamboatwedding. com) at the **Flamingo Hilton** and **Edgewater**. These cruises cost $11 for adults and $6 for children; dinner cruises ($30) are also available. At the **Riverside Resort** (© **702/298-2535**), you can take a tour on the 65-foot USS *Riverside* to Davis Dam. These last 1 hour and 20 minutes and cost $10 for adults and $6 for children.

If you'd rather look at natural surroundings instead of casino towers, consider booking a 6-hour jet-boat tour to the London Bridge with **London Bridge Jet Boat Tours** (© **888/505-3545** or 702/298-5498). On the way, the boat passes through scenic Topock Gorge. These powerful boats cruise at up to 40 mph and make the 58-mile, one-way trip in 2 hours. Round-trip fares are $52 for adults, $47 for seniors, and $32 for children 12 and under.

OUTDOOR PURSUITS
Back Bay Canoes & Kayaks, 1450 Newberry Dr., Bullhead City (© **888/ KAYAKEN** or 520/758-6242), offers full- and half-day river kayak trips in the Laughlin–Bullhead City area. Rates start at $25.

For information on fishing in nearby Lake Mohave, see the section on Lake Mead National Recreation Area, above. If you'd rather just feed the fish, check out the carp that hang out at the dock behind the Edgewater Hotel & Casino. There are machines dispensing carp chow so you can feed these piscine vacuums.

In Laughlin, golfers can play a round at the scenic and challenging **Emerald River Golf Course,** 1155 S. Casino Dr. (© **702/298-0061**), 2 miles south of Harrah's. Greens fees range from $30 to $80. The **Mojave Resort Golf Club,** 9905 Aha Macav Pkwy. (© **702/535-4653;** www.mojaveresort.com), adjacent to the Avi Resort & Casino, has wide, user-friendly fairways and charges greens fees of $62 to $72. In Bullhead City, try the **Desert Lakes Golf Course,** 5835 Desert Lakes Dr. (© **520/768-1000**), 15 miles south of town off Ariz. 95. Greens fees range from $65 to $75 and are usually lower during the hot summer months. There are also three 9-hole courses near Bullhead City. These include **Riverview Resort & Golf Club,** 2000 E. Ramar Rd. (© **520/ 763-1818**); **Chaparral Country Club,** 1260 E. Mohave Dr. (© **520/ 758-6330**); and **Willow Springs Golf Course,** 8011 Hwy. 95, Mohave Valley (© **520/768-4414**).

Bird-watching is excellent in **Havasu National Wildlife Refuge,** a wintering area for many species of waterfowl. However, much of this refuge lies within the scenic Topock Gorge and is accessible only by boat. The most accessible birding areas are along the marshes in the vicinity of the communities of Golden Shores and Topock, which are both north of the I-40 bridge over the Colorado. Topock Gorge, one of the most scenic stretches of the lower Colorado River, is a 15-mile stretch of the Colorado River bordered by multicolored cliffs that rise up from the river.

WHERE TO STAY
IN BULLHEAD CITY
Bullhead City has numerous budget chain motels, including a **Days Inn** (© **800/329-7466**) and a **Super 8** (© **800/800-8000**).

IN LAUGHLIN, NEVADA
Laughlin, Nevada, currently has 10 huge hotel-and-casino complexes, eight of which are right on the west bank of the Colorado River (the ninth is across the street from the river, and the 10th is on the river but several miles south of

town). All offer cheap rooms (usually $15–$30 on weeknights) to lure potential gamblers. In addition to huge casinos with hundreds of slot machines and every sort of gaming table, these hotels have several restaurants (with ridiculously low prices in at least one restaurant, which usually has long lines), bars and lounges (usually with live country or pop music nightly), swimming pools, video arcades for kids, ferry service to parking lots on the Arizona side of the river, valet parking, room service, car-rental desks, airport shuttles, gift shops, and gaming classes. The only real difference between most of these places is the theme each has adopted for its decor.

Should you wish to stay at one of these hotels, here's the information you'll need:

- **Avi Hotel & Casino,** 10000 Aha Macav Pkwy., Laughlin, NV 89029 (© 800/284-2946 or 702/535-5555; www.avicasino.com)
- **Colorado Belle Hotel & Casino,** 2100 S. Casino Dr., Laughlin, NV 89028 (© 800/47-RIVER or 702/298-4000; www.coloradobelle.com)
- **Edgewater Hotel & Casino,** 2020 S. Casino Dr., Laughlin, NV 89029 (© 800/67-RIVER or 702/298-2453; www.edgewater-casino.com)
- **Flamingo Hilton,** 1900 S. Casino Dr., Laughlin, NV 89029 (© 800/ FLAMINGO or 702/298-5111; www.flamingolaughlin.com)
- **Golden Nugget,** 2300 S. Casino Dr., Laughlin, NV 89029 (© 800/ 237-1739 or 702/298-7111)
- **Harrah's Laughlin,** 2900 S. Casino Dr., Laughlin, NV 89029 (© 800/ HARRAHS or 702/298-4600; www.harrahs.com)
- **Pioneer Hotel & Gambling Hall,** 2200 S. Casino Dr., P.O. Box 29664, Laughlin, NV 89029 (© 800/634-3469 or 702/298-2442; www. pioneerlaughlin.com)
- **Ramada Express,** 2121 S. Casino Dr., Laughlin, NV 89029 (© 800/ 243-6846 or 702/298-4200; www.ramadaexpress.com)
- **River Palms Resort & Casino,** 2700 S. Casino Dr., Laughlin, NV 89028 (© 800/835-7904 or 702/298-2242; www.rvrpalm.com)
- **Riverside Resort Hotel & Casino,** 1650 S. Casino Dr. (P.O. Box 500), Laughlin, NV 89029 (© 800/227-3849 or 702/298-2535; www. riverside.com)

WHERE TO DINE
The dozens of inexpensive casino hotel restaurants are usually the top choice of visitors to Laughlin and Bullhead City. Cheap steaks, prime rib, and all-you-can-eat buffets are the specialties of these places.

4 Lake Havasu & the London Bridge

200 miles NW of Phoenix; 60 miles S of Bullhead City; 61 miles S of Kingman; 150 miles S of Las Vegas

Once upon a time London Bridge really was falling down, but that was before Robert McCulloch, founder of Lake Havasu City, hit upon the brilliant idea of buying the bridge and having it shipped to his undertouristed little planned community in the middle of the Arizona desert. That was more than 30 years ago, and today the London Bridge is still standing. Here in its desert setting on the shores of Lake Havasu, it looks for all the world like a strange mirage. An unlikely place for a bit of British heritage, true, but the London Bridge has turned Lake Havasu City into one of Arizona's most popular tourist destinations.

Lake Havasu was formed in 1938 by the building of the Parker Dam, but it wasn't until 1963 that McCulloch founded the town of Lake Havasu City. Not too many people were keen on spending time out in this remote corner of the desert, where summer temperatures are often over 110°F. Despite its name, Lake Havasu City at the time was little more than an expanse of desert with a few mobile homes on it. It was then that McCulloch began looking for ways to attract more people to his little "city" on the lake. His solution proved to be a stroke of genius.

Lake Havasu City attracts an odd mix of visitors. In winter, the town is filled with retirees, and you'll rarely see anyone under the age of 60. On weekends, during the summer, and over spring breaks, Lake Havasu City is popular with Arizona college students. In fact, the city has become something of a Fort Lauderdale in the desert, and businesses cater primarily to young partiers. Be prepared for a lot of noise if you're here on a weekend or a holiday. Summers bring out the water-ski and personal-watercraft crowds.

ESSENTIALS

GETTING THERE   From Phoenix, take I-10 west to Ariz. 95 north. From Las Vegas, take U.S. 95 south to I-40 east to Ariz. 95 south.

America West (© **800/235-9292**) has regular flights to Lake Havasu City from Phoenix. The **Havasu/Vegas Express** (© **800/459-4884** or 520/453-4884) operates a shuttle van between Lake Havasu City and Las Vegas. Fares are $49 one way and $87 round-trip.

VISITOR INFORMATION   For more information on this area, contact the **Lake Havasu Tourism Bureau** (© **800/242-8278** or 520/453-3444; www.golakehavasu.com). The **Lake Havasu Chamber of Commerce** runs a tourist information center at 420 English Village (© **520/855-5655**).

GETTING AROUND   Taxi (actually shared-ride) service is available from **City Transit Service** (© **520/453-7600**). For car rentals, try **Avis** (© **800/831-2847** or 520/764-3001), **Enterprise** (© **800/736-8622** or 520/453-0033), or **Hertz** (© **800/654-3131** or 520/764-3994).

LONDON BRIDGE

Back in the mid-1960s, the British government decided to sell the London Bridge, which was indeed falling down—or, more correctly, sinking—into the Thames River because of too much heavy car and truck traffic. McCulloch and his partner paid $2,460,000 for the famous bridge; had it shipped 10,000 miles to Long Beach, California; and then trucked it to Lake Havasu City. Reconstruction of the bridge was begun in 1968, and the grand reopening was held in 1971. Oddly enough, the 900-foot-long bridge was not built over water; it just connected desert to more desert on a peninsula jutting into Lake Havasu. It wasn't until after the bridge was rebuilt that a mile-long channel was dredged through the base of the peninsula, thus creating an island offshore from Lake Havasu City.

The London Bridge has a long history, although the bridge that now stands in Arizona is not very old by British standards. The first bridge over the Thames River in London was probably a pontoon bridge built by the Romans in A.D. 43. The first written record of a London Bridge comes from the mention of a suspected witch being drowned at the bridge in 984. In 1176, the first stone bridge over the Thames was built. They just don't build 'em like that bridge anymore—it lasted for more than 600 years but was eventually replaced in 1824 by the bridge that now stands in Lake Havasu City.

Moments Canoeing the Colorado

Paddling down a desert river is a very special experience: rocks and cactus on the banks and cool waters beneath your boat. If you're interested in a scenic canoe tour, there are a couple of canoe rental/tour companies in the area. Both provide boats, paddles, life jackets, maps, and shuttles to put-in and take-out points, but most often no guide. **Western Arizona Canoe and Kayak Outfitter** (© 520/855-6414; www.azwacko.com) offers kayak trips through the beautiful and rugged Topock Gorge, where you can see ancient petroglyphs and possibly bighorn sheep. Per-person trip prices are $39 for self-guided and $44 for guided (with a minimum of four to six persons). **Jerkwater Canoe Company** (© 800/421-7803 or 520/768-7753; www.jerkwater.com) offers a similar Topock Gorge trip and also arranges other canoe trips of varying lengths. Jerkwater's Topock Gorge self-guided trip is $35 per person ($45 for a kayak rental). Another popular trip is through Black Canyon, but advance planning (6 months to 1 year) is required to get the necessary permit. It's easier to get a permit for Black Canyon midweek than on a weekend. Some trips include additional overnight campground or bunkhouse bed-and-breakfast fees.

At the base of the bridge sits **English Village,** which is done up in proper English style and has shops, restaurants, and a waterfront promenade. You'll find several cruise boats and boat-rental docks here.

LAND, RIVER & LAKE TOURS

Several companies offer different types of boat tours on Lake Havasu. **Bluewater Charters** (© 888/855-7171 or 520/855-7171) offers jet-boat tours that leave from the London Bridge and spend 2 hours cruising up the Colorado River to the Topock Gorge, a scenic area 25 miles from Lake Havasu City. The tours are $35 for adults, $32 for seniors, $17.50 for children 10 to 16, and free for children 9 and under.

You can also cruise on the *Dixie Belle* (© 520/453-6776), a small replica paddle-wheel riverboat. Cruises are $12 for adults and $5 for children 6 to 12.

One of the most interesting and beautiful boat-tour destinations is Copper Canyon, a flooded canyon 9 miles from Lake Havasu City. The *Kon Tiki* (© 520/453-6776), a pontoon boat berthed at English Village, makes the trip regularly and charges $10 for adults and $5 for children 6 to 12.

To explore the desert surrounding Lake Havasu City, arrange a four-wheel-drive tour with **Outback Off-Road Adventures** (© 520/680-6151), which charges $65 for a half-day tour and $130 for a full-day tour.

WATERSPORTS

While the London Bridge is what made Lake Havasu City, these days watersports on 45-mile-long Lake Havasu are the area's real draw. Whether you want to go for a swim, take a leisurely pedal-boat ride under the London Bridge, try parasailing, or spend the day water-skiing, there are plenty of places to get wet.

London Bridge Beach is the area's best. It's located in a county park behind the Island Inn Resort, off West McCulloch Boulevard. This park has a sandy beach, lots of palm trees, and views of both the London Bridge and the distant desert mountains. There are also picnic tables and a snack bar, which make this park a great place to spend the day. There are more beaches at the **Windsor Beach Unit of Lake Havasu State Park** (© 520/855-2784), 2 miles north of the London Bridge, and **Cattail Cove State Park** (© 520/855-1223), 15 miles south of Lake Havasu City. Lake Havasu State Park also has 20 miles of shoreline to the south of Lake Havasu City, but there are no roads to this shoreline. If you have your own boat, you'll find lots of secluded little beaches.

The cheapest way to get out on the water in Lake Havasu also happens to involve the greatest expenditure of energy. At the **Fun Center,** in English Village (© 520/453-4386), you can rent pedal boats and aqua cycles for $15 an hour. If kayaking or canoeing is more your style, contact **Western Arizona Canoe and Kayak Outfitter** (© 520/855-6414; www.azwacko.com), with rates beginning at $25 a day.

If you didn't bring your own boat, you can rent one at **Blue Water Boat Rentals,** in English Village beside the bridge (© 520/453-9613 or 520/855-7171). The company offers rentals of ski boats (starting at $280 per day) and pontoon boats (from $220 per day). Boats are also available at **Fun Time Boat Rentals,** 1633 Industrial Blvd. (© 800/680-1003 or 520/680-1003). Ski boats come with water skis or knee boards.

If your main reason for getting out on the water is to catch some fish, you'll likely come away from a visit to Lake Havasu with plenty of fish stories to tell. Striped bass, also known as stripers, are the favorite quarry of anglers here. These fish have been known to reach almost 60 pounds in these waters, so be sure to bring the heavy tackle. Largemouth bass in the 2- to 4-pound range are also fairly common, and giant channel catfish of up to 35 pounds have been caught in Topock Marsh. The best fishing starts in midspring when the water begins to warm up, but there is also good winter fishing.

GOLF

Lake Havasu City has four courses, all of which are open to the public. Panoramic views are to be had from each of the courses here, and there's enough variety to accommodate golfers of any skill level.

London Bridge Golf Club, 2400 Club House Dr. (© 520/855-2719), with two 18-hole courses, is the area's premier championship course. High-season greens fees (with cart) top out at $79 on the West Course and $53 on the East Course. The **Havasu Island Golf Course,** 1040 McCulloch Blvd. (© 520/855-5585), is a 4,012-yard, par-61 executive course with lots of water hazards. The nine-hole **Bridgewater Links,** 1477 Queen's Bay Rd. (© 520/855-4777), at the London Bridge Resort, is the most accessible and easiest of the area courses.

Golfers also won't want to miss the **Emerald Canyon Golf Course** ★, 7351 Riverside Dr., Parker (© 520/667-3366), about 30 miles south of Lake Havasu City. This municipal course is the most spectacular in the region and plays through rugged canyons and past red-rock cliffs, from which there are views of the Colorado River. One hole even has you hitting your ball off a cliff to a green 200 feet below! Greens fees range from around $30 to $45. Also in Parker is the **Havasu Springs Resort** course (© 520/667-3361), which some people claim is the hardest little nine-hole, par-three course in the state. It's atop a rocky outcropping with steep drop-offs all around. Greens fees are only $5 to $8 for nine holes.

WHERE TO STAY
HOUSEBOATS

Havasu Springs Resort *Kids*   One of the most popular ways to enjoy Lake Havasu is on a rented houseboat. You can spend your days motoring from one good fishing or swimming hole to the next, and there are beaches and secluded coves where you can drop anchor and stay for days. If you feel like doing a bit of sightseeing or shopping, you can cruise right up to the London Bridge. Houseboats come in several sizes and sleep 10 to 12 people.

2581 Hwy. 95, Parker, AZ 85344. © 520/667-3361. Fax 520/667-1098. www.havasusprings.com. Mar to early Sept $1,855–$2,432 per week; early Sept to Feb $1,166–$1,690 per week. No credit cards. *In room:* Kitchen, coffeemaker, no phone.

HOTELS & MOTELS

In addition to the accommodations listed here, Lake Havasu City has numerous budget chain motels, including **Motel 6, Super 8,** and **Days Inn.**

Bridgeview Motel   If you're just looking for a clean and inexpensive place to stay, this motel fits the bill. It's also quiet (usually), and rooms even have views of the bridge, which is within walking distance.

101 London Bridge Rd., Lake Havasu City, AZ 86403. © 520/855-5559. Fax 520/855-5564. 37 units. $40–$70 double (higher on holidays). MC, V. **Amenities:** Small outdoor pool. *In room:* A/C, TV.

Island Inn   The Island Inn is across the London Bridge from downtown and has one of the nicest hotel settings in Lake Havasu City. Although it's not right on the water, it is close to one of the area's best public beaches. The rooms are large and seem to have seen a lot of wear and tear. Ask for a room with a balcony; units on the upper floors have the better views (and higher prices).

1300 W. McCulloch Blvd., Lake Havasu City, AZ 86403. © 800/243-9955 or 520/680-0606. Fax 520/680-4218. www.rentor.com/hotels/islanlin.htm. 117 units. Mar–Oct $65–$115 double, $130–$180 suite; Nov–Feb $49–$59 double, $98–$147 suite. AE, DC, DISC, MC, V. Pets accepted with extra charge. **Amenities:** Restaurant, lounge; outdoor pool; Jacuzzi. *In room:* A/C, TV.

London Bridge Resort *★*   Merrie Olde England was once the theme here, with Tudor half-timbers jumbled up with turrets, towers, ramparts, and crenelations. However, England is giving way to the tropics and the desert as the resort strives to please its young, partying clientele (who tend to make a lot of noise and leave the hotel looking much the worse for wear). Although the bridge is just out the hotel's back door, and a replica of Britain's gold State Coach is inside the lobby, guests seem more interested in the three pools and the tropical-theme outdoor nightclub. The one- and two-bedroom units are large and have gotten a Southwestern face-lift as the hotel has converted to time-share ownership.

1477 Queens Bay, Lake Havasu City, AZ 86403. © 800/624-7939 or 520/855-0888. Fax 520/855-5404. www.londonbridgeresort.com. 122 units. Sept–Feb $69–$239 condo; Mar–Aug $159–$289 condo. AE, DISC, MC, V. **Amenities:** Restaurant (American), 2 lounges; 9-hole executive golf course; tennis court; 3 pools; Jacuzzi; coin-op laundry. *In room:* A/C, TV/VCR, fridge, coffeemaker, hair dryer.

CAMPGROUNDS

In the Lake Havasu City area, there are two state park campgrounds. **Lake Havasu State Park's Windsor Beach Unit** (© 520/855-2784) is 2 miles north of the London Bridge on London Bridge Road, while **Cattail Cove State Park** (© 520/855-1223) is 15 miles south of Lake Havasu City off Ariz. 95. The former campground has no hookups and charges $12 per night per vehicle, and the latter charges $15 for a full hookup. Reservations are not accepted. In addition to sites in these campgrounds, there are about 160 boat-in campsites within Lake Havasu and Cattail Cove state parks.

WHERE TO DINE

Chico's Tecate Grill *Finds* MEXICAN   This Mexican fast-food place is great for a quick, cheap bite to eat. The carne asada and chicken carbón are excellent, and there's a fresh salsa bar for you to do your own doctoring of your meal.

In the Basha's Center, 1641 McCulloch Blvd. C 520/680-7010. Main courses $2.50–$7.50. MC, V. Sun–Thurs 6:30am–9pm; Fri–Sat 6:30am–10pm.

London Bridge Brewery & Restaurant PUB FARE/STEAKHOUSE   If you find yourself powerless to resist the overwhelming old English kitsch in Lake Havasu City, head to this "traditional" English pub at the foot of the London Bridge. While the interior does a respectable job of re-creating merry old England, the sun-washed patio is pure Arizona. You'll find a few English dishes on the menu, but seafood, steaks, pizza, and pasta are more common. The restaurant also has its own brewpub.

422 English Village. C 520/855-8782. Reservations recommended. Main courses $7–$17. AE, DC, DISC, MC, V. Sun–Thurs 11am–9 or 10pm; Fri–Sat 11am–midnight.

Shugrue's *Kids* STEAKHOUSE/SEAFOOD   Located just across the London Bridge from the English Village shopping complex, Shugrue's seems to be popular as much for its view of the London Bridge as for its food. Offerings include seafood, prime rib, burgers, sandwiches, and a short list of pastas. This place is a favorite of vacationing retirees and families—there's also a children's menu.

1425 McCulloch Blvd. (at the Island Mall). C 520/453-1400. Reservations recommended. Main courses $7–$23. AE, DC, MC, V. Daily 11am–3pm and 4:30–10pm (sometimes later on weekend nights).

DRIVING DOWN TO YUMA
THE PARKER AREA

About 16 miles south of Lake Havasu City stands the **Parker Dam,** which holds back the waters of Lake Havasu and is said to be the deepest dam in the world because 73% of its 320-foot height is below the riverbed. Beginning just above the dam and stretching south to the town of Parker is one of the most beautiful stretches of the lower Colorado River. Just before you reach the dam, you'll come to the **Bill Williams National Wildlife Refuge** (C 520/667-4144), which preserves the lower reaches of the Bill Williams River. This refuge offers some of the best bird-watching in western Arizona. Keep your eyes open for vermilion flycatchers, Yuma clapper rails, soras, Swainson's hawks, and white-faced ibises.

Continuing south, you'll reach a dam overlook and the Take-Off Point boat launch, where you can also do some fishing from shore. Below the dam, the river becomes narrow and red-rock canyon walls close in. Although this narrow gorge is lined with mobile-home parks, the most beautiful sections have been preserved in two units of **Buckskin Mountain State Park** (C 520/667-3231; www.pr.state.az.us). Both units—Buckskin Point and River Island—have campgrounds ($15 for campsites and $20 for cabanas at Buckskin and $12 campsites at River Island) as well as day-use areas ($6) that include river beaches and hiking trails leading into the Buckskin Mountains. Reservations for camping are not accepted. In this area is also the spectacular Emerald Canyon Golf Course (see "Golf," above, for details).

For more information on the Parker area, contact the **Parker Area Chamber of Commerce,** 1217 California Ave., Parker (C 520/669-2174; www.arizonaguide. com/parker).

WHERE TO STAY

Blue Water Resort and Casino ★★ Located 37 miles south of Lake Havasu City, this riverside casino resort is western Arizona's most impressive hotel. The only other accommodations that come close are the casino hotels in nearby Laughlin, Nevada. Even if you aren't interested in spending your time at the slot machines, you'll find something here that appeals. There's a big indoor pool complex (with water slide) designed to resemble ancient ruins, a marina, and a mile of riverfront land, miniature golf, a movie theater, and a theater for live entertainment. Guest rooms are all close to the water, which means nice river views but also traffic noise from all the ski boats. Furnishings are standard motel modern.

11300 Resort Dr., Parker, AZ 85344. ✆ 888/243-3360 or 520/669-7000. www.bluewaterfun.com. 200 units. $59–$79 double. AE, DISC, MC, V. **Amenities:** 3 restaurants, snack bars; 4 pools; miniature golf; exercise room; Jacuzzi; shopping arcade; room service; laundry service. *In room:* A/C, TV, coffeemaker, hair dryer.

THE QUARTZSITE AREA

For much of the year, the community of **Quartzsite** is little more than a few truck stops at an interstate off-ramp. The population explodes each year with the annual influx of winter visitors (also known as snowbirds), and from early January to mid-February it's the site of numerous gem-and-mineral shows that attract more than a million rock hounds. Among these shows is the **Quartzsite Pow Wow,** which is held in late January and is one of the largest gem-and-mineral shows in the country. During the winter months, Quartzsite sprouts thousands of vendor stalls, as flea markets and the like are erected along the town's main streets. A variety of interesting food makes it a great place to stop for lunch or dinner. For more information, contact the **Quartzsite Chamber of Commerce,** 1490 Main Event Lane (✆ **520/927-5600;** www.quartzsitechamber.com).

For information on parking your RV in the desert outside Quartzsite, contact the **Bureau of Land Management,** Yuma Field Office, 2555 East Gila Ridge Rd., Yuma (✆ **520/317-3200;** www.az.blm.gov). Alternatively, you can get information and camping permits at the Long-Term Visitor Area entrance stations just south of Quartzsite on U.S. 95. The season here runs September 15 to April 15, with permits going for $100 for the season and $20 for 7 consecutive days.

There are only three places in Arizona where palm trees grow wild, and if you'd like to visit one of these spots, watch for the Palm Canyon turnoff 18 miles south of Quartzsite. Palm Canyon lies within the boundaries of the **Kofa National Wildlife Refuge,** which was formed primarily to protect the desert

---

⌒ *Finds* The Bouse Fisherman

If ancient rock art interests you, be sure to watch for Plomosa Road as you travel between Parker and Quartzsite. Off this road, you'll find a 30-foot-long intaglio (or geoglyph) known as the **Bouse Fisherman.** This primitive image of a person spearing fish was formed by scratching away the rocky crust of the desert soil. Its origin and age are unknown, but it is believed to have been created centuries ago by native peoples and may depict the god Kumastamo, who created the Colorado River by thrusting a spear into the ground. To find it, drive 8 miles up Plomosa Road, which is approximately 6 miles north of Quartzsite, and watch for a wide parking area on the north side of the road. From here, follow the trail for a quarter of a mile over a small hill.

bighorn sheep that live here in the rugged Kofa Mountains. The palms are 8 miles off U.S. 95 in a narrow canyon a short walk from the end of the well-graded gravel road, and although there are only a couple of dozen trees, the hike to see them provides an opportunity to experience these mountains up close. Keep your eyes peeled for desert bighorn sheep. Incidentally, the Kofa Mountains took their name from the King of Arizona Mine. For maps and more information, contact the **Kofa National Wildlife Refuge,** 356 W. First St., Yuma (© **520/783-7861;** http://southwest.fws.gov/refuges/arizona/kofa.html).

5 Yuma ⍟

180 miles SW of Phoenix; 180 miles E of San Diego; 240 miles W of Tucson

Although you may have never heard of Yuma, it was once one of the most important towns in the region, known as the Rome of the Southwest because all roads led to Yuma Crossing—the shallow spot along the Colorado River where Yuma was founded. Quechan Indians, Spanish missionaries and explorers, Kit Carson and his mountain men, '49ers heading for the gold fields of California, pioneers, and soldiers all passed through this narrow spot on the lower Colorado River. Despite its location in the middle of the desert, Yuma became a busy port town during the 1850s as shallow-draft steamboats traveled up the Colorado River from the Gulf of California. From here, during the Apache wars of the 1870s and 1880s, military supplies were transported overland to the many forts and camps throughout the Southwest. When the railroad pushed westward into California in the 1870s, it passed through Yuma. Even today, I-8, which connects San Diego with Tucson and Phoenix, crosses the Colorado at Yuma.

Even hotter than Phoenix, Yuma often records summer temperatures in excess of 120°F. However, the flip side of furnacelike summer heat is the warmest and sunniest winter climate in the nation. This has made Yuma the winter destination of tens of thousands of snowbirds (retired winter visitors), who drive their RVs to Yuma from as far away as Canada.

However, despite having more than a dozen golf courses and two important historic sites, Yuma has had to struggle to attract visitors. For whatever reason, many people just don't take this city seriously as a winter vacation destination. In the hopes of luring more people off the interstate, Yuma has in the past few years been working hard to restore its downtown historic buildings, expand its historic sites, and preserve its natural setting on the Colorado River.

ESSENTIALS
GETTING THERE   Yuma is on I-8, which runs from San Diego, California, to Casa Grande, Arizona. There's **Amtrak** (© **800/872-7245**) passenger service to Yuma from Los Angeles and New Orleans. The station is on Gila Street.

The Yuma Airport is at 2191 32nd St. and is served from Phoenix by **Mesa Airlines** (© **800/637-2247**), an affiliate of America West, and from Los Angeles by **United Express** (© **800/241-6522**).

VISITOR INFORMATION   Contact the **Yuma Convention and Visitors Bureau,** 377 S. Main St. (© **800/293-0071** or 520/783-0071; www.visityuma.com).

GETTING AROUND   For a taxi, call **Yuma City Cab** (© **520/782-0111**). Rental cars are available from **Avis** (© **800/831-2847** or 520/726-5737), **Budget** (© **800/527-0700** or 520/344-1822), **Enterprise** (© **800/325-8007** or 520/344-5444), and **Hertz** (© **800/654-3131** or 520/726-5160).

SPECIAL EVENTS The Yuma area is a major producer of lettuce, and celebrates this in the **Lettuce Festival** held in late January. **Yuma Crossing Day,** in late February, features historical reenactments, historic site tours, and train rides.

HISTORIC SITES

Arizona Historical Society Century House Museum If you'd like to find out more about pioneer life in Yuma, stop by this territorial-period home, which is full of historic photographs and artifacts and surrounded by lush gardens and aviaries full of exotic birds. Adjacent to the museum is the Garden Cafe, an excellent lunch spot.

240 S. Madison Ave. (𝒞 520/782-1841. Free admission; $2 suggested donation. Tues–Sat 10am–4pm.

Yuma Crossing State Historic Park ✪ In 1865, Yuma Crossing, the narrow spot in the Colorado River where the town of Yuma sprang up, became the site of the military's Quartermaster Depot. Yuma was a busy river port during this time, and after supplies shipped from California were unloaded, they went to military posts throughout the region. When the railroad arrived in Yuma in 1877, the Quartermaster Depot began losing its importance in the regional supply network, and by 1883, the depot was closed. Today, the depot's large wooden buildings have been restored, and although they are now set back from the current channel of the Colorado River, it's easy to imagine being stationed at this hot and dusty outpost in the days before air-conditioning. Exhibits tell the story of those who lived and worked at Yuma Crossing. In late 2000, President Clinton designated Yuma Crossing a National Heritage Area.

201 N. Fourth Ave. (at the Colorado River). (𝒞 520/329-0471. www.pr.state.az.us. Admission $3 adults, $2 children 7–13. Daily 10am–5pm (May–Oct closed Tues–Wed). Closed Christmas.

Yuma Territorial Prison State Historic Park ✪ Yuma is one of the hottest places in the world, so it comes as no surprise the Arizona Territory chose this bleak spot for a prison (although there is a nice view of the confluence of the Gila and Colorado rivers from Prison Hill). The prison first housed convicts in 1876, but operated for only 33 years before being replaced by a larger prison. Despite the thick stone walls and iron bars, this was considered a model penal institution in its day. It even had its own electric-generating plant and ventilation system. The prison museum has some interesting displays, including photos of many of the 3,049 men and 29 women who were incarcerated at Yuma over the years.

1 Prison Hill Rd. (𝒞 520/783-4771. www.pr.state.az.us. Admission $3 adults, $2 children 7–13. Daily 8am–5pm. Closed Christmas.

DOWNTOWN YUMA

Historic downtown Yuma isn't exactly a bustling place, and it doesn't abound in historic flavor, but the south-of-the-border atmosphere is worth a visit. Huge well-shaped ficus trees provide deep shade, and at the center of the shopping district is a plaza similar to those found in towns all over Mexico. Funky and inexpensive crafts and antiques shops occupy an occasional storefront, and, down a landscaped alleyway off Main Street (at 224 Main St., across from Lutes Casino), there's a potpourri of small tourist-oriented stores. Just off Main Street, you'll also find two pottery studio/galleries: **One Percent Gallery,** 78 W. Second St. (𝒞 520/782-1934), and **Colorado River Pottery,** 67 W. Second St. (𝒞 520/ 343-0413). Also nearby are two interesting shops housed in restored adobe buildings. **Picaflor,** 206 First Ave. (𝒞 520/782-6535), sells Mexican decorative items, while **The Bee's Knees,** 226 S. First Ave. (𝒞 520/329-8545), features all manor of unusual stuff for kids, from the latest Harry Potter action figures to designer fashions and kids' furniture. Within just a couple of blocks of downtown, you can play in the sand or go for a stroll along the Colorado River at **Colorado River Crossing Beach Park.** The park is at the north end of Madison Avenue.

DATES & DESERT TOURING

Date palms, which are among the most ancient of cultivated tree crops and which were grown in the Middle East as far back as 3000 B.C., flourish in the heat of the Arizona desert. Here in Yuma, you'll find **Ehrlich's Date Garden,** 868 Ave. B (✆ **520/783-4778**), which sells nearly a dozen varieties of organically grown dates, as well as organic oranges. Prices are incredibly low, and the old-fashioned fruit stand is open daily from 9am to 5pm (but closed mid-May through Aug).

The Colorado River has been the lifeblood of the Southwestern desert for centuries, and today there's a wealth of history along its banks. **Yuma River Tours,** 1920 Arizona Ave. (✆ **520/783-4400;** www.yumarivertopurs.com), operates narrated jet-boat tours from Yuma to the Imperial Wildlife Refuge (great bird-watching) and an extended trip to Draper. Along the way, you'll learn about the homesteaders, boatmen, Native Americans, and miners who once relied on the Colorado River. Tours, including lunch, cost $52 to $69. Alternatively, you can take a 3-hour paddle-wheel trip on the *Colorado King I* (✆ **520/ 782-2412;** www.coloradoking.com). Tours are $27 to $42 for adults and $20 to $25 for children 12 and under.

While the river was the reason for Yuma's existence, it was the railroad that finally forced the town to abandon its connection to the Colorado. Today, you can ride the rails on the historic **Yuma Valley Railway** (✆ **520/783-3456**), which offers 34-mile excursions along the Colorado River between November and May. You may spot birds and other wildlife on the banks of the river, and you'll get views of Mexico across the river and rich agricultural lands on this side. Passengers ride in a 1922 Pullman coach. Fares are $13 for adults, $12 for seniors, and $7 for children 4 to 16. Dinner excursions are also available.

If you're a bird-watcher, an angler, or a canoeist, you'll want to spend some time along the Colorado River north of Yuma. Here you'll find the **Imperial and Cibola National Wildlife Refuges,** comprised of extensive marshes and shallow lakes alongside the river. Plenty of bird species, good fishing and canoeing, and several campgrounds make it a popular area. For more information, contact the **Imperial Refuge** (✆ **520/783-3371;** http://southwest.fws.gov) or the **Cibola Refuge** (✆ **520/857-3253;** http://southwest.fws.gov).

One of the best ways to explore the Imperial National Wildlife Refuge is by canoe. You can rent one from **Martinez Lake Resort** (✆ **800/876-7004** or 520/783-9589) for $32 a day, plus shuttle and delivery charges. Both 1- and 2-day canoe trips are possible along this stretch of the lower Colorado, which features rugged, colorful mountains and quiet backwater areas.

Bird-watchers will want to head out to the **Betty's Kitchen Wildlife and Interpretive Area** and the adjacent **Mittry Lake.** To get here, take U.S. 95 east out of town, turn north on Avenue 7E, and continue 9 miles, at which point the road turns to gravel. Turn left in a quarter-mile to reach Betty's Kitchen; continue straight on the gravel road to reach Mittry Lake. Fall and spring migration are some of the best times of year for birding at these spots; many waterfowl winter in the area as well.

GOLF

While the golf courses are not nearly as impressive as those at the resorts in Phoenix and Tucson, there are certainly plenty of them, and you can't beat the winter climate. The courses cater primarily to the long-term visitors who descend on this area every winter. The **Mesa del Sol Golf Club,** 12213 Calle del Cid (℗ **520/342-1283**), off I-8 at the Fortuna Road exit, is the most challenging local course open to the public. On the other hand, the **Desert Hills Golf Course,** 1245 W. Desert Hills Dr. (℗ **520/344-GOLF**), has been rated the best municipal course in the state. Other area courses include the **Arroyo Dunes Golf Course,** 32nd Street and Avenue A (℗ **520/726-8350**), and the **Cocopah Bend RV Resort,** 6800 Strand Ave. (℗ **520/343-1663**). The **Ironwood Public Golf Course,** 2945 W. Eighth St. (℗ **520/343-1466**), is worth a round if you're in the mood for only a quick nine holes.

WHERE TO STAY
MODERATE

Best Western Coronado Motor Hotel ⭐ With its red-tile roofs, whitewashed walls, and archways, this Mission-Revival building on the edge of downtown is the picture of a mid-20th-century motel—but rooms are as up-to-date as you would expect from a major chain. The convenient location puts you within walking distance of several good restaurants, Yuma Crossing State Historic Park, the Century House Museum, and the Yuma Valley Railway.

233 Fourth Ave., Yuma, AZ 85364. ℗ **800/528-1234** or 520/783-4453. Fax 520/782-7487. www.bestwestern. com. 86 units. $69–$79 double. Rates include continental breakfast. AE, DISC, MC, V. Pets accepted. **Amenities:** Restaurant; 2 outdoor pools; Jacuzzi; coin-op laundry. *In room:* A/C, TV, dataport, hair dryer, iron.

La Fuente Inn & Suites Conveniently located just off the interstate, this appealing hotel is done in Spanish-colonial style with red-tile roof, pink stucco walls, and a fountain out front, and the theme continues in the lobby, which has rustic furnishings and a tile floor. French doors open onto the pool terrace and a large courtyard, around which the guest rooms are arranged. Standard units feature modern motel furnishings, while the well-designed suites offer much more space. The Spanish styling and pleasant courtyard pool area set this place apart from other off-ramp hotels in Yuma.

1513 E. 16th St., Yuma, AZ 85365. ℗ **800/841-1814** or 520/329-1814. Fax 520/343-2671. www.lafuenteinn. com. 96 units. $78–$140 double. Rates include continental breakfast and evening happy hour. AE, DC, DISC, MC, V. **Amenities:** Courtyard pool; exercise room; access to nearby health club; Jacuzzi; business center; coin-op laundry. *In room:* A/C, TV, dataport, fridge, coffeemaker, hair dryer.

Shilo Inn ⭐ Located on the edge of town overlooking farmland and desert, the Shilo Inn is Yuma's most luxurious hotel, and the neatly manicured gardens provide an oasis of greenery in this dry landscape. The guest rooms contains comfortable chairs, couches, and patios, as well as such extras as microwaves and VCRs. The more expensive rooms are those with a view of the desert. For long-term stays, ask for a suite with kitchenette. The casual dining room offers both indoor and terrace dining, and a lounge often has live music on weekends.

1550 S. Castle Dome Ave., Yuma, AZ 85365-1702. ℗ **800/222-2244** or 520/782-9511. Fax 520/783-1538. www.shiloinns.com. 134 units. $75–$150 double; $129–$241 suite. Rates include full breakfast. AE, DC, DISC, MC, V. Small supervised pets accepted ($10). **Amenities:** Restaurant; lounge; large outdoor pool; exercise room; Jacuzzi; sauna; steam room; room service; coin-op laundry; laundry service; dry cleaning. *In room:* A/C, TV/VCR, dataport, fridge, coffeemaker, hair dryer.

INEXPENSIVE

In addition to numerous older budget motels, Yuma has several newer chain motels, including two branches of **Motel 6** (② **800/4-MOTEL-6**) and a **Super 8** (② **800/800-8000**).

WHERE TO DINE

The Garden Cafe ⋆⋆ BREAKFAST/SANDWICHES/SALADS   In back of the Century House Museum is Yuma's favorite breakfast and lunch spot. Set amid quiet terraced gardens and large aviaries full of singing birds, the Garden Cafe provides a welcome respite from Yuma's heat. On the hottest days, misters spray the air with a gentle fog that keeps the gardens cool. There's also an indoor dining area. The menu consists of various delicious sandwiches, daily special quiches, salads, and rich desserts. Pancakes with lingonberry sauce are a breakfast specialty. On Sunday, there's a brunch buffet. This place is a favorite among retirees and the ladies-who-lunch crowd.

250 Madison Ave. ② **520/783-1491**. Main courses $5–$8.25. AE, MC, V. Tues–Fri 9am–2:30pm; Sat 8–11am and 11:30am–2:30pm; Sun 8am–2:30pm. Closed late May to early Oct.

Lutes Casino BURGERS/SANDWICHES *Kids*   You won't find any slot machines or poker tables at Lutes Casino anymore, just lots of very serious domino players. Today Lute's is a dark and cavernous pool hall, but it's better known as a family restaurant serving the best hamburgers in town. You don't need to see a menu—just walk in and ask for a special, or *especial* (this is a bilingual joint). What you'll get is a cheeseburger/hot dog combo. Then cover your special with Lute's own secret-recipe hot sauce to make it truly special.

221 S. Main St. ② **520/782-2192**. www.lutescasino.com. Sandwiches and burgers $3.25–$5.25. No credit cards. Mon–Fri 10am–8pm; Fri–Sat 10am–9pm; Sun 10am–6pm; sometimes closes earlier.

River City Grill ⋆⋆ INTERNATIONAL   With its hip, big-city decor, colorful exterior paint job, and long red-meat-free menu, this restaurant is definitely a novelty in Yuma. But the lines out the door are testimony to the fact that this town obviously craves just such a dining experience. Despite the location far from saltwater, seafood dominates the menu. The crab cakes with spicy peanut sauce are a must for a starter, and the tequila snapper is an excellent entree choice. Flavor combinations range all over the globe: Vietnamese spring rolls, Mediterranean salad, shrimp pad Thai, teriyaki-grilled salmon, jerk chicken.

600 W. Third St. ② **520/782-7988**. Reservations highly recommended. Main courses $12–$20. MC, V. Mon–Sat 5–10pm.

Appendix:
Arizona in Depth

Despite the searing summer temperatures, the desolate deserts, and the lack of water, people have been lured to Arizona for generations. In the 16th century, the Spanish came looking for gold—but settled for saving souls. In the 19th century, cattle ranchers came (despite frightful tales of spiny cactus forests) and found that a few corners of the state actually had lush grasslands. At the same time, sidetracked '49ers were scouring the hills for gold (and found more than the Spanish did). However, boomtowns—both cattle and mining—soon went bust. Despite occasional big strikes (such as the silver strike at Tombstone), mining didn't prove itself until the early 20th century, and even then, the mother lode was not gold or silver, but copper, which Arizona has in such abundance that it is called the Copper State.

In the 1920s and 1930s, Arizona struck a new vein of gold. The railroads made travel to the state easy, and the word of the mild winter climate spread to colder corners of the nation. Among the first "vacationers" were people suffering from tuberculosis. These "lungers," as they were known, rested and recuperated in the dry desert air. It didn't take long for the perfectly healthy to realize that they, too, could enjoy winter in Arizona, and wintering in the desert soon became fashionable with wealthy northerners.

Today it's still the golden sun that lures people to Arizona. Scottsdale, Phoenix, Tucson, and Sedona are home to some of the most luxurious and expensive resorts in the country, and more are under construction. The state has seen a massive influx of retirees, many of whom have found the few pockets of Arizona where the climate is absolutely perfect—not too hot, not too cold, and plenty of sunshine.

Although it's the Grand Canyon that attracts the most visitors to Arizona, the state has plenty of other natural wonders. The largest meteorite crater, the painted desert, the spectacular red-rock country of Sedona, the sandstone buttes of Monument Valley, and the "forests" of saguaro cacti are just a few of the state's other natural spectacles.

The human hand has also left its mark on Arizona. More than 1,000 years ago, the Anasazi, Sinagua, and Hohokam tribes built villages on mesas, in valleys, and in the steep cliff walls of deep canyons. In more recent years, much larger structures have risen in canyons across the state. The Hoover and Glen Canyon dams on the Colorado River are among the largest dams in the country and have created the nation's largest and most spectacular reservoirs, although at the expense of the rich riparian areas that once filled the now flooded desert canyons. Today these reservoirs are among the state's most popular destinations, especially with Arizonans, who flock to the water with an amazing variety of high-powered watercraft.

Just as compelling as its sunshine, resorts, and reservoirs are the tall tales of Arizona's fascinating history. This is the Wild West, the land of cowboys and Indians, of prospectors and ghost towns, coyotes and rattlesnakes. Scratch the glossy surface of modern, urbanized Arizona and you'll strike real gold—the story of the American West.

1 The Natural Environment

Although the very mention of Arizona may cause some people to turn the air-conditioning on full blast, this state is much more than a searing landscape of cactus and creosote bush. From the baking shores of the lower Colorado River to the snowcapped heights of the San Francisco Peaks, Arizona encompasses virtually every North American climatic zone. Cactus flowers bloom in spring, and mountain wildflowers have their turn in summer. In autumn, the aspens color the White Mountains golden, and in winter, snows blanket the higher elevations from the North Rim of the Grand Canyon to the Mexican border.

But it's the Sonoran Desert, with its massive saguaro cacti, that most people associate with Arizona, and it is here in the desert that the state's two largest cities—Phoenix and Tucson—are to be found. The Sonoran Desert is among the world's most biologically diverse deserts. This is due in large part to the relatively plentiful rains in the region. In the Arizona desert, rain falls during both the winter and the late summer. This latter rainy season, when clamorous thunderstorms send flash floods surging down arroyos, is known as the monsoon season and is the most dramatic time of year in the desert. The sunsets are unforgettable, but then so, too, is the heat and humidity.

Before the coming of dams and deep wells, many Arizona rivers and streams flowed year-round and nurtured a surprising variety of plants and animals. Today, however, only a few rivers and creeks still flow unaltered through the desert. They include Sonoita and Aravaipa creeks and the San Pedro, Verde, and Hassayampa rivers. The green riparian areas along these watercourses are characterized by the rare cottonwood-willow forest and serve as magnets for wildlife, harboring rare birds as well as fish species unique to Arizona.

The saguaro cactus, which can stand 40 feet tall and weigh several tons, is the Sonoran Desert's most conspicuous native inhabitant. Massive and many-armed, these are the cacti of comic strips and Hollywood Westerns. This desert is also home to many other lesser-known species of cactus, including organ pipe cactus (closely related to the saguaro), barrel cactus, and various species of prickly pears and chollas. Despite their spiny defenses, cacti are still a source of food and shelter for many species of desert animals. Bats sip the nectar from saguaro flowers, and in the process act as pollinators. Javelinas (collared peccaries), which are similar to wild pigs, chow down on the prickly pear fruit—spines and all. Gila woodpeckers nest in holes in saguaro trunks, while cactus wrens build their nests in the branches of the cholla cactus.

Just as cacti have adapted to the desert, so have the animals that live here. Many desert animals spend sweltering days in burrows and venture out only in the cool of the night. Under cover of darkness, coyotes howl, rattlesnakes and great horned owls hunt kangaroo rats, and javelinas root about for anything edible. Gila lizards, among the only poisonous lizards in the world, drag their ungainly bodies through the dust, while tarantulas tiptoe silently in search of unwary insects.

Outside the desert regions, there is great diversity as well. In the southern part of the state, small mountain ranges rise abruptly from the desert floor, creating refuges for plants and animals that require cooler climates. It is these so-called sky islands that harbor the greatest varieties of bird species in the continental United States. Birds from both warm and cold climates find homes in such oases as Ramsey, Madera, and Cave Creek canyons.

Although rugged mountain ranges crisscross the state, only a few rise to such heights that they support actual forests. Among these are the Santa Catalinas

Arizona: Hollywood Back Lot

Spectacular landscapes, rugged deserts, ghost towns, and the cowboy mystique have, over the years, made Arizona the location for hundreds of films. From obscure B Westerns starring long-forgotten singing cowboys to the seminal works of John Ford, Arizona has provided a stunning backdrop to stories of life in the Wild West. This state has become so associated with the Old West that Europeans, Asians, and Australians come from halfway around the world to walk where John Wayne once swaggered and where Clint Eastwood cultivated his outlaw image.

Arizona has represented the past, the present, and the future, and the state's landscape is so varied that it has doubled for Texas, Kansas, Mexico, foreign planets, a postapocalyptic earth, and even New York. Production companies working on movies, television shows, and commercials have traveled to every corner of the state to find just the right setting for their work.

In 1939, a set was built in Tucson for the filming of the movie *Arizona*, and when the shooting was done, the set was left to be used in other productions. Today this mock-Western town is known as Old Tucson Studios and is still used for film and video productions. Movies that have been filmed here include *Tombstone;* John Wayne's *Rio Lobo, Rio Bravo,* and *El Dorado;* Clint Eastwood's *The Outlaw Josey Wales;* Kirk Douglas's *Gunfight at the O.K. Corral;* and Paul Newman's *The Life and Times of Judge Roy Bean.*

Although John Ford was not the first to film at Monument Valley, he made this otherworldly landscape a trademark of his filmmaking, using the valley as the backdrop for such movies as *Stagecoach, She Wore a Yellow Ribbon, My Darling Clementine, Rio Grande,* and *The Searchers.* Other Westerns filmed here have included *How the West Was Won, The Legend of the Lone Ranger,* and *Mackenna's Gold.* The valley has shown up in such non-Western films as *Back to the Future III, 2001: A Space Odyssey, Thelma and Louise,* and *Forrest Gump.* The red rocks of Sedona have also attracted many filmmakers over the years. *Broken Arrow, 3:10 to Yuma, The Riders of the Purple Sage,* and *The Call of the Canyon* were all filmed in Sedona and nearby Oak Creek Canyon.

The area around the small town of Patagonia, in southeastern Arizona, has served as a backdrop for quite a few films, including *Oklahoma!, Red River, McClintock, Broken Lance, David and Bathsheba,* and *A Star Is Born,* and television programs such as *Little House on the Prairie, The Young Riders,* and *Red Badge of Courage.*

outside Tucson, the White Mountains along the state's eastern border, and the San Francisco Peaks north of Flagstaff. However, it's atop the Mogollon Rim and the Kaibab Plateau that the ponderosa pine forests cover the greatest areas. The Mogollon Rim is a 2,000-foot-high escarpment that stretches from central Arizona all the way into New Mexico. The ponderosa pine forest here is the largest in the world, and is dotted with lakes well known for their fishing. The Mogollon Rim area is also home to large herds of elk. At over 8,000 feet in elevation, the Kaibab Plateau is even higher than the Mogollon Rim; it is through this plateau that the Grand Canyon cuts its mighty chasm.

2 Arizona Today

Combining aspects of Native American, Hispanic, and European cultures, Arizona is one of the most culturally diverse states in the country. Here the Old West and the "New West" coexist. While the wealthy residents of Scottsdale raise Arabian horses as investments, the Navajos of the Four Corners region still raise sheep for sustenance and wool, herding their flocks from the backs of hardworking horses. Vacationers on Lake Powell water-ski through flooded canyons while cowboys in the southeast corner of the state still ride the range, mending fences and rounding up cattle.

Although Arizonans are today more likely to drive Hondas and Toyotas than to ride pintos and appaloosas, Western wear is still the preferred fashion of rich and poor alike. Cowboy boots, cowboy hats, blue jeans, and bolo ties are acceptable attire at almost any function in the state. Horses are still used on ranches, but most are kept simply for recreational or investment purposes. In Scottsdale, one of the nation's centers of Arabian-horse breeding, horse auctions attract a well-heeled (read lizard-skin–booted) crowd, and horses sell for tens of thousands of dollars. Even the state's dude ranches, which now call themselves "guest ranches," have changed their image, and many are as likely to offer tennis and swimming as horseback riding.

A long legacy of movies being filmed here has further blurred the line between the real West and the Hollywood West. More city slickers wander the streets of the Old Tucson movie set and videotape shootouts at the O.K. Corral than ever saddle up a palomino or ride herd on a cattle drive. Even dinner has been raised to a cowboy entertainment form at Arizona's many Wild West steakhouses, where families are entertained by cowboy bands, staged gunfights, hayrides, and singalongs, all in the name of reliving the glory days of "cowboys and Indians."

For Arizona's Indians, those were days of hardship and misery, and today the state's many tribes continue to strive for the sort of economic well-being enjoyed by the state's nonnative population. Traditional ways are still alive, but tribes struggle to preserve their unique cultures—their languages, religious beliefs and ceremonies, livelihoods, and architecture.

Arizona is home to the largest Indian reservation in the country—the Navajo nation—as well as nearly two dozen smaller reservations. As elsewhere in the United States, poverty and alcoholism are major problems on Arizona reservations. However, several of the state's tribes have, through their arts and crafts, managed to both preserve some of their traditional culture and share it with nonnatives. Among these tribes are the Navajo, known for their rugs and silver jewelry; the Hopi, known for their pottery and kachinas; the Zuni, known for their inlaid stone jewelry; and the Tohono O'odham, known for their baskets.

Lately, however, many nonnatives have been visiting reservations not out of an interest in learning about another culture, but to gamble. Throughout the state, casinos have opened on reservation land, and despite the controversies surrounding such enterprises, many native peoples are finally seeing some income on their once-impoverished reservations.

Many of the people who visit these new casinos are retirees, who are among the fastest-growing segment of Arizona's population. The state's mild winter climate has attracted tens of thousands of retirees over the past few decades. Many of these winter residents, known as snowbirds, park their RVs outside such warm spots as Yuma and Quartzsite. Others have come to stay, settling in retirement communities such as Sun City and Green Valley.

This graying of the population, combined with strong ranching and mining industries, has made Arizona one of the most conservative of states. Although by today's standards Barry Goldwater could almost be considered a liberal, his conservative politics were so much a part of the Arizona mindset that the state kept him in the Senate for 30 years.

Arizona's environmental politics have been somewhat contentious in recent years. Although many people think of the desert as a wasteland in need of transformation, others see it as a fragile ecosystem that has been endangered by the encroachment of civilization. Saguaro cacti throughout the state are protected by law, but the deserts they grow in are not. In Tucson, environmentalists have for several years been fighting (with limited success) to stop the suburban sprawl that's pushing farther and farther into saguaro country. The balance in this battle tipped in favor of preservation when rare ferruginous pygmy owls were found nesting in the Tucson area.

Way up at the north end of the state, remote Grand Canyon National Park is suffering from its own popularity. With more than five million visitors a year, the park now sees summer traffic jams and parking problems that have made a visit an exercise in patience. The national park has begun using alternative-fuel buses for transporting visitors around the South Rim and Grand Canyon Village; there is also a plan to build a light-rail system to shuttle visitors into the park from a parking lot outside the park's boundaries. Such a system would solve the parking problems within the park, but questions about the cost have now stalled implementation.

In his last year in office, President Clinton signed legislation creating five new national monuments in Arizona. The Grand Canyon–Parashant National Monument, in the northwest corner of the state adjacent to Grand Canyon National Park, preserves one of the most remote and inhospitable regions of the state. To the north of Grand Canyon National Park, near Glen Canyon National Recreation Area, is the Vermillion Cliffs National Monument. The Agua Fria National Monument, north of Phoenix, preserves hundreds of archaeological sites. Sonoran Desert National Monument, 40 to 60 miles southwest of Phoenix, encompasses some of the most pristine areas of the Sonoran Desert, while Ironwoods National Monument, 40 to 50 miles northwest of Tucson, preserves an area of the Sonoran Desert noteworthy for its 800-year-old ironwood trees. At this time, none of these monuments have anything in the way of visitor facilities. Because these monuments were all created by President Clinton under the Antiquities Act, there has been much opposition in the Republican administration and it is not certain whether they will even survive President Bush's time in office.

Efforts at preserving the state's environment make it clear that Arizonans value the outdoors, but a ski boat in every driveway doesn't mean the arts are ignored. Although it hasn't been too many years since evening entertainment in Arizona meant dance-hall girls or a harmonica by the campfire, Phoenix and Tucson have become centers for the visual and performing arts. The two cities share an opera company and a ballet company, and the Valley of the Sun is home to a number of symphony orchestras and theater companies.

Small towns around the state are also supporting the arts. Whole communities such as Jerome, Tubac, and Bisbee, all nearly ghost towns at one time, have been reborn as arts communities, and where miners and outlaws once walked, artists now offer their creations for sale.

Tourism continues to boom in Arizona, and after a decade-long construction lull, new resorts have once again been opening in both the Valley of the Sun and Tucson. In particular, the north Scottsdale area, which has experienced a residential building boom in recent years, is now seeing the construction of luxury resorts. Downtown Phoenix has positioned itself as the state's sports and entertainment mecca, with Bank One Ballpark, the America West Arena, and numerous sports bars, nightclubs, and even a combination barbecue joint and sports bar operated by former rock star Alice Cooper. The Arizona Cardinals will also be getting a new football stadium in a few years and will no longer have to play at Arizona State University's Sun Devil Stadium.

In Arizona today, the New West and the Old West are coming to grips with each other. Hopi perform their age-old dances atop their mesas. SUVs and convertible sports cars jockey for parking spaces at glitzy shopping centers in Phoenix and Tucson. Grizzled wranglers lead vacationing Germans on horseback rides across open range. Ranchers find they have something in common with environmentalists—saving Arizona's ranch lands. What all these people have in common is a love of sunshine, which, of course, Arizona has in abundance.

3 History 101

Over the past 5 centuries, the land now known as Arizona has been the homeland of various Indian tribes as well as part of New Spain, Mexico, and the United States. Early explorers and settlers saw little profit in the desert wasteland, but time proved them wrong: Mineral resources, cattle grazing, and cotton (after dams began providing irrigation water) all became important income sources. In the 20th century, the economy moved from the three Cs (copper, cattle, and cotton) to a service-based economy, with tourism as one of its major resources.

EARLY HISTORY Arizona is the site of North America's oldest cultures and one of the two longest continuously inhabited settlements in the United States (the Hopi village of Oraibi). The region's human habitation actually dates back more than 11,000 years, to the time when Paleo-Indians known as the Clovis people inhabited southeastern Arizona. Stone

Dateline

- 9700 B.C. Paleo-Indians (the Clovis people) in southeastern Arizona are among the earliest recorded inhabitants of North America.
- A.D. 200 The Anasazi people move into Canyon de Chelly.
- 450 Hohokam peoples farm the Salt and Gila river valleys, eventually building 600 miles of irrigation canals.
- 650 The Sinagua cultivate land northeast of present-day Flagstaff.
- 1100s Hopi tribes build Oraibi village, the oldest continuously occupied village in the United States; the Anasazi build cliff dwellings in Canyon de Chelly; the Sinagua build Wupatki.
- 1250 The Sinagua abandon Wupatki and other pueblos.
- 1300 The Anasazi abandon cliff dwellings in Canyon de Chelly and Tsegi Canyon.
- 1350 The Hohokam build Casa Grande in the Gila River valley.
- 1400s The Navajo people migrate south from Canada to northeastern Arizona.

continues

tools and arrowheads of the type credited to the Clovis have been found in southeastern Arizona, and a mammoth-kill site has become an important source of information about these people, some of the earliest inhabitants of North America.

Few records exist of the next 9,000 years of Arizona's history, but by about A.D. 200, wandering bands of hunter-gatherers began living in Canyon de Chelly in the north. These people would come to be known as the Anasazi, a Navajo word that means "the ancient ones." The earliest Anasazi period, from A.D. 200 to 700, is called the Basket Maker period because of the numbers of baskets that have been found in Anasazi ruins from this time. During this period, the Anasazi gave up hunting and gathering and took up agriculture, growing corn, beans, squash, and cotton on the canyon floors in northeastern Arizona. In recent years, the term *Anasazi* has been replaced with "ancestral Puebloan," which is considered a more appropriate description of the people who built the many pueblos (villages) scattered across northern Arizona.

During the Pueblo period, between 700 and 1300, the Anasazi began building multistory pueblos and cliff dwellings. Despite decades of research, it is still unknown why the Anasazi began living in niches and caves high on the cliff walls of the region's canyons. It may have been to conserve farmland as their population grew and required larger harvests, or for protection from flash floods or attacks by hostile neighbors. Whatever the reason, the Anasazi cliff dwellings were all abandoned by 1300. It's unclear why the villages were abandoned, but a study of tree rings indicates that the region experienced a severe drought between 1276 and 1299, which suggests the Anasazi left in search of more fertile farmland. Keet Seel and

- 1450 The Hohokam abandon lowland desert villages; the Sinagua abandon Verde Valley villages.
- 1539 Marcos de Niza ventures into present-day Arizona from Mexico (New Spain) in search of the Seven Cities of Cíbola.
- 1540s Francisco Vásquez de Coronado leads an expedition to Arizona in search of gold.
- 1691 Jesuit Fr. Eusebio Kino begins converting Native Americans.
- 1751 The mission of Tumacacori and the presidio of Tubac, the first European settlement in Arizona, are established.
- 1776 A Spanish garrison is established in Tucson to protect the mission of San Xavier del Bac.
- 1821 Mexico gains independence from Spain and takes control of Arizona.
- 1848 Most of present-day Arizona is ceded to the United States following the Mexican-American War.
- 1853 In the Gadsden Purchase, the United States acquires the remainder of Arizona from Mexico.
- 1862 Arizona becomes the Confederate Territory of Arizona but is reclaimed by the Union later that same year.
- 1863 Arizona becomes a U.S. territory.
- 1869 Maj. John Wesley Powell explores the Grand Canyon by boat.
- 1880 Southern Pacific Railroad arrives in Tucson.
- 1881 Shootout at the O.K. Corral.
- 1886 Geronimo surrenders to the U.S. Army.
- 1911 Theodore Roosevelt Dam, on the Salt River, enables irrigation and development of the desert.
- 1912 Arizona becomes the 48th state.
- 1919 Grand Canyon National Park established.
- 1936 Hoover Dam is completed.
- 1948 Arizona Indians receive the right to vote.
- 1981 Arizona judge Sandra Day O'Connor becomes the first woman appointed to the U.S. Supreme Court.
- 1991 A California jury finds Charles Keating guilty of defrauding Arizona investors who had deposited funds with Lincoln Savings and Loan.

continues

Betatakin, at Navajo National Monument, and the many ruins in Canyon de Chelly, are Arizona's best-preserved Anasazi ruins.

During the Anasazi Basket Maker period, another culture was beginning to develop in the fertile plateau northeast of present-day Flagstaff and

- 1997 Gov. Fife Symington is convicted of bank fraud and resigns as governor.
- 1998 Bank One Ballpark, with retractable roof, opens in Phoenix.
- 2000–2001 Pres. Bill Clinton creates five new national monuments in Arizona.

southward into the Verde River valley. The Sinagua, a Spanish name that means "without water," built their stone pueblos primarily on hills and mesas such as those at Tuzigoot near Clarkdale and Wupatki near Flagstaff. They also built cliff dwellings at places such as Walnut Canyon and Montezuma Castle. By the mid–13th century, Wupatki had been abandoned, and by the early 15th century, Walnut Canyon and pueblos in the lower Verde Valley region had been abandoned.

By A.D. 450, the Hohokam culture, from whom the Sinagua most likely learned irrigation, had begun to farm the Gila and Salt river valleys between Phoenix and Casa Grande. Over a period of 1,000 years, they constructed a 600-mile network of irrigation canals, some of which can still be seen today. Because the Hohokam built their homes of earth, few Hohokam ruins remain. However, one building, the Casa Grande ruin, has been well preserved, and throughout the desert the Hohokam left petroglyphs (rock carvings) as a lasting reminder that they once dwelt in this region. By the 1450s, the tribe had abandoned its villages and disappeared without a sign, hence the name Hohokam, a Tohono O'odham word meaning "all used up" or "the people who have gone." Archaeologists believe that the irrigation of desert soil for hundreds of years had left a thick crust of alkali on the surface, which made further farming impossible.

HISPANIC HERITAGE   The first Europeans to visit the region may have been a motley crew of shipwrecked Spaniards among whom was a black man named Estévan de Dorantes. This unfortunate group spent 8 years wandering from a beach in Florida to a Spanish village in Mexico. These wanderers arrived back in Spanish territory with a fantastic story of seven cities so rich in gold and jewels that the inhabitants even decorated their doorways with jewels. No one is sure whether they actually passed through Arizona, but their story convinced the viceroy of New Spain (Mexico) to send a small expedition, led by Fr. Marcos de Niza and Estévan de Dorantes, into the region. Father de Niza's report of finding the fabled Seven Cities of Cíbola inspired Don Francisco Vásquez de Coronado to set off in search of wealth. Instead of fabulously wealthy cities, Coronado found only pueblos of stone and mud. A subordinate expedition led by Garcia Lopez de Cárdenas stumbled upon the Grand Canyon, while another group of Coronado's men, led by Don Pedro de Tovar, visited the Hopi mesas.

In the 150 years that followed, only a handful of Spaniards visited Arizona. In the 1580s and 1600s, Antonio de Espejo and Juan de Oñate explored northern and central Arizona and found indications that there were mineral riches in the region. In the 1670s, the Franciscans founded several missions among the Hopi pueblos, but the Pueblo Revolt of 1680 obliterated this small Spanish presence.

In 1687, Fr. Eusebio Francisco Kino, a German-educated Italian Jesuit, began establishing missions in the Sonoran Desert region of northern New Spain. In 1691, he visited the Pima village of Tumacacori. Father Kino taught the inhabitants European farming techniques, planted fruit trees, and gave the natives cattle, sheep, and goats to raise. However, it was not until 1751, in response to a

Pima rebellion, that the permanent mission of Tumacacori and the presidio (military post) of Tubac were built. Together these two Spanish outposts became the first European settlements in Arizona.

In 1775, a group of settlers led by Juan Bautista de Anza set out from Tubac to find an overland route to California, and in 1776, this group founded the city of San Francisco. That same year, the Tubac presidio was moved to Tucson. As early as 1692, Father Kino had visited the Tucson area and by 1700 had laid out the foundations for the first church at the mission of San Xavier del Bac. It was not until sometime around 1783 that construction of the present church, known as the White Dove of the Desert, began.

In 1821, Mexico won its independence from Spain, and Tucson, with only 65 inhabitants, became part of Mexico. Mexico at that time extended all the way to northern California, but in 1848, most of this land, except for a small section of southern Arizona that included Tucson, became U.S. territory in the wake of the Mexican-American War. Five years later, in 1853, Mexico sold the remainder of southern Arizona to the United States in a transaction known as the Gadsden Purchase.

INDIAN CONFLICTS   At the time the Spanish arrived in Arizona, the tribes living in the southern lowland deserts were peaceful farmers, but in the mountains of the east lived the Apache, a hunting-and-gathering tribe that frequently raided neighboring tribes. In the north, the Navajo, relatively recent immigrants to the region, fought over land with the neighboring Ute and Hopi (who were also fighting among themselves).

Coronado's expedition through Arizona and into New Mexico and Kansas was to seek gold. To that end he attacked one pueblo, killed the inhabitants of another, and forced still others to abandon their villages. Spanish-Indian relations were never to improve, and the Spanish were forced to occupy their new lands with a strong military presence. Around 1600, 300 Spanish settlers moved into the Four Corners region, which at the time supported a large population of Navajo. The Spanish raided Navajo villages to take slaves, and angry Navajo responded by stealing Spanish horses and cattle.

For several decades in the mid-1600s, missionaries were tolerated in the Hopi pueblos, but the Pueblo tribes revolted in 1680, killing the missionaries and destroying the missions. Encroachment by farmers and miners moving into the Santa Cruz Valley in the south caused the Pima people to stage a similar uprising in 1751, attacking and burning the mission at Tubac. This revolt led to the establishment of the presidio at Tubac that same year. When the military garrison moved to Tucson, Tubac was quickly abandoned because of frequent raids by Apaches. In 1781, the Yuman tribe, whose land at the confluence of the Colorado and Gila rivers had become a Spanish settlement, staged a similar uprising that wiped out the settlement at Yuma.

By the time Arizona became part of the United States, it was the Navajo and the Apache who were proving most resistant to white settlers. In 1864, the U.S. Army, under the leadership of Col. Kit Carson, forced the Navajo to surrender by destroying their winter food supplies, and then shipped the survivors to an internment camp in New Mexico. Within 5 years they were returned to their land, although they were forced to live on a reservation.

The Apache resisted white settlement 20 years longer than the Navajo did. Skillful guerrilla fighters, the Apache, under the leadership of Geronimo and Cochise, attacked settlers, forts, and towns despite the presence of U.S. Army troops sent to protect the settlers. Geronimo and Cochise were the leaders of the last resistant bands of rebellious Apache. Cochise eventually died in his Chiricahua Mountains homeland, while Geronimo was finally forced to surrender in 1886. Geronimo and many of his followers were subsequently relocated to Florida by the U.S. government. Open conflicts between whites and Indians finally came to an end.

TERRITORIAL DAYS   In 1846, the United States went to war with Mexico, which at the time extended all the way to northern California and included parts of Colorado, Wyoming, and New Mexico. When the war ended, the United States claimed almost all the land extending from Texas to northern California. This newly acquired land, called the New Mexico Territory, had its capital at Santa Fe. The land south of the Gila River, which included Tucson, was still part of Mexico, but when surveys determined that this land was the best route for a railroad from southern Mississippi to southern California, the U.S. government negotiated the Gadsden Purchase. In 1853, this land purchase established the current Arizona-Mexico border.

When the California Gold Rush began in 1849, many hopeful miners crossed Arizona en route to the goldfields, and some stayed to seek mineral riches in Arizona. Despite the ever-increasing numbers of settlers, the U.S. Congress refused to create a separate Arizona Territory. When the Civil War broke out, Arizonans, angered by Congress's inaction on their request to become a separate territory, sided with the Confederacy; in 1862, Arizona was proclaimed the Confederate Territory of Arizona. Although Union troops easily defeated the Confederate troops who had occupied Tucson, this dissension convinced Congress, in 1863, to create the Arizona Territory.

The capital of the new territory was temporarily established at Fort Whipple near Prescott, but later the same year was moved to Prescott, and in 1867 to Tucson. Ten years later, Prescott again became the capital, which it remained for another 12 years before the seat of government moved finally to Phoenix, which is today the Arizona state capital.

During this period, mining flourished, and although small amounts of gold and silver were discovered, copper became the source of Arizona's economic wealth. With each mineral strike, a new mining town would boom, and when the ore ran out, the town would be abandoned. These towns were infamous for their gambling halls, bordellos, saloons, and shootouts in the streets. Tombstone and Bisbee became the largest towns in the state and were known as the wildest towns between New Orleans and San Francisco.

In 1867, farmers in the newly founded town of Phoenix began irrigating their fields using canals that had been dug centuries earlier by the Hohokam. In the 1870s, ranching became another important source of revenue in the territory, particularly in the southeastern and northwestern parts of the state. In the 1880s, the railroads finally arrived, and life in Arizona began to change drastically. Suddenly the mineral resources and cattle of the region were accessible to the East.

STATEHOOD & THE 20TH CENTURY   By the beginning of the 20th century, Arizonans were trying to convince Congress to make the territory a state. Congress balked at the requests, but finally in 1910 allowed the territorial government to draw up a state constitution. Territorial legislators were progressive thinkers, and the draft of Arizona's state constitution included clauses for the recall of elected officials. Pres. William Howard Taft vetoed the bill that would have made Arizona a state because he opposed the recall of judges. Arizona politicians removed the controversial clause, and on February 14, 1912,

Arizona became the 48th state. One of the new state legislature's first acts was to reinstate the clause providing for the recall of judges.

Much of Washington's opposition to Arizona's statehood had been based on the belief that Arizona could never support economic development. This belief was changed in 1911 by one of the most important events in state history—the completion of the Roosevelt Dam (later to be renamed the Theodore Roosevelt Dam) on the Salt River. The dam provided irrigation water to the Valley of the Sun and tamed the violent floods of the river. The introduction of water to the heart of Arizona's vast desert enabled large-scale agriculture and industry. Over the next decades, more dams were built throughout Arizona. Completed in 1936, the Hoover Dam on the Colorado River became the largest concrete dam in the western hemisphere and formed the biggest man-made reservoir in North America. Arizona's dams would eventually provide not only water and electricity but also recreation areas.

Despite labor problems, copper mining increased throughout the 1920s and 1930s, and with the onset of World War II, the mines boomed as military munitions manufacturing increased the demand for copper. However, within a few years after the war, many mines were shut down. Arizona is still littered with old mining ghost towns that boomed and then went bust. A few towns, such as Jerome, Bisbee, and Chloride, managed to hang on after the mines shut down and were eventually rediscovered by artists, writers, and retirees. Bisbee and Jerome are now major tourist attractions known for their many art galleries.

World War II created demand for beef, leather, and cotton (which became the state's most important crop). During the war, clear desert skies proved ideal for training pilots, and several military bases were established in the state. Phoenix's population doubled during the war years, and after the war ended, many veterans returned with their families. However, it would take the invention of air-conditioning to truly open up the desert to major population growth.

During the postwar years, Arizona attracted a number of large manufacturing industries and slowly moved away from its agricultural economic base. Today electronics manufacturing, aerospace engineering, and other high-tech industries provide employment for thousands of Arizonans. The largest segment of the economy, however, is now in the service industries, with tourism playing a crucial role.

Even by the 1920s, Arizona had become a winter destination for the wealthy, and the Grand Canyon, declared a national park in 1919, lured more and more visitors every year. The clear, dry air attracted people suffering from allergies and lung ailments, and Arizona became known as a healthful place. Guest ranches of the 1930s eventually gave way to the resorts of the 1990s. Today Scottsdale and Phoenix boast the greatest concentration of resorts in the United States. In addition, tens of thousands of retirees from as far north as Canada make Arizona their winter home and play a crucial role in the state's economy.

Continued population growth throughout the 20th century created an ever greater demand for water. Despite the damming of virtually all of Arizona's rivers, the state still suffered from insufficient water supplies in the south-central population centers of Phoenix and Tucson. It would take the construction of the controversial and expensive Central Arizona Project (CAP) aqueduct to carry water from the Colorado River over mountains and deserts and deliver it where it was wanted. Construction on the CAP began in 1974, and in 1985 water from the project finally began irrigating fields near Phoenix. In 1992, the CAP reached Tucson. With the populations of Phoenix, Tucson, and Las Vegas skyrocketing, the future of Colorado River water usage may again become a question for hot debate.

By the 1960s, Arizona had become an urban state with all the problems confronting other areas around the nation. The once-healthful air of Phoenix now rivals that of Los Angeles for the thickness of its smog. Allergy sufferers are plagued by pollen from the nondesert plants that have been introduced to make this desert region look more lush and inviting. The state's economy is still growing, though. High-tech companies continue to locate within Arizona, and the continued influx of both retirees and Californians fleeing earthquakes and urban problems is giving the state new energy and new ideas.

4 A Look at Local Arts & Crafts

Although Santa Fe has for many years claimed the Southwest arts spotlight, Arizona, too, is a mecca for artists and art collectors. The Cowboy Artists of America, an organization of artists dedicated to capturing the lives and landscapes of the Old West, was formed in a tavern in Sedona in 1965 by Joe Beeler, George Phippen, Bob McLeod, Charlie Dye, John Hampton, and a few other local artists. Working primarily in oils and bronze, members of this organization depicted the lives of cowboys and Native Americans in their art, and today their work is sought by collectors throughout the country.

As more and more artists and craftspeople headed for Arizona, the towns in which they congregated came to be known as artists' colonies, and galleries sprang up to serve a growing number of visitors. Although Sedona is probably the best known of these communities, others include the former mining towns of Jerome and Bisbee, along with Tubac, the first Spanish settlement in Arizona. All three have numerous galleries and crafts shops. It is upscale Scottsdale, though, that has the state's highest concentration of art galleries.

Red-rock canyons, pensive Indians, hardworking cowboys, desert wildflowers, majestic mesas, and stately saguaros have been the themes of the 20th century's representational artists of Arizona. Although contemporary abstract art can be found in museums and galleries, the style pioneered by Frederic Remington and Charles M. Russell in the early 20th century still dominates the Arizona art scene. Remington, Russell, and those who followed in their footsteps romanticized the West, imbuing their depictions of cowboys, Indians, settlers, and soldiers with mythic proportions that would be taken up by Hollywood.

Further back, even before the first Spanish explorers arrived in Arizona, the ancient Anasazi were creating an artistic legacy in their intricately woven baskets, painted pottery, and cryptic petroglyphs and pictographs. In recent years, both contemporary Native American and nonnative artists have been drawing on Anasazi designs for their works. Today's Hopi, Navajo, and Zuni artisans have become well known for their jewelry, which is made of silver and semiprecious stones, primarily turquoise. The Hopi now carve images of their traditional kachinas for commercial distribution, and the Navajo continue to weave traditional patterns in their rugs. The Zuni, noted for their skill in carving stone, have focused on their traditional animal fetishes. And since the founding of the Santa Fe Indian School in 1932, and later the Institute of American Indian Art, Indian artists have ventured into the realm of painting. Hopi artist Fred Kabotie and his son, Michael Kabotie, are among the best-known Native American painters.

Collectors, and those with a casual interest in Southwestern art, will find local arts and crafts available in every corner of the state. From exclusive Scottsdale galleries to roadside stands on the Navajo Reservation, Arizona arts and crafts are ubiquitous. The best places to look for Southwestern and cowboy (or Western) art are Scottsdale, Tucson, Sedona, Tubac, and Jerome. Native American crafts can be found in these same towns, but it's somewhat more rewarding to visit trading posts and reservation studios and shops.

The best known of the trading posts are the Hubbell Trading Post in Ganado and the Cameron Trading Post in Cameron, but there are trading posts all over the state, many of which offer excellent selection and quality. Keep in mind that no matter where you shop for Native American arts and crafts, you'll find that prices are high.

The Indian tribes of Arizona tend to have one or two specialty crafts that they produce with consummate skill. Many of these crafts were disappearing when the first traders came to the reservations more than a century ago. Today most of the crafts are alive and well, but primarily as collectibles, not as items for everyday use. Prices are high because of the many hours that go into creating these items—what you're buying is handmade, using techniques that sometimes go back for generations.

Keep in mind that you can avoid paying sales tax if you live outside Arizona and have your purchase shipped directly to your home. On a high-ticket item such as a Navajo rug, you could save quite a bit. It's a good idea to make your jewelry purchases from reputable stores rather than from roadside stalls, of which there are many in the Four Corners region; many of these stalls sell cheap imitation Indian jewelry.

For a discussion of individual native crafts, see "A Native American Crafts Primer," in chapter 7, "The Four Corners Region: Land of the Hopi & Navajo."

5 Recommended Books

HISTORY   Marshall Trimble and Joe Beeler's *Roadside History of Arizona* (Mountain Press Publishing, 1986) is an ideal book to take along on a driving tour of the state. It goes road by road and discusses events that happened in the area. If you're interested in learning more about the infamous shootout at the O.K. Corral, read Paula Mitchell Marks's *And Die in the West: The Story of the O.K. Corral Gunfight* (University of Oklahoma Press, 1996). This is a very objective, non-Hollywood look at the most glorified and glamorized shootout in Western history.

THE GRAND CANYON/COLORADO RIVER   John Wesley Powell's diary produced the first published account (1869) of traveling through the Grand Canyon. Today his writings still provide a fascinating glimpse into the canyon and the first trip through it. *The Exploration of the Colorado River and Its Canyons* (Penguin, 1997), with an introduction by Wallace Stegner, is a recent republishing of Powell's writings. Stegner, with Bernard Devoto, writes about Powell in his *Beyond the Hundredth Meridian: John Wesley Powell and the Second Opening of the West* (Penguin, 1992).

For an interesting account of the recent human history of the canyon, read Stephen J. Pyne's *How the Canyon Became Grand* (Viking Penguin, 1999), which focuses on the explorers, writers, and artists who have contributed to our current concept of the canyon. *The Man Who Walked through Time* (Vintage, 1989), by Colin Fletcher, is a narrative of one man's hike through the rugged inner canyon. In *Down the River* (Dutton, 1991), Western environmentalist Edward Abbey chronicles many of his trips down the Colorado and other Southwest rivers. Among the essays here are descriptions of Glen Canyon before

Lake Powell was created. *Travelers' Tales Grand Canyon* (Travelers' Tales, 1999), provides a wide range of perspectives on the Grand Canyon experience. In this book, you'll find essays by Edward Abbey, Colin Fletcher, Barry Lopez, and many others.

Water rights and human impact on the deserts of the Southwest have raised many controversies in the 20th century, none more heated than those centering on the Colorado River. *Cadillac Desert: The American West and Its Disappearing Water* (Penguin, 1993), by Marc Reisner, focuses on the West's insatiable need for water. *A River No More: The Colorado River and the West* (University of California Press, 1996), by Philip L. Fradkin, addresses the fate of the Colorado River.

NATURAL HISTORY/THE OUTDOORS   Anyone the least bit curious about the plants and animals of the Sonoran Desert should be sure to acquire *A Natural History of the Sonoran Desert* (Arizona–Sonora Desert Museum Press, 2000). Cactus, wildflowers, tarantulas, roadrunners—they're all here and described in very readable detail. You'll likely get much more out of a trip to the desert with this book at your side. Halka Chronic's *Roadside Geology of Arizona* (Mountain Press Publishing, 1998) is another handy book to keep in the car. If you're a hiker, you'll find Scott S. Warren's *100 Hikes in Arizona* (The Mountaineers, 1994) another invaluable traveling companion.

FICTION   Tony Hillerman is perhaps the best-known contemporary author whose books rely on Arizona settings. Hillerman's murder mysteries are almost all set on the Navajo Reservation in the Four Corners area and include many references to actual locations that can be seen by visitors. Among Hillerman's Navajo mysteries are *Hunting Badger, The First Eagle, Sacred Clowns, Coyote Waits, Thief of Time, The Blessing Way, Listening Woman, The Ghostway,* and *The Fallen Man.*

Barbara Kingsolver, a biologist and social activist, has set several of her novels either partly or entirely in Arizona. *The Bean Trees, Pigs in Heaven,* and *Animal Dreams* are peopled by Anglo, Indian, and Hispanic characters, allowing for quirky, humorous narratives with social and political overtones that provide insights into Arizona's cultural mélange. Kingsolver's nonfiction works include *High Tide in Tucson* (HarperPerennial, 1996) and *Holding the Line: Women in the Great Arizona Mine Strike of 1983* (HarperPerennial, 1997). The former is a collection of essays, many of which focus on the author's life in Tucson, while the latter is an account of a copper-mine strike.

Edward Abbey's *The Monkey Wrench Gang* (HarperPerennial, 2000) and *Hayduke Lives!* (Little, Brown, 1991) are tales of an unlikely gang of ecoterrorists determined to preserve the wildernesses of the Southwest, including parts of northern Arizona. The former book helped inspire the founding of the radical Earth First! movement.

Zane Grey spent many years living in north-central Arizona and based many of his western novels on life in this region of the state. Among his books are *Riders of the Purple Sage, The Vanishing American, Call of the Canyon, The Arizona Clan,* and *To the Last Man.*

TRAVEL   If you're particularly interested in Native American art and crafts, you may want to search out a copy of *Trading Post Guidebook* (Northland Publishing, 1995), by Patrick Eddington and Susan Makov, an invaluable guide to trading posts, artists' studios, galleries, and museums in the Four Corners region.

Index

See also Accommodations index, below.

Let Us Hear From You!

Dear Frommer's Reader,

You are our greatest resource in keeping our guides relevant, timely, and lively. We'd love to hear from you about your travel experiences—good or bad. Want to recommend a great restaurant or a hotel off the beaten path—or register a complaint? Any thoughts on how to improve the guide itself?

Please use this page to share your thoughts with me and mail it to the address below. Or if you like, send a FAX or e-mail me at frommersfeedback@hungryminds.com. And so that we can thank you—and keep you up on the latest developments in travel—we invite you to sign up for a free daily Frommer's e-mail travel update. Just write your e-mail address on the back of this page. Also, if you'd like to take a moment to answer a few questions about yourself to help us improve our guides, please complete the following quick survey. (We'll keep that information confidential.)

Thanks for your insights.

Yours sincerely,

Michael Spring

Michael Spring, *Publisher*

Name (Optional) _____

Address _____

_____

City _____ **State** _____ **ZIP** _____

Name of Frommer's Travel Guide _____

Comments _____

_____

_____

_____

_____

_____

_____

_____

Please tell us a little about yourself so that we can serve you and the Frommer's community better. We will keep this information confidential.

Age: ( )18-24; ( )25-39; ( )40-49; ( )50-55; ( )Over 55

Income: ( )Under $25,000; ( )$25,000-$50,000; ( )$50,000-$100,000; ( )Over $100,000

I am: ( )Single, never married; ( )Married, with children; ( )Married, without children; ( )Divorced; ( )Widowed

Number of people in my household: ( )1; ( )2; ( )3; ( )4; ( )5 or more

Number of people in my household under 18: ( )1; ( )2; ( )3; ( )4; ( )5 or more

I am ( )a student; ( )employed full-time; ( )employed part-time; ( )not employed at this time; ( )retired; ( )other

I took ( )0; ( )1; ( )2; ( )3; ( )4 or more leisure trips in the past 12 months

My last vacation was ( )a weekend; ( )1 week; ( )2 weeks; ( )3 or more weeks

My last vacation was to ( )the U.S.; ( )Canada; ( )Mexico; ( )Europe; ( )Asia; ( )South America; ( )Central America; ( )The Caribbean; ( )Africa; ( )Middle East; ( )Australia/New Zealand

( )I would; ( )would not buy a Frommer's Travel Guide for business travel

I access the Internet ( )at home; ( )at work; ( )both; ( )I do not use the Internet

I used the Internet to do research for my last trip. ( )Yes; ( )No

I used the Internet to book accommodations or air travel on my last trip. ( )Yes; ( )No

My favorite travel site is ( )frommers.com; ( )travelocity.com; ( )expedia.com;
other_____

I use Frommer's Travel Guides ( )always; ( )sometimes; ( )seldom

I usually buy ( )1; ( )2; ( )more than 2 guides when I travel
Other guides I use include _____

What's the most important thing we could do to improve Frommer's Travel Guides?

_____

_____

_____

_____

Yes, please send me a daily e-mail travel update. My e-mail address is

_____

Mail to: Michael Spring, Publisher and Vice President, Frommer's Travel Guides
909 Third Ave., New York, NY 10022   FAX: 212.884.5432

FROMMER'S® COMPLETE TRAVEL GUIDES

Alaska
Amsterdam
Argentina & Chile
Arizona
Atlanta
Australia
Austria
Bahamas
Barcelona, Madrid & Seville
Beijing
Belgium, Holland &
  Luxembourg
Bermuda
Boston
British Columbia & the
  Canadian Rockies
Budapest & the Best of Hungary
California
Canada
Cancún, Cozumel & the
  Yucatán
Cape Cod, Nantucket &
  Martha's Vineyard
Caribbean
Caribbean Cruises & Ports
  of Call
Caribbean Ports of Call
Carolinas & Georgia
Chicago
China
Colorado
Costa Rica
Denmark
Denver, Boulder & Colorado
  Springs
England
Europe

European Cruises & Ports of Call
Florida
France
Germany
Greece
Greek Islands
Hawaii
Hong Kong
Honolulu, Waikiki & Oahu
Ireland
Israel
Italy
Jamaica
Japan
Las Vegas
London
Los Angeles
Maryland & Delaware
Maui
Mexico
Montana & Wyoming
Montréal & Québec City
Munich & the Bavarian Alps
Nashville & Memphis
Nepal
New England
New Mexico
New Orleans
New York City
New Zealand
Nova Scotia, New Brunswick &
  Prince Edward Island
Oregon
Paris
Philadelphia & the Amish
  Country
Portugal

Prague & the Best of the Czech
  Republic
Provence & the Riviera
Puerto Rico
Rome
San Antonio & Austin
San Diego
San Francisco
Santa Fe, Taos & Albuquerque
Scandinavia
Scotland
Seattle & Portland
Shanghai
Singapore & Malaysia
South Africa
Southeast Asia
South Florida
South Pacific
Spain
Sweden
Switzerland
Texas
Thailand
Tokyo
Toronto
Tuscany & Umbria
USA
Utah
Vancouver & Victoria
Vermont, New Hampshire
  & Maine
Vienna & the Danube Valley
Virgin Islands
Virginia
Walt Disney World & Orlando
Washington, D.C.
Washington State

FROMMER'S® DOLLAR-A-DAY GUIDES

Australia from $50 a Day
California from $70 a Day
Caribbean from $70 a Day
England from $70 a Day
Europe from $70 a Day

Florida from $70 a Day
Hawaii from $70 a Day
Ireland from $60 a Day
Italy from $70 a Day
London from $85 a Day

New York from $80 a Day
Paris from $80 a Day
San Francisco from $60 a Day
Washington, D.C.,
  from $70 a Day

FROMMER'S® PORTABLE GUIDES

Acapulco, Ixtapa &
  Zihuatanejo
Alaska Cruises & Ports
  of Call
Amsterdam
Australia's Great Barrier Reef
Bahamas
Baja & Los Cabos
Berlin
Boston
California Wine Country
Charleston & Savannah
Chicago

Dublin
Hawaii: The Big Island
Hong Kong
Houston
Las Vegas
London
Los Angeles
Maine Coast
Maui
Miami
New Orleans
New York City
Paris

Phoenix & Scottsdale
Portland
Puerto Rico
Puerto Vallarta, Manzanillo &
  Guadalajara
San Diego
San Francisco
Seattle
Sydney
Tampa & St. Petersburg
Vancouver
Venice
Washington, D.C.

FROMMER'S® NATIONAL PARK GUIDES

Family Vacations in the
  National Parks
Grand Canyon

National Parks of the American
  West
Rocky Mountain
Yellowstone & Grand Teton

Yosemite & Sequoia/
  Kings Canyon
Zion & Bryce Canyon

FROMMER'S® MEMORABLE WALKS

Chicago	New York	San Francisco
London	Paris	Washington, D.C.

FROMMER'S® GREAT OUTDOOR GUIDES

Arizona & New Mexico	Northern California	Southern New England
New England	Southern California & Baja	Vermont & New Hampshire

FROMMER'S® BORN TO SHOP GUIDES

Born to Shop: France	Born to Shop: Italy	Born to Shop: New York
Born to Shop: Hong Kong, Shanghai & Beijing	Born to Shop: London	Born to Shop: Paris

FROMMER'S® IRREVERENT GUIDES

Amsterdam	Los Angeles	Seattle & Portland
Boston	Manhattan	Vancouver
Chicago	New Orleans	Walt Disney World
Las Vegas	Paris	Washington, D.C.
London	San Francisco	

FROMMER'S® BEST-LOVED DRIVING TOURS

America	France	New England
Britain	Germany	Scotland
California	Ireland	Spain
Florida	Italy	Western Europe

THE UNOFFICIAL GUIDES®

Bed & Breakfasts in California	Golf Vacations in the Eastern U.S.	New Orleans
Bed & Breakfasts in New England	The Great Smokey & Blue Ridge Mountains	New York City
Bed & Breakfasts in the Northwest	Inside Disney	Paris
Bed & Breakfasts in Southeast	Hawaii	San Francisco
Beyond Disney	Las Vegas	Skiing in the West
Branson, Missouri	London	Southeast with Kids
California with Kids	Mid-Atlantic with Kids	Walt Disney World
Chicago	Mini Las Vegas	Walt Disney World for Grown-ups
Cruises	Mini-Mickey	Walt Disney World for Kids
Disneyland	New England with Kids	Washington, D.C.
Florida with Kids		World's Best Diving Vacations

SPECIAL-INTEREST TITLES

Frommer's Britain's Best Bed & Breakfasts and Country Inns
Frommer's France's Best Bed & Breakfasts and Country Inns
Frommer's Italy's Best Bed & Breakfasts and Country Inns
Frommer's Caribbean Hideaways
Frommer's Adventure Guide to Australia & New Zealand
Frommer's Adventure Guide to Central America
Frommer's Adventure Guide to India & Pakistan
Frommer's Adventure Guide to South America
Frommer's Adventure Guide to Southeast Asia
Frommer's Adventure Guide to Southern Africa
Frommer's Gay & Lesbian Europe
Frommer's Exploring America by RV
Hanging Out in England

Hanging Out in Europe
Hanging Out in France
Hanging Out in Ireland
Hanging Out in Italy
Hanging Out in Spain
Israel Past & Present
Frommer's The Moon
Frommer's New York City with Kids
The New York Times' Guide to Unforgettable Weekends
Places Rated Almanac
Retirement Places Rated
Frommer's Road Atlas Britain
Frommer's Road Atlas Europe
Frommer's Washington, D.C., with Kids
Frommer's What the Airlines Never Tell You